DIALECTIC SPIRITUALISM

BOOKS by
His Divine Grace
A.C. Bhaktivedanta Swami Prabhupāda

Bhagavad-gītā As It Is
Śrīmad Bhāgavatam, Cantos 1-10 (29 vols.)
Śrī Caitanya-caritāmṛta (17 vols.)
Teachings of Lord Caitanya
The Nectar of Devotion (Bhakti-rasāmṛta-sindhu)
The Nectar of Instruction
Śrī Īśopaniṣad
Easy Journey to Other Planets
Kṛṣṇa Consciousness: The Topmost Yoga System
Kṛṣṇa, the Supreme Personality of Godhead (3 vols.)
Perfect Questions, Perfect Answers
Teachings of Lord Kapila, the Son of Devahūti
Transcendental Teachings of Prahlād Mahārāja
Teachings of Queen Kuntī
Kṛṣṇa, the Reservoir of Pleasure
The Science of Self-Realization
The Path of Perfection
Life Comes From Life
The Perfection of Yoga
Beyond Birth and Death
On the Way to Kṛṣṇa
Rāja-vidyā: The King of Knowledge
Elevation to Kṛṣṇa Consciousness
Kṛṣṇa Consciousness: The Matchless Gift
Back to Godhead Magazine (founder)

A complete catalog is available upon request.

New Vrindaban Community
RD 1, Box 319
Moundsville, W.Va. 26041

DIALECTIC SPIRITUALISM

A VEDIC VIEW OF WESTERN PHILOSOPHY

HIS DIVINE GRACE A.C. BHAKTIVEDANTA
SWAMI PRABHUPĀDA

PRABHUPĀDA BOOKS

Readers interested in the subject matter of this book are invited to visit the New Vrindaban Community, Home of Prabhupāda's Palace of Gold, Hare Kṛṣṇa Ridge, Moundsville, W. Va., or to correspond with the Secretary.

c/o New Vrindaban
RD 1, Box 319
Moundsville, W. Va. 26041

First Printing: 50,000 copies

Printed in Singapore

Library of Congress Catalog Card No. 85-090424

International Standard Book Number: 0-932215-02-5

Contents

FOREWORD
by
His Divine Grace Kīrtanānanda Swami Bhaktipāda

The idea for this book first emerged in 1973, when Śrīla Prabhupāda began asking his secretary, Śyāmasundara dāsa adhikārī (Sam Speerstra), about Western philosophy. Śyāmasundara would try to state succinctly the major ideas of certain philosophers, and Śrīla Prabhupāda would give the Vedic view. As Śrīla Prabhupāda travelled throughout the world preaching Kṛṣṇa consciousness, this process continued, until finally, in 1976, Prabhupāda's editor, Hayagrīva dāsa adhikārī (Professor Howard Wheeler), supplied further questions for Prabhupāda and completed the editing. Then Śrīla Prabhupāda gave the book its title: *Dialectic Spiritualism: A Vedic View of Western Philosophy*, and said, "Print it."

Almost immediately some people objected that since professional scholars had not presented the material to Śrīla Prabhupāda, there might be some discrepancies. When the manuscript was shown to a philosophy professor, he called it "a treatise against philosophy," and "an unscholarly punch in the nose." Then, when Śrīla Prabhupāda left this mortal world in November, 1977, the book's future became uncertain. One student tried to restate the questions. Then another tried, only to conclude that it would be better to start all over. But Śrīla Prabhupāda was no longer present, and the extensive work, on which he had spent so much time, remained unavailable to the world. Finally, in 1984, Hayagrīva resolved to print Śrīla Prabhupāda's last great opus *as it is*, and for this we are all greatly indebted.

Whatever the criticisms, they are rendered insignificant in the light of Śrīla Prabhupāda's brilliant insights into the problems of Western philosophy and his lucid expositories of the Vedic view. Much of the confusion arises from a difference in methodology and perspective. For many Westerners, philosophy is a kind of armchair speculation, an intellectual game; but for the follower of the Vedas, it is a matter of life and death. Or, more precisely, it is the recognition of the absolute need to stop the repetition of birth and death. For Śrīla Prabhupāda, real philosophy deals with applying Absolute Knowledge in our daily lives, consciously, moment by moment. "We should act in such a way that we have to think of Kṛṣṇa all the time," he said. "For instance, we are discussing the philosophy of Socrates in order to strengthen our Kṛṣṇa consciousness. Therefore the ultimate goal is Kṛṣṇa. Otherwise we are not interested in criticizing or accepting anyone's philosophy. We are neutral."

Obviously, this is not the goal of Western philosophy, which tends to see man as "the measure of all things" in a physical, humanistic universe. Western thought has always encouraged self-reliance and individualism, which are reflected even in today's street philosophy: "Do your own thing."

The Vedic view clashes fiercely with such relativistic thinking. Far from celebrating the authority of the individual mind, or the autonomy and ascendence of reason, the Vedas point out the four fundamental defects of conditioned souls. Śrīla Prabhupāda made this point clear:

> Of course, in European philosophy there is an attempt at more independent thought, but such independent thinking is not approved by the followers of the Vedas. The Vedic followers receive knowledge directly from authorities. They do not speculate. We cannot attain knowledge through speculation because everyone is imperfect.... According to the Vedic system, we receive knowledge from Vyāsadeva, Nārada, and Śrī Kṛṣṇa Himself. This knowledge is perfect because these personalities are not subjected to the four defects of all conditioned living entities: the tendency to commit mistakes, to be illusioned, to have imperfect senses, and to cheat.... We therefore have to receive knowledge from those who are liberated. This is the Vedic process. If we receive knowledge from Kṛṣṇa, there cannot be any mistake, nor any question of illusion. Our senses may be imperfect, but Kṛṣṇa's senses are perfect; therefore whatever Kṛṣṇa says, we accept, and that acceptance is our perfection.

With these defects, a conditioned human being, cannot possibly present perfect knowledge. Therefore he is reduced to wrangling. As Śrīla Prabhupāda often observed, "Being a big philosopher, a *muni*, means refuting the theories of others and setting up your own conclusions as supreme." There is no end to this process, nor is there perfection. "It is said that a philosopher is not a philosopher unless he differs from other philosophers," Śrīla Prabhupāda said when discussing Descartes. "If one is to be a great philosopher, he has to defy all his predecessors. Scientists also work in the same way. If we try to find out whose statement is true, we have a great deal of difficulty. Therefore the Vedic *śāstras* enjoin that we follow the personalities who have realized God...If we follow the *ācāryas* in the disciplic succession, our path is clear."

Perfect knowledge can come only from a perfect source, the reservoir of knowledge, God Himself. Such knowledge is imparted by the Supreme and comes down by the *paramparā* process, the line of true disciplic succession, from one realized soul to another.

Śrīla Prabhupāda explains the Vedic method in this way:

> Every word we hear has a meaning behind it. As soon as we hear the word "water," there is a substance—water—behind the word. Similarly, as soon as we hear the word "God," there is a meaning to it. If we receive that meaning and explanation of "God" from God Himself, then it is perfect. But if we speculate about the meaning of "God," it is imperfect. *Bhagavad-gītā*, which is the science of God, is spoken by the Personality of Godhead Himself. This is perfect knowledge. Mental speculators, or so-called philosophers who are researching for what is actually God, will never understand the nature of God. The science of God has to be understood in disciplic succession from Brahmā, who was first instructed about knowledge of God from God Himself. (*Śrīmad-Bhāgavatam*, Purport, 3.26.33)

This does not mean, however, that the human mind is reduced to that of a robot. The mind is useful for acceptance and rejection, and one's intelligence is measured by his power of discrimination. But in the presence of the Supreme Absolute Truth, nothing is to be rejected, and discrimination has no meaning. Therefore perfect knowledge must be accepted from a perfect source. Still, history shows that thought is dynamic and progressive, and the great reformers—Vālmīki, Vyāsadeva, Socrates, Jesus, Mohammed, and Caitanya Mahāprabhu—all declare, directly or indirectly, that they have come not to destroy the Law of God, but to fulfill it. Such great souls are not content to accept something simply because it is handed down by tradition. Indeed, tradition has often proved untrustworthy, for in the course of time, and influenced by common men, its purity is lost. "This supreme science was thus received through the chain of disciplic succession, and the saintly kings understood it in that way," Lord Kṛṣṇa tells Arjuna. "But in course of time, the succession was broken, and therefore the science as it is appears to be lost." (*Bg.* 4.2) For this reason, Lord Kṛṣṇa again spoke *Bhagavad-gītā*, reestablishing the true disciplic succession (*paramparā).*

Some have charged that this approach is more theosophic than philosophic. But why arbitrarily force an either/or situation? Kṛṣṇa consciousness is the happy marriage of theology and philosophy. As Śrīla Prabhupāda often said, "Religion without philosophy is sentimental and therefore fanatical; and philosophy without religion is mental speculation." However, the rejection of mental speculation does not extend to sincere philosophical speculation, which is a legitimate activity of the mind. The difference is like that between pure, fresh milk and milk contaminated by the poisonous fangs of a serpent. Philosophical speculation is the attempt to understand the Lord and His energies by using all the faculties which God has so kindly given us, whereas mental speculation is the proud attempt to use those faculties, which rightly belong to the Lord, *against* the Lord. Philosophical speculation leads to greater and greater awareness and appreciation of the Supreme Personality of Godhead, whereas mental speculation always comes to the atheistic conclusion of the voidists: God is void and we are void, therefore let us eat, drink, and be merry, for tomorrow we die.

For example, trying to understand how the Supreme Personality of Godhead enters into the creation, maintains it, and destroys it, is proper philosophical speculation. In this sincere attempt, the previous *ācāryas* and the holy scriptures can guide us. But trying to figure out the origin of everything solely by the power of the tiny human brain, without referring to God or His representatives (*guru-sādhu-śāstra*), is useless mental speculation. We may speculate in this fashion for billions of years and still not arrive at the Absolute Truth, the Supreme Personality of Godhead, who lies beyond the purview of finite thought.

It is precisely on this point of the centrality of the Personality of Godhead that the Vedic observer differs radically from his Western counterpart. Both Eastern and Western philosophy wrestle with the same problems: birth, death, reincarnation, liberation, the nature of God and the soul, the creation, good and evil, human responsibility, free will, karma, material vs. spiritual, and so on. By and large, Western thinkers are pantheistic and impersonalistic. Even great theists like Aquinas and Augustine have ultimately considered the personal aspect to be a manifestation of the impersonal principle. The impersonalism of Plato and Aristotle are indeed deeply engrained in Western thought. This is not some strange coincidence, but the result of a basic difference in methodology. Only when a sincere devotee surrenders to God does God agree to reveal Himself. "One can understand the Supreme Personality as He is only by devotional service," Lord Kṛṣṇa says (*Bg*. 18.55). Surrender to God is a prerequisite for knowing God. Śrīla Prabhupāda often remarked that when we speak of surrender, we necessarily predicate a person. According to the Vedas, the attributes and nature of that person can be known only through the person Himself. There is no room for imagination, myth, human reasoning, speculation, anthropomorphism, or whatever. In knowledge of the Personality of Godhead, Western philosophy has proved sadly deficient, as Carl Jung observed:

> **Hayagrīva dāsa:** Seeing that philosophies and theologies could not give him a clear picture of God's personality, Jung concludes: "What is wrong with these philosophers? I wondered. Evidently they know of God only by hearsay."
>
> **Śrīla Prabhupāda:** Yes, that is also our complaint. None of the philosophers

we have discussed has given us any clear idea of God. Because they are speculating, they cannot give concrete, clear information. As far as we are concerned, our understanding of God is clear because we receive the information given by God Himself to the world.

In Western philosophy, personalism is an unknown territory, approached only in Socrates's instructions from Diotima in *The Symposium,* wherein Socrates was enjoined to contemplate and converse with beauty absolute, beauty simple, divine, true, unpolluted, real and wondrous. It is the same territory before which Jung stood longing for a guru. It is the borderline of the finite individual soul awaiting revelation. Personalism necessitates revelation, for the Supreme Personality of Godhead can be affirmed only by the personal descent of the Divine.

Dialectic Spiritualism should not be seen as an academic attempt at comparative philosophy, but as a devotee's informal, spontaneous response to various Western philosophers. Each philosopher is viewed in his own existential loneliness, without reference to historical influences. Each faces the eternal Vedas alone. Sometimes we may imagine the court of the Last Judgement. By his own words, each man stands praised or condemned. There is no consideration for personality, no allowance for time or place. For the academician bent on the historicity of a thought, this doubtlessly seems unfair and arbitrary, but it is typically Vedic. Our thoughts and deeds are fixed in eternal time. We are responsible for even our most random, idle, or uncharacteristic statements.

Far from being detrimental, Śrīla Prabhupāda's unfamiliarity with formal Western philosophy evoked the most genuine and candid responses. Of all the philosophers, he agreed most with Socrates, whom he considered Brahman realized. He often quoted Socrates's answer to the question of what should be done with him after his death: "Well, you have to catch me first. But as for my body, you can dispose of that as you like." Still, Prabhupāda considered Socrates an impersonalist because he had no specific information of the Supreme Personality of Godhead, despite his speaking of the form of Absolute Beauty. Plato, being Socrates's disciple, also ranked high in Prabhupāda's Vedic eyes, particularly for his view of the soul and reincarnation. But Prabhupāda disagreed with his recommendation of uniform education and universal military training.

Aristotle was severely criticized for his view that the souls of animals are not immortal. There are not two types of souls, mortal and immortal, as Aristotle contends. This pernicious doctrine was carried even further by Augustine, who argued that since animals do not possess an immortal soul, "they are meant for our use, dead or alive. It only remains for us to apply the commandment, 'Thou shalt not kill' to man alone, oneself and others." Strange words from a so-called saint! Unfortunately, this became the standard Christian doctrine: since animals have no souls, it is all right to kill and eat them.

Śrīla Prabhupāda felt that Plotinus, following Plato's footsteps, presented a basically sound philosophy of the soul, particularly of the *jīvātmā's* relation with the One, but, of course, Plotinus's "One" was impersonal. Prabhupāda disagreed with Origen's theory that souls are created. If they are created, how can they be immortal? "Never was there a time when I did not exist, nor you, nor all these kings," Kṛṣṇa tells Arjuna. "Nor in the future shall any of us cease to be." (*Bg.* 2.12) The theory of the creation of a "human soul" at the moment of conception was also accepted by Aquinas, and thus became official Catholic doctrine. The belief that each individual human soul is created at a point in time, lives his life, and thereafter is saved or damned eternally, excludes the possibility of reincarnation.

By denying reincarnation, Augustine and Aquinas broke with the Platonic tradition, and made it difficult for subsequent philosophers to understand evil in the world. If there is no transmigration of souls, where is Divine Justice? How can we account for fortune and misfortune? Why is one man pious, knowledgeable, beautiful, or opulent, and another man impious, ignorant, deformed, or poor? Why, on the basis of one finite lifetime, is one man eternally saved and another eternally damned? Why is God so arbitrary, so unmerciful? Having rejected the possibilities of transmigration and karma, Western philosophers have been troubled all the way down to Mill, Dewey, and Sartre. Because evil exists, they argue, either God's power is limited, or He is not all good, or He does not exist at all.

In their confrontation with the Vedic version, some of the philosophers scored high, some low, some in between. Ranking high as first-class philosophers were Socrates, Plato, Plotinus, Origen, Scotus, Descartes, Pascal, and Bergson. Śrīla Prabhupāda also liked the psychologist Carl Jung ("He seems the most sensible."). After these, ranked Aquinas, Locke, Berkeley, Spinoza, Leibnitz, Kant, Schopenhauer, Alexander, Nietzsche, James, and Kierkegaard. In low regard, for various reasons, were Aristotle, Augustine, Fichte, Bacon, and Huxley. Conflicting most with Vedic thought were Machiavelli, Hume, Hegel, Hobbes, Darwin,

Mill, Comte, Marx, Dewey, Sartre, and Freud.

Ultimately, no Western philosopher can measure up to the high standard of the Vedic ideal. In contrast, Śrīla Prabhupāda emerges as the emissary of a higher source, for he is Lord Kṛṣṇa's pure devotee. It is not as though he alone were speaking; rather, an unbroken line of disciplic succession speaks through him, delivering the pure knowledge of the Vedas intact. When he called the book "A Vedic view of Western philosophy," Śrīla Prabhupāda humbly said, "Yes, *Vedic* view. After all, what is my personal view worth?"

Although *Dialectic Spiritualism* marks a clashing of different knowledge-acquiring processes, the inductive and deductive, we reach the mutual understanding that arises from all fruitful confrontations: a clarification of positions, from which points of agreement and contention can be discerned. Thus the book is valuable to students of all schools of philosophy and theology. If the reader chooses to accept Śrīla Prabhupāda's conclusion that God has manifested Himself in sound (*śabdāvatāra*)—that is, in the Vedas, of which *Bhagavad-gītā* is the essence—he will have a standard by which every thought can be judged. Viewed thus, the book takes on new and profound perspectives. It is *Dialectic Spiritualism* read in the spirit of the dialectic itself.

PREFACE

idaṁ hi puṁsas tapasaḥ śrutasya vā
sviṣṭasya sūktasya ca buddhi-dattayoḥ
avicyuto 'rthaḥ kavibhir nirūpito
yad-uttamaśloka-guṇānuvarṇanam

TRANSLATION

Learned sages have definitely concluded that the infallible fruit of knowledge, austerity, Vedic study, sacrifice, the chanting of hymns, and charity is found in the transcendental descriptions of the qualities of the Lord, who is defined in choice poetry. (*Śrīmad-Bhāgavatam* 1.5.22)

PURPORT

The human intellect is developed for advancement in art, science, philosophy, physics, chemistry, psychology, economics, politics, and other fields. Through the culture of knowledge, humanity can attain the perfection of life, which culminates in the realization of the Supreme Being, Viṣṇu. The *śruti* therefore advises the learned to aspire for the service of Lord Viṣṇu. Unfortunately, when people are enamored by the external beauty of *viṣṇu-māyā*, they do not understand that perfection, or self-realization, depends on Viṣṇu. *Viṣṇu-māyā* means sense enjoyment, which is transient and miserable. Those who are entrapped by *viṣṇu-māyā* utilize their knowledge for sense enjoyment. Śrī Nārada Muni, however, has explained that all phenomena in the universe emanate from the Lord because the Lord, through His inconceivable energies, has set in motion the actions and reactions of the creation. Everything has come into being out of His energy; everything rests on His energy, and after annihilation, everything merges into Him. Therefore nothing is different from the Lord, although the Lord is always different from His creation.

When knowledge is applied in the service of the Lord, the process of advancement becomes absolute. The Supreme Personality of Godhead and His transcendental name, fame, and glory are all nondifferent from Him; therefore all sages and devotees of the Lord have recommended that art, science, philosophy, physics, chemistry, psychology, and other branches of knowledge be wholly and solely applied in the Lord's service. Art, literature, poetry, and music may be used in glorifying the Lord. Poets and other celebrated litterateurs are generally engaged in writing of sensuous themes, but if they turn towards the service of the Lord, they can describe the Lord's transcendental pastimes. Vālmīki was a great poet, and Vyāsadeva was a great writer, and both completely engaged themselves in delineating the transcendental activities of the Lord, and by so doing, they have become immortal. Similarly, science and philosophy should also be applied in the service of the Lord. Advanced people are eager to understand the Absolute Truth through the medium of science, and therefore scientists should endeavor to prove the Lord's existence on a scientific basis. Philosophy should also aim to establish the Supreme Truth as sentient and all-powerful. Indeed, all other branches of knowledge should similarly be engaged in the Lord's service. This is also affirmed by *Bhagavad-gītā.* All knowledge not engaged in the Lord's service is but nescience. Advanced knowledge should be utilized to establish the glories of the Lord, and that is the real import of this verse. Scientific knowledge and other branches of knowledge engaged in the Lord's service are all factually *hari-kīrtana*, glorification of the Lord.

I

THE GREEK FOUNDATION

Socrates
(470?-399 B.C.)

Hayagrīva dāsa: When a student of Socrates once said, "I cannot refute you, Socrates," Socrates replied, "Say, rather, that you cannot refute the truth, for Socrates is easily refuted." He thus considered the Absolute Truth transcendental to mental speculation and personal opinion.
Śrīla Prabhupāda: That is correct. If we accept Kṛṣṇa, God, as the supreme authority, the Absolute Truth, we cannot refute what He says. Kṛṣṇa, or God, is by definition supreme perfection, and philosophy is perfect when it is in harmony with Him. This is our position. The philosophy of this Kṛṣṇa consciousness movement is religious because it is concerned with carrying out the orders of God. That is the sum and substance of religion. It is not possible to manufacture a religion. In *Bhagavad-gītā* and *Śrīmad-Bhāgavatam,* manufactured religion is called *dharma-kaitava,* just another form of cheating. Our basic principle is given in *Śrīmad-Bhāgavatam:*

dharmaṁ tu sākṣād bhagavat-praṇītaṁ
na vai vidur ṛṣayo nāpi devāḥ
na siddha-mukhyā asurā manuṣyāḥ

kuto nu vidyādhara-cāraṇādayaḥ

"Real religious principles are enacted by the Supreme Personality of Godhead. Although fully situated in the mode of goodness, even the great *ṛṣis* who occupy the topmost planets cannot ascertain the real religious principles, nor can the demigods, nor the leaders of Siddhaloka, to say nothing of the *asuras*, ordinary human beings, Vidyādharas and Cāraṇas." (*Bhāg.* 6.3.19) The word "dharma" refers to the orders given by God, and if we follow those orders, we are following dharma. An individual citizen cannot manufacture laws, because laws are given by the government. Our perfection is in following the orders of God cent per cent. Those who have no conception of God or His orders may manufacture religious systems, but our system is different.

Śyāmasundara dāsa: It seems that Socrates was more or less a *dhyāna-yogī* because he thought that we could arrive at the truth by approaching a subject from every mental angle until there was nothing left but the truth.

Śrīla Prabhupāda: He was a *muni*, a great thinker. However, the real truth comes to such a *muni* by that process after many, many births. As stated in *Bhagavad-gītā:*

bahūnāṁ janmanām ante
jñānavān māṁ prapadyate
vāsudevaḥ sarvam iti
sa mahātmā sudurlabhaḥ

"After many births and deaths, he who is actually in knowledge surrenders unto Me, knowing Me to be the cause of all causes and all that is. Such a great soul is very rare." (*Bg.* 7.19)

These people are known as *jñānavān*, wise men, and after many births, they surrender themselves to Kṛṣṇa. They do not do so blindly, but knowing that the Supreme Personality of Godhead is the source of everything. However, this process of self-searching for knowledge takes time. If we take the instructions of Kṛṣṇa directly and surrender unto Him, we save time and many, many births.

Śyāmasundara dāsa: Socrates believed that the soul, which is tied up with intelligence, carries knowledge from existence to existence. The truth can be evoked through the *maieutic* method, the Socratic dialectic. Since someone can make us understand the truth and admit it, we must have known the truth in a previous existence. Thus our intelligence is eternal.

Śrīla Prabhupāda: Yes, because the soul is eternal, the intelligence, mind, and senses are also eternal. However, they are all now covered by a material coating, which must be cleansed. Once this material coating is washed away, the real mind, intelligence, and senses will emerge. That is stated in the *Nārada-Pañcarātra: tat paratvena nirmalam.* The purificatory process necessitates being in touch with the transcendental loving service of the Lord. This means chanting the Hare Kṛṣṇa *mahā-mantra.* Caitanya Mahāprabhu said: *ceto-darpaṇa-mārjanam (Śikṣāṣṭaka* 1). "We must cleanse the heart." All misconceptions come from misunderstanding. We are all part and parcel of God, yet somehow or other we have forgotten this. Previously, our service was rendered to God, but now we are rendering service to something illusory. This is māyā. Whether liberated or conditioned, our constitutional position is to render service. In the material world, we work according to our different capacities—as a politician, an industrialist, a thinker, a poet, or whatever. But if we are not connected with Kṛṣṇa, all of this is māyā. When we perform our duty in order to develop Kṛṣṇa consciousness, our very same duty enables liberation from this bondage. In any case, both life and knowledge are continuous. Consequently, one person can acquire knowledge very quickly, whereas another cannot. This is proof of continuity.

Śyāmasundara dāsa: In a dialogue with Socrates, Protagoras said, "Truth is relative. It is only a matter of opinion." Socrates then asked, "Do you mean that truth is mere subjective opinion?" Protagoras replied, "Exactly. What is true for you is true for you, and what is true for me is true for me. Thus truth is subjective." Socrates then asked, "Do you really mean that my opinion is true by virtue of its being my opinion?" Protagoras said, "Indeed I do." Socrates then said, "My opinion is that truth is absolute, not subjective, and that you, Protagoras, are absolutely in error. Since this is my opinion, you must grant that it is true according to your philosophy." Protagoras then admitted, "You are quite correct, Socrates." Through this kind of dialogue, or dialectic, Socrates would logically convince many people.

Śrīla Prabhupāda: That is what we are also doing. The Absolute Truth is true for everyone, and the relative truth is relative to a particular position. The relative truth depends on the Absolute Truth, which is the summum bonum. God is the Absolute Truth, and the material world is relative truth. Because the material world is God's energy, it appears to be real or true, just as the reflection of the sun in water emits some light. That reflection is not absolute, and as soon as the sun sets, that light will disappear. Since relative truth is a reflection of the Absolute Truth, *Śrīmad-Bhāgavatam* states: *satyaṁ paraṁ dhīmahi.* "I worship the Absolute Truth." (*Bhāg.* 1.1.1) The Absolute Truth is Kṛṣṇa, Vāsudeva. *Oṁ namo bhagavate vāsudevāya.* This cosmic manifestation is relative truth; it is a manifestation of Kṛṣṇa's external energy. If Kṛṣṇa withdrew His energy, the universal creation would not exist. In another sense, Kṛṣṇa and Kṛṣṇa's energy are not different. We cannot separate heat from fire; heat is also fire, yet heat is not fire. This is the position of relative truth. As soon as we experience heat, we understand that there is fire. Yet we cannot say that heat is fire. Relative truth is like heat because it stands on the strength of the Absolute Truth, just as heat stands on the strength of fire. Because the Absolute is true, relative truth also appears to be true, although it has no independent existence. A mirage appears to be water because in actuality there is such a thing as water. Similarly, this material world appears attractive because there is an all-attractive spiritual world.

Hayagrīva dāsa: According to Socrates, the real pursuit of man is the search for the Absolute Good. Basically, Socrates is an impersonalist because he does not ultimately define this Absolute Good as a person, nor does he give it a personal name.

Śrīla Prabhupāda: That is the preliminary stage of understanding the Absolute, known as Brahman realization, realization of the impersonal feature. When one is further advanced, he attains Paramātmā realization, realization of the localized feature, whereby he realizes that God is everywhere. It is a fact that God is everywhere, but at the same time God has His own abode. *Goloka eva nivasaty akhilātma bhūtaḥ (Brahma-saṁhitā* 5.37). God is a person, and He has His own abode and associates. Although He is in His abode, He is present everywhere, within every atom. *Aṇḍāntara-stha-paramāṇu-cayāntara-stham (Brahma-saṁhitā* 5.35). Like other impersonalists, Socrates cannot understand how God, through His potency, can remain in His own abode and simultaneously be present in every atom. The material world is His expansion, His energy.

bhūmir āpo'nalo vāyuḥ
khaṁ mano buddhir eva ca
ahaṅkāra itīyaṁ me
bhinnā prakṛtir aṣṭadhā

"Earth, water, fire, air, ether, mind, intelligence, and false ego—altogether these eight comprise My separated material energies." (*Bg.* 7.4) Because His energy is expanded everywhere, He can be present everywhere. Although the energy and the energetic are nondifferent, we cannot say that they are not distinct. They are simultaneously one and different. This is the perfect philosophy of *acintya-bhedābheda-tattva.*

Hayagrīva dāsa: The Good of which Socrates speaks is different from *sattva-guṇa*. In *The Republic*, Socrates says that it is the Good which gives truth to the objects of knowledge and the very power of knowing to him who knows them. He speaks of the Form of essential goodness as the cause of knowledge and truth. Although we may consider the Good to be an object of knowledge, it would be better if we regarded it as being beyond truth and knowledge and of higher value. Both knowledge and truth are therefore to be regarded as like unto the Good, but it is incorrect to identify either with the Good. He believes that the Good must hold a higher place of honor. Objects of knowledge derive their very being and reality from the Good, which is beyond being itself and surpasses it in dignity and power.

Śrīla Prabhupāda: *Sattva-guṇa*, the mode of goodness, is a position from which we can receive knowledge. Knowledge cannot be received from the platform of passion and ignorance. If we hear about Kṛṣṇa, or God, we are gradually freed from the clutches of darkness and passion. Then we can come to the platform of *sattva-guṇa*, and when we are perfectly situated there, we are beyond the lower modes. *Śrīmad-Bhāgavatam* says:

naṣṭa-prāyeṣv abhadreṣu
nityaṁ bhāgavata-sevayā
bhagavaty uttama-śloke
bhaktir bhavati naiṣṭhikī

tadā rajas-tamo-bhāvāḥ
kāma-lobhādayaś ca ye
ceta etair anāviddhaṁ
sthitaṁ sattve prasīdati

"By regularly hearing the *Bhāgavatam* and rendering service unto the pure devotee, all that is troublesome to the heart is practically destroyed, and loving service unto the glorious Lord, who is praised with transcendental songs, is established as an irrevocable fact. At the time loving service is established in the heart, the modes of passion (*rajas*), and ignorance (*tamas*), and lust and desire (*kāma*), disappear from the heart. Then the devotee is established in goodness, and he becomes happy." (*Bhāg*. 1.2.18-19)

This process may be gradual, but it is certain. The more we hear about Kṛṣṇa, the more we become purified. Purification means freedom from the attacks of greed and passion. Then we can become happy. From the *brahma-bhūta* platform, we can realize ourselves and then realize God.

So before realizing the Supreme Good, we must first come to the platform of *sattva-guṇa*, goodness. Therefore we have regulations prohibiting illicit sex, meat eating, intoxication, and gambling. Ultimately, we must transcend even the mode of goodness through *bhakti*. Then we become liberated, gradually develop love of God, and regain our original state.

nirodho 'syānuśayanam
ātmanaḥ saha śaktibhiḥ
muktir hitvānyathā rūpaṁ
sva-rūpeṇa vyavasthitiḥ

"When the living entity, along with his conditional living tendency, merges with the mystic lying down of the Mahā-viṣṇu, it is called the winding up of the cosmic manifestation. Liberation is the permanent situation of the form of the living entity after giving up the changeable material gross and subtle bodies." (*Bhāg*. 2.10.6) This means giving up all material engagements and rendering full service to Kṛṣṇa. Then we attain the state where māyā cannot touch us. If we keep in touch with Kṛṣṇa, māyā has no jurisdiction.

daivī hy eṣā guṇamayī
mama māyā duratyayā
mām eva ye prapadyante
māyām etāṁ taranti te

"This divine energy of Mine, consisting of the three modes of material nature, is difficult to overcome. But those who have surrendered unto Me can easily cross beyond it." (*Bg*. 7.14) This is perfection.

Hayagrīva dāsa: Socrates taught a process of liberation comparable to that of *dhyāna-yoga*. For him, liberation meant freedom from passion, and he approved the saying *gnothi seauton*—"Know thyself." By knowing ourselves through meditation, or insight, we can gain self-control, and by being self-controlled, we can attain happiness.

Śrīla Prabhupāda: Yes, that is a fact. Meditation means analyzing the self and searching for the Absolute Truth. That is described in the Vedic literatures: *dhyānāvasthita-tad-gatena manasā paśyanti yaṁ yoginaḥ* (*Bhāg*. 12.13.1).Through meditation, the yogī sees the Supreme Truth (Kṛṣṇa, or God) within himself. Kṛṣṇa is there. The yogī consults with Kṛṣṇa, and Kṛṣṇa advises him. That is the relationship Kṛṣṇa has with the yogī. *Buddhi-yogaṁ dadāmyaham*. When one is purified, he is always seeing Kṛṣṇa within himself. This is confirmed in *Brahma-saṁhitā*:

premāñjana-cchurita-bhakti-vilocanena
santaḥ sadaiva hṛdayeṣu vilokayanti

yaṁ śyāmasundaram acintya-guṇa-svarūpaṁ
govindam ādi-puruṣaṁ tam ahaṁ bhajāmi

"I worship the primeval Lord, Govinda, who is always seen by the devotee whose eyes are anointed with the pulp of love. He is seen in His eternal form of Śyāmasundara situated within the heart of the devotee." (*Brahma-saṁhitā* 5.38) Thus an advanced saintly person is always seeing Kṛṣṇa. In this verse, the word *śyāma* means "blackish," but at the same time extraordinarily beautiful. The word *acintya* means that He has unlimited qualities. Although He is situated everywhere, as Govinda He is always dancing in Vṛndāvana with the *gopīs*. In Vṛndāvana, Kṛṣṇa plays with His friends, and sometimes, acting as a naughty boy, teases His mother. These pastimes of the Supreme Person are described in *Śrīmad-Bhāgavatam*.

Śyāmasundara dāsa: As far as we know, Socrates was a self-taught man. Is it possible for a person to be self-taught? That is, can self-knowledge be attained through meditation, or introspection?

Śrīla Prabhupāda: Yes. Ordinarily, everyone thinks according to the bodily conception. If I begin to study the different parts of my body and seriously begin to consider what I am, I will gradually arrive at the study of the soul. If I ask myself, "Am I this hand?" the answer will be, "No, I am not this hand. Rather, this is *my* hand." I can thus continue analyzing each part of the body and discover that all the parts are mine but that I am different. Through this method of self-study, any intelligent man can see that he is not the body. This is the first lesson of *Bhagavad-gītā:*

dehino 'smin yathā dehe
kaumāraṁ yauvanaṁ jarā
tathā dehāntara-prāptir
dhīras tatra na muhyati

"As the embodied soul continually passes, in this body, from boyhood to youth to old age, the soul similarly passes into another body at death. The self-realized soul is not bewildered by such a change." (*Bg.* 2.13)

At one time I had the body of a child, but now that body is no longer existing. Still, I am aware that I possessed such a body; therefore from this I can deduce that I am something other than the body. I may rent an apartment, but I do not identify with it. The body may be mine, but I am not the body. By this kind of introspection, a man can teach himself the distinction between the body and the soul.

As far as being completely self-taught—according to *Bhagavad-gītā* and the Vedic conception, life is continuous. Since we are always acquiring experience, we cannot say that Socrates was self-taught. Rather, in his previous lives he cultivated knowledge, and this knowledge is continuing. That is a fact. Otherwise, why is one man intelligent and another man ignorant? This is due to continuity.

Hayagrīva dāsa: Socrates believed that through meditation, a person can attain knowledge, and through knowledge he can become virtuous. When he is virtuous, he acts in the right way, and by so doing, becomes happy. Therefore the enlightened man is meditative, knowledgeable, and virtuous. He is also happy because he acts properly.

Śrīla Prabhupāda: Yes, that is confirmed in *Bhagavad-gītā:*

brahma-bhūtaḥ prasannātmā
na śocati na kāṅkṣati
samaḥ sarveṣu bhūteṣu
mad-bhaktiṁ labhate parām

"One who is thus transcendentally situated at once realizes the Supreme Brahman. He never laments nor desires to have anything; he is equally disposed to every living entity. In that state, he attains pure devotional service unto Me." (*Bg.* 18. 54) When one is self-realized, he immediately becomes happy, joyful (*prasannātmā*). This is because he is properly situated. A person may labor a long time under some mistaken idea, but when he finally comes to the proper conclusion, he becomes very happy. He thinks, "Oh, what a fool I was, going on so long in such a mistaken way." Thus a self-realized person is happy. Happiness means that you no longer have to think of attaining things. For instance, Dhruva Mahārāja told the Lord: *Svāmin kṛtārtho 'smi.* "I don't want any material benediction." Prahlāda Mahārāja also said, "My Lord, I don't want any material benefits. I have seen my father, who was such a big materialist that even the demigods were afraid of him, destroyed by You within a second. Therefore I am not after these things." Real knowledge means that you no longer hanker. The *karmīs, jñānīs,* and yogīs are all hankering after something. The *karmīs* want material wealth, beautiful women and good positions. If one is not hankering for what one does not have, he is lamenting for what he has lost. The *jñānīs* are also hankering, expecting to become one with God and merge into His existence. The yogīs are hankering after some magical powers to befool others into thinking that they have become God. In India, some yogīs convince people that they can manufacture gold and fly in the sky, and foolish people believe them. Even if a yogī can fly, there are many birds flying. What is the difference? An intelligent person can understand this. If a person says that he can walk on water, thousands of fools will come to see him. People will even pay ten rupees just to see a man bark like a dog, not thinking that there are many dogs barking anyway. In any case, people are always hankering and lamenting, but the devotee is fully satisfied in the service of the Lord. The devotee doesn't hanker for anything, nor does he lament.

Hayagrīva dāsa: Through *jñāna,* the path of meditation, it seems that Socrates realized Brahman. Could he also have realized Paramātmā?

Śrīla Prabhupāda: Yes.

Hayagrīva dāsa: But what of the realization of Bhagavān, Kṛṣṇa? I thought that Kṛṣṇa can be realized only through *bhakti.*

Śrīla Prabhupāda: Yes, no one can enter into Kṛṣṇa's abode without being a purified *bhakta.* That is stated in *Bhagavad-gītā:*

bhaktyā mām abhijānāti
yāvān yaś cāsmi tattvataḥ
tato māṁ tattvato jñātvā
viśate tad-anantaram

"One can understand the Supreme Personality as He is only by devotional service. And when one is in full consciousness of the Supreme Lord by such devotion, he can enter into the kingdom of God." (*Bg.* 18.55) Kṛṣṇa never says that He can be understood by *jñāna,* karma, or yoga. The personal abode of Kṛṣṇa is especially reserved for the *bhaktas,* and the *jñānīs,* yogīs, and *karmīs* cannot go there.

Śyāmasundara dāsa: When you say that Kṛṣṇa consciousness is the ultimate goal of life, does this mean always being conscious of Kṛṣṇa?

Śrīla Prabhupāda: Yes, we should always be thinking of Kṛṣṇa. We should act in such a way that we have to think of Kṛṣṇa all the time. For instance, we are discussing the philosophy of Socrates in order to strengthen our Kṛṣṇa consciousness. Therefore the ultimate goal is Kṛṣṇa. Otherwise, we are not interested in criticizing or accepting anyone's philosophy. We are neutral.

Śyāmasundara dāsa: So the proper use of intelligence is to guide everything in such a way that we become Kṛṣṇa conscious?

Śrīla Prabhupāda: That is it. Without Kṛṣṇa consciousness, we remain on the mental platform. Being on the mental platform means hovering. On that platform, we are not fixed. It is the business of the mind to accept this and reject that, but when we are fixed in Kṛṣṇa consciousness, we are no longer subjected to the mind's accepting and rejecting.

Śyāmasundara dāsa: Right conduct then becomes automatic?
Śrīla Prabhupāda: Yes. As soon as the mind wanders, we should immediately drag it back to concentrate on Kṛṣṇa. While chanting, our mind sometimes wanders far away, but when we become conscious of this, we should immediately bring the mind back to hear the sound vibration of Hare Kṛṣṇa. That is called *yoga-abhyās*, the practice of yoga. We should not allow the mind to wander elsewhere. We should simply chant and hear. That is the best yoga system.
Hayagrīva dāsa: In addition to believing in the value of insight, or meditation, Socrates also believed that knowledge can be imparted from one person to another. He therefore asserted the importance of a guru, which he himself was for many people. Sometimes, posing as an ignorant person, Socrates would question his disciples. He would not offer the answers but would try to draw them out of his disciples, a process known as the *maieutic* method. He considered himself to be a kind of midwife drawing the truth from the repository of the soul.
Śrīla Prabhupāda: This is similar to our method because we say that you must approach a guru in order to learn the truth. This is the instruction given in all the Vedic scriptures. In *Bhagavad-gītā*, Lord Kṛṣṇa Himself advises:

tad viddhi praṇipātena
paripraśnena sevayā
upadekṣyanti te jñānaṁ
jñāninas tattva-darśinaḥ

"Just try to learn the truth by approaching a spiritual master. Inquire from him submissively and render service unto him. The self-realized soul can impart knowledge unto you because he has seen the truth." (*Bg.* 4.34) A guru who knows the truth is one who has seen the truth. People say, "Can you show me God?" It is a natural tendency to want to know something by direct perception. This is possible by advanced devotion. As I have already explained: *santaḥ sadaiva hṛdayeṣu vilokayanti*. The realized devotee is constantly seeing the Supreme Personality of Godhead, Śyāmasundara. You can constantly see the Supreme Lord as Paramātmā sitting within your heart, and you can take advice from Him. Kṛṣṇa also confirms this: *buddhi-yogaṁ dadāmyaham*. Yoga means concentrating the mind in order to see the Supersoul within. Therefore you have to control the activities of the senses and withdraw them from material engagement. When your concentration is perfect, when your mind is focused on Paramātmā, you always see Him. In *Bhagavad-gītā*, Kṛṣṇa says:

yoginām api sarveṣāṁ
mad-gatenāntarātmanā
śraddhāvān bhajate yo māṁ
sa me yuktatamo mataḥ

'And of all yogīs, he who always abides in Me with great faith, worshipping Me in transcendental loving service, is most intimately united with Me in yoga and is the highest of all." (*Bg*. 6.47) The perfect yogī sees God constantly within. That is perfection. The process that Socrates used gave his disciples a good chance to develop their understanding. When a parent raises his child, he first of all takes his hand and teaches him how to walk. Sometimes he gives the child freedom to walk on his own, although he may sometimes fall down. The father then encourages the child, saying, "Ah, you are doing very nicely. Stand up again and walk." Similarly, the guru gives his disciple the chance to think properly in order to go back home, back to Godhead. Sometimes, when a person comes to argue, the guru says, "All right, what do you consider important?" In this way, the person's position is understood. An expert teacher knows how to capture a fool. First, let the fool go on and speak all sorts of nonsense. Then he can understand where he is having difficulty. That is also a process.

Śyāmasundara dāsa: Socrates recommended good association because if one is to develop good qualities, he must associate with those who are virtuous and similarly interested.

Śrīla Prabhupāda: That is very valuable. Without good association, we cannot develop Kṛṣṇa consciousness. Narottama dāsa Ṭhākura sings: *Tādera caraṇa-sebi-bhakta-sane bās janame janame hoy ei abhilāṣ*. "My dear Lord, please allow me to live with those devotees who serve the lotus feet of the six Gosvamis. This is my desire, life after life." (*Nāma-saṅkīrtana* 7) The aim of this Kṛṣṇa consciousness movement is to create a society in which devotees can associate with one another.

Hayagrīva dāsa: It has been said that Socrates's philosophy is primarily a philosophy of ethics, pointing to the way of action in the world. *Jñāna*, or knowledge in itself, is not sufficient. It must be applied, and must serve as a basis for activity.

Śrīla Prabhupāda: Yes, ethics form the basic principle of purification. We cannot be purified unless we know what is moral and what is immoral. Unfortunately, everything in this material world is more or less immoral, but we still have to distinguish between good and bad. Therefore we have regulative principles. By following them, we can come to the spiritual platform and transcend the influence of the three modes of material nature. Passion is the binding force in the material world. In a prison, prisoners are sometimes shackled, and similarly, material nature provides the shackles of sex life to bind us to this material world. This is the mode of *rajas*, passion. In *Bhagavad-gītā*, Kṛṣṇa says:

kāma eṣa krodha eṣa
rajoguṇa-samudbhavaḥ
mahā-śano mahā-pāpmā
viddhy enam iha vairiṇam

"It is lust only, Arjuna, which is born of contact with the material mode of passion and later transformed into wrath, and which is the all-devouring sinful enemy of this world." (*Bg.* 3.37) *Rajo-guṇa*, the mode of passion, includes *kāma*, lusty desires. When our lusty desires are not fulfilled, we become angry (*krodha*). All this binds us to the material world. As stated in *Śrīmad-Bhāgavatam:*

tadā rajas-tamo-bhāvāḥ
kāma-lobhādayaś ca ye
ceta etair anāviddhaṁ
sthitaṁ sattve prasīdati

"As soon as irrevocable loving service is established in the heart, the effect of nature's modes of passion and ignorance, such as lust, desire, and hankering, disappear from the heart. Then the devotee is established in goodness, and he becomes completely happy." (*Bhāg.* 1.2.19) When we are subjected to the lower material modes (*rajo-guṇa* and *tamo-guṇa*), we become greedy and lusty. Ethics provide a way to escape the clutches of greed and lust. Then we can come to the platform of goodness and from there attain the spiritual platform.

Hayagrīva dāsa: Is meditation in itself sufficient to transcend these lower modes?

Śrīla Prabhupāda: Yes. If we seek the Supersoul within, our meditation is perfect. But if we manufacture something in the name of transcendental meditation in order to bluff others, it is useless.

Śyāmasundara dāsa: Socrates believed that ignorance results in bad actions, and that the knowledgeable man will automatically act properly.

Śrīla Prabhupāda: When an ignorant child touches fire and is burned, he cries. His distress is due to ignorance. An intelligent person will not touch fire because he knows its properties. Thus ignorance is the cause of bondage and suffering. It is due to ignorance that people commit many sinful activities and become entangled.

Śyāmasundara dāsa: Does this mean that when people are enlightened with proper knowledge, they will automatically become good?
Śrīla Prabhupāda: Yes. It is stated in *Bhagavad-gītā:*

yathaidhāṁsi samiddho 'gnir
bhasmasāt kurute 'rjuna
jñānāgniḥ sarva-karmāṇi
bhasmasāt kurute tathā

"As the blazing fire turns firewood to ashes, O Arjuna, so does the fire of knowledge burn to ashes all reactions to material activities." (*Bg.* 4.37) The fire of knowledge consumes all sinful activities. To this end, there is need for education. People are born ignorant, and education is needed to remove their ignorance. Since they are born illusioned by the bodily conception, people act like animals. They therefore have to be educated to understand that they are different from the material body.
Śyāmasundara dāsa: Why is it that some people who receive this knowledge later reject it?
Śrīla Prabhupāda: Then it is not perfect knowledge. When one actually receives perfect knowledge, he becomes good. This is a fact. If one is not good, it is because he has not received perfect knowledge.
Śyāmasundara dāsa: Is there not a class of men that is always evil?
Śrīla Prabhupāda: No.
Śyāmasundara dāsa: Can any man be made good?
Śrīla Prabhupāda: Certainly, because the soul is by nature good. The living entity is covered by the inferior modes of material nature, by passion and ignorance. When he is cleansed of this covering, his goodness will emerge. The soul is originally good because it is part and parcel of God, and God is all good. That which is part and parcel of gold is also gold. Although the soul is covered by matter, the soul is all good. When a sharpened knife is covered by rust, it loses its sharpness. If we remove the rust, the knife will once again be sharp.
Śyāmasundara dāsa: Does the existence of evil in the world mean that there is absolute evil?
Śrīla Prabhupāda: Absolute evil means forgetfulness of the Absolute Truth. Kṛṣṇa is the Absolute Truth, and lack of Kṛṣṇa consciousness is absolute evil. In terms of the absolute evil, we may say that this is good and that is bad, but all this is mental concoction.
Śyāmasundara dāsa: Generally speaking, Socrates was more concerned with God as a moral reality than as a personal conception.
Śrīla Prabhupāda: Moral reality is necessarily personal. If a man is

moral, we say that he is honest. If he follows no moral principles, we say that he is dishonest. Thus morality and immorality refer to a person. How can we deny personal morality?
Śyāmasundara dāsa: Then if God is pure morality, He must be a person.
Śrīla Prabhupāda: Certainly. All good. God is good, and this means that He is full of morality.
Śyāmasundara dāsa: Socrates taught that good deeds bring happiness and that to perform them is the real goal of life.
Śrīla Prabhupāda: That is the law of karma. If I work hard in this life, I earn money. If I study hard, I acquire an education. However, if I neither work nor study, I remain poor and uneducated. This is the law of karma. According to the Vedic *varṇāśrama-dharma*, society is divided into four castes: *brāhmaṇa, kṣatriya, vaiśya,* and *śūdra.* Each caste has its particular duty, but that duty is connected to God's service. In other words, everyone can satisfy the Supreme Lord by performing his duty. By walking, the legs perform their duty, and by touching or holding, the hands perform their duty. Every part of the body performs a duty alotted to it. Similarly, we are all part and parcel of God, and if we do our duty, we are serving God. This is the system of *varṇāśrama-dharma.* Kṛṣṇa Himself says in *Bhagavad-gītā:*

cātur-varṇyaṁ mayā sṛṣṭaṁ
guṇa karma-vibhāgaśaḥ

"According to the three modes of material nature and the work ascribed to them, the four divisions of human society were created by Me." (*Bg.* 4.13)

It is further stated:

yataḥ pravṛttir bhūtānāṁ
yena sarvam idaṁ tatam
svakarmaṇā tam abhyarcya
siddhiṁ vindati mānavaḥ

"By worship of the Lord, who is the source of all beings, and who is all pervading, man can, in the performance of his own duty, attain perfection." (*Bg.* 18.46) Thus the respective duties of the *brāhmaṇa, kṣatriya, vaiśya,* or *śūdra* can be dovetailed to the service of the Lord, and by doing so, any man can attain perfection.
Śyāmasundara dāsa: Is moral improvement the highest goal of mankind, or is there something higher?
Śrīla Prabhupāda: First of all, we must understand what morality is. Morality means discharging our prescribed duties without hindering others in the execution of their duties. That is morality.

Śyāmasundara dāsa: What do you consider the shortcomings of a philosophy devoted to moral improvement and knowing oneself through pure reason alone?

Śrīla Prabhupāda: Knowing oneself through pure reason alone will take time. Of course, in European philosophy, there is an attempt at more independent thought, but such independent thinking is not approved by the followers of the Vedas. The Vedic followers receive knowledge directly from authorities. They do not speculate. We cannot attain knowledge through speculation because everyone is imperfect. A person may be proud of seeing, but he does not know that his eyesight is conditioned. Unless there is sunlight, he cannot see. Therefore, what is the intrinsic value of eyesight? We should not be very proud of seeing or thinking because our senses are imperfect. We therefore have to receive knowledge from the perfect. In this way, we save time.

According to the Vedic system, we receive knowledge from Vyāsadeva, Nārada, and Śrī Kṛṣṇa Himself. This knowledge is perfect because these personalities are not subjected to the four defects of conditioned living entities. The conditioned living entity has a tendency to commit mistakes, to be illusioned, to have imperfect senses, and to cheat. These are the four imperfections of conditional life. We therefore have to receive knowledge from those who are liberated. This is the Vedic process. If we receive knowledge from Kṛṣṇa, there cannot be any mistake, nor any question of illusion. Our senses may be imperfect, but Kṛṣṇa's senses are perfect; therefore whatever Kṛṣṇa says, we accept, and that acceptance is our perfection. A person may search for years to find out who his father is, but the immediate answer is available through his mother. The best way to solve this problem is by directly asking the mother. Similarly, all knowledge received from the perfect liberated person or from the mother Vedas is perfect.

Śyāmasundara dāsa: Socrates's emphasis was on humanity and ethical action. He said that our lives should be composed of good deeds because we can attain the highest perfection by being virtuous.

Śrīla Prabhupāda: Yes, to do good work is also recommended in *Śrīmad-Bhāgavatam*. It is possible to go home, back to Godhead, if we always work for the benefit of others. This Kṛṣṇa consciousness movement means benefitting others twenty-four hours a day. People are lacking knowledge of God, and we are preaching this knowledge. This is the highest humanitarian work: to elevate the ignorant to the platform of knowledge.

Śyāmasundara dāsa: But wouldn't you say that there is something more than moral improvement? Isn't that just a by-product of something else?

Śrīla Prabhupāda: Yes, real improvement is realizing God and our relationship with Him. In order to come to this platform, morality or purity is required. God is pure, and unless we are also pure, we cannot approach God. Therefore we are prohibiting meat eating, illicit sex, intoxication, and gambling. These are immoral habits that are always keeping us impure. Unless we abandon these impure habits, we cannot progress in Kṛṣṇa consciousness.
Śyāmasundara dāsa: Then morality is just a qualification for becoming God conscious, isn't it?
Śrīla Prabhupāda: If we take to Kṛṣṇa consciousness, we automatically become moral. On the one hand, we have to observe the regulative moral principles, and on the other hand we have to develop our tendency to serve Kṛṣṇa more and more. By serving Kṛṣṇa, we become moral. However, if we try to be moral without serving Kṛṣṇa, we will fail. Therefore so-called followers of morality are always frustrated. The goal is transcendental to human morality. We have to come to the platform of Kṛṣṇa consciousness in order to be truly moral. According to *Śrīmad-Bhāgavatam:*

yasyāsti bhaktir bhagavaty akiñcanā
sarvair guṇais tatra samāsate surāḥ
harāv abhaktasya kuto mahad-guṇā
manorathenāsati dhāvato bahiḥ

"All the demigods and their exalted qualities, such as religion, knowledge, and renunciation, become manifest in the body of one who has developed unalloyed devotion for the Supreme Personality of Godhead, Vāsudeva. On the other hand, a person devoid of devotional service and engaged in material activities has no good qualities. Even if he is adept at the practice of mystic yoga or the honest endeavor of maintaining his family and relatives, he must be driven by his own mental speculations and must engage in the service of the Lord's external energy. How can there be any good qualities in such a man?" (*Bhāg.* 5.18.12)

The conclusion is that we cannot be moral without being devotees. We may artificially try to be moral, but ultimately we will fail.
Śyāmasundara dāsa: By virtue of his intelligence, Socrates could keep his passions controlled, but most people do not have such intellectual strength. They are not able to control themselves rationally and act properly. How does Kṛṣṇa consciousness help in this endeavor?
Śrīla Prabhupāda: Kṛṣṇa consciousness purifies the intelligence, the mind, and the senses. Since everything is purified, there is no chance in being employed in anything but Kṛṣṇa consciousness. Anyone can do

this under the proper guidance, whereas not everyone can do as Socrates did. The common man does not have sufficient intelligence to control himself without spiritual exercise. Yet, despite his intelligence, Socrates had no clear conception of God. In *Bhagavad-gītā*, Arjuna tells Śrī Kṛṣṇa:

paraṁ brahma paraṁ dhāma
pavitraṁ paramaṁ bhavān
puruṣaṁ śāśvataṁ divyam
ādi-devam ajaṁ vibhum

"You are the Supreme Brahman, the ultimate, the supreme abode and purifier, the Absolute Truth, and the eternal Divine Person. You are the primal God, transcendental and original, and You are the unborn and all-pervading beauty." (*Bg.* 10.12)

The word *pavitram* means "the purest." This includes all morality. Acting in Kṛṣṇa consciousness is the best morality, and this is supported in *Bhagavad-gītā:*

api cet sudurācāro
bhajate mām ananya-bhāk
sādhur eva sa mantavyaḥ
samyag vyavasito hi saḥ

"Even if one commits the most abominable actions, if he is engaged in devotional service, he is to be considered saintly because he is properly situated." (*Bg.* 9.30) Even if a person is considered immoral from the mundane point of view, he should be regarded as moral if he acts on the platform of Kṛṣṇa consciousness. Sometimes a person in Kṛṣṇa consciousness may appear to act immorally. For instance, in the dead of night, the young cowherd girls of Vṛndāvana left their husbands and fathers to go to the forest to see Kṛṣṇa. From the materialistic point of view, this is immoral, but because their actions were connected with Kṛṣṇa, they are considered highly moral. By nature, Arjuna was not inclined to kill, even at the risk of his kingdom, but Kṛṣṇa wanted him to fight; therefore Arjuna entered the battle and acted morally, even though he was killing people.

Śyāmasundara dāsa: Then, you are saying that morality is absolute as long as it is in relation with Kṛṣṇa?

Śrīla Prabhupāda: If Kṛṣṇa or His representative says, "Do this," that act is moral. We cannot create morality. We cannot say, "I am a devotee of Kṛṣṇa; therefore I can kill." No. We cannot do anything unless we receive a direct order.

Śyāmasundara dāsa: But can leading a life that is honest, or based on

doing good to others, lead us to ultimate happiness?
Śrīla Prabhupāda: Unless we are Kṛṣṇa conscious, there is no meaning to honesty and morality. They are artificial. People are always saying, "This is mine." But our accepting proprietorship is actually immoral because nothing belongs to us. *Īśāvāsyam idaṁ sarvam* (*Īśopaniṣad* 1). Everything belongs to Kṛṣṇa. We cannot say, "This table is mine. This wife is mine. This house is mine." It is immoral to claim another's property as our own.
Śyāmasundara dāsa: Socrates defines right as that which is beneficial to others, and wrong as that which does harm to others.
Śrīla Prabhupāda: That is a general definition, but we should know what is beneficial for others. Kṛṣṇa consciousness is beneficial, and anything else is not beneficial.
Śyāmasundara dāsa: For instance, he states that stealing, lying, cheating, hating, and other evils, are absolutely bad. Yet if there is a necessity to cheat or lie in order to serve Kṛṣṇa, would that be bad?
Śrīla Prabhupāda: Cheating and lying are not necessary. By cheating, we cannot serve Kṛṣṇa. That is not the principle. However, if Kṛṣṇa directly orders us to cheat, that is a different matter. But we cannot create that order. We cannot say, "Because I am Kṛṣṇa conscious, it is all right for me to cheat." No. However, once Kṛṣṇa asked Yudhiṣṭhira to go tell Droṇācārya that his son was dead, although his son was not. This was a kind of cheating, but because Kṛṣṇa directly ordered it, it was all right. Orders from Kṛṣṇa are transcendental to everything—morality and immorality. In Kṛṣṇa consciousness, there is neither morality nor immorality. There is simply good.
Hayagrīva dāsa: The Athenian government accused Socrates of fostering atheism and blaspheming the gods because he felt that worship of the demigods in the Greek pantheon did not lead to self-realization.
Śrīla Prabhupāda: Yes, Socrates was right. Worship of the demigods is also discouraged in *Bhagavad-gītā:*

kāmais tais tair hṛta-jñānāḥ
prapadyante'nya-devatāḥ
taṁ taṁ niyamam āsthāya
prakṛtyā niyatāḥ svayā

"Those whose minds are distorted by material desires surrender unto demigods and follow the particular rules and regulations of worship according to their own natures." (*Bg.* 7.20) Demigods are worshipped out of lust for some material benefit by one who has lost his intelligence (*hṛta-jñāna*). You may worship the demigod Sarasvatī, the goddess of learning, and thereby become a great scholar, but how long will you remain a scholar? When your body dies, your scholarly knowledge is finished. Then you have to accept another body and act accordingly. So how will scholastic knowledge help you? However, if you worship God Himself, the results are different.

janma karma ca me divyam
evaṁ yo vetti tattvataḥ
tyaktvā dehaṁ punar janma
naiti mām eti so'rjuna

"One who knows the transcendental nature of My appearance and activities does not, upon leaving the body, take his birth again in this material world, but attains My eternal abode, O Arjuna." (*Bg.* 4.9) To worship God means to know God. Knowing God means understanding how material nature is working under His directions. Kṛṣṇa says:

mayādhyakṣena prakṛtiḥ
sūyate sa-carācaram
hetunānena kaunteya
jagad viparivartate

"This material nature is working under My direction, O son of Kuntī, and it is producing all moving and unmoving beings. By its rule this manifestation is created and annihilated again and again." (*Bg.* 9.10) Because impersonalists cannot understand how a person can direct the wonderful activities of material nature, they remain impersonalists. But actually God is a person, and this is the understanding we get from *Bhagavad-gītā:*

mattaḥ parataraṁ nānyat
kiñcid asti dhanañjaya
mayi sarvam idaṁ protaṁ
sūtre maṇi-gaṇā iva

"O conqueror of wealth [Arjuna], there is no Truth superior to Me. Everything rests upon Me, as pearls are strung on a thread." (*Bg.* 7.7) The word *mattaḥ* refers to a person.

ahaṁ sarvasya prabhavo
mattaḥ sarvaṁ pravartate
iti matvā bhajante māṁ
budhā bhāva-samanvitāḥ

"I am the source of all spiritual and material worlds. Everything emanates from Me. The wise who know this perfectly engage in My devotional service and worship Me with all their hearts." (*Bg.* 10.8)

The *Vedānta-sūtra* also confirms that the Absolute Truth is a person, and when Arjuna understood *Bhagavad-gītā*, he addressed Kṛṣṇa as *paraṁ brahma paraṁ dhāma pavitraṁ paramaṁ bhavān.* "You are the Supreme Brahman, the ultimate, the supreme abode and purifier, the Absolute Truth, and the eternal Divine Person." (*Bg.* 10.12) Understanding the Absolute Truth means understanding the three features of the Absolute Truth: the impersonal, the localized, and the personal.

vadanti tat tattva-vidas
tattvaṁ yaj jñānam advayam
brahmeti paramātmeti
bhagavān iti śabdyate

"Learned transcendentalists who know the Absolute Truth call this nondual substance Brahman, Paramātmā, and Bhagavān." (*Bhāg.* 1.2.11) The Absolute Truth is one, but there are different features. One mountain seen from different distances appears different. From a far distance, the Absolute Truth appears impersonal, but as you approach, you see Paramātmā present everywhere. When you come even nearer, you can perceive Bhagavān, the Supreme Person.

Śyāmasundara dāsa: Socrates deliberately took poison in order not to contradict himself. The government told him that if he retracted his statements, he could live, but he preferred to be a martyr for his own beliefs.

Śrīla Prabhupāda: It is good that he stuck to his point, yet regrettable that he lived in a society that would not permit him to think independently. Therefore he was obliged to die. In that sense, Socrates was a great soul. Although he appeared in a society that was not very advanced, he was nonetheless a great philosopher.

Hayagrīva dāsa: Socrates considered the contemplation of beauty to be an activity of the wise man, but relative beauty in the mundane world is simply a reflection of absolute beauty. In the same way, good in the relative world is but a reflection of the absolute good. In any case, absolute good or beauty is transcendental.

Śrīla Prabhupāda: Yes, that is also our view. Beauty, knowledge, strength, wealth, fame, and renunciation are all transcendental. In this material world, everything is a perverted reflection. A foolish animal may run after a mirage in the desert, thinking it water, but a sane man knows better. Although there is no water in the desert, we cannot conclude that there is no water at all. Water certainly exists. Similarly, real happiness, beauty, knowledge, strength, and the other opulences exist in the spiritual world, but here they are only reflected pervertedly. Generally, people have no information of the spiritual world; therefore they have to imagine something spiritual. They do not understand that this material world is imaginary.

janma karma ca me divyam
evaṁ yo vetti tattvataḥ
tyaktvā dehaṁ punar janma
naiti mām eti so'rjuna

"One who knows the transcendental nature of My appearance and activities does not, upon leaving the body, take his birth again in this material world, but attains My eternal abode, O Arjuna." (*Bg.* 4.9) Although people are reading *Bhagavad-gītā*, they cannot understand this very simple point. After giving up the material body, the devotee goes to Kṛṣṇa. Of course, the Christians say that after death, one goes to heaven or hell, and to some extent that is a fact. If we understand Kṛṣṇa in this lifetime, we can go to Kṛṣṇa's eternal abode; otherwise, we remain in this material world to undergo the same cycle of birth and death. That is hell.

Hayagrīva dāsa: At the conclusion of *The Republic*, Socrates gives the analogy of humanity living within a dark cave. The self-realized teacher has seen the light outside the cave. When he returns to the cave to inform the people that they are in darkness, many consider him crazy for speaking of such a thing as the light outside. Thus the teacher often puts himself in a very dangerous position.

Śrīla Prabhupāda: That is a fact. We often give the example of a frog within a dark well, thinking that his well is everything. When he is informed that there is an Atlantic Ocean, he cannot conceive of such a great quantity of water. Those who are in the dark well of material existence are surprised to hear that there is light outside. Everyone in the material world is suffering in the dark well of material existence, and we are throwing down this rope called Kṛṣṇa consciousness. If people do not catch hold, what can we do? If you are fortunate, you can capture the Lord with the help of the teacher, but it is up to you to catch hold of the rope. Everyone is trying to get out of the misery of material existence. Therefore Kṛṣṇa says:

sarva-dharmān parityajya
mām ekaṁ śaranaṁ vraja
ahaṁ tvāṁ sarva-pāpebhyo
mokṣayiṣyāmi mā śucaḥ

"Abandon all varieties of religion and just surrender unto Me. I shall deliver you from all sinful reaction. Do not fear." (*Bg.* 18.66) Still, due to obstinance, people refuse, or do not believe Him. The Vedas also tell us, "Don't remain in the dark well. Come out into the light." Unfortunately, people want to become perfect and yet remain in the dark well. This material universe is by nature dark, and therefore Kṛṣṇa has supplied the sun and moon for light. Yet there is Kṛṣṇa's kingdom, which is different, as Kṛṣṇa Himself tells us in *Bhagavad-gītā:*

na tad bhāsayate sūryo
na śaśāṅko na pāvakaḥ
yad gatvā na nivartante
tad dhāma paramaṁ mama

"That abode of Mine is not illumined by the sun or moon, nor by electricity. One who reaches it never returns to this material world." (*Bg.* 15.6) In Kṛṣṇa's kingdom there is no need for sun, moon, or electricity. His kingdom is all effulgent. In the darkness of this material world, the only happiness is in sleep and sex. As stated in *Śrīmad-Bhāgavatam:*

śrotavyādīni rājendra
nṛṇāṁ santi sahasraśaḥ
apaśyatām ātma-tattvaṁ
gṛheṣu gṛha-medhinām

nidrayā hriyate naktaṁ
vyavāyena ca vā vayaḥ
divā cārthehayā rājan
kuṭumba-bharaṇena vā

"Those who are materially engrossed, being blind to the knowledge of ultimate truth, are interested in hearing about many different subjects, O Emperor. The lifetime of such envious householders is passed at night either in sleeping or in sex indulgence, and in the day either in making money or maintaining family members." (*Bhāg.* 2.1.2-3)

Materialists spend much time reading newspapers, novels, and magazines. They have many forms of engagement because they are ignorant of self-realization. They think that life simply means living in a family surrounded by their wife, children, and friends. They work hard during the day for money, racing their cars at breakneck speed, and at night they either sleep or enjoy sex. This is just like the life of a hog constantly searching for stool. Yet all of this is taking place in the name of civilization. This kind of hoggish civilization is condemned in the Vedic literatures. Kṛṣṇa advises us to produce grains, eat fruits, vegetables, drink milk, and cultivate Kṛṣṇa consciousness. In this way, we can become happy.

Hayagrīva dāsa: Socrates speaks of everyone sitting in the cave, watching a kind of cinema composed of imitation forms.

Śrīla Prabhupāda: This means that people are in darkness, and everything seen in darkness is not clear. Therefore the Vedic version is: "Don't remain in darkness. Come to the light." That light is the guru.

om ajñāna-timirāndhasya jñānāñjana-śalākayā
cakṣur unmīlitaṁ yena tasmai śrī-gurave namaḥ

"I was born in the darkest ignorance, and my spiritual master opened my eyes with the torch of knowledge. I offer my respectful obeisances unto him." (*Śrī Guru Praṇāma*)

Plato
(427-347 B.C.)

Hayagrīva dāsa: For Plato, the spiritual world is not a mental conception; rather, truth is the same as ultimate reality, the ideal or the highest good, and it is from this that all manifestations and cognitions flow. Plato uses the word *eidos* (idea) in order to denote a subject's primordial existence, its archetypal shape. Doesn't Kṛṣṇa use the word *bījam* [seed] in much the same way?

Śrīla Prabhupāda: Yes. *Bījaṁ māṁ sarva-bhūtānām.* "I am the original seed of all existences." (*Bg.* 7.10) In the Tenth Chapter of *Bhagavad-gītā*, Kṛṣṇa also states: *mattaḥ sarvaṁ pravartate.* "I am the source of all spiritual and material worlds. Everything emanates from Me." (*Bg.* 10.8) Whether we speak of the spiritual or material world, everything emanates from Kṛṣṇa, the origin of all manifestations. The origin is what is factual. God has two energies—material and spiritual. This is also described in *Bhagavad-gītā:*

bhūmir āpo 'nalo vāyuḥ
khaṁ mano buddhir eva ca
ahaṅkāra itīyaṁ me
bhinnā prakṛtir aṣṭadhā

apareyam itas tv anyāṁ
prakṛtiṁ viddhi me parām
jīva-bhūtāṁ mahā-bāho
yayedaṁ dhāryate jagat

etad yonīni bhūtāni
sarvāṇīty upadhāraya
ahaṁ kṛtsnasya jagataḥ
prabhavaḥ pralayas tathā

"Earth, water, fire, air, ether, mind, intelligence, and false ego—altogether these eight comprise My separated material energies. Besides this inferior nature, O mighty-armed Arjuna, there is a superior energy of Mine, which is all living entities who are struggling with material nature and sustaining the universe. Of all that is material and all that is spiritual in this world, know for certain that I am both its origin and dissolution." (*Bg.* 7.4-6)

Gross matter, as well as the subtle mind, intelligence, and ego, are Kṛṣṇa's separated material energies. The living entity, the individual soul (*jīva*) is also Kṛṣṇa's energy, but he is superior to the material energy. When we make a comparative study of Kṛṣṇa's energies, we find that one energy is superior and that another is inferior, but because both energies are coming from the Absolute Truth, there is no difference. In a higher sense, they are all one. In the material world, everything is created, maintained, and then annihilated, but in the spiritual world, this is not the case. Although the body is created, maintained, and annihilated, the soul is not.

na jāyate mriyate vā kadācin
nāyaṁ bhūtvā bhavitā vā na bhūyaḥ
ajo nityaḥ śāśvato'yaṁ purāṇo
na hanyate hanyamāne śarīre

"For the soul, there is never birth nor death. Nor having once been, does he ever cease to be. He is unborn, eternal, ever-existing, undying, and primeval. He is not slain when the body is slain." (*Bg.* 2.20) At death, the soul may take on another body, but one who is perfect goes directly to Kṛṣṇa.

janma karma ca me divyam
evaṁ yo vetti tattvataḥ
tyaktvā dehaṁ punar janma
naiti mām eti so'rjuna

"One who knows the transcendental nature of My appearance and activities does not, upon leaving the body, take his birth again in this material world, but attains My eternal abode, O Arjuna." (*Bg.* 4.9)

Or, one may go to the higher planetary systems, or the lower, or one may remain in the middle systems. In any case, it is better to go back to Godhead. This is the course of one who is intelligent.

yānti deva-vratā devān
pitṛn yānti pitṛ-vratāḥ
bhūtāni yānti bhūtejyā
yānti mad-yājino'pi mām

"Those who worship the demigods will take birth among the demigods; those who worship ghosts and spirits will take birth among such beings; those who worship ancestors go to the ancestors; and those who worship Me will live with Me." (*Bg.* 9.25)

Hayagrīva dāsa: What Plato is saying is that everything that exists has its seed or essence (*eidos*).

Śrīla Prabhupāda: That seed is originally with Kṛṣṇa. For instance, before its manifestation, a tree is but a seed. Yet within that seed the whole tree is present. If you sow the seed of a rose plant, roses will manifest. If you sow the seed of a mango tree, a mango tree will manifest. It is not an idea but a fact. The tree is there, but it is not developed. Although it is unmanifest, it is more than an idea.

Śyāmasundara dāsa: The senses perceive the changing phenomenal world, but according to Plato, the noumenal world is perceived by the mind. It is this world that is absolute, ideal, permanent, and universal. Would you say that ultimate reality is ideal in this Platonic sense?

Śrīla Prabhupāda: Not ideal—factual. *Paraṁ satyaṁ dhīmahi.* "We offer our obeisances unto the Absolute Truth." This relative world is a perverted reflection of the absolute world. It is just like a shadow. A tree reflected in the water may appear to be exactly like the tree itself, but it is a perverted reflection. The actual tree is there. Similarly, this relative world is a reflection of the absolute world. In the beginning of *Śrīmad-Bhāgavatam*, it is clearly stated that this manifested creation, which is but a reflection, has its beginning in the Supreme Personality of Godhead:

janmādy asya yato 'nvayād itarataś cārtheṣv abhijñaḥ svarāṭ
tene brahma hṛdā ya ādi-kavaye muhyanti yat sūrayaḥ
tejo-vāri-mṛdāṁ yathā vinimayo yatra tri-sargo 'mṛṣā
dhāmnā svena sadā nirasta-kuhakaṁ satyaṁ paraṁ dhīmahi

"I meditate upon Lord Śrī Kṛṣṇa because He is the Absolute Truth and the primeval cause of all causes of the creation, sustenance, and destruction of the manifested universes. He is directly and indirectly conscious of all manifestations, and He is independent because there is no other cause beyond Him. It is He only who first imparted the Vedic knowledge unto the heart of Brahmājī, the original living being. By Him, even the great sages and demigods are placed into illusion, as one is bewildered by the illusory representations of water seen in fire, or land seen on water. Only because of Him do the material universes, temporarily manifested by the reactions of the three modes of nature, appear factual, although they are unreal. I therefore meditate upon Him, Lord Śrī Kṛṣṇa, who is eternally existent in the transcendental abode, which is forever free from the illusory representations of the material world. I meditate upon Him, for He is the Absolute Truth." (*Bhāg.* 1.1.1)

In *Bhagavad-gītā*, the example of the banyan tree is given:

ūrdhva-mūlam adhaḥ-śākham
aśvatthaṁ prāhur avyayam
chandāṁsi yasya parṇāni
yas taṁ veda sa veda-vit

"There is a banyan tree which has its roots upward and its branches down, and whose leaves are the Vedic hymns. One who knows this tree is the knower of the Vedas." (*Bg.* 15.1) The tree of the phenomenal world has its roots upward, which indicates that it is but a reflection of the real tree. The real tree is there, but because the tree perceived in the phenomenal world is a reflection, it is perverted. So the absolute world is a fact, but we cannot arrive at it by speculation. Our process is to know about the absolute world from the absolute person. That is the difference between our process and Plato's. Plato wants to reach the absolute point through the dialectic process. We, however, receive information from *Bhagavad-gītā* that there is a superior world or nature which exists even after this phenomenal cosmic manifestation is annihilated.

paras tasmāt tu bhāvo'nyo
'vyakto 'vyaktāt sanātanaḥ
yaḥ sa sarveṣu bhūteṣu
naśyatsu na vinaśyati

"Yet there is another nature, which is eternal and is transcendental to this manifested and unmanifested matter. It is supreme and is never annihilated. When all in this world is annihilated, that part remains as it is." (*Bg.* 8.20)

Hayagrīva dāsa: Plato considered the material world restricted to limitations of time and space, but the spiritual world transcends both.

Śrīla Prabhupāda: Yes.

Hayagrīva dāsa: He also believed that time began with the creation of the material world. How does this relate to the Vedic version?
Śrīla Prabhupāda: Time is eternal. The past, present, and future are three features of time, but they are relative. Your past, present, and future are not the same as those of Brahmā. Brahmā lives for millions of years, and within this span we may have many pasts, presents, and futures. These are relative according to the person, but time itself is eternal. Is that clear? Past, present, and future are relative according to the body, but time has no past, present, or future.
Hayagrīva dāsa: Plato considered material nature, or *prakṛti*, to have always been existing in a chaotic state. God takes matter and fashions it into form in order to create the universe.
Śrīla Prabhupāda: More precisely, Kṛṣṇa sets *prakṛti* in motion, and the products are manifesting automatically. A printer may set up a press in such a way that many magazines can be printed completely. The seeds, or *bījams*, are created by God in such a way that creations are manifest automatically. These seeds are God's machines. He has created these seeds only. The seed of the entire universe is coming from Him. *Yasyaika niśvasita kālam athāvalambya* (*Brahma-saṁhitā* 5.48). When God breathes, millions of seeds of universes emanate from His body, and we call this creation. When He inhales, they return, and we call this annihilation. Things are manifest or unmanifest depending on His breathing. When He exhales, everything is manifest. When He inhales, everything is finished. Only a fool thinks that God's breathing and our breathing are the same. *Bhagavad-gītā* says:

avajānanti māṁ mūḍhā
mānusiṁ tanum āśritam
paraṁ bhāvam ajānanto
mama bhūta-maheśvaram

"Fools deride Me when I descend in the human form. They do not know My transcendental nature and My supreme dominion over all that be." (*Bg*. 9.11) Even Lord Brahmā and Lord Indra were bewildered to see that this cowherd boy is God Himself.
Śyāmasundara dāsa: Plato's word for God is *demiurge*, which in Greek means master builder, architect, or hand-worker.
Śrīla Prabhupāda: In Sanskrit this is called *sṛṣti-kartā*, but this conception is secondary. Lord Brahmā is *sṛṣti-kartā*, and Brahmā is inspired by Kṛṣṇa. The original master, Kṛṣṇa, is not *sṛṣti-kartā* because He does not do anything directly. As stated in the Vedas: *svā-bhāvikī jñāna-bala-kriyā ca*. "His potencies are multifarious, and thus His deeds are au-

tomatically performed as a natural sequence." (*Śvetāśvatara-upaniṣad* 6.8). As soon as He wants something done, it is actualized. *Sa aikṣata—sa imāl lokān asrjata* (*Aitareya-upaniṣad* 1.1.1-2). When He glances at matter, creation takes place immediately. His energy is so perfect that simply by willing and glancing, everything is immediately and perfectly created. For instance, this flower is Kṛṣṇa's energy. It requires a highly talented brain to color it and adjust it in such a way, but it is growing automatically. This is the way of Kṛṣṇa's energy. This flower is a very small thing, but the entire cosmic manifestation is created on the same basis. *Parāsya śaktir vividhaiva śrūyate.* Kṛṣṇa has multi-energies, fine and subtle. As soon as Kṛṣṇa thinks, "This thing must come into being immediately," that thing is prepared by so many subtle energies. Kṛṣṇa doesn't have to do anything with His hands. He simply desires something, and it is created. Lord Brahmā is supposed to be the direct creator of the universe, but there are millions of universes and millions of Brahmās. There are also millions of suns and other luminaries. There is no limit, and all this material creation is but the energy of Kṛṣṇa.

Śyāmasundara dāsa: Plato conceives of God as the essence of perfection, the supreme ideal, and the supreme good.

Śrīla Prabhupāda: According to Parāśara Muni, perfection belongs to Him who has complete knowledge, wealth, beauty, power, fame, and renunciation. God has everything in full, and there is no vacancy in Him.

Śyāmasundara dāsa: Plato's philosophy points to a personal conception, but there is no idea of what God looks like, or what He says.

Śrīla Prabhupāda: The Vedic literatures not only present this person but describe Him.

veṇuṁ kvaṇantam aravinda-dalāyatākṣaṁ
barhāvataṁsam asitāmbuda-sundarāṅgam
kandarpa-koṭi-kamanīya-viśeṣa-śobhaṁ
govindam ādi-puruṣaṁ tam ahaṁ bhajāmi

"I worship Govinda, the primeval Lord, who is adept in playing on His flute, whose blossoming eyes are like lotus petals, whose head is bedecked with a peacock's feather, whose figure of beauty is tinged with the hue of blue clouds, and whose unique loveliness charms millions of Cupids." (*Brahma-saṁhitā* 5.30) In this way, Lord Kṛṣṇa's form and activities are concretely described. In the Vedas, everything is factual. Plato thinks that the creator may be a person, but he does not know what kind of person He is, nor does he know of His engagements.

Hayagrīva dāsa: Later, in *The Republic*, in the allegory of the cave mentioned before, Socrates states that in the world of knowledge, the last thing to be perceived, and only with great difficulty, is the essential form of goodness. He considers this form to be the cause of whatever is right and good. He states that without having had a vision of this form, one cannot act with wisdom, neither in his own life, nor in matters of state. Here again, form is mentioned, but not personality.

Śrīla Prabhupāda: That is contradictory. As soon as we understand that there are instructions from God, we must understand that there is form, and when we understand that there is form, we must understand that there is personality. In *Bhagavad-gītā*, Kṛṣṇa tells Arjuna:

na tv evāhaṁ jātu nāsaṁ
na tvaṁ neme janādhipāḥ
na caiva na bhaviṣyāmaḥ
sarve vayam ataḥ param

"Never was there a time when I did not exist, nor you, nor all these kings; nor in the future shall any of us cease to be." (*Bg*. 2.12) This means that in the past, present, and future, Kṛṣṇa, Arjuna, and all other living entities exist as personalities and have form. There is no question of formlessness. Kṛṣṇa never said that in the past we were formless and that only in the present we have form. Rather, He condemns the impersonal version that says when God takes on form, that form is illusion, māyā.

avyaktaṁ vyaktim āpannaṁ
manyante mām abuddhayaḥ
paraṁ bhāvam ajānanto
mamāvyayam anuttamam

"Unintelligent men, who know Me not, think that I have assumed this form and personality. Due to their small knowledge, they do not know My higher nature, which is changeless and supreme." (*Bg*. 7.24) In this way, the impersonalists who claim that God is ultimately formless are condemned as *abuddhayah*, unintelligent. When one maintains that God accepts a body composed of māyā, he is called a Māyāvādī.

Śyāmasundara dāsa: For Plato, God is the ideal of every object, the ideal representation of everything. The individual soul is therefore a tiny portion of this ideal.

Śrīla Prabhupāda: The material world is a perverted reflection of the spiritual world. For instance, in this material world there is love, the sex urge. This is also present in the spiritual world, but it is present in its perfection. There is beauty, and there is attraction between Kṛṣṇa, a young boy, and Rādhārāṇī, a young girl. But that attraction is perfection.

In this world, that attraction is reflected in a perverted way. A young boy and girl fall in love, become frustrated, and separate. Therefore this is called perverted. Nonetheless, reality is there, and in reality there is no separation. It is perfect. That love is so nice that it is increasing pleasure.
Śyāmasundara dāsa: Plato called love in the material world lust, or sensual love. There was also ideal, Platonic love, or intellectual love. By this, one observes the soul in a person and loves that soul, not the body.
Śrīla Prabhupāda: Yes, spiritual love is factual. It is stated in *Bhagavad-gītā:*

vidyā-vinaya-sampanne
brāhmaṇe gavi hastini
śuni caiva śvapāke ca
paṇḍitāḥ sama-darśinaḥ

"The humble sage, by virtue of true knowledge, sees with equal vision a learned and gentle *brāhmaṇa,* a cow, an elephant, a dog, and a dog-eater [outcaste]." (*Bg.* 5.18) The learned person sees all these living entities with an equal vision because he does not see the outward covering. He sees the spirit soul within everyone. When we talk to a person, we do not talk to that person's dress but to the person himself. Similarly, those who are learned do not distinguish between outward bodies. The outward body has developed according to the karma of the living entity, but it is ephemeral. It is the soul that is real.
Hayagrīva dāsa: For Plato, perfection within the world of the senses can never be attained.
Śrīla Prabhupada: Yes, that is correct. Everything material has some defect. In *Bhagavad-gītā,* Kṛṣṇa tells Arjuna:

saha-jaṁ karma kaunteya
sa-doṣam api na tyajet
sarvārambhā hi doṣena
dhūmenāgnir ivāvṛtāḥ

"Every endeavor is covered by some sort of fault, just as fire is covered by smoke. Therefore one should not give up the work which is born of his nature, O son of Kuntī, even if such work is full of fault." (*Bg.* 18.48) If we execute our prescribed duties according to the *śāstras,* we can still attain perfection, even though there are some defects. Through Kṛṣṇa consciousness, everyone can become perfect, regardless of his situation. A *brāhmaṇa* may give knowledge, a *kṣatriya* may give protection, a *vaiśya* may provide food, and a *śūdra* may provide general help for everyone. Although there may be imperfections in the execution of our duty, perfection can be attained by following the injunctions.

Śyāmasundara dāsa: Plato perceives man's soul in a marginal, intermediate position between two worlds. The soul belongs to the ideal world, but he has taken on a material body.

Śrīla Prabhupāda: Yes, we agree that the conditioned soul is marginal energy. He can have a spiritual body or a material body, but until he is trained in acquiring a spiritual body, he will have to have a material body. However, when he engages in devotional service, his so-called material body is transformed into a spiritual body. For instance, if you put an iron rod into fire, it becomes red hot, and when it is red hot, it is no longer iron but fire. Similarly, when you are fully Kṛṣṇa conscious, your body is no longer material but spiritual.

Hayagrīva dāsa: Plato believed that God put intelligence in the soul, and the soul in the body, in order that He might be the creator of a work which is by nature best.

Śrīla Prabhupāda: We say that the living entity is part and parcel of God.

mamaivāṁśo jīva-loke
jīva-bhūtaḥ sanātanaḥ

"The living entities in this conditioned world are My eternal, fragmental parts." (*Bg.* 15.7) The living entity almost has all the qualities of God, but he has them in minute quantity. We may create large airplanes and take some credit, but we cannot create a fiery ball like the sun and have it float in space. That is the difference between God and us. By God's power, millions and millions of planets are floating in space. We may manufacture some things out of the materials given by God, but we cannot create these materials. For instance, it is not possible to manufacture gold, although God has created so many gold mines.

Śyāmasundara dāsa: Plato reasoned that the soul, being eternal, must have existed previously in the ideal world, where it learned about eternal principles. Because we can recollect the eternal ideas quite easily, they are latent, or dormant within us.

Śrīla Prabhupāda: The soul is eternally spiritual, and therefore all goodness resides in it. But due to contact with matter, the soul becomes conditioned. When the soul engages in his original work by rendering service to Kṛṣṇa, he immediately attains all spiritual qualities.

Śyāmasundara dāsa: For Plato, the longing for immortality is inborn. Man is yearning to realize this perfection.

Śrīla Prabhupāda: Yes, we desire to live eternally because we are in fact eternal. The living entity does not like changing material bodies. Birth and death are a botheration. He is afraid of taking birth, and he is afraid of dying, but he does not know how to get rid of these botherations. However, according to *Bhagavad-gītā* (4.9), as soon as we understand Kṛṣṇa, we immediately transcend this transmigration.

Hayagrīva dāsa: Plato perceives that every object in the universe is made with some purpose, and its ideal goal is to move toward the ideal in which its archetype or essence resides. According to the Vedic version, Kṛṣṇa is the all-attractive object of the universe; therefore all things must be moving toward Him. How is it that the individual soul apparently turns from Kṛṣṇa to participate in the world of birth and death?

Śrīla Prabhupāda: That is due to māyā, illusion. He should not have deviated, but due to the influence of māyā, he is deviating and consequently suffering. Therefore Kṛṣṇa says, *sarva-dharmān parityajya mām ekam (Bg.* 18.66). "Stop this material plan making, surrender unto Me, and do what I say. Then you will be happy." This is very practical. According to *Bhagavad-gītā,* the living entities are now forgetful of their relationship with God. They have taken on these material bodies because they have a desire to imitate God. They cannot be God, but simply imitations. A woman may dress like a man, but she cannot become a man despite her dress. The living entity, being part and parcel of God, may believe that he is just like God, the supreme enjoyer, and he may think, "I shall enjoy myself." However, because he is not the actual enjoyer, he is given a false platform for enjoying. That platform is the material world. On this false platform, the individual soul experiences frustration. It cannot be said that this frustration is one step forward towards his real life. If one is actually intelligent, he thinks, "Why am I being frustrated? What is real perfection?" This is the beginning of the *Vedānta-sūtra: athāto brahma-jijñāsā.* When he becomes frustrated with the material world, the living entity asks, "What is Brahman?" For instance, Sanātana Gosvāmī was a finance minister, but when he became frustrated, he approached Caitanya Mahāprabhu. Our real life begins when we become frustrated with material existence and approach a real spiritual master. If we do not do this, we will certainly be frustrated in whatever we attempt in this material world. *Śrīmad-Bhāgavatam* says:

parābhavas tāvad abodha-jāto
yāvan na jijñāsata ātma-tattvam
yāvat kriyās tāvad idaṁ mano vai
karmātmakaṁ yena śarīra-bandhaḥ

"As long as one does not inquire about the spiritual values of life, one is defeated and subjected to miseries arising from ignorance. Be it sinful or pious, karma has its resultant actions. If a person is engaged in any kind of karma, his mind is called *karmātmaka*, colored with fruitive activity. As long as the mind is impure, consciousness is unclear, and as long as one is absorbed in fruitive activity, he has to accept a material body." (*Bhāg.* 5.5.5)

In ignorance, the living entity tries to approach the ideal life, but he is ultimately defeated. He must come to the point of understanding himself. When he understands what he is, he knows, "I am not matter; I am spirit." When he understands this, he begins to make spiritual inquiries, and by this, he can again return home, back to Godhead.

Śyāmasundara dāsa: Plato believes that we must mold our lives in such a way as to attain perfection.

Śrīla Prabhupāda: That is Kṛṣṇa consciousness, devotional service. We are the eternal servants of God, of Kṛṣṇa, and as long as we are in the material world, we should be trained to serve God. As soon as our apprenticeship is completed, we are promoted to the spiritual world to render the same service in fact. We are chanting here, and in the spiritual world we will also be chanting. We are serving here, and there we will also be serving. However, here we experience a probational apprenticeship. There, that service is factual. But even though this is an apprenticeship, because devotional service is absolute, it is not different from the real world. Therefore if one engages in devotional service, he is already liberated. His very activities are liberated; they are not at all material. One who does not know anything about devotional service thinks, "Oh, what are they doing? Why are they chanting? Anyone can chant. How is this spiritual?" People do not know that the names of Kṛṣṇa are as good as Kṛṣṇa. They are absolute.

Śyāmasundara dāsa: Socrates maintained that one must become perfectly good, but he gives no clear idea of just how this is done.

Śrīla Prabhupāda: Being perfectly good means acting for the perfectly good, Kṛṣṇa. In Kṛṣṇa consciousness, we are given an actual occupation by which we can become perfectly good. The activities of a person in Kṛṣṇa consciousness appear to be perfectly good even to a materialistic person. Anyone can appreciate the good character and qualifications of devotees. *Yasyāsti bhaktir bhagavaty akiñcanā (Bhāg.* 5.18.12). If one has developed Kṛṣṇa consciousness, he will manifest all the good qualities of the demigods. This is a test to tell how we are advancing toward perfection. These qualities will be visible even in this material world. This is not simply a question of the ideal, the inaccessible. This can be factually experienced. And the devotee does not want anything other than engagement in Kṛṣṇa consciousness. He doesn't want material sense gratification at all. That is perfection.

Hayagrīva dāsa: For Plato, perfect happiness lies in attempting to become godly. Insofar as man is godly, he is ethical. Evil forces within man combat his efforts to attain this ultimate goal. But Plato was not a determinist; he emphasized freedom of the will, and insisted that evil acts are due to man's failure to meet his responsibilities. Evil does not come from God, who is all good.

Śrīla Prabhupāda: Everything comes from God, but we have to make our choice. Both the university and the prison are government institutions, but the prison is meant for criminals, and the university for scholars. The government spends money to maintain both institutions, but we make our choice either to go to prison or the university. That is the minute independence present in every human being. In *Bhagavad-gītā*, Kṛṣṇa says:

samo'haṁ sarva-bhūteṣu
na me dveṣyo'sti na priyaḥ
ye bhajanti tu māṁ bhaktyā
mayi te teṣu cāpy aham

"I envy no one, nor am I partial to anyone. I am equal to all. But whoever renders service unto Me in devotion is a friend, is in Me, and I am also a friend to him." (*Bg*. 9.29) It is not that out of envy God makes someone unhappy and someone else happy. This is not God's business. Happiness and unhappiness are our creation. The government does not tell us to become criminals, but it is our fault if we become criminals and suffer. Of course, God is ultimately responsible. God gives us suffering or happiness, but we create the situation which is made into fact by the potency of God.

Hayagrīva dāsa: Plato conceives of death as being the end of the sensory life of the individual, his thoughts, perceptions, and experiences. The individual then returns to the ideal world from which he came.

Śrīla Prabhupāda: This means that he believes in the eternity of the soul. There are three stages: awakening, dreaming, and deep sleep, or unconsciousness. When a man dies, he goes from the awakening state into the dreaming state, and then enters the state of deep sleep. Transmigration means that he gives up the gross body and carries the subtle body—the mind, intelligence, and false ego—into another body. Until the other body is properly prepared, he remains in a state of deep sleep. When the body is prepared after seven months (for the human being), he then regains consciousness. At this point, he thinks, "O my Lord, why am I put into this situation? Why am I packed tightly in this womb?"

In the womb, he feels very uncomfortable, and if he is pious, he prays to God for relief. At this time, he promises God that he will become a devotee. When he comes out of the womb, the different stages of life begin: childhood, youth, manhood, middle age, old age, and then again death. It is like a flower that goes through different stages. In the beginning, the flower is only a bud, and it eventually blossoms and looks very beautiful. By gradually developing our Kṛṣṇa consciousness, the beauty of our life can eventually be manifest.

Hayagrīva dāsa: Plato also stressed the process of remembering. For instance, a boy may be ignorant of a certain subject, but a teacher can elicit answers from him that will suggest that he acquired this certain knowledge in a previous existence.

Śrīla Prabhupāda: Yes, and therefore we find that some students are more intelligent than others. Why is this? One student can grasp the subject very quickly, while another cannot.

pūrvābhyāsena tenaiva
hriyate hy avaśo'pi saḥ

"By virtue of the divine consciousness of his previous life, he automatically becomes attracted to the yogic principles, even without seeking them." (*Bg.* 6.44) Some men may be born in rich families and may acquire a good education, whereas others may be born in poor families and remain uneducated. If one is extraordinarily rich, educated, aristocratic, and beautiful, we should understand that he is reaping the results of his previous good activities. In any case, regardless of one's position in this world, everyone has to be educated to Kṛṣṇa consciousness. In this sense, everyone has an equal opportunity. As stated in *Śrīmad-Bhāgavatam*:

kirāta-hūṇāndhra-pulinda-pulkaśā
ābhīra-śumbhā yavanāḥ khasādayaḥ
ye'nye ca pāpā yad-apāśrayāśrayāḥ
śudhyanti tasmai prabhaviṣṇave namaḥ

"Kirāta, Hūna, Āndhra, Pulinda, Pulkaśa, Ābhīra, Śumbha, Yavana, and the Khasa races, and even others who are addicted to sinful acts, can be purified by taking shelter of the devotees of the Lord due to His being the supreme power. I beg to offer my respectful obeisances unto Him." (*Bhāg.* 2.4.18) So even if one has the body of an aborigine, he can be trained in Kṛṣṇa consciousness because that consciousness is on the platform of the soul.

Hayagrīva dāsa: Concerning education, it is stated in *The Republic*: "The soul of every man possesses the power of learning the truth and the organ to see it with. Just as one might have to turn the whole body around for the eye to see light instead of darkness, so the entire soul must be turned away from this changing world, until its eye can bear to contemplate reality and that supreme splendor which we have called the Good. Hence there may well be an art whose aim would be to affect this very thing: the conversion of the soul, in the readiest way. Not to put the power of sight into the soul's eye, which already has it, but to insure that, instead of looking in the wrong direction, it is turned the way it ought to be."

Śrīla Prabhupāda: That is the purpose of this Kṛṣṇa consciousness movement. It is certainly an art. It is a process of purifying the senses. When the senses are purified, our main objective is attained. We do not say that sensory activities are to be stopped. They are to be redirected. Presently, the eyes are seeing things material. The eyes want to see beautiful objects, and we say, "Yes, you can see the beautiful form of Kṛṣṇa." The tongue wants to taste palatable food, and we say, "Yes, you can take this Kṛṣṇa *prasādam*, but do not eat meat or other foods you cannot offer to Kṛṣṇa." Everything is given; we simply have to purify the senses. According to *Bhagavad-gītā:*

viṣayā vinivartante
nirāhārasya dehinaḥ
rasa-varjaṁ raso'py asya
paraṁ dṛṣṭvā nivartate

"The embodied soul may be restricted from sense enjoyment, though the taste for sense objects remains. But, ceasing such engagements by experiencing a higher taste, he is fixed in consciousness." (*Bg.* 2.59)

Hayagrīva dāsa: Neither Socrates nor Plato ever mentions service to God, though they speak of the contemplation of God's reality, or the supreme splendor, or good. It is always contemplation or meditation that is stressed, as in *jñāna-yoga.*

Śrīla Prabhupāda: This is but one process of knowing God, and it may be partially helpful to know God as He is. However, when we come to know God, we understand, "He is great, and I am small." It is the duty of the small to serve the great. That is nature's way. Everyone is serving in one way or another, but when we realize that we are servants and not the master, we realize our real position. It is our natural position to serve. If someone doesn't have a family to serve, he keeps a dozen dogs and serves them. Especially in Western countries, we see that in old age, when one has no children, he keeps two or three dogs and tries to serve them. Our position as servant is always there, but when we think that we are masters, we are illusioned. The word māyā means that we are serving while thinking that we are masters. Māyā means "that which is not," or, "that which is not factual." Through meditation, when we become realized, we can understand, "Oh, I am a servant. Presently I am serving māyā, illusion. Now let me serve Kṛṣṇa." This is perfection. The spiritual master engages us from the very beginning in the service of God. Then we can attain perfection quickly.

Hayagrīva dāsa: In *The Republic*, Plato constructs an ideal state in which the leaders possess nothing of their own, neither property nor family. He felt that people should live together in a community where wives and children are held in common to guard against corruption, bribery, and nepotism in government. Elite philosophers should mate with women of high qualities in order to produce the best children for positions of responsibility. How does this correspond to the Vedic version?

Śrīla Prabhupāda: According to Vedic civilization, a man should accept a wife for *putra*, for sons. *Putra-piṇḍa-prayojanam.* A *putra*, or son, should offer *piṇḍa* so that after death the father will be elevated if he is in an undesirable position. Marriage is for begetting good sons who will deliver one from the fire of hell. Therefore the *śrāddha* ceremony is there because even if the father is in hell, he will be delivered. It is the son who offers the *śrāddha* oblation, and this is his duty. Therefore one accepts a wife for *putra*, a good son, not for sex enjoyment. One who utilizes his sex life in a religious way will get a good son who can deliver him. Therefore Kṛṣṇa says in *Bhagavad-gītā: dharmāviruddho bhūteṣu kāmo'smi bharatarṣabha.* "I am sex life which is not contrary to religious principles." (*Bg.* 7.11) Sex contrary to religious principle is sense gratification that leads us into a hellish condition. Therefore, according to Vedic civilization , we should marry and beget good progeny. Although my Guru Mahārāja was a *sannyāsī brahmacārī*, he used to say, "If I could produce really Kṛṣṇa conscious children, I would have sex a hundred times. But why should I have sex just to produce cats and dogs?" The *śāstras* also say:

gurur na sa syāt sva-jano na sa syāt
pitā na sa syāj jananī na sā syāt
daivaṁ na tat syān na patiś ca sa syān
na mocayed yaḥ samupeta-mṛtyum

"One who cannot deliver his dependents from the path of repeated birth and death should never become a spiritual master, a father, a husband, a mother, or a worshipable demigod." (*Bhāg.* 5.5.18) It is the duty of the father and mother to rescue their children from the cycle of birth and death. If one can do this, he can in turn be rescued by his *putra* if he happens to fall into a hellish condition.

Śyāmasundara dāsa: Plato believed that the perfect state should be organized in such a way that men can strive for the ideal. He equates political activity with moral endeavor, and he says that the ruler of the state must be a wise man (philosopher king), or a group of wise men. In a perfect society, each individual functions to his best capacity according to his natural abilities. This leads to the most harmonious type of society.

Śrīla Prabhupāda: This idea is also found in *Bhagavad-gītā*, in which Kṛṣṇa says that the ideal society is a society of four *varṇas: brāhmaṇa, kṣatriya, vaiśya*, and *śūdra*. In human society, as well as animal society, every living being is under the influence of the modes of material nature—*sattva-guṇa, rajo-guṇa*, and *tamo-guṇa*—that is, goodness, passion, and ignorance. By dividing men according to these qualities, society can be perfect. If a man in the mode of ignorance assumes a philosopher's post, havoc will result. Nor can we have a philosopher work as an ordinary laborer. There must be some scientific division in order to perfect society. According to the Vedas, the *brāhmaṇas*, the most intelligent men interested in transcendental knowledge and philosophy, should be given a topmost post, and the *kṣatriyas*, the administrators, should work under their instructions. The administrators should see that there is law and order and that everyone is doing his duty. The next section is the productive class, the *vaiśyas*, who are engaged in agriculture and cow protection. There are also the *śūdras*, the common laborers, who work for the benefit of the other sections. Of course, now there is industrialization, and large scale industry means exploitation. Such industry was unknown to Vedic civilization. Then, people lived by agriculture and cow protection. If there are healthy cows and enough milk, everyone can get grains, fruits, vegetables, and other foods. That is sufficient in itself. Unfortunately, modern civilization has taken to animal eating, and this is barbarous. This is not even human.

Ideal society is a society of *brāhmaṇas, kṣatriyas, vaiśyas*, and *śūdras*. In *Śrīmad-Bhāgavatam*, these divisions are compared to the body: the head, the arms, the belly, and the legs. All parts of the body are meant to keep the body fit. Comparatively, the head is more important than the legs. However, without the help of the legs, the body cannot properly work. The head must give the directions to the body to go to this place or that, but if the legs are unfit to walk, the body cannot move. Therefore there must be cooperation, and this cooperation is found in the ideal state. Nowadays, rascals, fools, and asses are being voted in as administrators. If a person can secure a vote in some way or another, he is given the post of an administrator, even though he may be rascal number one. So what can be done? For this reason, people cannot be happy.

The ideal state functions under the directions of the *brāhmaṇas*. The *brāhmaṇas* themselves are not personally interested in political affairs or administration because they have a higher duty. Presently, because the head is missing, the social body is a dead body. The head is very important, and our Kṛṣṇa consciousness movement is attempting to create some *brāhmaṇas* who can properly direct society. The administrators will be able to rule very nicely under the instructions of the philosophers and theologians—that is, God conscious people. A person who is theistic will never condone the opening of slaughterhouses. Because there are many rascals heading the government, animal slaughter is allowed. When Mahārāja Parīkṣit saw the personification of Kali trying to kill a cow, he immediately drew his sword and said, "Who are you? Why are you trying to kill this cow?" That was a real king.

Śyāmasundara dāsa: A similar social structure was also observed by Plato. However, he advocated three divisions instead of four. The guardians were men of wisdom who ruled and governed. The warriors were courageous, and they protected the others. The artisans performed their services obediently and were motivated to work by their need to satisfy their appetites. In addition, he saw in man a threefold division of intelligence, courage, and appetite, which correspond to the modes of goodness, passion, and ignorance possessed by the soul.

Śrīla Prabhupāda: The soul does not possess three qualities. That is a mistake. The soul is by nature pure, but due to his contact with the modes of material nature, he is dressed differently. This Kṛṣṇa consciousness movement aims at removing this material dress. Therefore our first instruction is, "You are not this body."

Hayagrīva dāsa: In *The Republic*, Plato states that the best form of government is an enlightened monarchy.

Śrīla Prabhupāda: Yes, we agree. *Evaṁ paramparā-prāptam imaṁ rājarṣayo viduḥ*. "This supreme science was received through the chain of disciplic succession, and the saintly kings understood it in that way." (*Bg*. 4.2) A *rājarṣi* is a saintly king who is an ideal ruler. We offer respect to Mahārāja Yudhiṣṭhira, Mahārāja Parīkṣit, and Lord Rāmacandra because they set examples as ideal kings.

Hayagrīva dāsa: Plato maintained that when a monarchy degenerates, it becomes a tyranny. When an aristocratic rule deteriorates, it becomes an oligarchy, a government ruled by corrupt men. He considered democracy to be one of the worst forms of government because when it deteriorates, it degenerates to mob rule.

Śrīla Prabhupāda: Yes, that is now the case. Instead of one saintly king, there are many thousands of so-called kings who are looting the people's hard-earned money by income tax and other means. In the Vedic system, however, there was a way to keep the monarchy from degenerating into tyranny. The monarch was guided by a counsel of learned men, *brāhmaṇas*, great saintly persons. Even Mahārāja Yudhiṣṭhira and Lord Rāmacandra were guided by *brāhmaṇas*. It was the duty of the monarch to act according to the decisions of the learned scholars, *brāhmaṇas*, and *sādhus*, saintly persons. When Vena Mahārāja was not ruling properly, the *brāhmaṇas* came and advised him to act otherwise. When he refused, they cursed him, and he died. The great Pṛthu Mahārāja was his son. A great sage is required to occupy the role of a monarch. Then everything is perfect in government. The present democratic systems are ludicrous because they are composed of rascals who simply bribe one another. When they attain their post, they plunder and take bribes. If the head of the state can understand *Bhagavad-gītā*, his government will be automatically perfect. Formerly, *Bhagavad-gītā* was explained to the monarchs for that reason. *Imaṁ rājarṣayo viduḥ (Bg.* 4.2).

Śyāmasundara dāsa: Plato's system was somewhat democratic in that he felt that everyone should be given a chance to occupy the different posts.

Śrīla Prabhupāda: You can also say that we are democratic because we are giving even the lowest *caṇḍāla* a chance to become a *brāhmaṇa* by becoming Kṛṣṇa conscious. As soon as one becomes Kṛṣṇa conscious, he can be elevated to the highest position, even though he may be born in a family of *caṇḍālas*.

aho bata śvapaco'to garīyān
yaj-jihvāgre vartate nāma tubhyam
tepus tapas te juhuvuḥ sasnur āryā
brahmānūcur nāma gṛṇanti ye te

"O my Lord, a person who is chanting Your holy name, although born of a low family like that of a *caṇḍala* [dog eater], is situated on the highest platform of self-realization. Such a person must have performed all kinds of penances and sacrifices according to Vedic rituals and studied the Vedic literatures many, many times after taking his bath in all the holy places of pilgrimage. Such a person is considered to be the best of the Āryan family." (*Bhāg.* 3.33.7)

Also, in *Bhagavad-gītā*, it is stated:

māṁ hi pārtha vyapāśritya
ye'pi syuḥ pāpa-yonayaḥ
striyo vaiśyās tathā śūdrās
te'pi yānti parāṁ gatim

"O son of Pṛthā, those who take shelter in Me, though they be of lower birth—women, *vaiśyas* [merchants], as well as *śūdras* [workers]—can approach the supreme destination." (*Bg.* 9.32) Kṛṣṇa says that everyone can go back home, back to Godhead. *Samo'haṁ sarva bhūteṣu.* "I am equal to everyone. Everyone can come to Me." (*Bg.* 9.29) There is no hindrance.

Śyāmasundara dāsa: Plato believed that the state should train its citizens to become virtuous. According to his system of education, the first three years of life were spent playing and training the body. From age three to six, the children were taught religious stories. From seven to ten, they were taught gymnastics; from ten to thirteen, reading and writing; from fourteen to sixteen, poetry and music; from sixteen to eighteen, mathematics; and from eighteen to twenty, military drill. From that time on, those who were scientific and philosophical remained in school until they were thirty-five. If they were warriors, they engaged in military exercises.

Śrīla Prabhupāda: Was this educational program for all men, or were there different types of education for different men?

Śyāmasundara dāsa: No, this applied to all.

Śrīla Prabhupāda: Oh, this is not desirable. If a boy is intelligent and inclined to philosophy and theology, why should he be made to take military training?

Śyāmasundara dāsa: Well, according to Plato's system, everyone took two years of military drill.

Śrīla Prabhupāda: But why waste two years? We cannot even waste two days.

Śyāmasundara dāsa: This type of education was designed in order to determine a person's category. It is not that one belongs to a particular class according to qualifications.

Śrīla Prabhupāda: Yes, we also say that, but that tendency or disposition is to be ascertained by the spiritual master, by the teacher who trains the boy. The teacher should be able to see whether a boy is fit for military training, for administration, or for philosophy. It is not that everyone should take the same training. One should be trained fully according to his particular tendency. If a boy is by nature inclined to philosophical study, why should he waste his time in the military? And if he is by nature inclined to military training, why should he waste his time with other studies? Arjuna belonged to a *kṣatriya* family, and this family was trained in the military. The Pāṇḍavas were never trained as philosophers. Droṇācārya was their master and teacher, and although he was a *brāhmaṇa*, he taught them the military science, not *brahma-vidyā*. *Brahma-vidyā is* theology, philosophy. It is not that everyone should be trained in everything; that is a waste of time. If a student is inclined toward production, business, or agriculture, he should be trained in those fields. If he is philosophical, he should be trained as a philosopher. If he is militaristic, he should be trained as a warrior. And if he is simply dull, he should remain a *śūdra*, a laborer. These four classes are selected by their symptoms and qualifications. Nārada Muni also says that one should be selected according to qualifications. Even if one is born in a *brāhmaṇa* family, he should be considered a *śūdra* if his qualifications are such. And if one is born in a *śūdra* family, he should be considered a *brāhmaṇa* if his symptoms are brahminical. It is not that everyone should be regarded in the same way. The spiritual master should be expert enough to recognize the tendencies of the student, and the student should immediately be trained in that line. This will bring about perfection.

Śyāmasundara dāsa: According to Plato's system, this tendency won't emerge unless one practices everything.

Śrīla Prabhupāda: No, that is wrong because the soul is continuous; therefore the soul retains some tendencies from his previous birth. According to Vedic culture, immediately after a boy's birth, astrological calculations were made. Astrology can help if there is a first-class astrologer who can tell what line a boy is coming from and how he should be trained. Of course, logical and physical symptoms are considered. If a boy does not fulfill the role assigned, he can be transferred to another class. Generally, it is ascertained from birth whether a child has a particular tendency, but this tendency may change according to circumstance. Someone may have brahminical training in a previous birth, and the symptoms may be exhibited, but he should not think that because he has taken birth in a *brāhmaṇa* family that he is automatically a *brāhmaṇa*. It is not a question of birth but of qualification.

Śyāmasundara dāsa: Then what would you say is the purpose of the state, of all these social orders, and the state government?

Śrīla Prabhupāda: The ultimate purpose is to make everyone Kṛṣṇa conscious. That is the perfection of life. The entire social structure should be molded with this aim in view. Of course, this is not possible for everyone. All students in a university do not receive the Ph. D. degree, but the idea of perfection is to pass the Ph.D. examination. The professors of the university should be maintained, although there are not many high caliber students to pass their classes. It is not that the university should close its higher classes. Similarly, an institution like this Kṛṣṇa Consciousness Society should be maintained to make at least a small percentage of the population Kṛṣṇa conscious.

Śyāmasundara dāsa: So the goal of government should be to enable everyone to become Kṛṣṇa conscious?

Śrīla Prabhupāda: Yes, Kṛṣṇa consciousness is the highest goal. Everyone should help and take advantage of this. Regardless of our social position, we can come to the temple and worship God. The instructions are for everyone, and *prasādam* is distributed to everyone; therefore there is no difficulty. Everyone can contribute to this Kṛṣṇa consciousness movement. The *brāhmaṇas* can contribute their intelligence, the *kṣatriyas* their charity, the *vaiśyas* grains, milk, fruits, and flowers, and the *śūdras* bodily service. By such joint cooperation, everyone attains the same goal—the highest perfection.

Aristotle
(384-322 B.C.)

Hayagrīva dāsa: Plato made a sharp distinction between the material and spiritual universes, but this dualism is not expressed by Aristotle. Since matter is simply one of God's energies, the finite reflects the infinite. Matter is a potency in the process of realizing itself.
Śrīla Prabhupāda: Aristotle may know something of God's energies, but our point is that we can know everything about God from God Himself. Then our knowledge is perfect. In *Bhagavad-gītā*, Kṛṣṇa says:

mayy āsakta-manāḥ pārtha
yogaṁ yuñjan mad-āśrayaḥ
asaṁśayaṁ samagraṁ māṁ
yathā jñāsyasi tac chṛṇu

"Now hear, O son of Pṛthā, how by practicing yoga in full consciousness of Me, with mind attached to Me, you can know Me in full, free from doubt." (*Bg.* 7.1) This is the process of Kṛṣṇa consciousness. Of course, we may speculate about God, and if we just think of God, that will help to some extent. If we are in darkness, we may speculate and concoct ideas about the sun. This is one kind of knowledge. However, if we come out of the darkness and see the sun, if we come to the light, our knowledge is complete. We may contemplate the sun in darkness, but the best process is to come into the sunshine and see for ourselves.

Hayagrīva dāsa: Aristotle does not believe that material objects are trying to realize God, as Plato does, but that God is realizing Himself through material objects, and God does this in a variegated and infinite way. God realizes the potentiality of a flower, or of a man, by creating a flower or a man perceivable by the material senses. So, in a sense, the world is more real to Aristotle than to Plato.

Śrīla Prabhupāda: Since God has created the material world with all its variety, He is in full awareness of how to act properly. That is God's perfection. He knows how to do everything perfectly and in a natural way. A child naturally knows how to put food into his mouth. He does not have to learn this. God's knowledge of everything is already there. It is not that He has to receive this knowledge through some source, or by creating. He is already fully aware of these things. He doesn't have to realize Himself or His potentiality through matter.

Hayagrīva dāsa: Aristotle would say that a flower is real because it has its basis in the ultimate reality, God.

Śrīla Prabhupāda: If God is the ultimate reality, how is it He is not in full knowledge of everything at all times? There is no question of realizing Himself through matter.

Hayagrīva dāsa: Plato would say that a flower is but a shadow of reality. Which point of view would be closer to the Vedic version?

Śrīla Prabhupāda: Whatever is in the material world is but a perverted reflection of the spiritual world. It is our experience that in the material world, objects are created, but in the spiritual world, nothing is created. Everything is there everlastingly.

Śyāmasundara dāsa: Aristotle says that imperfection is inherent in the substance matter. Because man is made of matter, he must be imperfect.

Śrīla Prabhupāda: Man is not made of matter but is covered by matter. Man is made of spirit. If God is spirit, man is also spirit. In the Bible, it is also said that man is made in the image of God; therefore man is originally perfect. A person is generally supposed to be healthy, but if he falls into a diseased condition, it is not his imperfection. It is something external that has attacked a healthy man. According to his original nature, man is healthy.

Śyāmasundara dāsa: For Aristotle, the goal of action is to realize our potential and attain the greatest happiness or pleasure. Since God created man for self-realization, it is realization that will bring him satisfaction.

Śrīla Prabhupāda: This means that in the beginning God created man imperfect. Otherwise, why is there need for self-realization?
Śyāmasundara dāsa: A piece of wood has the potential to become fire. It is not fire until it is kindled. Man is similar.
Śrīla Prabhupāda: We say that the living entity is part and parcel of God, and if God is all good, the living entity is also all good. A part of gold cannot be iron; it also must be gold. However, the part is not equal to the whole. A gold earring is also gold, but it is not as great as the gold mine. Nevertheless, the quality of the gold earring and the quality of gold in the gold mine are the same. If God is perfect, the living entity must also be perfect in quality. If God has the quality of goodness, the living entity must have it also. Why should he be imperfect? That would indicate that God is unjust. Why should God create something that has to come to the perfectional point by realization?
Śyāmasundara dāsa: Aristotle would say that the activities of the mind are pure and perfect, but that those of the body and matter are impure and imperfect. Therefore one must realize himself through the activities of the mind alone.
Śrīla Prabhupāda: No, the mind is never perfect. The mind's business is to accept this and reject that, and therefore it is very flickering. The mind is subtler than the body, but the mind is not the soul, nor is the mind perfect. Above the mind there is intelligence, and above the intelligence there is the soul. That soul is perfect in quality, and it has all the qualities of God in minute quantity.
Śyāmasundara dāsa: By mind, Aristotle means the rational faculty of intelligence.
Śrīla Prabhupāda: Intelligence is above the mind. Intelligence controls the mind, and intelligence is of the soul. Therefore the whole background is the soul.
Śyāmasundara dāsa: The mind must act or contemplate in accordance with logic. Logic is defined as the method of drawing correct inferences.
Śrīla Prabhupāda: The mind may logically accept something and again logically reject it. Where, then, is perfect logic?
Śyāmasundara dāsa: Perfect logic is simply a method for finding the truth.
Śrīla Prabhupāda: But the mind is constantly accepting and rejecting. How can it ascertain the truth according to logic? If our authority is the mind, does this mean that the mind of everyone is an authority? The mind may constantly search, but it will never be successful because the truth is beyond its reach. A follower of the Vedas does not accept this speculative method as a path to truth or perfection.

Hayagrīva dāsa: For both Plato and Aristotle, God is known by reason, not by revelation or religious experiences.
Śrīla Prabhupāda: We are all limited, and God is unlimited; therefore we cannot understand God by our limited sensory powers. Consequently, God must be known by revelation.

ataḥ śrī-kṛṣṇa-nāmādi
na bhaved grāhyam indriyaiḥ
sevonmukhe hi jihvādau
svayam eva sphuraty adaḥ

"Material senses cannot appreciate Kṛṣṇa's holy name, form, qualities, and pastimes. When a conditioned soul is awakened to Kṛṣṇa consciousness and renders service by using his tongue to chant the Lord's holy name and taste the remnants of the Lord's food, the tongue is purified, and one gradually comes to understand who Kṛṣṇa really is." (*Bhakti-ramsāmṛta-sindhu* 1.2.234) It is not possible to know God by mental speculation. When we engage in His service, He reveals Himself. Śrī Kṛṣṇa says:

nāhaṁ prakāśaḥ sarvasya
yoga-māyā-samāvṛtaḥ
mūḍho'yaṁ nābhijānāti
loko mām ajam avyayam

"I am never manifest to the foolish and unintelligent. For them I am covered by My eternal creative potency [*yoga-māyā*]; and so the deluded world knows Me not, who am unborn and infallible." (*Bg*. 7.25) It is a fact that unless God reveals Himself, He is not known. Therefore He appears, and great authorities like Vyāsadeva, Nārada, Śukadeva Gosvāmī, Rāmānujācārya, Madhvācārya, and Caitanya Mahāprabhu—great scholars and transcendentalists—accept Him as He reveals Himself. Arjuna saw God face to face, and he accepted Him. When we are freed by our service, God reveals Himself.
Hayagrīva dāsa: Well, Aristotle emphasizes man's use of reason, and he sees man's happiness depending on acting in a rational way, which is the way of virtue and intellectual insight. There is a suggestion of sense control, but no *bhakti*. Is it possible to attain happiness simply by controlling the senses with the mind?
Śrīla Prabhupāda: Yes, and that is the process of becoming a human being. Animals are ignorant of this process, and they act only for their sense gratification. Their only business is eating, sleeping, mating, and defending. Through proper guidance, a human being can engage in con-

templation, but he should be guided by authorities, otherwise he may contemplate with his limited senses for many millions of years and not be able to understand God.

Hayagrīva dāsa: But for happiness, or *ānanda,* isn't *bhakti* essential?

Śrīla Prabhupāda: God is full *ānanda,* full bliss. *Sac-cid-ānanda.* He is eternal and in full knowledge of everything. Unless we come in contact with God, there is no question of *ānanda. Raso vai saḥ.* From the Vedic literatures, we understand that God is the unlimited reservoir of all pleasure; consequently, when we come in contact with God, we will taste that pleasure. Material pleasure is only a perverted reflection of the real pleasure.

Śyāmasundara dāsa: Rather than personal guidance, Aristotle emphasized rational logic.

Śrīla Prabhupāda: Yes, but when you are guided, you have to sacrifice your logic to accept the superior logic of your guide.

Śyāmasundara dāsa: He felt that the mind can be its own guide.

Śrīla Prabhupāda: As I said, the mind will carry you this way and that. In *Bhagavad-gītā,* Arjuna says that the mind is more difficult to control than the wind. If a horse is not controlled, if it is allowed to run at will, it will cause some disaster. When the horse is guided, it can take you to your destination. We should therefore know how to control the mind by the intelligence.

Śyāmasundara dāsa: But because the mind is an aspect of God, we find our perfection or happiness in the contemplation of God.

Śrīla Prabhupāda: Everything is an aspect of God. In *Bhagavad-gītā,* Kṛṣṇa points out that He has eight separated energies. So why stress the mind? Because we have lost God's association, we are all searching after Him. We are struggling, but we do not know why. This is due to ignorance. If, by good fortune, we chance to meet a bona fide guru, the guru can inform us, "You are searching after God. This is the way. You only have to follow." It is then that we can become happy.

Śyāmasundara dāsa: Aristotle believed that the truth is inherent or innate within everything. For him, truth is the agreement of knowledge with reality. It corresponds with things in the objective world.

Śrīla Prabhupāda: If truth is within everything, then it must be drawn out. However, it is not drawn out by matter but by spirit. This means that the help of a superior energy is necessary. According to *Bhagavad-gītā,* the living entity is the superior energy, and matter is the inferior. It is the inferior energy that must be controlled by the superior. Both God and the living entities are eternal, but God is the Supreme Eternal. Living entities are *nitya-kṛṣṇa-dāsa,* eternal servants of God. When they tend to disobey God, they suffer. If we want to use our logic, we can understand that through our independent action, we have failed. Therefore we must take the advice of superior intelligence. That advice is given in *Bhagavad-gītā*. It is not that we can attain the truth through our own independent speculation. If we want to know who our father is, we may speculate forever, but it is much simpler to ask our mother. Otherwise we may go on searching and searching for millions of years and never know. What is the point in all this vain research? We should conclude that insofar as we are in the material, illusory condition, it is our duty to take help from God or His representative, who does not set forth anything that is not originally spoken by God. For instance, God says, "Surrender unto Me," and God's representative says, "Surrender unto God." If a rascal says, "I am God," he should be kicked. The living entities are part and parcel of God, and a part can never become the whole. A real representative of God acknowledges himself as the servant of God, and he requests everyone to surrender unto God. For perfect knowledge, we have to take guidance either directly from God, as Arjuna did, or from God's representative. Then we will be successful in ascertaining the truth.

Hayagrīva dāsa: Aristotle outlines three different conceptions of the soul: one, the soul itself is a separate substance; two, the body is but the instrument of the soul; and three, the soul is the actual form of the body.

Śrīla Prabhupāda: The body is like the clothes of the soul, and our clothes are designed to fit our body. A coat has arms because we have arms, and pants have legs because we have legs. So the body is like the coat and pants of the soul, and since the body has form, the soul also has the same form. The cloth, which is the body, originally has no shape, but when it comes into contact with the soul, it assumes a shape.

Śyāmasundara dāsa: It appears that Aristotle equates the soul with the intelligence.

Śrīla Prabhupāda: The soul has intelligence, but his intelligence is misused if it is limited to the mind. The intelligence should rise above the mind. The mind is superior to gross matter, the intelligence is superior to the mind, and the soul is superior to the intelligence. Superior to the soul is the ultimate cause of the soul, the Supreme Lord.

Śyāmasundara dāsa: Because he equates the soul's immortality with reason, Aristotle believes that it is only the rational soul, the human soul, that is immortal. Animals also have souls, but he saw them limited to sense, desire, and animation.

Śrīla Prabhupāda: Animals are also rational. If a dog enters my room, and I say, "Out!" the dog immediately understands and goes away. How can we say that there is no rationality at work? If I place my finger before an ant, that ant will turn away immediately. If you give a cow meat, the cow will not touch it. The cow understands that its food consists of grasses and grains. Animals have rationality, but one aspect of rationality is lacking: an animal cannot think of God. This is the main difference between animals and men. A man's rationality is so developed that he can think of God, whereas an animal cannot. But we should not think that the souls of animals are not immortal. This theory has given the Christians a basis for killing animals, but they cannot prove that an animal's soul is irrational or mortal. A man eats, sleeps, defends, and mates, and an animal does the same. So what is the difference?

Śyāmasundara dāsa: Perhaps the difference is one of mental activity. A man has the capacity to think in a more complicated way.

Śrīla Prabhupāda: But mental activity means accepting and rejecting. Animals also accept and reject; therefore they have mental activity.

Śyāmasundara dāsa: But what of developed intelligence?

Śrīla Prabhupāda: Of course, man has a more highly developed intelligence, but we should not think that an animal has no intelligence at all. The father has more intelligence than his small child, but this is because the child has not grown to attain that standard. Similarly, an animal is making progress up the evolutionary scale. It has intelligence, but it is not highly developed. Plants, animals, and men possess consciousness. It has been proven by Doctor Jagadish Candra Bose that a tree is conscious of your cutting it. However, the tree does not feel it very much. If you hit an animal, the animal feels it more, and if you hit a man, a man feels it even more than an animal. It is a question of developed consciousness, of developed intelligence. That development has to do with the body. As soon as you receive the body of a tree, your consciousness is plugged up. It is not so active. When you attain the human form, consciousness is more developed, and that developed consciousness should be further developed so that you can come to Kṛṣṇa consciousness, which is the highest perfection of the living entity.

Śyāmasundara dāsa: Aristotle conceived of the soul as having a dual nature. There is an individual soul, which awakens at birth and acquires impressions during one's lifetime. Thus it grows and develops, but it is not eternal. It is subject to conditioning. It is like the souls of animals. Then there is also a rational soul, the active soul, which is eternal, though not perfect. This is man's motivating principle and purpose for living.

Śrīla Prabhupāda: Kṛṣṇa is the eternal, changeless soul. In *Bhagavad-*

gītā, Kṛṣṇa tells Arjuna:

bahūni me vyatītāni
janmāni tava cārjuna
tāny ahaṁ veda sarvāṇi
na tvaṁ vettha parantapa

"Many, many births both you and I have passed. I can remember all of them, but you cannot, O subduer of the enemy!" (*Bg.* 4.5) That is the real meaning of eternity—eternal knowledge. Thus there are two kinds of souls: the Supersoul (Paramātmā), who is Kṛṣṇa Himself, and the ordinary soul (*jīva*), which is possessed by every living entity.

Śyāmasundara dāsa: For Aristotle, the rational soul is eternal, yet he says that it is not perfect.

Śrīla Prabhupāda: This means that he has to accept two souls, one perfect and rational, and another imperfect and irrational. The soul that is perfect and rational is Kṛṣṇa, the Supersoul.

Śyāmasundara dāsa: He doesn't say anything about the Supersoul accompanying the individual soul.

Śrīla Prabhupāda: That is because he does not know. He suggests that there is a dual nature, but he has no idea. The dual nature he refers to is not of the soul but the mind. The soul is one. When you are on the mental platform, it appears that the soul has a dual nature, but when the soul's perfection is attained, you think only of Kṛṣṇa. There is no question of duality.

Hayagrīva dāsa: In *Politics*, Aristotle writes: "The beauty of the body is seen, but the beauty of the soul is not seen." Is this true?

Śrīla Prabhupāda: The beauty of the soul is real, and the beauty of the body is superficial. In the material world, we see many ugly and many beautiful bodies, but here ugliness and beauty are artificial. The beauty of the soul, however, is real, not artificial. Unless we see the beauty of the Supersoul, Kṛṣṇa, we have no idea what actual beauty is. Therefore the devotees want to see the beauty of Kṛṣṇa, not the artificial beauty of this material world.

Hayagrīva dāsa: Is there no correspondence between a beautiful body and a beautiful soul? Aren't they linked by karma?

Śrīla Prabhupāda: There is some correspondence because we say that this material world is a perverted reflection of the spiritual. Originally, the soul is beautiful, but here that beauty is covered. We can only have a glimpse of the real beauty from the material covering, but we have to wait in order to see the actual beauty of the soul. That beauty is the real form of the body.

Hayagrīva dāsa: It is said that Socrates was physically ugly but that he had a very beautiful soul, and consequently people were attracted to him.

Śrīla Prabhupāda: In India, it is said that the quail is black and ugly like a crow, but when it sings, its song is so beautiful that people are attracted. The beauty of the body is secondary, and the beauty of the soul is primary. A beautiful man who is a fool is beautiful only as long as he does not speak. As soon as he speaks, we can understand his actual position. Essentially, external beauty is useless. If an ugly man speaks well, he attracts many people, and if a beautiful man speaks nonsense, no one cares for him. Real attraction is one thing, and artificial attraction is another.

Śyāmasundara dāsa: In man's search for truth, the role of logic is paramount. According to Aristotle's principle of contradiction, a proposition cannot be both true and false at the same time.

Śrīla Prabhupāda: That is on the relative platform. At one time we may accept something to be true, and at another time we may reject it as untrue. On the mental platform we cannot know what is true and what is not. Therefore we have to learn the truth from the Supreme Truth. Truth is truth. It is not subject to speculation. In *Bhagavad-gītā*, Kṛṣṇa says that after many lives of speculation, the man of wisdom surrenders unto the Supreme Absolute Truth. In the beginning, a man may employ deductive logic, but in the end, he surrenders. He comes to the conclusion: *Vāsudevaḥ sarvam iti (Bg.* 7.19). "God is everything; therefore I must surrender." This is the perfection and ultimate end of the mental processes of speculation. That is, speculation is abandoned.

Śyāmasundara dāsa: Aristotle more or less utilizes the process of *sāṅkhya-yoga* by analyzing objects and placing them into general categories. These categories become more and more general until one reaches the final cause, or ultimate category.

Śrīla Prabhupāda: Yes, this is the process of *neti-neti*, by which one eventually hopes to attain Brahman by understanding what Brahman is not. According to this process, one goes through the universe saying *neti-neti*, "This is not Brahman, that is not Brahman. This is not truth, that is not truth." This is the same inductive process. For instance, if you want to determine whether or not man is mortal, you may search from man to man and conclude whether each man is mortal or not. In this way, you can go on indefinitely seeing that all men are dying. Then why not accept the fact that man is mortal? In your attempt to find an immortal man, you are bound to be frustrated. You will only find mortality. This is the result of the *neti-neti* process.

Śyāmasundara dāsa: The idea is that through this process, we can come to the final cause, the final category.
Śrīla Prabhupāda: The final category is that we are part and parcel of God. That's all.
Śyāmasundara dāsa: Aristotle believed that matter as such has an inherent design. If it did not, it would be devoid of shape or form. Brute matter has to be activated; otherwise it would remain in a dormant state of nonexistence. Matter must be acted upon from without in order to be realized.
Śrīla Prabhupāda: This means that the Supreme Absolute must have form. *Īśvaraḥ paramaḥ kṛṣṇaḥ sac-cid-ānanda-vigrahaḥ* (*Brahma-saṁhitā* 5.1). The word *vigraha* indicates form. That form is not dead but is the activating spirit. Kṛṣṇa's form is *sac-cid-ānanda*, eternal, fully cognizant, and blissful. Our bodies are neither fully cognizant nor fully blissful, but Kṛṣṇa's is. He knows past, present, and future, and He is always happy. Our knowledge is limited, and we are always full of anxieties.
Śyāmasundara dāsa: For Aristotle, a form has innate purpose, or *entelechy*. Therefore all matter has some form for its actualization. The world is an unfolding of phenomena realizing itself. In other words, nature has a purpose.
Śrīla Prabhupāda: We agree with this. According to *Padma Purāṇa*, there are 8,400,000 various forms, and none of them are accidental. By karma, one receives a particular type of form. Brahmā receives his form according to his karma, and the dog or cat receives his form according to his. There is no question of accident. Nature unfolds in accordance with a plan, by virtue of which these various forms are existing.

yas tv indra-gopam athavendram aho sva-karma-
bandhānurūpa-phala-bhājanam ātanoti
karmāṇi nirdahati kintu ca bhakti-bhājāṁ
govindam ādi-puruṣaṁ tam ahaṁ bhajāmi

"Let me offer my respectful obeisances unto the original Personality of Godhead, Govinda, who regulates the sufferings and enjoyments of fruitive activity for everyone: from the heavenly King Indra down to the smallest insect [*indra-gopa*]. That very Personality of Godhead destroys the fruitive karma of one engaged in devotional service." (*Brahma-saṁhitā* 5.54) From Indra down to *indra-gopa*, a microscopic germ, all living entities are working out the results of their karma. If one's karma is good, he attains a higher form; if it is not good, he attains a lower form.
Śyāmasundara dāsa: Aristotle also believed that everything is designed

by God for the attainment of some particular objective. This indicates a grand scheme.

Śrīla Prabhupāda: This is the process of evolution. The living entity passes from one species to another, from trees to vegetables, to insects, to fish, birds, beasts, and humans. In the human form, evolution is fully manifest. It is like a flower unfolding from a bud. When the living entity attains the human form, his proper duty is to understand his lost relationship with God. If he misses this opportunity, he may regress. Aristotle is correct therefore in saying that everything has a purpose. The whole creative process aims at bringing the living entity back to Godhead.

Śyāmasundara dāsa: Does everything eventually come to that point?

Śrīla Prabhupāda: As a human being, you can properly utilize your consciousness, or you can misuse it. That is up to you. Kṛṣṇa gives Arjuna instructions and then tells him that the decision is up to him. Under the orders of Kṛṣṇa, nature has brought you through so many species. Now, as a human, you have a choice whether to return to God or again undergo the cycle of birth and death. If you are fortunate, you make the proper choice according to the instructions of the spiritual master and Kṛṣṇa. Then your life is successful.

Śyāmasundara dāsa: Aristotle sees a hierarchy of forms extending from minerals, vegetables, animals, to human beings, and ultimately God, who is pure form and pure act. God is devoid of all potentiality, or materiality.

Śrīla Prabhupāda: There is no guarantee that we will move upwards in that hierarchy. It is a fact that the individual soul transmigrates from one form to another, but how can you say that the next form you attain will be closer to perfection? If you have a human form in this life, there is no guarantee that you will get a higher form in the next. You accept another form just as you accept another dress. That dress may be valuable, or of no value whatsoever. I get a dress according to the price I pay, and I accept a form according to my work.

Śyāmasundara dāsa: But in order to attain perfection, we must move toward God. This is the goal for which the living entity is initially created.

Śrīla Prabhupāda: This is very expertly explained in Vedic literature as karma, *akarma*, and *vikarma*. You bring about your own form. You enjoy or suffer according to your work. In any case, a material form is never perfect because it undergoes six changes. It is born, grows, it stays for a while, it leaves some by-products, dwindles, and then vanishes. When your form vanishes, you have to take on another form, which also undergoes the same processes. When a form vanishes, it decomposes, and various elements return to nature. Water returns to water, earth

returns to earth, air returns to air, and so forth.
Śyāmasundara dāsa: Aristotle's God is the unmoved mover. He is perfect, and He wants nothing. He does not have to actualize Himself because He is completely actualized.
Śrīla Prabhupāda: We also agree that God is all perfect. Parāśara Muni defines God as the totality of wisdom, strength, wealth, fame, beauty, and renunciation. All these qualities are possessed by Kṛṣṇa in full, and when Kṛṣṇa was present, anyone could see that He was all perfect. One who is perfect can rule others, and we accept the leadership of a person according to his degree of perfection. If one is not somewhat wise, beautiful, wealthy, and so forth, why should we accept him as a leader? One who is supremely perfect in all these qualities is the supreme leader. That is natural. Since Kṛṣṇa is supremely perfect, we should accept Him as our leader.
Śyāmasundara dāsa: Aristotle sees God as pure thought (*nous*). God's life is the life of the mind, but God does not need to do anything to further perfect Himself.
Śrīla Prabhupāda: When he says that God is mind, what does he mean? Does he have some conception of God's personality? God must be a person. Otherwise, how could He think?
Śyāmasundara dāsa: Aristotle sees God as constantly engaged in self-contemplation.
Śrīla Prabhupāda: Does this mean that when one is perfect, he engages in no activity? Does God simply sit down and meditate? If so, what is the difference between a stone and God? A stone sits; it has no activity. How is inactivity perfection? Kṛṣṇa never meditates, yet when He speaks, He delivers perfect knowledge. Kṛṣṇa enacts various pastimes: He fights with demons, protects His devotees, dances with the *gopīs*, and delivers words of enlightenment. There is no question of God sitting down like a stone and engaging in self-meditation.
Śyāmasundara dāsa: But is it not possible to meditate while acting?
Śrīla Prabhupāda: Certainly, but God doesn't have to meditate. Why should He meditate? He is perfect. Meditation means coming from the imperfect stage to the perfect stage. Since God is perfect to begin with, what business does He have meditating? Everything is actualized by His will alone.
Śyāmasundara dāsa: Doesn't He contemplate His own activities?
Śrīla Prabhupāda: Why should He if He is perfect? Aristotle recommends that a man should meditate to become perfect. This meditation presupposes imperfection. Contemplation is recommended for living en-

tities, but we should understand that whatever God desires or wills immediately comes into being. This information is given in the Vedas. *Parāsya śaktir vividhaiva śrūyate.* God's multi-energies are so powerful that everything is immediately actualized as soon as He desires.
Śyāmasundara dāsa: But what about the meditations of the Buddha?
Śrīla Prabhupāda: Buddha's mission was different. He was setting an example for miscreants who were engaged in mischievous activities. He was recommending that they sit down and meditate, just as you tell a mischievous child to sit in a corner and be quiet.
Śyāmasundara dāsa: Well, Aristotle isn't saying that we should put an end to our activities. Rather, we should always contemplate God.
Śrīla Prabhupāda: That is our process, as recommended by *Śrīmad-Bhāgavatam:*

śravaṇaṁ kīrtanaṁ viṣṇoḥ
smaraṇaṁ pāda-sevanam
arcanaṁ vandanaṁ dāsyaṁ
sakhyam ātma-nivedanam
iti puṁsārpitā viṣṇau
bhaktiś cen nava-lakṣanā
kriyeta bhagavaty addhā
tan manye 'dhītam uttamam

"Hearing and chanting about the transcendental holy name, form, qualities, paraphernalia, and pastimes of Lord Viṣṇu, remembering them, serving the lotus feet of the Lord, offering the Lord respectful worship with sixteen types of paraphernalia, offering prayers to the Lord, becoming His servant, considering the Lord one's best friend, and surrendering everything unto Him [in other words, serving Him with the body, mind, and words]—these nine processes are accepted as pure devotional service. One who has dedicated his life to the service of Kṛṣṇa through these nine methods should be understood to be the most learned person, for he has acquired complete knowledge." (*Bhāg.* 7.5.23-24)

We should always think of Viṣṇu. Kṛṣṇa consciousness means remembering Kṛṣṇa and acting for Him. When you sweep Kṛṣṇa's temple, you remember Kṛṣṇa. When you cook for Kṛṣṇa, you remember Kṛṣṇa. When you talk about Kṛṣṇa, you remember Kṛṣṇa. This is also the process recommended in *Bhagavad-gītā.* The topmost yogī is always thinking of Kṛṣṇa.

yoginām api sarveṣāṁ
mad-gatenāntarātmanā
śraddhāvān bhajate yo māṁ

sa me yuktatamo mataḥ

"And of all yogīs, he who always abides in Me with great faith, worshipping Me in transcendental loving service, is most intimately united with Me in yoga and is the highest of all." (*Bg.* 6.47)

Hayagrīva dāsa: For Aristotle, God essentially does not have any knowledge of the world, and consequently He cannot return the love He receives. He neither loves nor cares for mankind.

Śrīla Prabhupāda: What kind of God is this? If one knows nothing of God, one should not speak of God. God certainly reciprocates. As we offer our love to God, He responds and cooperates accordingly. In *Bhagavad-gītā*, Kṛṣṇa says:

ye yathā māṁ prapadyante
tāṁs tathaiva bhajāmy aham
mama vartmānuvartante
manuṣyāḥ pārtha sarvaśaḥ

"All of them—as they surrender unto Me—I reward accordingly. Everyone follows My path in all respects, O son of Pṛthā." (*Bg.* 4.11) When we fully surrender to God in loving service, we can understand God's nature.

Hayagrīva dāsa: For Aristotle, God is loved by everything in the universe, and He attracts all objects in the universe just as a magnet attracts nails. Everything is striving toward Him and longing for Him, but there is no mention of Him as a person. Yet Aristotle speaks of God as pure form. Would this be an imagined form like that of the Māyāvādīs?

Śrīla Prabhupāda: Yes, it appears that Aristotle is Māyāvādī. One has to speculate if he does not receive perfect knowledge from God Himself. Unless God is all attractive, how can He be God? Therefore the word "Kṛṣṇa," which means "all attractive," is the perfect name for God because God is attracting everyone. In Vṛndāvana, He attracts His parents, the cowherd boys and girls, the animals, the fruits and flowers, the water—everything. You have read the descriptions of how the water of the Yamunā stopped flowing as soon as she saw Kṛṣṇa. So even the water was attracted to Kṛṣṇa.

Śyāmasundara dāsa: Aristotle believed that thought and activity are one with God. There is no dualism because God is pure act and pure thought.

Śrīla Prabhupāda: Yes, that is so. God only needs to think of a thing for that thing to be created or actualized. God's thinking, feeling, willing, and acting are the same. Because I am imperfect, when I think of something, it may or may not happen, but whenever God thinks something, it takes place. Because Kṛṣṇa thought that the battle of Kurukṣetra should take place, there was no stopping it. At first, Arjuna declined to fight, but Kṛṣṇa plainly told him that whether he fought or not, most of the people there were destined to die. He therefore told Arjuna to become an instrument and take the credit for killing them. No one can check whatever God decides. It doesn't matter whether you help God or not, but it is for your interest that you become His instrument.

Śyāmasundara dāsa: Aristotle says that one should perform his activities in such a way that he is always contemplating God.

Śrīla Prabhupāda: Yes, that is the process of *bhakti*. Unless one is a devotee, how can he constantly think of God? Rūpa Gosvāmī gives the example of a woman who has a paramour other than her husband. She performs her household chores very nicely, but she is always thinking, "When will my lover come at night?" If it is possible to think of someone like this all the time materially, why not spiritually? It is a question of practice. Despite engaging in so many different types of work, you can think of God incessantly. Now, Aristotle may have some conception of God, but he has no clear idea of Kṛṣṇa's personality. We can think specifically and concretely of God because we receive information from Vedic literature that God is a person and appears a certain way. In *Bhagavad-gītā*, it is stated that impersonalists experience a great deal of trouble because they have no clear idea of God.

kleśo'dhikataras teṣām
avyaktāsakta-cetasām
avyaktā hi gatir duḥkhaṁ
dehavadbhir avāpyate

"For those whose minds are attached to the unmanifested, impersonal feature of the Supreme, advancement is very troublesome. To make progress in that discipline is always difficult for those who are embodied." (*Bg.* 12.5) If you have no conception of God's form, your attempt to realize God will be very difficult.

Śyāmasundara dāsa: Aristotle conceives of God as the greatest good, as pure thought. When we act, we should always contemplate the good. In this way, we can lead a godly life.

Śrīla Prabhupāda: You cannot contemplate the good unless you are guided by the good. Arjuna, for instance, was guided by the Supreme Good; therefore despite his activity, which was fighting, he performed the greatest good.

Śyāmasundara dāsa: Aristotle believes that there is a grand design in the universe because everything is evolving from one form to another to realize its most perfect form. Everything is being attracted by the most perfect form.

Śrīla Prabhupāda: Does he say that there is only one perfect form, or a variety of perfect forms? What does he mean? Is everyone striving to come to the perfect form? Is that form one or various?

Śyāmasundara dāsa: Well, since each material form is designed by God and moves toward God in its longing for perfection, there must be a variety of forms.

Śrīla Prabhupāda: If that is the case, it tallies with the Vedic conception. We say that Kṛṣṇa and His associates are perfect; therefore this flower, for instance, attains its perfect form when it is in Kṛṣṇa-loka, Kṛṣṇa's planet. Everything in Kṛṣṇa-loka is perfect because everything there is directly related to Kṛṣṇa. Consequently, in Kṛṣṇa-loka, the Yamunā River, the Vṛndāvana forest, the flowers, the beasts, the birds, and the men and women are nondifferent from Kṛṣṇa.

ānanda-cinmaya-rasa-pratibhāvitabhis
tābhir ya eva nija-rūpatayā kalābhiḥ
goloka eva nivasaty akhilātma-bhūto
govindam ādi-puruṣaṁ tam ahaṁ bhajāmi

"I worship Govinda, the primeval Lord, who resides in His own realm, Goloka, with Rādhā, who resembles His own spiritual figure and who embodies the ecstatic potency [*hlādinī*]. Their companions are Her confidantes, who embody extensions of Her bodily form, and who are imbued and permeated with ever-blissful spiritual *rasa.*" *(Brahma-saṁhitā* 5.37)

When Brahmā stole all the cowherd boys and calves, Kṛṣṇa immediately expanded Himself into many cowherd boys and calves, each with different features and mentalities. The mothers of the cowherd boys could not understand that their real sons had been stolen. Because Kṛṣṇa was substituting for them, the mothers' love for their sons increased. Thus Kṛṣṇa can expand Himself in many ways—as cows, calves, trees, boys, girls, and so on. Yet Kṛṣṇa is still one.

Śyāmasundara dāsa: Aristotle would say that since God has a spiritual form, He is without plurality in the sense that He is composed of no parts. In other words, He is pure spirit.

Śrīla Prabhupāda: Yes, God is one without plurality. The sun may be visible to millions of persons, still the sun is one. At noon, millions of men may claim, "The sun is over my head," but does this mean that everyone has a different sun? No, the sun is one, but the sun can represent itself variously.

Śyāmasundara dāsa: Aristotle gave two arguments for God's existence.

One is that there is a design in the universe, and a design presupposes a designer. The other holds that there must be a first cause, a cause of all causes.

Śrīla Prabhupāda: That is so. A designer moreover presupposes a person. Kṛṣṇa explains in *Bhagavad-gītā:*

mayādhyakṣeṇa prakṛtiḥ
sūyate sa-carācaram
hetunānena kaunteya
jagad viparivartate

"This material nature is working under My direction, O son of Kuntī, and it is producing all moving and unmoving beings. By its rule, this manifestation is created and annihilated again and again." (*Bg.* 9.10) Kṛṣṇa is also the directing cause, the *puruṣa*, the cause of all causes. *Anādir ādir govindaḥ sarva-kāraṇa-kāraṇam.* "Govinda [Kṛṣṇa] is the origin of all. He has no other origin, and He is the prime cause of all causes." (*Brahma-saṁhitā* 5.1)

Hayagrīva dāsa: In *Nicomachean Ethics*, Aristotle writes: "Moral excellence is concerned with pleasure and pain; it is pleasure that makes us perform base action, and pain that prevents us from acting nobly. For that reason, as Plato says, men must be reared from childhood to feel pleasure and pain at the proper things. This is proper education." How does this correspond to the Vedic view of education?

Śrīla Prabhupāda: According to the Vedic view, there is no pleasure in this material world. We may make all kinds of arrangements for pleasure, but we may suddenly have to die. So where is the pleasure? If we make arrangements for pleasure and then do not enjoy it, we are disappointed. We are constantly trying to attain pleasure by inventing so many contrivances, but because we are controlled by some superior force, we may at any moment be kicked out of our house of pleasure. The conclusion is that there is no pleasure in this material world. Pleasure here is an illusion, a mirage. In a desert, you may hallucinate water, but ultimately you will die of thirst.

Śyāmasundara dāsa: For Aristotle, virtue is the golden mean, or that activity between two extreme activities. By his intelligence, man can perceive and act upon that golden mean. Ultimately, all virtues are summed up in the virtue of justice, which means doing the right thing for everyone concerned so that everyone's rights will be protected.

Śrīla Prabhupāda: But if everyone's rights are to be protected, how can you kill animals? Why shouldn't animals have the right to live? According to the Vedic conception, even if you kill one ant unconsciously, you are responsible. Because we are killing so many ants and microbes unconsciously, we therefore have to perform *pañca-yajña*, sacrifice. We may consciously avoid killing animals, but we may be unconsciously killing many. Therefore, in either case, sacrifice is compulsory.

Śyāmasundara dāsa: Aristotle believes that virtue can be analyzed, that any situation can be analyzed by the intelligence, and then that intelligence can be applied to correct action.

Śrīla Prabhupāda: By intelligence he should try to understand whether or not animals have souls. If an animal doesn't have a soul, how is it he is acting like a human being? He is eating, sleeping, mating and defending. How can you say he has no soul? The life symptoms are the same.

Śyāmasundara dāsa: He equates the immortal soul with rational activity.

Śrīla Prabhupāda: Well, animals have rational activities. I have already explained this. A philosopher certainly must know the symptoms of the soul, and these must be defined. We receive perfect information on this subject from *Bhagavad-gītā*, when Kṛṣṇa says:

sarva-yoniṣu kaunteya
mūrtayaḥ sambhavanti yāḥ
tāsāṁ brahma mahad yonir
ahaṁ bīja-pradaḥ pitā

"It should be understood that all species of life, O son of Kuntī, are made possible by birth in this material nature, and that I am the seed-giving father." (*Bg.* 14.4)

Does this mean that God is the father only of human beings? For instance, the Jews say that they are the only selected people of God. But what kind of God is this who selects some people and condemns others? This is God: Kṛṣṇa says, *sarva-yoni.* "I am the father of all species of life." Everyone is God's son. How can I kill and eat any living entity? He is my brother in any case. Suppose a man has five sons, and two of them are fools. Does this mean that the intelligent sons have the right to kill and eat the foolish ones? Would the father like this? Who would ask the father, "Father, these two sons are fools and useless rascals. So let us cut them to pieces and eat them."? Will the father agree to this? Or will the state agree? And why should God agree?

Śyāmasundara dāsa: Aristotle claims that one can use his intelligence to practice virtue, but you once said that because a thief considers theft a virtue, he can use his intelligence to steal.

Śrīla Prabhupāda: Yes, a thief's intelligence has been described as *duṣkṛtina*. The word *kṛti* means "very meritorious," and the word *duṣ* means "misapplied." Is that virtuous when one's intelligence is misapplied? When merit and intelligence are properly used for the proper activity, that is virtue. Such activity will not entangle a man. That is intelligence and virtue.

Śyāmasundara dāsa: Ambition is one of the Aristotelean virtues, but one can have the ambition to steal.

Śrīla Prabhupāda: Yes, it was Hitler's ambition to become total ruler of Europe. He killed many people and then finally killed himself. So what was all this ambition worth? All these politicians are very ambitious, but they are ambitious to unlawfully encroach upon the rights of others. We should have the ambition to become the sincere servant of God. That is real ambition.

Śyāmasundara dāsa: Among virtues, Aristotle includes courage, temperance, liberality, magnificence, and ambition.

Śrīla Prabhupāda: What is the magnificence of killing animals? How can you have no kindness for poor animals and yet talk of magnificence? *Harāv abhaktasya (Bhāg.* 5.18.12). If your ultimate conclusion is not God consciousness, you have no good qualities. You can be neither a scientist, nor a philosopher, because you are *narādhama,* hovering on the mental platform. Thus you concoct so many theories.

Śyāmasundara dāsa: As far as Aristotle's social philosophy is concerned, he says that man is basically a political and social animal and that he must exist in some society in order to fulfill himself. Men live together to transcend their crude natural condition and arrive at a civilized culture of ethical and intellectual life.

Śrīla Prabhupāda: If that is done, that is all right, but he is philosophizing that animals have no souls. Following his philosophy, people are saying, "Let's kill the animals and eat them." So what is the benefit of this grouping together in a society? We should instead group together to cultivate knowledge of God. This is what is required. What is the use in living together just to plunder other nations and kill other living entities? Such a group is a group of rogues and gangsters. Even today in the United Nations people are grouping together and planning to encroach upon one another. So what is the point in all these groups of gangsters?

Śyāmasundara dāsa: Aristotle is talking about the ideal way a state or a political body should be organized. He says that ideally a state should be formed in order to educate men to the highest level.

Śrīla Prabhupāda: But if we do not know what is education, or if we do not know the highest level of education, or if we do not even know the primary principles of a virtuous life, how can we speak of such things? Therefore we should be very careful to take bona fide guidance. According to Vedic civilization, Manu is the law-giver, and he is considered perfect. Manu, for instance, states that a woman should not be given independence. Now, certain groups are asking, "Why not?" Thus there is a confrontation, and Manu is surely being attacked, but Manu's conception is right in any case. Instruction should be taken from liberated persons. What can a group of fools do? One liberated personality like Manu can give the right directions. Presently, in the name of independence, there is havoc.

Śyāmasundara dāsa: Aristotle's state would be tightly controlled either by a monarch or a group of men intellectually and morally superior. These would guide the rest of the people.

Śrīla Prabhupāda: Yes, that would be very nice. Unless one is morally superior, he cannot guide. Nowadays, in democracies, all kinds of rascals are voted into positions of authority. What is the use in such groups?

Śyāmasundara dāsa: Aristotle condemns democracy because in a democracy each person strives for his own self-interest.

Śrīla Prabhupāda: Yes, that is going on. Monarchy is good if the monarch is trained in such a way that he can rule properly. That was the Vedic system. Even then, the monarch was controlled by great sages. In a proper government, the *brāhmaṇas* and sages should form an advisory committee. They should not participate in politics. The *kṣatriyas*, who are ambitious to rule, should rule under the guidance of the *brāhmaṇas* and sages. Mahārāja Yudhiṣṭhira was very pious, and people were very happy because he acted under the guidance of *brāhmaṇas* and sages. Formerly, the monarch was guided by priestly, religious, or saintly people. That was very nice. This Kṛṣṇa consciousness movement can guide society, but presently society is in such a state that it does not even want to consider the importance of this movement. This is unfortunate. Still, we have to struggle to spread Kṛṣṇa consciousness because we are representatives of Kṛṣṇa, and Kṛṣṇa's desires are our commands.

II
THE EARLY THEISTS

Plotinus

(205?-270 A.D.)

Hayagrīva dāsa: Plotinus, as well as Origen, studied philosophy in Alexandria under the supposed founder of Neo-Platonism, Ammonius Saccas. Plotinus ascribed to a theory of emanation, which holds that the soul emanates from the intelligence just as the intelligence emanates from the One. The intelligence (*nous*) is multiple and yet one at the same time. The One is omnipresent, devoid of multiplicity, impersonal, and transcendental. For Plotinus, there is a kind of hierarchy headed by the One, to which the intelligence and individual souls are subordinate.
Śrīla Prabhupāda: According to the Vedic conception, the Supreme Absolute Truth is one. The individual souls are of the same quality as the Supreme One, but they are fragmental parts, and they emanate from Him. The individual souls have the same intelligence and mind, but their jurisdiction is limited. As individual souls, we are present, but we are not omnipresent. God is omnipresent. We have some knowledge, but we are not omniscient. We are not dull matter, but are sentient beings. The Supreme One has all spiritual qualities in full, whereas we have them in minute quantity. We are like sparks, and the Supreme One is like a great fire. That is our constitutional position in relation to the One.

When sparks fly away from a great fire, they are extinguished. When we turn from the One, our illumination is obscured, and we are enveloped in māyā, darkness. If we revive our relationship with the One, we can revive our illuminating power, which is our spiritual power, and live with the Supreme One in a peaceful, eternal life of bliss.

Hayagrīva dāsa: Plotinus was an impersonalist in that he believed that by attributing qualities to God, we necessarily limit Him. Although the One is transcendental, there is no multiplicity in Him. At the same time, God is the cause of all multiplicities.

Śrīla Prabhupāda: According to the Vedic conception, the Supreme One is the cause of all living entities.

nityo nityānāṁ cetanaś cetanānām
eko bahūnāṁ yo vidadhāti kāmān
tam ātmasthaṁ ye'nupaśyanti dhīrās
teṣāṁ śāntiḥ śāśvatī netareṣām

(*Katha* 2.2.13)

In the *Kaṭha Upaniṣad*, as well as the *Śvetāśvatara Upaniṣad*, it is said that the Supreme Personality of Godhead maintains innumerable living entities. He is the Supreme Eternal Being. Among eternal living beings, He is the chief. He has unlimited transcendental qualities and is therefore omnipresent, omniscient, and omnipotent. If He did not have these qualities, He could not be perfect. He is the unlimited cause of everything, and, being unlimited, cannot be limited. I do not know what Plotinus means when he says that God's attributes are limiting. In no way can God be limited. Everything is Brahman unlimitedly. *Mat-sthāni sarva-bhūtāni (Bg.* 9.4). Everything emanates from Him, and everything rests on Him. Considered impersonally, God is everywhere, and considered personally, He is localized. The impersonal effulgence, however, emanates from the person. This is verified by *Bhagavad-gītā:*

brahmaṇo hi pratiṣṭhāham
amṛtasyāvyayasya ca
śāsvatasya ca dharmasya
sukhasyaikāntikasya ca

"And I am the basis of the impersonal Brahman, which is the constitutional position of ultimate happiness, and which is immortal, imperishable, and eternal." (*Bg*. 14.27)

Although the sun is situated in one place, its rays are distributed throughout the universe; similarly, the Supreme Lord unlimitedly expands His transcendental impersonal feature, the *brahmajyoti*. If we consider the personality, it may appear that He is limited, but He is not.

Through His energies, He is unlimited.

vadanti tat tattva-vidas
tattvaṁ yaj jñānam advayam
brahmeti paramātmeti
bhagavān iti śabdyate

"Learned transcendentalists who know the Absolute Truth call this non-dual substance Brahman, Paramātmā, and Bhagavān." (*Bhāg.* 1.2.11) The impersonal feature is all-pervading. The localized aspect, the Paramātmā, is also omnipresent, living within the hearts of all living entities. The personal feature, the Paramātmā, is even within every atom and is thus worshipped by the devotee. When the devotee is present, the Supreme Lord is also personally present, although He resides in Goloka Vṛndāvana. That is the nature of His omnipresence. No one can calculate the distance to Goloka Vṛndāvana, but when a devotee like Prahlāda is in danger, the Supreme Lord is immediately present. He can protect His devotee even though He be trillions of miles away. This is the meaning of omnipresence.

Hayagrīva dāsa: Although Plotinus believed that God is present in all objects throughout the universe, God remains distinct from all created things and also transcendental to them. Thus God is more than all pervading.

Śrīla Prabhupāda: That is clearly explained in *Bhagavad-gītā:*

mayā tatam idaṁ sarvaṁ
jagad avyakta-mūrtinā
mat-sthāni sarva-bhūtāni
na cāhaṁ teṣv avasthitaḥ

na ca mat-sthāni bhūtāni
paśya me yogam aiśvaram
bhūta-bhṛn na ca bhūta-stho
mamātmā bhūta-bhāvanaḥ

yathākāśa-sthito nityaṁ
vāyuḥ sarvatra-go mahān
tathā sarvāṇi bhūtāni
mat-sthānīty upadhāraya

"By Me, in My unmanifested form, this entire universe is pervaded. All beings are in Me, but I am not in them. And yet everything that is created does not rest in Me. Behold My mystic opulence! Although I am the maintainer of all living entities, and although I am everywhere, still My Self is the very source of creation. As the mighty wind, blowing everywhere, always rests in ethereal space, know that in the same manner all beings rest in Me." (*Bg.* 9.4-6)

Hayagrīva dāsa: Plotinus envisioned the individual souls existing in different states: some embodied, others unembodied. Some are celestial and do not suffer, whereas others are terrestrial. In any case, they are all individuals.

Śrīla Prabhupāda: No one can count the number of souls. They have the same qualities possessed by the One, but they have them in minute quantity. Some of these souls have fallen into the material atmosphere, whereas others, called *nitya-mukta*, are everlastingly liberated. The *nitya-muktas* are never conditioned. These souls that have fallen into this material world in order to gratify their senses are called *nitya-baddha*, eternally conditioned. By "eternal," we mean that no one can estimate the amount of time the conditioned soul has to spend within the material world. The creation goes on perpetually; sometimes it is manifest and sometimes not. Without Kṛṣṇa consciousness, the conditioned souls continue to exist within the material world. Before the creation, the conditioned soul is present in a dormant condition, and when the manifestation comes out from the Mahā-viṣṇu, the individual soul awakens. For the deliverance of such conditioned souls, the Supreme Personality of Godhead descends Himself, or sends His incarnation or devotee to call the *nitya-baddhas* back home, back to Godhead. Those who are fortunate take advantage of this. Those who are unfortunate are not interested and thus remain conditioned within this material world. The material world is created and annihilated, and the conditioned souls suffer in this cycle.

Hayagrīva dāsa: Plotinus believed that the soul is eternal and incorporeal in men, animals, and even plants. In this, he differed from many other philosophers at the time.

Śrīla Prabhupāda: It is also the Vedic conclusion (*sarva-yoniṣu*) that the living soul, which is part and parcel of God, is present in all different life species. Those who are foolish think the animal has no soul, but there is no rational basis for this belief. An animal may be less intelligent than a man, just as a child may be less intelligent than his father, but this does not mean that no soul is present. This type of mentality is ruining civilization. People have become so degraded that they even think that an embryo has no soul. From Kṛṣṇa we understand that everyone has a soul and that the soul is undoubtedly present in all different life forms. The individual soul evolves from a lower type of body to a higher one, and this is the meaning of spiritual evolution. Once in the human form, the individual soul can understand the teachings of *Bhagavad-gītā*, and, if he likes, surrender to the Supreme Lord and return to the Godhead. If he does not care to do so, he remains in this material world to undergo the tribulations of repeated birth, old age, disease, and death. Thus he takes on another corporeal body.

Hayagrīva dāsa: Plotinus sees the soul as returning to God, the One, through three stages. In the first, the individual soul must learn detachment from the material world. In the second, he separates himself from the reasoning process itself. This is the highest point that philosophy or mental speculation can attain. In the third stage, the intellect transcends itself into the realm of the unknown, the One. Plotinus writes: "Because it is intellect, it contemplates what it contemplates [the One] by reasoning of that in it which is not intellect."

Śrīla Prabhupāda: According to the Vedas, there are also three stages: karma, *jñāna*, and yoga. The *karmīs* try to improve their condition by material science and education. Some try to go to the heavenly planets by performing pious activities. Superior to the *karmīs* are the *jñānīs*, who speculate on the Absolute Truth and conclude that God is impersonal. The yogīs attempt to acquire some mystic powers by practicing the mystic yoga system. By this system, they acquire *aṣṭa-siddhi*, eight different perfections. They can become lighter than the lightest, smaller than the smallest, bigger than the biggest, and so on. Real yoga, however, means seeing the Supreme within the core of the heart. All three processes require a strenuous endeavor. The supreme process is *bhakti-yoga*, whereby one simply surrenders to the Supreme. The Supreme One gives the *bhakti-yogī* the intelligence by which he can be freed from material entanglement.

teṣāṁ satata-yuktānāṁ
bhajatāṁ prīti-pūrvakam
dadāmi buddhi-yogaṁ taṁ
yena mām upayānti te

"To those who are constantly devoted and worship Me with love, I give the understanding by which they can come to Me." (*Bg.* 10.10)

Hayagrīva dāsa: For Plotinus, matter is evil in the sense that it imprisons the soul, yet the visible cosmos is beautiful. Evil does not arise from the creator.

Śrīla Prabhupāda: Yes, being attracted by this illusory energy, the individual soul comes here for sense gratification. The Supreme Lord does not desire him to come, but he comes propelled by his personal desires.

God gives the living entity freedom, and in the beginning, the conditioned living entity begins life from a very exalted position in this material world. Sometimes he has the powers of a Brahmā, but due to material activities, he becomes entangled and degraded. He can thus fall from the position of a Brahmā to that of a worm in stool. Therefore we find so many different species. Degradation and elevation are thus taking place, and the living entity is sometimes elevated and sometimes degraded. In this way, he suffers. When he understands that degradation and elevation are perpetually taking place, and are the cause of his suffering, he begins to seek for the Supreme One, Kṛṣṇa. By the grace of Kṛṣṇa, he gets a bona fide spiritual master, and by the mercy of both, he gets a chance to engage in devotional service. With a little effort and sincerity, the conditioned living entity attains perfection in devotional service and returns back to Godhead.

Hayagrīva dāsa: Although most of Plotinus's philosophy deals with the impersonal aspect, he writes, "Let us flee to the beloved fatherland. The fatherland for us is there whence we have come. There is the Father."

Śrīla Prabhupāda: As long as we speculate, we will be confused and will not know whether the Supreme Absolute Truth is personal or impersonal. However, when there is a question of love between the Absolute and the individual souls, there must be a personal conception. In truth, God is a person, Kṛṣṇa. When the living entity, by the mercy of Kṛṣṇa, contacts a devotee, his impersonal conceptions are subordinated to the personal aspect, and he worships Kṛṣṇa and His devotee.

Hayagrīva dāsa: Concerning the soul's conditioning, or fall, Plotinus believes that the human soul never entirely leaves the intelligible or spiritual realm.

Śrīla Prabhupāda: Because the living entity is an eternal spiritual being, he is not a product of this material world. He is part and parcel of the Supreme One, but he is embodied by the material elements. As the material elements change, he becomes old. When our clothes no longer fit, or if they wear out, we have to acquire new ones. Material life means change, but as spirit souls, we are eternal and changeless. Material life is not very happy because it is always changing. Whether we are in a comfortable or miserable condition, our condition will change for better or worse. In any case, we have to save ourselves from the repetition of changing bodies. If we want to remain in our original spiritual form, we have to take to Kṛṣṇa consciousness.

Hayagrīva dāsa: Plotinus writes: "If the souls remain in the intelligible realm with the Soul, they are beyond harm, and share in the Soul's governance. They are like kings who live with the high King and govern with him and like him, and do not come down from the palace.... But there comes a point at which they come down from this state, cosmic in its dimensions, to one of individuality. They wish to become independent....When a soul remains for long in this withdrawal in estrangement from the whole, with never a glance toward the intelligible, it becomes a thing fragmented, isolated, and weak...."

Śrīla Prabhupāda: Yes, that is his falldown and the beginning of his material tribulations. As long as the living entity is maintained in the material world, he thinks of material happiness, and, according to nature's law, he accepts a variety of bodies. Although conditioned, the spirit soul remains part and parcel of the Supreme Lord. Yet according to the circumstance, he thinks in terms of a particular body. He thinks that he is a dog, a man, an aquatic, and so on. According to material considerations, one thinks himself an American, Indian, Hindu, Moslem, male, or female. All these designations are due to the body, and when one understands that he is different from the body, he begins his spiritual education. Understanding himself as the eternal part and parcel of God leads to liberation. When one advances, he understands that the Supreme Truth is the Supreme Person, Kṛṣṇa. He then engages in Kṛṣṇa's service, and that is his actual spiritual life. Kṛṣṇa lives in the Vaikuṇṭha planets in the spiritual world, and the devotee can be promoted to any of these planets, or to the supreme planet, Goloka Vṛndāvana. Once he is there, he is happy as an associate of Kṛṣṇa, and he can enjoy life eternally.

Hayagrīva dāsa: Plotinus conceives of the soul as basically having two parts, a lower part directed toward the corporeal, and a higher part directed toward the spiritual.

Śrīla Prabhupāda: Yes, and that means that the soul is prone to fall. Because the individual soul is very minute, there is the tendency to fall, just as a small spark may fall from a fire. Because we are only minute particles of God, we can become entangled by His material external energy. An unintelligent man may commit some crime and go to jail, but we should not think that he has been created for the purpose of going to jail. It is said that those who descend into the material world are less intelligent because they think that they can enjoy life independent of Kṛṣṇa. A rich man's son may think that he can live independent of his father, but that is his foolishness. The Supreme Father is full in all opulences , and if we live under His care, we naturally live very comfortably. When an intelligent man realizes that he is the son of Kṛṣṇa, he thinks,

"Let me go back to my Father." This is the proper use of intelligence. An intelligent person knows perfectly well that he will be happy with Kṛṣṇa and unhappy without Him. Learning this is part of the Kṛṣṇa consciousness process. Without Kṛṣṇa consciousness, a man cannot be happy.

Hayagrīva dāsa: Plotinus also believes that the cosmic order awards and punishes everyone according to merit.

Śrīla Prabhupāda: When a father sees that his son has gone astray, he tries to bring him back home, either through punishment or some other way. This is the duty of an affectionate father. Those who are foolishly suffering in the material world are being punished for the purposes of correction. This is to bring the living entity to his proper position. If one is sufficiently intelligent, he surrenders to Kṛṣṇa, revives his old constitutional position, and attains the spiritual platform of bliss and knowledge.

Hayagrīva dāsa: Plotinus uses the following metaphor: "We are like a chorus that allows the audience to distract its attention from the conductor. If, however, we were to turn towards our conductor, we would sing as we should and would really be with him. We're always around the One. If we were not, we would dissolve and cease to exist. Yet our gaze does not remain fixed upon the One. When we look at it, we then attain the end of our desires and find rest. Then it is that, all discord past, we dance an inspired dance around it. In this dance, the soul looks upon the source of life, the source of the Intelligence, the root of Being, the cause of the Good, the root of the Soul. All these entities emanate from the One without any lessening, for it is not a material mask."

Śrīla Prabhupāda: Yes, that is a good metaphor. God is an individual, and the countless souls are also individuals. Sometimes they sing in tune, and sometimes their attention is diverted by the audience. When this happens, they fall out of tune. Similarly, when we divert our attention to the illusory energy, we fall down. Of course, we remain part and parcel of the Supreme Lord, but the influence of material energy covers us, and we identify with the gross elements life after life. We identify with the body, which is but a changing dress. Therefore we must first of all understand that we are not the gross material covering. This is taught in the very beginning of *Bhagavad-gītā*, wherein Kṛṣṇa explains to Arjuna that since he is not the body, he should not consider the battle from a material, bodily platform. Our identity is that of spirit soul, part and parcel of the Supreme Spirit. We should therefore act according to His directions. By doing so, we become freed from material designations and gradually develop our Kṛṣṇa consciousness.

Hayagrīva dāsa: Plotinus accounts for the soul's conditioning in this way: "How is it, then, that souls forget the divinity that begot them? This evil that has befallen them has its source in self-will, in being born, in becoming different, and desiring to be independent. Once having tasted the pleasures of independence, they use their freedom to go any direction that leads away from their origin. And when they have gone a great distance, they even forget that they came from it."

Śrīla Prabhupāda: That is correct. The more one turns from Kṛṣṇa, the more degraded one becomes. I have already explained that the living entity may begin his life as Lord Brahmā and eventually become so degraded that he becomes a worm in stool. Again, by nature's way, one may evolve to the human form, which gives him a chance to understand how he has fallen from his original position. By taking to Kṛṣṇa consciousness, he can put an end to this transmigration. Everyone has to give up the material body, but when a devotee gives up his body, he does not have to accept another. He is immediately transferred to the spiritual world. *Mām eti (Bg.*4.9). "He comes to Me." For a devotee, death means giving up the material body and remaining in the original, spiritual body. It is said that whether a devotee lives or dies, his business is the same: devotional service. Those who are degraded in material life—like butchers, who daily cut the throats of many animals—are advised, "Don't live, and don't die." This is because their present life is abominable, and their future life will be filled with suffering. The devotee is liberated because he is indifferent to living or dying. He is *jīvan-mukta,* which indicates that although his body is rotting in the material world, he is liberated. In *Bhagavad-gītā,* Kṛṣṇa affirms that His devotee is not subject to the modes of material nature.

daivī hy eṣā guṇamayī
mama māyā duratyayā
mām eva ye prapadyante
māyām etāṁ taranti te

"This divine energy of Mine, consisting of the three modes of material nature, is difficult to overcome, but those who have surrendered unto Me can easily cross beyond it." (*Bg.* 7.14) The devotee is therefore situated on the Brahman platform. It is our constitutional position to serve: either māyā or Kṛṣṇa. *Jīvera 'svarūpa' haya—kṛṣṇera 'nitya-dāsa'.* Caitanya Mahāprabhu has given our real identity as being the eternal servant of Kṛṣṇa. Presently everyone is rendering service to his family, community, nation, and so on. When this service is rendered cent per cent to Kṛṣṇa, we are liberated. Due to a poor fund of knowledge, impersonalists think that *mukti*, liberation, means inactivity, but there is no basis for this belief. The soul is naturally active, and because the soul is within the body, the body is engaged in many activities. The body in itself is inactive, but it acts because the soul is present. When we give up the bodily conception, why should activities stop? Māyāvādīs cannot understand that the active principle is the soul. When the active principle leaves the body, the body is called dead. Even if one is liberated from the material body, he must act. That is also explained in the *Bhakti-śāstra:*

sarvopādhi-vinirmuktaṁ
tat-paratvena nirmalam
hṛṣīkeṇa hṛṣīkeśa-
sevanaṁ bhaktir ucyate

"*Bhakti*, or devotional service, means engaging all our senses in the service of the Lord, the Supreme Personality of Godhead, the master of all the senses. When the spirit soul renders service unto the Supreme, there are two side effects. He is freed from all material designations, and, simply by being employed in the service of the Lord, his senses are purified." (*Nārada-pañcarātra*)

Hayagrīva dāsa: Plotinus writes: "A soul in such a condition [of forgetfulness] can be turned about and led back to the world above and the supreme existent, the One. This can be done by a two-fold discipline: By showing it the low value of the things it esteems at present, and by informing—reminding!—it of its nature and worth."

Śrīla Prabhupāda: Yes, this is the process. One may understand or not, but if one is engaged in Kṛṣṇa's service under the direction of the spiritual master, he automatically gives up the service of māyā and is liberated.

viṣayā vinivartante
nirāhārasya dehinaḥ
rasa-varjaṁ raso'py asya
paraṁ dṛṣṭvā nivartate

"The embodied soul may be restricted from sense enjoyment, though the taste for sense objects remains. But, ceasing such engagements by experiencing a higher taste, he is fixed in consciousness." (*Bg.* 2.59) However, if he again voluntarily accepts māyā's service, he again becomes conditioned. By rendering service to Kṛṣṇa under the guidance of a bona fide spiritual master, we can come to understand all that need be known. The devotees do not speculate about their position; they know it by the grace of Kṛṣṇa.

teṣāṁ satata-yuktānāṁ
bhajatāṁ prīti-pūrvakam
dadāmi buddhi-yogaṁ taṁ
yena mām upayānti te

teṣām evānukampārtham
aham ajñāna-jaṁ tamaḥ
nāśayāmy ātma-bhāvastho
jñāna-dīpena bhāsvatā

"To those who are constantly devoted and worship Me with love, I give the understanding by which they can come to Me. Out of compassion for them, I, dwelling in their hearts, destroy with the shining lamp of knowledge, the darkness born of ignorance." (*Bg.* 10.10-11)

Origen
(185?-254?)

Hayagrīva dāsa: Origen is generally considered the founder of formal Christian philosophy, because he was the first to attempt to establish Christianity on the basis of philosophy as well as faith. He believed that the ultimate spiritual reality consists of the supreme, infinite Person, God, as well as individual personalities. Ultimate reality may be defined as the relationships of persons with one another and with the infinite Person Himself. In this view, Origen differs from the Greeks, who were basically impersonalists.
Śrīla Prabhupāda: Our Vedic conception is almost the same. Individual souls, which we call living entities, are always present, and each one of them has an intimate relationship with the Supreme Personality of Godhead. In material conditional life, the living entity has forgotten this relationship. By rendering devotional service, he attains the liberated position and at that time revives his relationship with the Supreme Personality of Godhead.
Hayagrīva dāsa: Origen ascribed to a doctrine of the Trinity, in which God the Father is supreme. God the Son, called the *Logos*, is subordinate to the Father. It is the Son who brings the material world into existence.

That is, God the Father is not the direct creator; rather, it is the Son who creates directly, like Lord Brahmā. The third aspect of the Trinity is the Holy Spirit, who is subordinate to the Son. According to Origen, all three of these aspects are divine and co-eternal. They have always existed simultaneously as the Trinity of God.

Śrīla Prabhupāda: According to the Vedas, Kṛṣṇa is the original Personality of Godhead. As confirmed by *Bhagavad-gītā: ahaṁ sarvasya prabhavaḥ.* "I am the source of all spiritual and material worlds." (*Bg.* 10.8) Whether you call this origin the Father, Son, or Holy Spirit, it doesn't matter. The Supreme Personality of Godhead is the origin. According to the Vedic conception, there are two types of expansion: God's personal expansions, called *Viṣṇu-tattva,* and His partial part-and-parcel expansions called *jīva-tattva.* There are many varieties of personal expansions: *puruṣa-avatāras, śaktyāveśa-avatāras, manvantara-avatāras,* and so on. For the creation of this material world, the Lord expands as Brahmā, Viṣṇu, and Maheśvara (Śiva). Viṣṇu is a personal expansion, and Brahmā is a *jīva-tattva* expansion. Between the personal *Viṣṇu-tattva* expansion and the *jīva-tattva* expansion is a kind of intermediate expansion called Śiva, or Maheśvara. The material ingredients are given, and Brahmā creates the particular creation. Viṣṇu maintains the creation, and Lord Siva annihilates it. It is the nature of the external potency to be created, maintained, and dissolved. More detailed information is given in the *Caitanya-caritāmṛta.* In any case, the *jīvas,* or living entities, are all considered to be sons of God. They are situated in one of two positions: liberated or conditioned. Those who are liberated can personally associate with the Supreme Personality of Godhead, and those who are conditioned within this material world have forgotten the Supreme Lord. Therefore they suffer within this material world in different bodily forms. They can be elevated, however, through the practice of Kṛṣṇa consciousness under the guidance of the *śāstras* and the bona fide guru.

Hayagrīva dāsa: Origen believed that it is through the combined working of divine grace and man's free will that the individual soul attains perfection, which consists of attaining a personal relationship with the infinite Person.

Śrīla Prabhupāda: Yes, and that is called *bhakti-mārga.* The Absolute Truth is manifested in three features: Brahman, Paramātmā, and Bhagavān. Bhagavān is the personal feature, and the Paramātmā, situated in everyone's heart, may be compared to the Holy Spirit. The Brahman feature is present everywhere. The highest perfection of spiritual life includes the understanding of the personal feature of the Lord. When one understands Bhagavān, one engages in His service. In this way, the living entity is situated in his original constitutional position and is eternally blissful.

Hayagrīva dāsa: Origen considered that just as man's free will precipitated his fall, man's free will can also bring about salvation. Man can return to God by practicing material detachment. Such detachment can be made possible by help from the *Logos*, the Christ.

Śrīla Prabhupāda: Yes, that is also our conception. The fallen soul is transmigrating within this material world, up and down in different forms of life. When his consciousness is sufficiently developed, he can be enlightened by God, who gives him instructions in the *Bhagavad-gītā*. Through the spiritual master's help, he can attain full enlightenment. When he understands his transcendental position of bliss, he automatically gives up material bodily attachments. Then he attains freedom. The living entity attains his normal, constitutional position when he is properly situated in his spiritual identity and engaged in the service of the Lord.

Hayagrīva dāsa: Origen believed that all the elements found in the material body are also found in the spiritual body, which he called the "interior man." Origen writes: "There are two men in each of us.... As every exterior man has for homonym the interior man, so it is for all his members, and one can say that every member of the exterior man can be found under this name in the interior man...." Thus for every sense that we possess in the exterior body, there is a corresponding sense in the interior, or spiritual body.

Śrīla Prabhupāda: The spirit soul is now within this material body, but originally the spirit soul had no material body. The spiritual body of the spirit soul is eternally existing. The material body is simply a coating of the spiritual body. The material body is cut, like a suit, according to the spiritual body. The material elements—earth, water, air, fire, etc.—become like a clay when mixed together, and they coat the spiritual body. It is because the spiritual body has a shape that the material body also takes a shape. In actuality, the material body has nothing to do with the spiritual body; it is but a kind of contamination causing the suffering of the spirit soul. As soon as the spirit soul is coated with this material contamination, he identifies himself with the coating and forgets his real spiritual body. That is called māyā, ignorance, or illusion. This ignorance continues as long as we are not fully Kṛṣṇa conscious. When we become fully Kṛṣṇa conscious, we understand that the material body is but the external coating and that we are different. When we attain this uncontaminated understanding, we arrive at what is called the *brahma-bhūta* platform. When the spirit soul, which is Brahman, is under the illusion of the material bodily conditioning, we are on the *jīva-bhūta* platform. *Brahma-bhūta* is attained when we no longer identify with the material body but with the spirit soul within. When we come to this platform, we become joyful.

brahma-bhūtaḥ prasannātmā
na śocati na kāṅkṣati
samaḥ sarveṣu bhūteṣu
mad-bhaktiṁ labhate parām

"One who is thus transcendentally situated at once realizes the Supreme Brahman. He never laments nor desires to have anything; he is equally disposed to every living entity. In that state, he attains pure devotional service unto Me." (*Bg.* 18.54) In this position, one sees all living entities as spirit souls; he does not see the outward covering. When he sees a dog, he sees a spirit soul covered by the body of a dog. This state is also described in *Bhagavad-gītā.*

vidyā-vinaya-sampanne
brāhmaṇe gavi hastini
śuni caiva śvapāke ca
paṇḍitāḥ sama-darśinaḥ

"The humble sage, by virtue of true knowledge, sees with equal vision a learned and gentle *brāhmaṇa*, a cow, an elephant, a dog, and a dog-eater [outcaste]." (*Bg.* 5.18) When one is in the body of an animal, he cannot understand his spiritual identity. This identity can best be realized in a human civilization in which the *varṇāśrama* system is practiced. This system divides life into four *āśramas (brāhmaṇa, kṣatriya, vaiśya,* and *śūdra*), and four *varṇas (brahmacārī, gṛhastha, vānaprastha,* and *sannyāsī).* The highest position is that of a *brāhmaṇa-sannyāsī*, a platform from which one may best realize his original constitutional position, act accordingly, and thus attain deliverance, or *mukti. Mukti* means understanding our constitutional position and acting accordingly. Conditional life, a life of bondage, means identifying with the body and acting on the bodily platform. On the *mukti* platform, our activities differ from those enacted on the conditional platform. Devotional service is rendered from the *mukti* platform. If we engage in devotional service, we maintain our spiritual identity and are therefore liberated, even though inhabiting the conditional, material body.

Hayagrīva dāsa: Origen also believed that the interior man, or the spiritual body, also has spiritual senses that enable the soul to taste, see, touch, and contemplate the things of God.
Śrīla Prabhupāda: Yes. That is devotional life.
Hayagrīva dāsa: During his lifetime, Origen was a famous teacher and was very much in demand. For him, preaching meant explaining the words of God and no more. He believed that a preacher must first be a man of prayer and must be in contact with God. He should not pray for material goods but for a better understanding of the scriptures.
Śrīla Prabhupāda: Yes, that is a real preacher. As explained in Vedic literatures: *śravaṇam, kīrtanam.* First of all, we become perfect by hearing. This is called *śravaṇam.* When we are thus situated by hearing perfectly from an authorized person, our next stage begins: *kīrtana,* preaching. In this material world, everyone is hearing something from someone else. In order to pass examinations, a student must hear his professor. Then, in his own right, he can become a professor himself. If we hear from a spiritualized person, we become perfect and can become real preachers. We should preach about Viṣṇu for Viṣṇu, not for any person within this material world. We should hear and preach about the Supreme Person, the transcendental Personality of Godhead. That is the duty of a liberated soul.
Hayagrīva dāsa: As far as contradictions and seeming absurdities in scripture are concerned, Origen considered them to be stumbling blocks permitted to exist by God in order for man to pass beyond the literal meaning. He writes that "everything in scripture has a spiritual meaning, but not all of it has a literal meaning."
Śrīla Prabhupāda: Generally speaking, every word in scripture has a literal meaning, but people cannot understand it properly because they do not hear from the proper person. They interpret instead. There is no need to interpret the words of God. Sometimes the words of God cannot be understood by an ordinary person; therefore we may require the transparent medium of the guru. Since the guru is fully cognizant of the words spoken by God, we are advised to receive the words of the scriptures through the guru. There is no ambiguity in the words of God, but due to our imperfect knowledge, we sometimes cannot understand. Not understanding, we try to interpret, but because we are imperfect, our interpretations are also imperfect. The purport is that the words of God, the scriptures, should be understood from a person who has realized God.
Hayagrīva dāsa: For Origen, there are two rebirths. The first is a baptism, which is something like a mystical union between Christ and the

soul. Baptism marked the first stage in spiritual life: from there, one could regress or progress. Baptism is compared to a shadow of the ultimate rebirth, which is complete purification and rebirth in the spiritual world with Christ. When the soul is reborn with Christ, it receives a spiritual body like Christ and beholds Christ face to face.

Śrīla Prabhupāda: What is the position of Christ?

Hayagrīva dāsa: He is seated at the right hand of the Father in the kingdom of God.

Śrīla Prabhupāda: But when Christ was present on earth, many people saw him.

Hayagrīva dāsa: They saw him in many different ways, just as the people saw Kṛṣṇa in many different ways.

Śrīla Prabhupāda: Is it that Christ is seen in his full spiritual body?

Hayagrīva dāsa: When the soul is reborn with Christ, it beholds Christ's spiritual body through its spiritual senses.

Śrīla Prabhupāda: Yes. We also think in this way.

Hayagrīva dāsa: Origen did not believe that the individual soul has been existing from all eternity. It was created. He writes: "The rational natures that were made in the beginning did not always exist; they came into being when they were created."

Śrīla Prabhupāda: That is not correct. Both the living entity and God are simultaneously eternally existing, and the living entity is part and parcel of God. Although eternally existing, the living entity is changing his body. *Na hanyate hanyamāne śarīre (Bg.* 2.20). One body after another is being created and destroyed, but the living being is eternally existing. So we disagree when Origen says that the soul is created. Our spiritual identity is never created. That is the difference between spirit and matter. Material things are created, but the spiritual is without beginning.

na tv evāhaṁ jātu nāsaṁ
na tvaṁ neme janādhipāḥ
na caiva na bhaviṣyāmaḥ
sarve vayam ataḥ param

"Never was there a time when I did not exist, nor you, nor all these kings; nor in the future shall any of us cease to be." (*Bg.* 2.12)

Hayagrīva dāsa: Origen differed from later Church doctrine in his belief in transmigration. Although he believed that the soul was originally created, he also believed that it transmigrated because it could always refuse to give itself to God. So he saw the individual soul as possibly rising and falling perpetually on the evolutionary scale. Later Church doctrine held that one's choice for eternity is made in this one lifetime. As Origen saw it, the individual soul, falling short of the ultimate goal, is reincarnated again and again.

Śrīla Prabhupāda: Yes, that is the Vedic version. Unless one is liberated and goes to the kingdom of God, he must transmigrate from one material body to another. The material body grows, remains for some time, reproduces, grows old, and becomes useless. Then the living entity has to leave one body for another. Once in a new body, he again attempts to fulfill his desires, and again he goes through the process of dying and accepting another material body. This is the process of transmigration.

Hayagrīva dāsa: It is interesting that neither Origen nor Christ rejected transmigration. It wasn't until Augustine that it was denied.

Śrīla Prabhupāda: Transmigration is a fact. A person cannot wear the same clothes all of his life. Our clothes become old and useless, and we have to change them. The living being is certainly eternal, but he has to accept a material body for material sense gratification, and such a body cannot endure perpetually. All of this is thoroughly explained in *Bhagavad-gītā.*

dehino'smin yathā dehe
kaumāraṁ yauvanaṁ jarā
tathā dehāntara-prāptir
dhīras tatra na muhyati

"As the embodied soul continually passes, in this body, from boyhood to youth to old age, the soul similarly passes into another body at death. The self-realized soul is not bewildered by such a change." (*Bg*. 2.13)

śarīraṁ yad avāpnoti
yac cāpy utkrāmatīśvaraḥ
gṛhītvaitāni saṁyāti
vāyur gandhān ivāśayāt

"The living entity in the material world carries his different conceptions of life from one body to another as the air carries aromas." (*Bg*. 15.8)

Augustine
(354-430)

Hayagrīva dāsa: Augustine considered the soul to be spiritual and incorporeal, but he also believed that the soul of the individual does not exist prior to birth. The soul attains its immortality only at death, and then goes on to live through eternity.
Śrīla Prabhupāda: If the soul is created, how is it immortal? How can the soul sometimes not be eternal?
Hayagrīva dāsa: Augustine would say that the soul is immortal after it is created, but that at a certain point it is brought into being.
Śrīla Prabhupāda: Then what does he consider death to be?
Hayagrīva dāsa: Augustine recognizes two types of death: physical death, wherein the soul leaves the body; and soul-death, which is the death experienced by the soul when God abandons it. When one is damned, he faces not only physical death but spiritual soul-death as well.
Śrīla Prabhupāda: Figuratively speaking, when one forgets his position, he undergoes a kind of death, but the soul is eternal. What Augustine calls spiritual death is forgetfulness. When one is unconscious, he forgets his identity, but when one is dead, he cannot revive his consciousness. Of course, until one acquires his freedom from material existence,

he is spiritually dead, even though existing in the material form. Forgetfulness of our real identity is a kind of death. When we are alive to God consciousness, we are actually alive. In any case, the soul is eternal and survives the annihilation of the body.

Hayagrīva dāsa: Augustine would consider that in some cases the forgetful stage is eternal.

Śrīla Prabhupāda: It is not. Our consciousness can always be revived, and that is the conviction of this Kṛṣṇa consciousness movement. We say that a man is unconscious when he is sleeping, but if you call him again and again, the sound of his name enters his ear, and he awakes. Similarly, this process of chanting the Hare Kṛṣṇa *mahā-mantra* awakens us to spiritual consciousness. Then we can live a spiritual life.

Hayagrīva dāsa: Augustine would say that God eternally abandons the damned soul to eternal perdition.

Śrīla Prabhupāda: He may be "eternally abandoned" in the sense that he may remain forgetful for millions of years. It may seem eternal, but our spiritual consciousness can be revived at any moment by good association, by the method of hearing and chanting. Devotional service therefore begins with *śravaṇam*, hearing. In the beginning, especially, hearing is very important. If we hear the truth from a self-realized soul, we can awake to spiritual life and remain spiritually alive in devotional service.

Hayagrīva dāsa: In *The City of God,* Augustine refers to two cities, or societies: one demonic, and the other divine. In one city, love of God and the spirit is the unifying factor; and in the other, love of the world and the flesh is dominant. Augustine writes: "These are two loves, the one of which is holy, the other unholy; one social, the other individualistic; the one is subject to God, the other sets itself up as a rival to God."

Śrīla Prabhupāda: A similar allegory is given in *Śrīmad-Bhāgavatam.* The body is likened to a city, and the soul is likened to the king of that city. The body has nine gates, and the king can leave the city through these gates. These detailed descriptions are given in *Śrīmad-Bhāgavatam.*

Hayagrīva dāsa: Augustine seems to admit the transcendence of God, but not His omnipresence as the Paramātmā accompanying each individual soul. He writes: "God is not the soul of all things, but the maker of all souls."

Śrīla Prabhupāda: Then how is God all pervading? The Paramātmā is accepted as the Supersoul both in *Brahma-saṁhitā* and in *Bhagavad-gītā.*

upadraṣṭānumantā ca

bhartā bhoktā maheśvaraḥ
paramātmeti cāpy ukto
dehe'smin puruṣaḥ paraḥ

"Yet in this body there is another, a transcendental enjoyer who is the Lord, the supreme proprietor, who exists as the overseer and permitter, and who is known as the Supersoul." (*Bg.* 13.23) God is present in every atom.

viṣṭabhyāham idaṁ kṛtsnam
ekāṁśena sthito jagat

"With a single fragment of Myself, I pervade and support this entire universe." (*Bg.* 10.42)

vadanti tat tattva-vidas
tattvaṁ yaj jñānam advayam
brahmeti paramātmeti
bhagavān iti śabdyate

"Learned transcendentalists who know the Absolute Truth call this non-dual substance Brahman, Paramātmā, and Bhagavān." (*Bhāg.* 1.2.11) Certainly God has the potency of omnipresence. This cannot be denied.

Hayagrīva dāsa: Augustine disagrees with Origen's contention that the body is like a prison. He writes: "If the opinion of Origen and his followers were true—that matter was created that souls might be enclosed in bodies, as in penitentiaries for the punishment of sin—then the higher and lighter bodies should have been for those whose sins were slight, and the lower and heavier ones for those whose crimes were great."

Śrīla Prabhupāda: The soul is essentially part and parcel of God, but is imprisoned in different types of bodies. In *Bhagavad-gītā*, Kṛṣṇa says:

sarva-yoniṣu kaunteya
mūrtayaḥ sambhavanti yāḥ
tāsāṁ brahma mahad yonir
ahaṁ bīja-pradaḥ pitā

"It should be understood that all species of life, O son of Kuntī, are made possible by birth in this material nature, and that I am the seed-giving father." (*Bg.* 14.4) From material nature, the mother, different species are coming. They are found in earth, water, air, and even fire. The individual souls, however, are part and parcel of the Supreme, who impregnates them within this material world. The living entity then comes out into the material world through the womb of some mother. It appears that the soul is coming out of matter, but it is not composed of matter.

The souls, always part and parcel of God, assume different types of bodies according to pious or impious activities or desires. The desires of the soul determine higher or lower bodies. In any case, the soul is the same. It is therefore said that those who are advanced in spiritual consciousness see the same soul in each and every body, be it the body of a dog, or a *brāhmaṇa*.

vidyā-vinaya-sampanne
brāhmaṇe gavi hastini
śuni caiva śvapāke ca
paṇḍitāḥ sama-darśinaḥ

"The humble sage, by virtue of true knowledge, sees with equal vision a learned and gentle *brāhmaṇa*, a cow, an elephant, a dog, and a dog-eater [outcaste]." (*Bg*. 5.18)

Hayagrīva dāsa: Augustine looked on Adam as the root of mankind. He writes: "God knew how good it would be for this community often to recall that the human race had its roots in one man, precisely to show how pleasing it is to God that men, though many, should be one."

Śrīla Prabhupāda: Our Vedic conception is similar. We say that mankind has come from Manu. From Manu, we get the Sanskrit word *mānuṣaḥ*, which means "coming from Manu," or "human being." Manu himself comes from Brahmā, who is the first living being. Thus living beings come from other living beings, not from matter. Brahmā, in his turn, comes from the Supreme Lord as *rajo-guṇa avatāra*. Indeed, Brahmā is the incarnation of *rajo-guṇa*, the mode of passion. All living beings ultimately come from the supreme living Being.

Hayagrīva dāsa: Like Origen, Augustine considered the soul to be created at a particular time, but unlike Origen, he rejected reincarnation: "Let these Platonists stop threatening us with reincarnation as punishment for our souls. Reincarnation is ridiculous. There is no such thing as a return to this life for the punishment of souls. If our creation, even as mortals, is due to God, how can the return to bodies, which are gifts of God, be punishment?"

Śrīla Prabhupāda: Does he think that the assumption of the body of a hog or similar lower creature is not punishment? Why does one person get the body of King Indra or Lord Brahmā, and another the body of a pig or insect? How does he explain the body of a pig? If the body is a gift from God, it can also be a punishment from God. When one is rewarded, he gets the body of a Brahmā or a King Indra, and if he is punished, he gets the body of a pig.

Hayagrīva dāsa: What about the body of a man? Is that a gift or

punishment?
Śrīla Prabhupāda: There are many men who are well situated, and others who are suffering. Suffering and enjoyment take place according to the body. As explained in *Bhagavad-gītā:*

mātrā-sparśās tu kaunteya
śītoṣṇa-sukha-duḥkha-dāḥ
āgamāpāyino'nityās
tāṁs titikṣasva bhārata

"O son of Kuntī, the nonpermanent appearance of happiness and distress, and their disappearance in due course, are like the appearance of winter and summer seasons. They arise from sense perception, O scion of Bharata, and one must learn to tolerate them without being disturbed." (*Bg*. 2.14) An old man may perceive cold very acutely, whereas a young child may not perceive it. Perception is relative to the body. An animal may go naked and not feel the cold, whereas a man cannot. Thus the body is a source of suffering and enjoyment. Or we may consider this punishment and reward.
Hayagrīva dāsa: For Augustine, the soul of each individual man is not necessarily condemned to earth due to his own desire or sin, but due to the original sin of Adam, the first man. He writes: "When the first couple [Adam and Eve] were punished by the judgement of God, the whole human race...was present in the first man. And what was born was not human nature as it was originally created, but as it became after the first parents' sin and punishment—as far, at least, as concerns the origin of sin and death." In this sense, the individual partakes of the karma of the entire race.
Śrīla Prabhupāda: If this is the case, why does he call the body a gift? Why does he say that it is not punishment? The original man was punished, as well as the man after him, and so on. Sometimes a father's disease is inherited by the son. Is this not a form of punishment?
Hayagrīva dāsa: Then the human form is a punishment in itself?
Śrīla Prabhupāda: Yes. At the same time, you can consider human life a gift because it is given by God. We should think that if God has given us this body for our punishment, it is His mercy, because by undergoing punishment we may become purified and progress toward God. Devotees think in this way. Although the body is a form of punishment, we consider it a reward because by undergoing the punishment, we are progressing toward God realization. Even when the body is given by God for our correction, it can thus be considered a gift.
Hayagrīva dāsa: For Augustine, the physical body precedes the spiritual:

"What is sown a natural body, arises a spiritual body. If there is a natural body, there is also a spiritual body.... But it is not the spiritual that comes first, but the physical. The first man was of the earth, earthly; the second man is from heaven, heavenly.... But the body which, of the life-giving spirit, will become spiritual and immortal will under no condition be able to die. It will be immortal, just as the created soul is immortal."

Śrīla Prabhupāda: Why does he speak of immortality in connection with man only? Every living entity has an immortal body. As we said, entering the mortal body is a kind of punishment. The individual undergoes an evolutionary process from lower to higher species. Every soul is part and parcel of God, but due to some sinful activity, the living entity comes into this material world. In the Bible, it is said that due to disobedience to God, Adam and Eve lost paradise and had to come into the material world. The soul belongs to the paradise in heaven, the planets of Kṛṣṇa, but somehow or other he has fallen into this material world and has taken on a body. According to our activities, we are elevated or degraded as a demigod, human being, animal, tree, or plant. In any case, the soul is always aloof from the material body. This is confirmed by Vedic literatures. Our actual spiritual life begins when we are freed from material contamination, or transmigration.

Hayagrīva dāsa: Concerning peace, Augustine writes: "Peace between a mortal man and his Maker consists in ordered obedience, guided by faith, under God's eternal law; peace between man and man consists in regulated fellowship.... The peace of the heavenly city lies in a perfectly ordered and harmonious communion of those who find their joy in God and in one another in God. Peace in its final sense is the calm that comes of order."

Śrīla Prabhupāda: Peace means coming in contact with the Supreme Personality of Godhead. A man in ignorance thinks that he is the enjoyer of this world, but when he contacts the Supreme Personality of Godhead, the supreme controller, he understands that God is the enjoyer. We are servants meant to supply enjoyment to God. A servant supplies the needs of his master. Actually, the master has no needs, but he enjoys the company of his servants, who in turn enjoy his company. A public servant is very happy when he receives a good government job, and a master is happy to acquire a very faithful servant. This is the relationship between the individual soul and God, and when this relationship is destroyed, it is said that the individual soul exists in māyā. When the relationship is restored, the individual is situated in his spiritual consciousness, which we call Kṛṣṇa consciousness, by which he understands that the supreme God is the actual enjoyer and proprietor as well as the Supreme Being. When we understand God's transcendental qualities, we become happy and attain peace.

Hayagrīva dāsa: Augustine felt that neither activity nor meditation should be exclusive but should complement one another: "No man must be so committed to contemplation as, in his contemplation, to give no thought to his neighbor's needs, nor so absorbed in action as to dispense with the contemplation of God."

Śrīla Prabhupāda: Unless you think of God, how can you be active in the service of God? Real meditation is meditation on the Supreme Personality of Godhead, or the Supersoul within the core of the heart. Activity and meditation should go together, however. If we sit down and think of God, it is commendable, but if we work for God as God desires, our position is superior. If you love me and simply sit and think of me, that is commendable. That may be considered meditation. However, if you love me, it is better that you carry out my orders. That is more important.

Hayagrīva dāsa: Augustine conceived of a spiritual world in which the movements of the spiritual bodies "will be of such unimaginable beauty that I dare not say more than this: There will be such poise, such grace, such beauty as become a place where nothing unbecoming can be found. Wherever the spirit wills, there, in a flash, the body will be.... God will be the source of every satisfaction. He will be the consummation of all our desiring, the object of our unending vision, of our unlessening love, of our unwearying praise.... The souls in bliss will still possess freedom of will, though sin will have no power to tempt them."

Śrīla Prabhupāda: Yes, sin cannot touch one who remains in contact with God. According to our desires, we associate with the modes of material nature and acquire different types of bodies. Nature, the agent of Kṛṣṇa, affords us facilities by giving us a body, which is like a machine. When a son insists, "Father, give me a cycle," the affectionate father complies. This is a typical relationship between a father and his son. As explained in *Bhagavad-gītā:*

īśvaraḥ sarva-bhūtānāṁ
hṛd-deśe'rjuna tiṣṭhati
bhrāmayan sarva-bhūtāni
yantrārūḍhāni māyayā

"The Supreme Lord is situated in everyone's heart, O Arjuna, and is directing the wanderings of all living entities, who are seated as on a machine, made of the material energy." (*Bg.* 18.61) The Supreme Father, Kṛṣṇa, is within the core of everyone's heart. As the living entity desires, the Father supplies a body manufactured by material nature. This body is destined to suffer, but the spiritual bodies in the Vaikuṇṭhas are not subject to birth, old age, disease, or death, nor the threefold miseries. They are eternal and full of knowledge and bliss.

Hayagrīva dāsa: For Augustine, the mind, reason, and the soul are one and the same.

Śrīla Prabhupāda: No, these are different identities. The mind acts according to the intelligence, but the intelligence of different living entities differs. Similarly, minds also differ. A dog's intelligence is not equal to that of a human being, but this is not to say that the dog does not have a soul. The soul is placed in different bodies that have different types of intelligence and different ways of thinking, acting, feeling, and willing. So the mind and intelligence differ according to the body, but the soul remains the same.

Hayagrīva dāsa: By identifying the soul with mind and reason, Augustine could justify killing animals. He writes: "Indeed, some people try to stretch the prohibition ['Thou shalt not kill.'] to cover beasts and cattle, and make it unlawful to kill any such animal. But then, why not include plants and anything rooted in and feeding on the soil?...Putting this nonsense aside, we do not apply 'Thou shalt not kill' to plants, because they have no sensation; nor to irrational animals that fly, swim, walk, or creep, because they are linked to us by no association or common bond. By the creator's wise ordinance, they are meant for our use, dead or alive. It only remains for us to apply the commandment, 'Thou shalt not kill' to man alone, oneself and others."

Śrīla Prabhupāda: The Bible says, "Thou shalt not kill," without qualification. Our Vedic philosophy admits that one living entity serves as food for another living entity. That is natural. As stated in *Śrīmad-Bhāgavatam,* those animals who have hands eat animals without hands. The four-legged animals eat animals that cannot move, as well as plants and vegetables. Thus the weak is food for the strong. This is a natural law. Our Kṛṣṇa consciousness philosophy, however, is not based on the view that plant life is less sensitive than animal life, or animal life is less sensitive than human life. We consider all human beings, animals, plants, and trees to be living entities, spirit souls. We may eat an animal or a vegetable—whatever the case, we must inevitably eat some living entity. It therefore becomes a question of selection. Apart from vegetarian or nonvegetarian diets, we are basically concerned with Kṛṣṇa *prasādam*. We take only the remnants of whatever Kṛṣṇa eats. In *Bhagavad-gītā*, Kṛṣṇa says:

patraṁ puṣpaṁ phalaṁ toyaṁ
yo me bhaktyā prayacchati
tad ahaṁ bhakty-upahṛtam
aśnāmi prayatātmanaḥ

"If one offers Me with love and devotion a leaf, a flower, fruit, or water, I will accept it." (*Bg.* 9.26) This is our philosophy. We are concerned with taking the remnants of Kṛṣṇa's food, which we call *prasādam*, mercy. We should not touch meat or anything else not offerable to Kṛṣṇa.

yajña-śiṣṭāśinaḥ santo
mucyante sarva-kilbiṣaiḥ
bhuñjate te tv aghaṁ pāpā
ye pacanty ātma-kāraṇāt

"The devotees of the Lord are released from all kinds of sins because they eat food which is offered first for sacrifice. Others, who prepare food for personal sense enjoyment, verily eat only sin." (*Bg.* 3.13)

III
SCHOLASTICISM

Thomas Aquinas
(1225?-1274)

Hayagrīva dāsa: Thomas Aquinas compiled the entire Church doctrine in *Summa Theologiae*, which constitutes the official philosophy of the Roman Catholic Church. Aquinas did not make Augustine's sharp distinction between the material and spiritual worlds, or between secular society and the city of God. For him, both material and spiritual creations have their origin in God. At the same time, he admits that the spiritual world is superior to the material.
Śrīla Prabhupāda: When we speak of "material world" we refer to that which is temporary. Some philosophers like the Māyāvādīs claim that the material world is false, but we Vaiṣṇavas prefer to say that it is temporary or illusory. It is a reflection of the spiritual world, but in itself it has no reality. We therefore sometimes compare the material world to a mirage in the desert. In the material world, there is no happiness, but the transcendental bliss and happiness existing in the spiritual world are reflected here. Unintelligent people chase after this illusory happiness, forgetting the real happiness that is in spiritual life.
Hayagrīva dāsa: Aquinas agreed with both the statements of Anselm and Abelard: "I believe in order that I may understand," and, "I under-

stand in order that I may believe." Thus reason and revelation complement one another as a means to truth.

Śrīla Prabhupāda: Since human reason is not perfect, revelation is also needed. The truth is attained through logic, philosophy, and revelation. According to the Vaiṣṇava tradition, we arrive at the truth through the guru, the spiritual master, who is accepted as the representative of the Absolute Truth, the Personality of Godhead. He transmits the message of the truth because he has seen the Absolute Truth through the disciplic succession. If we accept the bona fide spiritual master and please him by submissive service, by virtue of his mercy and pleasure, we can understand God and the spiritual world by revelation. We therefore offer our respects to the spiritual master in the prayer:

yasya prasādād bhagavat-prasādo
yasyāprasādān na gatiḥ kuto 'pi
dhyāyan stuvaṁs tasya yaśas tri-sandhyaṁ
vande guroḥ śrī-caraṇāravindam

"By the mercy of the spiritual master, one receives the benediction of Kṛṣṇa. Without the grace of the spiritual master, one cannot make any advancement. Therefore, I should always remember and praise the spiritual master, offering respectful obeisances unto his lotus feet at least three times a day." (*Śrī Gurv-aṣṭaka* 8) We can understand God if we please the spiritual master, who carries the Lord's message without speculation. It is stated: *sevonmukhe hi jihvādau svayam eva sphuraty adaḥ (Padma Purāṇa)*. When we engage our senses in the Lord's service, the Lord is revealed.

Hayagrīva dāsa: For Aquinas, God is the only single essence that consists of pure form. He felt that matter is only a potential, and, in order to be real, must assume a certain shape or form. In other words, the living entity has to acquire an individual form in order to actualize himself. When matter unites with form, the form gives individuality and personality.

Śrīla Prabhupāda: Matter in itself has no form; it is the spirit soul that has form. Matter is a covering for the actual form of the spirit soul. Because the soul has form, matter appears to have form. Matter is like cloth that is cut to fit the body. In the spiritual world, however, everything has form: God and the spirit souls.

Hayagrīva dāsa: Aquinas believed that only God and the angels have nonmaterial form. There is no difference between God's form and God's spiritual Self.

Śrīla Prabhupāda: Both the individual souls and God have form. That is real form. Material form is but a covering for the spiritual body.
Hayagrīva dāsa: Aquinas set forth five basic arguments for God's existence: first, God necessarily exists as the first cause; second, the material world cannot create itself but needs something external, or spiritual, to create it; third, because the world exists, there must be a creator; fourth, since there is relative perfection in the world, there must be absolute perfection underlying it; and fifth, since the creation has design and purpose, there must be a designer who planned it.
Śrīla Prabhupāda: We also honor these arguments. Also, without a father and mother, children cannot be brought into existence. Modern philosophers do not consider this strongest argument. According to *Brahma-saṁhitā*, everything has a cause, and God is the ultimate cause.

īśvaraḥ paramaḥ kṛṣṇaḥ
sac-cid-ānanda-vigrahaḥ
anādir ādir govindaḥ
sarva-kāraṇa-kāraṇam

"Kṛṣṇa, who is known as Govinda, is the Supreme Godhead. He has an eternal, blissful, spiritual body. He is the origin of all. He has no other origin, and He is the prime cause of all causes." (*Brahma-saṁhitā* 5.1)
Hayagrīva dāsa: He also states that the relative perfection we find here necessitates an absolute perfection.
Śrīla Prabhupāda: Yes, the spiritual world is absolute perfection, and this temporary material world is but a reflection of that spiritual world. Whatever perfection we find in this material world is derived from the spiritual world. *Janmādy asya yataḥ*. According to *Vedānta-sūtra*, whatever is generated comes from the Absolute Truth.
Hayagrīva dāsa: Today, some scientists even admit Aquinas's argument that since nothing can create itself in this material world, something external, or spiritual, is required for initial creation.
Śrīla Prabhupāda: Yes, a mountain cannot create anything, but a human being can give form to a stone. A mountain may be very large, but it remains a stone incapable of giving shape to anything.
Hayagrīva dāsa: Unlike Plato and Aristotle, Aquinas maintained that God created the universe out of nothing.
Śrīla Prabhupāda: No, the universe is created by God, certainly, but God and His energies are always there. You cannot logically say that the universe was created out of nothing.
Hayagrīva dāsa: Aquinas would contend that since the material universe

could not have arisen out of God's spiritual nature, it had to be created out of nothing.

Śrīla Prabhupāda: Material nature is also an energy of God's. As Kṛṣṇa states in the *Bhagavad-gītā:*

bhūmir āpo'nalo vāyuḥ
khaṁ mano buddhir eva ca
ahaṅkāra itīyaṁ me
bhinnā prakṛtir aṣṭadhā

"Earth, water, fire, air, ether, mind, intelligence, and false ego—altogether, these eight comprise My separated material energies." (*Bg.* 7.4) All of these emanate from God, and therefore they are not unreal. They are considered inferior because they are God's separated material energies. The sound that comes from a tape recorder may sound exactly like the original person's voice. The sound is not the person's voice itself, but it has come from the person. If one cannot see where the sound is coming from, one may suppose that the person is actually speaking, although the person may be far away. Similarly, the material world is an expansion of the Supreme Lord's energy, and we should not think that it has been brought into existence out of nothing. It has emanated from the Supreme Truth, but it is the inferior, separated energy. The superior energy is found in the spiritual world, which is the world of reality. In any case, we cannot agree that the material world has come from nothing.

Hayagrīva dāsa: Well, Aquinas would say that it was created by God out of nothing.

Śrīla Prabhupāda: You cannot say that God's energy is nothing. His energy is exhibited and is eternally existing with Him. God's energy must be there. If God doesn't have energy, how can He be God?

na tasya kāryaṁ karaṇaṁ ca vidyate
na tat-samaś cābhyadhikaś ca dṛśyate
parāsya śaktir vividhaiva śrūyate
svā-bhāvikī jñāna-bala-kriyā ca

"He does not possess bodily form like that of an ordinary living entity. There is no difference between His body and His soul. He is absolute. All His senses are transcendental. Any one of His senses can perform the action of any other sense. Therefore, no one is greater than Him, or equal to Him. His potencies are multifarious, and thus His deeds are automatically performed as a natural sequence." (*Śvetāśvatara Upaniṣad*, 6.8) God has multi-energies, and the material energy is but one. Since God is everything, you cannot say that the material universe comes from nothing.

Hayagrīva dāsa: Like Augustine, Aquinas believed that sin and man are concomitant. Due to Adam's original sin, all men require salvation, which can be obtained only through God's grace. But the individual has to assent by his free will for God 's grace to function.

Śrīla Prabhupāda: Yes, we call that assent *bhakti,* devotional service.

ataḥ śrī-kṛṣṇa-nāmādi
na bhaved grāhyam indriyaiḥ
sevonmukhe hi jihvādau
svayam eva sphuraty adaḥ

"Material senses cannot appreciate Kṛṣṇa's holy name, form, qualities, and pastimes. When a conditioned soul is awakened to Kṛṣṇa consciousness and renders service by using his tongue to chant the Lord's holy name, and taste the remnants of the Lord's food, the tongue is purified, and one gradually comes to understand who Kṛṣṇa really is." (*Padma Purāṇa*)

Bhakti is our eternal engagement, and when we engage in our eternal activities, we attain salvation, or liberation. When we engage in false activities, we are in illusion, māyā. *Mukti,* liberation, means remaining in our constitutional position. In the material world, we engage in many different activities, but they all refer to the material body. In the spiritual world, the spirit engages in the Lord's service, and this is liberation, or salvation.

Hayagrīva dāsa: Aquinas considered sins to be both venial and mortal. A venial sin is one that can be pardoned, but a mortal sin cannot. A mortal sin stains the soul.

Śrīla Prabhupāda: When a living entity disobeys the orders of God, he is put into this material world, and that is his punishment. He either rectifies himself by good association, or undergoes transmigration. By taking on one body after another, he is subject to the tribulations of material existence. The soul is not stained, but he can participate in sinful activity. Although you cannot mix oil and water, oil floating on water is carried away by water. As soon as we are in contact with material nature, we come under the clutches of the material world.

prakṛteḥ kriyamāṇāni
guṇaiḥ karmāṇi sarvaśaḥ
ahaṅkāra-vimūḍhātmā
kartāham iti manyate

"The bewildered spirit soul, under the influence of the three modes of material nature, thinks himself to be the doer of activities, which are in actuality carried out by nature." (*Bg.* 3.27) As soon as the living entity enters the material world, he loses his own power. He is completely under the clutches of material nature. Oil never mixes with water, but it may be carried away by the waves.

Hayagrīva dāsa: Aquinas felt that the monastic vows of poverty, celibacy, and obedience give a direct path to God, but he did not think that these austerities were meant for the masses of men. He looked on life as a pilgrimage through the world of the senses to the spiritual world of God, from imperfection to perfection, and the monastic vows are meant to help us on this path.

Śrīla Prabhupāda: Yes, according to the Vedic instructions, we must take to the path of *tapasya*, voluntary self-denial. *Tapasā brahmacaryena. Tapasya,* or austerity, begins with *brahmacarya,* celibacy. We must first learn to control the sex urge. That is the beginning of *tapasya.* We must control the senses and the mind, then we should give everything that we have to the Lord's service. By following the path of truth and remaining clean, we can practice yoga. In this way, it is possible to advance toward the spiritual kingdom. All of this can be realized, however, by engaging in devotional service. If we become devotees of Kṛṣṇa, we automatically attain the benefits of austerities without having to make a separate effort. By one stroke, devotional service, we can acquire the benefits of all the other processes.

Hayagrīva dāsa: Aquinas did not believe in a soul per se as being divorced from a particular form. God did not create a soul capable of inhabiting any body or form; rather, He created an angelic soul, a human soul, an animal soul, or a plant soul. Here again, we find the conception of the soul's creation.

Śrīla Prabhupāda: The soul is not created but is eternally existing along with God. The soul has the independence to turn from God, in which case he becomes like a spark falling from a great fire. When the spark is separated, it loses its illumination. In any case, the individual soul is always there. The master and His servants are there eternally. We cannot say that the parts of a body are separately created. As soon as the body is present, all the parts are there with it. The soul is never created, and it never dies. This is confirmed in the very beginning of *Bhagavad-gītā:*

na jāyate mriyate vā kadācin
nāyaṁ bhūtvā bhavitā vā na bhūyaḥ
ajo nityaḥ śāśvato'yaṁ purāṇo
na hanyate hanyamāne śarīre

"For the soul there is never birth nor death. Nor, having once been, does he ever cease to be. He is unborn, eternal, ever-existing, undying, and primeval. He is not slain when the body is slain." (*Bg.* 2.20) It may appear that the soul comes into existence and dies, but this is because he has accepted the material body. When the material body dies, the soul transfers to another body. When the soul is liberated, he doesn't have to accept another material body. He can return home, back to Godhead, in his original spiritual body. The soul was never created but is always existing with God. If we say that the soul was created, the question may be raised whether or not God, the Supreme Soul, was also created. Of course, this is not the case. God is eternal, and His parts and parcels are also eternal. The difference is that God never accepts a material body, whereas the individual soul, being but a small particle, sometimes succumbs to the material energy.

Hayagrīva dāsa: Is the soul eternally existing with God in a spiritual form?

Śrīla Prabhupāda: Yes.

Hayagrīva dāsa: So the soul has a form that is incorruptible. Is this not also the form of the material body?

Śrīla Prabhupāda: The material body is an imitation. It is false. Because the spiritual body has form, the material body, which is a coating, takes on form. As I have already explained, a cloth originally has no form, but a tailor can cut the cloth to fit a form. In actuality, this material form is illusory. It originally has no form. It takes on form for a while, and when it becomes old and useless, it returns to its original position. In *Bhagavad-gītā* (18.61), the body is compared to a machine. The soul has his own form, but he is given a machine, the body, which he uses to wander throughout the universe, attempting to enjoy himself.

Hayagrīva dāsa: I think that part of the problem is that Augustine and Aquinas could not conceive of a spiritual form. When they speak of form, they think that matter must necessarily be involved. Aquinas followed the Augustinian and Platonic doctrines maintaining that if the soul is independent from matter, man loses his basic unity. He saw man as both body and soul. A man is a particular type of soul in a specific body.

Śrīla Prabhupāda: When you are dressed, it appears that you are not different from your clothes. Your clothes move just as you do, but you are completely different.

Hayagrīva dāsa: Aquinas did not believe that the living entity has pure spiritual form as such. Matter is necessary to give the soul form.

Śrīla Prabhupāda: No. He has his original form.

Hayagrīva dāsa: Is this the form of the body?

Śrīla Prabhupāda: It is the form of the spirit. The body takes on form because the spirit has form. Matter has no form, but it coats the spiritual

form of the soul and thus takes on form.
Hayagrīva dāsa: Aquinas considered sex to be meant exclusively for the begetting of children, and the parents are responsible for giving their children a spiritual education.
Śrīla Prabhupāda: That is also the Vedic injunction. You should not beget children unless you can liberate them from the cycle of birth and death.

gurur na sa syāt sva-jano na sa syāt
pitā na sa syāj jananī na sā syāt
daivaṁ na tat syān na patiś ca sa syān
na mocayed yaḥ samupeta-mṛtyum

"One who cannot deliver his dependents from the path of repeated birth and death should never become a spiritual master, a father, a husband, a mother, or a worshipable demigod." (*Bhāg.* 5.5.18)
Hayagrīva dāsa: Aquinas argued that sex for reasons other than propagation is "repugnant to the good of nature, which is the conservation of the species." Considering today's overpopulation, does this argument still hold?
Śrīla Prabhupāda: The conservation of the species doesn't enter into it. Illicit sex is sinful because it is for sense gratification instead of the begetting of children. Sense gratification in any form is sinful.
Hayagrīva dāsa: Concerning the state, Aquinas believed like Plato in an enlightened monarchy, but in certain cases, he felt that it is not necessary for man to obey human laws if these laws are opposed to human welfare and are instruments of violence.
Śrīla Prabhupāda: Yes, but first of all we must know what our welfare is. Unfortunately, as materialistic education advances, we are missing the aim of life. Life's aim is declared openly in the *Vedānta-sūtra: athāto brahma-jijñāsā.* Life is meant for understanding the Absolute Truth. Vedic civilization is based on this principle, but modern civilization has deviated and is devoting itself to that which cannot possibly relieve us from the tribulations of birth, old age, disease, and death. So-called scientific advancement has not solved life's real problems. Although we are eternal, we are presently subjected to birth and death. In this age of Kali-yuga, people are slow to learn about self-realization. People create their own way of life, and they are unfortunate and disturbed.
Hayagrīva dāsa: Aquinas concludes that if the laws of God and man conflict, we should obey the laws of God.
Śrīla Prabhupāda: Yes. We can also obey the man who obeys the laws of God. It is useless to obey an imperfect person. That is the blind follow-

ing the blind. If the leader does not follow the instructions of the supreme controller, he is necessarily blind, and he cannot lead. Why should we risk our lives by following blind men who believe that they are knowledgeable but are not? We should instead decide to take lessons from the Supreme Person, Kṛṣṇa, who knows everything perfectly. Kṛṣṇa knows past, present, and future, and what is for our benefit.

Hayagrīva dāsa: For Aquinas, all earthly powers exist only by God's permission. Since the Church is God's emissary on earth, the Church should control secular power as well. He felt that secular rulers should remain subservient to the Church, which should be able to excommunicate a monarch and dethrone him.

Śrīla Prabhupāda: World activities should be regulated so that God is the ultimate goal of understanding. Although the Church, or the *brāhmaṇas*, may not directly carry out administrative activities, the government should function under their supervision and instructions. That is the Vedic system. The administrators, the *kṣatriyas*, used to take instructions from the *brāhmaṇas*, who could deliver a spiritual message. It is mentioned in *Bhagavad-gītā* (4.1) that millions of years ago, Kṛṣṇa instructed the sun god in the yoga of *Bhagavad-gītā*. The sun god is the origin of the *kṣatriyas*. If the king follows the instructions of the Vedas or other scriptures through the *brāhmaṇas*, or through a bona fide church, he is not only a king but a saintly person as well. The *kṣatriyas* should follow the orders of the *brāhmaṇas*, and the *vaiśyas* should follow the orders of the *kṣatriyas*. The *śūdras* should follow the instructions of the three superior orders.

Hayagrīva dāsa: Concerning the beauty of God, Aquinas writes: "God is beautiful in Himself and not in relation to some limited terminus....It is clear that the beauty of all things is derived from the divine beauty....God wishes to multiply His own beauty as far as possible, that is to say, by the communication of His likeness. Indeed, all things are made in order to imitate divine beauty in some fashion."

Śrīla Prabhupāda: Yes, God is the reservoir of all knowledge, beauty, strength, fame, renunciation, and wealth. God is the reservoir of everything, and therefore whatever we see that is beautiful emanates from a very minute part of God's beauty.

yad yad vibhūtimat sattvaṁ
śrīmad ūrjitam eva vā
tad tad evāvagaccha tvaṁ
mama tejo'ṁśa-sambhavam

"Know that all beautiful, glorious, and mighty creations spring from but a spark of My splendor." (*Bg.* 10.41)

Hayagrīva dāsa: Concerning the relationship between theology and philosophy, Aquinas writes: "As sacred doctrine is based on the light of faith, so is philosophy founded on the natural light of reason.... If any point among the statements of the philosophers is found contrary to faith, this is not philosophy but rather an abuse of philosophy, resulting from a defect in reasoning."

Śrīla Prabhupāda: Yes, that is correct. Due to material conditional life, every man is defective. The philosophy of defective people cannot help society. Perfect philosophy comes from one who is in contact with the Supreme Personality of Godhead, and such philosophy is beneficial. Speculative philosophers base their beliefs on imagination.

Hayagrīva dāsa: Aquinas concluded that divine revelation is absolutely necessary because very few men can arrive at the truth through the philosophical method. It is a path full of errors, and the journey takes a long time.

Śrīla Prabhupāda: Yes, that is a fact. We should directly contact the Supreme Person, Kṛṣṇa, who has complete knowledge. We should understand His instructions and try to follow them.

Hayagrīva dāsa: Aquinas believed that the author of sacred scriptures can be only God Himself, who can not only "adjust words to their meaning, which even man can do, but also adjust things in themselves." Also, scriptures are not restricted to one meaning.

Śrīla Prabhupāda: The meaning of scriptures is one, but the interpretations may be different. In the Bible it is stated that God created the universe, and that is a fact. One may conjecture that the universe was created out of some chunk, or whatever, but we should not interpret scripture in this way. We present *Bhagavad-gītā* as it is without interpretation or motive. We cannot change the words of God. Unfortunately, many interpreters have spoiled the God consciousness of society.

Hayagrīva dāsa: In this, Aquinas seems to differ from the official Catholic doctrine, which admits only the Pope's interpretation. For him, the scriptures may contain many meanings according to our degree of realization.

Śrīla Prabhupāda: The meaning is one, but if we are not realized, we may interpret many meanings. It is stated both in the Bible and *Bhagavad-gītā* that God created the universe.

ahaṁ sarvasya prabhavo

mattaḥ sarvaṁ pravartate

"I am the source of all spiritual and material worlds. Everything emanates from Me." (*Bg.* 10.8) If it is a fact that everything is an emanation of God's energy, why should we accept a second meaning or interpretation? What is the possible second meaning?

Hayagrīva dāsa: Well, in the Bible it is stated that after creating the universe, God walked through paradise in the afternoon. Aquinas would consider this to have an interior, or metaphorical, meaning.

Śrīla Prabhupāda: If God can create, He can also walk, speak, touch, and see. If God is a person, why is a second meaning necessary? What could it possibly be?

Hayagrīva dāsa: Impersonal speculation.

Śrīla Prabhupāda: If God is the creator of all things, He must be a person. Things appear to come from secondary causes, but actually everything is created by the Supreme Creator.

Hayagrīva dāsa: Aquinas seems to have encouraged individual interpretation. He writes: "It belongs to the dignity of divine scripture to contain many meanings in one text, so that it may be appropriate to the various understandings of men for each man to marvel at the fact that he can find the truth that he has conceived in his own mind expressed in divine scripture."

Śrīla Prabhupāda: No. If one's mind is perfect, he may give a meaning, but, according to our conviction, if one is perfect, why should he try to change the word of God? And if one is imperfect, what is the value of his change?

Hayagrīva dāsa: Aquinas doesn't say "change."

Śrīla Prabhupāda: Interpretation means change. If man is imperfect, how can he change the words of God? If the words can be changed, they are not perfect. So there will be doubt whether the words are spoken by God or by an imperfect person.

Hayagrīva dāsa: The many different Protestant faiths resulted from such individual interpretation. It's surprising to find this viewpoint in Aquinas.

Śrīla Prabhupāda: As soon as you interpret or change the scripture, the scripture loses its authority. Then another man will come and interpret things in his own way. Another will come and then another, and in this way the original purport of the scripture is lost.

Hayagrīva dāsa: Aquinas believed that it is not possible to see God in this life. He writes: "God cannot be seen in His essence by one who is merely man, except he be separated from this mortal life....The divine essence cannot be known through the nature of material things."

Śrīla Prabhupāda: What does he mean by divine essence? For us, God's divine essence is personal. When one cannot conceive of the Personality of Godhead, he sees the impersonal feature everywhere. When one advances further, he sees God as the Paramātmā within his heart. That is the result of yoga meditation. Finally, if one is truly advanced, he can see God face to face. When Kṛṣṇa came, people saw Him face to face. Christians accept Christ as the son of God, and when he came, people saw him face to face. Does Aquinas think that Christ is not the divine essence of God?

Hayagrīva dāsa: For a Christian, Christ must be the divine essence.

Śrīla Prabhupāda: And didn't many people see him? Then how can Aquinas say that God cannot be seen?

Hayagrīva dāsa: It's difficult to tell whether Aquinas is basically impersonalist or personalist.

Śrīla Prabhupāda: That means that he is speculating.

Hayagrīva dāsa: He writes about the personal feature in this way: "Because God's nature has all perfection and thus every kind of perfection should be attributed to Him, it is fitting to use the word 'person' to speak of God; yet when used of God it is not used exactly as it is of creatures but in a higher sense....Certainly the dignity of divine nature surpasses every nature, and thus it is entirely suitable to speak of God as a 'person.'" Aquinas is no more specific than this.

Śrīla Prabhupāda: Christ is accepted as the son of God, and if the son can be seen, why can't the Father be seen? If Christ is the son of God, who is God? In *Bhagavad-gītā*, Kṛṣṇa says: *ahaṁ sarvasya prabhavaḥ*. "Everything is emanating from Me." (*Bg.* 10.8) Christ says that he is the son of God, and this means that he emanates from God. Just as he has his personality, God also has His personality. Therefore we refer to Kṛṣṇa as the Supreme Personality of Godhead.

Hayagrīva dāsa: Concerning God's names, Aquinas writes: "Yet since God is simple and subsisting, we attribute to Him simple and abstract names to signify His simplicity, and concrete names to signify His subsistence and perfection; although both these kinds of names fail to express His mode of being, because our intellect does not know Him in this life as He is."

Śrīla Prabhupāda: One of God's attributes is being. Similarly, one of His attributes is attraction. God attracts everything. The word "Kṛṣṇa" means "all attractive." What, then, is wrong with addressing God as Kṛṣṇa? Because Kṛṣṇa is the enjoyer of Rādhārāṇī, His name is Rādhikā-ramaṇa. Because He exists, He is called the Supreme Being. In one sense, God has no name, but in another sense He has millions of names according to His activities.

Hayagrīva dāsa: Aquinas maintains that although the names apply to God to signify one reality, they are not synonymous because they signify that reality under diverse aspects.

Śrīla Prabhupāda: God's names are there because He has different features and activities.

Hayagrīva dāsa: But Aquinas asserts that no name belongs to God in the same sense that it belongs to creatures.

Śrīla Prabhupāda: The names of creatures are also derived from God. For instance, Hayagrīva appeared as the horse incarnation, and therefore a devotee is named Hayagrīva dāsa, which means "servant of God." This name is not created; it refers to the activities of God.

Hayagrīva dāsa: Aquinas believed that names of God that imply relation to creatures are predicated of God temporarily. He writes: "Though God is prior to the creature, still, because the signification of 'Lord' includes the idea of a servant and vice versa, these two relative terms, Lord and servant, are simultaneous by nature. Hence God was not 'Lord' until He had a creature subject to Himself....Thus names which import relation to creatures are applied to God temporarily, and not from eternity, since God is outside the whole order of creation."

Śrīla Prabhupāda: God is always existing as the Lord, and His servants are existing everlastingly with Him. How can He be the Lord without a servant? How can it be that God has no servants?

Hayagrīva dāsa: Well, the contention is that creatures were created at one point in time, and before that, God must have been by Himself.

Śrīla Prabhupāda: That is a material idea. It is the material world that is created, not the spiritual world. The spiritual world and God are existing everlastingly. The bodies of creatures in this material world are created, but God is always in the spiritual world with countless servants. According to our philosophy, there is no limit to living entities. Those who do not like to serve are put into this material world. As far as our identity as eternal servant is concerned, that is eternal, whether we are in the material or spiritual world. If we do not serve God in the spiritual world, we come down into the material world to serve the illusory energy of God. In any case, God is always master, and the living entity always servant. In the material world, the living entity, although a servant, is thinking of himself as a master. This is a false conception that creates many disturbances. This forgetfulness or misconception is not possible in the spiritual world. There, the self-realized souls know their position as eternal servants of God, the eternal spiritual master.

Hayagrīva dāsa: Aquinas felt that the less determinate God's name, the more universal and absolute it is. He therefore believed that the most proper name for God is "He who is."
Śrīla Prabhupāda: Why? If God is active and has created the entire universe, what is wrong in addressing Him according to His activities and attributes?
Hayagrīva dāsa: Aquinas claims that the very essence of God is the sheer fact of His being, the fact that He is.
Śrīla Prabhupāda: He is, certainly, but "He is" means that He is existing in His abode with His servants, playmates, hobbies, and paraphernalia. Everything is there. We must ask what is the meaning or nature of His being.
Hayagrīva dāsa: It seems that Aquinas was basically impersonalist.
Śrīla Prabhupāda: No. He could not determine whether God is personal or impersonal. His inclination was to serve God as a person, but he had no clear conception of His personality. Therefore he speculates.
Hayagrīva dāsa: In the Vedas, is there an equivalent to "He who is?"
Śrīla Prabhupāda: *Oṁ tat sat* is impersonal. This mantra, however, can also be extended as *oṁ namo bhagavate vāsudevāya.* The word *vāsudeva* means "one who lives everywhere," and refers to Bhagavān, the Supreme Personality of Godhead. God is both personal and impersonal, but the impersonal feature is secondary. According to Bhagavān Śrī Kṛṣṇa in *Bhagavad-gītā:*

brahmaṇo hi pratiṣṭhāham
amṛtasyāvyayasya ca
śāśvatasya ca dharmasya
sukhasyaikāntikasya ca

"And I am the basis of the impersonal Brahman, which is the constitutional position of ultimate happiness, and which is immortal, imperishable, and eternal." (*Bg.* 14.27) What is the purport to that?
Hayagrīva dāsa [reading]: "The constitution of Brahman is the beginning of transcendental realization. Paramātmā, the Supersoul, is the middle, the second stage in transcendental realization, and the Supreme Personality of Godhead is the ultimate realization of the Absolute Truth."
Śrīla Prabhupāda: That is divine essence.
Hayagrīva dāsa: Aquinas was perhaps the most prolific of the Church writers. His *Summa Theologiae* still serves as official Roman Catholic doctrine. Since the words of Christ are often allegorical, they have always been open to many different interpretations.

Śrīla Prabhupāda: That is not very good.
Hayagrīva dāsa: Christ used a lot of parables to simplify a transcendental message. For instance, he likened the word of the kingdom of God to a seed that sometimes falls among thorns, or on rocky land, and even somtimes in a fertile place, where it grows.
Śrīla Prabhupāda: A similar description is given in the *Upaniṣads*, wherein the living entity is compared to a spark, and God to the fire. When the sparks are in the fire, they are illuminated, but when they fall from the fire, their position is different. The sparks may fall on rock, in the water, or on the ground, just as the living entity may fall into the modes—*sattva-guṇa*, *rajo-guṇa*, and *tamo-guṇa*—within the material world.

John Duns Scotus
(1265?-1308)

Hayagrīva dāsa: Scotus, a Thirteenth Century Scotsman, was Thomas Aquinas's principal antagonist. Whereas Aquinas emphasized the intellect, Scotus emphasized what he called the primacy of will. The will is even superior to the intellect, and this is true for both God and man. Scotus felt that if this were not the case, the will would not be free but would be controlled by the intellect, which is exterior to the soul.
Śrīla Prabhupāda: According to the Vedic understanding, intelligence, or intellect, is superior to the mind, and superior to the intelligence is the ego. The mind is superior to the gross senses and controls them.

indriyāṇi parāṇy āhur
indriyebhyaḥ paraṁ manaḥ
manasas tu parā buddhir
yo buddheḥ paratas tu saḥ

"The working senses are superior to dull matter; mind is higher than the senses; intelligence is still higher than the mind; and he [the soul] is even higher than the intelligence." (*Bg*. 3.42)

If the mind acts intelligently, the senses can be utilized for self-realization. If the mind does not act intelligently, the senses act for material sense gratification. This is the conclusion of *Bhagavad-gītā*.

bandhur ātmātmanas tasya
yenātmaivātmanā jitaḥ
anātmanas tu śatrutve
vartetātmaiva śatruvat

"For him who has conquered the mind, the mind is the best of friends; but for one who has failed to do so, his very mind will be the greatest enemy." (*Bg.* 6.6)

A dog also has a mind, but his intelligence is inferior to that of human beings. When a dog sees some eatables, he will come for them, although his master may drive him away. If he has a little intelligence, he goes away when his master tells him to, but due to his limited intelligence, after a few minutes he may return. He has a mind capable of remembering that there is something eatable for him, but he hasn't sufficient intelligence to know that the food is forbidden. That is the difference between the mind and the intelligence. Therefore, according to the Vedic understanding, intelligence is superior to the mind.

Hayagrīva dāsa: Where does the will enter?

Śrīla Prabhupāda: Thinking, feeling, and willing are activities of the mind, and are within the mind.

Hayagrīva dāsa: Scotus believes that everything is subordinate to the divine will.

Śrīla Prabhupāda: Of course, because the divine will is always perfect. Whatever is divine is perfect and flawless. Whatever the Supreme Divine Personality wills actually becomes a fact. Our thinking, feeling, and willing differ from the supreme will of the Personality of Godhead. Our mind proposes, and God disposes. We may express our will, but unless our desires are sanctioned by the will of the Supreme, they cannot be fulfilled. Despite our willing to live to a certain age, for instance, we cannot do so if God does not will us to. In every sphere of activity, we express our will, but our will must be sanctioned by the supreme will in order to be successful. Therefore God's will is called supreme.

Hayagrīva dāsa: Scotus would say that everything is good because it is sustained by God's absolute will. God's killing is good, for instance, simply because God wills it to be so.

Śrīla Prabhupāda: Yes. Because God is perfect, whatever He does is perfect.

Hayagrīva dāsa: Scotus's view is in opposition to that of Aquinas, who would say that everything is subordinate to the divine intelligence.

Śrīla Prabhupāda: But what does he understand by the divine intelligence? In relation to us, divine intelligence is this: We living entities are eternal servants of God, but we have wanted to become God ourselves, master of everything. Ignorance, or māyā, thus differs from divine intelligence. In the ignorance of materialism, people work very hard to become monarchs of all they survey. All this is taking place under various "ism's." We are thinking that we are proprietors, but the Supreme Lord is the only factual proprietor.

īśāvāsyam idaṁ sarvaṁ
yat kiñca jagatyāṁ jagat
tena tyaktena bhuñjīthā
mā gṛdhaḥ kasya svid dhanam

"Everything animate or inanimate that is within the universe is controlled and owned by the Lord. One should therefore accept only those things necessary for himself, which are set aside as his quota, and one should not accept other things, knowing well to whom they belong." (*Īśopaniṣad* 1)

Hayagrīva dāsa: Scotus believes that there is an interplay of the will and the intellect because before we will something to be, we must first know the facts about it. Despite this counterplay, Scotus maintains that the will alone is the total cause of volition in the will.

Śrīla Prabhupāda: Yes, that is thinking, feeling, and willing. When we are ignorant, we think our will is supreme. So-called philosophers like to say, "I think," or "I believe," but this is not perfect knowledge. Perfect knowledge is thinking as God Himself thinks.

Hayagrīva dāsa: Scotus affirmed that it was the Church's unfailing authority that provided the criterion of truth. Church dogma was sacred, and philosophy was naturally subordinate to it. Revelation was behind all Church dogma, and therefore sacred dogma is not open for debate.

Śrīla Prabhupāda: If by "church" we mean an institution wherein we can learn about God, then philosophy is certainly subordinate. In such a Church, we can learn what God Himself is, what He is willing, and how He is acting. We may learn this either from the Bible or another scripture. However, if the Church is polluted by imperfect interpretation, and there are different factions, the truth is lost. At such a time, the authority of Christ is no longer imparted. People become free to think and act as they like, and thus God's kingdom is lost.

Hayagrīva dāsa: Because the *paramparā* is broken?

Śrīla Prabhupāda: Yes. The Church is the supreme authority provided that it maintains itself in exactly the same way and does not deviate from its beginning. As soon as we interpret and divide, the message is lost.

Hayagrīva dāsa: The Protestants claimed that the *paramparā* of the

Catholic Church was broken, therefore they broke from Catholicism and fragmented into many different sects.

Śrīla Prabhupāda: Yes, they condemned the Catholic Church because its *paramparā* was broken, but they concluded, "Let us also break." Those who first broke away from the message as it is and those who followed them by breaking away themselves are both to blame. Since the original solidarity of the Christian religion is broken, the Christian religion is dwindling and losing its importance.

Hayagrīva dāsa: For Scotus, apart from being a human being, each individual is also a specific personality. The individual is the ultimate reality because prior to existence he existed in essence in the mind of God.

Śrīla Prabhupāda: The real fact is that the living entity is eternal, and the material world is created to satisfy his false existence, which is called false ego (*ahaṅkāra*). The individual is thinking that he is independent and can act independent of God. That is the beginning of paradise lost, of Adam's fall. When Adam and Eve thought that they could do something independently, they were condemned. Every living entity is the eternal servant of God, and he must act according to the desire or will of the Supreme Lord. When he deviates from this principle, he is lost. Losing paradise, he comes into the material world, and God gives him certain facilities to act, but says, "If you act according to this system, you can come back to Me. If you do not follow this system, you go down and down." That is the process of transmigration, the rotation of the cycle of birth and death. This is all due to disobeying God. When the living entity hears the instructions of the Supreme Lord, he again revives his original constitutional position and returns home, back to Godhead.

sarva-dharmān parityajya
mām ekaṁ śaraṇaṁ vraja
ahaṁ tvāṁ sarva-pāpebhyo
mokṣayiṣyāmi mā śucaḥ

"Abandon all varieties of religion and just surrender unto Me. I shall deliver you from all sinful reaction. Do not fear." (*Bg.* 18.66)

Hayagrīva dāsa: Aquinas believed that the angels—what the Vedas might call *devas*—have pure spiritual forms, but Scotus argues that only God Himself has a purely spiritual form since only God is perfect essence.

Śrīla Prabhupāda: Yes, since God exists in His spiritual form, He never falls down; therefore He is sometimes called Acyuta. When a person falls from his original, spiritual position, he is *cyuta*, fallen. God, however, is Acyuta because He is not subject to falling down.

Hayagrīva dāsa: Scotus rejects the method of negation, the *neti-neti*

process, as being of no particular value. Knowledge of God must be positive, and negative concepts only presuppose a positive concept.
Śrīla Prabhupāda: Yes, the *neti-neti* process is for those who are still speculating. This is an indirect process by which one negates everything material. Positive understanding means taking direct knowledge from God Himself.

mattaḥ parataraṁ nānyat
kiñcid asti dhanañjaya
mayi sarvam idaṁ protaṁ
sūtre maṇi-gaṇā iva

"O conqueror of wealth [Arjuna], there is no Truth superior to Me. Everything rests upon Me, as pearls are strung on a thread." (*Bg.* 7.7) If we accept the words of God, we save ourselves much labor. We cannot understand God by speculation, but still we are inclined to speculate. But knowing God perfectly is knowing God beyond a doubt. Kṛṣṇa tells Arjuna:

mayy āsakta-manāḥ pārtha
yogaṁ yuñjan mad-āśrayaḥ
asaṁśayaṁ samagraṁ māṁ
yathā jñāsyasi tac chṛṇu

"Now hear, O son of Pṛthā, how by practicing yoga in full consciousness of Me, with mind attached to Me, you can know Me in full, free from doubt." (*Bg.* 7.1) The word *asaṁśayam* means "without a doubt," and *samagram* means "complete." Following Kṛṣṇa and trying to understand Him is called *bhakti-yoga,* and such yoga is possible for one who is actually attached to Kṛṣṇa. Therefore our first business is learning how to be attached to Kṛṣṇa (*mayy āsakta-manāḥ pārtha).* There are nine different aspects of *bhakti-yoga: śravaṇaṁ kīrtanaṁ viṣṇoḥ smaraṇam,* etc. Of these, *śravaṇam* (hearing), and *kīrtanam* (chanting), are most important. Then there is remembering, worshipping in the temple according to the regulations, rising early in the morning, offering *ārātrika,* and so forth. This is the process of *bhakti-yoga* meant to increase our devotion for Kṛṣṇa. When attachment increases, we become very obedient and always engage devotedly in His service. When Kṛṣṇa sees that we are obeying Him, He reveals Himself.

teṣāṁ satata-yuktānāṁ
bhajatāṁ prīti-pūrvakam
dadāmi buddhi-yogaṁ taṁ
yena māṁ upayānti te

"To those who are constantly devoted and worship Me with love, I give

the understanding by which they can come to Me." (*Bg.* 10.10) These are the words of Śrī Kṛṣṇa speaking directly to Arjuna, and we take this to be a perfect statement. What is the purport I give to this in *Bhagavad-gītā As It Is?*
Hayagrīva dāsa [reading]: "In this verse the word *buddhi-yogam* is very significant. We may remember that in the Second Chapter, the Lord, instructing Arjuna, said that He had spoken to him of many things, and that He would instruct him in the way of *buddhi-yoga*. Now *buddhi-yoga* is explained. *Buddhi-yoga* itself is action in Kṛṣṇa consciousness; that is the highest intelligence. *Buddhi* means intelligence, and *yogam* means mystic activities, or mystic elevation. When one tries to go back home, back to Godhead, and takes fully to Kṛṣṇa consciousness in devotional service, his action is called *buddhi-yogam*. In other words, *buddhi-yogam* is the process by which one gets out of the entanglement of this material world. The ultimate goal of progress is Kṛṣṇa. People do not know this; therefore the association of devotees and a bona fide spiritual master is important. One should know that the goal is Kṛṣṇa, and when the goal is assigned, then the path is slowly but progressively traversed and the ultimate goal reached.

"When a person knows the goal of life but is addicted to the fruits of activities, he is acting in *karma-yoga*. When he knows that the goal is Kṛṣṇa, but he takes pleasure in mental speculations to understand Kṛṣṇa, he is acting in *jñāna-yoga*. And when he knows the goal and seeks Kṛṣṇa completely in Kṛṣṇa consciousness and devotional service, he is acting in *bhakti-yoga*, or *buddhi-yoga*, which is the complete yoga. This complete yoga is the highest perfectional stage of life.

"A person may have a bona fide spiritual master and may be attached to a spiritual organization, but still, if he is not intelligent enough to make progress, then Kṛṣṇa from within gives him instructions so that he may ultimately come to Him without difficulty. The qualification is that a person always engage himself in Kṛṣṇa consciousness and with love and devotion render all kinds of services. He should perform some sort of work for Kṛṣṇa, and that work should be with love. If a devotee is intelligent enough, he will make progress on the path of self- realization. If one is sincere and devoted to the activities of devotional service, the Lord gives him a chance to make progress and ultimately attain to Him."
Śrīla Prabhupāda: So this is the process in summary.
Hayagrīva dāsa: Scotus argued for the existence of God on the basis of primary cause, but he felt that the proposition "God exists" is not of much use unless we understand what God is and know something of His nature.

Śrīla Prabhupāda: God is the Supreme Father, and He has created everything within our experience. When we are convinced that there is certainly a creator, we can make further progress to understand the nature of that creator. Is He animate or inanimate? Is He matter, or a living being? Further analysis takes up from this point, but first we must understand that God is the creator. That is very well explained in *Bhagavad-gītā:*

sarva-yoniṣu kaunteya
mūrtayaḥ sambhavanti yāḥ
tāsāṁ brahma mahad yonir
ahaṁ bīja-pradaḥ pitā

"It should be understood that all species of life, O son of Kuntī, are made possible by birth in this material nature, and that I am the seed-giving father." (*Bg.* 14.4) Everything is coming from the womb (*yoni*) of material nature. If the earth or material nature is the mother, there must be a father. Of course, atheists think that a mother can give birth without a father, but that thinking is most unnatural. One next asks, "Who is my father? What is his position? How does he talk? How does he live?" First we must understand that there is a creator father, and then we can understand His nature. This understanding must be beyond a doubt (*asaṁśayam*).

Hayagrīva dāsa: Scotus was also opposed to Aquinas in his belief that the human soul can be separated from the body, and when it is separated, it is not changed at all. When the soul is united with the body, it activates the body, but the soul itself is beyond corruption. The individual soul is incapable of destroying itself or giving itself being.

Śrīla Prabhupāda: The individual soul is always separate from the body. That is the Vedic injunction: *asaṅgo hyayaṁ puruṣa iti (Bṛhad āraṇyakopanīṣat* 4.3.16). If the body actually mixed with the soul, how could the soul give up one body and accept another? The soul is always aloof from the body, from its material formation. The living entity, the *jīva-soul,* is always *asaṅga*, incorruptible.

IV
RENAISSANCE THOUGHT

Niccolo Machiavelli
(1469-1527)

Hayagrīva dāsa: Machiavelli has been called the most influential political philosopher of the Renaissance, and his philosophy of politics has influenced rulers down to modern times. He is typical of the Renaissance in that he turned from the subjects of the Church fathers—such as God, heaven, and salvation—to concentrate on man and nature. The Renaissance marked a decline in the Church's power, and philosophy began a process of secularization. Machiavelli himself admitted that his most famous work, *The Prince*, does not apply to a Utopian state composed of good citizens; rather, it is an unscrupulous philosophy that applies to corrupt citizens. *The Prince* is a guidebook for a tyrant, and it contains the advice he chose to impart to the ruling Medici family. It is a justification for immoral actions. Power is the ultimate goal, and in the quest for power, the end justifies the means. Success in attaining power makes one the object of obedience and respect. Failure is the only sin.
Śrīla Prabhupāda: So, this is politics, the occupation of *kṣatriyas*. In *Bhagavad-gītā*, the qualities of a *kṣatriya* are given:

śauryaṁ tejo dhṛtir dākṣyaṁ
yuddhe cāpy apalāyanam

dānam īśvara-bhāvaś ca
kṣātraṁ karma svabhāva-jam

"Heroism, power, determination, resourcefulness, courage in battle, generosity, and leadership are the qualities of work for the *kṣatriyas*." (*Bg*. 18.43) Of course, in modern politics, the king or president does not come onto the battlefield to exhibit his courage. He simply appears when there is a battle of words, but when there is an actual battle, he remains in a secluded place and lets the citizens fight. And he institutes a draft board to assure that they will. According to the Vedic system, however, when there is a fight, the king or president must be present on the battlefield and should lead the fight himself so that his men will be encouraged. This is called *yuddhe cāpy apalāyanam*. The leader of a nation should fight with all his ability and be determined either to gain victory in the battle, or lay down his life. *Bhagavad-gītā* itself is a guidebook for *kṣatriyas* and was originally spoken to the sun-god millions of years ago. Sometimes, people try to interpret *Bhagavad-gītā* as a philosophy of nonviolence, but in politics there must be violence, because the king must emerge victorious. It is stated in the Vedas that if the king is victorious, he will be respected. Strength must be there. Apart from this, the chief of state must also be charitable, and formerly all the great kings performed big *yajñas*, sacrifices.

annād bhavanti bhūtāni
parjanyād anna-sambhavaḥ
yajñād bhavati parjanyo
yajñaḥ karma-samudbhavaḥ

"All living bodies subsist on food grains, which are produced from rains. Rains are produced by performance of *yajña* [sacrifice], and *yajña* is born of prescribed duties." (*Bg*. 3.14) When sufficient sacrifices are performed by the royal head of government, rainfall results. Power in itself is not sufficient. One must be powerful enough to fully satisfy the citizens by supplying them sufficient grains so that men and animals can eat and be satisfied. This is an ability that the politician or prince should have. He should be not only powerful but charitable as well. Taxes exacted from the citizens should be properly utilized in performing sacrifices. Of course, it is not possible to perform *yajñas* today as previously. Formerly, they used to sacrifice tons of ghee and grain in the fire, but today that is impractical. The best *yajña* for today is *saṅkīrtana-yajña* propagated by this Kṛṣṇa consciousness movement. The heads of state should encourage this.

Hayagrīva dāsa: Machiavelli felt that the prince must at least exhibit five basic virtues, whether he has them or not. These are mercy, faith, integrity, humanity, and religion. He writes: "It is not necessary for a prince to have all the above-mentioned qualities, but it is very necessary to seem to have them. I would even be so bold as to say that to possess them and always to practice them is dangerous, but to appear to possess them is useful. Thus it is well to seem merciful, faithful, humane, sincere, religious, and also to be so; but you must have your mind so disposed that, when it is needful to be otherwise, you can change to the opposite qualities."

Śrīla Prabhupāda: Well, Machiavelli may think like that, but unless a prince or king possesses all these qualities, he is unworthy. If he is unworthy, he cannot remain a prince because he is situated artificially. Because the kings lacked the proper qualities, monarchy is finished today, and democracy has become prominent. In Indian history, however, there were kings like Mahārāja Parīkṣit, who actually possessed all good qualities. When Parīkṣit Mahārāja went on a tour of his kingdom and saw a black man attempting to kill a cow, the Mahārāja immediately drew his sword and said, "Who is this person trying to kill a cow in my kingdom? He must be punished." A king must exhibit such determination to give protection to all the inhabitants of his kingdom. At the present moment, governments are not offering protection for animals. They are killing cows, although cows are supplying milk from which we can make wonderful preparations. This is Kali-yuga, and the government does not exhibit good sense in any field. Since the government is unworthy of governing, there is chaos throughout the world. According to Vedic civilization, the king is worshipped as God in human form and is therefore called Naradeva. If the good qualities are lacking in a king, he can no longer be considered Naradeva, and he cannot rule for very long, because his rule is artificial. Therefore in Kali-yuga, the royal order is finished.

Hayagrīva dāsa: Machiavelli didn't say that this is the way political life ought to be. Rather, since this is the way political life is at present, this is the best way a prince can rule.

Śrīla Prabhupāda: Our principles should be the same, whether in the past, present, or future. Kṛṣṇa delivered *Bhagavad-gītā* millions of years ago to the king of the sun, Vivasvān. Five thousand years ago He repeated these same principles to Arjuna on the battlefield of Kurukṣetra. It is not that the principles have changed. Whether one is a prince, president, or whatever, the ruling principles should be maintained. Then the people will benefit. It is said that when Mahārāja Yudhiṣṭhira ruled, the people suffered neither from intense heat nor intense cold. There was regular rainfall, and people were free from all anxiety. Such is an ideal kingdom in which the people are happy in all respects.

Hayagrīva dāsa: Machiavelli thought that the ruler should take the sins of the state upon himself, just as Christ took upon himself the sins of the world.

Śrīla Prabhupāda: But if the ruler himself is sinful, how can he assume the sins of others?

Hayagrīva dāsa: Well, Machiavelli felt that evil in politics was a necessity. He writes: "A man who wishes to make a profession of goodness in everything must necessarily come to grief among so many who are not good."

Śrīla Prabhupāda: But if one is not good himself, how can he introduce anything that is good? Presently, in India, there are many people claiming to be big *mahātmās*, religionists, scholars, and politicians, but they cannot even protect the cows. *Bhagavad-gītā* says:

kṛṣi-gorakṣya-vāṇijyaṁ
vaiśya-karma svabhāva-jam

"Farming, cow protection, and business are the qualities of work for the *vaiśyas*." (*Bg.* 18.44) It is at least the duty of the state to protect the cow, which is a special animal. It is the king's duty to protect the welfare of all citizens, including the cows. If the king or president does no more than sit in an exalted position, the people will not be happy. Even in America, the people dragged their president down when they were discontent with him. In any case, the head of state must be ideal and exhibit the ideal princely characteristics.

Hayagrīva dāsa: Machiavelli suggested that since the people usually desire peace, the prince should promote peace in his public addresses. On the other hand, the army always prefers war, which gives opportunities for promotion, and the prince should also appease the militarists. Although publicly promoting peace, the prince can break his promise whenever necessary to start a war abroad, especially when there is trouble at home.

Śrīla Prabhupāda: No one can introduce peace unless he is educated in God consciousness. It is stated in *Bhagavad-gītā:*

bhoktāraṁ yajña-tapasāṁ
sarva-loka-maheśvaram
suhṛdaṁ sarva-bhūtānāṁ
jñātvā māṁ śāntim ṛcchati

"The sages, knowing Me as the ultimate purpose of all sacrifices and austerities, the Supreme Lord of all planets and demigods, and the benefactor and well-wisher of all living entities, attain peace from the pangs of material miseries." (*Bg.* 5.29) The king should not think of his kingdom as his property or his father's property. Rather, knowing himself to be the representative of the Supreme Father, he must understand that the state belongs to the Supreme Father. He is a representative whose duty is to protect the state and the citizens. The proprietor of the state is God Himself. There is not a spot of land throughout the universe that is not owned by the Supreme Personality of Godhead; therefore all property should be engaged for the satisfaction of God. *Bhoktāraṁ yajña-tapasām.* Everything must be carried out for the satisfaction of the Supreme Lord, and this is ideal activity for all societies.

ataḥ pumbhir dvija-śreṣṭhā
varṇāśrama-vibhāgaśaḥ
svanuṣṭhitasya dharmasya
saṁsiddhir hari-toṣaṇam

"O best among the twiceborn, it is therefore concluded that the highest perfection one can achieve, by discharging his prescribed duties [dharma] according to caste divisions and orders of life, is to please the Lord Hari." (*Bhāg.* 1.2.13) According to the *śāstras*, there are social divisions—*brāhmaṇa, kṣatriya, vaiśya,* and *śūdra*—and these divisions allow for proper management. It is the king's duty to divide human society according to the *varṇāśrama-dharma.* There should be genuine *brāhmaṇas, kṣatriyas, vaiśyas, śūdras, brahmacārīs, gṛhasthas, vānaprasthas,* and *sannyāsīs.* No one should cheat but should carry out his duty accordingly. The king must know what is sin so that he can take precautions against it. But if he supports sinful activities—for instance, if he maintains a slaughterhouse—how can he become sinless? The *śāstras* say that the king attains political power by pious activities, but if he does not give security to the citizens, he loses his power automatically.

Hayagrīva dāsa: Machiavelli certainly believed that the people should be protected, but he also believed in the use of power and might. If there are internal difficulties, they must be put down by force. If this proves impossible, the prince should divert people's attention by starting a war abroad. He even felt that it was better to go to war than to remain neutral because a neutral nation is hated by the loser and not respected by the winner. Consequently, he praised power and war.

Śrīla Prabhupāda: He praises war because he cannot manage internally. That is most inhumane.

Hayagrīva dāsa: "Trouble at home, war abroad" is one of his most famous points.

Śrīla Prabhupāda: Yes, and sometimes the governments create artificial restlessness and poverty. We have seen in 1940, when the Second World War was going on, that the government created an artificial famine in order to get men to fight. People who didn't work had no alternative but to join the military. The government increased the price of food, and I remember the price of rice jumping from six rupees to ten rupees. The very next day, the price rose to twenty rupees. Then it jumped again to fifty rupees, whereas formerly it was only six. This is all the results of politics. When the government is not pious or strong, this will go on, and the people will be unhappy.
Hayagrīva dāsa: Machiavelli's view of man was very cynical. He wrote: "In constituting and legislating for a commonwealth, it must be taken for granted that all men are wicked."
Śrīla Prabhupāda: This is not philosophy, considering all men wicked.
Hayagrīva dāsa: Well, he considered that men are so created that they desire all things, although they cannot acquire them. Men are never satisfied. As soon as they have one thing, they crave another.
Śrīla Prabhupāda: Therefore it is the duty of the government to introduce Kṛṣṇa consciousness so that the people can know the way of peace and happiness.
Hayagrīva dāsa: As long as the prince benefitted the people, they would be entirely his.
Śrīla Prabhupāda: But he must know how to benefit them.
Hayagrīva dāsa: Machiavelli was very fond of speaking of "the common good," and he set love of country and the common good above the Christian love of God.
Śrīla Prabhupāda: But what is his common good? He is thinking that people must have enough to eat, but it is for the common good of everyone to love God. Love of God is for everyone, and God is one. When we become lovers of God, our lives are perfected.
Hayagrīva dāsa: But if the people are basically wicked, he argued, a strong prince is necessary to control them.
Śrīla Prabhupāda: Why should the people remain wicked? It is the king's duty to see that all the citizens become gentlemen. He should not allow them to remain wicked. The educational, social, and religious systems should be so perfect that the people become God conscious. At least a sector of the people, the *brāhmaṇas*, should be perfect.
Hayagrīva dāsa: But he felt that if the prince were perfectly virtuous or truthful in all cases, he couldn't possibly survive in the political world.
Śrīla Prabhupāda: That is why there are social divisions: *brāhmaṇas*, *kṣatriyas*, *vaiśyas*, and *śūdras*. It is not possible for everyone to be truth-

ful, but at least a section of the people should be ideal so that others can take advantage of their good advice. It is not that everyone is in the same position, nor that everyone should join the military. Only those who are interested in fighting should join the military.

Hayagrīva dāsa: Machiavelli recommended compulsory military service as a primary form of education for everyone.

Śrīla Prabhupāda: Nothing is meant for everyone. There must be divisions. Machiavelli had no idea that brahminical training is absolutely necessary for intelligent men.

Hayagrīva dāsa: Since youth should especially become used to hardships, he considered war as a form of education.

Śrīla Prabhupāda: Well, any education requires hardships, and to become a *brāhmaṇa* or *brahmacārī* requires the greatest hardships. In any case, there must be educational divisions, just as there are divisions in the human body: the head, arms, belly, and legs. Military education is education of the arms, but where is the education for the brain? Unless the head is educated, how will the arms act?

Hayagrīva dāsa: Machiavelli recommended a democratic republic for a society consisting of virtuous people. In such a state, the ruler must obtain the people's consent. But he considered such a society to be purely Utopian.

Śrīla Prabhupāda: Yes, a completely virtuous society is Utopian in this age. It is not possible. Yet a section of the population can be ideally virtuous, and the remainder may take lessons from them. It is not possible for everyone to become a *brāhmaṇa*, but a few can be trained. The sky may be full of stars, but one moon is all that is necessary. If the populace consists of fools and rascals, how can anything be managed? There must be at least a section that shines like the moon.

Hayagrīva dāsa: This cynical view of mankind was partially based on the Christian doctrine—or at least on the doctrine of Augustine—which held that man is by nature corrupt. Whereas Augustine believed in the saving grace of God, Machiavelli believed in man's willpower to overcome bad fortune.

Śrīla Prabhupāda: But who adjusts good and bad fortune? If we consider good and bad fortune, we must consider a dispenser, a supreme power or controller, and that supreme power is God. Therefore people should be educated in God consciousness by reading transcendental literatures like *Bhagavad-gītā* and *Śrīmad-Bhāgavatam.*

Hayagrīva dāsa: Machiavelli's attitude toward religion has greatly influenced modern governments. He considered religion to be a department of the state; it should not be separate in the sense that it should not compete.

Śrīla Prabhupāda: In that I agree. It is the government's duty to give protection to religion, and if that religion is scientific, the state will be sound. America is presently strong in many respects, and now America must become strong in God consciousness. It is very good to write, "In God We Trust," but we must also know who God is and why we should trust in Him. We are therefore trying to introduce this science of God, Kṛṣṇa consciousness.

Hayagrīva dāsa: Machiavelli felt that as long as religion is not detrimental to the state, the state may accept it as valid. But in one sense, religion is subordinate to the state.

Śrīla Prabhupāda: Of course, they are separate, but the state must know what religion is and how to introduce it to the general public. There is no question of blind faith. The government is maintaining many different departments: an engineering department, medical department, military department, and so forth. Similarly, a religious department may be subordinate to the state because all other departments are subordinate, but religion must be based on scientific knowledge. If the state takes advantage of the Vedic literatures, it can introduce a scientific system of religion. Then the people will be knowledgeable and happy.

Hayagrīva dāsa: For Machiavelli, the only sin is not acting for the common good. First, the ruler must protect the citizens from physical harm. Citizens are happy when they obey the laws, follow customs, and pray to God.

Śrīla Prabhupāda: If the ruler must first of all protect the citizens from physical harm, how can he advocate animal slaughter? Animals are also subjects because they are born in a country. A citizen is anyone who is born in a state. So how can a ruler discriminate between one type of citizen and another? If he discriminates, he cannot speak of common good. He can only say "man's good." According to the common good, animals as well as men are protected.

Hayagrīva dāsa: Machiavelli placed love of country and the common good above everything else. He rarely uses the word "God" or "Providence," but prefers the word "fortune." It is fortune that plays tricks on men and changes friends into enemies.

Śrīla Prabhupāda: If God is fortune, who is misfortune? Since God is the supreme controller, He is both fortune and misfortune. When you act wrongly, punishment comes from God, and when you act properly, the reward comes from God.

Hayagrīva dāsa: Love of country transcends everything religious and

moral, so that one may even lose his own soul for his country's sake. Indeed, Machiavelli wrote: "I love my country more than my soul."
Śrīla Prabhupāda: But how long will he remain in his country?
Hayagrīva dāsa: Well, he remained from 1469 to 1527.
Śrīla Prabhupāda: So what is that? Time and the soul are eternal. Such deification of one's country is not very intelligent.

Francis Bacon
(1561-1626)

Hayagrīva dāsa: Francis Bacon is generally acknowledged as the founding father of modern science in England, and although he did not work in a modern laboratory like today's scientists, he inspired what has become known as the scientific method. He believed that science could give man a mastery over nature that would improve his life on this earth. For Bacon, science was not simply an intellectual or academic undertaking, but a utilitarian one.

Śrīla Prabhupāda: It is erroneous for Bacon or any other scientist to think that science can control nature. It is not possible to control birth, old age, disease, and death. During our lifetime, we may be able to make some changes and give some facilities, but that is not the ultimate end.

Hayagrīva dāsa: Bacon disliked mental speculation about God because we cannot expect God to conform to our own conception. Due to God's infinitude, no conception of God can be unbelievable. By and large, Bacon relegated theology to the realm of faith, and science to the realm of knowledge of the world.

Śrīla Prabhupāda: It is good to be a master architect and make a house with all modern facilities, but if these facilities cause us to forget life's real aim, we have lost a great deal. It is better to remain without facilities, evacuate in the field, and bathe in the river, than overly concern ourselves with modern amenities, facilities for a pampered life. If we forget our real business—how to revive God consciousness—we have not advanced but regressed.

Hayagrīva dāsa: Bacon did not conceive of science as being a disunifying factor as far as religion or God is concerned. Rather, he believed that science could enable civilization to progress. It could be a binding force between man and God.

Śrīla Prabhupāda: That is certainly a very good idea, but many modern scientists are denying the existence of God. Many are claiming that God is dead, that there is no need of God, or that we can manufacture God and man in our own way.

Hayagrīva dāsa: Bacon considered some knowledge to be supernatural in that it comes from God, whereas other forms of knowledge are attained through man's own attempts. He admits that the material senses are imperfect and act like false mirrors, which distort the actual world. Thus men are constantly being deceived.

Śrīla Prabhupāda: Yes, although they are advancing the cause of material science, they are forgetting God in the process. This is most degrading. Men should prove by scientific methods that God exists and is doing everything. Scientists should use a scientific method to understand how the supreme intelligent Being is working. God's scientific knowledge is perfect, and knowledge that complies with this is very good. But if men have a little knowledge and defy the existence of God, their knowledge is useless. So their little knowledge has become a dangerous thing.

Hayagrīva dāsa: Bacon says something very much like this. He writes: "It is true, that a little philosophy inclineth man's mind to atheism; but depth in philosophy bringeth men's minds about to religion."

Śrīla Prabhupāda: Yes. Kṛṣṇa says in *Bhagavad-gītā:*

sarva-yoniṣu kaunteya
mūrtayaḥ sambhavanti yāḥ
tāsāṁ brahma mahad yonir
ahaṁ bīja-pradaḥ pitā

"It should be understood that all species of life, O son of Kuntī, are made possible by birth in this material nature, and that I am the seed-giving father." (*Bg.* 14.4) If we have a little intelligence and think about this verse, we can understand that all living entities are coming from some womb. Since everyone is the child of some mother, there must be a father. When we are grown, we must understand our father, his property, and his desire. How can we deny a universal father?

Hayagrīva dāsa: This is Bacon's conclusion: "For a while, the mind of man looketh upon second causes scattered, it may sometimes rest in them, and go no further; but when it beholdeth the chain of them, confederate and linked together, it must needs fly to Providence and Deity."

Śrīla Prabhupāda: Yes. This is the version given in *Bhagavad-gītā*.

ahaṁ sarvasya prabhavo
mattaḥ sarvaṁ pravartate

"I am the origin of everything. Everything is emanating from Me." (*Bg.* 10.8) The *Vedanta-sūtra* also states: *janmādyasya yataḥ*. "The Supreme Being is He from whom everything is emanating." It is a fact that there must be a source of everything, and it is the business of philosophy to find that original source. It is neither scientific nor philosophic to try to obscure or ignore the original source.

Hayagrīva dāsa: Concerning superstition, Bacon writes: "It were better to have no opinion of God at all than such an opinion as is unworthy of Him. For one is unbelief, and the other is contumely."

Śrīla Prabhupāda: Why should we remain superstitious? Why not introduce education whereby everyone can understand God and His nature? We are trying to establish such an institution with this Kṛṣṇa consciousness movement. If the government participates and cooperates, the masses of people can understand this science of God and benefit.

Hayagrīva dāsa: Bacon distinguished between sects and religions. Sects change, but true religion "is built upon the rock; the rest are tossed on the waves of time...."

Śrīla Prabhupāda: Real religion comes directly from God because religion is the law of God. Therefore we must philosophically and scientifically understand God and His law. That is the perfection of knowledge.

Hayagrīva dāsa: Many of the Indian sects are successful in America because their leaders do not impose any restrictions.

Śrīla Prabhupāda: They have no conception of God. They come for some material profit, and this is revealed in the course of time.

Hayagrīva dāsa: Bacon also believed in the divine right of kings, maintaining that the king is empowered by God to make laws. He also felt that a national church could best provide for the people's spiritual needs.

Śrīla Prabhupāda: Therefore it is necessary that the king be so trained as not to misuse his power. According to the Vedic system, the king was educated to abide by the instructions of saintly persons, *brāhmaṇas*. The *brāhmaṇas* would advise, and the king would follow their desire. If a king misuses his power, he is good for nothing. His monarchy will be abolished, and the people will replace it with something else.

Thomas Hobbes
(1588-1679)

Śyāmasundara dāsa: It is Hobbes who declared, "Whatever exists is matter, and whatever changes is motion." For him, mental or spiritual entities are not realities in their own right, but are merely by-products of matter. Spirit and mind perish when the material basis is destroyed.
Śrīla Prabhupāda: Spirit is not a combination of material conditions. If so, why not combine matter in such a way as to produce living spirit, living forms?
Hayagrīva dāsa: Hobbes believed that a "substance incorporeal" is contradictory because nothing exists in the world but bodies. He defined God as "a most pure, simple, invisible, spirit corporeal."
Śrīla Prabhupāda: Why invisible? When Kṛṣṇa came, He was certainly visible, for Arjuna was talking to Him face to face. God's visibility or invisibility depends on God's own good will. He is visible to one who is competent or perfect. Not only was He visible to Arjuna, but He reciprocated by answering Arjuna's questions. If we become qualified like Arjuna, we can see God and talk with Him. Then God will give direct instructions. God is invisible for one who is imperfect, but for one who is perfect, He is certainly visible.

Śyāmasundara dāsa: Empiricists maintain that the only proof we have of anything is through our senses.

Śrīla Prabhupāda: We say that since the senses are imperfect, whatever you believe through them is imperfect. This is very simple. When the sun rises in the morning, it is many millions of miles away, but can a child tell how far away it is? Who can really tell how far away the sun is?

Śyāmasundara dāsa: They have invented certain instruments to measure distance.

Śrīla Prabhupāda: Therefore they have learned from some authority. Because they could not measure with their own senses, they have turned to instruments. But we should take the help of the expert instrument driver, Śrī Kṛṣṇa. What is the value of our senses if they are imperfect?

Śyāmasundara dāsa: So the mind or soul is not simply a physiological system?

Śrīla Prabhupāda: The soul is a different energy. Heat and light emanate from the same source, fire. Nonetheless, heat is not light, and light is not heat. Sometimes we may feel heat, but that does not mean that there is light. Sometimes we may have light, but that does not mean that there is heat. Still, heat and light come from the same source.

Śyāmasundara dāsa: How is it that the soul and mind are different from the body?

Śrīla Prabhupāda: They are not different, but they are being manifested in different phases. At the moment, we are experiencing sunshine, and we are feeling heat from the sun, but if we approach the sun, we feel much more intense heat. If we approach very closely, we will be disintegrated.

Śyāmasundara dāsa: But how is it that the soul is not produced by the body? How do we know that it is not a mere by-product?

Śrīla Prabhupāda: At death, all the physical parts of the body are present. But why is the man dead? What is missing? His heart may be present, but why is it not beating? All the parts of the body may be present, yet you can see that the body is dead. What is it that is missing?

Śyāmasundara dāsa: Impulses are no longer being sent from the brain to the heart.

Śrīla Prabhupāda: But why has the brain stopped? The brain's construction is all there. What is missing? Why not replace what is missing? If you are a mechanic, and the machine stops, you should be able to find the defect and immediately repair it. But no one has been able to do this with the body, no scientist or philosopher. They cannot meet such a challenge.

Hayagrīva dāsa: Hobbes is best known as a political philosopher, and in his most famous work, *The Leviathan,* he set forth his socio-political theories, as Machiavelli had done in *The Prince*. Hobbes's ruling body, or monarch, his "mortal god," who was under the immortal God, was the Leviathan, who would rule above the law. Now, according to the Vedic conception, is the king, or head of state, above the law?

Śrīla Prabhupāda: No. The king is also under the law. As we understand it from *Bhagavad-gītā*, Śrī Kṛṣṇa imparted His laws to the sun god. Since the sun god followed these laws, he is, compared to a common man, a supremely elevated being. The king is supposed to be the representative of God in the state, and the king's perfection lies in following the laws of Kṛṣṇa. If the king follows the order of Kṛṣṇa, the king's orders are final. In *Bhagavad-gītā* (4.1-2), Kṛṣṇa says that He originally imparted the laws of *Bhagavad-gītā* to the sun god, Vivasvān, who imparted them to Manu, the father of man, who in turn imparted them to Ikṣvaku, and in this way *Bhagavad-gītā* was received via disciplic succession and imparted to the *rājarṣis*, the saintly kings. If the king rules according to *Bhagavad-gītā*, he cannot be subjected to any other law. If the king follows the laws given by God, he is above mundane laws and conventions.

Hayagrīva dāsa: Hobbes compares man to a machine ultimately made by God, but he does not consider this machine to be controlled directly by God but by the Leviathan, the king or ruler.

Śrīla Prabhupāda: No. God is situated in everyone's heart, and every moment He is witnessing the actions of the soul. He knows what the soul desires, and He sees how the soul is manipulating the machine of the body. This is clearly explained in *Bhagavad-gītā:*

īśvaraḥ sarva-bhūtānāṁ
hṛd-deśe'rjuna tiṣṭhati
bhrāmayan sarva-bhūtāni
yantrārūḍhāni māyayā

"The Supreme Lord is situated in everyone's heart, O Arjuna, and is directing the wanderings of all living entities, who are seated as on a machine, made of the material energy." (*Bg.* 18.61) If a person wants to enjoy this material world as a human being, God gives him the opportunity to become a human being, and if he wants to enjoy it as a dog, God gives him the body of a dog. This is all God's mercy. As long as the individual living entity wants to enjoy this material world, God gives all facility through a particular body. The body itself is material and is supplied by *prakṛti*, material nature. The machine is composed of material ingredients supplied by *prakṛti*, which follows the orders of Kṛṣṇa, and it is given for the enjoyment of the living entity. The living entity, or *jīva,* sits in that machine and travels, just as a person travels in a car. He receives a particular machine in some species on some planet. There are innumerable planets, and over eight million different species. Due to his contact with material nature, the living entity desires so many things, and God is so merciful that He supplies all facilities. At the same time, God is a friend to everyone, and when the *jīva* is prepared to understand ultimate happiness from God, God says, "Give up all your nonsensical plans and surrender unto Me." This is the living entity's perfection, and if he does not come to this perfect stage, he will constantly desire so many things. God will then supply an unlimited number of machines to go here and there, and up and down, within this universe. Either you go up, or you come down. When you come down, you enter the lower species, and when you go up, you enter the higher species. These include the demigods like Lord Indra and Lord Brahmā. There are different types of life, and some endure millions of years, while others endure only a few moments. In any case, every opportunity is given by the Supreme Lord because He is the supreme controller. Man proposes, and God disposes. As long as we continue to propose this and that, we'll never be happy, but when we agree to comply with God's plans, we will attain happiness.

Hayagrīva dāsa: Hobbes would say that since warfare is perpetual, and the struggle for existence goes on and on, the Leviathan is necessary. It is the fear of death that drives men together into a social contract, and it is the Leviathan who places everything under a common power and authority. This Leviathan is like God's representative or lieutenant, who has sovereignty under God.

Śrīla Prabhupāda: Yes, that is the perfection of monarchy. Therefore the king is called *nṛpadeva,* or *naradeva,* God in human form.

Śyāmasundara dāsa: For Hobbes, the Leviathan must be sufficiently strong to enforce the social contract, the law. It is he who can punish anyone who does not live up to his end of the bargain. In this way, society and peace will be preserved.

Śrīla Prabhupāda: But who is the right man? Since men are always defective, how is this possible? This means that we have to accept a man or an authority who is infallible, who is beyond suspicion.

Śyāmasundara dāsa: Yes, and therefore Hobbes says that such a man must be something like a mortal god. If such a mortal god cannot be found, a government has to be instituted.

Śrīla Prabhupāda: Such a man has to be the direct representative of God. He not only has to understand what is written in the scriptures; he has to follow the instructions as well. This is the exalted position of the bona fide spiritual master.

sākṣād-dharitvena samasta-śāstrair
uktas tathā bhāvyata eva sadbhiḥ
kintu prabhor yaḥ priya eva tasya
vande guroḥ śrī-caraṇāravindam

"The spiritual master is to be honored as much as the Supreme Lord, because he is the most confidential servitor of the Lord. This is acknowledged in all revealed scriptures and followed by all authorities. Therefore I offer my respectful obeisances unto the lotus feet of such a spiritual master, who is a bona fide representative of Śrī Hari [Kṛṣṇa]." (*Śrī Gurv-aṣṭaka*, 7) The spiritual master, or guru, is the direct representative of Kṛṣṇa because he is the most confidential servant of Kṛṣṇa. Therefore his position is as good as Kṛṣṇa's. He renders the most confidential service by trying to bring everyone to Kṛṣṇa consciousness. Unless we come to that position, we will never be happy. Hobbes says that we have to find some sort of mortal god, but such a person must be one who actually knows God. We have to understand the qualifications of the bona fide guru from the Vedas. Then we have to approach the guru submissively. The guru is expert in transcendental Vedic knowledge, and he has fully given himself to Kṛṣṇa. He is no longer disturbed by anything material. He is full in Brahman realization, and he is free from all material contamination. These are some of the preliminary qualifications of a godly man, but since Hobbes did not know these qualifications, he could never find such a man. Even when Kṛṣṇa Himself was present, not everyone could understand that He was the Supreme Personality of Godhead. How will we be able to find the godly man unless we know what is God and what is a godly man? In order to find this out, we have to approach *Bhagavad-gītā;* otherwise our knowledge will remain imperfect.

Śyāmasundara dāsa: In Hobbes's case, a godly man is only necessary insofar as he is required to maintain peace.

Śrīla Prabhupāda: But since godly men cannot be found, peace is maintained for a while, and then again there is disturbance. Social contracts can never be absolute because things are always changing. A certain social condition may prevail for a while, but in fifty years it will be totally different. How can we make a social contract that will never change? It is not possible in the material world. In the Vaikuṇṭha-loka, the spiritual sky, the social condition never changes. It is eternal. The inhabitants there are pleased to be with Kṛṣṇa and dance, eat, play, and live with Him. That condition is eternal, *nitya-siddha*. Kṛṣṇa is always there, and He is always

tending *surabhi* cows. He is always playing on His flute, and He is always dancing with His friends, the *gopīs*. Our business should be to enter into that eternal play, and that is the process of Kṛṣṇa consciousness.
Hayagrīva dāsa: Hobbes claims that the Leviathan could not only be an individual but also a group of individuals.
Śrīla Prabhupāda: Yes, a group of individuals can run the government provided they are devotees. But if this group is composed of rogues and rascals, it cannot represent God. Representatives of God abide by the laws of God.

dharmaṁ tu sākṣād bhagavat-praṇītaṁ
na vai vidur ṛṣayo nāpi devaḥ
na siddha-mukhyā asurā manuṣyāḥ
kuto nu vidyādhara-cāraṇādayaḥ

"Real religious principles are enacted by the Supreme Personality of Godhead. Although fully situated in the mode of goodness, even the great *ṛṣis* who occupy the topmost planets cannot ascertain the real religious principles, nor can the demigods, or the leaders of Siddhaloka, to say nothing of the *asuras*, ordinary human beings, Vidyādharas and Cāraṇas." (*Bhāg*. 6.3.19) Actual religion, or law, consists of what God Himself says. If we manufacture our own laws, without referring to God's program, we will ultimately fail.
Hayagrīva dāsa: In *Leviathan*, Hobbes writes: "Some men have pretended for their disobedience to their sovereign a new covenant, made not with men but with God, and this also is unjust; for there is no covenant with God but by mediation of somebody that represents God's person, which none does but God's lieutenent, who has this sovereignty under God." But might not this argument of divine right be used by a tyrant to discourage his subjects from rebelling? What guidelines are there to assure against this?
Śrīla Prabhupāda: Everything depends on the king's accepting the absolute instructions of God. In the Vedic civilization, the king absolutely followed the regulations given by God. The king's activities were confirmed by saintly persons, sages, and then they were carried out. It was not that the king acted whimsically. There was always an advisory board composed of saintly persons, who knew the Vedas very well. The sages used to guide the monarch, and therefore the monarch was the absolute governing body. The ministers helped, but the king was educated by God's direct instructions. For instance, Kṛṣṇa gave direct instructions to the sun god (*Bg*. 4.1). According to Vedic tradition, there are two

kṣatriya (administrative) families: one coming from the sun god (*sūrya-vaṁśa*), and one coming from the moon god (*candra-vaṁśa*). *Sūrya*, the sun god, is the original *kṣatriya*, and from him came Vaivasvata Manu. This is the age of Vaivasvata Manu, and from him came his son Ikṣvāku. Kṛṣṇa's instructions are explicitly given in *Bhagavad-gītā*, and if governments throughout the world take them up, they will attain perfection. Then there will be no disturbances, and there will be peace and happiness. That will make a perfect world. Kṛṣṇa has given instructions in all fields of activity, but people are so foolish due to their demoniac tendencies that they attempt to manufacture their own standards. If the heads of state are degraded either individually or collectively, how can there be good government?

Śyāmasundara dāsa: Hobbes contends that in the natural state, man is like all other animals. Might makes right, and the strongest always prevail. Therefore it is necessary that man form a social contract and volunteer to restrict natural liberties for the sake of self-preservation.

Śrīla Prabhupāda: That is not natural liberty but ghostly liberty. There are many haunted people, and in their unnatural condition they are falsely thinking, "I am God." The natural condition is to think, "I am God's servant." Any condition devoid of Kṛṣṇa consciousness is unnatural. Kṛṣṇa is the supreme, and I am His subordinate. My business is to render service unto Him. This is the natural position.

Śyāmasundara dāsa: Yet when men group together in a society to preserve themselves, they make a contract to the effect that they will not kill one another.

Śrīla Prabhupāda: Why not a group of asses? What is their utility? Do you mean to say that because a group of asses congregate that some good will come of it? These rogues are always making contracts after a big war. After World War I, they made a contract through the League of Nations, and that failed. Then they had a Second World War, and they formed the United Nations and made more contracts. Eventually that will all be dissolved again. These contracts and compromises may serve some purposes for the time being, but ultimately they are useless.

Śyāmasundara dāsa: Men in society volunteer, "I will not kill you or steal your property if you will not kill me or steal my property."

Śrīla Prabhupāda: Yes, that is the thieves' contract. But, after all, if you remain a thief, what is the improvement? Thieves may steal some valuable things, and afterwards they congregate and say, "Let's divide the property honestly." Thieves are all dishonest, although they talk of honesty among themselves. Originally, everyone immigrated to America,

and the whole land was stolen from the Indians. Now the thieves have formed a government and will not allow outsiders in without visas and passports and so many things. This is the kind of morality that is going on.
Śyāmasundara dāsa: Hobbes's social contract was something like the converse of the Golden Rule: "Do not do unto others what you would not have them do unto you."
Śrīla Prabhupāda: That was also Buddha's theory. Lord Buddha pointed out that if someone hurts us, we feel pain. Why, therefore, should we hurt others? Of course, third and fourth-class men have to be taught in this way. But in *Bhagavad-gītā,* Kṛṣṇa tells Arjuna, "Kill them!" Does this mean that Kṛṣṇa's position is reduced? It is a question of the intelligence of the men involved.
Śyāmasundara dāsa: Well, Hobbes is trying to determine how society can live peacefully.
Śrīla Prabhupāda: Yes, people have tried many times but have always failed. There cannot be any peace in this material world. Kṛṣṇa says plainly:

ābrahma-bhuvanāl lokāḥ
punar āvartino'rjuna
mām upetya tu kaunteya
punar janma na vidyate

"From the highest planet in the material world down to the lowest, all are places of misery wherein repeated birth and death take place. But one who attains to My abode, O son of Kuntī, never takes birth again." (*Bg.* 8.16) Since this is a place of misery, how can we establish peace here? We cannot. The material universe is structured in such a way that peace is not possible. As Śrīla Viśvanātha Cakravartī Ṭhākura says: *saṁsara-dāvānala-līḍha-loka (Śrī Gurv-aṣṭaka,* 1). This material world is exactly like a blazing forest fire. No one wants fire in a forest, but it takes place naturally. No one wants to fight, but fighting takes place. How can you check it simply by making a contract? We are thinking that the material world is a nice place to live, but this is like a man thinking that stool is nice because it has been dried in the sun. If the stool is soft, it is not so good. But in either case, it is stool. *Padaṁ padaṁ yad vipadāṁ na teṣām (Bhāg.* 10.14.58). In this world, there is danger at every step. Throughout history, people have tried to make contracts for peace, but it is not possible. One may refuse to submit to Kṛṣṇa, but nature will not allow this. If we do not submit to Kṛṣṇa, nature will punish us so that we will finally be obliged to submit to Him. That is nature's law. If we voluntarily submit to Kṛṣṇa, that is for our benefit, but if we do not, nature's laws are so stringent that they will always give us trouble, and at the end we will be obliged to agree: *vāsudevaḥ sarvam iti.* "Vāsudeva, Kṛṣṇa, is everything." (*Bg.* 7.19) If, after many births of struggle, we have to come to this point, why waste our time? Why not surrender to Kṛṣṇa immediately? Otherwise, we will go on suffering according to nature's law.

Śyāmasundara dāsa: Hobbes is called a utilitarian because he accepts a thing only if it's pragmatic or useful.

Śrīla Prabhupāda: That is relative. A child is satisfied if you give him five rupees, but if you give his father five rupees, the man will think, "What is the use of this?" So the utility of five rupees is relative. Hobbes's conception of utility is not the same as Kṛṣṇa's conception. Arjuna was thinking that he was speaking like a very learned man, but immediately Kṛṣṇa told him that he was not (*Bg.* 2.11). All this is relative. The hog thinks that he is in a comfortable position and is eating very nicely, but he is eating stool and living in garbage. Crows believe one thing, and swans believe another. An imperfect man like Hobbes may believe one thing to be pragmatic, but one who is perfect may consider something totally different to be pragmatic.

Śyāmasundara dāsa: Hobbes accepted religion only as a practical instrument. He says that it doesn't have any real value as a science but that it may be used by the state to pacify the people or to keep them confused.

Śrīla Prabhupāda: This means that he does not know what religion is. Of course, some people have made religion into a certain type of faith, but actually religion means one's inherent characteristic. Religion is to the living entity what sweetness is to sugar. It is an inherent characteristic that cannot be separated. Every living entity is rendering service to someone. Everyone is subordinate to someone else, or to his senses. It is the characteristic of the living entity to be subordinate and to render service. In *Bhagavad-gītā,* Kṛṣṇa says, "Surrender unto Me." (*Bg.* 18.66) That is our first business, but we are too busy trying to become Kṛṣṇa. Therefore we say, "I am God," or, "You are God," or, "We are all God." The living entity is not the Supreme God, but he is playing that way. When a man is haunted by ghosts, he says many nonsensical things. Similarly, when the living entity is under the clutches of the material energy, he speaks in such a way.

Śyāmasundara dāsa: What about this idea of utility? What do you think of something being accepted only as long as it is useful?

Śrīla Prabhupāda: It is our foolishness that we accept something temporarily useful. Our real desire is to have eternal life. We want something

that is eternally useful, but in the material world we are always being frustrated. We want to live here permanently, but nature will not allow this. Even if there is no disturbance in the form of war, we will still not be allowed to remain.
Śyāmasundara dāsa: A utilitarian would say that a thing should be used only insofar as it is required for some time. Then something else can be used, and in this way we can adjust things indefinitely.
Śrīla Prabhupāda: But another point is that no one wants anything to change. Why? People want permanence because they are seeking their eternal, spiritual nature.
Śyāmasundara dāsa: Hobbes might say that although we may be seeking something eternal, we may employ temporary things just as long as they are useful.
Śrīla Prabhupāda: First of all, we must know what our eternal life is; then we can try to use everything favorable to further that end. Kṛṣṇa is the ultimate goal, and whatever is favorable in helping us toward Him should be accepted. That is real utilitarianism. For instance, Arjuna said, "What should I do? Kill or not kill? Kṛṣṇa wants me to kill. All right, I'll kill." This is utilitarianism.
Śyāmasundara dāsa: For Hobbes, the goal is a peaceful society.
Śrīla Prabhupāda: That is not possible. The goal should be the advancement of Kṛṣṇa consciousness. Then peace will follow automatically.
Śyāmasundara dāsa: His utilitarianism means the acceptance of whatever is favorable for the preservation of society.
Śrīla Prabhupāda: In any case, society cannot be preserved. So many societies have come and gone. British society. Roman society. Greek society. Only Kṛṣṇa's society is eternal. Knowing this is intelligence. *Nitya-līlā praviṣṭa.* "Now he has entered the eternal society of Kṛṣṇa." This is what we say when our guru passes away. We are accepting Kṛṣṇa as the Supreme and glorifying Him here on earth. This same process will go on there in the spiritual sky, in Kṛṣṇa's abode. However, there it will take place in a perfect way. Here we are just practicing.

V
RATIONALISM

Rene Descartes
(1596-1650)

Hayagrīva dāsa: In *Meditations on First Philosophy*, Descartes writes: "The power of forming a good judgement and of distinguishing the true from the false, which is called good sense or reason, is by nature equal in all men.... God has given to each of us some light with which to distinguish truth from error." Is he speaking of the Supersoul, or another form of intellection?
Śrīla Prabhupāda: The Supersoul is one thing, and reasoning is another. Still, reasoning should be there. For instance, through reasoning, we can understand that the body is just a lump of matter composed of skin, bone, muscle, blood, stool, urine, and so forth. Through our reasoning power, we can ask if a combination of these ingredients can bestow life, and we can come to understand that life is different from a lump of matter.
Śyāmasundara dāsa: For Descartes, all truth can be derived from reason, which is superior to and independent of sense experience. Knowledge is deductible from self-evident concepts, or innate, necessary ideas. In other words, he disagrees with those empiricists who believe that truth can be derived only from sense experience.
Śrīla Prabhupāda: We cannot understand God through sense experi-

ence, but through our reason we can understand that there is God. We can reason, "I have my father, and my father also has a father, who has a father, and so on. Therefore there must be a Supreme Father." God is the supreme and original Father, and by reasoning we can understand that He exists. Similarly, we can also understand by reasoning that God is the creator. We see that everything has a maker, a creator, and we can conclude that this great cosmic manifestation also has a creator. This is reasoning, but rascals speculate that in the beginning there was a big chunk of matter and an explosion, or whatever, that started the universe. But if there were an explosion, there must have been some explosive, and if there were some explosive, there must have been some worker to set it off. Otherwise, how did the chunk of matter explode? Through our reason we can perceive that everything has some creator or cause.

Hayagrīva dāsa: Descartes claims that good sense or reason is by nature equal in all men, but doesn't the reasoning power differ?

Śrīla Prabhupāda: Yes, otherwise why is one man intelligent and another ignorant? When, through reasoning, one concludes that the living force within the body is different from the body itself, he is on the human platform. If he considers life to be nothing more than a combination of material ingredients, he remains an animal. That is the verdict of the Vedas.

yasyātma-buddhiḥ kuṇape trī-dhātuke
sva-dhīḥ kalatrādiṣu bhauma ijya-dhīḥ
yat-tīrtha-buddhiḥ salile na karhicij
janeṣv abhijñeṣu sa eva go-kharaḥ

"A human being who identifies this body made of three elements with his self, who considers the by-products of the body to be his kinsmen, who considers the land of birth worshipable, and who goes to the place of pilgrimage simply to take a bath rather than meet men of transcendental knowledge there, is to be considered like an ass or a cow." (*Bhāg.* 10.84.13) If one thinks that he is the body, he is no better than an animal. So through reasoning, we can conclude that the soul is not this and not that. This is the *neti-neti* process. We then have to continue our search and ask, "What is soul? What is Brahman?" We can then conclude that Brahman is the origin of matter and that matter is developed by the soul. That is the Vedic conclusion in the *Vedānta-sūtra.* The act of sex, for instance, cannot bring about pregnancy unless a soul is present. People may have sex many times, and no pregnancy may result. You may sow a seed, and a tree may develop, but if you fry that seed before sowing it, it will not fructify because it is unsuitable for the soul to remain. The conclusion is that the soul is the basis of matter. Although the soul cannot be perceived materially, it is certainly there. Yet its presence can be understood by its symptoms, which are consciousness and bodily development. Just as the individual soul is the living force that gives life to the body, God is the supreme living force that gives life to the entire cosmic manifestation.

Śyāmasundara dāsa: Descartes's method involved searching within one's self for a basis of truth. That basis he found to be self-consciousness. He concluded that first of all, I exist, and then reasoned that God exists necessarily.

Śrīla Prabhupāda: Yes. I exist, my father exists, my grandfather exists, and so on; therefore God exists. In Sanskrit, we use the word *ahaṅkāra*, "I am." At the present moment, we exist, but our conception of existence is incorrect. We are thinking, "I exist through my body." We do not understand how it is we exist. By reasoning and understanding, we have to come to know that we are spirit soul and not the body. It is the spirit soul that exists. By reasoning, we can understand that we existed as a child, as a young man, and as an old man, and that after the body is finished, we will continue to exist. I still exist, and I have passed through many bodies, and by reasoning I can conclude that even after this body is destroyed, I will continue to exist. It is stated in *Bhagavad-gītā:*

na jāyate mriyate vā kadācin
nāyaṁ bhūtvā bhavitā vā na bhūyaḥ
ajo nityaḥ śāśvato 'yaṁ purāṇo
na hanyate hanyamāne śarīre

"For the soul there is never birth nor death. Nor having once been, does he ever cease to be. He is unborn, eternal, ever-existing, undying, and primeval. He is not slain when the body is slain." (*Bg.* 2.20) Even when the body is annihilated, the spirit soul continues. We can arrive at this conclusion through experience, and our experience can be confirmed by the *śāstras*. This can also be concluded by reason. If this is supported in so many ways, it is a fact.

Śyāmasundara dāsa: Descartes claims that truth must be self-evident and innate, like the intuitive knowledge "I exist."

Śrīla Prabhupāda: This is innate knowledge: I exist now, I existed in the past, and I shall continue to exist in the future. This is also confirmed by *Bhagavad-gītā:*

na tv evāhaṁ jātu nāsaṁ
na tvaṁ neme janādhipāḥ

na caiva na bhaviṣyāmaḥ
sarve vayam ataḥ param

"Never was there a time when I did not exist, nor you, nor all these kings; nor in the future shall any of us cease to be." (*Bg.* 2.12) This is confirmed by Kṛṣṇa, and my reasoning also agrees. The body changes during one lifetime. As I exist in a body that is different now from my childhood body, in the future I will continue to exist in a different body.

Śyāmasundara dāsa: For Descartes, whatever is clear and distinct—such as the mind's consciousness of itself—must be true.

Śrīla Prabhupāda: Yes, this is true. I think in this way, and this is corroborated by authoritative scriptures and confirmed by the *ācāryas.* It is not that we think in a whimsical way. Śrī Kṛṣṇa, Śrī Caitanya Mahāprabhu, and all the *ācāryas* agree; therefore there is no doubt.

Hayagrīva dāsa: In *Meditations on First Philosophy*, Descartes further writes: "I fall into error because the power which God has given me of distinguishing the true from the false is not in me an infinite power." If we can never be certain that we can distinguish truth from error, where does certainty lie?

Śrīla Prabhupāda: Certainty is in Kṛṣṇa because He is absolute. He is infinite, and we are finite. The soul is finite Brahman, and the infinite Brahman is God. All religions accept the fact that God is the Supreme Father and that all living entities are His sons. Our existence is based on the mercy of the Supreme Father, and we can reach this conclusion by reasoning.

Śyāmasundara dāsa: Descartes claims that the elementary truths of consciousness are innate in man's personality and that they provide man with immediate and rational proof.

Śrīla Prabhupāda: Yes, that is a fact. Because I am part and parcel of the Supreme Perfection, I am minutely perfect. A particle of gold may be minute, but it is gold nonetheless. Because I am part and parcel of the Supreme Perfection, I am perfect in minute quantity. Of course, I cannot become as great; that is the difference. We are qualitatively one with God and quantitatively different. All of the qualities found in God are also found in us in minute quantity. Due to association with māyā, we have become imperfect. The whole process is to return to the perfectional point through Kṛṣṇa consciousness, and that is called *mukti*, liberation. When we are situated in our original form, we attain perfection.

Śyāmasundara dāsa: Descartes says that the alleged truths which appear to our senses are unreliable and that only innate ideas are clear and unmuddled by the senses because they are derived from our own nature.

Śrīla Prabhupāda: Is it that the truth has to be established by oneself and not by others?
Śyāmasundara dāsa: He first searched within himself to find some innate basis for truth. First of all, he discovered that "I am."
Śrīla Prabhupāda: Ages ago, there were many people who could understand this. A fool thinks that all others are fools. A deaf man will talk very softly because he thinks that the sound he is making is sufficient. He has no other experience. Everyone thinks that all others are like himself. It is not that Descartes was the first man to realize the identification of the self, "I am." This awareness has been existing a very long time. Kṛṣṇa says:

aham evāsam evāgre
nānyad yat sad-asat param
paścād ahaṁ yad etac ca
yo'vaśiṣyeta so'smy aham

"Brahma, it is I, the Personality of Godhead, who was existing before the creation when there was nothing but Myself. Nor was there the material nature, the cause of this creation. That which you see now is also I, the Personality of Godhead, and after annihilation what remains will also be I, the Personality of Godhead." (*Bhāg*. 2.9.33) This is Kṛṣṇa talking about the creation, but we can also say the same. We existed before these bodies were created, and we will continue to exist when these bodies are annihilated. However, our business involves these little bodies, and Kṛṣṇa's business involves the whole universe. That is the difference. So this conception of "I" is present in God as well as in the living entity. What is so new about all this?
Hayagrīva dāsa: Descartes considers God a substance that is infinite, immutable, independent, all-knowing, and all-powerful. He is the creator of all things. Descartes writes: "Perhaps all those perfections which I am attributing to God are in some fashion potentially in me, although they do not show themselves, or issue an action."
Śrīla Prabhupāda: I have often explained that the qualities that are infinitely present in God are finitely present in the living entities. For instance, the creative force is also within us, and we can create an airplane that can fly. However, we cannot create another planet that can float in space. Although we may be able to create so many wonderful devices, we are still finite. The creative power is present both in God and in the living entities because the living entities are part and parcel of God. God's knowledge is total, and our knowledge lies only within our limited sphere. God knows everything, and we know some things. The

difference was pointed out by Kṛṣṇa in *Bhagavad-gītā:*

vedāhaṁ samatītāni
vartamānāni cārjuna
bhaviṣyāṇi ca bhūtāni
māṁ tu veda na kaścana

"O Arjuna, as the Supreme Personality of Godhead, I know everything that has happened in the past, all that is happening in the present, and all things that are yet to come. I also know all living entities, but Me no one knows." (*Bg.* 7.26)

Śyāmasundara dāsa: Descartes worked with a four-part methodology which is now called Cartesian methodology. First of all, one is never to accept anything as true which is not known truly and distinctly to be true.

Śrīla Prabhupāda: Of course it is commendable not to accept anything blindly, but if you do not have the intelligence to understand, you have to consult one who is intelligent.

Śyāmasundara dāsa: He felt that the truth must be as clear and distinct as mathematical proof.

Śrīla Prabhupāda: That is good provided one is a mathematician, but if one is a plowman, what can he understand about mathematics?

Śyāmasundara dāsa: According to Descartes, it was up to those who could understand mathematics to chalk out the truth and pass it on to those less intelligent.

Śrīla Prabhupāda: In other words, higher truth cannot be understood by everyone. We have to accept the truth from authorities. Therefore we take the Vedas as truth. *Śruti-pramānam.* When the Vedas give evidence, we accept it whether we understand it or not.

Śyāmasundara dāsa: The second part of his methodology involved dividing the complex into simpler and simpler parts in order to arrive at a solution. In this way, the whole will be proved.

Śrīla Prabhupāda: But one must be expert in analysis. If I give you a typewriter to fix, and you know nothing about the machine, you will open it up, see all the parts, and not know how to adjust it. It is easy to open the machine up, but it is very difficult to adjust it.

Śyāmasundara dāsa: The third part involved arranging ideas from the simplest to the more complex according to the sequence of events.

Śrīla Prabhupāda: First of all, we must understand that we are spirit soul. That is the first step in our process. We must first understand ourselves and how we are existing despite these changes of bodies. We have to study ourselves as masters of our bodies. Then we can conclude that for the universal body there is another source. That is the Supersoul, or God. Just as my body is existing due to my presence, the gigantic *virāṭ* body exists due to the presence of the Supersoul. Everything in the universe is constantly looking fresh and new; therefore there must be a large soul maintaining it. This is confirmed by the Vedas: *aṇḍāntara-stha-paramāṇu-cayāntara-stham (Brahma-saṁhitā* 5.35). God is all-pervasive as Brahman, and He is also within the smallest atom. By His plenary expansion, God pervades the entire universe. According to the Vedas, there are different manifestations of God: Mahā-viṣṇu, Kāraṇodakaśāyī-viṣṇu, Garbhodakaśāyī-viṣṇu, and Kṣīrodakaśāyī-viṣṇu. What is the difficulty in understanding this? In large lamps and small lamps there is the same electricity. The Māyāvādī philosophers consider only the similitude; they do not take the varieties into account. God is all-pervasive, but there is variety.

Śyāmasundara dāsa: How is it that we create the body by our presence?

Śrīla Prabhupāda: You create your body by your work. A dog has created his body according to his desire, and a tiger creates his body according to his. In any case, the soul is the same. The learned man, the *paṇḍita,* does not see the external varieties, but the soul within. According to their desires and activities, souls are acquiring different bodies; therefore there are 8,400,000 different types of bodies. Kṛṣṇa claims all of these as His sons. *Ahaṁ bīja-pradaḥ pitā.* "I am the seed-giving father." (*Bg.* 14.4) Kṛṣṇa, the Father of all, gives the seed, but the son creates his own situation. Some of His sons are very rich, some very poor, some are great scientists and philosophers, and some are simply rascals. When a child is born, the father does not say, "You become a rascal," or, "You become a scientist," or whatever. The father sees them all as his sons.

Śyāmasundara dāsa: The fourth part of Cartesian methodology involves taking into account the most detailed points and making sure that nothing is omitted.

Śrīla Prabhupāda: Yes, that is knowledge. For instance, we are considering the details when we consider the difference between the Supreme Lord and ourselves.

Śyāmasundara dāsa: And we can place everything in the scheme of Kṛṣṇa's creation?

Śrīla Prabhupāda: Yes. Kṛṣṇa says *ahaṁ sarvasya prabhavaḥ.* "I am the origin of all." (*Bg.* 10.8) Kṛṣṇa says that He is the *bīja,* the seed or soul, the spiritual spark of all living entities.

Śyāmasundara dāsa: Descartes also suggested rules of conduct which everyone should follow. He felt that we should obey the laws and customs

of our nation, religious faith, and family tradition, and should avoid extreme behavior.
Śrīla Prabhupāda: That is a good proposal. Actually, family tradition is respected in Vedic civilization. In *Bhagavad-gītā*, Arjuna argues:

kula-kṣaye praṇaśyanti
kula-dharmāḥ sanātanāḥ
dharme naṣṭe kulaṁ kṛtsnam
adharmo'bhibhavaty uta

"With the destruction of dynasty, the eternal family tradition is vanquished, and thus the rest of the family becomes involved in irreligious practice." (*Bg*. 1.39) This means that Arjuna was respecting family tradition, but Kṛṣṇa pointed out that this consideration was material. It really has no spiritual value. Therefore Kṛṣṇa chastised Arjuna, telling him that he was situated on the material platform. Arjuna was lamenting over things for which a learned man does not lament. So, perhaps Descartes made these propositions for ordinary men, but they are not for those who are highly elevated or spiritually advanced.
Śyāmasundara dāsa: Descartes considered these practical rules for daily conduct. He also believed that we should stand by the convictions we have formed and be resolute in the course of action we have chosen.
Śrīla Prabhupāda: This could also be a dog's obstinacy. However, if our final conclusion is true, then this obstinacy is nice. But if we have not reached the final goal, the Absolute Truth, such obstinacy is an impediment to advancement. This should not be generally applied because in the neophyte stage, we must be flexible. In the advanced stage, when we are firmly situated in the truth, it is, of course, good to stand by our convictions. That is determination. For instance, we have understood that Kṛṣṇa is the Supreme Personality of Godhead. No one can change us in this conviction. In the Christian system, they say that only Jesus Christ can help one go back to Godhead. That was meant for those whom Jesus Christ instructed because Jesus Christ saw that if the people left him, they would go to ruination. He saw that these inferior people had to stick to him in order to progress. Lord Buddha rejected the Vedas, but this does not mean that Vedic authority is diminished. The men to whom he spoke were not able to understand the authority of the Vedas, and they were misusing the Vedic rituals. This is all relative truth, but Absolute Truth is different. Relative truth is within Absolute Truth, but Absolute Truth is independent of relative truth.
Śyāmasundara dāsa: According to Descartes, we should adapt ourselves

and our ambitions to our environment and fortune, instead of defying them. In other words, we should be satisfied with what we have and utilize it to the best of our ability.

Śrīla Prabhupāda: That is nice. In Vedic civilization, for instance, there is no great endeavor for economic development. In India, you will still find villagers satisfied with whatever they have. There are even street sweepers who are great devotees. After they work, they bathe, put on *tilaka*, and sit down to chant and worship the Deity. Why should we be unnecessarily ambitious? Better to be satisfied.

Śyāmasundara dāsa: Descartes also believed that we should carefully choose the life work which is best for our personal selves.

Śrīla Prabhupāda: Well, if you are given that freedom, a drunkard will say that the best thing is to drink and sleep. Everyone has his own program, which he thinks is the best. So who will judge what is best? According to Vivekananda's philosophy, whatever philosophy you select is all right. That is nonsense.

Hayagrīva dāsa: In the same *Meditations on First Philosophy*, Descartes writes: "It is not in truth an imperfection in God that He has given me the freedom of assenting or not assenting to things of which He has not placed a clear and distinct knowledge in my understanding. On the other hand, it is an imperfection in me that I do not use this freedom right...." But then, why doesn't God give us the understanding by which we can choose properly in all cases? Why can't we have free will and at the same time infallible judgement?

Śrīla Prabhupāda: Free will means that you can act wrongly. Unless there is a chance of your acting properly or improperly, there is no question of free will. If I only act in one way, I have no freedom. We have freedom because we can sometimes act improperly.

Hayagrīva dāsa: In other words, freedom means that a man may know better, yet still act wrongly?

Śrīla Prabhupāda: Yes, that is free will: the freedom to misuse free will. A thief may know that stealing is bad, yet he steals. That is his free will in action. He cannot check his greed, despite his knowing that he is acting improperly and that he will be punished. He knows all the repercussions that result from stealing, yet he steals and misuses his free will. So unless there is a possibility of misusing our free will, there is no question of freedom.

Hayagrīva dāsa: In the *Meditations*, Descartes maintains that when one does not know God, he really has no perfect knowledge of anything, and when he knows God, he knows everything else.

Śrīla Prabhupāda: Yes, and knowledge of God means following the instructions of God. In *Bhagavad-gītā,* Kṛṣṇa imparts the most confidential knowledge to Arjuna, but it is ultimately up to Arjuna to accept it or reject it. At the conclusion of *Bhagavad-gītā,* Kṛṣṇa tells him:

iti te jñānam ākhyātaṁ
guhyād guhyataraṁ mayā
vimṛśyaitad aśeṣeṇa
yathecchasi tathā kuru

"Thus I have explained to you the most confidential of all knowledge. Deliberate on this fully, and then do what you wish to do." (*Bg.* 18.63) This is free will. It depends on the individual whether to act according to the instructions of God or according to his own whims and sensual inclinations.

Hayagrīva dāsa: Descartes further writes: "I see that the certainty in truth of all knowledge depends on knowledge of the true God, and that before I knew Him I could have no perfect knowledge of any other thing. And now that I know Him, I have the means of acquiring a perfect knowledge of innumerable things...." Descartes goes on to conclude that since God is all good, He would not deceive him in matters pertaining to the Godhead.

Śrīla Prabhupāda: If he follows God's instructions and has real knowledge of God, he will never be misled, but if he selects a false God, or if he has not met the real God, he is subject to being misled. To save him from this danger, God imparts instructions in *Bhagavad-gītā.* Whoever follows these instructions will be perfect. If we receive knowledge of the soul from God, there is no chance in being mistaken. As soon as we think in our own way, we are subject to error because we are imperfect and finite. Kṛṣṇa precisely says that the soul is within the body, and if we accept this, we can immediately understand that the soul is different from the body. Kṛṣṇa says that the owner of the body is the soul within the body, and immediately the false impression that one is the body, which is a fool's conclusion, should be eradicated. The light is there, but those who do not accept it prefer to live as fools and speculate.

Śyāmasundara dāsa: It was Descartes's contention that the most perfect and highest emotion is intellectual love of God.

Śrīla Prabhupāda: That is also confirmed in *Bhagavad-gītā.* Kṛṣṇa says that the *jñānī-bhakta,* the intelligent *bhakta,* is very dear to Him.

teṣāṁ jñānī nitya-yukta
eka-bhaktir viśiṣyate

priyo hi jñānino' tyartham
ahaṁ sa ca mama priyaḥ

"Of these, the wise one who is in full knowledge in union with Me through pure devotional service is the best. For I am very dear to him, and he is dear to Me." (*Bg*. 7.17) An unintelligent devotee may accept the principles today, and leave tomorrow. A person who accepts the Kṛṣṇa conscious philosophy intelligently is very rare. We should not accept it by sentiment, but by intelligence.

Śyāmasundara dāsa: For Descartes, real happiness arises from consciousness of perfection.

Śrīla Prabhupāda: Yes, that consciousness is Kṛṣṇa consciousness, the awareness that God is the supreme and that I am His eternal servant. This consciousness is happiness, and it is confirmed by *Bhagavad-gītā*. When Dhruva Mahārāja was offered all the riches in the world by Kuvera, the treasurer of the demigods, he said, "Please benedict me so that I may have unflinching faith in the lotus feet of Kṛṣṇa." That is proper intelligence. Similarly, when Prahlāda Mahārāja was offered whatever he wanted by Lord Nṛsiṁhadeva, he said, "What should I ask from You? My father was a great materialist, so great that the demigods were afraid of his anger, yet You have finished him in one second. What then is the value of this material power and opulence? Please engage me in the service of Your servants. That is all I want."

Śyāmasundara dāsa: Descartes maintains that a man is virtuous insofar as his reason controls his passion.

Śrīla Prabhupāda: Yes, if one can control his passions somehow or other, he is freed from many troubles.

viṣayā vinivartante
nirāhārasya dehinaḥ
rasa-varjaṁ raso'py asya
paraṁ dṛṣṭvā nivartate

"The embodied soul may be restricted from sense enjoyment, though the taste for sense objects remains. But, ceasing such such engagements by experiencing a higher taste, he is fixed in consciousness." (*Bg*. 2.59) People are suffering due to their passionate activities. Therefore there are many Vedic rules and regulations governing action. If we can subdue our passionate impulses, we can save ourselves a great deal of trouble. Due to passion, one becomes a drunkard, engages in illicit sex, gambles, and acts unreasonably. If one can check his passion by reason, he can save himself from the greatest danger.

Śyāmasundara dāsa: Descartes had a great reverence for theology, the science of God, because he felt that it was an open road to heaven for everyone, the intelligent and unintelligent alike. For Descartes, theology is concerned with real truths that transcend human reason.
Śrīla Prabhupāda: This means that we have to take the truth from the revealed scriptures. Every revealed scripture gives some hint of an understanding of God.
Śyāmasundara dāsa: First of all, Descartes tried to find some basis for truth. Then he came to the proof of the existence of God. As far as philosophy is concerned, he maintained that it lacks certainty and that its tenets are always subject to dispute.
Śrīla Prabhupāda: Yes, we agree with that. It is said that a philosopher is not a philosopher unless he differs from other philosophers. If one is to be a great philosopher, he has to defy all his predecessors. Scientists also work in the same way. If we try to find out whose statement is true, we have a great deal of difficulty. Therefore the Vedic *śāstras* enjoin that we follow the personalities who have realized God, and therefore we follow Prahlāda Mahārāja, Dhruva Mahārāja, Vyāsadeva, Lord Brahmā, Lord Śiva, Kapila-deva, the twelve *mahājanas*, and their followers, the followers of Brahmā's disciplic succession, the Brahma-*sampradāya*, the Rudra-*sampradāya*, the Viṣṇusvāmī-*sampradāya*, the Rāmānuja-*sampradāya*, and so on. If we follow the *ācāryas* in the disciplic succession, our path is clear.
Śyāmasundara dāsa: Descartes felt that because science is based on philosophical principles which have no basis in themselves, science is not worthy of our cultivation. He condemns people for using scientific technology to make more money. He said, "I am resolved no longer to seek any science other than knowledge of myself."
Śrīla Prabhupāda: Yes, but he had no guru.
Śyāmasundara dāsa: No, he didn't accept a guru. He accepted only what he could know through self-realization, the innate truths that he discovered in himself by meditation. First, he came to the understanding that I am, and later he concluded that because I am, God is.
Śrīla Prabhupāda: That is a nice conclusion.
Śyāmasundara dāsa: He had an obsession for the need of absolute certainty because he felt that all the conclusions of the philosophers before him were dubious. He believed that every idea must be subjected to doubt until the truth or falsity can be ascertained, just as a mathematical formula can be ascertained. Every idea must be subjected to cross examination.

Śrīla Prabhupāda: But when will these doubts be finished? Your standard of understanding self-evident truths may be different from mine. So what is the standard? He must give some standard.
Śyāmasundara dāsa: When Descartes meditated on the first philosophy, he concluded, *cogito ergo sum*, "I think; therefore I exist." He felt that everything was subject to doubt with the exception of the act of doubting itself. Since doubting is a part of thinking, the act of thinking is an undeniable experience. Therefore he concluded that because I doubt, I think, and because I think, I exist.
Śrīla Prabhupāda: That is a good argument. If I do not exist, how can I think? But is he condemning doubt or accepting doubt? What is his position?
Śyāmasundara dāsa: He accepts doubt as the only real fact. Because I can doubt that my hand exists, it may be a hallucination, a dream. I can doubt that everything perceived exists because it may all be a dream, but the fact that I am doubting cannot be doubted.
Śrīla Prabhupāda: So what is his conclusion? Should one stop doubting or continue doubting? If I doubt everything, I may come to the truth and then doubt the truth.
Śyāmasundara dāsa: His point is that the truth cannot be doubted, but that to discover the truth, we have to doubt everything. When we come to the truth, the truth will be undoubtable.
Śrīla Prabhupāda: But how do you come to the truth if your business is simply doubting? How will you ever stop doubting?
Śyāmasundara dāsa: Well, I cannot doubt that I am, that I exist. That truth is undoubtable. So he proceeds from there to the fact that since I exist, God exists.
Śrīla Prabhupāda: Then his point is that by doubting, we come to a point where there is no more doubt. That is good. Doubt in the beginning, then the truth as the conclusion. But in any case, that doubt must be resolved. I doubt because I am imperfect and because my knowledge is imperfect. So another question is how we can obtain perfection. As long as we are imperfect, there will be doubt.
Śyāmasundara dāsa: He says that even though I am imperfect, there exists perfect knowledge, or a self-conscious awareness of perfect ideas within myself. Knowledge of the perfect is innate within me, and I can know it through meditation.
Śrīla Prabhupāda: That is also acceptable.
Śyāmasundara dāsa: Because I understand that I think, I can establish existence of my soul beyond all doubt.

Śrīla Prabhupāda: Everyone thinks. Everyone is there, and everyone has a soul. There are countless souls, and this has to be accepted.
Śyāmasundara dāsa: What about a blade of grass, for instance?
Śrīla Prabhupāda: Yes, it has a way of thinking. That has to be accepted. It is not that we have souls and that the grass has no soul, or that animals have no souls. Jagadish Candra Bose has proved by a machine that plants can feel and think. "I think, therefore I am" is a good proposition because everyone thinks and everyone exists. There are 8,400,000 species of living entities, and they are all thinking, and they all have individual souls.
Hayagrīva dāsa: There is a lot of conjecture in Descartes concerning the location of the soul. In his *Meditations,* he writes: "Although the soul is joined to the whole body, there is yet a certain part in which it exercises its functions more particularly than in all the others; and that is usually believed to be the brain, or possibly the heart; the brain, because it is with it that the organs of sense are connected, and the heart because it is apparently in it that we experience the passions." Descartes then goes on to conclude that the soul is situated in a small appendage of the brain called the pineal body.
Śrīla Prabhupāda: This speculation means that he has no definite information. Therefore we have to accept God's instructions. In *Bhagavad-gītā,* Kṛṣṇa specifically states:

īśvaraḥ sarva-bhūtānāṁ
hṛd-deśe'rjuna tiṣṭhati

"The Supreme Lord is situated in everyone's heart, O Arjuna." (*Bg.* 18.61) There are two kinds of *īśvaras,* controllers. One is the individual living entity, the *jīva,* and the other is the Supreme Living Being, the Paramātmā, or Supersoul. From the Vedas, we understand that both are sitting together within this body, which is compared to a tree. Both the Supersoul and the individual soul are living within the heart.
Hayagrīva dāsa: But at the same time, doesn't the soul pervade the whole body?
Śrīla Prabhupāda: Yes. That is also explained in *Bhagavad-gītā:*

yathā prakāśayaty ekaḥ
kṛtsnaṁ lokam imaṁ raviḥ
kṣetraṁ kṣetrī tathā kṛtsnaṁ
prakāśayati bhārata

"O son of Bharata, as the sun alone illuminates all this universe, so does the living entity, one within the body, illuminate the entire body by consciousness." (*Bg.* 13.34) This is the illumination of the soul. It is like the sun, which is situated in one particular location, yet its illumination is spread everywhere. Similarly, although the soul is situated within the heart, his illumination is characterized by what we call consciousness. As soon as the soul leaves the heart, consciousness is immediately absent from the entire body. At one moment, there may be consciousness, and at the next moment there may be no consciousness at all. When there is no consciousness, one may hack the body to pieces, and no pain will be felt. This is because something is missing, and that something is the soul. When the soul is gone, consciousness is absent from the body. Both the individual soul and individual consciousness are immortal. Under the influence of māyā, the illusory energy, our consciousness is absorbed in many material things: society, nationality, sex life, speculation, and so forth. Kṛṣṇa consciousness means purifying the consciousness so that it will remain fixed only on Kṛṣṇa.

Hayagrīva dāsa: Descartes writes: "I know that brutes do many things better than we do, but I am not surprised at it; for that also goes to prove that they act by force of nature. If they could think as we do, they would have an immortal soul as well as we. But this is not likely, because there is no reason for believing it of some animals without believing it of all, and there are many of them too imperfect to make it possible to believe it of them, such as oysters, sponges, etc."

Śrīla Prabhupāda: First of all, living entities do not act by force of nature, but by force of God. Even in the heart of the brute, God is also present. God is within all, and He gives us instructions so that we can advance. When we attain the platform of human life, we have the alternative to refuse God's instructions. Lower life forms do not have the power to refuse.

Hayagrīva dāsa: You have just said that whatever grows has a soul, including the grass.

Śrīla Prabhupāda: Yes, in a dormant stage. For instance, a child has a soul, but it is not yet developed because the body is not yet developed. According to the body and circumstances, the soul acts.

Hayagrīva dāsa: Descartes equated the mind, the higher mental processes, with the soul. He believed in an incorporeal, immortal, human mind, which has been mysteriously injected somewhere into the body.

Śrīla Prabhupāda: No, the mind is not the soul but an instrument through which the soul acts. The mind is rejecting and accepting according to the dictations of the soul. Although I walk with my legs, I do not consider myself to be my legs. Although I think with my mind, I am not my mind. Some philosophers identify the mind with the self, and this is a mistake. Intelligence is subtler than the mind, and the mind is subtler than the senses. The gross senses can be seen, but the center of the senses, the mind, cannot be seen. Therefore it is called subtle. The mind is guided by the intelligence, which is even subtler. The background of that intelligence is the soul. The mind is the instrument by which we think, but that instrument is not "I."

Hayagrīva dāsa: For Descartes, animals are mere machines that react. He felt that they have no souls or minds, and hence no consciousness at all, and the basis for this view is ratiocination, language. In other words, because they have no language, they simply act as machines.

Śrīla Prabhupāda: They have languages, but you do not understand them.

Hayagrīva dāsa: Scientists claim to be able to communicate verbally with dolphins.

Śrīla Prabhupāda: That may be, but Kṛṣṇa was speaking with everyone, even with the birds. When one *gopī* went to the Yamunā to bathe, she was surprised to see that Kṛṣṇa was speaking with the birds. Because Kṛṣṇa is God, He can understand everyone's language. That is a qualification described in the *Nectar of Devotion* as *vāvadūka*. When a human being can understand many languages, he is called a linguist. Another name for Kṛṣṇa is *vāvadūka*, which indicates that He can understand everyone's language, even the languages of the birds and bees. That is the potency of God.

Śyāmasundara dāsa: Descartes considers five basic ideas to be inherent within every man, ideas which every man knows without having to verify. One is that God is innate to us as our own soul.

Śrīla Prabhupāda: Yes, this is because we are part and parcel of God. For instance, in the material world, everyone knows that he has a father. This is common knowledge.

Śyāmasundara dāsa: Secondly, it is impossible for something to originate out of nothing; every effect must have a cause, and therefore there is a cause of everything.

Śrīla Prabhupāda: Yes, we have discussed this. That ultimate cause is Kṛṣṇa. We do not accept the Māyāvādī philosophy because they philosophize in a negative way to try to make the ultimate truth zero.

Śyāmasundara dāsa: Thirdly, it is impossible for a thing to exist and not exist at the same time.

Śrīla Prabhupāda: Who protests this? Who says that something can exist and not exist simultaneously? Who is he trying to refute?

Śyāmasundara dāsa: He is not refuting anyone. He says that this is an innate idea that we know for certain without having to verify.

Śrīla Prabhupāda: This body is a temporary manifestation, and this soul is always existing. Eventually, this body will not exist, but the owner of the body is eternal and existing eternally. If something is a temporary manifestation, we can say that it is simultaneously existing and not existing. On the material platform, everything is existing and not existing because it is temporary. For instance, we are existing in this room right now, but at the next moment we may not be existing. The whole cosmic manifestation is like that. As stated in *Bhagavad-gītā:*

nāsato vidyate bhāvo
nābhāvo vidyate sataḥ
ubhayor api dṛṣṭo 'ntas
tv anayos tattva-darśibhiḥ

"Those who are seers of the truth have concluded that of the nonexistent there is no endurance, and of the existent there is no cessation. This seers have concluded by studying the nature of both." (*Bg.* 2.16) Because the soul is never created, the soul never dies. Everything that is born must die.

Śyāmasundara dāsa: Descartes's fourth innate idea is that whatever is done can never be undone.

Śrīla Prabhupāda: Karma cannot be undone. However, it can change. In *Bhagavad-gītā*, Kṛṣṇa tells us to abandon all varieties of religion and just surrender unto Him. If we do so, He will relieve us of all the reactions of karma. (*Bg.* 18.66) So in this sense it is not a fact that what is done cannot be undone.

Śyāmasundara dāsa: Descartes is thinking in the realm of the physical. After I throw a ball, that ball can never be unthrown.

Śrīla Prabhupāda: That is a child's knowledge, not a philosopher's. Direct perception is childish. A child believes so many things by direct perception. I remember that when I first saw a train in Calcutta, I thought that within the engine there must have been horses, otherwise the train could not have run. This kind of thinking is not really philosophy. Of course, it is a part of philosophy because all philosophers are nature's children. Therefore they think in that way.

Śyāmasundara dāsa: Descartes's fifth principle is that we cannot be nonexistent as long as we are thinking.

Śrīla Prabhupāda: We have already discussed this. Everyone thinks, and therefore everyone is a soul.

Śyāmasundara dāsa: Descartes also gives two arguments for the exist-

ence of God. First, an innate idea of an infinite being necessitates the existence of that infinite being because a finite being could not possibly create such an idea. In other words, because I can think of the infinite, the infinite must exist. The infinite must have put that thought in my head.
Śrīla Prabhupāda: There are many ways of thinking of the infinite. The voidists think of the infinite as zero, void. Descartes may be thinking in one way, but someone else may be thinking in another.
Śyāmasundara dāsa: Descartes argues that because we can conceive of perfection, perfection must be there.
Śrīla Prabhupāda: Yes, but just because I am thinking of something does not mean that it exists. Everyone is thinking in his own way. Who will decide which way of thinking is correct? Who will judge? Therefore we ultimately have to accept the confirmation of authorities. If our thinking is confirmed by the authorities, it is all right; otherwise it cannot be accepted.
Śyāmasundara dāsa: Descartes was thinking more in terms of mathematics. If we begin counting, we can conceive of numbers stretching to infinity. So the fact that one can think of infinity necessitates the infinite.
Śrīla Prabhupāda: But the voidists are thinking that the infinite is zero. Some mathematicians calculate that infinity means zero.
Śyāmasundara dāsa: Secondly, God is an absolutely perfect being, and perfection necessarily implies existence. Since God's existence is the same as His essence, He must exist.
Śrīla Prabhupāda: That is our proposition. We say that Kṛṣṇa is the sum total of all wealth, knowledge, fame, power, beauty, and renunciation. Because these opulences are attractive, and Kṛṣṇa has them in full, Kṛṣṇa is all-attractive. All these attractive qualities must be there in Kṛṣṇa in totality. That is Parāśara Muni's definition of God.
Śyāmasundara dāsa: This is similar to Descartes's contention that perfect beauty and wisdom must exist somewhere because we can conceive of the fact.
Śrīla Prabhupāda: *Īśvaraḥ paramaḥ kṛṣṇaḥ (Brahma-saṁhitā* 5.1). No one is richer, more famous, wiser, more beautiful, or more powerful than Kṛṣṇa. Kṛṣṇa is the sum total of all qualities; therefore He is complete. Because we are part and parcel of the complete, we can think of the complete. Because I am the son of my father, I can think of my father. Similarly, Kṛṣṇa is the Father of all living entities, and every living entity has the power to offer his respects to God. Unfortunately, the living entity

is artificially educated by society not to obey God, and that is the cause of his suffering.

Śyāmasundara dāsa: When Descartes inspects reality, he concludes that reality consists of substances. He defines substance as "a thing which exists in such a way as to stand in need of nothing beyond itself." He says that there is only one absolutely independent substance—God. All other substances are created by Him. There are also two types of substances—matter and spirit.

Śrīla Prabhupāda: This is all described in *Bhagavad-gītā.* The summum bonum substance is Kṛṣṇa, and everything emanates from Him. All these emanations can be divided into two categories: inferior and superior. The inferior energy is matter, and the superior energy is spirit. Everything that we see or experience is a combination of the inferior and superior energies. Since these energies emanate from Kṛṣṇa, Kṛṣṇa is the origin of everything, the cause of all causes.

Śyāmasundara dāsa: Descartes states that the chief attribute of this spirit or soul is consciousness.

Śrīla Prabhupāda: That is so.

Śyāmasundara dāsa: And the chief attribute of the body is extension. Both the body and mind are finite and depend upon God for their existence, whereas God is completely independent.

Śrīla Prabhupāda: *Jīvera 'svarūpa' haya-kṛṣṇera 'nitya-dāsa' (Caitanya-caritāmṛta, Madh.* 20.108). Therefore every living entity is the eternal servant of God, or Kṛṣṇa. Since we all depend upon Kṛṣṇa for our existence, it is our duty to please Him. That is the process of *bhakti.* In the material world, we see that we depend upon our employer for our salary. Therefore we always have to please him. *Eko bahūnāṁ yo vidadhāti kāmān (Kaṭha-upaniṣad* 2.2.13). God is providing everything for everyone. So why not please Him? Our only duty is to please Him, and that process is perfectly manifested in Vṛndāvana. It is in Vṛndāvana that everyone is trying to please Kṛṣṇa, and because they are trying to please Him, they are happy. Kṛṣṇa in turn is pleasing them.

jaya rādhā-mādhava kuñja-bihārī
gopī-jana-vallabha giri-vara-dhārī
jaśodā-nandana braja-jana-rañjana
jāmuna-tīra-vana-cārī

"Kṛṣṇa is the lover of Rādhā. He displays many amorous pastimes in the groves of Vṛndāvana. He is the lover of the cowherd maidens of Vraja, the holder of the great hill named Govardhana, the beloved son of mother

Yaśodā, the delighter of the inhabitants of Vraja, and He wanders in the forests along the banks of the River Yamunā." (from Bhaktivinoda Ṭhakura's *Gītāvalī*) Kṛṣṇa engages in pleasing the *gopījana*, and the *gopījana* is engaged in pleasing Kṛṣṇa. That is the perfect relationship. In a perfect family, the head of the family tries to please all the members by providing them with food, shelter, clothing, and everything else. Therefore he works hard to please them, and their duty is to please him. When the father comes home, the wife and sons try to please him, and that makes the perfect home. Similarly, God is the original creator, and we are all subordinates maintained by Him. Our only duty is to please Him, and if He is pleased, we will all remain pleased. If we pour water on the root of a tree, all the parts of the tree—the leaves and flowers and branches—are nourished. The process of *bhakti-yoga* is the process of pleasing the Lord. This is our only business, and as long as we take to some other business, we are in māyā. We have no other business. The living entity who does not serve Kṛṣṇa is in māyā and is diseased, and the living entity who is constantly engaged in Kṛṣṇa's service is liberated and situated in his constitutional position. If anyone within the creation is not cooperating with God or not satisfying the senses of the Lord, he is not in his normal condition. It is the function of this Kṛṣṇa consciousness movement to engage everyone in Kṛṣṇa's service and bring everyone to his normal condition. People are suffering because they are in an abnormal condition.

Śyāmasundara dāsa: Descartes believed that God's truth is the basis for our knowledge of the truth, and that God is truth.

Śrīla Prabhupāda: Since God is truth, everything is emanating from the truth. We are trying to employ everything in the service of the truth. Because God is truth, we do not say that the world is false. The Māyāvādīs claim that the world is false, but we say that it is temporary. For instance, this flower is the creation of God. It therefore cannot be false; it is truth. It should therefore be employed in the service of the truth, and that is our reason for offering it to Kṛṣṇa. Suppose you work very hard to make something beautiful, and then you bring it to me, and I say, "Oh, it is all false." Will you be pleased with me? You will say, "What is this nonsense? I have travelled so far and have made such a beautiful thing, and he says it is false." Similarly, since God has created such a wonderful universe, why should we say that it is false? Our philosophy is that the universe is God's creation and therefore should be employed in God's service. For instance, we are using this tape recorder to record this conversation. It is being used for Kṛṣṇa. We do not say, "Oh, it is false. It is material. We won't use it." That is the position of the Jains, who do not take advantage of these things. We say, rather, that we can use these devices, but not for our personal sense gratification. That is real *vairāgya*, detachment.

Śyāmasundara dāsa: Descartes maintains that we can know and understand truth because God is true. This is the basis for our knowledge. God's existence assures us that this external world is not a fiction.

Śrīla Prabhupāda: This is what I was explaining. Because God is truth, His creation cannot be untrue. It is untrue when I see everything devoid of God. If I see this table as unrelated to God, it is untruth. However, when I see this table as a product of God's energy, I am seeing it in the proper way. In other words, I am seeing God. One who has no sense of God sees the table as a temporary creation, something produced by nature's law. He sees that it comes from zero, and that it will return to zero, and that ultimately it is zero, false. We do not say this. We do not say that Kṛṣṇa is zero but that this table comes from Kṛṣṇa's energy. Kṛṣṇa's energy is not zero, and the table is not zero. Whatever is within our experience has some relationship with Kṛṣṇa. The vision of that relationship is Kṛṣṇa consciousness. Generally, people have no vision of Kṛṣṇa. Their only vision is that of their family, their wife, their children, their this and their that. That is māyā.

Śyāmasundara dāsa: If people see nothing in relation to Kṛṣṇa, how can they justify saying that it is all a dream, that it is unreal?

Śrīla Prabhupāda: Because they cannot understand the beginning, they say that it is a temporary manifestation. People may say that this tree has come out of nothing and that when the tree dies, it will again become nothing. However, this tree has not come out of nothing, but from a seed, and Kṛṣṇa says, *ahaṁ bīja-pradaḥ pitā*. "I am the original seed of all existences." (*Bg*. 14.4) In a cinema, an image comes from a small hole, and we see it expanded on the screen. When the projector stops, the pictures on the screen cease to exist. People may say that these pictures come from nothing, but actually they are focused by the projector that projects the film, and behind that film there is an actual performance. Similarly, the material world is a perverted reflection of the spiritual world. That spiritual world is reality, not zero. When we see a photograph, we understand that it is an image of something actual. This material world is like something being played on a screen. Therefore the Māyāvādī philosophers say that it is false. In one sense, it is false, in that the show is not an actual performance. But it is a reflection of the original play under a different process. Because the original play is not

within our vision, we are thinking that the projection on the screen has come from zero. However, one who knows things as they are knows that the projection has come from reality, even though it is temporary and not permanently existing. In other words, the reality is the basis of what is being shown. When we see this, there is no question of anything being false.
Śyāmasundara dāsa: Descartes sees matter operating like a machine under mechanical laws. The sum total of all motion in the world is always constant; it neither increases nor decreases. However, he claims that the soul is unaffected by mechanical causes and is therefore immortal.
Śrīla Prabhupāda: Yet somehow or other he has been put into this mechanical process.
Śyāmasundara dāsa: Yes, and this was Descartes's problem. He could not understand how spirit and matter interact, how the nondimensional, nonextended spirit can have a three dimensional body.
Śrīla Prabhupāda: When you are on the land and fall into the water, your struggle begins. This means that on land you are safe, but somehow or other you have fallen into this material struggle. Spirit is spirit, and matter is matter, but now they have come in contact with one another. We have caused this contact because we have misused our independence. A boy may stand firmly beside the water, but if he wants to enjoy the water, he may fall in. If he cannot manage to swim, he is lost. This is our position. The spirit soul has a spiritual body, but he accepts a foreign body. The spirit soul has a body, and his business is to enjoy life, but because he falls within the jurisdiction of matter, he cannot enjoy his labor. As long as he is within water, there is no possibility of happiness.
Śyāmasundara dāsa: Does the spiritual body have dimensions? Does it exist in space?
Śrīla Prabhupāda: Yes, it has dimensions. It has length, breadth, and everything. Otherwise, how can we say that it is one ten-thousandth of the tip of a hair? In other words, there is measurement, but that measurement is beyond our imagination. The soul is something different. It is inconceivable. If the spirit soul has no body, how can the material body develop? A material body is like a coat molded in the form of the spiritual body. You cannot make a dress without measuring the body.
Śyāmasundara dāsa: Then the spiritual body is very small?
Śrīla Prabhupāda: You cannot imagine it. Because the materialists cannot see or measure the spiritual body, they say that it does not exist.
Śyāmasundara dāsa: Descartes says that the soul exists, but not that it occupies space.

Śrīla Prabhupāda: This means that his conception of space is limited. The material body is a body that has a beginning and an end. Your coat is made at a certain date. The spiritual body is changing dress from one material body to another, just as you change your clothes.
Śyāmasundara dāsa: After the soul has fallen into matter, can it be delivered through proper knowledge?
Śrīla Prabhupāda: Yes, that is the purpose of this Kṛṣṇa consciousness movement. Even if a person is an expert swimmer, how long can he swim? He will eventually succumb because he is in a fallen condition. However, if one is elevated just one inch above the water, he is immediately safe. The water may remain in its position, but he is transcendental to it. This transcendental position is Kṛṣṇa consciousness.
Śyāmasundara dāsa: In other words, the spirit soul can rise above matter, above the water.
Śrīla Prabhupāda: Yes, just like a flying fish. This fish may swim within the water, but suddenly he may fly over it. As soon as you become Kṛṣṇa conscious, you can fly over the water of material existence. Then you can gradually come to land.
Śyāmasundara dāsa: If the spirit is unlimited and has unlimited power, how does it fall within matter?
Śrīla Prabhupāda: It does not have unlimited power. Its power is so great that in the material sense it is unlimited, but actually it is not unlimited.
Śyāmasundara dāsa: How is it able to be confined by something as limited as a body?
Śrīla Prabhupāda: I have already explained this. It is like falling into the water. As spirit soul, we have nothing to do with this material body, but somehow or other we have come in contact with it. There is a cause, but instead of finding out this cause, we should realize that we are in a dangerous position.
Śyāmasundara dāsa: But if the spirit has great power, and the body has limited power, how is it that this limited power is able to hold onto the great power, to capture it and keep it?
Śrīla Prabhupāda: The material energy is Kṛṣṇa's energy, and each and every energy of Kṛṣṇa is as great as Kṛṣṇa. Therefore Kṛṣṇa says in *Bhagavad-gītā:*

daivī hy eṣā guṇamayī
mama māyā duratyayā
mām eva ye prapadyante
māyām etāṁ taranti te

"This divine energy of Mine, consisting of the three modes of material nature, is difficult to overcome. But those who have surrendered unto Me can easily cross beyond it." (*Bg*. 7.14)

Śyāmasundara dāsa: In other words, it is sometimes stronger than the spiritual energy?

Śrīla Prabhupāda: When you come in contact with the material energy without a specific purpose, it is stronger. Kṛṣṇa's representative comes into the material energy in order to preach. Although he is within the material energy, he is not under its control. But if you come in contact with material energy without serving Kṛṣṇa's purpose, you suffer. For instance, in a jail there are many superintendents and government officials. There are also prisoners. However, their conditions differ. We cannot say that because they are all in jail that they are all suffering in the same way. The superintendent is there because he is serving the government's purpose. Therefore he is not subject to the laws of the jail. When you are in the service of Kṛṣṇa, you are no longer under the laws of māyā. You are liberated.

Śyāmasundara dāsa: So the prisoners who have forgotten their real service have been weakened?

Śrīla Prabhupāda: Yes, because they have disobeyed and have forgotten their subordinate position. They want to be independent of the state, and therefore they have been put into jail.

Śyāmasundara dāsa: Then for them, the material energy is stronger.

Śrīla Prabhupāda: Yes. It is stronger for them. Those who are conditioned and are serving the material energy cannot escape through their own endeavor. They are dependent on the mercy of Kṛṣṇa and His representatives.

Blaise Pascal
(1623-1666)

Hayagrīva dāsa: Pascal saw man situated in the universe between two extremes: infinity and nothingness. Man has a body like the animals, and an intellect like the angels or demigods. As such, he is neither a demigod nor an animal but somewhere between the two. He is intelligent enough to know that he is in a miserable situation, despite his great desire to be happy. Man engages in all kinds of pastimes and diversions to forget his misery, but nothing ultimately helps. What man once possessed and now has lost is perfect happiness. All men suffer and complain, despite their situation, and Pascal believed that the emptiness felt by man can only be filled by God.
Śrīla Prabhupāda: Yes, life after life, the living entity strives for happiness, but he only becomes more morose because he does not take shelter of Kṛṣṇa. He manufactures new ways to sport. He dives in the water, and flies in the air, and God is supplying him all facilities. If you want to fly, become a bird. If you want to dive, become a fish. Sometimes, after making many attempts to be happy, the living entity gives up his planmaking and surrenders to Kṛṣṇa. Kṛṣṇa says, "Surrender unto Me, and I will make you happy." God comes personally as Lord Rāmacandra,

Lord Kṛṣṇa, and Lord Caitanya Mahāprabhu to give instructions how to surrender and attain happiness.

Hayagrīva dāsa: Whereas Descartes emphasized the importance of reason, Pascal believed that the principles that are understood by the heart are absolutely certain and adequate to overcome all skepticism and doubt. Is this because the Supersoul speaks within the heart?

Śrīla Prabhupāda: Yes. As Kṛṣṇa says in *Bhagavad-gītā:*

teṣāṁ satata-yuktānāṁ
bhajatāṁ prīti-pūrvakam
dadāmi buddhi-yogaṁ taṁ
yena mām upayānti te

"To those who are constantly devoted and worship Me with love, I give the understanding by which they can come to Me." (*Bg.* 10.10) Every living entity is living with God, but out of ignorance he does not know this. As we have stated before, there are two birds situated in the tree of the body. One bird is enjoying the fruits of the tree, while the other bird is witnessing. God gives instructions whereby we can return home, but nondevotees will not accept these instructions. A devotee strictly follows the orders of God, but the demoniac act according to their own whims, even though knowing God's desires. There is no doubt that God is giving instructions. Instructions are given externally through God's agent, the spiritual master, and through the scriptures. Instructions are given internally through the conscience, the Supersoul.

Śyāmasundara dāsa: Pascal was a mystic who believed very deeply in God, but he was also a skeptic in the sense that he believed that we cannot prove the existence of God by our reason or any other way. Therefore he emphasized that we have to believe in God with our heart.

Śrīla Prabhupāda: Yes, that is a fact. You cannot prove the existence of God by your material senses.

ataḥ śrī-kṛṣṇa-nāmādi
na bhaved grāhyam indriyaiḥ
sevonmukhe hi jihvādau
svayam eva sphuraty adaḥ

"Material senses cannot appreciate Kṛṣṇa's holy name, form, qualities and pastimes. When a conditioned soul is awakened to Kṛṣṇa consciousness and renders service by using his tongue to chant the Lord's holy name and taste the remnants of the Lord's food, the tongue is purified, and one gradually comes to understand who Kṛṣṇa really is." (*Padma Purāṇa*) The senses are incompetent to appreciate God, but if you are anxious to know God, you should render Him service. Then He will let you know what He is. The more we engage in God's service, the more He reveals. He cannot be perceived by our senses; therefore His name is *adhokṣaja,* which means that He is beyond our sense perception. We worship the Deity of God in the temple, but the gross materialist with his sense perception can never understand that the Deity is God. He will say that it is simply a stone carving. Therefore we have to believe in God with our heart. Because the atheist does not believe in God with his heart, he sees only a piece of stone.

Śyāmasundara dāsa: Pascal says that the heart has reasons which the mind does not know.

Śrīla Prabhupāda: Yes, the mind is an instrument; it is not something final. For instance, the brain is instrumental just like this tape recorder. Behind the mind there is the intelligence, and behind the intelligence there is the soul.

Hayagrīva dāsa: Pascal ascribed to the doctrine of original sin, which holds that at one time man fell from grace by committing some sin or other, and this fall from grace accounts for his present position between the angels and the beasts. In other words, original sin accounts for man's encagement in matter.

Śrīla Prábhupāda: Yes. This is also our philosophy.

Hayagrīva dāsa: What was this original sin?

Śrīla Prabhupāda: Disobedience—refusing to serve Kṛṣṇa. Sometimes a servant thinks, "Why am I serving this master? I myself must become a master." The living entity is eternally part and parcel of God, and his duty is to serve God. When he thinks, "Why should I serve God? I shall enjoy myself instead," he brings about his downfall. Original sin means refusing to serve God and attempting instead to become God. Māyāvādīs, for instance, are still attempting to become God, despite their knowledge and philosophy. If by meditation or some material effort, we can become God, what is the meaning of God? It is not possible to become God. The attempt to become God is the original sin, the beginning of sinful life.

Hayagrīva dāsa: Pascal believed that it is impossible for man to understand the universe or his position in it. We cannot look for certainty or stability in the material world because our reasoning powers are always being deceived. Therefore man must surrender to the dictates of his heart and to God.

Śrīla Prabhupāda: Yes, that is our position. We are not depending on the heart, however, because the dictations of the heart are not appreciated by nondevotees. Direct instructions are given in *Bhagavad-*

gītā and explained by the spiritual master. If we take the advice of God and His representative, we will not be misled.

Hayagrīva dāsa: Of all things in the world, Pascal considered this to be the strangest: "A man spends many days and nights in rage and despair over the loss of his job or for some imaginary insult to his honor, yet he does not consider with anxiety and emotion that he will lose everything by death. It is a monstrous thing to see in the same heart and at the same time this sensibility to trifles and the strange insensibility to the greatest objects (death). It is an incomprehensible enchantment, and a supernatural slumber, which indicates as its cause an all-powerful force."

Śrīla Prabhupāda: Yes, according to *Bhagavad-gītā,* when one does not believe in God, or when one disobeys God's orders, God comes as death. Then all power, pride, imagination, and plans are broken. After this, one may attain the body of an animal because in his life he acted like an animal. This is the process of transmigration. This is suffering.

Hayagrīva dāsa: Pascal writes: "If we submit everything to reason, our religion will have no mysterious and supernatural element. If we offend the principles of reason, our religion will be absurd and ridiculous."

Śrīla Prabhupāda: Yes that is a fact. The orders of God constitute religion, and if we carry out these orders, we are religious. Pseudo-religions, religions that cheat, are condemned in *Śrīmad-Bhāgavatam.* Any religious system which has no conception of God and which annually changes its resolutions is not a religion but a farce.

Hayagrīva dāsa: Pascal seems to be saying that we should not accept our faith blindly, but at the same time we should not expect everything to be comprehensible to our understanding.

Śrīla Prabhupāda: Yes. A father may tell his child to do something, although the child may not comprehend it. In any case, we understand that the father's plans are complete and good for the son. If the son says, "No, I don't wish to do this," he may fall down. God's orders constitute religion, but there is no question of blind following. We must understand God's nature and realize that He is all perfect. In this way, we can understand that whatever He says is also perfect and that we should therefore accept it. If we apply our finite reasoning and try to change God's instructions according to our whims, we will suffer.

Śyāmasundara dāsa: Pascal claims that by faith we have to make a forced option, or what he calls a religious wager. We either have to cast our lot on the side of God—in which case we have nothing to lose in this life and everything to gain in the next—or we deny God and jeopardize our eternal position.

Śrīla Prabhupāda: That is our argument. If there are two people, and neither has experience of God, one may say that there is no God, and the other may say that there is God. So both must be given a chance. The one who says that there is no God dismisses the whole case, but the one who says that there is a God must become cautious. He cannot work irresponsibly. If there is a God, he cannot run risks. Actually, both are taking risks because neither knows for certain that there is a God. However, it is preferable that one believe.
Śyāmasundara dāsa: Pascal says that there is a fifty-fifty chance.
Śrīla Prabhupāda: Yes, so take the fifty percent chance in favor.
Śyāmasundara dāsa: Pascal also advocated that. We have nothing to lose and everything to gain.
Śrīla Prabhupāda: Yes. We also advise people to chant Hare Kṛṣṇa. Since you have nothing to lose and everything to gain, why not chant?
Śyāmasundara dāsa: Pascal's religious wager rests upon the assumption that God will punish the individual who refuses to believe in Him, and reward the one who believes.
Śrīla Prabhupāda: Well, God is the Supreme Person who rewards and punishes. Lord Viṣṇu has four hands holding four symbolic objects. Two hands are for punishment, and two for protection. The conch shell and lotus give protection to the devotees, and the club and disc punish the nondevotees.
Hayagrīva dāsa: Pascal writes: "Man is great in that he knows himself to be miserable. A tree does not know itself to be miserable.... These miseries prove man's greatness. They are the miseries of a great lord, a deposed king."
Śrīla Prabhupāda: Yes. *Śrīmad-Bhāgavatam* points out that we are trying to live long, but a tree lives longer. Does this mean that the tree has attained perfection? Does perfection mean longevity? We may analyze life's conditions in this way in order to understand that perfection means coming to God consciousness and understanding God and our relationship with Him.
Hayagrīva dāsa: For Pascal, knowledge can be attained only by curbing the passions, submitting to God, and accepting God's revelation. He considered himself a Christian.
Śrīla Prabhupāda: Yes, without religion, one is an animal. Amongst animals, there is no discussion of God and no sense of religion. Presently, society is becoming degraded because governments are forbidding the discussion of God in schools and colleges. This causes increased suffering.
Hayagrīva dāsa: Although Pascal was considered a great philosopher,

he concluded that philosophy in itself only leads to skepticism. Faith is needed. "Hear God" was his favorite motto.
Śrīla Prabhupāda: Philosophy means understanding the truth. Sometimes philosophers spend their time speculating about sex and thus become degraded. Sex is present in animals as well as man. Sex is not life itself; it is only a symptom of life. If we emphasize only this symptom, the results are not philosophy. Philosophy means finding out the Absolute Truth. The real subject of philosophy is Brahman, Paramātmā, and Bhagavān.

Benedict Spinoza
(1632-1677)

Hayagrīva dāsa: Spinoza asserts that God cannot be a remote cause of the creation. He sees the creation flowing from God just as conclusions flow from principles in mathematics. God is free to create, but He is the immanent cause; the creation is but an extension.
Śrīla Prabhupāda: Yes, because He creates through His energy. As stated in *Bhagavad-gītā:*

bhūmir āpo'nalo vāyuḥ
khaṁ mano buddhir eva ca
ahaṅkāra itīyaṁ me
bhinnā prakṛtir aṣṭadhā

"Earth, water, fire, air, ether, mind, intelligence, and false ego—altogether these eight comprise My separated material energies." (*Bg.* 7.4) The material world is composed of these eight material elements, and because it is made out of God's energy, it is called the creation of God. More directly, however, it is His energies that create the material universe. The ingredients come from Him, and *prakṛti*, nature, creates. God is both the remote and immanent cause of the creation because the elements are God's energies.

Śyāmasundara dāsa: Spinoza sees God as the universal principle that binds together all the relationships in the material world.

Śrīla Prabhupāda: If God is nothing but a principle, He has no personal activity. Is it that Spinoza is an impersonalist?

Śyāmasundara dāsa: He states that God is the sum total of everything.

Śrīla Prabhupāda: Certainly God is everything, but why shouldn't we utilize discrimination? By saying that God is a principle like light, we imply that God is like a material thing. According to him, what is man's position in relationship with God?

Śyāmasundara dāsa: He states that the infinite universe is like a machine, yet all things are conditioned to exist in a particular way, and this is necessitated by the divine nature.

Śrīla Prabhupāda: Everything may be like a machine, but a machine is devised by a person. So according to him, who is God? Is God the machine, or the person who devises the machine?

Śyāmasundara dāsa: For him, God is the absolute universal principle behind everything. God is a thinking thing.

Śrīla Prabhupāda: If He is thinking, He must be the creator of that machine.

Śyāmasundara dāsa: Yes, he says that God is the creator, but we cannot know anything beyond the fact that God is that thinking and extended thing. Because we are aware of mind and matter, God must be thinking, and God must have extension. He claims that man cannot know more than that about God. Extension means that God takes up space.

Śrīla Prabhupada: If God is everything, He must exist in space. That is understood. But it must also be understood that if God is thinking, He is a person. How can He simply be a principle? How can we say that God is nothing but a principle and yet is thinking? The sun is working according to certain principles. It has to be at a certain place at a certain time. There is no question of thinking. If I say that the sun, which is a principle, is thinking, I am contradicting myself. If God is reason, God is a person, not a principle. Has Spinoza not explained what that principle is?

Śyāmasundara dāsa: He says that everything is God, and that God is everything.

Śrīla Prabhupāda: That is logical, but what is his conception of God? Is He a person or not? According to the Vedic version, the person is the origin, and the impersonal aspect is secondary. God is a person, and His influence or His supremacy is in everything.

īśāvāsyam idaṁ sarvaṁ
yat kiñca jagatyāṁ jagat
tena tyaktena bhuñjīthā
mā gṛdhaḥ kasya svid dhanam

"Everything animate or inanimate that is within the universe is controlled and owned by the Lord. One should therefore accept only those things necessary for himself, which are set aside as his quota, and one should not accept other things, knowing well to whom they belong." (*Īśopaniṣad* 1) Everything is made of God's energy, and therefore indirectly everything is God. Yet at the same time, everything is not God. That is Caitanya Mahāprabhu's philosophy of *acintya-bhedābheda-tattva:* everything is simultaneously one with and different from God. Everything is God, but at the same time, we are not worshipping this table. We are worshipping the personal God. Although everything is God, we cannot necessarily conceive of God in everything.

Śyāmasundara dāsa: Spinoza says that we can appreciate God by intellectually appreciating all of His creation and therefore understanding that God is the perfect principle behind everything. In this way, we can have an intellectual love for Him.

Śrīla Prabhupāda: God is a person, otherwise why are we worshipping the Deity? What is the difference between the Deity and this table? God has a personal form, but this table is not that form. Everything is the manifestation of God's energy. The Viṣṇu Purāṇa gives the example of fire, which expands as light and heat. Light and heat are nothing but fire, but at the same time, light and heat are not fire. They are simultaneously one and different. God is everything, but everything is not God. This table is God in the sense that it is part of God, but we cannot worship this table. In *Bhagavad-gītā*, Kṛṣṇa says:

mayā tatam idaṁ sarvaṁ
jagad avyakta-mūrtinā
mat-sthāni sarva-bhūtāni
na cāhaṁ teṣv avasthitaḥ

"By Me, in My unmanifested form, this entire universe is pervaded. All beings are in Me, but I am not in them." (*Bg.* 9.4) For instance, in the solar system, everything is resting on the sun's energy, but everything is not the sun. The sunshine is different from the sun, yet the sunshine is nothing but the sun. It is simultaneously one and different. This is perfect philosophy. Everything that is manifest is due to God, and when God withdraws His energy, there is no existence. It is insufficient to understand God simply as a principle. Spinoza says that God is a principle, but actually God is the Supreme Person. God expands His energy, and that energy is His principle.

Śyāmasundara dāsa: God is identical with the substance of the world, the stuff the world is made of.

Śrīla Prabhupāda: Yes, you cannot separate the energy from the energetic. That is one fact, but at the same time you cannot say that the sunshine is the same as the sun. It is identical and at the same time different.

Śyāmasundara dāsa: In a sense, Spinoza would agree in that he says there is a God who is substance but who also has an infinite number of attributes unknown to man.

Śrīla Prabhupāda: That's all right, but the attributes are simultaneously God and not God. There is substance and category. Gold is the substance, and a gold ring is the category. The gold ring is certainly gold, but the original substance gold is different.

Śyāmasundara dāsa: Spinoza would call God the substance and the things of this world the categories. Because the categories are made of the substance, they are all God.

Śrīla Prabhupāda: This clay pot is made of earth, but would you say that it is the whole earth? You may call it earthly, just as you may call the creation godly. That is pantheism.

Hayagrīva dāsa: Spinoza writes: "The more we understand individual objects, the more we understand God." Is this the proper process? Or is it that the more we understand God, the more we understand individual objects?

Śrīla Prabhupāda: Everything is related to God. In the material world, for instance, things are composed of the five gross elements, which are expansions of God's energies. An intelligent person sees everything in relation to God's expansions of energy. A devotee does not look on anything as being separate from God. Since he is a lover of God, he wants to engage everything in God's service because he understands that everything is God's property. The *asuras* have no conception of God, nor do they obey or love Him. The demoniac living entity thinks that the material world is created for his enjoyment. He does not see the material world as an expansion of God's energy. One who uses material products for his personal benefit is called a thief because he does not acknowledge the proprietorship of the creator, God. If we do not consider everything to be *prasāda,* the mercy of God, we become thieves subject to punishment. The conclusion is that the devotee sees every material object related to God and tries to use everything for God's benefit.

Hayagrīva dāsa: The emphasis in Spinoza is on intellectual knowledge of God through self-knowledge. He writes: "He who knows himself and knows his affections clearly and distinctly— and that with the accompaniment of the idea of God—is joyous, for he knows and loves God." Through knowledge of the self, we can come to know something of God. In this way, man can be happy and love God. There is no mention of service, however.

Śrīla Prabhupāda: Love means service. When a mother loves her child, she renders him service.

dadāti pratigṛhnāti
guhyam ākhyāti pṛcchati
bhuṅkte bhojayate caiva
ṣaḍ-vidhaṁ prīti-lakṣaṇam

"Offering gifts in charity, accepting charitable gifts, revealing one's mind in confidence, inquiring confidentially, accepting *prasāda,* and offering *prasāda* are the six symptoms of love shared by one devotee and another." (*Śrī Upadeśāmṛta* 4) Love means giving to one's beloved and also accepting some gift from him. *Dadāti pratigṛhnati.* Love means feeding one's beloved and also taking food from him. It means disclosing one's mind to him, and understanding his mind also. There are six reciprocal relationships in love. Love includes service.

Hayagrīva dāsa: Spinoza's God is basically not personal. His love for God is more intellectual or philosophical than religious. He takes the typical impersonalist stand in his belief in the identity of the individual soul with God. This is not to say that he believed that the individual soul is infinite but that it is not distinct from God. He writes: "Thus that love of the soul is a part of the infinite love with which God loves Himself." He sees the soul's intellectual love of God, and God's love for the individual soul, to be one and the same.

Śrīla Prabhupāda: There are five kinds of love: *śānta, dāsya, sākhya, vātsalya,* and *mādhurya.* In the beginning, there is love in awe and adoration (*śānta*), and one thinks, "Oh, God is so great. God is everything." When the soul understands God's unlimited potencies, the soul adores Him, and that adoration is also love. When our love advances, we serve God as a servant serves his master (*dāsya*). As the service becomes more intimate, friendship is established, and a reciprocal relationship of service is developed. This is the kind of service one friend renders to another. As this develops, the love turns into paternal love (*vātsalya*), and this expands into conjugal love (*mādhurya*). Thus there are different stages of love of God, and Spinoza only touches the beginning one: adoration and appreciation of God's powerful expansions. That is commendable, but when this love expands, it reaches the platforms of *dāsya*, *sākhya*, *vātsalya*, and *mādhurya-rasa*.

Hayagrīva dāsa: It appears that Spinoza believes in the Paramātmā present within all beings but not in the *jīva* accompanying the Paramātmā. Is this not a typical impersonalist position?

Śrīla Prabhupāda: This means that he does not know what is love. If God loves the living entity, He must be both well-wisher and friend. Because God expands Himself unlimitedly, He lives in the living entity. This is the conclusion of *Bhagavad-gītā:*

īśvaraḥ sarva-bhūtānāṁ
hṛd-deśe'rjuna tiṣṭhati

"The Supreme Lord is situated in everyone's heart, O Arjuna." (*Bg.* 18.61) The *Upaniṣads* also give the example of two birds sitting on a tree. One bird is eating the fruit of that tree, and the other is simply witnessing. The bird that witnesses is God, the Paramātmā. Thus God, the Paramātmā, and the individual soul, the *jīvātmā*, live together on the same tree of the body. This is confirmed throughout the Vedic literature.

sarvasya cāhaṁ hṛdi sanniviṣṭho
mattaḥ smṛtir jñānam apohanaṁ ca

"I am seated in everyone's heart, and from Me come remembrance, knowledge, and forgetfulness." (*Bg.* 15.15) God reminds the living entity that unless Brahman is present, he cannot remember anything. The Paramātmā is always there with the *jīvātmā*.

Hayagrīva dāsa: Spinoza does not believe that God has a body because "by body we understand a certain quantity possessing length, breadth, and depth, limited by some fixed form; and that to attribute these to God, a being absolutely infinite, is the greatest absurdity."

Śrīla Prabhupāda: God has a body, but it is not like this material body, which is limited. Spinoza's view comes from imperfect knowledge of God's spiritual qualities. It is confirmed in Vedic literatures that God has a body: *sac-cid-ānanda-vigraha. Vigraha* means "body" or "form." God's form is eternal, and He is all-aware. *Sac-cit.* He is also always blissful. The material body is neither eternal nor blissful, nor all-aware, and therefore it is different from God's body, which possesses different qualities and is all spiritual.

Hayagrīva dāsa: Concerning the individual material body, Spinoza asserts that each soul coincides with its body. That is, the soul acquires the body that befits it. However, the soul can progress beyond bodies to come to know spiritual truths by turning toward God rather than the material world, or, as Spinoza would put it, God's "extensions."

Śrīla Prabhupāda: The extension or expansion is also God, but at the same time, God is not personally present in the extension. The extension or expansion comes from the person. We might compare the expansions to the government and the person to the governor. The government is under the control of the governor, just as the impersonal expansion of God is under the control of the Supreme Person, Kṛṣṇa. Pantheism says that because everything is God, God Himself has no individual personal existence. To say that everything is God and that God is no more than everything is a material conception. In the material world, if you tear a piece of paper into pieces and throw the pieces away, the original paper is lost. The spiritual conception is different. God may expand Himself unlimitedly through His extensions, but He still remains complete in His own person.

Hayagrīva dāsa: Spinoza believed that as long as man is composed of body and soul, he will be under the mode of passion, and as long as the soul is confined to the body, the living entity will necessarily be attached to the physical world.

Śrīla Prabhupāda: Yes, we call this māyā, forgetfulness. The real aim of life, however, is to learn how to distinguish the soul from the material body so that when they separate, we may remain in our original, spiritual form. As long as we are attached to the material body, we have to continue to transmigrate from one body to another. If we give up our attachment to the material body, we are liberated from transmigration, and this is called *mukti*. It is possible to remain in our spiritual body by always thinking of God. That is the real meaning of meditation. This is confirmed by Śrī Kṛṣṇa in *Bhagavad-gītā:*

manmanā bhava mad-bhakto
mad-yājī māṁ namaskuru
mām evaiṣyasi satyaṁ te
pratijāne priyo'si me

"Always think of Me and become My devotee. Worship Me and offer your homage unto Me. Thus you will come to Me without fail. I promise you this because you are My very dear friend." (*Bg*. 18.65)

Hayagrīva dāsa: Spinoza considered good and evil to relate only to man. They have no basis in God, who is beyond both.

Śrīla Prabhupāda: But if everything is in God, as Spinoza thinks, what is man's position? God is there, but what is the position of evil? Evil is there, but he says that there is no evil in God. If this is the case, where does evil come from? According to the Vedas, good and evil also emanate from God. It is said that evil is His back, and that good is His front.

Śyāmasundara dāsa: Since the absolute reality is perfect, error and evil do not really exist because they would imply imperfection. According to Spinoza, since everything is God, everything must be perfect.

Śrīla Prabhupāda: *Pūrṇāt pūrṇam udacyate (Īśopaniṣad,* Invocation). Everything that is produced from the perfect is also perfect. Because God is perfect, the expansions of God are also perfect. If things are perfect in themselves, as long as we keep them in a perfect state, they are perfect. Because material nature is temporary, in the course of time it will become imperfect.

Śyāmasundara dāsa: Spinoza says that imperfection or error arises from a partial view of the whole. They are not viewed under the aspect of the eternal.

Śrīla Prabhupāda: In *Bhagavad-gītā,* Kṛṣṇa says that when the material energy is wound up, it again enters into Him. In the material world, everything is temporary, and everything will eventually be annihilated.

sarva-bhūtāni kaunteya
prakṛtiṁ yānti māmikām
kalpa-kṣaye punas tāni
kalpādau visṛjāmy aham

"O son of Kuntī, at the end of the millennium, every material manifestation enters into My nature, and at the beginning of another millennium, by My potency I again create." (*Bg.* 9.7) This body will eventually catch some disease, and there will be some so-called imperfection. You cannot consider that disease or imperfection is not in perfect order. This cosmic manifestation is created by Lord Brahmā, maintained by Lord Viṣṇu, and annihilated by Lord Śiva. There is perfect order here, and this annihilation is also perfect. Thus in a larger sense you can also say that when the body grows old, catches some disease, and dies, these events are also in perfect order. From one point of view, we may see birth, old age, disease and death as imperfections, but actually they are in perfect order. In order to fulfill the whole plan, there must be some

disease, or some destruction. We cannot call this imperfection. The plan of destruction is there from the beginning, and that plan is perfect.
Śyāmasundara dāsa: Spinoza says that we err because we cannot see the whole.
Śrīla Prabhupāda: Yes, the mistake is also in perfect order. For instance, it was the plan of Kṛṣṇa that so many warriors die on the battlefield of Kurukṣetra. That was all in perfect order because it was all planned by God. *Parāsya śaktir vividhaiva śrūyate (Śvetāśvatara Upaniṣad* 6.8). The Vedas say that the energies of the Lord are multifarious, and just as God is perfect, His energies are also perfect.
Śyāmasundara dāsa: For Spinoza, evil is due to ignorance, an inability to see reality in its entirety, which is all good because it is God.
Śrīla Prabhupāda: Yes, evil is due to ignorance. That is a fact. In a higher sense, there is no evil. Ignorance may be considered the cause of evil.
Hayagrīva dāsa: In his *Ethics*, Spinoza writes: "Properly speaking, God loves no one and hates no one; for God is not affected with any emotion of joy or sorrow, and consequently, He neither loves nor hates anyone."
Śrīla Prabhupāda: Yes, and therefore He is called *ātmārāma*. Being complete in Himself, He doesn't require anything from anyone. However, He states in *Bhagavad-gītā:*

patraṁ puṣpaṁ phalaṁ toyaṁ
yo me bhaktyā prayacchati
tad ahaṁ bhakty-upahṛtam
aśnāmi prayatātmanaḥ

"If one offers Me with love and devotion a leaf, a flower, fruit, or water, I will accept it." (*Bg.* 9.26) It is not for God's benefit that He accepts the offering of His devotee; rather, it is for the devotee's benefit to offer something out of love so that his love for God will develop. If we are decorated, our reflection in the mirror is automatically decorated. If we are God's reflections, we also become decorated if God is decorated.
Hayagrīva dāsa: When Kṛṣṇa destroys demons, does He do so without passion or hatred?
Śrīla Prabhupāda: Yes. He kills demons for their benefit.
Hayagrīva dāsa: Spinoza writes: "No sorrow can exist with the accompanying idea of God. No one can hate God."
Śrīla Prabhupāda: By nature, God is always full of pleasure. He is *sac-cid-ānanda*. He is the very source of pleasure. When Kṛṣṇa dances with the *gopīs*, He appears very pleasing, and when He kills a demon, He appears very pleasing also. It is not that He is morose when He

destroys a demon. He knows that He is not killing the demon, but awarding him salvation.

Hayagrīva dāsa: What about the contention that no one can hate God? What of Kaṁsa and others?

Śrīla Prabhupāda: Hatred of God is demoniac. Naturally, the living entity is in love with God, and he certainly should love God, but when he is in māyā, he considers himself separate from God. Instead of loving Him, he begins to consider God a competitor and hindrance to sense gratification. It is then that he thinks of avoiding God, or killing Him. The living entity then thinks, "I will become an absolute sense gratifier." In this way, he becomes demoniac.

Śyāmasundara dāsa: Spinoza defines the supreme virtue to be understanding God.

Śrīla Prabhupāda: Yes. Therefore *Bhagavad-gītā* says:

bahūnāṁ janmanām ante
jñānavān māṁ prapadyate
vāsudevaḥ sarvam iti
sa mahātmā sudurlabhaḥ

"After many births and deaths, he who is actually in knowledge surrenders unto Me, knowing Me to be the cause of all causes and all there is. Such a great soul is very rare." (*Bg.* 7.19) Unless we come to that point, our knowledge is necessarily imperfect.

Śyāmasundara dāsa: Spinoza's idea of understanding God is understanding nature. This is because he believes that God reveals Himself in nature.

Śrīla Prabhupāda: Yes, just as in order to understand the sun, we have to understand the sunshine. If we study nature, *daiva-śakti,* we can get some idea of God. Those who are just beginning to understand God are nature worshippers. They cannot go directly to God. The study of nature is the first stage of understanding God.

Śyāmasundara dāsa: Spinoza stresses the importance of the intellect, which allows a man to understand the laws of his own personality and thereby control his emotions.

Śrīla Prabhupāda: What does he mean by the emotions?

Śyāmasundara dāsa: Acting emotionally means acting instinctively by one's senses without intelligent consideration.

Śrīla Prabhupāda: A madman acts according to his emotions. But what is the source of these emotions? Unless there are emotions in the whole substance, how can emotions exist? There must be emotions in the whole.

The substance is the origin, and therefore emotion is a category. Unless emotions are already there in the substance, how can they be manifest? How can you neglect your emotions? If emotions exist in the substance, they have some purpose. Why is he trying to negate his emotions?
Śyāmasundara dāsa: He thinks that emotions will only lead one to error.
Śrīla Prabhupāda: Whatever the case, emotions are concomitant factors in the substance. Every madman also has a mind just as a sane man, but the sane man does not commit mistakes because his mind is in order. Similarly, when emotions are not in order, they lead to trouble, but when emotions are in order, they serve a purpose and are proper. Spinoza does not know this?
Śyāmasundara dāsa: He claims that the intelligence can direct the emotions.
Śrīla Prabhupāda: Love of God is an emotion. One may cry in the perfectional stage of devotional service. When Caitanya Mahāprabhu threw Himself into the ocean, that was an emotional act, but that was also a perfect act. According to his emotions, Caitanya Mahāprabhu was considering one moment to be like a *yuga*, like forty-three million years. This was because He was feeling separation from Kṛṣṇa. When we feel separation from Govinda, Kṛṣṇa, our emotions are in perfect order. That is the perfection of life. However, when the emotions are misused, that is māyā.
Śyāmasundara dāsa: Spinoza believes that by nourishing our intelligence, we can will things accordingly. First of all, our will should be subordinate to our intelligence.
Śrīla Prabhupāda: It is already subordinate to our intelligence.
Śyāmasundara dāsa: But in a madman, is it not reversed?
Śrīla Prabhupāda: A madman actually loses his intelligence. He thinks wildly. This is due to derangement, to a loss of intelligence.
Śyāmasundara dāsa: Spinoza says that God's intelligence controls His will.
Śrīla Prabhupāda: That is a different thing. In God, there is no such distinction. There is no distinction between God's body, soul, mind, and intelligence. In Him, everything is absolute. You cannot say that this is God's intelligence, or that this is God's mind. If you make these distinctions, how can you say that God is absolute? In the relative material world, there are such distinctions. We say that this is the intelligence, this is the mind, this is the soul, and so on, but in the spiritual world, there are no such distinctions. Everything is spirit.
Śyāmasundara dāsa: For Spinoza, nature and God are one, and the moral and the natural are the same.

Śrīla Prabhupāda: Sexual desire is a part of nature. Why is it sometimes called immoral?
Śyāmasundara dāsa: It is immoral when it is unnatural.
Śrīla Prabhupāda: Then we must distinguish between what is natural and unnatural. Whatever is done in God's service is natural and moral, and whatever is not done in His service is unnatural and immoral. Everything in nature is for the satisfaction of God. God has created this flower, and this flower should therefore be employed in God's service. That is moral. As soon as you take this flower for your own sense enjoyment, that is immoral.
Śyāmasundara dāsa: Spinoza states that man should act for his own self-preservation because this is a natural law.
Śrīla Prabhupāda: All preservation depends on God; therefore self-preservation means surrendering to God. A child can preserve himself by surrendering to his parents' will, but if he acts independently, he may be in trouble. If we do not surrender to God, there is no question of preservation. In *Bhagavad-gītā*, Kṛṣṇa says:

sarva-karmāṇy api sadā
kurvāṇo mad-vyapāśrayaḥ
mat-prasādād avāpnoti
śāśvataṁ padam avyayam

"Though engaged in all kinds of activities, My devotee, under My protection, reaches the eternal and imperishable abode by My grace." (*Bg*. 18.56) Kṛṣṇa tells Arjuna to surrender unto Him. "I will give you all protection." Without Kṛṣṇa, we can not protect ourselves. When Lord Rāmacandra wanted to kill Rāvaṇa, no one could preserve him, not even Lord Śiva or Goddess Durgā. Although there was a huge arrangement for the slaughter of the Pāṇḍavas, no one could kill them because they were protected by Kṛṣṇa. Self-preservation means taking shelter of Kṛṣṇa and depending on Him. *Rākhe kṛṣṇa māreke māre kṛṣṇa rākheke*. "If Kṛṣṇa protects one, who can kill him? And if Kṛṣṇa wants to kill one, who can protect him?" Just surrender unto Kṛṣṇa, and you will never be destroyed. That is self-preservation. Kṛṣṇa tells Arjuna: *kaunteya pratijānīhi na me bhaktaḥ praṇaśyati*. "O son of Kuntī, declare it boldly that My devotee never perishes." (*Bg*. 9.31).
Śyāmasundara dāsa: Spinoza believes that the more we understand reality, the more we understand God.
Śrīla Prabhupāda: This is because God is reality, and forgetfulness of God is illusion. Illusion is also God, but in illusion we forget God;

therefore it is not real. Sunshine and darkness are both reality because they exist side by side. Wherever there is light, there is also shadow. How can we say that the shadow is not reality? It is māyā, but because māyā attacks the individual soul, Kṛṣṇa is forgotten. In that sense, illusion or the unreal is also reality.

Śyāmasundara dāsa: But in illusion we forget the reality, the light.

Śrīla Prabhupāda: Yes. But this is so-called illusion. It is darkness, the atmosphere in which Kṛṣṇa is forgotten. Māyā is the shadow of darkness, yet even if we come under the shadow of darkness, reality remains. That atmosphere of the unreal is existing side by side with the real. Kṛṣṇa states, "Māyā is Mine." (*Bg*. 9.10) It is created by God; therefore how can it be unreal? Kṛṣṇa is reality, and everything dovetailed to Kṛṣṇa is reality. Therefore māyā, or the unreal, is also Kṛṣṇa. However, when we are in Kṛṣṇa consciousness, we are situated in reality. This material world is called the unreal, but if we are Kṛṣṇa conscious, there is nothing unreal.

Śyāmasundara dāsa: Because there is no forgetfulness?

Śrīla Prabhupāda: Yes. As long as you are engaged in the service of Kṛṣṇa, there is nothing unreal for you.

Śyāmasundara dāsa: Spinoza also believed that man, by subordinating his spirit to natural necessity, finds perfect peace.

Śrīla Prabhupāda: Yes, that natural necessity means surrender unto Kṛṣṇa. Kṛṣṇa is the Supersoul, and naturally if I surrender unto Him, I will find perfect peace.

tam eva śaraṇaṁ gaccha
sarva-bhāvena bhārata
tat prasādāt parāṁ śāntiṁ
sthānaṁ prāpsyasi śāśvatam

"O scion of Bharata, surrender unto Him utterly. By His grace you will attain transcendental peace and the supreme and eternal abode." (*Bg*. 18.62)

Gottfried von Leibnitz
(1646-1716)

Śyāmasundara dāsa: Leibnitz was a German mathematician and philosopher who maintained that in the universe, every act has a purpose, and the purpose of the universe is to realize the goal set forth by God.

Śrīla Prabhupāda: Yes, actually the goal is to reach God. The ignorant do not know this. Instead, they are hoping for something that can never be realized. This is the version of *Śrīmad-Bhāgavatam:*

na te viduḥ svārtha-gatiṁ hi viṣṇuṁ
durāśayā ye bahir-artha-māninaḥ
andhā yathāndhair upanīyamānās
te 'pīśa-tantryām uru-dāmni baddhāḥ

"Persons who are strongly entrapped by the consciousness of enjoying material life, and who have therefore accepted as their leader or guru a similar blind man attached to external sense objects, cannot understand that the goal of life is to return home, back to Godhead, and to engage in the service of Lord Viṣṇu. As blind men guided by another blind man miss the right path and fall into a ditch, materially attached men led by another materially attached man are bound by the ropes of fruitive labor, which are made of very strong cords, and they continue again and again in materialistic life, suffering the threefold miseries." (*Bhāg.* 7.5.31) Throughout history, people have been trying to adjust situations by manipulating the material, external energy, but they do not know that they are bound fast by the laws of material nature. No one can violate the laws of nature. As Caitanya Mahāprabhu explained:

kṛṣṇa bhuli' sei jīva anādi-bahirmukha
ataeva māyā tāre deya saṁsāra-duḥkha

"Forgetting Kṛṣṇa, the living entity has been attracted by the external feature from time immemorial. Therefore the illusory energy [māyā] gives him all kinds of misery in his material existence." (*Caitanya-caritāmṛta*, Madh. 20.117) Māyā, the illusory energy, ties the living entity by his neck, just as one ties a dog. The dog thinks, "I am very happy and free. My master is controlling me." In *Bhagavad-gītā*, it is also stated:

prakṛteḥ kriyamāṇāni
guṇaiḥ karmāṇi sarvaśaḥ
ahaṅkāra-vimūḍhātmā
kartāham iti manyate

"The bewildered spirit soul, under the influence of the three modes of material nature, thinks himself to be the doer of activities, which are in actuality carried out by nature." (*Bg.* 3.27) *Prakṛti*, material nature, is controlling the living entity by her different modes, but in ignorance the living entity is thinking, "I am inventing, I am acting, I am progressing." This is called māyā, illusion. No one can progress or improve without Kṛṣṇa consciousness. The living entities have come into this material world because they wanted to imitate Kṛṣṇa. Therefore they have been given a chance to engage in so-called enjoyment. At the same time, Kṛṣṇa is so kind that He has given them the Vedas, the right directions. He says, "All right, if you want to enjoy, enjoy in this way so that one day you may come back to Me." If a child insists on acting improperly, the father may be very careful in giving him what he wants, and at the same time directing him.

There are two kinds of activities. One is *pravṛtti*, by which we become very much attached to the material world. By the other type of activity, *nivṛtti*, we become detached. Both activities are mentioned in the Vedas. However, there is a plan. Because the living entities have forgotten or disobeyed Kṛṣṇa and are trying to enjoy life by imitating Him, they are placed into this material world. Under the supervision of the superintendent of this material world, Durgā, these living entities can return home, back to Godhead. That is the plan, and there is really no other. Every one of us has to go back home, back to Godhead. If we do so immediately and voluntarily, we save time; otherwise we waste time. We have to come to this point. Therefore *Bhagavad-gītā* says: *bahūnāṁ janmanām ante (Bg.* 7.19). After struggling for many births, the wise man surrenders unto Kṛṣṇa. The final point is surrender, and māyā gives the living entity trouble in many different ways so that he will eventually come to this point. When he becomes frustrated in his attempts at sense gratification, it should be understood that he is receiving special favor. When Kṛṣṇa is anxious to reform the living entity, He bestows His mercy by first of all taking away all his money. This is a special favor. The living entity always wants to delay, but by special favor Kṛṣṇa draws the living entity to Him by force. This is explained in *Caitanya-caritāmṛta.* The living entity wants Kṛṣṇa, or God, but at the same time he wants to enjoy the material world. This is inconsistent, because desiring God means rejecting the material world. Sometimes the living entity is caught between these two desires, and when Kṛṣṇa sees this, He places him in a hopeless condition. He takes away all his money, and then the living entity sees that all his so-called relatives and friends turn from him, saying, "Oh, this man is useless. He has no money." In this hopeless condition, the living entity surrenders to Kṛṣṇa.

All beings are trying to be happy in this material world, but it is nature's plan to give them trouble. In other words, every attempt at happiness will be frustrated so that eventually the living entity will turn to Kṛṣṇa. This is the plan: to bring the living entity back home, back to Godhead. This plan does not apply to just a few living entities. It is not that some will remain here and others will go back to Godhead. No, the whole plan is that everyone must come back to Godhead. Some living entities are very obstinate, just like bad boys. The father says, "Come on," but the boy says, "No, I'll not go." It is then the father's business to drag him. At the end of *Bhagavad-gītā*, Kṛṣṇa says:

sarva-guhyatamaṁ bhūyaḥ
śṛṇu me paramaṁ vacaḥ
iṣṭo'si me dṛḍham iti
tato vakṣyāmi te hitam

"Because you are My very dear friend, I am speaking to you the most confidential part of knowledge. Hear this from Me, for it is for your benefit." (*Bg*. 18.64) Then He says, "Surrender unto Me, and I will give you all protection." (*Bg.* 18.66) In *Bhagavad-gītā*, Kṛṣṇa instructed Arjuna in *karma-yoga*, *jñāna-yoga*, and other yogas, but His final instruction was to surrender.

Śyāmasundara dāsa: Leibnitz agrees that the mechanics of nature serve to fulfill God's purposes.

Śrīla Prabhupāda: Yes, that's it. All the laws of nature are working under Kṛṣṇa's direction.

mayādhyakṣeṇa prakṛtiḥ
sūyate sa-carācaram
hetunānena kaunteya
jagad viparivartate

"This material nature is working under My direction, O son of Kuntī, and it is producing all moving and unmoving beings. By its rule this manifestation is created and annihilated again and again." (*Bg.* 9.10) Material nature is the goddess Durgā. It is she who is the superintendent of the fort. Material nature is like a fort which no one can leave. Durgā is the confidential maidservant of Kṛṣṇa, but she has a very thankless task of punishing the demoniac living entities, who are thinking, "I will worship my mother Durgā," not knowing that her engagement is punishment. She is not an ordinary mother. She gives the demonic living entity whatever he wants. "Give me money. Give me a good wife. Give me reputation. Give me strength." Goddess Durgā says, "All right, take these things, but at the same time you will be frustrated with them." On the one hand, the living entity is given whatever he wants, and on the other there is frustration and punishment. This is nature's law, and nature is functioning under the instructions of Kṛṣṇa. The living entity in the material world has revolted against Kṛṣṇa. He wants to imitate Kṛṣṇa and become the enjoyer; therefore Kṛṣṇa gives him all the resources of material enjoyment, but at the same time He punishes him. The goddess Durgā is so powerful that she can create, maintain, and dissolve, but she is working just like a shadow. A shadow does not move independently. The movement is coming from Kṛṣṇa. A fool thinks that material nature is there for his enjoyment. This is the materialistic view. When he sees a flower, he thinks, "Nature has produced this flower for me. Everything is for me." In the Bible, it is stated that animals are placed under the dominion or protection of men, but men mistakenly think, "They are given to us to kill and eat." If I entrust you to someone, is it proper that he eat you? What kind of intelligence is this? This is all due to a lack of Kṛṣṇa consciousness.

Śyāmasundara dāsa: Leibnitz believed that truth could be represented by an exact, mathematical science of symbols, which could form a universal language, a linguistic calculus. He believed in a rational world and an empirical world, and that each stood opposed to the other. He felt that each had its own truth, which applied to itself, and that each had to be understood according to its own logic. Thus for Leibnitz, there are two kinds of truth. One is the truth of reason, which is a priori. This is innate knowledge which we have prior to and independent of our experience in the material world. The other truth is a posteriori, which is knowledge acquired from experience. This is accidental knowledge in the sense that it is not necessary.
Śrīla Prabhupāda: The real truth is that God has a plan, and one has to be taught that plan by one who knows it. This is explained in *Caitanya-caritāmṛta:*

nitya-siddha kṛṣṇa-prema 'sādhya' kabhu naya
śravaṇādi-śuddha-citte karaye udaya

"Pure love for Kṛṣṇa is eternally established in the hearts of living entities. It is not something to be gained from another source. When the heart is purified by hearing and chanting, the living entity naturally awakens." (*Caitanya-caritāmṛta*, Madh. 22.107) The truth is there, but we have forgotten it. Through the process of chanting and hearing, we can revive the truth, which is that we are eternal servants of Kṛṣṇa. The living entity is good by nature because he is part and parcel of the supreme good, but due to material association, he has become conditioned. Now we have to again draw forth this goodness through the process of Kṛṣṇa consciousness.
Śyāmasundara dāsa: As an innate, or a priori truth, Leibnitz gives the example of a triangle: three angles of a triangle must always equal two right angles. This is a truth of reason which is necessarily permanent. The other type of truth is gathered by experience and is called accidental, or unnecessary. For example, we see that snow is white, but it is also possible that snow may be red.
Śrīla Prabhupāda: It is also experienced that the three angles of a triangle must always equal two right angles.
Śyāmasundara dāsa: But this truth exists independently.
Śrīla Prabhupāda: How is that? Not everyone knows how a triangle is formed. Only when you study geometry do you understand. You cannot ask any child or any man who has no knowledge of geometry.
Śyāmasundara dāsa: Whether the man knows it or not, this truth exists.

Śrīla Prabhupāda: But truth by definition exists. It is not this truth or that truth. You may know it or not, but truth exists. So why is he using this particular example?
Śyāmasundara dāsa: Because there is also another kind of truth, which may say that snow is white, but that truth is not absolute because snow could conceivably be red. However, a triangle must always have certain innate properties. That is a necessary truth.
Śrīla Prabhupāda: Any mathematical calculation is like that. Why use this example? Two plus two equals four. That is always the truth according to mathematical principles.
Śyāmasundara dāsa: Leibnitz was trying to prove that there are certain truths that we cannot deny, that exist independent of our knowledge, and that are fundamental. There are other truths, like snow is white, which may or may not be true because our senses deceive us.
Śrīla Prabhupāda: But that is due to our defective senses. It is a fact that snow is white. Now why should it be red? In any case, we have no experience of red snow. Pure snow is white by nature. It may assume another color due to contact with something else, but actually it is white. It is an innate truth that the three angles of a triangle must always equal two right angles, and it is also an innate truth that snow is white, that water is liquid, that stone is hard, and that sugar is sweet. These are fundamental truths that cannot be changed. Similarly, the living entity is the eternal servant of God, and that is his natural position. Water may become hard due to temperature changes, but as soon as the temperature rises, the water again turns into a liquid. Thus the liquidity of water is the truth, the constitutional position of water, because water by definition is a liquid. Similarly, the whiteness of snow is truth, and the servitude of the living entity is truth. In the conditional world, the living entity serves māyā, and that is not truth. We cannot consider that there are two types of truth. Truth is one. What we take to be not truth is māyā. There cannot be two truths. Māyā has no existence, but it appears to be true or factual due to our imperfect senses. A shadow has no existence, but it resembles whatever projects it. In the mirror, you may see your face in exactly the same way that it exists, but that is not truth. The truth is one, and there cannot be two. What is taken for truth at the present moment is called māyā.
Śyāmasundara dāsa: Leibnitz says that innate truths are governed by the principle of contradiction. That is, the opposite of the truth is impossible to conceive.
Śrīla Prabhupāda: The opposite is māyā.

Śyāmasundara dāsa: For instance, it is impossible to conceive that the three angles of a triangle cannot equal two right angles.
Śrīla Prabhupāda: My point is that there are not two types of truth. When you think that there are, you are mistaken. When you think that two plus two equals five, you are mistaken. Two plus two is always four, and that is the truth. Similarly, snow is always white, and when you think that snow is red, it is the same as thinking that two plus two equals five. It is an untruth. You cannot say that the whiteness of snow is another type of truth. You may make a mistake by thinking snow to be red, but this mistake cannot invalidate the truth that snow is white or that water is liquid. There is one truth, and any other truth is but a shadow. It is not true. Our language must be exact. You can see your face in the mirror as exactly the same, but it is a shadow only; therefore it is not truth. You cannot say that the reflection of your face in the mirror is another type of truth.
Śyāmasundara dāsa: Leibnitz would call this type of truth conditional truth.
Śrīla Prabhupāda: That conditional truth is not the truth. For instance, the living entity is trying to become master of the material world. He thinks, "I am monarch of all I survey." That is not the truth. The truth is that he is the eternal servant of God. You cannot say that because he is trying to imitate God that he is God. There cannot be a second God. God is one, and that is the Absolute Truth. Our point is that we do not accept the proposition that truth is two. There are relative truths, but Kṛṣṇa is the Absolute Truth. Kṛṣṇa is the substance, and everything is emanating from Kṛṣṇa by Kṛṣṇa's energy. Water is one of Kṛṣṇa's energies, but that energy is not the Absolute Truth. Water is always a liquid, but that is relative truth. Absolute Truth is one. Leibnitz should more precisely say that there is Absolute Truth and relative truth, not that there are two types of truth.
Śyāmasundara dāsa: According to Leibnitz's law of continuity, everything in nature goes by steps and not leaps. In other words, there are no gaps in nature. Everything is connected, and there is gradual differentiation.
Śrīla Prabhupāda: No, there are two processes: gradual and immediate. Of course, in one sense everything is gradual, but if the gradual process takes place quickly, it appears immediate. For instance, if you want to go to the top of the building, you can go step by step, and that is gradual. But you may also take an elevator, which may take just a second. The process of elevation is the same, but one takes place very quickly, and the other is gradual. Foolish people say that a flower is created by nature,

but in fact the flower is growing due to the energy of Kṛṣṇa. His energy is so perfect that He doesn't have to take a brush and canvas and try to paint a flower like an artist. The flower appears and grows automatically. Kṛṣṇa is so powerful that whatever He desires immediately happens. This process is very quick, and it appears to be magical. Still, the process is there.

Śyāmasundara dāsa: Leibnitz sees in nature a combination of forces or activities at work. According to the law of motion, there is an uninterrupted series of regularly progressive changes in a body as it moves. If a ball rolls along the floor, it goes progressively, without gaps or sudden changes.

Śrīla Prabhupāda: I explained that. The complete motion is part of the same process. However, the ball has no power to move of itself. If you push it in one way, it will roll slowly, and if you push it in another way, it will roll quickly. All these wonderful processes are happening in material nature due to the will of the Supreme. The process takes place automatically, but it is initially pushed by God, who created this material nature. In the beginning, material nature was unmanifest. Gradually, the three qualities or modes came into being, and by the interaction of the modes, many manifestations arose. First there was space, then sky, then sound, one after another. Kṛṣṇa's push is so perfect that everything comes into being automatically in perfect order. Foolish people think that everything comes about automatically without an initial push, without a background. Therefore they think there is no God. This cosmic manifestation has not come about automatically. Kṛṣṇa is the creator, and He gives nature its original purpose. A potter may make a clay pot on a wheel, but the wheel is not the original cause of the pot. It is the potter who gives force to the wheel. Foolish people think that the wheel moves automatically, but behind the wheel's movement there is the potter who gives it force. There is no question of nature creating independently. Everything results from God, Kṛṣṇa.

As soon as you speak of a process, you imply that everything is linked together, that one event follows another. That is nature's way. The first creation is the *mahat-tattva,* the sum total of material energy. Then there is an interaction of the three *guṇas*, qualities, and then there is mind, ego, and intelligence. In this way, creation takes place. This is explained in the Second Canto of *Śrīmad-Bhāgavatam.* The Supreme Lord impregnates matter, *prakṛti*, by glancing at her. In the material world, one has to impregnate by the sexual process, but in the Vedas it is stated that Kṛṣṇa impregnated the total material energy simply by His glance. This is due to His omnipotence. When Kṛṣṇa throws His glance toward material nature, material nature is immediately activated, and events begin to happen. So the original cause of the creation is Kṛṣṇa's glance. Materialists cannot understand how Kṛṣṇa can set material nature into motion just by glancing at it, but that is due to their material conception.

Śyāmasundara dāsa: Leibnitz says that space and time are mere appearances and that the ultimate reality is different.

Śrīla Prabhupāda: The ultimate reality is Kṛṣṇa, *sarva-kāraṇa-kāraṇam (Brahma-saṁhitā* 5.1), the cause of all causes.

Śyāmasundara dāsa: Leibnitz calls the ultimate entities monads. The word "monad" means "unity," or, "oneness." He says that the stuff out of which even atoms are made are all monads, the ultimate particles.

Śrīla Prabhupāda: That small particle is not final. Within that particle there is Kṛṣṇa. *Aṇḍāntara-stha-paramāṇu-cayāntara-stham (Brahma-saṁhitā* 5.35).

Śyāmasundara dāsa: Leibnitz says that these monads are individual, conscious, active, and alive, and that they range in quality from the lowest type (matter) through the higher types, such as souls, to the highest, which is God.

Śrīla Prabhupāda: Does he state that within the atom there is the soul?

Śyāmasundara dāsa: His theory is that even the atoms are composed of these monads, which possess activity, consciousness, individuality, and other inherent qualities. The monad is the force or activity that constitutes the essence of a substance.

Śrīla Prabhupāda: We understand from *Brahma-saṁhitā* that Kṛṣṇa is within the atom. That is Kṛṣṇa who is the substance, the summum bonum. He is smaller than the smallest, and is within everything. That is His all-pervasive nature.

Śyāmasundara dāsa: Then how are the individualities accounted for?

Śrīla Prabhupāda: Every individual soul is awarded a portion of independence because each is part and parcel of God. Thus he has the quality of independence, but in minute quantity. That is his individuality. We consider the atom to be the smallest particle of matter, but we say that Kṛṣṇa is the force within the atom. Leibnitz is suggesting that some force or power exists, but we are directly saying that the force or power is Kṛṣṇa.

Śyāmasundara dāsa: But he says that the force or power in each atom is individual, separate, different.

Śrīla Prabhupāda: Yes, that is so. By His omnipotence, Kṛṣṇa can expand Himself in innumerable forms. *Advaitam acyutam anādim ananta*

rūpam (Brahma-saṁhita 5.33). The word *ananta* means unlimited, and it is clearly said *aṇḍāntara-stham:* He is within the atom.
Śyāmasundara dāsa: Is he within each atom as an individual entity different from every other entity?
Śrīla Prabhupāda: Yes. If Kṛṣṇa is there, He is individual. There are varieties of atoms, and sometimes they are combined together.
Śyāmasundara dāsa: How is each Kṛṣṇa different? How is it He is an individual in each of the atoms?
Śrīla Prabhupāda: Why is He not an individual? Kṛṣṇa is always an individual. He is always a person, the Supreme Person, and He can expand Himself innumerably.
Śyāmasundara dāsa: And is Paramātmā a person?
Śrīla Prabhupāda: Yes, every expansion is a person. We are all atomic expansions of Kṛṣṇa, and we are all individual persons. Paramātmā is another expansion, but that is a different kind of expansion.
Śyāmasundara dāsa: Is the *jīvātmā*, the individual soul, also a person?
Śrīla Prabhupāda: Yes. If he were not a person, then how would you account for the differences? We are all different persons. You may agree with my opinion or not, but in any case you are an individual. Kṛṣṇa is also an individual. *Nityo nityānām.* There are innumerable individual souls, but He is the supreme individual person. Now Leibnitz may say that within the atom there is a monad, or whatever—you could call it by any name you want—but within the atom the force is Kṛṣṇa.
Śyāmasundara dāsa: Leibnitz maintains that the lowest type of monad is found within material atoms, and then they progress to higher monads, which are souls.
Śrīla Prabhupāda: Directly we say Kṛṣṇa, and that is automatically spiritual.
Śyāmasundara dāsa: He says that each monad has an inner or mental activity, a spiritual life.
Śrīla Prabhupāda: As soon as we say Kṛṣṇa, we include everything.
Śyāmasundara dāsa: So even within material atoms, there is a spiritual life, a spiritual force?
Śrīla Prabhupāda: Yes, force means spiritual force.
Śyāmasundara dāsa: He says that all bodies are ultimate quantums of force, and that the essential nature of all bodies is force.
Śrīla Prabhupāda: Yes, that force is the spiritual soul. Without the spirit soul, the body has no force. It is a dead body.
Śyāmasundara dāsa: But even within the dead body there are forces. There is the force of decomposition.

Śrīla Prabhupāda: Kṛṣṇa is within the atom, and the body is a combination of so many atoms; therefore the force for creating other living entities is also there even in the process of decomposition. When the individual soul's force is stopped within a particular body, we call that body a dead body. Still, Kṛṣṇa's force is there because the body is a combination of atoms.

Śyāmasundara dāsa: He says that what is manifested to our senses, what occupies space and exists in time, is only an effect of the basic nature, which is transcendental to the physical nature. Physical nature is just an effect of a higher nature.

Śrīla Prabhupāda: Physical nature is a by-product. As I have explained, according to your desire, you receive or create a body. Physical nature is subservient to the soul.

Śyāmasundara dāsa: According to Leibnitz, these monads create bodies.

Śrīla Prabhupāda: Yes, at the time of death, you think in a certain way, and your next body is created. Therefore you create your next body according to your karma.

Śyāmasundara dāsa: But does the monad of a hydrogen molecule, for instance, create its own body? Does it only accidentally become part of a water molecule?

Śrīla Prabhupāda: Nothing is accidental.

Śyāmasundara dāsa: Then does it also desire to become a water molecule? Does the hydrogen desire to combine with oxygen and become water?

Śrīla Prabhupāda: No. The ultimate desire is of Kṛṣṇa. If you take it in that way, Kṛṣṇa is within every atom, and therefore Kṛṣṇa wants whatever is to be. Therefore He wills that these two elements become one, and therefore the molecules combine to create water, or whatever. Thus there is a creation, and again there is another creation, and so on. In any case, the ultimate brain governing all creation is Kṛṣṇa.

Śyāmasundara dāsa: But does the hydrogen molecule have an independent desire?

Śrīla Prabhupāda: No, because Kṛṣṇa is within the atoms, they combine. It is not that the atoms as matter are individually willing to combine; rather, because Kṛṣṇa is within the atoms, He knows that by certain combinations, certain creations will result.

Śyāmasundara dāsa: But does the individual soul have a little independence to choose?

Śrīla Prabhupāda: No. *Bhagavad-gītā* states that when the individual soul wants to act, Kṛṣṇa gives the orders. Man proposes, and God disposes.

Śyāmasundara dāsa: So we have no free will?

Śrīla Prabhupāda: Not without the sanction of Kṛṣṇa. Without Him, we cannot do anything. Therefore He is the ultimate cause.

Śyāmasundara dāsa: But I thought you have been saying that we have a little independence.

Śrīla Prabhupāda: We have the independence in the sense that we may deny or affirm, but unless Kṛṣṇa sanctions, we cannot do anything.

Śyāmasundara dāsa: If we desire something, we take a body because of that desire. Now, can a hydrogen molecule desire to become a part of water and be given a body accordingly? Does it have the independence to desire something?

Śrīla Prabhupāda: As far as we understand from the Vedas—*aṇḍāntara-stha paramāṇu-cayāntara-stham (Brahma-saṁhitā* 5.35)—Kṛṣṇa is within the *paramāṇu.* It is not stated that the soul is within the *paramāṇu.*

Śyāmasundara dāsa: Then the individual soul is not present within the atom?

Śrīla Prabhupāda: No. But Kṛṣṇa is present.

Śyāmasundara dāsa: Then Leibnitz's view does not accord with the Vedas?

Śrīla Prabhupāda: No.

Śyāmasundara dāsa: Is this because he states that in matter there is also this kind of individuality?

Śrīla Prabhupāda: That individuality is in Kṛṣṇa. As I have stated, Kṛṣṇa knows that a certain element will be formed when so many atoms combine. It is not the individual soul enacting this, but Kṛṣṇa Himself directly.

Śyāmasundara dāsa: But when we refer to the living entities, the individual soul is also there?

Śrīla Prabhupāda: Yes, the individual soul is within the body. Both are present within the body: Kṛṣṇa and the individual soul.

Śyāmasundara dāsa: According to Leibnitz, substance is defined as being capable of action.

Śrīla Prabhupāda: Substance is original, and extensions are categories. Since substance is the original cause, He is completely able to act. To be means to act. Without activity, what is the meaning of existence?

Śyāmasundara dāsa: Leibnitz states that the monads change in their appearance because their inner desire compels them to pass from one phenomenal representation to another.

Śrīla Prabhupāda: The monad does not change, but the mind changes. At any rate, I do not know what Leibnitz means by monads. He is simply complicating matters.

Śyāmasundara dāsa: By definition, the monad is a small unit, a unity, which is the substance behind everything, even the atom.

Śrīla Prabhupāda: That is Kṛṣṇa. Kṛṣṇa is fully independent.

Śyāmasundara dāsa: Yet Leibnitz says that a monad changes his appearance according to his desires.

Śrīla Prabhupāda: That is the case for the individual souls, but Kṛṣṇa is not like that. Kṛṣṇa is *acyuta*. He does not change. It is Kṛṣṇa who creates the entire cosmic energy. By His plan and devices, so many creations are divided into different parts, and they change. Material objects change according to the will of God, Kṛṣṇa. These individual monads are more precisely the Supersoul existing within matter, within the atom.

Śyāmasundara dāsa: Leibnitz would say that each particle of Supersoul, or each monad, is self-contained, that there is no loss or gain of force.

Śrīla Prabhupāda: Yes, each is eternal.

Hayagrīva dāsa: Concerning the relationship between the soul and body, Leibnitz writes: "Insofar as the soul has perfection and distinct thoughts, God has accomodated the body to the soul, and has arranged beforehand that the body is impelled to execute its orders."

Śrīla Prabhupāda: Yes, it is explained in *Bhagavad-gītā* (18.61) that the body is like a machine. Because the soul wants to walk or move in a certain way, he is given this instrument. The soul has particular desires, and God gratifies these desires through His material agent, a particular type of body. Therefore there are birds flying, fish swimming, animals hunting in forests, men in cities, and so on. According to *Padma Purāṇa*, there are 8,400,000 different bodies created to gratify the desires of the soul. Thus the machine of the body is supplied by nature under the orders of God.

Hayagrīva dāsa: For Leibnitz, in that the soul is perfect, it controls the body. However, "insofar as the soul is imperfect and its perceptions are confused, God has accomodated the soul to the body, in such a sort that the soul is swayed by the passions arising out of corporeal representations."

Śrīla Prabhupāda: Yes, it is explained in *Bhagavad-gītā* that the soul in the material world is influenced by the three modes of material nature.

na tad asti pṛthivyāṁ vā
divi deveṣu vā punaḥ
sattvaṁ prakṛti-jair muktaṁ
yad ebhiḥ syāt tribhir guṇaiḥ

"There is no being existing, either here or among the demigods in the higher planetary systems, which is freed from the three modes of material nature." (*Bg.* 18.40) He receives a particular type of body according to

his position in respect to the modes. If his appetite is insatiable and his eating indiscriminate, he receives the body of a pig. If he wants to kill and eat bloody meat, he gets the body of a tiger. If he wants to eat Kṛṣṇa *prasādam*, he is given the body of a *brāhmaṇa*. Thus we receive different types of bodies according to our desires. People attempt to gratify their desires because they think that by doing so they will be happy. Unfortunately, people do not know that they will be happy only by completely abiding by the orders of God. Kṛṣṇa comes personally to request the living entity to abandon his material desires and act according to God's orders.
Hayagrīva dāsa: In *Monadology*, Leibnitz writes: "The soul changes its body only gradually and by degrees, so that it is never deprived of all its organs at once. There is often a metamorphosis in animals, but never metempsychosis or transmigration of souls."
Śrīla Prabhupāda: What is his understanding of the soul?
Hayagrīva dāsa: He believes that it is not possible for souls to be entirely separate from bodies. For living entities, a body must always accompany the soul.
Śrīla Prabhupāda: According to Vedic understanding, the body changes, but the soul remains eternal. Even in one lifetime we can see that our material body is changing from childhood to youth to old age, yet the soul remains the same. When the body dies, the soul takes on another body. This is the first lesson of *Bhagavad-gītā*. If the soul is distinct from the body, it is nonsensical to say that a soul cannot exist without a body.
Hayagrīva dāsa: Leibnitz elaborates on this: "There is, strictly speaking, neither absolute birth nor complete death consisting in the separation of the soul from the body. What we call birth is development or growth, and what we call death is envelopment and diminution."
Śrīla Prabhupāda: But that is the process of transmigration. Why does he deny it? The diminution is temporary. The living entity is not dead; he goes on to develop another body.
Hayagrīva dāsa: He seems to be saying that as soon as the human soul leaves the body, it must immediately enter another body.
Śrīla Prabhupāda: Yes, that is the case, but that is the process of transmigration. So why does he deny transmigration?
Hayagrīva dāsa: Well, he denies the existence of the soul apart from some form of material body. He writes: "God alone is wholly without body."
Śrīla Prabhupāda: Yes, that is, He has no material body. He does not transmigrate. According to *Bhagavad-gītā*, *mūḍhas*, fools, consider Kṛṣṇa's body to be like that of a human being.

avajānanti māṁ mūḍhā
mānuṣīṁ tanum āśritam
paraṁ bhāvam ajānanto
mama bhūta-maheśvaram

"Fools deride Me when I descend in the human form. They do not know My transcendental nature and My supreme dominion over all that be." (*Bg.* 9.11) Kṛṣṇa does not change His body as an ordinary living entity does. He is the Supreme Person. Because He does not change His body, He remembers everything in the past. When we receive a body, we do not remember our past lives, but Kṛṣṇa remembers because His body never changes. God is without a body in the sense that He has no material body.

Śyāmasundara dāsa: According to his doctrine of preestablished harmony, Leibnitz likens the soul and the body to two perfectly synchronized clocks, both going at the same speed but both separate.

Śrīla Prabhupāda: Yes, the soul is different from the body, but the body is manifest due to the soul's desire. The body is the instrument of the soul.

Śyāmasundara dāsa: Does the body ever affect the soul?

Śrīla Prabhupāda: The soul is unaffected by the body, but the body is helping the soul to fulfill its desires. I am using this microphone to serve my purposes, but this microphone is not influencing me. It is not that this microphone wills that I dictate this or that. The body is a combination of atoms. If Kṛṣṇa is within the atoms, the monads of the atoms and the monad in the body are different. If the monad is a small united particle, Leibnitz is speaking of the Supersoul. Although the Supersoul appears innumerable, it is in actuality one. As stated in *Īśopaniṣad:*

yasmin sarvāṇi bhūtāny
ātmaivābhūd vijānataḥ
tatra ko mohaḥ kaḥ śoka
ekatvam anupaśyataḥ

"One who always sees all living entities as spiritual sparks, in quality one with the Lord, becomes a true knower of things, and there is no illusion or anxiety for him." (*Īśopaniṣad* 7) Although we find the Supersoul all-pervasive, there is but one. Kṛṣṇa says in *Bhagavad-gītā:*

samaṁ sarveṣu bhūteṣu
tiṣṭhantaṁ parameśvaram
vinaśyatsv avinaśyantaṁ
yaḥ paśyati sa paśyati

"One who sees the Supersoul accompanying the individual soul in all bodies and who understands that neither the soul nor the Supersoul is ever destroyed, actually sees." (*Bg.* 13.28) The devotee always sees all things in Kṛṣṇa, and Kṛṣṇa in all things. That is the true vision of oneness.

Śyāmasundara dāsa: Leibnitz believes that God creates the principle of preestablished harmony, that He sets the two clocks in motion and synchronizes them. The body is acting, but the soul is independent. It is not really affected by the body.

Śrīla Prabhupāda: We also agree to that, but why use the example of clocks? Why not analyze the relationship between the body and the soul? You cannot consider them separately, because they are combined. The fallacy of this analogy is that two individual clocks are not combined at any point.

Śyāmasundara dāsa: The common point is their synchronization.

Śrīla Prabhupāda: But eventually one clock will go faster than the other. You cannot consider the body and soul as completely separate entities working independent of one another. It is stated in the Vedic *śāstras* that the soul is the master of the body; therefore you cannot say that the body is working independently. If I tell my body to place this hand here, my hand will move to this spot. It is not that suddenly my hand moves without my desire.

Śyāmasundara dāsa: Leibnitz would say that the act of your desiring and the act of the hand moving are simultaneous but separate.

Śrīla Prabhupāda: In Sanskrit, this argument is called *kākatālīya-nyāya*. Once, when a crow flew into a *tāl* tree, the fruit on that tree immediately fell to the ground. One observer said that the crow lighted on the tree first, and then the fruit fell, and the other observer said that the fruit fell before the crow could light. This kind of argument has no value. We say that if Kṛṣṇa so desires, a stone can float on the water, despite the law of gravitation. Although the law of gravitation is working here, there are so many huge planets floating in space. All these laws act according to Kṛṣṇa's desire. By the law of gravitation, all these planets would have fallen into the causal ocean and hit the Garbhodakaśāyī-viṣṇu in the head because He is lying on that ocean. But by His order all these planets are floating in space. Similarly, if God so desires, a rock may fall into the water, but the water will not give way. The rock will simply float. Since God is the ultimate monad, this is possible. Whatever God wills will come into effect.

Śyāmasundara dāsa: Leibnitz admits that the monads are spiritual in nature and therefore immortal.

Śrīla Prabhupāda: Yes, we agree to that. Both Kṛṣṇa and the living entity are spiritual. Ultimately, everything is spiritual because everything is Kṛṣṇa's energy. If Kṛṣṇa is the original cause, matter can be changed into spirit, and spirit into matter. Electricity may be used to heat or to cool, but in either case, the original energy is electricity. Similarly, the original cause is Kṛṣṇa; therefore He has the power to change matter into spirit, or spirit into matter.

Śyāmasundara dāsa: He states that unlike the other monads, God is absolute necessity and eternal truth, and He is governed by the law of contradiction. That is to say, it is impossible to conceive of no God.

Śrīla Prabhupāda: The atheists say that there is no God, although God is there. Unless God is there, where is the idea of God coming from? The atheist refuses to accept God. Similarly, the impersonalists refuse to accept a Supreme Personality of Godhead. Unless the idea of personality is there, how can they consider God to be impersonal? All this is due to frustration.

Hayagrīva dāsa: Leibnitz pictures a city of God very much like that of Augustine. He writes: "God is the monarch of the most perfect republic composed of all the spirits, and the happiness of this city of God is His principal purpose."

Śrīla Prabhupāda: Yes. If everyone becomes Kṛṣṇa conscious and acts according to the instructions of Kṛṣṇa, this hellish world will become the city of God.

Hayagrīva dāsa: Leibnitz further writes: "We must not therefore doubt that God so ordained everything that spirits not only shall live forever, because this is unavoidable, but that they shall also preserve forever their moral quality, so that His city may never lose a person."

Śrīla Prabhupāda: Yes, this is Vaikuṇṭha consciousness. As stated in *Bhagavad-gītā:*

avyakto'kṣara ity uktas
tam āhuḥ paramāṁ gatim
yaṁ prāpya na nivartante
tad dhāma paramaṁ mama

"That supreme abode is called unmanifested and infallible, and it is the supreme destination. When one goes there, he never comes back. That is My supreme abode." (*Bg*. 8.21) That spiritual sky, or city of God, is well known to Vedic students.

Hayagrīva dāsa: Leibnitz did not believe that the city of God is divorced from the natural world. In *Monadology*, he writes: "The assembly of all spirits must compose the city of God, that is, the most perfect state possible and of the most perfect of monarchs [God]. This city of God, this truly universal monarchy, is a moral world within the natural world, and the highest and most divine of the works of God."

Śrīla Prabhupāda: Yes, and we can realize this city immediately if we come to the proper consciousness that this planet does not belong to any particular nation but to God Himself. If people accept this principle, the entire world will become the city of God. Presently, the United Nations is attempting to settle all the problems of the world, but the leaders themselves have an animalistic mentality. They are thinking, "I am this body, I am American, or Indian, or whatever." People must give up these designations and understand their real identity as part and parcel of God. The entire planet belongs to God. We are His sons, and it is possible for us to live peacefully understanding that our Father is supplying us everything. If there is scarcity, it is due to improper distribution. If everyone abides by the orders of God, and everything produced is divided among the sons of God, there no question of scarcity. Since people are denying the actual fact that everything belongs to God, and since they are hoarding goods, there is scarcity. If people want to remain in animal consciousness, they will continue to suffer. Once they come to Kṛṣṇa consciousness, they will realize the city of God, even within this material world.

Śyāmasundara dāsa: Leibnitz also states that the world could have been otherwise if God so desired, but that He chose this particular arrangement as the best possible.

Śrīla Prabhupāda: Yes, God can do as He likes, but this world was not exactly planned by God. It is given to the living entities who want to imitate God. The plan is shaped according to the desires of the living entities who want to lord it over material nature. This is not God's plan. This material world is like a prison supported by the government because there are criminals. It is God's plan that all the living entities in the material world give up their striving and return home, back to Godhead.

Śyāmasundara dāsa: But from the standpoint of the ingredients of this world, is this the best possible world?

Śrīla Prabhupāda: The spiritual world is the best possible world. This planet earth is not a very good planet; there are many other planets even in the material world thousands of times better. The higher you go in the planetary systems, the more comforts and amenities you find. The next planetary system is a thousand times superior to this one, and the planetary system above that is a thousand times superior still. In Brahmaloka, the highest planet, twelve hours of Brahmā's day are beyond our comprehension.

Śyāmasundara dāsa: Leibnitz accepts the conditions of this material world as being the best we can hope for, the best of a bad bargain.
Śrīla Prabhupāda: But *Bhagavad-gītā* states that this is a place of misery:

ābrahma-bhuvanāl lokāḥ
punar āvartino'rjuna
mām upetya tu kaunteya
punar janma na vidyate

"From the highest planet in the material world down to the lowest, all are places of misery wherein repeated birth and death take place. But one who attains to My abode, O son of Kuntī, never takes birth again." (*Bg.* 8.16) This place is meant for suffering. We cannot stay here for very long, even if we agree to stay in such an uncomfortable situation. We have to change our body and go to a higher or lower situation. On the whole, material life is miserable. There is no question of happiness.
Śyāmasundara dāsa: He also states that because there is more good than evil in this world, the creation of this world is justified.
Śrīla Prabhupāda: Well, there is good and evil according to our angle of vision. A devotee sees this material world as good. In the material world, people are always complaining and are in a distressed condition, but a devotee sees that there is really no distressed condition. Everything is happiness because he lives with Kṛṣṇa. Because he dovetails everything with Kṛṣṇa, including himself, for him there is no misery.
Śyāmasundara dāsa: He also says that if the world had not been worth creating, God would not have created it. The fact that He created it makes it worth creating.
Śrīla Prabhupāda: Yes, that is stated in the Vedas:

oṁ pūrṇam adaḥ pūrṇam idaṁ
pūrṇāt pūrṇam udacyate
pūrṇasya pūrṇam ādāya
pūrṇam evāvaśiṣyate

"The Personality of Godhead is perfect and complete, and because He is completely perfect, all emanations from Him, such as this phenomenal world, are perfectly equipped as complete wholes. Whatever is produced of the complete whole is also complete in itself. Because He is the complete whole, even though so many complete units emanate from Him, He remains the complete balance." (*Īśopaniṣad,* Invocation) The creator is complete, and the creation is also complete. Nothing incomplete can be created by the complete. In that sense, everything that is wanted in this world is here. The arrangement is complete.

VI
BRITISH EMPIRICISM

John Locke
(1632-1704)

Hayagrīva dāsa: In *Essay Concerning Human Understanding*, Locke writes: "This argument of universal consent, which is made use of to prove innate principles, seems to me a demonstration that there are none such because there are none to which all mankind give a universal consent." That is, it cannot be argued that all people have an innate or inborn idea of God. But do innate ideas have to be universal? Might they not differ from person to person?

Śrīla Prabhupāda: Innate ideas depend on the development of our consciousness. Animals have no innate idea of God due to their undeveloped consciousness. In every human society, however, men have some innate idea of a superior power. For instance, even aborigines offer obeisances when they see lightning. The offering of obeisances to something wonderful or powerful is innate in man. The consciousness of offering respects is not developed in animals. When we have developed this innate idea to its fullest extent, we are Kṛṣṇa conscious.

Hayagrīva dāsa: Wouldn't it be better to say that the living entity is born with certain tendencies, which carry over from the previous life, and that all he needs is to meet with some stimulus in order for them to be manifest?

Śrīla Prabhupāda: Yes. For instance, when an animal is born, it naturally searches for the nipples of its mother. This means that the animal has had experience in a previous life, and therefore knows how to find food. Although the animal may not be able to see, it knows how to search for its food by virtue of past experience. This proves the eternal continuity of the soul. Presently, I am living in this room, and if I go away for ten years, then return, I can still remember where the bathroom and living room are. This remembrance is due to my having lived here before. In material life, the living entity passes through different species, or forms.

Hayagrīva dāsa: Locke would argue that the idea of Kṛṣṇa is not innate because it is not universally assented to. Since not everyone acknowledges that Kṛṣṇa is God, Locke would say that the idea is not inborn in the mind.

Śrīla Prabhupāda: In the material world, different living entities have different ideas. The ideas of a person with developed consciousness are different from those of a person with undeveloped consciousness. If someone is Kṛṣṇa conscious shortly after his birth, we are to understand that he has previously contemplated Kṛṣṇa. In *Bhagavad-gītā*, Śrī Kṛṣṇa says:

tatra taṁ buddhi-saṁyogaṁ
labhate paurva-dehikam
yatate ca tato bhūyaḥ
saṁsiddhau kuru-nandana

"On taking such a birth, he again revives the divine consciousness of his previous life, and he tries to make further progress in order to achieve complete success." (*Bg.* 6.43) Our culture of Kṛṣṇa consciousness is never lost; it grows until it is perfected. Therefore Kṛṣṇa says:

nehābhikrama-nāśo'sti
pratyavāyo na vidyate
svalpam apy asya dharmasya
trāyate mahato bhayāt

"In this endeavor there is no loss or diminution, and a little advancement on this path can protect one from the most dangerous type of fear." (*Bg.* 2.40) We have the example of Ajāmila, who cultivated Kṛṣṇa consciousness in the beginning of his life, and then fell down and became the greatest debauchee. Yet at the end of his life, he again remembered Nārāyaṇa and attained salvation.

Śyāmasundara dāsa: Locke maintains that there are two basic ideas: those which come from sensations, external experience, and those provided by inner reflection.

Śrīla Prabhupāda: That is known as *pratyakṣa pramāṇa*. However, we have to go higher. *Pratyakṣa, paro'kṣa, anumāna, adhokṣaja, and aparājita*. These are different stages of knowledge. *Pratyakṣa* means direct knowledge, *paro'kṣa* is knowledge received from others, and *anumāna*, inference, is knowledge acquired after judging direct knowledge and knowledge received from authorities. *Adhokṣaja* is knowledge beyond the limits of direct perception. *Aparājita* is spiritual knowledge. All the stages of knowledge advance toward spiritual knowledge. Direct perception is material.

Śyāmasundara dāsa: Locke states that the mind can reflect only after it has acquired some sense experience. In other words, only after acquiring some knowledge of this world through the senses can we have thoughts and ideas.

Śrīla Prabhupāda: Yes, but my ideas may not always be true. I may have experience of gold and a mountain, and I may dream of a golden mountain, but a golden mountain does not exist in the external world.

Śyāmasundara dāsa: Locke distinguished between simple ideas and complex ideas. There are four types of simple ideas: those we perceive from one sense, such as sound, touch, and so on; those we receive from two or more senses, such as motion or space; those we receive by reflection, such as remembering, reasoning, knowing, and believing; and those we receive from both sensation and reflection, ideas of existence, or unity.

Śrīla Prabhupāda: These all arise out of different material conditions. For instance, how do we experience ether? By sound. We can neither see nor touch ether. As the material condition changes, the sense perception also changes. We can sense air and water by touch, fire by form, and fragrance by smell. In the beginning, the living entity has his mind, intelligence, and ego, but presently the mind, intelligence and ego are false, just as this present body is false. The spirit soul has a body, but this body is covered. Similarly, the mind, ego, and intelligence are covered by material conditioning. When they are uncovered, we acquire our pure mind, pure intelligence, and pure identity. Devotional service means bringing the soul to his original, pure condition. In Kṛṣṇa consciousness, everything is pure: pure mind, pure intelligence, and pure ego. *Tat-paratvena nirmalam (Nārada-pañcarātra)*. Everything is purified when it is connected with the supreme spirit. When we are purified, we have nothing to do with the material mind, body, intelligence, or ego. We are purely spiritual.

Śyāmasundara dāsa: Locke is trying to find a basis for knowledge beginning with sense perception. He states that the mind receives knowledge from the senses and is able to reflect on this.
Śrīla Prabhupāda: Yes, we agree that the mind receives knowledge through the senses. Then there is thinking, feeling, and willing. There is also judgment and work. We receive many impressions and then plan something. We think and feel, and then we put the plan into action. That action is the process of work.
Śyāmasundara dāsa: Locke states that these simple ideas combine to form complex or abstract ideas like the conception of God. This is an enlargement upon the simple ideas of existence, knowledge, time, power, and so on. We combine these to make a complex idea like the idea of God.
Śrīla Prabhupāda: God is not a complex idea but a perfect idea. However, God is so great that He is naturally complex to the ordinary man.
Śyāmasundara dāsa: Locke states that there are three types of complex ideas: that which depends upon substances like roundness, hardness, and so on; that which is a relation between one idea and another, agreeing or disagreeing with another; and that which is a substance or body subsisting by itself and providing the basis for experience. Because we can know only the quality of a substance, we cannot know what the substance itself is, nor where it comes from, nor how it is produced. The nature of ultimate reality cannot be known or proved.
Śrīla Prabhupāda: It is a fact that it cannot be known by such mental speculation, but it can be known from a person who knows it. Locke may not know, but someone else may know. Everyone thinks that others are like himself. Because he does not know, he thinks that others do not know. But that is not a fact. There may be someone who knows.

tad-vijñānārthaṁ sa gurum evābhigacchet
samit-pāṇiḥ śrotriyaṁ brahma-niṣṭham

"In order to learn the transcendental science, one must approach the bona fide spiritual master in disciplic succession, who is fixed in the Absolute Truth." (*Muṇḍaka Upaniṣad* 1.2.12) The Vedas tell us to seek out the person who knows. That is the bona fide guru. Caitanya Mahāprabhu says that such a guru is one who knows that the ultimate reality is Kṛṣṇa. That is the most important qualification.

kibā vipra, kibā nyāsī, śūdra kene naya
yei kṛṣṇa-tattva-vettā, sei 'guru' haya

"Whether one is a *brāhmaṇa*, a *sannyāsī*, or a *śūdra*—regardless of what he is—he can become a spiritual master if he knows the science of Kṛṣṇa." (*Caitanya-caritāmṛta*, Madh. 8.128)

Śyāmasundara dāsa: Locke claims that objective reality has primary qualities that are inseparable from the object itself, just as the color red is inseparable from a red object.

Śrīla Prabhupāda: We say that which cannot be separated is called dharma. Dharma is the particular characteristic of a particular thing. For every living entity, dharma means rendering service to Kṛṣṇa, the supreme. That is liberation and the perfection of life.

Hayagrīva dāsa: Some people claim to remember events from their previous lives. How are these reminiscences different from innate ideas?

Śrīla Prabhupāda: An innate idea is inevitable. The idea that God is great and that I am controlled is innate everywhere, but sometimes out of ignorance, one tries to become God. That is not possible. That is māyā, and one simply suffers. It is an innate idea with the living entity that he is a servant and that God is great.

Hayagrīva dāsa: Locke further writes: "The knowledge of our own being we have by intuition. The existence of God, reason clearly makes known to us. We have a more certain knowledge of the existence of a God than of anything our senses can discover." How is this? If this is the case, how is it that some men have no conception of God?

Śrīla Prabhupāda: Everyone has some conception of God, but under the spell of māyā, the living entity tries to cover that conception. How can any sane man deny God's existence? Some superior power must be present to create the vast ocean, land, and sky. No one can avoid some conception of God, but one can artificially and foolishly attempt to avoid it. This is called atheism, and this will not endure. One's foolishness will ultimately be exposed.

Śrīla Prabhupāda: Locke recommends four tests to know whether knowledge is true, by which we can perceive agreement or disagreement between ideas.

Śrīla Prabhupāda: Whether we agree or not, truth is truth. There is no question of my agreement or disagreement.

Śyāmasundara dāsa: We can objectively study something to see if there is agreement or disagreement. It is not that knowledge depends on our subjective opinion. There must be some scientific proof.

Śrīla Prabhupāda: Our test of truth is Vedic evidence. For instance, it is stated in the Vedas that cow stool is pure. We accept this as true. We cannot reach this conclusion by argument.

Śyāmasundara dāsa: Locke states that God must be a thinking being

because matter, which is senseless, could never produce sense experience, perception, and thoughts.
Śrīla Prabhupāda: Certainly. By definition, God has full knowledge of everything. Kṛṣṇa says:

vedāhaṁ samatītāni
vartamānāni cārjuna
bhaviṣyāṇi ca bhūtāni
māṁ tu veda na kaścana

"O Arjuna, as the Supreme Personality of Godhead, I know everything that has happened in the past, all that is happening in the present, and all things that are yet to come. I also know all living entities, but Me no one knows." (*Bg.* 7.26) Kṛṣṇa also told Arjuna that millions of years ago He instructed the sun god in the philosophy of *Bhagavad-gītā*. Kṛṣṇa also points out that Arjuna took birth with Him, but that Arjuna had forgotten. Kṛṣṇa knows everything. That is the meaning of omniscience.
Śyāmasundara dāsa: Locke also says that since there are no innate ideas, moral, religious, and political values must be regarded as products of experience.
Śrīla Prabhupāda: We should understand what is the best experience. For instance, we consider Manu to be the authority on political and social affairs. *Manur ikṣvākave'bravīt (Bg.* 4.1). Manu instructed his son Ikṣvāku. If this depends on experience, we should accept perfect, unadulterated experience.
Śyāmasundara dāsa: He states that values must obey the will of God as expressed in natural law, the laws upon which men agree, such as social contracts, and the established traditions, customs, and opinions of mankind. He states that our laws must be obeyed in such a way that we will exist in harmony.
Śrīla Prabhupāda: And what is that harmony? Perfect harmony is in knowing that we are part and parcel of God. In this body, there are different parts, and each part has a particular function. When each part performs its function, the body is harmonious. The hand is meant for touching, lifting, and grasping, but if the hand says, "I shall walk," there is disharmony. Being part and parcel of God, we have a particular function. If we fulfill that function, there is harmony. If we do not, there is disharmony. The law of nature means working in harmony with the desire of God.

mayādhyakṣeṇa prakṛtiḥ
sūyate sa-carācaram

hetunānena kaunteya
jagad viparivartate

"This material nature is working under My direction, O son of Kuntī, and it is producing all moving and unmoving beings. By its rule this manifestation is created and annihilated again and again." (*Bg.* 9.10) Under Kṛṣṇa's superintendence, everything is functioning in harmony. Events do not happen blindly. In any organization, there is a supreme authority under whose orders everything moves in harmony. Harmony means that there must be some supreme superintendent. It is generally said that obedience is the first law of discipline. There cannot be harmony without obedience.

Śyāmasundara dāsa: Locke would say that we have to obey the laws of nature.

Śrīla Prabhupāda: Everyone is obeying the laws of nature. *Yasyājñayā bhramati. Brahma-saṁhitā* (5.52) states that the sun is moving in its orbit fixed by the law of Govinda. The ocean has certain limitations fixed by the Supreme. All nature is functioning according to the law of God.

Śyāmasundara dāsa: Locke believes that we must also obey the laws upon which we agree, that is, the social contract.

Śrīla Prabhupāda: This is the law: we must surrender to Kṛṣṇa. When we agree to the laws of the Supreme, that is religion.

Śyāmasundara dāsa: Men agree socially not to steal one another's property, or to kill one another. Shouldn't we obey these laws of man?

Śrīla Prabhupāda: Men's laws are imitations of God's laws. God's law states: *īśāvāsyam idaṁ sarvam.* "Everything animate or inanimate that is within the universe is controlled and owned by the Lord." (*Īśopaniṣad* 1) Every living entity is the son of God, and he has the right to live at the cost of God. Everyone is eating food supplied by God. The animals are eating their food. The cow is eating grass, but why should we kill the cow? This is against God's law. We have rice, grains, fruits, vegetables, and so on. These are for us. Tigers do not come to eat our fruits or grains, so why should we kill tigers? A tiger is not encroaching upon our rights.

Hayagrīva dāsa: Locke argues on behalf of private property given to man by God. He believes that a man may have stewardship over a certain amount of property. Is this in compliance with the Īśopaniṣadic version?

Śrīla Prabhupāda: Yes. *Tena tyaktena bhuñjīthā.* "One should therefore accept only those things necessary for himself, which are set aside as his quota." (*Īśopaniṣad* 1) Everything belongs to God. A father may have many sons and be the ultimate proprietor of his house, yet he gives different rooms to his sons. The obedient son is satisfied with what his father has alloted him. The disobedient son simply wants to disturb his other brothers, and so he claims their rooms. This creates chaos and confusion in the world. The United Nations has been formed to unify nations, but they have not succeeded. People continue to encroach on one another's property, and therefore there is no peace. If we accept God as the supreme proprietor, and are satisfied with the allotment He has given us, there will be no trouble. Unfortunately, we are not satisfied.

Śyāmasundara dāsa: According to Locke's utilitarian ethic, happiness is the greatest good, and obedience to the moral law results in happiness.

Śrīla Prabhupāda: But the difficulty is that here in this material world, happiness is temporary. And even if we follow moral laws, other people will give us trouble. There are people who don't care whether you are moral or immoral. *Bhagavad-gītā* confirms that this is not a place of happiness. *Duḥkhālayam aśāśvatam.* "This temporary world is full of miseries." (*Bg.* 8.15) Therefore we have to find where real happiness exists. That is the spiritual world. Happiness here is only another illusion. It is not possible. If Kṛṣṇa Himself says that this is a place of misery, how can we find happiness here? In *Bhagavad-gītā*, Kṛṣṇa speaks of real happiness:

sukham ātyantikaṁ yat tad
buddhi-grāhyam atīndriyam
vetti yatra na caivāyaṁ
sthitaś calati tattvataḥ

"In that joyous state, one is situated in boundless transcendental happiness and enjoys himself through transcendental senses. Established thus, one never departs from the truth, and upon gaining this, he thinks there is no greater gain." (*Bg.* 6.21) Real happiness is beyond the senses. It is *atīndriya*. In other words, we have to purify our senses in order to attain it. This is also confirmed by Ṛṣabhadeva:

nāyaṁ deho deha-bhājāṁ nṛloke
kaṣṭān kāmān arhate viḍ-bhujāṁ ye
tapo divyaṁ putrakā yena sattvaṁ
śuddhyed yasmād brahma-saukhyaṁ tv anantam

"Of all the living entities who have accepted material bodies in this world, one who has been awarded this human form should not work hard day and night for sense gratification, which is available even for dogs and hogs that eat stool. One should engage in penance and austerity to attain the divine position of devotional service. By such activity, one's heart is purified, and when one attains this position, he attains eternal, blissful life, which is transcendental to material happiness and which continues forever." (*Bhāg.* 5.5.1) Presently, our existence is impure. If a man is suffering from jaundice, he tastes sweet things as bitter. In order to taste real happiness, we have to purify our senses. Materialists think that as soon as they have sexual intercourse, they will be happy, but that is not real happiness. We cannot even enjoy that happiness. The conclusion is that we should not seek happiness like cats, dogs, and hogs, but as human beings. This means *tapasya,* purification of the senses. First we must be cured of this material disease, then we can taste real happiness in our healthy life. A sane man knows that he is spirit soul covered by a material coating. So let this coating be washed away by devotional service. *Tat-paratvena nirmalam (Nārada-pañcarātra).* When we engage in devotional service, we remove the false coating, and our real senses emerge. We enjoy those real senses by serving Kṛṣṇa.

Śyāmasundara dāsa: Locke also says that all men are born free and equal in the state of nature and that they have formed a social contract; therefore the government must be based on and subject to the mutual consent of all the citizens.

Śrīla Prabhupāda: That agreement can be reached when everyone is situated on the spiritual platform. On the material platform, people are subject to the three modes of material nature: goodness, passion, and ignorance. How can the vote of a God conscious man and the vote of a drunkard be equal? Equality is not possible unless everyone comes to the spiritual platform.

Śyāmasundara dāsa: Is it true that all men are born free and equal?

Śrīla Prabhupāda: Yes, that is a fact. If we are not free, how can we commit sin? Committing sin means that we have the freedom to commit sins. And equality means that we all have small independence. We are equal in the sense that we can properly utilize or misuse our independence. Because we all have independence, we are equal. If we misuse it, we go downward, and if we use it properly, we go upward. In the use of our independence, we have equal rights.

George Berkeley
(1685-1753)

Hayagrīva dāsa: Berkeley seems to argue against objective reality. For instance, three men standing in a field looking at a tree could all have different impressions or ideas of the tree. The problem is that although there are three different impressions of the tree, there is no tree as such. Now, how does the tree as such exist? In the mind of God? Is it possible for a conditioned living entity to perceive the suchness or essence of anything?

Śrīla Prabhupāda: Since everything is God, or an expansion of God's energy, how can a tree or anything else exist independent of God? A clay pot is not different from earth. Since there is nothing but God's energy, how can we avoid God? Since nothing can exist independent of God, whatever we see must refer to God. As soon as we see a clay pot, we remember the potter. God is not only the original creator; He is the ingredient, the category, and the original substance as well. According to the Vedic conception, God is everything. That is a nondual conception. If you separate anything from God, you cannot say, *sarvaṁ khalv idaṁ brahma (Chāndogya Upaniṣad* 3.14.1). "Everything is Brahman." Everything refers to God, and everything is God's property; therefore whatever exists should be utilized for God's service, and that is the object of our Kṛṣṇa consciousness movement.

Śyāmasundara dāsa: Berkeley maintained that nothing exists outside perception. Matter is simply perceived. For instance, this table is only an immaterial substance which enters my mind. It is not made of matter.

Śrīla Prabhupāda: Then what is your mind? Is the mind also immaterial? This is the Śūnyavādī position. They believe that everything is zero.

Śyāmasundara dāsa: Berkeley says that everything is spiritual, not zero.

Śrīla Prabhupāda: The spiritual is not an idea but a fact. The Śūnyavādīs cannot understand how spirit has form. They have no idea of *sac-cid-ānanda-vigraha,* our spiritual form of bliss. They really have no idea of spiritual existence.

Śyāmasundara dāsa: Berkeley says that everything has form, but that it is not made of matter.

Śrīla Prabhupāda: That is nice. Everything has form. It is not necessary that the form be material. We say that God has a spiritual form.

Śyāmasundara dāsa: But Berkeley goes so far as to say that everything is made of spirit.

Śrīla Prabhupāda: Yes, in the higher sense, everything is spirit. We always say that materialism means forgetfulness of Kṛṣṇa. As soon as we dovetail everything to Kṛṣṇa, nothing is material but spiritual.

Śyāmasundara dāsa: Berkeley uses the example of a book on a table. The only way the book exists is through the idea or sense impression in the mind. It doesn't enter the mind as matter but as spirit, something immaterial.

Śrīla Prabhupāda: If it is not matter, it is spirit. If everything is spirit, why distinguish between the idea of the book and the book?

Śyāmasundara dāsa: Well, for him there is no difference.

Śrīla Prabhupāda: But he explains that the book is not material. If everything is spiritual, the idea is spiritual as well as the book. Why make the distinction? *Sarvaṁ khalv idaṁ brahma (Chāndogya Upaniṣad* 3.14.1). If everything is Brahman, why make these distinctions between the idea of the book and the book? Why is he trying so hard to attempt to explain?

Śyāmasundara dāsa: He also states that God creates all objects.

Śrīla Prabhupāda: Yes, that's right, and because God creates all objects, there is no object that is not true. We cannot say that something false comes from something true. If God is truth, then whatever emanates from God is also truth. It is Māyāvādī philosophy to say that everything that we are seeing is false. *Brahma satyaṁ jagan mithyā.*

Śyāmasundara dāsa: No, he says it is real because God perceives it.
Śrīla Prabhupāda: If it is real, and my idea of it is real, then everything is real. Why make these distinctions? Our philosophy is that there cannot be these distinctions. If the world emanates from God, can it be false? If everything is spiritual, why does he make the distinction in saying that it is not matter, that it is something else? As soon as we bring up the subject of matter, we imply that matter is something separately existing. In other words, there is duality. As soon as you say that this is not matter, you are making matter into something that is not true. If everything emanates from God and is true, there is no question of there being anything that is not true. If everything is spiritual, we cannot make these distinctions. When he says, "This is not matter," he implies that there is matter somewhere. If everything is spirit, there is no question of material existence.
Śyāmasundara dāsa: He says that there are two types of objects: those which we actively sense, perceive, and experience, and those which are passively sensed, perceived, and experienced. Both are basically the same because they are equally spiritual.
Śrīla Prabhupāda: But two types means duality. How does he distinguish between this type and that type? He distinguishes between the senses and the objects of the senses. If everything is spiritual, we can say that there is spiritual variety. But the senses and the objects of the senses are all real.
Śyāmasundara dāsa: No, he says that they are real and made of spirit. They are not real in the sense that they are made of matter.
Śrīla Prabhupāda: I do not understand this logic. If everything is spirit, why is he making these distinctions? There is no need to make such distinctions if you are spiritually realized. Rather, you can say that these are spiritual varieties. For instance, you can say that stone is not water, that air is not stone, that water is not air, and so on. These are all spiritual varieties. The exact Sanskrit word is *saviśeṣa,* which indicates that everything is spirit but that there is variety.
Śyāmasundara dāsa: Berkeley says that if no one experiences a thing, not even God, then it cannot exist. Things can exist only when they are perceived by God.
Śrīla Prabhupāda: This means in one word that there is no existence except God, that nothing exists but God.
Śyāmasundara dāsa: He uses the example of the far side of the North Star. We will never be able to perceive it from our viewpoint, but because God can perceive it, it must exist.
Śrīla Prabhupāda: That's nice. The idea that something does not exist

because I cannot perceive it is not very logical. I may not perceive many things, but that does not mean that they do not exist. In the beginning, this is what I understood you to say Berkeley was saying. That kind of logic is contradictory. God's perception is different. He is unlimited, and we are limited. Since He is unlimited, His perception is unlimited; therefore there are unlimited varieties of existence that we have not even perceived. We cannot say that objects do not exist just because we cannot perceive them.

Śyāmasundara dāsa: He says that objects exist because of perception, whether it is God's perception or ours.

Śrīla Prabhupāda: God's perception is another thing. Perception means *cetana. Nityo nityānāṁ cetanaś cetanānām (Kaṭha Upaniṣad,* 2.2.13) The word *cetana* means "living." We are living, and God is also living, but He is the supreme living entity. We are the subordinate entities. Our perception is limited, and God's perception is unlimited. It is admitted that everything exists due to God's perception. Many objects exist that are not within our experience or perception. However, God experiences everything. In *Bhagavad-gītā,* Kṛṣṇa says that He knows everything, past, present, and future (*Bg.* 7.26). Nothing is beyond His experience.

Śyāmasundara dāsa: He says that because God experiences all objects, objects are rendered potentially perceptible to human minds.

Śrīla Prabhupāda: That's all right, because as we advance in Kṛṣṇa consciousness, we experience objects through God, not directly. That is stated in the Vedas: *yasmin vijñate sarvam eva vijñataṁ bhavanti.* God experiences all things, and if we receive our experience from God, we are advanced. We are preaching that people should receive their experience, their perception, through Kṛṣṇa. We shouldn't try to speculate because speculation is always imperfect. We are searching after the original source of everything, and Kṛṣṇa says: *ahaṁ sarvasya prabhavaḥ (Bg.* 10.8). Kṛṣṇa is the root of all emanations, of all creation. The conclusion should be that we should receive our experience through God; therefore we accept the experience of the Vedas. The Vedas were spoken by God, and they contain knowledge given by God. The word *veda* means knowledge, and the knowledge of the Vedas is perfect. The Vedic system is *śruti-pramāṇam.* As soon as an experience is corroborated or verified by Vedic statement, it is perfect. There is no need to philosophize. If we can receive perfect knowledge directly from the Vedas, why should we speculate? Why should we take so much unnecessary trouble?

dharmaḥ svanuṣṭhitaḥ puṁsāṁ

viṣvaksena-kathāsu yaḥ
notpādayed yadi ratiṁ
śrama eva hi kevalam

"Duties [dharma] executed by men, regardless of occupation, are only so much labor if they do not provoke attraction for the message of the Supreme Lord." (*Bhāg.* 1.2.8) My speculation is always imperfect because I am imperfect.

Śyāmasundara dāsa: There is an inherent tendency in men to want to experience something first hand rather than through someone else.

Śrīla Prabhupāda: From the beginning of our lives, we are experiencing things through authority. A child receives experience by asking his parents. A child knows nothing about fire, and he wants to touch it because it is red. However, he receives knowledge from his parents that he shouldn't touch fire. In this way, he comes to understand certain basic laws of nature. The Vedas tell us that in order to know the transcendental science of Kṛṣṇa, we must approach a guru. We cannot speculate about God, the spiritual world, and spiritual life.

Śyāmasundara dāsa: Berkeley says that the world is real because if it were not real, we could not experience it.

Śrīla Prabhupāda: That is also our version. The world is real because it was created by God. But the Māyāvādīs say that the world is unreal. *Brahma satyaṁ jagan mithyā.*

Śyāmasundara dāsa: He states that the only way we can know that this table exists is through our senses, but these sense impressions are subtle, not material.

Śrīla Prabhupāda: Instead of saying that they are not material, he should say that they are abstract. Abstract is the original position. The Śūnyavādīs cannot understand the abstract; therefore they say that the abstract is zero, nothing. But the abstract is not nothing.

Śyāmasundara dāsa: Berkeley says that if this table were composed of matter, we would not be able to experience it because the only objects capable of entering our experience must be sensitive substances.

Śrīla Prabhupāda: Kṛṣṇa is nondifferent from everything because everything is Kṛṣṇa. Fools look at the Deity and say, "This is not Kṛṣṇa, this is stone." Because a fool cannot see anything but stone, God appears to him as stone. Unfortunate atheists make these distinctions. They will say, "Everything is Brahman, but not this stone Deity." Or, they will say, "Why go to the temple to worship when God is everywhere?" What they are saying is that God is everywhere, but not in the temple. This means that they have no clear idea. We see that everything has form. Are we to assume that we have form and God hasn't? Impersonalists have no conception of Kṛṣṇa's original form. Kṛṣṇa very kindly and mercifully appears before us so that we can experience Him. Ultimately, there is no distinction between matter and spirit, but because at the present moment I cannot conceive of spiritual form, God appears in the form of the Deity. Kṛṣṇa says:

kleśo'dhikataras teṣām
avyaktāsakta-cetasām
avyaktā hi gatir duḥkhaṁ
dehavadbhir avāpyate

"For those whose minds are attached to the unmanifested, impersonal feature of the Supreme, advancement is very troublesome. To make progress in that discipline is always difficult for those who are embodied." (*Bg.* 12.5) People are going through unnecessary labor in order to meditate on something impersonal. Because they have no idea of God, they superficially say, "Everything is God." Still, they cannot see God in the temple in His *arca-vigraha* form. They cannot understand why all the *ācāryas* like Rāmānujācārya and Madhvācārya have established these temples. Are these *ācāryas* simply fools? There has been Deity worship since time immemorial. Are all the people who have participated in Deity worship fools?

Śyāmasundara dāsa: Berkeley says that spirit is the only genuine substance, that there is no substance that exists without thinking. In other words, there is thinking involved even in objects like this table. This table is made of spirit, and spirit is thinking and thoughtful.

Śrīla Prabhupāda: That's nice. His conclusion is that everything is Brahman because thinking is also Brahman. At the present moment, we cannot perceive the spiritual; therefore God, out of His unlimited kindness, comes to us in a small, tangible, concrete form that we can dress, feed, and handle. We cannot say that this form is different from God.

arcye viṣṇau śilādhīr guruṣu
nara-matir vaiṣṇave jāti-buddhiḥ

"One who considers the *arca-mūrti* or worshipable Deity of Lord Viṣṇu to be stone, the spiritual master to be an ordinary human being, and a Vaiṣṇava to belong to a particular caste or creed, is possessed of hellish intelligence and is doomed." (*Padma Purāṇa*) It is horrible to think of these spiritual things in a material way. We should always offer respect and consider that Kṛṣṇa is present. We should not think that the Deity is simply stone and cannot hear or see. There are sixty-four items mentioned in *Nectar of Devotion (Bhakti-rasāmṛta-sindhu)* that guide us in Deity worship.

Hayagrīva dāsa: In his last dialogue, Berkeley writes: "The apprehension of a distant Deity naturally disposes men to be negligent of their moral actions, which they would be more cautious of in case they thought Him immediately present and acting on their minds without the interposition of matter, or unthinking second causes."

Śrīla Prabhupāda: The Vedic *śāstras* say that God is everywhere; He is not distant. In Queen Kuntī's prayers, it is said that God is both distant and near. God's proximity is manifest in His Paramātmā feature. He is living in everyone's heart. *Īśvaraḥ sarva-bhūtānāṁ hṛd-deśe 'rjuna tiṣṭhati (Bg.* 18.61). If He is within our heart, how can He be distant? At the same time, He is present in His personal feature in Goloka Vṛndāvana, which is far, far beyond this material existence. That is God's all-pervasive quality. Although He is far, far away, He is still very near. The sun may be very far away, but its light is present in my room. Similarly, God is both far away and also within my heart. One who is expert in seeing God sees Him in both ways. *Goloka eva nivasaty akhilātma bhūtaḥ (Brahma-saṁhitā* 5.37). Although He is living in His own abode, eternally enjoying Himself with His associates, He is still present everywhere. That is God.

Hayagrīva dāsa: In what way is God concerned with the moral or immoral actions of man? Is God indifferent to them, or has He simply set the laws of nature in motion, allowing men to follow their own course and reap the fruits of their own karma?

Śrīla Prabhupāda: Because we have disobeyed God, we are thrown into this material world and placed under the supervision of material nature for correction. As long as we are in the material world, there is a distinction between what is moral and immoral. Actually, moral and immoral have no meaning, but in the material world, we have conceptions of them. When we are in the spiritual world, there is no conception of immorality. For instance, the *gopīs* went to see Kṛṣṇa in the dead of night, and ordinarily this is considered immoral, but because they were going to see Kṛṣṇa, it was not immoral. In one sense, in the spiritual world everything is moral. In the material world there is duality in order for the material creation to work properly.

Śyāmasundara dāsa: Berkeley gives two arguments for the existence of God: first, the things we perceive in our waking state are more vivid than those things we imagine or dream about, and this is because God's mind

is activating these things.
Śrīla Prabhupāda: We accept that. God is the superior mind, and because God sees, we can see. Because God walks, we can walk. This is also admitted in *Brahma-saṁhitā: yasya prabhā prabhavato jagadaṇḍa-koṭi (Brahma-saṁhitā* 5.40). Due to the bodily effulgence of Kṛṣṇa, many universes have come into being. In these universes, there are many varieties, many planets, and on each of the planets are many different living entities. All these varieties are there because they are emanating from Kṛṣṇa.
Śyāmasundara dāsa: Secondly, the things we perceive do not obey our wishes as our imaginations do, but resist them because they obey the will of God. God's will is arbitrary, and we cannot predict it.
Śrīla Prabhupāda: Therefore it is better to always obey the orders of God. If we do what God says, we are perfect. In any case, there is no need for all this speculation. The basic proof of God is God. Kṛṣṇa says, "I am God," and Nārada, Vyāsadeva, and Arjuna agree, "Yes, You are God." If we accept Kṛṣṇa as God, we save ourselves much labor. Why speculate? In the causal ocean, the Mahā-viṣṇu is inhaling and exhaling, and many universes are being manifest and then destroyed by His breathing. When He breathes out, all the universes are created, and when He breathes in, they all return to His body. This entire creation is the dream of God, Mahā-viṣṇu.
Śyāmasundara dāsa: Berkeley would maintain that our dreams are imperfect, and when we open our eyes, we see that everything is perfect; therefore there must be a perfect person, a perfect dreamer.
Śrīla Prabhupāda: But when we open our eyes and see perfection, that is also dreaming. But the dreaming of the perfect is perfect also. That is absolute. Unless we accept the absolute, how can we say that His dream is perfect? The dream of the absolute is also perfect.
Śyāmasundara dāsa: He also asserts a doctrine of divine arbitrariness. Because God's will is arbitrary, we cannot predict what will happen.
Śrīla Prabhupāda: That is correct. Therefore a Vaiṣṇava says, "If Kṛṣṇa wills, I will do this." He never says, "I will do this." If Kṛṣṇa so desires, a thing will be done. A Vaiṣṇava always considers himself helpless without God. As far as we are concerned, we are always incapable.
Śyāmasundara dāsa: Berkeley states that our repeated experience will discern the regular activity or will of God, and that by experiencing nature, we can understand that God's will is regular. In other words, we can come to understand the habits of God by observing the laws of nature.
Śrīla Prabhupāda: Yes, Kṛṣṇa says in *Bhagavad-gītā* that nature is

working under His direction (*Bg.* 9.10). Nature is not blind. Because it is working under the direction of God, it is perfect.
Śyāmasundara dāsa: He also states that there is no necessary connection between cause and effect, but that things follow one another in sequence in time.
Śrīla Prabhupāda: If there is no cause, why does he say that effect follows cause in a sequential order? This is contradictory. The supreme cause is Kṛṣṇa, the cause of all causes. In that sense, we cannot say that there is no cause. The ultimate cause is the supreme, and to Kṛṣṇa there is no difference between cause and effect. Since He is the supreme cause, He affects everything. In the absolute sense, there is no difference between cause and effect.
Śyāmasundara dāsa: As an example, he would say that a rock falling in the water will not necessarily splash, but that it regularly follows in sequence that it will splash.
Śrīla Prabhupāda: But we say that if God does not will this, it will not happen. It is all dependent on the supreme will. It is not necessary for the rock to splash. It is not compulsory. If God so wills, it will simply float. We admit that everything is affected by the will of God; therefore our best course is to depend totally on His will.

David Hume
(1711-1776)

Hayagrīva dāsa: Abstract objects, relations, space, time, and matter are all considered by Hume to be mind-dependent perceptions. For him, perceptions or impressions are all there is. He rejected revealed religion, which he considered dogmatic, and accepted "natural religion" instead, a religion wherein the existence of God can be proved or even shown to be probable by argument and reason. According to Hume, we really know nothing of God; at the most we can know only of people's ideas of God, and these are but perceptions.

Śrīla Prabhupāda: What is that natural religion?

Hayagrīva dāsa: Hume writes: "The whole course of nature raises one hymn to the praises of its creator. I have found a Deity, and here I stop my enquiry. Let those go further who are wiser or more enterprising."

Śrīla Prabhupāda: He admits that the senses are imperfect, and at the same time that there is a God. Now, if our senses are imperfect, how can we imagine God to be like this or that? If God explains Himself, why should we not accept His version?

Hayagrīva dāsa: In *Dialogues Concerning Natural Religion*, Hume opposes the search for God in the ideal world. He writes: "Why not stop at the material world? How can we satisfy ourselves without going on ad infinitum?...If the material world rests upon a similar ideal world, this ideal world must rest upon some other, and so on without end. It were better, therefore, never to look beyond the present material world. By supposing it to contain the principle of its order within itself, we really assert it to be God, and the sooner we arrive at the divine being, so much the better. When you go one step beyond the mundane system, you only excite an inquisitive humor which it is impossible ever to satisfy."

Śrīla Prabhupāda: The material world by definition is full of misery, and those who are advanced therefore search for another world where there is no misery. Everyone is searching for a happy world that is permanent, and that search is not unnatural. There is such a world, and since it exists, why should we not hanker after it? If we look at the world objectively, we can see that no one is really happy—that is, unless he is an animal. Animals do not know what is happiness or distress. They remain satisfied in any condition. A man, however, feels pain more acutely.

Hayagrīva dāsa: Hume felt that the sooner we find God the better, and therefore he opposed going beyond the mundane system in search of Him.

Śrīla Prabhupāda: You cannot find God in your present conditional state. You may glimpse the fact that there is God, but you cannot understand His forms and pastimes by speculation. Therefore revelation is there for those fortunate people who are seriously searching for God. God is living within, and when we are serious, He reveals Himself. It is also possible to learn about God directly from a person who knows God. *Bhagavad-gītā* is God's direct revelation, and if we try to understand it, we can understand what God is.

Śyāmasundara dāsa: Hume maintains that all that we are, all that we know, is merely a sequence of ideas.

Śrīla Prabhupāda: But behind the ideas there must be a fact. Otherwise, how can we have the ideas?

Śyāmasundara dāsa: He separates facts from ideas. For instance, I may think that this table is red, but I may be wrong; it could be brown.

Śrīla Prabhupāda: Your idea may be incorrect, but actually the table has some color, be it red, yellow, or whatever. If you have some eye disease, you cannot determine the color, but one whose eyes are not diseased can tell you. Because our eyes are diseased and we cannot see things properly, we have to receive knowledge from one who is not diseased. Hume is wrong when he says that there is no possibility of

attaining right knowledge.
Śyāmasundara dāsa: He admits that the external world is full of concrete objects, but he thinks that we are also one of those objects because the self is "nothing but a bundle or collection of different perceptions, which succeed each other with inconceivable rapidity and are in a perpetual flux and movement." Our consciousness is composed of only our observations of material nature.
Śrīla Prabhupāda: That is so far as direct perception is concerned, but indirect perception is different. It may be taken from authorities.
Śyāmasundara dāsa: Hume distrusts all authority. For him, the only certainty is found in mathematical proofs and immediate sense perceptions. We can perceive that there is time and space, but this is the only knowledge that he will admit.
Śrīla Prabhupāda: And beyond time and space?
Śyāmasundara dāsa: We cannot know anything.
Śrīla Prabhupāda: Perhaps you cannot, but there is a process whereby we can know. We cannot say that beyond the mind there is no time or perception. There are insects that are born in the evening and die in the morning, and during that time they experience a lifespan. For a man, this is only twelve hours of life, but the insect cannot live beyond that time. From *Bhagavad-gītā* we understand that Brahmā lives for many thousands of years, and that compared to him we are like insects. Everything is relative: our lifespan, knowledge, and perception. We are small human beings, and what is impossible for us is not necessarily impossible for others. Hume is talking from the relative platform.
Śyāmasundara dāsa: He believes that objects are only relative, not that there is anything absolute.
Śrīla Prabhupāda: But as soon as he speaks of relative, he posits the existence of the absolute. If there is no absolute, how can we have the conception of an object being relative?
Śyāmasundara dāsa: He believes that things exist only in relation to one another.
Śrīla Prabhupāda: Then what is the supreme relation?
Śyāmasundara dāsa: He doesn't admit one.
Śrīla Prabhupāda: According to logic, at the end of all relative truths there is Absolute Truth, the summum bonum. But if Hume denies substance, he has no idea of the summum bonum, the ultimate substance.
Śyāmasundara dāsa: Hume says that an object like an apple consists only of certain sensory qualities, like sweetness or color, and that the individual consists of only a series of mental activities, not of a soul

capable of creating experiences.
Śrīla Prabhupāda: Inert objects have certain qualities, but the living entity possesses senses by which he can appreciate those qualities. He is therefore superior to inert matter. Because the living entity has senses, he can appreciate sense objects. We have eyes with which we can see color and perceive beauty.
Hayagrīva dāsa: Hume is famous for his skepticism. He rejected revealed scriptures and looked toward science instead.
Śrīla Prabhupāda: If he preaches skepticism, why should we believe his words? If he does not believe the statements of others, why should others accept his statements?
Śyāmasundara dāsa: Hume postulates three laws whereby perceptions are associated or connected with one another. First, according to his principle of resemblance, a picture, for instance, makes us think of the original. Secondly, according to the principle of contiguity, if I mention a room in this building, I think of other rooms also. Third, according to the principle of cause and effect, if I think of a wound, I automatically think of pain. Thus he suggests that our whole being consists of such a stream of ideas and associations, which follow one another perpetually.
Śrīla Prabhupāda: This is the nature of the relative world. We cannot understand what a father is without understanding what a son is. We cannot conceive of a husband without a wife.
Śyāmasundara dāsa: Hume denies the existence of an ultimate reality, asserting that only the phenomena of the senses exists.
Śrīla Prabhupāda: But where do these phenomena come from? If there are phenomena, there must be noumena.
Śyāmasundara dāsa: Hume suggests that it is possible that the world has existed since eternity and that therefore no first cause is required.
Śrīla Prabhupāda: But what about the manifestation of past, present, and future? Why does death take place if there is no cause?
Śyāmasundara dāsa: The body is like a machine which is born and dies.
Śrīla Prabhupāda: When you say machine, you automatically presuppose the beginning of the machine. In other words, the machine must be made by someone.
Śyāmasundara dāsa: The machines may be like the seasons. They may come and go.
Śrīla Prabhupāda: Yes, they may come and go, and then come again, but what is the meaning of this?
Śyāmasundara dāsa: They may be eternally existing facts without cause

or creator. Hume says that we may believe in a creator if we like, but this is based on mere probability, not knowledge. We may think as we like.
Śrīla Prabhupāda: Well, he goes on talking as he likes. In other words, you can speak all kinds of nonsense, and I can too. You are right, and I am right, and everything is right.
Śyāmasundara dāsa: Hume divided human understanding into two categories: relationships among ideas and relationships among facts. The first involves mathematics. Two plus two equals four is true whether it refers to something existing in nature or not. According to the relationships among facts, this is a knowledge to be assumed on the basis of sense experience. According to the information we have based on sense perceptions, we believe that the sun will rise tomorrow. However, there is a possibility that the world will end, and the sun will not rise tomorrow.
Śrīla Prabhupāda: Why is this so? Who makes this possible or impossible? The sun may rise, or the sun may not rise. Is this accidental, or is this according to someone's will?
Śyāmasundara dāsa: Hume would say that it is accidental.
Śrīla Prabhupāda: Nothing is accidental. Everything is symmetrical. According to Kṛṣṇa in *Bhagavad-gītā*, everything in nature is working under His direction. The sun rises because God has so ordained it. If God does not ordain it, the sun will not rise. It is not accidental at all.
Śyāmasundara dāsa: Hume denies cause and effect relationships. We associate friction with heat, but he says that it is a mistake to assume that friction causes heat. For him, there is merely a repetition of two incidents. The effect may habitually attend the cause, but it is not necessarily its consequence. There is only association, not cause and effect.
Śrīla Prabhupāda: But who made the laws of association? The association may be accidental, but as soon as there is friction, there is heat. This means that in nature there is a systematic law.
Śyāmasundara dāsa: Hume would say that this law is not ultimate reality but mere probability.
Śrīla Prabhupāda: Nonetheless, there are physical laws. The sequence of these laws may differ because they are created by someone who can change them. A legislature may assemble today and pass a certain law, but tomorrow it may assemble again and nullify that law. Similarly, a supreme will makes these laws, and He can also nullify or change them. As far as you are concerned, when there is friction, there is heat. It is not that we can rub our hands together without experiencing a sensation of heat. This means that we are subject to the supreme will. God gives

us a chance to speak all kinds of nonsense, but He can stop us immediately. At any instant, our tongue may be in a dead body. The supreme will gives us the freedom to talk in this way or that, and concoct all kinds of philosophies, but at any moment He can put an end to all of this. Thus the supreme will is the ultimate cause of all causes.

Śyāmasundara dāsa: Hume rejected the idea of absolute matter and the conception of the soul as a substance. He also rejected the utility of scientific laws and moral principles as objective realities. He claims that all religious ideas are relative, maintaining that there is no certainty in religious matters.

Śrīla Prabhupāda: Religion means love of God, and there are different religious processes. If we ultimately develop love of God, we have realized the first and most important factor of religion. If love of God is absent, what passes for religion is not really religion. It is simply a show.

Śyāmasundara dāsa: Hume states that even the idea of God is merely probable but not certain.

Śrīla Prabhupāda: We do not agree to that. As soon as we speak of authority, we posit the existence of a supreme authority. We call that supreme authority God.

Śyāmasundara dāsa: Hume would say that we would have to accept the authority of our senses.

Śrīla Prabhupāda: The senses are imperfect, and God is beyond the senses. We cannot see God, touch Him, or hear Him because our senses are imperfect. A man with imperfect senses says that there is no God, but those who have cleansed their senses can see God, touch Him, and talk with Him.

Śyāmasundara dāsa: Hume denies the existence of miracles.

Śrīla Prabhupāda: One thing may be a miracle for one person and not for another. An electric fan may seem like a miracle for a child, but not for his father. So our conception of miracles is also relative.

Hayagrīva dāsa: On this subject, Hume writes: "All the new discoveries in astronomy, which prove the immense grandeur and magnificence of the works of nature, are so many additional arguments for a Deity, according to the true system of theism." In this way, Hume rejects the necessity or desirability of miracles as well as the conception of a God transcendental to His creation. He states that it is not the being of God that is in question, but God's nature, which cannot be ascertained through study of the universe itself. However, if the universe can only be studied by imperfect senses, what is the value of our conclusion?

How can we ever come to know the nature of God?
Śrīla Prabhupāda: According to our Vedic philosophy, the nature of God can be explained by God Himself. In *Bhagavad-gītā*, Kṛṣṇa tells Arjuna:

mattaḥ parataraṁ nānyat
kiñcid asti dhanañjaya
mayi sarvam idaṁ protaṁ
sūtre maṇi-gaṇā iva

"O conqueror of wealth, there is no Truth superior to Me. Everything rests upon Me, as pearls are strung on a thread." (*Bg.* 7.7) We accept this as a fact, because it is not possible for anyone to be greater than God. It is God's nature to be the greatest in everything: wealth, fame, power, beauty, knowledge, and renunciation. If we can find one who is garnished with such greatness, we have found God. These qualities are found in Kṛṣṇa, and therefore we accept Kṛṣṇa as the Supreme Lord.
Hayagrīva dāsa: In *Dialogues Concerning Natural Religion,* Hume writes: "All religious systems, it is confessed, are subject to great and insuperable difficulties. Each disputant triumphs in his turn, while he carries on an offensive war and exposes the absurdities, barbarities and pernicious tenets of his antagonists. But all of them, on the whole, prepare a complete triumph for the skeptic, who tells them that no system ought ever be embraced....A total suspense of judgement is here our only reasonable recourse."
Śrīla Prabhupāda: We do not accept this. We believe that we can know God from God Himself. Religion refers to the principles given by God. If there are no directions given by God, there is no religion. Religion is not a kind of blind faith; it is factual because it is given by God Himself. If you know God and follow His instructions, you are religious.
Hayagrīva dāsa: Hume did believe that religion is necessary. He says that religion, however corrupted, is still better than no religion at all.
Śrīla Prabhupāda: We agree to that, but religion without philosophy and logic is simply sentiment. That will not help us. Real religion is given by Śrī Kṛṣṇa.

man-manā bhava mad-bhakto
mad-yājī māṁ namaskuru
māṁ evaiṣyasi yuktvaivam
ātmānaṁ mat-parāyaṇaḥ

"Engage your mind always in thinking of Me, offer obeisances and worship Me. Being completely absorbed in Me, surely you will come to Me." (*Bg.* 9.34) If we always think of God, we will become purified. Religion means meditating upon God and thinking of Him. Therefore temple worship is necessary to facilitate our constantly thinking of God. But if we do not know of God's form, how can we offer Him worship? How can we think of Him? We then have to construct a pseudo religion, and this kind of religion will not help us.

Hayagrīva dāsa: Hume's conception of religion is utilitarian and social. He writes: "The proper office of religion is to regulate the heart of man, humanize their conduct, infuse the spirit of temperance, order, and obedience...."

Śrīla Prabhupāda: We also say that religion is the greatest welfare work for all humanity. For instance, religion forbids illicit sex, and if people indulge in illicit sex, society will become chaotic. If we continue eating meat, we revolt against God's will because God is the father of all living entities. When other foods are available, why should we kill animals to eat meat? When there is a wife, why should we have illicit sex? A religious man is necessarily a man of good character. If we are God conscious, all good qualities are automatically manifest. A devotee can sacrifice his own interests because he is a devotee. Others cannot do this.

Hayagrīva dāsa: Hume felt that one must first be a philosophical skeptic before accepting the revealed truths of religion. Ultimately, he insists that these truths can be accepted only on faith, not experience or reason.

Śrīla Prabhupāda: Why not on reason? We can use our reason to consider that everything has some proprietor and that it is quite reasonable that this vast universe also has a proprietor. Is there a fault in this logic? Of course, now astronomers are saying that in the beginning there was a chunk, but where did that chunk come from? Where did gas come from? Where did fire come from? There is a proprietor, and He is described in *Bhagavad-gītā*. *Mayādhyakṣeṇa prakṛtiḥ* (*Bg.* 9.10). It is completely illogical to think that there is no universal proprietor.

Hayagrīva dāsa: As far as we can ascertain, Hume personally had no religion, no faith in the Christian or any other God. He also rejected the contention that argument or reason could justify a faith. He is a skeptic who denies the possibility of attaining certainty outside of a mere sequence of perceptions or ideas.

Śrīla Prabhupāda: In other words, all statements are to be rejected except his.

Hayagrīva dāsa: Well, he claims that man cannot know ultimate reality or possess knowledge of anything beyond a mere awareness of phenomenal, sensory images.

Śrīla Prabhupāda: If man cannot possess knowledge, why should we accept Hume's knowledge? It is better to stop the search for knowledge altogether, is it not? Why does Hume bother to write so many books? He is simply trying to set up his own system as supreme. But a skeptic has no foundation for anything.

Śyāmasundara dāsa: Hume says that if we like, we can attribute the order and design of the world to an architect, but as far as he is concerned, there is no proof that a superior architect exists.

Śrīla Prabhupāda: If something is artistic and systematic, we must admit that there is some intelligence behind it. We have no other experience. According to our experience, things do not work well without some brain behind them. When we see that the cosmic manifestation is systematic, we must admit that there is a guiding intelligence.

Śyāmasundara dāsa: He feels that if such an architect exists, he must be responsible for evil in nature. He therefore concludes that God is either finite or imperfect. If He were perfect, there would be no evil, and if He were infinite in power, He could eliminate it.

Śrīla Prabhupāda: God is absolute, and for Him there is no evil. For Him, there is only good, otherwise He could not be called absolute. What we think is evil, is good to God. A father may slap his child, and that child may cry. For the child, this is evil, but for the father, this is good, because he thinks, "I have done right. Although he is crying, he will not commit this same mistake again." Chastisement may sometimes appear evil, but that is relative to our position. Whose opinion are we to take?

Śyāmasundara dāsa: Hume would say that this means that God is limited.

Śrīla Prabhupāda: That is nonsense. If God is limited, He cannot be God.

Śyāmasundara dāsa: The logic is that God must be limited in His goodness to allow evil to exist.

Śrīla Prabhupāda: God is unlimitedly good.

Śyāmasundara dāsa: Then God must be limited in His power because He cannot eliminate evil.

Śrīla Prabhupāda: No. Evil works under His guidance. God controls both good and evil; therefore He is called the supreme controller. He is not limited in any way. The exact word used in Sanskrit is *ananta*, unlimited. God is *advaitam acyutam anantam:* nondual, infallible, and un-

limited.
Śyāmasundara dāsa: Concerning world morality, Hume maintains that morality consists of values formulated by the individual for himself as a matter of personal opinion. Each man may do as his conscience dictates.
Śrīla Prabhupāda: One man may say that his conscience dictates this, and another that his conscience dictates something else. Therefore there is no agreement.
Śyāmasundara dāsa: However, in society, Hume would say that moral values are relative to public opinion.
Śrīla Prabhupāda: Then we have to accept the opinion of the majority. This is democracy.
Śyāmasundara dāsa: Yet Hume admits that it is up to the individual whether to accept public opinion or reject it. Although the law is there, and society agrees to it, it is still up to the individual to follow it or not.
Śrīla Prabhupāda: If you do not follow the law, you will be punished by the state. So we can conclude that independent thinking is not absolute. It is also relative.
Śyāmasundara dāsa: Hume would say that it is not logic or reason that determines morality, but sentiment.
Śrīla Prabhupāda: We cannot decide what is moral or immoral. Only the supreme will can decide that.
Śyāmasundara dāsa: It is the sentiment of the individual that decides. A person should act according to the way he feels at the moment, according to his personal opinion.
Śrīla Prabhupāda: You may be satisfied with your personal opinion, but if it is not approved by others in society, you are living in a fool's paradise.
Śyāmasundara dāsa: The remedy for this is social. We should try to change the laws or opinions of the state so that they will comply with a certain type of morality. If I think that something is right, but the state says that it is wrong, I should act politically to change it.
Śrīla Prabhupāda: But public opinion and individual opinion are not final. Above them is the supreme will of Kṛṣṇa, and that ultimately determines what is moral or immoral.
Śyāmasundara dāsa: Hume believed that moral sentiments enhance the social good, whereas immoral attitudes are egotistic and anti-social.
Śrīla Prabhupāda: In any case, for him the social body is the authority. Ultimately, we have to depend on some authority for all sanction. We propose that the supreme authority is Kṛṣṇa, and that whatever He sanctions is moral, and whatever He does not sanction is immoral. Arjuna was thinking that it was moral to be nonviolent on the battlefield of

Kurukṣetra, but Kṛṣṇa told him otherwise. Instead of depending on the social, political, or communal body to determine morality, we should depend on the supreme will of the supreme authority. We maintain that all morality is relative to Kṛṣṇa's sanction. Killing is considered immoral, but because Kṛṣṇa ordered Arjuna to fight, Arjuna's killing was not immoral. When our actions are approved by the supreme authority, we are moral. If our acts are not approved by the supreme authority, we are immoral. Morality and immorality have no fixed position. When something is approved by Kṛṣṇa, it is moral. Thus what is considered immoral may actually be moral, and vice versa, depending on the orders or desires of Kṛṣṇa. In a war, a soldier may kill many human beings and be awarded many medals for this, but if he kills one person when he returns home, he is considered immoral, and he is hanged. Even on the mundane platform, morality and immorality depend on the sanction of the state. The state says, "It is moral that you kill this man because he is an enemy." And the state also says, "If you kill, you will be hanged." In this way, people accept authority. Everything in the universe depends on Kṛṣṇa's will, on His authority. In the beginning of *Bhagavad-gītā*, Kṛṣṇa says that He comes to reestablish religious principles (*Bg.* 4.8), but at the conclusion He states that one should reject all religious principles and simply surrender unto Him and accept His order (18.66). This is the confidential teaching of *Bhagavad-gītā*. In any case, He is the ultimate authority, and surrender unto Him is the ultimate religious principle.

Śyāmasundara dāsa: Hume lays the groundwork for permissiveness in modern society because he leaves it up to the individual to choose a specific ethical attitude. In other words, to do as he pleases.

Śrīla Prabhupāda: But this is not possible because no one can do as he pleases. In life, there are many stumbling blocks. A person may propose a certain action, but his proposal may not be practical. We cannot act independently. Otherwise, there will be chaos. There must be some authority.

VII
GERMAN IDEALISM

Immanuel Kant
(1724-1804)

Śyāmasundara dāsa: In *Critique of Pure Reason,* Kant asks the fundamental question, "How are a priori synthetic judgments possible?" How can we apprehend the relationship between cause and effect? Where does this facility come from? What is the source of knowledge? He proposes that one knowledge-acquiring process, the transcendental aesthetic, synthesizes sense experience through the concepts of time and space. The mind acts upon sensory perceptions and applies time and space relations to them. Knowledge of time and space is a priori, prior to and independent of sense experience. It is an internal creation of the mind. Even before we sense anything, we have an idea of time and space.

Śrīla Prabhupāda: He speaks of the transcendental aesthetic, but we understand the real meaning of transcendental to be beyond the senses—that is, referring to something not in our experience. We have to receive this knowledge from higher authority, *paramparā,* a source beyond the reach of the material senses. By sense perception, we have no knowledge of the spiritual world, but in *Bhagavad-gītā,* Kṛṣṇa says that there is another nature, a spiritual nature, which is beyond this material nature (*Bg.* 8.20). We have to understand this through transcendental knowledge; we cannot experience it.

ataḥ śrī-kṛṣṇa-nāmādi
na bhaved grāhyam indriyaiḥ
sevonmukhe hi jihvādau
svayam eva sphuraty adaḥ

"Material senses cannot appreciate Kṛṣṇa's holy name, form, qualities, and pastimes. When a conditioned soul is awakened to Kṛṣṇa consciousness and renders service by using his tongue to chant the Lord's holy name and taste the remnants of the Lord's food, the tongue is purified, and one gradually comes to understand who Kṛṣṇa really is." (*Padma Purāṇa*). The names, qualities, pastimes, and nature of God cannot be understood by these material senses, but if we engage in God's service, they will all be revealed. Vaikuṇṭha and Goloka Vṛndāvana, Kṛṣṇa's abode, will then be confirmed. These truths are revealed gradually; they are not abruptly understood. Common men cannot understand the meaning of going back to Godhead. They say, "What nonsense is this?" They cannot understand because it is transcendental, beyond the reach of the gross senses. It is revealed knowledge. If one becomes submissive and engages in the service of the Lord and the spiritual master, all these truths will be revealed. No one can mislead a person who receives knowledge through revelation. From *Bhagavad-gītā*, we understand that there is a transcendental abode, *cintāmaṇi*, and we cannot forget this even if offered a great fortune to forget. On the other hand, if we offer a person a million dollars to believe in the transcendental abode, he will not believe in it. Transcendental knowledge is not a matter of speculation. It is received from higher authority. As we progress in *bhakti-yoga*, these things become clear.

Hayagrīva dāsa: Kant strongly advocated the right and duty of every man to judge for himself in religious and secular matters. "Have courage to make use of your own intellect" was his motto. He emphasized individual freedom and the ability of man to intuit the truth.

Śrīla Prabhupāda: Does this mean that whatever anyone does is perfectly right? If we are given that freedom, then anyone can do as he likes.

Hayagrīva dāsa: At the same time, Kant considered the Bible to be the best vehicle for the instruction of the public in a truly moral religion.

Śrīla Prabhupāda: This means that he has accepted some authority. Where is his freedom then?

Hayagrīva dāsa: The individual can intuit truths within, but can be helped from without by scripture.

Śrīla Prabhupāda: This means that we should not be totally independent. We should be dependent on some authority, and that authority should be recognized. Then knowledge is possible. That is Vaiṣṇavism.
Śyāmasundara dāsa: Descartes believed that knowledge comes through innate ideas, and Hume opposed this by saying that knowledge comes from sense experience. Kant tries to unify these extremes.
Śrīla Prabhupāda: Knowledge comes from purified sense experience. That is *sevā*. I may see Kṛṣṇa, whereas others may see a stone. This means that my eyes and vision are different.

premāñjana-cchurita-bhakti-vilocanena
santaḥ sadaiva hṛdayeṣu vilokayanti
yaṁ śyāmasundaram acintya-guṇa-svarūpaṁ
govindam ādi-puruṣaṁ tam ahaṁ bhajāmi

"I worship the primeval Lord, Govinda, who is always seen by the devotee whose eyes are anointed with the pulp of love. He is seen in His eternal form of Śyāmasundara situated within the heart of the devotee." (*Brahma-saṁhitā*, 5.38) When our eyes are anointed with the ointment of love of God, we can truly see. The same applies to the rest of the senses. Unless our senses are purified, we can neither see nor know.
Śyāmasundara dāsa: In *Critique of Pure Reason*, Kant wrote: "Thoughts without content are empty, perceptions without conceptions are blind....Understanding can perceive nothing, the senses can think nothing. Knowledge arises only from their united action."
Śrīla Prabhupāda: When you try to understand through the senses, that is called *pratyakṣa*. There is knowledge through direct perception, *pratyakṣa*, and knowledge received from higher authorities, *paro'kṣa*. When we apply our senses and come to the same conclusion, that is *anumāna*. For instance, a higher authority says that there is a spiritual world. Now, how can we come to this conclusion? Obviously, we have to apply our senses. We can reason, "I am a combination of spirit and matter. That is a fact. However, I cannot see the spirit at the present moment, but I know that there is spirit." If we understand that there is a material world, we can also understand that there is a spiritual world. We can arrive at this conclusion by applying our senses and reason. If a material world is possible, certainly a spiritual world is possible. This is preliminary knowledge. When we see a dead body, we understand that something is missing. We see this with our senses, and from higher authority, from *Bhagavad-gītā*, we understand that this something that is missing is eternal.

avināśi tu tad viddhi
yena sarvam idaṁ tatam
vināśam avyayasyāsya
na kaścit kartum arhati

"Know that which pervades the entire body is indestructible. No one is able to destroy the imperishable soul." (*Bg.* 2.17) That consciousness is spread throughout the body. It is eternal and spiritual. Through our sense experience, we can also understand that the body is constantly changing from the body of a child to that of an old man, and that this consciousness is continuing. Despite the different bodily changes, consciousness is enduring. The basic principles of knowledge are received from higher authorities, just as preliminary mathematical information is given by the teacher when he informs the student that two plus two equals four. God has given us reason, senses, and consciousness, and by applying them, we can arrive at the proper conclusion.

Hayagrīva dāsa: In *Critique of Judgement*, Kant writes: "Absolutely no human reason...can hope to understand the production of even a blade of grass by mere mechanical causes. That crude matter should have originally formed itself according to mechanical laws, that life should have sprung from the nature of what is lifeless, that matter should have been able to dispose itself into the form of a self-maintaining purpose—is contradictory to reason."

Śrīla Prabhupāda: Yes, and therefore we have to learn from an authority, from one who is cognizant and knows things as they are. Matter certainly cannot combine itself without a brain behind it, and that brain is the Supreme Lord, God. It is unreasonable to think that matter automatically combines independent of intelligence to form the sun, moon, and other planets.

Śyāmasundara dāsa: If we are unable to receive knowledge from a higher authority, is it possible to have it innately inside of us?

Śrīla Prabhupāda: Innate knowledge is knowledge that is already there. We say that Kṛṣṇa is the *caitya-guru* because Kṛṣṇa is within. Kṛṣṇa is everything both inside and outside. Within, He is the Paramātmā, the Supersoul, and outside He is the spiritual master and the *śāstra*, the scripture. Kṛṣṇa is trying to help the conditioned soul in both ways: from within and without. It is therefore said that the spiritual master is the representative of Kṛṣṇa because Kṛṣṇa appears outside as the spiritual master. Inside, He is personally present as Paramātmā.

Śyāmasundara dāsa: For Kant, the second knowledge-attaining process is the transcendental analytic. First, the mind applies the concept of time and space. Then it applies the categories of quantity, cause and effect, quality, modality, and so on.

Śrīla Prabhupāda: That is all right.

Śyāmasundara dāsa: The third process is the transcendental dialectic, whereby the human mind seeks to understand everything. But since sensory information is inadequate, the mind tries to go beyond sense experience.

Śrīla Prabhupāda: How is that?

Śyāmasundara dāsa: The mind is aware that there is an ultimate reality, a thing in itself, a noumenon, which produces each phenomenon. But because the mind is not equipped to sense this ultimate reality, the mind must forever remain agnostic.

Śrīla Prabhupāda: Why agnostic? He should go to higher authorities. If we hear a sound on the roof, we may speculate that the sound is this or that, but with our imperfect senses we cannot ascertain what made the sound. But if someone is actually on the roof, he can tell us, "The sound was made by this." Why should we remain satisfied with an agnostic position? We should satisfy ourselves by asking, "Is there someone on the roof?" If someone says, "Yes, I am here," then we can ask him what made the sound. Therefore the Vedas enjoin: *tad-vijñānārthaṁ sa gurum evābhigacchet (Muṇḍaka Upaniṣad* 1.2.12). In order to understand what is beyond the senses, we must approach a spiritual master who can impart information. When we actually want to understand transcendental subjects, we must approach a guru. And what is a guru?

tasmād guruṁ prapadyeta
jijñāsuḥ śreya uttamam
śābde pare ca niṣṇātaṁ
brahmaṇy upaśamāśrayam

"Any person who is seriously desirous of achieving real happiness must seek out a bona fide spiritual master and take shelter of him by initiation. A spiritual master must have realized the conclusion of the scriptures by deliberation and arguments and thus be able to convince others of these conclusions. Such great personalities who have taken complete shelter of the Supreme Godhead, leaving aside all material considerations, are to be understood as bona fide spiritual masters ." (*Bhāg.* 11.3.21) A guru is one who is well versed in the Vedic literatures, *śruti.* And how can we understand that he is? *Brahmaṇy upaśamāśrayam.* One who knows the Vedas forgets everything material and concerns himself only with spirit soul.

Śyāmasundara dāsa: Kant was just exploring the possibility that although we cannot know ultimate reality by our senses, the mind nevertheless wants to know it.

Śrīla Prabhupāda: But that is misleading. No one can ascertain the Absolute Truth by mental speculation. That is impossible. The *śāstras* state: *panthāstu koṭi-śata-vatsara-sampragamyaḥ (Brahma-saṁhitā* 5.34). Even if we travel at the speed of mind for thousands of years, we cannot find Kṛṣṇa. If this is the case, a man, who lives the utmost for only a hundred years, cannot understand Kṛṣṇa through his material senses. The material attempt will be futile. The Vedas say that the devotee who has received a little grace from Kṛṣṇa's lotus feet can understand Him. Others will speculate for millions of years to no end. Kṛṣṇa can be understood only through the grace of Kṛṣṇa. Because the devotee is engaged in Kṛṣṇa's service, Kṛṣṇa reveals Himself.

Hayagrīva dāsa: Kant would also say that we cannot experience God through our senses but only through faith and intuitive reason. Speculative reason is unable to attain to a sure or adequate conception of God.

Śrīla Prabhupāda: That is correct: it is not possible to understand God by mental speculation. When God explains Himself, we can understand Him. The devotees can accept the Supreme Personality of Godhead and His instructions, but a nondevotee or atheist, unable to understand, simply speculates. It is not possible for a speculator to reach the vicinity of God. We can understand God only by God's mercy, which is bestowed by a pure devotee surrendered to God. In *Bhagavad-gītā*, Kṛṣṇa explicitly states:

nāhaṁ prakāśaḥ sarvasya
yoga-māyā-samāvṛtaḥ
mūḍho'yaṁ nābhijānāti
loko mām ajam avyayam

"I am never manifest to the foolish and unintelligent. For them, I am covered by My eternal creative potency (*yoga-māyā*); and so the deluded world knows Me not, who am unborn and infallible." (*Bg.* 7.25) Revelation means that God opens the curtain for His devotee. The sun is in the sky all the time, but at night it is obscured. By God's mercy, the sun rises in the morning, and everyone can immediately see the light. At night, we may speculate about the sun, but when the sun rises in the morning, we can immediately understand what the sun is.

Śyāmasundara dāsa: Kant maintains that the mental speculators try to reconstruct ultimate reality by applying mundane categories to it. They attempt through the mind to create what they believe to be the real world.

Śrīla Prabhupāda: For mental speculators, the real world is nothing more than the negation of this world. This is voidism. In this world, we experience that everything is material. The mental speculator's materialistic thinking induces him to conclude that the spiritual must be the opposite of the material. Since the material has form, the spiritual must be formless, or void. This is typical materialistic thinking. He thinks, "Since this is not truth, the opposite must be truth."
Śyāmasundara dāsa: Kant says that "the world is my representation." That is, this real world becomes an ideal construction in the mind of man.
Śrīla Prabhupāda: We try to construct an ideal world, but we are frustrated here because everything is temporary; therefore we can understand that the ideal must be eternal. No one wants to die; we all want to live. However, this is hopeless because the body is not eternal. Therefore we understand that in the ideal world, the body is eternal.
Hayagrīva dāsa: Kant acknowledges that there is a design in nature but that man, not being able to know the total design, cannot know for certain whether there is a designer. The design, as man sees it, does not necessarily prove the existence of the designer. His existence can only be intuited.
Śrīla Prabhupāda: As soon as we see pottery, we immediately understand that there is a potter. It is impossible for pottery to be made any other way.
Hayagrīva dāsa: Kant maintains that due to the overwhelming effects of suffering and natural calamities, it is impossible for man to see nature's final end.
Śrīla Prabhupāda: Nature does not have a final end; nature is only an instrument. If I beat you with a stick, it is I, not the stick, that is beating you. When we receive pains and tribulations from nature, we should understand that nature is an instrument designed by God. *Śītoṣṇa-sukha-duḥkheṣu (Bg.* 12.18). By witnessing the changes of seasons, heat and cold, happiness and distress, we can understand that there is a designer or brain behind the functionings of material nature.

mayādhyakṣena prakṛtiḥ
sūyate sa-carācaram
hetunānena kaunteya
jagad viparivartate

"This material nature is working under My direction, O son of Kuntī, and it is producing all moving and unmoving beings. By its rule, this manifestation is created and annihilated again and again." (*Bg.* 9.10)

Hayagrīva dāsa: Kant would say that the design can be intuited but not known.

Śrīla Prabhupāda: To a foolish man, everything is unknown, but a man in knowledge knows everything from authority, or from direct perception. Some way or other, the knowledge is there. Something is unknown when one doesn't care to know, or doesn't want to receive the knowledge.

Śyāmasundara dāsa: When man realizes the futility of mental speculation, he attempts to create ideas about the universe which transcend the bounds of experience. For Kant, this is the third stage, the transcendental dialectic. These ideas belong to the realm of pure reason, or transcendental reason, and are not mere fictions. They spring from the very nature of reason itself.

Śrīla Prabhupāda: We are all seeking eternity. Because we understand that we are eternal souls, we know that this is not our place, and are therefore seeking the eternal world. The spirit soul does not feel comfortable within this material body. This is understood when we conclude that we must return to the spiritual world and attain a spiritual body. Information on how this is done is given in *Bhagavad-gītā,* wherein Kṛṣṇa says that one who understands Him and develops love for Him attains a spiritual body that will enable him to see God. If we are very anxious to see Kṛṣṇa and full in Kṛṣṇa consciousness, we will be transferred to Kṛṣṇa's abode at the time of death. This is Kṛṣṇa's promise in *Bhagavad-gītā.*

Śyāmasundara dāsa: Transcendental reasoning is in man to guide his understanding to clearer and wider knowledge. For instance, the idea of a Supreme Being is a regulative principle of reason because it tells us to view everything in the world as if it proceeded from a necessary cause, the Supreme Being.

Śrīla Prabhupāda: The Supreme Being is the cause of all causes.

Śyāmasundara dāsa: Kant says that it is the natural impulse of pure reason to perceive a total regularity in everything. To arrive at this total synthesis, the mind must suppose that there is a Supreme Being.

Śrīla Prabhupāda: This is confirming the statements of *Bhagavad-gītā.*

Śyāmasundara dāsa: He claims that it is impossible to arrive at the ultimate reality by pure reason alone because phenomena are endless.

Śrīla Prabhupāda: Therefore he has to accept Kṛṣṇa's assertions. He has to admit that he is puzzled with these various changes in phenomena. As soon as we come to Kṛṣṇa, we find out that Kṛṣṇa is behind the changing phenomena and that the universe is working under His direction. This is the perfect conclusion.

Śyāmasundara dāsa: According to Kant, when we examine material phenomena by our reason, we arrive at certain contradictions called antimonies—that is, two opposing statements regarded to be true.
Śrīla Prabhupāda: In Sanskrit, this is called *viruddhārtha*, words that mean both yes and no.
Śyāmasundara dāsa: For instance: "The world has a beginning in time, and is enclosed within limits of space." And, "The world has no beginning in time, and no limits in space, but is infinite." As far as reason is concerned, both conclusions are true.
Śrīla Prabhupāda: So how is this adjusted? The adjustment is given in *Bhagavad-gītā*, wherein Kṛṣṇa says that this phenomenal world of materials comes into existence, is annihilated, and then comes again into existence.

avyaktād vyaktayaḥ sarvāḥ
prabhavanty ahar-āgame
rātry-āgame pralīyante
tatraivāvyakta-saṁjñake

bhūta-grāmaḥ sa evāyaṁ
bhūtvā bhūtvā pralīyate
rātry-āgame'vaśaḥ pārtha
prabhavaty ahar-āgame

"When Brahmā's day is manifest, this multitude of living entities comes into being, and at the arrival of Brahmā's night, they are annihilated. Again and again the day comes, and this host of beings is active; and again the night falls, O Pārtha, and they are helplessly dissolved." (*Bg.* 8.18-19)
Śyāmasundara dāsa: Another antimony of Kant's is: "Every composite substance in the world is made up of simple parts, and nothing whatever exists but the simple, or what is composed out of the simple." And, "No composite thing in the world is made up of simple parts, nor does anything simple exist anywhere in the world."
Śrīla Prabhupāda: We say that the whole world is made of material energy, and this is the simplistic view. Now, there are many component parts of material energy: the *mahat-tattva*, the *pradhāna*, the *puruṣa*, the twenty-four elements, the five gross elements, eight subtle elements, the senses, the objects of the senses, and so forth. In this way, when we begin to analyze material energy, so many complications arise.
Śyāmasundara dāsa: Another antimony deals with causal relations: "Causality and conformity with laws of nature are not the only causality

from which all the phenomena of the world can be derived. To explain those phenomena, it is necessary to suppose that there is also a free causality." And, "There is no freedom, but all that comes to be in the world takes place entirely in accordance with laws of nature."

Śrīla Prabhupāda: He cannot explain the cause because he does not know it. The ultimate cause is Kṛṣṇa, God. Events may seem miraculous because we cannot understand how they are taking place. God's energy is so subtle that it works simply by His will. By His will, all processes in nature take place, but they take place so swiftly that we see them as miracles. Actually, there is no such thing as a miracle; we only see it as a miracle. Kṛṣṇa is floating many planets in space, and this may seem like a miracle, but to Kṛṣṇa it is not. Kṛṣṇa is known as Yogeśvara, the master of all mystic power.

Śyāmasundara dāsa: Another antimony questions the existence of an Absolute Being: "There exists an absolutely necessary being, which belongs to the world either as a part or as the cause." And, "There nowhere exists an absolutely necessary being, either in the world or outside, as its cause." Thus, according to reason, we can conclude that there is either a God or no God.

Śrīla Prabhupāda: What reasoning can support the nonexistence of God?

Śyāmasundara dāsa: We can conclude this by using the senses.

Śrīla Prabhupāda: But where do you get your senses?

Śyāmasundara dāsa: One could say that they are only a combination of matter.

Śrīla Prabhupāda: But where does this matter come from?

Śyāmasundara dāsa: According to material reasoning, one can say that there is no necessary cause.

Śrīla Prabhupāda: But we can see that matter is growing, coming into existence like a tree.

Śyāmasundara dāsa: It may have been eternally existing.

Śrīla Prabhupāda: How is that? A tree is not eternally existing. This brass pot is not eternally existing. Someone has made it.

Śyāmasundara dāsa: But the matter itself could have been eternally existing.

Śrīla Prabhupāda: But we can see that it is not only existing. It is growing. A tree is wood, and wood is matter. How is it growing? Similarly, our material bodies take birth at a certain moment, grow, reproduce, dwindle, and finally vanish. This is the nature of all matter. Everything starts out as a seed and grows from there. Now, where does the seed come from? Kṛṣṇa says, *bījaṁ māṁ sarva-bhūtānām.* "I am the original seed of all existences." (*Bg.* 7.10) Therefore Kṛṣṇa is the cause of everything.

Śyāmasundara dāsa: Kant's point is that these antimonies arise from the attempt by reason to apply its categories to the Absolute, the transcendent. But by mundane reasoning alone, we cannot approach the Absolute.

Śrīla Prabhupāda: By our reasoning, we can see that everything is growing and that the entire cosmic manifestation must have grown from a source.

Śyāmasundara dāsa: But this is transcendental reasoning.

Śrīla Prabhupāda: No, common reason. Everything is growing from a certain source; therefore this material world must have grown from a certain source. It is very simple.

Śyāmasundara dāsa: But some people can look at the seed of a tree and come to a different conclusion.

Śrīla Prabhupāda: Well, we also receive this information from authoritative literature, from the Vedas.

Śyāmasundara dāsa: Someone can apply material reasoning and arrive at a different conclusion.

Śrīla Prabhupāda: But is this reasoning proved by experience? Can a man prove that he is born without a father? How did the material body come into existence? How can one deny his father? How can one deny the cause? He cannot because his very existence is depending on some cause.

Śyāmasundara dāsa: Kant is simply saying that whenever we begin to speculate about the Absolute, we run into contradictions.

Śrīla Prabhupāda: Contradiction is due to imperfect knowledge. Unless we conclude that Kṛṣṇa is the cause of all causes, our knowledge is doomed to be imperfect. Vedic literature says that Kṛṣṇa glanced at material nature and impregnated her. Then so many products developed, including all these categories. Matter and spirit combined to bring this whole cosmic manifestation into existence.

Śyāmasundara dāsa: For Kant, cause and effect relationships are also a priori conceptions, mental creations, like time and space. Prior to sense experience, we have an idea of them.

Śrīla Prabhupāda: I take my birth at a certain time, and I die at a certain time. Time is existing before my birth, and it will continue to exist after my death. Similarly with space. This body is temporarily manifest in time, for a certain period considered my lifespan. During that time, I

occupy some space, and that is a temporary occupation. Time and space, however, are eternally there. At least, time is eternally there, because space is also born in time.
Śyāmasundara dāsa: How is that?
Śrīla Prabhupāda: We receive information from *Śrīmad-Bhāgavatam* that because this material space is also *ākāśa*, it is born of the finer, subtle mind and intelligence. These descriptions are given in *Śrīmad-Bhāgavatam*. Space is also created.
Śyāmasundara dāsa: Hume had said that cause and effect are habitual assumptions, that we naturally assume that a certain effect follows a certain cause but that the cause does not necessarily bring about the effect.
Śrīla Prabhupāda: We don't agree with that. There cannot be an effect without a cause. Let him prove first that there is an existence without a cause.
Śyāmasundara dāsa: Well, Hume gave the example of a footprint on the beach. Normally we can assume that a human being left the footprint.
Śrīla Prabhupāda: Why normally assume? If it is actually there, it is a fact.
Śyāmasundara dāsa: Possibly something else left the footprint. Someone could have made a cast of a foot, or some other possibility may exist.
Śrīla Prabhupāda: That is nonsense. Why should someone make a footprint to mislead you? But even if he does, that is the cause. The cause is that someone came to mislead you.
Śyāmasundara dāsa: Kant would say that when we see something, we intuitively understand the cause and effect relationship.
Śrīla Prabhupāda: You may or may not understand what the cause is, but there must be a cause. Without a cause, nothing can happen. People foolishly inquire when or why the living entity fell into material nature, but what is the use of this question? There is certainly a cause, but instead of trying to find out the cause, we should try to treat the disease. Why waste time?
Śyāmasundara dāsa: Kant concludes that because the mind imposes a priori laws upon nature as both necessary and universal, the mind is creative and does not come into the world a blank slate.
Śrīla Prabhupāda: It is a fact that the mind is creative. It creates and then rejects. That is the mind's business—*saṁkalpa-vikalpa*.
Śyāmasundara dāsa: Kant would say that apart from using the categories of thought—like quantity, quality, cause and effect, and modality—there is only mere guesswork and imperfect dogma. The mind is not

satisfied with this partial explanation; it wants to grasp reality in a comprehensive way. The mind wants to know something beyond these categories, and this is the realm of the transcendental dialectic.

Śrīla Prabhupāda: This inquisitiveness is actual philosophy. We are searching for the cause of all causes. A thoughtful man is naturally interested in the ultimate cause of everything. That is human nature. It is the *mahātmā* who searches after the ultimate cause and finds it. The *Vedānta-sūtra* therefore begins with the inquiry: *athāto brahma-jijñāsā.* "What is the ultimate cause? What is Brahman?" It answers: *janmādyasya yataḥ.* "Brahman is the supreme source from whom everything emanates." Unless we go to the supreme source, we cannot be satisfied. Those who approach this source through mental speculation attain the impersonal feature. From this point, they can make further advancement. In *Īśopaniṣad*, there is a prayer petitioning the Supreme:

hiraṇmayena pātreṇa
satyasyāpihitaṁ mukham
tat tvaṁ pūṣann apāvṛṇu
satya-dharmāya dṛṣtaye

"O my Lord, sustainer of all that lives, Your real face is covered by Your dazzling effulgence. Please remove that covering and reveal Yourself to Your pure devotee." (*Īśopaniṣad* 15) If we penetrate this impersonal Brahman, we will arrive at Kṛṣṇa, and then be satisfied. Therefore it is stated in *Bhagavad-gītā:*

bahūnāṁ janmanām ante
jñānavān māṁ prapadyate
vāsudevaḥ sarvam iti
sa mahātmā sudurlabhaḥ

"After many births and deaths, he who is actually in knowledge surrenders unto Me, knowing Me to be the cause of all causes and all that is. Such a great soul is very rare." (*Bg.* 7.19)

Śyāmasundara dāsa: Kant says that after the futile attempt to apply categorical analysis to transcendental knowledge, a man attempts to create other ideas about the universe which transcend sense experience.

Śrīla Prabhupāda: In other words, after failing to attain material knowledge, he attempts to attain transcendental knowledge. What is this?

Śyāmasundara dāsa: Rather, he fails to understand transcendental knowledge when applying the techniques of material knowledge.

Śrīla Prabhupāda: This means that he cannot approach transcendental knowledge with material senses. If this is not possible, how can he hope

to form valid ideas about transcendence?
Śyāmasundara dāsa: Through pure reason.
Śrīla Prabhupāda: He admits that the material senses cannot reach transcendence, but he is not clear about the meaning of this pure reason. If the senses are imperfect, and if your reasoning is fed by the senses, your reasoning is also imperfect.
Śyāmasundara dāsa: Kant maintains that reason can act a priori, separate or independent of the senses, to understand that there is God and a soul.
Śrīla Prabhupāda: That is possible.
Śyāmasundara dāsa: In fact, Kant recognizes three ideals of pure reason: the soul, the ultimate world, and God. These ideals transcend the bounds of sensory experience; they are innate and a priori.
Śrīla Prabhupāda: That is also true.

nitya-siddha kṛṣṇa-prema 'sādhya' kabhu naya
śravaṇādi-śuddha-citte karaye udaya

"Pure love for Kṛṣṇa is eternally established in the hearts of living entities. It is not something to be gained from another source. When the heart is purified by hearing and chanting, the living entity naturally awakens." (*Caitanya-caritāmṛta*, Madh. 22.107) It is our natural tendency to offer service to the Lord. Caitanya Mahāprabhu has also said that the living entity is God's eternal servant. The tendency to offer service is natural. Somehow or other, it has been covered by material ignorance.

Śyāmasundara dāsa: Whereas sense perception cannot provide any information about the soul and God, pure reason can provide us with certain conceptions, but not much more.
Śrīla Prabhupāda: We cannot know more by our personal attempt, but these subjects can be known by a process called *guru-paramparā*. When God speaks, it is possible to know. We hear from God in order to understand what, who, and where He is. In this way, our knowledge is perfect. According to Kant, we cannot attain reality or God through reason and the senses. That is a fact admitted in the Vedas. The word *vacanam* means "words," and *manaḥ* means "mind." We cannot reach the Supreme either by words or the mind.
Hayagrīva dāsa: Kant suggests that certain knowledge of God's existence would destroy a man's freedom and reduce human experience to a show of puppets frantically attempting to attain the favor of the Almighty. Thus uncertainty is a necessary ingredient for faith.
Śrīla Prabhupāda: Faith should not be blind. If it is, it is useless. We may believe in the government, but the government is not dependent on

faith. There is a government, and we are under the government's laws and therefore have to obey them . There is no question of faith. Similarly, one who knows God becomes dependent on Him, and that is not faith but fact. The devotee is happy depending on God. He knows that it is foolishness to think himself independent. A child voluntarily depends on his parents and is therefore happy.

Śyāmasundara dāsa: Since our knowledge is limited to mere phenomena, faith is necessary to acquire knowledge of God, freedom, and immortality.

Śrīla Prabhupāda: No, faith is not a fact but a compromise. It is good that he admits that we cannot approach God ultimately by our senses or reason, but faith alone also is not sufficient, not perfect. Western philosophers have created so many different faiths. One may believe in one faith, and another person in another, but this is faith, not fact. The fact is this: if we are convinced that there is a God and that He is omnipotent, we have to admit that by His omnipotence He can descend into the world. In *Bhagavad-gītā*, Kṛṣṇa says that He descends into the world for two reasons: to rectify the discrepancies in religion, and to please His devotees who are always anxious to see Him. Some people may say that God is partial, but He is not. God is kind both to His devotees and to the miscreants and demons. When the miscreants are killed by God, they attain immediate salvation, and when the devotees see God, they can understand His actual position. In Vṛndāvana, God displays Himself just as He does in the spiritual world. It is His nature to play with the cowherd boys and dance with the *gopīs*. When the devotees understand this, they become encouraged by knowing that after finishing the material body, they will return to Kṛṣṇa to join in His pastimes. This information is not only understood from the *śāstras*, but is actually demonstrated by Kṛṣṇa. Thus this knowledge is doubly confirmed. When we hear about God and His activities, we can also realize them because God is absolute. There is no difference between seeing Him and hearing about Him. In this way, true knowledge is attained. However expert a logician one may be, it is not possible by reason, logic, or mundane knowledge to approach the Supreme Absolute. It is possible to understand God only when He descends Himself, gives information about Himself, and displays His pastimes.

Śrīmad-Bhāgavatam is a chronicle of the descents of God. If we try to understand God through *Śrīmad-Bhāgavatam* or *Bhagavad-gītā*, we become a *bhāgavata*. In *Bhagavad-gītā*, God speaks about Himself and His activities, and *Śrīmad-Bhāgavatam* is a record of God's activities and pastimes. The first nine cantos are devoted to the understanding of

the transcendental nature of God, and the Tenth Canto is a chronicle of God's activities before the eyes of the people of the world. However, those who are miscreants will think that God is just a famous person, or a superhuman being, and that's all.
Hayagrīva dāsa: Concerning religion and faith, Kant writes: "There is only one (true) religion, but there can be faiths of several kinds. It is therefore more fitting to say, 'This man is of this or that faith (Jewish, Mohammedan, Catholic, Lutheran), than he is of this or that religion.'"
Śrīla Prabhupāda: That is correct. Since religion means obedience to God, it does not refer to some sect. People are trying to understand God in different ways, but these ways are not real religion; they are methods of understanding God. Religion begins when we have understood God and are rendering Him service.
Śyāmasundara dāsa: In *Critique of Practical Reason*, Kant affirmed that moral laws are necessary and universal objects of the human will and must be accepted as valid for everyone. We can know what is morally right a priori, by intuition.
Śrīla Prabhupāda: No. Morality is relative. It varies according to the development of a particular society. For instance, there are many immoral acts taking place in modern society, but no one cares. People go ahead and act as they please.
Śyāmasundara dāsa: Then there is no universal morality?
Śrīla Prabhupāda: Universal morality means obeying God. That's all.
Śyāmasundara dāsa: But are any of God's laws fixed?
Śrīla Prabhupāda: All laws are included if you obey God. That is universal morality.

manmanā bhava mad-bhakto
mad-yājī māṁ namaskuru
mām evaiṣyasi satyaṁ te
pratijāne priyo'si me

"Always think of me and become My devotee. Worship Me and offer your homage unto Me. Thus you will come to Me without fail. I promise you this because you are My very dear friend." (*Bg.* 18.65) This is the basis of morality. We must become Kṛṣṇa's servitor. Since so many immoral activities are being accepted as moral, how else can a person know what is moral and what is not?
Hayagrīva dāsa: Kant writes: "For a rational but finite being, the only thing possible is an endless progress from the lower to the higher degrees of moral perfection."

Śrīla Prabhupāda: This means that there is an endless struggle to understand real morality. This is not necessary. We need only accept the orders of God and follow them. That is ultimate reality.
Hayagrīva dāsa: What Kant means by morality is rather vague. He does not give specific outlines for action. Rather, he writes, "The moral individual is to do what is good only because it is good." According to his categorical imperative, man should act in such a way that the maxim of his actions might become the principle for universal law.
Śrīla Prabhupāda: But that is impossible for the individual soul. It is impossible for a conditioned living entity to do something that will be universally accepted.
Hayagrīva dāsa: Then man cannot establish a universal law by his own action?
Śrīla Prabhupāda: No. Only God can do so. Only God can say, *sarva-dharmān parityajya mām ekam.* "Abandon all varieties of religion and just surrender unto Me." (*Bg.* 18.66) If an individual conditioned soul says this, who will accept him?
Śyāmasundara dāsa: But Kant says that there are certain imperatives that we are born with.
Śrīla Prabhupāda: What are these? He should say specifically. The only universal imperative is that you should be obedient to God. That's all.
Hayagrīva dāsa: Kant rejects the traditional proofs of God's existence in order to clear the ground for his assertion that God is morally necessary in a moral universe. In this universe, every soul is an end in itself, and these individual souls are like citizens in a "kingdom of ends."
Śrīla Prabhupāda: Why does he use the word "kingdom" if he does not accept the king?
Hayagrīva dāsa: No, he would say that the king is a moral necessity in a moral universe. He simply rejects the traditional proofs.
Śrīla Prabhupāda: That's all right, but he sees the individual souls as ends in themselves. There is no question of such independence, because everything is part and parcel of the Supreme Personality of Godhead. God is behind nature, and if our morality denies the existence of God, what is its value? One man may think that animal killing is good, while another may think that it is immoral. So who is correct? There must be some authority to establish morality. Morality must have some background, otherwise it will change at any moment.
Hayagrīva dāsa: Kant also writes: "It does not enter men's heads that when they fulfill their duty to men (themselves and others), they are, by these very acts, performing God's commands and are therefore in all

their actions and abstentions, so far as these concern morality, perpetually in the service of God, and that it is absolutely impossible to serve God directly in any other way...."

Śrīla Prabhupāda: If man does not serve God, how can he know how to serve humanity? If he does not receive information from God about how to serve humanity, what is the value of his humanitarianism? The best way to serve mankind is to preach this message of *Bhagavad-gītā* so that everyone can become a faithful servant of God. When we are God's servants, we can render service not only to our fellow man but to all other living entities as well. However, if we manufacture our service, it is useless.

Hayagrīva dāsa: In the preface to one of his last works, *Religion Within the Limits of Reason Alone*, Kant seems to shift his position to say that morality "extends itself to the idea of a powerful moral Lawgiver, outside of mankind." Still, he believes that knowledge of God is ultimately uncertain.

Śrīla Prabhupāda: It is uncertain for one who does not have perfect knowledge. If you believe in God and know God, you can get perfect knowledge from Him. Then you'll become perfect.

Śyāmasundara dāsa: Ideally, for Kant, it is the moral obligation of everyone to obey the moral commands.

Śrīla Prabhupāda: Not moral commands, but the supreme command. As I said, what is moral for you may be immoral for others. One man's food is another's poison. If Kṛṣṇa tells Yudhiṣṭhira to lie, that lying is moral. Kṛṣṇa tells Arjuna to fight and kill, and that killing is moral. Morality means obeying God's order. Because your senses are imperfect, you cannot create morality. You cannot even know what is moral. Therefore you should follow the orders of Kṛṣṇa or His representative. The real categorical imperative is to obey the Supreme. That is morality, and anything else is immoral.

Śyāmasundara dāsa: Then we are not born with a priori knowledge of what is right?

Śrīla Prabhupāda: A priori in the sense that we know we have to obey Kṛṣṇa. That knowledge is manifest even in uncivilized men. When aborigines see a thunderbolt, they offer prayers. It is natural and inborn to offer obeisances.

Śyāmasundara dāsa: Kant says that it is not the act itself which is good or bad, but the will behind the act.

Śrīla Prabhupāda: Yes, but that will has to be developed. A child has will, but it has to be developed by his teacher. Everyone in the material world is in ignorance; therefore it is called a place of darkness. The Vedas advise: "Don't remain in darkness. Go to the light." The spiritual world is light. In the material world, since our will is in darkness, it is bound to be imperfect. The will has to be dragged to the light, and that requires superior help. We cannot think, "I am doing this for a good cause; therefore it is good." In this way, people manufacture all kinds of creeds and act in every way. Guidance is required. We must consult a superior authority for confirmation.

Hayagrīva dāsa: Kant believed that only man can be regarded as nature's own end, or highest product, because on earth only man is capable of complying with the categorical imperative, the moral law.

Śrīla Prabhupāda: But if nature creates man, then nature is supreme. However, nature is only dull matter.

bhūmir āpo'nalo vāyuḥ
khaṁ mano buddhir eva ca
ahaṅkāra itīyaṁ me
bhinnā prakṛtir aṣṭadhā

"Earth, water, fire, air, ether, mind, intelligence, and false ego—altogether these eight comprise My separated material energies." (*Bg.* 7.4) Human beings cannot create these things, nor can nature in itself create them. So how can nature create man? How can man be considered nature's own end or highest product? What is the logic in this philosophy?

Hayagrīva dāsa: Kant would say that man is nature's final end because man's moral nature alone is worthwhile.

Śrīla Prabhupāda: We object to his emphasizing that man is a product of nature. Nature itself cannot make man. Nature provides the body, just as a tailor provides a suit. This body is but the outward covering of the living entity. The living entity within the body is not created by material nature. He is part and parcel of God.

Śyāmasundara dāsa: Kant says that man belongs to "the kingdom of ends" because man is not just an object of utility but an end in himself. Since he alone possesses self-direction, or dignity, he should never stoop to sell himself like a commodity.

Śrīla Prabhupāda: And what is that end? Kant does not give any concrete example. Man's dignity is his inherent quality of obedience to the Supreme. It is that obedience that we should not sacrifice. We are not independent, but subordinate to God's will. Kant may be a strict moralist, but that is not the highest platform. We have to transcend even the moral principle to attain perfection. There is morality and immorality in the material world because there are the three modes of material nature operating: goodness, passion, and ignorance. Morality is on the platform of goodness. According to the transcendental, spiritual point of view, the entire material world is condemned. One may be a first-class prisoner, or a second-class prisoner, a *brāhmaṇa* or a *śūdra*. Whatever the case, one is still a conditioned soul. Of course, as far as conditional life is concerned, there is value in morality. Morality may help us come to the transcendental platform, but coming to that platform is not dependent on morality. It is independent of everything. Kṛṣṇa's order is above morality.

Śyāmasundara dāsa: But might not morality help us see behind the moral law and transcend it?

Śrīla Prabhupāda: Not necessarily. In *Bhagavad-gītā*, we find that Arjuna was trying to become moral by not killing his relatives, but that could not help him. Rather, by directly abiding by the orders of Kṛṣṇa, he transcended morality. So morality in itself does not always help.

Hayagrīva dāsa: Kant spoke of "the starry sky above, and the moral law within." This seems to echo Christ's teaching that "the kingdom of God is within you."

Śrīla Prabhupāda: Yes, if you are actually a lover of God and His instructions, the kingdom of God is within.

Śyāmasundara dāsa: Kant proposes that since the moral law cannot possibly be fulfilled within the limits of one lifetime, the soul must be immortal.

Śrīla Prabhupāda: That is a very good proposition. That is real evolution. Darwin had no idea of the existence of the soul, and he gave some theories about material evolution, which we do not accept. But there is spiritual evolution. Even though a devotee falls down, what he has earned in devotional service will never be lost. In the next life, he begins from that point. However, as far as material activities are concerned, they vanish with the change of body.

Śyāmasundara dāsa: Kant also proposes that since only God can insure the human endeavor for the supreme good, God's existence is a necessary postulate of practical reason.

Śrīla Prabhupāda: We have already explained this. Whatever devotional service is rendered in this life is taken up in the next. Who can give the living entity that chance but God? I may forget, but God does not forget. God is Paramātmā. He is within, and He knows what the living entity has done to this point.

Śyāmasundara dāsa: For Kant, the summum bonum is virtue combined

with happiness. Happiness is the knowledge of doing what is right.
Śrīla Prabhupāda: Happiness means spiritual happiness. There is no material happiness because whatever is material is temporary. Since the spirit soul is eternal, he must have spiritual happiness. That happiness is Kṛṣṇa consciousness. If you know that you are the eternal servant of Kṛṣṇa, and you are serving Kṛṣṇa, that service is your happiness. Even if your duty is painful, you are still happy because you know that you are acting for Kṛṣṇa.
Śyāmasundara dāsa: Kant points out that on earth, happiness does not necessarily accompany goodness; therefore there must be a God who sees that a virtuous man finds his deserved happiness in a future life. Without such justice, there would be no meaning to morality.
Śrīla Prabhupāda: Yes, in the last mantra of *Īśopaniṣad*, it is stated:

agne naya supathā rāya asmān
viśvāni deva vayunāni vidvān
yuyodhy asmaj juhurāṇam eno
bhuyiṣṭhāṁ te nama-uktiṁ vidhema

"O my Lord, powerful as fire, omnipotent One, now I offer You all obeisances, falling on the ground at Your feet. O my Lord, please lead me on the right path to reach You, and, since You know all that I have done in the past, please free me from the reactions to my past sins so that there will be no hindrance to my progress." (*Īśopaniṣad* 18) We should be very sincere in our service to God so that He will relieve us of the reactions of our karma. Unless there is a Supreme, what is the value of morality?
Śyāmasundara dāsa: Kant would say that in his earthly life, a man should not be motivated toward moral conduct out of any expectation of happiness, but out of a sense of duty, or reverence for the moral law.
Śrīla Prabhupāda: Yes, that means unmotivated service. It is not that we love Kṛṣṇa just to receive some benefit. It is our duty. That is pure morality. Knowing that we are part and parcel of Kṛṣṇa, we should render service to Kṛṣṇa without ulterior motivation.
Śyāmasundara dāsa: The goal of Kant's personal ethics is twofold: it is a person's duty to attain his own perfection and also to seek the happiness of others.
Śrīla Prabhupāda: Yes, that is Kṛṣṇa consciousness. A Kṛṣṇa conscious man is not happy thinking, "I have now contacted Kṛṣṇa; therefore my business is finished." Other living entities are also part and parcel of Kṛṣṇa, but due to misguidance, they are not serving Him. Consequently,

they are not attaining happiness. It is the duty of one who knows Kṛṣṇa to preach about Him out of mercy. Those who are satisfied just tending to their own personal spiritual life are not as highly elevated as those who try to enlighten others.
Śyāmasundara dāsa: Pure practical reason, the free will's ability to choose, takes priority over pure speculative reason, or theorizing about reality.
Śrīla Prabhupāda: Yes, it is not sufficient to merely understand that there is a God. We must render service to God. Our Kṛṣṇa consciousness movement means applying knowledge of Kṛṣṇa. If you are a devotee, you must demonstrate it. My Guru Mahārāja therefore condemned those who make a show of being devotees and spend all day and night within closed doors chanting Hare Kṛṣṇa. Sometimes such people smoke and have illicit sex because they are not mature in their devotional service. A neophyte should work for Kṛṣṇa; otherwise he will simply be a showbottle. We have to spread Caitanya Mahāprabhu's teachings all over the world.
Śyāmasundara dāsa: Kant concludes that self-realization is superior to mere philosophy.
Śrīla Prabhupāda: This Kṛṣṇa consciousness movement is a practical demonstration of this. Since we know that we are the eternal servants of Kṛṣṇa, we engage in His service. Kṛṣṇa wants it to be known that He is the Supreme Personality of Godhead. We may either accept this or not—that is all right with Kṛṣṇa—but it is our business to inform everyone that Kṛṣṇa is the Supreme Lord and that everyone else is His eternal servant. If we enlighten people in this way, we are engaged in Kṛṣṇa's service. It is not that we go to church and ask God, "Give us our daily bread." God is giving bread daily to everyone, even to birds and beasts; therefore it is not practical to ask God for what He is already supplying. According to our Vaiṣṇava philosophy, we must work for Kṛṣṇa. We are not just theorizing, but practicing.
Hayagrīva dāsa: Kant rejected church-going as a means to salvation. He states that "sensuous representation of God is contrary to the command of reason: 'Thou shalt not make unto thee any graven image,' etc."
Śrīla Prabhupāda: If someone imagines an image, that is not good. An image arises from the imagination. However, it is different to keep a photograph of your beloved. The photograph of your beloved is not imaginary. It is a fact.
Hayagrīva dāsa: Although rejecting prayer as an inner formal service to God, Kant believed that it is good to teach children to pray so that in

their early years they might accustom themselves to a life pleasing to God.

Śrīla Prabhupāda: Religion means pleasing God, and that is not restricted to children.

Hayagrīva dāsa: Concerning the Christian belief in the resurrection of the body, Kant writes: "For who is so fond of his body that he would wish to drag it about with him through all eternity if he could get on without it?"

Śrīla Prabhupāda: It is natural to want to retain one's body. Even though his life is abominable, a hog will cry when being captured or killed. He does not consider his body to be undesirable, although he is eating stool and living in a filthy place. It is natural to want to protect one's body perpetually, regardless of one's condition. This tendency is there because the living entity is eternal, and he is hankering after that eternity. It is his mistake to desire this eternity in a material body.

Śyāmasundara dāsa: In his book *Eternal Peace*, Kant asserts that there can be peace in the world if certain laws are followed.

Śrīla Prabhupāda: We often hear that peace can be attained, but it can be attained only when we understand that Kṛṣṇa is the factual proprietor of everything. We must accept Kṛṣṇa as our friend and understand that we are not the proprietors of anything. We must know that everything belongs to Kṛṣṇa if peace is to reign.

Hayagrīva dāsa: Concerning government, Kant writes: "An ethical commonwealth can be thought of only as a people under divine commands, as a people of God.... This would be a commonwealth wherein God would be the Lawgiver."

Śrīla Prabhupāda: If the king or president and the people abide by the orders of God, the state will be ideal.

Hayagrīva dāsa: Kant's state would be theocratic in its constitution; however, since priests receive gifts from God directly, they would construct an aristocratic government.

Śrīla Prabhupāda: A theocratic government is properly outlined in *Manu-saṁhitā*, given by Manu for the benefit of all human society.

Śyāmasundara dāsa: Kant believes that there should be a world state in which everyone can participate, and a system of international law regulating relationships between various nations or states.

Śrīla Prabhupāda: This is also our position, the proposition of the International Society for Kṛṣṇa Consciousness. There is one God, and there should be one state. If we can turn the majority of people to Kṛṣṇa consciousness, they will vote for Kṛṣṇa conscious people, and they will not be exploited. The principles that we are following individually can be

introduced on a larger scale.
Śyāmasundara dāsa: Kant believes that the leaders should follow the moral principles, but he rejects Plato's idea that the philosophers should be kings. Rather, they should serve as advisors only. Then they will be able to exercise good judgment.
Śrīla Prabhupāda: That is also the Vedic system. The *brāhmaṇas* advise the *kṣatriyas*. If the *brāhmaṇas* are empowered and try to administer, their philosophical qualities will be diminished. They should remain free and act only as advisors.

Johann Gottlieb Fichte (1762-1814)

Hayagrīva dāsa: Fichte is not as important as Kant or Hegel, but he is in the same tradition. He followed pretty much in the footsteps of Kant. In his first work, entitled *Our Belief in a Divine Government of the Universe*, he writes: "Our belief in a moral world order must be based on the concept of a supersensible world." That is, without the conception of a transcendental reality, morality in the world has no basis.
Śrīla Prabhupāda: First of all, he must define morality. He cannot do this simply by saying, "Our moral principles are...." It is not sufficient to imagine moral principles. Everyone is always saying, "This is moral, and this is immoral." There must be some standard. Following the Vedic scriptures, we say: *kṛṣi-gorakṣya-vāṇijyam (Bg.* 18.44). Cows should be protected. Others claim that cows should be killed in a religious place, in a mosque, synagogue, or whatever. So who is to say what is moral?
Hayagrīva dāsa: Following Kant, Fichte would emphasize inner reality, intuition, or conscience.
Śrīla Prabhupāda: Fichte may follow Kant, and I may follow Kṛṣṇa, but if there is a contradiction, who is to decide which is moral? Who

is to be our leader? How can we decide? In any case, we cannot avoid following some leader, be this leader Lenin, Kṛṣṇa, Kant, or whoever.

Hayagrīva dāsa: Fichte would emphasize the use of individual intuition, or conscience.

Śrīla Prabhupāda: Our conscience is determined according to our association. There is no standard conscience. The conscience of a drunkard says that drinking is good, and the conscience of a devotee says that chanting is good. So which are we to follow? We may follow one definition of God, and others may follow another definition. There must be some standard.

dharmaṁ tu sākṣād bhagavad-praṇītaṁ
na vai vidur ṛṣayo nāpi devaḥ
na siddha-mukhyā asurā manuṣyāḥ
kuto nu vidyādhara-cāraṇādayaḥ

"Real religious principles are enacted by the Supreme Personality of Godhead. Although fully situated in the mode of goodness, even the great *ṛṣis* who occupy the topmost planets cannot ascertain the real religious principles, nor can the demigods or the leaders of Siddhaloka, to say nothing of the *asuras*, ordinary human beings, Vidyādharas and Cāraṇas." (*Bhāg*. 6.3.19) The definition of God and the orders of God are standard. We cannot manufacture God or morality.

Hayagrīva dāsa: For Fichte, the world has no objective reality outside of its being an instrument for the enactment of duty. He sees the world of the senses as the "stuff of duty." He writes, "Our world is the centralized material of our duty....It is our duty that is revealed in the world of the senses."

Śrīla Prabhupāda: If there is no definition of duty, everyone can manufacture his own. Our standard is given by Lord Kṛṣṇa:

sarva-dharmān parityajya
mām ekaṁ śaraṇaṁ vraja
ahaṁ tvāṁ sarva-pāpebhyo
mokṣayiṣyāmi mā śucaḥ

"Abandon all varieties of religion and just surrender unto Me. I shall deliver you from all sinful reaction. Do not fear." (*Bg*. 18.66) So whatever duties have been manufactured should be given up. It is not necessary to go on speculating, because the instructions are very clear. For our standard, we refer to the Vedas. *Śabda-pramāṇam*. If our actions are approved by Vedic injunctions, they will meet the standard and be perfect.

Śyāmasundara dāsa: Fichte believes that the world is a rational unified system directed toward a purpose. It is not a mere machine.
Śrīla Prabhupāda: Yes, we agree to that. The material world is created for the pastimes of the conditioned soul, just as the spiritual world is manifest for the pastimes of Kṛṣṇa. Those who are eternally liberated and enjoy Kṛṣṇa are called *nitya-mukta.* The *nitya-baddha* is a soul conditioned by material nature. These souls, or *jīvas,* are given a chance to play as they like, and they have come here to satisfy their material senses. Ultimately, they should come to their real senses and understand that it is not their business to enjoy material sense objects here but to return home, back to Godhead. This is a good plan, and one who takes advantage of it does not deviate. If one follows the Vedic instructions concerning eating, sleeping, defending, and mating, he can become eligible to return to Godhead very quickly. However, those who manufacture their own way and go against the plan become implicated in *karma-bandhana.* The word *bandhana* means "to be implicated."
Śyāmasundara dāsa: Fichte claims that because the world is a rational system, reason has a very important place. Reason is a real entity or power which performs purposeful acts.
Śrīla Prabhupāda: Yes, that is so. Caitanya Mahāprabhu pointed out that the living entity is the eternal servant of Kṛṣṇa. If he utilizes his reason, he can understand very well what he is doing here. He can understand that he is receiving everything through his senses, and by acting in this way and that, has become a servant of his senses. People cannot master their senses, yet they are prepared to try to master the world, or society. The living entity is not the master, yet he artificially attempts to be master. We attain knowledge when we realize that we are not masters but the eternal servants of Kṛṣṇa. People are trying to serve their senses, their family, their country, society, dog, or whatever. This service is misplaced. By the use of reason, we can come to the understanding that we are eternal servants of Kṛṣṇa. When we abandon the service of the senses, of māyā, and take to Kṛṣṇa's service, we attain liberation, *mukti.*
Hayagrīva dāsa: Fichte believes that true atheism consists in "...refusing to obey the voice of one's conscience until one thinks that one can foresee the success of one's actions and thus elevating one's own judgment above that of God and in making oneself into God. He who wills to do evil in order to produce good is a godless person."
Śrīla Prabhupāda: If you do not know God or His orders, how can you verify your duty? Do you simply manufacture your duty? Anyone can

do that. First of all, you must understand what is meant by duty. Duty means following the orders given by your superior, but if you have no superior, if you have no conception of the Supreme and His order, how can you know your duty? Of course, you may imagine your duty. Is this what he advises?

Hayagrīva dāsa: He is vague on this point.

Śrīla Prabhupāda: Because he does not know. According to the Vedas, we have definite, prescribed duties. Society is divided into eight divisions comprising the *varṇāśrama-dharma.* There are four *varṇas (brāhmaṇa, kṣatriya, vaiśya,* and *śūdra),* and four *āśramas (brahmacārī, gṛhastha, vānaprastha,* and *sannyāsa).* Whatever you do, you must function according to one of these *varṇas* or *āśramas,* and there are duties prescribed for each. If you follow the principles that are set forth specifically for each stage of life, you are doing your duty.

Hayagrīva dāsa: For Fichte, our knowledge of God arises from the enactment of our duty.

Śrīla Prabhupāda: That is all right, but what is our duty? God must assign our duty for us to understand God by enacting our duty. But if we have no conception of God, how can we know what our duty is?

Śyāmasundara dāsa: For Fichte, self-consciousness is the basic principle of human knowledge and our means for searching out the Absolute.

Śrīla Prabhupāda: That self-consciousness should be "I am the eternal servant of Kṛṣṇa." This can be realized by practice, by education, and by study of the Vedas.

Śyāmasundara dāsa: Fichte believes that the philosopher's search for the truth begins with a demand for fulfillment—that is, "Think thyself!"

Śrīla Prabhupāda: We should think, "What am I?" By profound meditation, we can understand, "I am not this body but something else. I am eternal. I existed in the past, I exist now, and I will continue to exist in the future. Whatever I am doing now in the material world is separate and temporary. But what is my eternal duty?" If we understand our position and learn from a spiritual master that we are the eternal servants of Kṛṣṇa, we will take to Kṛṣṇa's service—that is, if we are sensible. In this way, we can attain a higher position.

Hayagrīva dāsa: Fichte was ambiguous and vague when he wrote of God as a personal being. He seemed to lean toward pantheism or impersonalism.

Śrīla Prabhupāda: If he is an impersonalist, he has no understanding of his master, God, who is giving him his duty.

Hayagrīva dāsa: He looked on the attribution of personality to God as simply a multiplication of oneself in one's own thoughts.

Śrīla Prabhupāda: If our understanding of God is only impersonal, where is God's leadership? Is there any question of leadership in impersonalism?

Hayagrīva dāsa: Well, he feels that if you attribute personality to God, you are projecting yourself onto God—that is, you are manufacturing God.

Śrīla Prabhupāda: We cannot manufacture God by giving Him imaginary attributes. Whatever attributes we ascribe to Him must be logical. For instance, we say, "God is great" because we have some conception of greatness, and we understand that greatness must be in God. Or we say that God is supremely wealthy, and that also is quite reasonable. We say that God is supreme, and that also logically follows. The attributes of God given by Parāśara Muni—knowledge, fame, wealth, strength, beauty, and renunciation—all combine to give a reasonable definition.

Hayagrīva dāsa: Like many other impersonalists, Fichte believes that if you attribute personality to God, you necessarily limit Him.

Śrīla Prabhupāda: He is thinking that God's personality is finite like his, and that is his mistake. Kṛṣṇa's personality is not like that of an ordinary man. As soon as it was necessary to protect the inhabitants of Vṛndāvana from the torrents of Indra, Kṛṣṇa immediately lifted Govardhana Hill to serve as an umbrella. When He did this, He appeared as a seven-year-old boy. He did not have to meditate for years in order to become God. Presently, rascals are meditating to try to become God, but what kind of God? God is always God. He is the transcendental personality, and there is no need for Him to meditate.

Hayagrīva dāsa: Fichte rejects the personality of God because he felt that "the concept of God as a separate substance is impossible and contradictory."

Śrīla Prabhupāda: Since God is everything, there is no question of separation. As stated in *Bhagavad-gītā:*

mayā tatam idaṁ sarvaṁ
jagad avyakta-mūrtinā
mat-sthāni sarva bhūtāni
na cāhaṁ teṣv avasthitaḥ

"By Me, in My unmanifested form, this entire universe is pervaded. All beings are in Me, but I am not in them." (*Bg.* 9.4) If everything is in God, how can He be separate?

Hayagrīva dāsa: He rejects God as a separate person.
Śrīla Prabhupāda: If God is everything, why is He not a separate person also? There is no question of rejection. If he admits that God is everything, how can he reject God's personality?
Hayagrīva dāsa: Since Fichte's pantheism would not admit that God is more than the creation, he would reject the transcendental personality.
Śrīla Prabhupāda: Then he is trying to create God after his own conceptions. But if he admits that God is everything, how can he reject God's transcendental personality? If God is everything, He is that which is transcendental, as well as what is not. Those who follow the Vedas do not reject any part of God. They see God in everything. *Īśāvāsyam idaṁ sarvam (Īśopaniṣad* 1). A real Vaiṣṇava sees everything related to God. If one thinks, "This is matter, and this is spirit," he is speculating. We have to see God in relation to everything. When we do not, everything becomes material. Materialism means forgetfulness of God.
Hayagrīva dāsa: Most people, including Fichte, would find it difficult to concentrate on the transcendental personality of Kṛṣṇa, especially when they know nothing about Kṛṣṇa.
Śrīla Prabhupāda: It requires a little intelligence and purification. Once the impurities are cleansed from the mirror of the mind, we can understand; otherwise, we think of God as a ordinary person.

ānanda-cinmaya-rasa-pratibhāvitābhis
tābhir ya eva nija-rūpatayā kalābhiḥ
goloka eva nivasaty akhilātma-bhūto
govindam ādi-puruṣaṁ tam ahaṁ bhajāmi

"I worship Govinda, the primeval Lord, who resides in His own realm, Goloka, with Rādhā, who resembles His own spiritual figure and who embodies the ecstatic potency [*hlādinī*]. Their companions are Her confidantes, who embody extensions of Her bodily form and who are imbued and permeated with ever-blissful spiritual *rasa*." (*Brahma-saṁhitā* 5.37) God is a person living in Goloka Vṛndāvana, dancing with the *gopīs,* and playing with the cowherd boys. Despite this, God is everywhere. It is not that because He is dancing, He has no time to go anywhere. Although He dances in Goloka Vṛndāvana, He is still present everywhere. *Īśvaraḥ sarva-bhūtānāṁ hṛd-deśe.* "The Supreme Lord is in everyone's heart." (*Bg.* 18.61) By His inconceivable potencies, God can be in one place and everywhere else simultaneously. This is the philosophy of *acintya-bhedābheda-tattva*—simultaneously, inconceivably one with the creation and different from it.

Hayagrīva dāsa: Although an impersonalist, Fichte is certainly not an inactivist. In *The Vocation of Man*, he writes: "Not merely to know, but according to thy knowledge to do, is thy vocation.... Not for idle contemplation of thyself, not for brooding over devout sensations—no, for action art thou here; thine action, and thine action alone, determines thy worth."

Śrīla Prabhupāda: Yes, and that is also the philosophy of our Kṛṣṇa consciousness movement, which maintains that we are meant for rendering daily service to Kṛṣṇa. We do not believe that you should simply sit down, smoke cigarettes, and speculate on God. What will be the use of such speculation? We advocate a practical life of action devoted to Kṛṣṇa.

Hayagrīva dāsa: In this, Fichte seems closer to Vaiṣṇavism than most impersonalists, who advocate inaction and meditation on the void. At the same time, how can you act without directing your action toward some person or specific goal?

Śrīla Prabhupāda: Even in India, the impersonalists have some activities. Śaṅkarācārya gives many *vairāgya* instructions, which are more difficult to perform than the Vaiṣṇava instructions. As far as Vaiṣṇavism is concerned, Caitanya Mahāprabhu taught through His personal example that there is no time for inactivity. We should not sit idly and gossip about God or imagine what He is like. Both personalists and impersonalists are fully engaged: the impersonalists in reading *Vedānta-sūtra*, and the personalists in rendering service unto the Supreme Personality of Godhead.

Śyāmasundara dāsa: Fichte says that in order to understand reality, reason must follow a process called the dialectical method, which involves thesis, antithesis, and synthesis. First comes the thesis, which fails to provide an adequate solution; this gives rise to an antithesis, the opposite, which is also inadequate; the dilemma is resolved by combining the two into a synthesis.

Śrīla Prabhupāda: The thesis is that I am trying to be master of this material world. The antithesis is that my spiritual master informs me that I am the eternal servant of God. The synthesis is that I become master and servant simultaneously, because by serving Kṛṣṇa, I master my senses.

Śyāmasundara dāsa: According to Fichte, the thesis is the ego; the antithesis is the non-ego; and the synthesis is the unification of ego and non-ego.

Śrīla Prabhupāda: The ego arises when I think, "I am the monarch of all I survey." The antithesis is, "I am not the monarch but the servant of my senses." Through the synthesis, I become a servant of Kṛṣṇa and simultaneously a master of the senses, a *svāmī*, or *gosvāmī*.

Śyāmasundara dāsa: For Fichte, this dialectical process is endless, for each synthesis in turn becomes a new thesis, etc. However, the ultimate synthesis is the Absolute, or God.

Śrīla Prabhupāda: It is explained in *Bhagavad-gītā* that those who attempt to attain God in this way, through the process of mental speculation, eventually attain God, but only after many lives. However, one who is intelligent immediately surrenders when he understands God to say, "Just surrender unto Me." This saves time. You can come to the ultimate synthesis, God, by immediately surrendering. If you can perfect your life immediately, why perpetuate this process?

Śyāmasundara dāsa: Fichte states that the original thesis, or the starting point, is the person and his consciousness, the ego. The antithesis is the object of consciousness, phenomena, the non-ego. The synthesis arises with the unification of the subject-object.

Śrīla Prabhupāda: The Vedas admit that there is direct knowledge, then knowledge received from authority. These combine to form transcendental, spiritual knowledge. At present, our ego is false because we are thinking, "I am matter. I am this body." When we come to real knowledge, we understand that we are spirit soul. This is our true identity. The function of the individual spirit soul is to eternally serve the supreme spirit soul, Kṛṣṇa.

Śyāmasundara dāsa: For Fichte, ultimate reality is the moral ego. This is the pure will, active reason, or the good.

Śrīla Prabhupāda: Yes, God is also the ego. We say, "I am," and God also says, "I am." However, God's "I am" is superior to ours. He is the eternal primal living force. We are also eternal living force, but we are subordinate.

Hayagrīva dāsa: Fichte considered faith to be the real basis of action. He felt that knowledge in itself was insufficient.

Śrīla Prabhupāda: Yes, faith must be there. We see faith exhibited even amongst the lower species. We see cygnets following their mother swan into the water to swim and play. Faith is quite natural.

Hayagrīva dāsa: In Kṛṣṇa consciousness, does faith or knowledge serve as the basis for action?

Śrīla Prabhupāda: In the last chapter of *Bhagavad-gītā,* Kṛṣṇa tells us to abandon everything and just surrender unto Him (*Bg.* 18.66). Now this requires full faith. If we speculate about this, we do not have faith. In *Caitanya-caritāmṛta*, faith is described:

śraddhā-śabde—viśvāsa kahe sudṛḍha niścaya
kṛṣṇe bhakti kaile sarva-karma kṛta haya

"By rendering transcendental loving service to Kṛṣṇa, one automatically performs all subsidiary activities. This confident, firm faith, favorable to the discharge of devotional service, is called *śraddhā*." (*Caitanya-caritāmṛta*, Madh. 22.62) Faith means believing firmly. If we have firm faith, we will become perfect by surrendering unto Kṛṣṇa. If we still have reservations, we cannot have firm faith. We may then ask how this faith comes to be, and to this, *Bhagavad-gītā* answers:

bahūnāṁ janmanām ante
jñānavān māṁ prapadyate
vāsudevaḥ sarvam iti
sa mahātmā sudurlabhaḥ

"After many births and deaths, he who is actually in knowledge surrenders unto Me, knowing Me to be the cause of all causes and all that is. Such a great soul is very rare." (*Bg.* 7.19) This faith, therefore, is not very easily come by. Piety is also required of a candidate. Kṛṣṇa appeared on the battlefield of Kurukṣetra five thousand years ago, and *Bhagavad-gītā* has recently been studied by many people like Gandhi, Dr. Radhakrishnan, Vivekananda, and Aurovinda. But where is their faith? They have taken advantage of *Bhagavad-gītā* by interpreting it according to their own pleasure. They have never taught complete surrender unto Kṛṣṇa. That requires firm faith in Kṛṣṇa. In any case, in this Kṛṣṇa consciousness movement, we are teaching our students how to capture Kṛṣṇa through firm faith. There are many faithless people, including yogīs and *svāmīs*, who are commenting on *Bhagavad-gītā*, but this is useless. In the beginning, there must be firm faith. Faith is the foundation. If the foundation is lost, how can a big building stand?

Hayagrīva dāsa: Fichte believes that faith is innate in all men. He writes: "So has it been with all men who have ever seen the light of the world. Without being conscious of it, they apprehend all the reality which has an existence for them through faith alone. This faith forces itself on them simultaneously with their existence. It is born with them. How could it be otherwise?"

Śrīla Prabhupāda: Yes, and this faith is also strengthened by experience. For instance, in the world we understand that everything has some proprietor. Since this is the case, why shouldn't the entire cosmic manifestation have a proprietor? We may not see the proprietor, but we accept His existence on faith.

Hayagrīva dāsa: Concerning the infallibility of conscience, Fichte writes: "This voice of my conscience announces to me precisely what I ought to do, and what leave undone, in every particular situation of life....To listen to it, to obey honestly and unreservedly...is my true vocation, the whole end and purpose of my existence."

Śrīla Prabhupāda: As soon as he says that he listens, he indicates that someone is speaking. That someone is God situated in everyone's heart and dictating. This is explained in *Bhagavad-gītā:*

īśvaraḥ sarva-bhūtānāṁ
hṛd-deśe'rjuna tiṣṭhati
bhrāmayan sarva-bhūtāni
yantrārūḍhāni māyayā

"The Supreme Lord is situated in everyone's heart, O Arjuna, and is directing the wanderings of all living entities, who are seated as on a machine, made of the material energy." (*Bg.* 18.61) Thus God is dictating to everyone. He is telling the thief, "You may go out and steal, but this is not good. If you are arrested, you'll be punished." That dictation is there, and if one disobeys and goes ahead and steals, he commits sin. God is there giving dictations within the heart, and we may either obey or disobey. If we obey, we become devotees. As I said before, the dictations come from the heart, and also from the scriptures and the spiritual master. If we regularly disobey, how can we be happy?

Hayagrīva dāsa: Fichte is typical of the impersonalist in his desire to merge into what he calls "the universal Ego." He feels that this should be our ultimate goal.

Śrīla Prabhupāda: In this material world, we all have some ego. We think, "I am the husband of this woman, I am the head of this family, I am the president of this state, and so on." These are different manifestations of ego. However, we cannot say, "I am the master of this entire universe. I am the universal ego." That is also called false ego.

Hayagrīva dāsa: Fichte thinks that we can go through the universe embracing and assimilating everything until we finally unify with the impersonal Absolute.

Śrīla Prabhupāda: As soon as we speak of "Absolute," there is no distinction between the impersonal and the personal. If there is a distinction, you are not referring to the Absolute. It is contradictory to speak of the "impersonal Absolute."

Hayagrīva dāsa: More precisely, Fichte would consider the original thesis to be one's own consciousness, or ego; the antithesis to be the object of consciousness, sense phenomena, or the non-ego; and the synthesis to be the unification of these opposites.

Śrīla Prabhupāda: He is distinguishing between the ego and non-ego, and between the personal and the impersonal, but in the Absolute, there are no such distinctions.

vadanti tat tattva-vidas
tattvaṁ yaj jñānam advayam
brahmeti paramātmeti
bhagavān iti śabdyate

"Learned transcendentalists who know the Absolute Truth call this nondual substance Brahman, Paramātmā, and Bhagavān." (*Bhāg.* 1.2.11) In the Absolute, there is no duality. When we search for the Absolute Truth, we may realize it in three different aspects: as Brahman, as Paramātmā, and as Bhagavān. Depending on our relationship to the Absolute, the Absolute appears in different ways, but this is not due to some inconsistency in the Absolute. The Absolute is always one, but due to our relative position, we see the Absolute as the impersonal all-pervading Brahman, as the localized Supersoul, or as the Supreme Personality of Godhead, Bhagavān. Ultimately, the Absolute is Bhagavān, and the impersonal feature is resting on Him. *Brahmaṇo hi pratiṣṭhāham.* "I am the basis of the impersonal Brahman." (*Bg.* 14.27) We may attempt to merge with the impersonal aspect, Brahman, but our position will not be permanent. As for merging or unifying with the Absolute Supreme Personality of Godhead, Bhagavān, this is not possible. It is not possible for the finite living entity to become the infinite God.

Georg Wilhelm Friedrich Hegel
(1770-1831)

Śyāmasundara dāsa: Hegel sought to synthesize other philosophies to arrive at the truth, and in so doing, he concluded that everything that exists is reason; what is real is rational, and what is rational is real.
Śrīla Prabhupāda: This means that he wanted to arrive at the Absolute in whom there is no duality. That is Kṛṣṇa. Kṛṣṇa says:

paritrāṇāya sādhūnāṁ
vināśāya ca duṣkṛtām
dharma-saṁsthāpanārthāya
sambhavāmi yuge yuge

"In order to deliver the pious and to annihilate the miscreants, as well as to reestablish the principles of religion, I appear Myself millennium after millennium." (*Bg*. 4.8) He comes to earth to protect the devotees and kill the demons. Although He actually did this, we should not think that He is partial. When He killed the great demon Pūtanā, for instance, Pūtanā attained a position like Kṛṣṇa's mother Yaśodā. Because Kṛṣṇa is Absolute, there is no difference between His loving Yaśodā and killing Pūtanā. Whatever He does is good: be it killing or loving. The two opposites are reconciled in Him. The Sanskrit word for this is *viruddārtha-*

sambandha.

Śyāmasundara dāsa: Hegel saw that his predecessors had become so increasingly abstract in trying to find out the nature of substance, that they had reduced substance to nothingness.

Śrīla Prabhupāda: This was due to ignorance. That is called *virasa*. When one cannot understand the nature or form of God through speculation, out of frustration he says, "Oh, there is no God."

Śyāmasundara dāsa: Hegel's predecessors analyzed an object into smaller and smaller parts until they arrived at a nonentity.

Śrīla Prabhupāda: The fact is that the Absolute cannot be divided into parts. In *Bhagavad-gītā* it is stated:

nainaṁ chindanti śastrāṇi
nainaṁ dahati pāvakaḥ
na cainaṁ kledayanty āpo
na śoṣayati mārutaḥ

"The soul can never be cut into pieces by any weapon, nor can he be burned by fire, nor moistened by water, nor withered by the wind." (*Bg.* 2.23) It is possible to cut a material thing into pieces, but it is impossible to divide a spiritual being. A spiritual being is inexhaustible. The Māyāvādīs think that since the Absolute is all-pervading, He has no form, but this is incorrect. The Absolute can maintain His form as He is and yet expand Himself. Kṛṣṇa says, *mayā tatam idaṁ sarvaṁ jagad avyakta-mūrtinā.* "By Me, in My unmanifested form, this entire universe is pervaded." (*Bg.* 9.4) Kṛṣṇa has three features: *brahmeti paramātmeti bhagavān iti śabdyate (Bhāg.* 1.2.11)—the impersonal, localized, and personal. Unless we come to understand this science, it is very difficult to know the forms of the Absolute Truth. One who is incompetent, who has a poor fund of knowledge, concludes that the Absolute Truth is *nirākāra*, void, but this is not so.

Śyāmasundara dāsa: Hegel wanted to reverse the trend from abstraction to concretion. He believed that every phenomenal object has its relationship with the whole, which is reality. To understand reality, we must examine all objects and relate them to the whole and to each other.

Śrīla Prabhupāda: That is our process. The whole is Kṛṣṇa, and everything is related to Kṛṣṇa. Because we see everything related to Kṛṣṇa, we do not artificially renounce anything, but try to utilize everything in the service of Kṛṣṇa. Although the Māyāvādī philosophers say that everything is Brahman, their process is *neti-neti*: "Not this, not that." In this way, the Māyāvādīs say that Kṛṣṇa and His worship are also māyā. Our philosophy is that everything is a manifestation of Kṛṣṇa's energy; the energy and the energetic are one. Nārada explained:

idaṁ hi viśvaṁ bhagavān ivetaro
yato jagat-sthāna-nirodha-sambhavāḥ
tad dhi svayaṁ veda bhavāṁs tathāpi te
prādeśa-mātraṁ bhavataḥ pradarśitam

"The Supreme Lord Personality of Godhead is Himself this cosmos, and still He is aloof from it. From Him only has this cosmic manifestation emanated, in Him it rests, and unto Him it enters after annihilation. Your good self knows all about this. I have given only a synopsis." (*Bhāg.* 1.5.20) The whole universe is Bhagavān, Kṛṣṇa, but it appears to be separate. How it is not separate can be understood through Kṛṣṇa consciousness. Ordinary men think of Kṛṣṇa and non-Kṛṣṇa, but there is no non-Kṛṣṇa. That is illusion. Everything is Kṛṣṇa.

Śyāmasundara dāsa: For Hegel, nothing can be separated from the spiritual whole because everything is related to it. For Kant, phenomenon is the mode in which things-in-themselves represent themselves to the individual.

Śrīla Prabhupāda: It is explained in *Bhagavad-gītā* that Kṛṣṇa has two energies: the spiritual and the material. His spiritual energy is described as superior, and His material energy as inferior. These designations are given for our consideration because we cannot understand otherwise, but the fact is that there is only one energy: the superior spiritual energy. When this spiritual energy is covered by ignorance, it is called material energy. The sky is naturally clear, and we can normally see the sun, but when there are clouds, we cannot see it. Still, the sun is there. When we cannot see Kṛṣṇa or understand Him, we experience what is called the material energy. The fact is that there is nothing material because everything is Kṛṣṇa.

Śyāmasundara dāsa: Hegel says that objects themselves are the spirit expressing itself in objective nature, whereas Kant maintains that the spirit expresses itself through objects. There is a distinction made between the spirit within the object expressing itself, and the spirit as the object.

Śrīla Prabhupāda: The object as it is is spirit. In one sense, the sunshine is not the sun, but at the same time, it is not different from the sun because it is the sun's heat and light. Therefore our philosophy is *acintya-bhedābheda-tattva:* simultaneously one and different. All these objects are actually spirit, but if we have no sense of Kṛṣṇa, we consider them to be material. Sometimes people criticize us for using material devices like dictaphones, typewriters, and airplanes, but we reply that these things are spiritual. If they are used for our sense gratification, they are material, but if used in relation to Kṛṣṇa, they are spiritual. It is the consciousness that is important. Rūpa Gosvāmī says:

anāsaktasya viṣayān
yathārham upayuñjataḥ
nirbandhaḥ kṛṣṇa-sambandhe
yuktaṁ vairāgyam ucyate

prāpañcikatayā buddhyā
hari-sambandhi-vastunaḥ
mumukṣubhiḥ parityāgo
vairāgyaṁ phalgu kathyate

"One is said to be situated in the fully renounced order of life if he lives in accordance with Kṛṣṇa consciousness. He should be without attachment for sense gratification and should accept only what is necessary for the upkeep of the body. On the other hand, one who renounces things which could be used in the service of Kṛṣṇa, under the pretext that such things are material, does not practice complete renunciation." (*Bhakti-rasāmṛta-sindhu* 1.2.255-256) Everything has its relationship with Kṛṣṇa. Rejecting everything as false is artificial renunciation. Our method is to renounce things for our sense gratification, but accept everything for Kṛṣṇa's satisfaction. Kṛṣṇa says:

māṁ ca yo'vyabhicāreṇa
bhakti-yogena sevate
sa guṇān samatītyaitān
brahma-bhūyāya kalpate

"One who engages in full devotional service, who does not fall down in any circumstances, at once transcends the modes of material nature and thus comes to the level of Brahman." (*Bg.* 14.26) As soon as we engage fully in devotional service, we are immediately spiritualized. When we are in devotional service, the spiritual quality of everything is revived. In truth, everything is spirit, but it is covered by our material consciousness, just as gold may be covered by mud. If we cleanse the heart, we immediately understand that things are spiritual. In material consciousness, we conceive of ourselves as Americans, Indians, men, women, and so on, but when we come to our spiritual consciousness, we realize, "I am Kṛṣṇa's servant." Thus we understand that we are spiritual. These material conceptions are like dreams. When we are dreaming, we may think that we are this or that, or that we are performing so many acts, but when we awake, we understand our real identity. Because we are part and parcel of Kṛṣṇa, we have no duty other than to serve Kṛṣṇa. When this consciousness comes, everything is spiritual.

Hayagrīva dāsa: In *Philosophy of Religion*, Hegel writes: "God is a living God, who is acting and working. Religion is a product of the divine spirit; it is not a discovery of man, but a work of divine operation and creation in Him [God]."

Śrīla Prabhupāda: Yes, it is very important to understand that a man cannot manufacture religion. We define religion as "the orders given by God." As stated in *Bhagavad-gītā:*

yadā yadā hi dharmasya
glānir bhavati bhārata
abhyutthānam adharmasya
tadātmānaṁ sṛjāmyaham

paritrāṇāya sādhūnāṁ
vināśāya ca duṣkṛtām
dharma-saṁsthāpanārthāya
sambhavāmi yuge yuge

"Whenever and wherever there is a decline in religious practice, O descendant of Bharata, and a predominant rise of irreligion—at that time, I descend Myself. In order to deliver the pious and to annihilate the miscreants, as well as to reestablish the principles of religion, I appear Myself millennium after millennium." (*Bg.* 4.7-8) This is religion. Religion rests on the orders of Kṛṣṇa, or God, and if you strictly follow Kṛṣṇa's instructions, you are religious, pious, and transcendental. If you defy Kṛṣṇa and manufacture your own religion, you are asuric, demoniac.

Śyāmasundara dāsa: According to Plato's and Kant's philosophy, these temporary objects are representations of an ideal. This table, for instance, represents or expresses the ideal table, but it is not the ideal itself.

Śrīla Prabhupāda: We also say that this material world is a perverted reflection of the spiritual world. It is like a mirage. Śrīdhara Svāmī said that it is due to the actuality of the spiritual world that this illusory world appears to be true. Because there is in reality a real table, we can perceive this table. Although the entire material creation is but a perverted reflection of the reality, people are enamored by it. People take this to be a real table, a real body, a real society, real happiness, and so on.

Śyāmasundara dāsa: Hegel would say that these are genuine externalizations of the reality, that this is a real table and that these are real objects. It is not that they are images of the real, but that they themselves are real.
Śrīla Prabhupāda: What does he mean by real? For us, reality means that which does and will exist. If this is not the case, it is not real.

nāsato vidyate bhāvo
nābhāvo vidyate sataḥ
ubhayor api dṛṣṭo'ntas
tv anayos tattva-darśibhiḥ

"Those who are seers of the truth have concluded that of the nonexistent there is no endurance, and of the existent there is no cessation. This seers have concluded by studying the nature of both." (*Bg.* 2.16) Reality refers to that which exists eternally. This table exists temporarily; therefore it cannot be classified as reality. It is like a dream or hallucination because it is temporary. We cannot say that a dream is real, although in a dream everything appears to be real.
Śyāmasundara dāsa: But isn't there a table on the spiritual platform? An absolute table?
Śrīla Prabhupāda: Yes, in Kṛṣṇa's abode there are tables, chairs, all kinds of furniture eternally existing. But these things are manifest here only temporarily.
Śyāmasundara dāsa: Which is correct? Does the spirit express itself in this object, or is it that the spirit is this object?
Śrīla Prabhupāda: The object is an expression of the spiritual energy. Whatever is manifest is the energy of Kṛṣṇa, but one energy is eternal, and another energy is temporary. That which is manifest temporarily is material, and that which is manifest eternally is spiritual.
Śyāmasundara dāsa: So, in that sense, can you say that this table is made of spirit, but at the same time is not?
Śrīla Prabhupāda: Originally, it is made of spirit in the sense that Kṛṣṇa is the whole spirit, and because it is Kṛṣṇa's energy, it is factually Kṛṣṇa. You may make various images out of clay. You may mold pots and bricks, and they may be manifest temporarily as pots and bricks, but originally they are clay, and when they are destroyed, they will again merge into their original condition. There are three conditions: the formless condition, the form, and again a merging into the formless. In *Śrīmad-Bhāgavatam*, Kṛṣṇa tells Lord Brahmā:

aham evāsam evāgre

nānyad yat sad-asat param
paścād ahaṁ yad etac ca
yo'vaśiṣyeta so'smy aham

"It is I, the Personality of Godhead, who was existing before the creation when there was nothing but Myself. Nor was there the material nature, the cause of this creation. That which you see now is also I, the Personality of Godhead, and after annihilation what remains will also be I, the Personality of Godhead." (*Bhāg.* 2.9.33) So, Kṛṣṇa existed in the beginning of the creation; He maintains the creation; and when the creation is annihilated, He continues to exist.

Śyāmasundara dāsa: Therefore the Māyāvādīs would say that this table is māyā?

Śrīla Prabhupāda: They say that it is māyā, but we say that it is temporary.

Śyāmasundara dāsa: But there's also a spiritual world full of form?

Śrīla Prabhupāda: Yes, but the Māyāvādīs do not know of this. What is the source of these forms? The *Vedānta-sūtra* states: *janmādy asya.* Form comes from the original source. These forms that we see here are not eternal forms. They are imitations, perverted reflections of eternal forms. A reflection is not eternal.

Śyāmasundara dāsa: Hegel says that these forms are not eternal but that the interaction of forms is an eternal process.

Śrīla Prabhupāda: A mirage is neither factual nor eternal, but there is factual and eternal water. Otherwise, how could anyone have a conception of water?

Śyāmasundara dāsa: But if the universe is rational and everything has a purpose, this temporary form is also spiritual because it has some kind of purpose.

Śrīla Prabhupāda: Yes, we are utilizing everything for Kṛṣṇa's purpose. Our proposal is to make the best use of a bad bargain.

Śyāmasundara dāsa: But what if a person doesn't know the purpose? Is the object still spiritual?

Śrīla Prabhupāda: Yes. Whether a person knows or does not know, fact is fact. We have only to receive knowledge from one who knows. All objects are spiritual, but one who does not have knowledge does not have the eyes to see that spirituality.

Śyāmasundara dāsa: Then, is God's plan unfolding itself everywhere, whether we understand it or not?

Śrīla Prabhupāda: Yes, He reveals Himself in *Bhagavad-gītā,* and He sends His representative to unfold His plan. The essence of things is spiritual, but our imperfect vision makes things material.

Śyāmasundara dāsa: Hegel believes that everything has a purpose, that the whole universe is rational, and that it is unfolding under the direction of reason, the spirit of the Absolute.

Śrīla Prabhupāda: Certainly. Only rascals think that there is no purpose in life, that everything is a result of chance.

Śyāmasundara dāsa: For Hegel, in order to understand this reality, we must examine the interrelationships of things.

Śrīla Prabhupāda: We are also teaching that. The origin of everything is Kṛṣṇa, and Kṛṣṇa's energetic expansions constitute everything.

parasya brahmaṇaḥ sākṣāj
jāta-vedo 'si havyavāṭ
devānāṁ puruṣāṅgānāṁ
yajñena puruṣaṁ yajeti

"O fire-god, you are a part of the Supreme Personality of Godhead, Hari, and you carry to Him all the offerings of sacrifices. Therefore we request you to offer to Him the sacrificial ingredients we are offering the demigods, for the Lord is the real enjoyer." (*Bhāg.* 5.20.17) Physical existence is heat and light, and these energies emanate from Kṛṣṇa, the original light. Everything material and spiritual is composed of heat and light. One who has eyes to see that which is spiritual can see.

Śyāmasundara dāsa: Hegel attempted to establish the relationship between concrete realities. Isolated facts, or moments, as he calls them, can never constitute the truth because the truth is the whole, an integrated unity that is organic and dynamic.

Śrīla Prabhupāda: Just by analyzing ourselves, we can understand that I, the soul, am existing and that my bodily features are changing. When things change, we call them material. The spirit soul exists in all conditions, and that is the difference between spirit and matter.

Śyāmasundara dāsa: Moments, factors in the organic whole, progress in an evolutionary way according to the course set by reason, which Hegel calls the *Welt Geist*, the World Spirit.

Śrīla Prabhupāda: That World Spirit is a person. Unless you accept a personal God, there is no question of reason. The reason guiding everything in the universe is explained in *Bhagavad-gītā: mayādhyakṣeṇa prakṛtiḥ*. "This material nature is working under My direction." (*Bg.* 9.10) Direction means reason; therefore as soon as you speak of reason, you must accept the Supreme Person who is directing everything according to His supreme reason.

Śyāmasundara dāsa: Would you say that all world events are expressions of this World Spirit, or world reason, unfolding itself? If so, what is the ultimate purpose of that plan?
Śrīla Prabhupāda: Yes, there is a plan, otherwise why would Kṛṣṇa say *adhyakṣeṇa*, superintendence? There is a plan, direction, and also reason. The living entities are part and parcel of Kṛṣṇa, and somehow or other they wanted to enjoy this material world. Therefore Kṛṣṇa has given them a chance, just as a father gives a chance to his small children to play. Kṛṣṇa says:

sarvasya cāhaṁ hṛdi sanniviṣṭho
mattaḥ smṛtir jñānam apohanaṁ ca

"I am seated in everyone's heart, and from Me come remembrance, knowledge, and forgetfulness." (*Bg.* 15.15) The whole plan is that Kṛṣṇa gives the living entity freedom to play and then again come home. He says, "All right, you want to play, but when you are tired of all this nonsense, give it up and come back to Me." This world is like a playground for conditioned souls, and the body is like a small field (*kṣetra*) on which the living entity wants to play.

idaṁ śarīraṁ kaunteya
kṣetram ity abhidhīyate
etad yo vetti taṁ prāhuḥ
kṣetrajñaḥ iti tad-vidaḥ

"This body, O son of Kuntī, is called the field, and one who knows this body is called the knower of the field." (*Bg.* 13.2) The material body is nothing but a field of action, and Kṛṣṇa says, "All right, utilize this field and enjoy yourself. When you are exhausted playing in this field, you can have another." In this way, the living entity is changing bodies, changing different fields of action.
Śyāmasundara dāsa: Is this play aimless, or is there gradual evolution?
Śrīla Prabhupāda: There is a goal. Kṛṣṇa gives us knowledge, and the Vedas are also there. Kṛṣṇa says, "This play is not very healthy; therefore I request that you give it up and come back to Me." This is the plan.
Śyāmasundara dāsa: According to the Hegelian dialectic, being and nothing are empty abstractions. Being is the thesis, nothing is the antithesis, and the synthesis is change, becoming.
Śrīla Prabhupāda: The question of becoming arises because we are now in this awkward, marginal position. Although I am eternal, I have been trapped by something mortal. Consequently, I am changing my position, and this is called transmigration. When I cease transmigrating, I attain

my own true being, which is eternal.

Śyāmasundara dāsa: Hegel believes that when the dialectic is exhausted, it reveals the whole, unified Absolute Truth. But since nature is constantly unfolding, guided by the World Spirit, the dialectic process continues indefinitely.

Śrīla Prabhupāda: In other words, you cannot find out the ultimate synthesis. Therefore you have to receive information from *śāstra*. The thesis is that the soul within the body is immortal, and the antithesis is that the body is mortal. The liberation of the soul from the body is the synthesis. When we understand that we are in an awkward position within this material world, we strive for liberation. Unless we understand that we are entrapped, there is no question of liberation.

Śyāmasundara dāsa: Hegel understood the Absolute Truth to be always changing and yet always permanent.

Śrīla Prabhupāda: The Absolute does not change. Even we are permanent. Being part and parcel of Kṛṣṇa, we are permanent even though we are moving about in these material bodies. Although Kṛṣṇa manifests Himself in various expansions, He remains the same.

Śyāmasundara dāsa: Hegel saw the Absolute Truth unfolding itself in history, biology, sociology, and other sciences.

Śrīla Prabhupāda: Kṛṣṇa is in the center of everything, and everything is emanating from Kṛṣṇa. Temporary manifestations come from Kṛṣṇa and then return to Kṛṣṇa. History is simply repetition.

Śyāmasundara dāsa: For Hegel, God, or the Absolute Truth, manifests in three forms: the idea-in-itself, the idea-for-itself, and the idea-in-and-for-itself.

Śrīla Prabhupāda: This means that he is trying to create God. For him, God is an idea. Is this his philosophy? The Māyāvādīs also believe that actually there is no God, that God is created by man's imagination, that He is impersonal or dead. So many people are busy creating God. Vivekananda, for instance, claimed Ramakrishna to be God.

Hayagrīva dāsa: In maintaining that God's essence is "thought and thinking"—despite whatever images God may assume—Hegel is basically an impersonalist. He writes: "God is in His very essence thought and thinking, however His image and configuration be determined otherwise."

Śrīla Prabhupāda: If God is Absolute, His image is also Absolute and also God. If God is Absolute, His words are also Absolute and are nondifferent from Him. The image of God worshipped in the temple is God Himself because God is Absolute. God says that earth, water, fire, and everything else is His energy, and even if we think that the image of God is made of stone, we must acknowledge that the stone is God's energy. Even though a copper wire may not be electricity, it carries electricity, and if you touch it, you will understand it to be nondifferent from electricity. We may think materially that an object is different from God, but spiritually, everything is God.

arcye viṣṇau śilādhīr guruṣu
nara-matir vaiṣṇave jāti-buddhiḥ

"One who considers the *arca-mūrti* or worshipable Deity of Lord Viṣṇu to be stone, the spiritual master to be an ordinary human being, and a Vaiṣṇava to belong to a particular caste or creed, is possessed of hellish intelligence and is doomed." (*Padma Purāṇa*) We should not look upon the Deity as something material, as stone (*śilā*). As soon as Caitanya Mahāprabhu saw the Jagannātha Deity, Caitanya Mahāprabhu immediately fainted. In order to realize God's omnipresence, we must be trained to follow God's instructions. It appears that Hegel is theorizing that God is an idea, but God is substance.

Śyāmasundara dāsa: And what do you mean by substance?

Śrīla Prabhupāda: Substance is something concrete. You may form an idea of a golden mountain, but there is a difference between that idea and the golden mountain itself. When you actually see and touch a golden mountain, it is a fact. That fact is substance.

Śyāmasundara dāsa: For Hegel, there is idea, substance, and the synthesis, which is spirit.

Śrīla Prabhupāda: According to our philosophy, spirit is realized in three phases: Brahman, Paramātmā, and Bhagavān. Realizing Brahman is like realizing the sunshine, which is impersonal. Realizing Paramātmā is like realizing the sun disc itself, which is localized. However, if we have the capacity to enter the sun, we will see the sun god himself, and this may be compared to Bhagavān realization, the personal feature of God. Once we realize the personal feature, we automatically understand the impersonal and localized features. According to *Brahma-saṁhitā* (5.40), the impersonal *brahmajyoti* is the bodily rays of Kṛṣṇa. Similarly, Paramātmā is the localized feature of Kṛṣṇa sitting in everyone's heart. The sun is one, not many, but it is capable of being reflected in countless waterpots. One who sees the sun's reflections in the pots may think, "Oh, there are millions of suns." One who has seen only the sunshine thinks of the sun impersonally. But when one knows the sun god, he has attained personal realization. The Supreme Personality of Godhead is a person, Śrī Kṛṣṇa. When you have a clear conception of God, you understand this. You cannot make God into an idea. Ideas arise because there is substance.

Śyāmasundara dāsa: Hegel uses the word "idea" to refer to rational form, which precedes material or physical form.

Śrīla Prabhupāda: It is stated in *Brahma-saṁhitā* that Kṛṣṇa, the Supreme Personality of Godhead, has form (*vigraha*), but what kind of form is this? *Īśvaraḥ paramaḥ kṛṣṇaḥ sac-cid-ānanda-vigrahaḥ.* "Kṛṣṇa is the Supreme Godhead, and He has an eternal, blissful, spiritual body." (*Brahma-saṁhitā* 5.1) *Sat* means eternal. Presently, we have bodies which are *asat*, temporary, but Kṛṣṇa's body is different from ours. The word *ānanda* means blissful; Kṛṣṇa is always blissful. And *cit* means knowledge; Kṛṣṇa knows everything. In this way, He is different from us. He is not an idea but substance itself.

Śyāmasundara dāsa: When we were discussing Plato, you agreed that the ideal precedes the physical representation.

Śrīla Prabhupāda: From the *śāstras* we learn that there is a spiritual world, and that this material world is a perverted reflection of that world. From the *śāstras* we also understand that the houses in the spiritual world are made of *cintāmaṇi. Cintāmaṇi prakara-sadmasu.* In this world, we have no experience of *cintāmaṇi* [philosophers' stone], a stone that turns other metals to gold, but we may have some idea by hearing from authorities. It is not that we manufacture or think up the spiritual world. In other words, we have ideas of substances which we may not have seen.

Śyāmasundara dāsa: For Hegel, spirit generates ideas and actualizes them.

Śrīla Prabhupāda: We say that everything comes from Kṛṣṇa. Why just ideas and substances? Why this or that? Why so many distinctions? Everything comes from Him. Unless there is substance in the spiritual world, nothing could exist. In the final analysis, we have to accept the fact that everything is emanating from the substance. *Janmādy asya.* All ideas can be traced back to the original substance, which is Kṛṣṇa. Therefore Kṛṣṇa says, "Everything is emanating from Me." If you attain Kṛṣṇa, therefore, you attain the ultimate substance. If you understand God, you understand everything.

Śyāmasundara dāsa: Then you would say that form precedes idea, not that idea precedes form?

Śrīla Prabhupāda: Yes, form precedes idea. Kṛṣṇa says, *sarvasya* *cāhaṁ hṛdi sanniviṣṭho mattaḥ smṛtir jñānam apohanaṁ ca.* "I am seated in everyone's heart, and from Me come remembrance, knowledge, and forgetfulness." (*Bg.* 15.15) As far as man is concerned, he cannot invent anything. He can only discover things that are already there.

Śyāmasundara dāsa: Hegel sees idea and substance opposing one another as thesis and antithesis; spirit is the synthesis containing both.

Śrīla Prabhupāda: Yes, we agree. *Viruddhārtha-sambandha.* Contradictory things are adjusted in Kṛṣṇa; therefore we say that Kṛṣṇa is inconceivable. He is simultaneously one with and different from His creation. Since it is impossible to conceive of these things in the material world, they are called inconceivable.

Śyāmasundara dāsa: Then, if we can conceive of something, must it exist somewhere?

Śrīla Prabhupāda: Yes. It is a fact that you cannot conceive of anything that does not have existence. In this material world, we understand that one plus one equals two, and that one minus one equals zero, but in the spiritual world, this law does not apply. There, one plus one equals one, and one minus one equals one.

Śyāmasundara dāsa: But what of the idea that God is evil? Can I conceive of this?

Śrīla Prabhupāda: Yes, God is also evil, but not according to our understanding. God is Absolute, and evil and good are reconciled in Him. We cannot say that because we think of God as evil that He is evil. Rather, we say that He is all good because He is Absolute.

Śyāmasundara dāsa: What of the idea that God does not exist?

Śrīla Prabhupāda: Yes, it is a fact that He does not exist as far as rascals are concerned. Since a rascal cannot understand God, God does not exist for him.

Śyāmasundara dāsa: What of the idea that I am God?

Śrīla Prabhupāda: That is also a fact because you are part and parcel of God. You may say, "I am an American," and President Nixon can also say, "I am an American," but this does not mean that you are President Nixon. It is madness to claim such a thing.

Hayagrīva dāsa: Concerning God and man, Hegel writes: "God is only God insofar as He knows Himself; His self-knowledge is moreover His consciousness of Himself in man, and man's knowledge of God, a knowledge that extends itself into the self-knowledge of man in God."

Śrīla Prabhupāda: If he accepts the existence of God and man, why does he not agree to receive knowledge of God from God Himself? Why speculate? To possess knowledge of God, man had best take knowledge from God Himself. Yet Hegel is opposed to receiving knowledge or instructions from an exterior source. It stands to reason that if you want to know about me and my nature, you had best take knowledge from me personally instead of speculating. In *Bhagavad-gītā*, God explains Himself, and if we accept this knowledge, which is given by God, our knowledge of God will be perfect. Why waste time speculating?

Hayagrīva dāsa: Perhaps without speculation, a philosopher wouldn't be able to write so many books.

Śrīla Prabhupāda: No. When you have perfect knowledge, you can write perfectly. Without perfect knowledge, your writings will simply be nonsensical. If there is any meaning in our books, it is there because we are not speculating about God but are understanding God from God Himself. This is the *paramparā* system. According to Viśvanātha Cakravartī Ṭhākura, *sākṣād-dharitvena samasta-śāstrair (Śrī Gurv-aṣṭaka* 7). All scriptures accept the guru, the spiritual master, as the Supreme Lord Himself because he does not concoct anything. He is the servant of God, and his knowledge is given by God. If Hegel accepts the fact that he is a man and that God exists, he should logically receive knowledge about God from God Himself.

Śyāmasundara dāsa: For Hegel, the absolute idea, the idea-in-and-for-itself, manifests itself in the objective mind in the form of laws, morality, and social ethics, and the free will develops in these areas.

Śrīla Prabhupāda: Yes, that is the field of the free will. As soon as we accept a controller, all these are manifest. Laws will come, morality will come, and social ethics will come. Since atheists do not accept the controller, they act immorally. Unless we have a platform on which to execute the free will, there is no meaning to free will. There must be some law, some system of morality. At the same time, Kṛṣṇa told Arjuna to do whatever he decides (*Bg.* 18.63). That is free will. After explaining *Bhagavad-gītā* to him, Kṛṣṇa told him that the choice was his.

Hayagrīva dāsa: Hegel placed a great deal of emphasis on human freedom. He accused the "Orientals," specificially the Hindus, of not knowing "that the spirit is free in itself or that man is free in himself. Because they do not know it, they are not free."

Śrīla Prabhupāda: He speaks of human freedom, but he is subjected to birth, old age, disease, and death. Where is his freedom when he dies?

Hayagrīva dāsa: Hegel writes that "only the Germanic nations have in and through Christianity achieved the consciousness that man qua man is free and that freedom of the spirit constitutes his very nature."

Śrīla Prabhupāda: According to the Christian religion, a man has the freedom either to go to heaven or to hell. That is, he has the freedom to make a choice. However, if he goes to hell, where is his freedom? Every citizen has the freedom either to live as a free citizen or to go to jail, but if one goes to jail, where is freedom? His freedom is dependent on someone else who gives him a chance to either remain free or go to prison. Our freedom is relative, and God is the supreme absolute controller. It is God who gives the living entity the freedom to make his choice. The living entity is never completely free, as God is.

Hayagrīva dāsa: Hegel criticized Hinduism as a theocracy in which man is handed laws from an exterior God; for Hegel, this is a blind following of an exterior will, a following not confirmed within the individual himself. He believed that man could best attain God through the exercise of his own free will.

Śrīla Prabhupāda: If this is the case, why can't animals attain God? They are also given a free will.

Hayagrīva dāsa: He claims that animals have no will.

Śrīla Prabhupāda: If they have no will, why do they go different directions?

Hayagrīva dāsa: Hegel even went further to say in *The Philosophy of Right and Law* that animals have no right to life because they have no will.

Śrīla Prabhupāda: First of all, you must determine what is life. Animals are eating, sleeping, defending, and mating just as we are. A small ant has all the life symptoms that we have. Who is to say that a man has more right to live than an ant? The life symptoms are the same.

Śyāmasundara dāsa: For Hegel, the individual conscience evaluates itself and sets its own standard of morality.

Śrīla Prabhupāda: Our morality is not like that because we accept morality from a higher authority. Our morality is standardized. Kṛṣṇa says, "Abandon all varieties of religion and just surrender unto Me." (*Bg.* 18.66) This is the morality we accept. The laws of man are imperfect, but God's are perfect. Why should we accept the imperfect advice of other men?

Śyāmasundara dāsa: Hegel sees the subjective mind dealing with inner experiences, the objective mind with exterior, and the absolute mind dealing with both, and uniting them.

Śrīla Prabhupāda: That is correct. Anyone can understand that this is the case with the Absolute.

Śyāmasundara dāsa: This Absolute expresses itself in three forms: art, religion, and philosophy. In art, the Absolute assumes the form we call

beauty.
Śrīla Prabhupāda: Yes, we define God as all beautiful.
Śyāmasundara dāsa: Hegel considers religion to be like an art form. Whereas philosophy conceives or thinks of the Absolute, religion represents or pictures it.
Śrīla Prabhupāda: Without a philosophical basis, religion is simply sentiment.
Śyāmasundara dāsa: He maintains that art is an expression of spirit.
Śrīla Prabhupāda: Well, everything is an expression of spirit. How is that a definition of art?
Śyāmasundara dāsa: What about a tree? Can we say that a tree is the artful display of the Absolute?
Śrīla Prabhupāda: Yes, a tree is also a form of art. Kṛṣṇa is the supreme artist also.
Śyāmasundara dāsa: The absolute mind expresses itself through religion, which presents the Absolute Truth as representations in our consciousness.
Śrīla Prabhupāda: Religion means accepting God. If he thinks that religion is a mere representation in our consciousness, he has no clear idea of religion. Abiding by the laws of God is religion.
Śyāmasundara dāsa: For Hegel, the highest form in which the Absolute manifests itself is philosophy, which is the synthesis of art and religion.
Śrīla Prabhupāda: Philosophy also means obeying the orders of God. Anything else is dry speculation. God says, "Thou shalt not kill." If we are religious, we stop killing. However, if we understand why we should not kill, we are philosophic. There are many people who accept Kṛṣṇa as God, but an advanced devotee understands Kṛṣṇa, and therefore he is very dear to Kṛṣṇa. But highest of all is love of Kṛṣṇa. The *gopīs* were not philosophers, but they loved Kṛṣṇa without ulterior consideration. Caitanya Mahāprabhu Himself expressed this love of Kṛṣṇa.
Śyāmasundara dāsa: Once, you said that even higher than philosophy is the practice of philosophy.
Śrīla Prabhupāda: Yes, the *gopīs* were practicing philosophy because they were loving Kṛṣṇa. Moreover, they were enjoying the results of philosophy.
Hayagrīva dāsa: Since the body is the soul's instrument, Hegel considered injury to the body to be injury to the person himself. In *The Philosophy of Right and Law*, he says: "It is but vain sophistry that says that the real person—the soul—cannot be injured by maltreatment offered to one's body.... Violence done to the body is really done to me."
Śrīla Prabhupāda: Then what is the justification for killing animals?

Hayagrīva dāsa: He would say that a person can possess his body because he can put his will into it. Animals, however, have no right to life because they do not put their will into the possession of their bodies.
Śrīla Prabhupāda: If that is the case, why do animals object when you kill them? What kind of philosophy is he expounding?
Hayagrīva dāsa: He says that mankind has the right of absolute proprietorship. He writes: "A thing belongs to the accidental first comer who gets it, because a second comer cannot take possession of what is already the property of another."
Śrīla Prabhupāda: In other words, might makes right. But consider, how would you take ownership of gold? First of all, you must hunt out gold that has no proprietor. You must inquire who the actual proprietor of the gold is. You may claim first proprietorship, but the gold was there in the first place. Whose property is it? Who made the gold and kept it before you came along?
Hayagrīva dāsa: Hegel would say that "the first comer is not legal owner by virtue of his being the first comer, but because he has free will." That is, it is mine because I put my will into it.
Śrīla Prabhupāda: That's all right, but someone made the gold and kept it before you went to capture it. Since this was the case, by willing it to be yours, or by taking it, you become a common thief, not a philosopher. Our claim to proprietorship is false because we are neither the creators nor maintainers of property.
Śyāmasundara dāsa: As far as action is concerned, activity in accordance with conscience is proper activity for Hegel.
Śrīla Prabhupāda: A thief becomes accustomed to stealing, and therefore his conscience says, "Yes, I must steal. It is my right." The conscience of a murderer tells him to murder. Originally, the Bible said, "Thou shalt not kill," but people have created a conscience by which they can think, "Yes, killing is all right." Conscience is created by association. If our association is good, we create a good conscience, and if it is bad, we create a bad conscience. There is no absolute standard for the conscience. Conscience means discriminating power.
Śyāmasundara dāsa: He maintains that there is an absolute conscience, which is pure rationality.
Śrīla Prabhupāda: Pure rationality is Kṛṣṇa consciousness. Unless we come to that platform, so-called conscience and philosophy have no value.
Śyāmasundara dāsa: Hegel believes that punishment for crime is justified because it vindicates justice and restores rights.

Śrīla Prabhupāda: Yes. Therefore when one kills an animal, he should be prepared to be killed. That is justice. According to the *Manu-saṁhitā*, it is justice to hang a murderer. It is unjust to save him because if he is not hanged in this life, he escapes justice, and has to suffer severely in the next. In order to be saved from many troubles in the next life, the murderer should be killed. The king who is hanging him is doing him justice in rendering a life for a life. But according to Vedic philosophy, if one kills an animal, he should also be prepared to be killed. A sane man would not run such a risk.

Śyāmasundara dāsa: If I observe in nature that living entities are killing one another to eat, it only seems rational that I should be able to eat animals.

Śrīla Prabhupāda: Well, Vedic philosophy also accepts the fact that one living being is food for another.

ahastāni sahastānām
apadāni catuṣ-padām
phalgūni tatra mahatāṁ
jīvo jīvasya jīvanam

"Those who are devoid of hands are prey for those who have hands; those devoid of legs are prey for the four-legged. The weak are the subsistence of the strong, and the general rule holds that one living being is food for another." (*Bhāg.* 1.13 .47) But this does not mean that you should kill your son and eat him. There must be discrimination. It is nature's law that we have to eat other living beings in order to exist; therefore we can eat fruit and vegetables. We can take these without killing the trees and plants. But if we eat animals, we have to kill them. The point is that we should act intelligently to make the best of a bad bargain. We take fruits, grains, vegetables, and milk products, and offer them to Kṛṣṇa. If there is any responsibility, it is Kṛṣṇa's. After offering the food to Kṛṣṇa, we then accept it as *prasādam.*

yajña-śiṣṭāśinaḥ santo
mucyante sarva-kilbiṣaiḥ
bhuñjate te tv aghaṁ pāpā
ye pacanty ātma-kāraṇāt

"The devotees of the Lord are released from all kinds of sins because they eat food which is offered first for sacrifice. Others, who prepare food for personal sense enjoyment, verily eat only sin." (*Bg.* 3.13) If you cook for yourself, you have to take all the responsibility for your sinful activity, even if you are a vegetarian. We therefore take the remnants of *yajña,*

sacrifice, and in this way we perform *yajña*. It is not that we prepare food directly for our own consumption.
Hayagrīva dāsa: Hegel was a strong believer in the right of man to choose his own occupation. He writes: "In the Platonic State, subjective freedom was of no account, since the government assigned to each individual his occupation. In many Oriental states, this assignment results from birth. The subjective choice which ought to be respected requires free choice by individuals."
Śrīla Prabhupāda: The occupations are already given, but you have the freedom to select one of them. Kṛṣṇa states in *Bhagavad-gītā:*

cātur-varṇyaṁ mayā sṛṣṭaṁ
guṇa karma-vibhāgaśaḥ

"According to the three modes of material nature and the work ascribed to them, the four divisions of human society were created by Me." (*Bg.* 4.13) One can make his selection according to his qualifications. A man can become an engineer, for instance, when he becomes qualified to do the work. The words used are *guṇa-karma:* the work is determined by one's qualities, not by birth. It is not that one automatically becomes a *brāhmaṇa* because he is born in a *brāhmaṇa* family. Rather, he has a better chance of being trained as a *brāhmaṇa* if his father is a *brāhmaṇa*, just as one stands a better chance of being trained as a musician or a cobbler if those are his father's occupations. However, it is not that a cobbler cannot become a *brāhmaṇa*. If he acquires the qualifications, he should be considered a *brāhmaṇa*. Nor is it that a *brāhmaṇa's* son necessarily becomes a *brāhmaṇa* without qualification. The point is that we must first attain the qualifications and then work accordingly.
Śyāmasundara dāsa: Concerning the state, Hegel writes: "The state is the realization of the ethical ideal.... We must therefore worship the state as the manifestation of the divine on earth."
Śrīla Prabhupāda: First, we have to understand the duty of the state. If it is accepted that the state is the representative of God, the state's first business is to make its citizens God conscious. Any state that neglects this duty should be immediately rejected as unqualified. The leader may either be a president or a king—it doesn't matter. In Vedic culture, the king is called *naradeva*, God in human form, and he is offered respect in that way. A king is respected because he is considered God's representative. We also present ourselves as Kṛṣṇa's representative. And what is our duty? To lift others to God consciousness.
Śyāmasundara dāsa: Hegel recommended a constitutional monarch to

be the executor for the World Spirit, but he was so vague that even Hitler could utilize his political philosophy to his ends.

Śrīla Prabhupāda: First of all, the monarch has to be educated. Hitler came not as a king but a usurper. Nowadays, any rascal can assume power. Because the leaders are not trained to protect the citizens, the whole world is in trouble. A leader can whimsically declare war and involve all the citizens. In Vedic monarchy, there is a kind of disciplic succession wherein the king trains his son, and in this way he can govern properly.

Śyāmasundara dāsa: According to Hegel, in a well-ordered monarchy, only the law has objective power; the king is simply the servant of the law.

Śrīla Prabhupāda: That is constitutional monarchy, a showbottle king. If a king is God conscious and is trained up properly and has complete power, he is a *rājarṣi*. In *Bhagavad-gītā*, it is mentioned that the ancient saintly kings had understood this science of Kṛṣṇa consciousness (*Bg.* 4.2). They were not ordinary men. The king was supposed to have been saintly. He had to understand the philosophy of *Bhagavad-gītā* and introduce an educational system so that the people could understand the science of God. That is the very first duty of the state and king. It is also stated in *Śrīmad-Bhāgavatam* that one should not become a head of state, a father, or a guru if he cannot save his wards from the imminent danger of death (*Bhāg.* 5.5.18). We are now entangled in repeated birth and death, and it is the state's duty to promote liberation from this cycle.

Śyāmasundara dāsa: Hegel considers it the purpose of the state and king to apply the moral law.

Śrīla Prabhupāda: That is the duty of the king, but the leaders in modern democratic states are concerned only with exacting taxes. It is stated in the *śāstras* that if the leaders keep the citizens morally blind and exact taxes from them, the leaders will go to ruination. Because they are sinfully earning money, they suffer in this life and the next. Similarly, when the guru accepts disciples, he takes the responsibility for their sinful reactions. When a king levies taxes, he takes a share of the sinful reactions of the citizens. If the citizens are pious, both the king and the citizens will profit. If not, if it is a case of the blind leading the blind, they will lead one another to hell. The main point is that the head of state should be a representative of God, and his duty should be to train citizens to become God conscious.

Śyāmasundara dāsa: Hegel also maintains that each state should be independent in itself and not be subordinate to other states.

Śrīla Prabhupāda: Every state may be independent in an individual capacity, but every state is dependent on God's order. If the states are representatives of God, how can they be independent?

Śyāmasundara dāsa: He claims that there is no higher body to judge the states, and that their differences must be settled by war.

Śrīla Prabhupāda: There is a higher authority if there is religion, philosophy, and learned *brāhmaṇas*.

Śyāmasundara dāsa: He can see no potential world authority.

Śrīla Prabhupāda: That is because the Vedic *varṇāśrama dharma* has been rejected. According to that system, the brahminical culture was superior to the *kṣatriya* culture. The *brāhmaṇas* are to advise the kings. Because people have rejected the Vedic system, they say that there is no authority.

Śyāmasundara dāsa: Well, there was no judge to settle the dispute between Rāma and Rāvaṇa, and that resulted in war.

Śrīla Prabhupāda: The judge was Lord Rāmacandra Himself. He is God.

Śyāmasundara dāsa: In a sense, Hegel glorifies war. "War protects the people from the corruption which an everlasting peace would bring upon them," he says.

Śrīla Prabhupāda: At the conclusion of the battle of Kurukṣetra, Sañjaya points out that wherever there is Kṛṣṇa, there will be victory (*Bg.* 18.78). If there is a war, the party that is God conscious will be victorious. If neither side is God conscious, it is a demonic war. It is not justified; it is just like a cat and dog fight. If we fight, we should fight on behalf of the Supreme God. That is called *dharma-yuddha*. Arjuna did not want to fight, but Kṛṣṇa told him, "I am on your side. Fight." Arjuna was victorious because God was on his side.

Śyāmasundara dāsa: For Hegel, because the conflict itself is purifying, it has some ethical value. He writes, "By war, the ethical health of the nation is preserved, and its finite aims uprooted."

Śrīla Prabhupāda: Then he wants continuous war? If that is the case, Hitler is a first-class man. But why is he condemned? Of course, in the material world, there are opposing elements, and therefore there must be war. It is not that war can be stopped. Rather, the party that has Kṛṣṇa's support will emerge victorious. We don't say that you can stop war, but that if you fight, you should fight on behalf of Kṛṣṇa.

Śyāmasundara dāsa: But what of Hegel's view that progress comes only through conflict, and that peace means stagnation?

Śrīla Prabhupāda: We do not agree that peace is stagnation. Our peace is working for Kṛṣṇa. That is real peace. We are educating people to understand that Kṛṣṇa is our friend, and this is not stagnation. Telling people about Kṛṣṇa is our peace.

Śyāmasundara dāsa: Are we not in a state of war with material nature, māyā?

Śrīla Prabhupāda: We don't fight with māyā. Those who are under māyā's clutches and who are being kicked by māyā are struggling with māyā. We have nothing to do with māyā.

daivī hy eṣā guṇamayī
mama māyā duratyayā
mām eva ye prapadyante
māyām etāṁ taranti te

"This divine energy of Mine, consisting of the three modes of material nature, is difficult to overcome. But those who have surrendered unto Me can easily cross beyond it." (*Bg.* 7.14) If māyā does not disturb us, what is the point of fighting?

Śyāmasundara dāsa: Hegel looks on world history as the supreme tribunal, the higher judge of events. History will bear out the worth of an empire and national policy.

Śrīla Prabhupāda: We say that whatever empire comes will certainly fall. There is no need to study history to know that. A godless empire will never endure.

Hayagrīva dāsa: Hegel considered history and theology to be intrinsic. History is "a justification of God," and tells the story of man's elevation to God. Without the history of man, God would be alone and lifeless. Since God is not transcendental but is manifest in the world, He depends on human history.

Śrīla Prabhupāda: But if God is dependent on human history, how can He be God? God is always independent. *Janmādy asya yato 'nvayād itarataś cārtheṣv abhijñaḥ sva-rāṭ (Bhāg.* 1.1.1). If He is dependent on anything, He is not God.

Hayagrīva dāsa: Does the history of man necessarily make any sense? Hegel looked on history as evolutionary.

Śrīla Prabhupāda: As soon as there is creation, there is history. This history will continue until the universe is annihilated. We may superficially consider history as existing from the beginning to the end of the universal manifestation, just as we may consider our personal history to extend from our birth to our death, but God is not subjected to such a history. It is not that God is created at a certain point and then annihilated. Since God is eternal, there is no question of history in respect to

Him. History is for the finite, for things that have a past, present, and future. Since there is no past, present, and future for God, there is no history. You must have a past, present, and future in order to have history.
Śyāmasundara dāsa: Hegel believes that the dominant nation in any epoch represents a dominant phase of the Absolute at that time. For instance, if the United States is currently predominant, the Absolute is being expressed through the United States.
Śrīla Prabhupāda: Aeons ago, the Absolute Truth was connected to the dominant nation. That is, to Mahārāja Parīkṣit. Because Mahārāja Parīkṣit and Mahārāja Yudhiṣṭhira were representing God, they could dominate the entire world. Now all that is lost, and today there are many small states that are not God conscious; therefore they are fighting each other like cats and dogs. Still, it is a fact that Vedic kings like Mahārāja Rāmacandra, Mahārāja Pṛthu, Mahārāja Yudhiṣṭhira, and Mahārāja Parīkṣit were actually representatives of God. In those days, one king ruled the entire world. Therefore there was no trouble.
Śyāmasundara dāsa: Could America's dominance in this century be attributed to God's will?
Śrīla Prabhupāda: Whenever we see some extraordinary power, we should understand that it is derived from God's power. We may therefore say that the predominance of America is due to God's favor. However, if Americans spread Kṛṣṇa consciousness and make their president Kṛṣṇa conscious, America will be God's empowered nation. Let the president be Kṛṣṇa conscious. Why not? Educate the American people to be Kṛṣṇa conscious and elect a Kṛṣṇa conscious president. This Kṛṣṇa consciousness movement is in your hands, and it is up to you to utilize it and become the factual leaders of the world. It was my mission to go to America and educate the Americans in Kṛṣṇa consciousness because I knew that if they become Kṛṣṇa conscious, the whole world will follow. You are young men, and this mission is in your hands. A few Communists like Stalin and Lenin formed a big Communist Party, and now this Party is dominating most of the world. It was started simply by a few men. Now many of you young Americans have understood this God conscious philosophy, and it is up to you to spread this movement. You should not become stagnant, thinking, "Now I have understood Kṛṣṇa consciousness. Now let me sit down and just chant Hare Kṛṣṇa." This is not desired. Go spread Kṛṣṇa consciousness, and in this way glorify your nation.
Śyāmasundara dāsa: According to Hegel's aesthetics, beauty is the Ab-

solute penetrating the world of the senses.
Śrīla Prabhupāda: Yes, Kṛṣṇa is the most beautiful. Because Kṛṣṇa is beautiful, even the chirping of a bird is beautiful. Kṛṣṇa is the reservoir of all pleasure and beauty. Beauty is appreciated in the world because beauty is one of Kṛṣṇa's qualities. Whatever little beauty we find in this material world is but the perverted reflection of Kṛṣṇa's beauty.
Śyāmasundara dāsa: Hegel feels that art is a combination of spiritual content and sensuous form, and that the artist should try to imbue his material forms with spiritual content.
Śrīla Prabhupāda: We agree with that. When we are painting pictures, playing music, or writing books, we are placing Kṛṣṇa at the center.
Śyāmasundara dāsa: Of all the arts, Hegel says, music and poetry are the highest.
Śrīla Prabhupāda: Yes, therefore we are writing many books. Vyāsadeva has written many great epics in praise of Kṛṣṇa. Lord Brahmā has written *Brahma-saṁhitā, cintāmaṇi prakara-sadmasu.* There are many poems in praise of Kṛṣṇa; therefore another name for Kṛṣṇa is Uttamaśloka, the greatest of poems. He is described in beautiful poetry in the Vedic literatures. It is not very important whether it is poetry or prose. Anything sublime is called poetry. It is not that it has to be written in meter.
Śyāmasundara dāsa: For Hegel, religion is pure thought put into form.
Śrīla Prabhupāda: He has no knowledge of what religion is. Religion is neither imagination nor pure thought. Religion is the order coming from the most pure. This cannot be imagined or created. We need only receive the instructions from the most pure. These are given in *Bhagavad-gītā.* We are not imagining this.
Hayagrīva dāsa: Hegel maintained that since God is necessarily manifest in the infinite, the incarnation is central to any religion. In order for God to be manifest, He has to incarnate as a finite man.
Śrīla Prabhupāda: If God becomes a mere man and is to be considered such, why should His instructions be followed?
Hayagrīva dāsa: Hegel did not believe in following any exterior will.
Śrīla Prabhupāda: This means that he is either godless, or that God has no meaning for him.
Hayagrīva dāsa: He interpreted the goal of Indian philosophy to be *nirvāṇa,* spiritual as well as physical extinction.
Śrīla Prabhupāda: Everyone acknowledges physical extinction, and as far as the spiritual is concerned, there is no such thing as extinction. The spirit is eternal.

na jāyate mriyate vā kadācin
nāyaṁ bhūtvā bhavitā vā na bhūyaḥ
ajo nityaḥ śāśvato'yaṁ purāṇo
na hanyate hanyamāne śarīre

"For the soul there is never birth nor death. Nor, having once been, does he ever cease to be. He is unborn, eternal, ever-existing, undying, and primeval. He is not slain when the body is slain." (*Bg.* 2.20) If the spirit is annihilated, how is it different from matter?

Śyāmasundara dāsa: Hegel believed that in the highest religion, God is seen as Father, Son, and all-pervasive Holy Spirit. Thus he considered Christianity to be the perfect religion.

Śrīla Prabhupāda: Is it perfect to say that God only has one son? If God is unlimited, why is He limited to only one son?

Śyāmasundara dāsa: Well, he claims that Christ represents nature, or the objective world, because Christ is God incarnate.

Śrīla Prabhupāda: When there is an incarnation of God as the son of God, and an incarnation of God as God Himself, which is superior? If God has begotten a son, God is a father, a person. How can a son be born of an impersonal father? What evidence do we have of such a thing ever happening?

Śyāmasundara dāsa: Hegel would like to have philosophy without religion because he saw religion as basically an encumbrance.

Śrīla Prabhupāda: Such a philosophy is simply mental speculation. If he claims that philosophy is superior to religion, then religion supported by philosophy is real religion; otherwise it is sentiment. As I stated before, the orders of God constitute religion. In *Bhagavad-gītā*, Kṛṣṇa says, "Surrender unto Me." This is religion. When we try to understand why Kṛṣṇa wants us to surrender unto Him, why we are obliged to surrender unto Him, we are in the realm of philosophy. When philosophy supports religion, it is perfect. It is neither sentiment, nor mental speculation.

Hayagrīva dāsa: In *The Phenomenology of the Spirit*, Hegel deprecates the use of plants and animals as objects of religion, considering it a kind of pantheism typical of Hinduism. How would worship of the *tulasī* plant or the cow differ?

Śrīla Prabhupāda: God has specifically said that among plants, He is the *tulasī*. It is not that the Hindus are worshipping just any plant. For instance, in *Bhagavad-gītā*, Kṛṣṇa says, *praṇavaḥ sarva-vedeṣu.* "I am the syllable *Oṁ* in the Vedic mantras." (*Bg.* 7.8) Therefore the word *Oṁ* is used in mantras, as in *oṁ tad viṣṇoḥ paramaṁ padam.* We know that *oṁkara* is God because God says so. God gives instructions on how He should be realized, and we have only to follow. What is the point in speculating? We can never understand the unlimited God by our limited speculation.

Hayagrīva dāsa: But if God is in all animals and in all plants, why concentrate on any particular ones? Why not worship all?

Śrīla Prabhupāda: That is especially prohibited. In *Bhagavad-gītā*, Kṛṣṇa says:

mayā tatam idaṁ sarvaṁ
jagad avyakta-mūrtinā
mat-sthāni sarva-bhūtāni
na cāhaṁ teṣv avasthitaḥ

"By Me, in My unmanifested form, this entire universe is pervaded. All beings are in Me, but I am not in them." (*Bg.* 9.4) The soul and the Supersoul exist within the body of a dog, but this does not mean that the barking of a dog is the word of God. Vivekananda said that we should worship *daridra*, the poor man in the street. He even used the word *daridra-nārāyaṇa*, indicating that Nārāyaṇa, God, has become poor, *daridra*. Although the body of a *daridra* rests in God, Nārāyaṇa, we should not consider his body to be the body of Nārāyaṇa. Everything in a government may rest on the orders of the king, but the king is not personally present everywhere. According to the *acintya-bhedābheda* philosophy, God is simultaneously one with and different from His creation. God is undoubtedly present in the heart of the *daridra*, the poor man, but we should not consider the *daridra* to be God. That is an impersonalist Māyāvādī mistake. That is pantheism.

Hayagrīva dāsa: When Lord Kṛṣṇa says that He is sex life according to dharma, does that mean that He can be perceived in that way?

Śrīla Prabhupāda: Yes, if one performs the Garbhādhāna ceremony to beget a Kṛṣṇa conscious child, Kṛṣṇa is remembered. It is the duty of the father to remember Kṛṣṇa while having sex, thinking, "Kṛṣṇa, give me a child who will be Your devotee." This kind of sex is for Kṛṣṇa, and is Kṛṣṇa, but if one has sex for his own sense enjoyment, that is demoniac.

Hayagrīva dāsa: But isn't Kṛṣṇa present nonetheless?

Śrīla Prabhupāda: Kṛṣṇa is always present, but when we hold the Garbhādhāna ceremony to beget a Kṛṣṇa conscious child, we remember Kṛṣṇa. The rules and regulations for the Garbhādhāna ceremony are given in the *Śrīmad-Bhāgavatam*. As soon as society abandons this ceremony, people become degraded.

Hayagrīva dāsa: So the philosophy behind reverence for the *tulasī* plant and the cow, or the sexual ceremony, is that these can bring remembrance of Kṛṣṇa.
Śrīla Prabhupāda: Yes. Kṛṣṇa says:

satataṁ kīrtayanto māṁ
yatantaś ca dṛḍha-vratāḥ
namasyantaś ca māṁ bhaktyā
nitya-yuktā upāsate

"Always chanting My glories, endeavoring with great determination, bowing down before Me, these great souls perpetually worship Me with devotion." (*Bg*. 9.14) If somehow or other you always think of Kṛṣṇa, you become Kṛṣṇa conscious.
Hayagrīva dāsa: Is it that you shouldn't think of Kṛṣṇa in any other way? For instance, as a palm tree?
Śrīla Prabhupāda: When Kṛṣṇa says that among trees He is the *tulasī*, or whatever, we should simply accept it. For instance, He says, *raso'ham apsu kaunteya*. "I am the taste of water." (*Bg*. 7.8) When we follow these instructions, we think, "I am drinking water and am feeling satisfaction. This satisfaction is Kṛṣṇa." In this way, we can remember Him.
Hayagrīva dāsa: Hegel mistook this for pantheism.
Śrīla Prabhupāda: He is mistaken in so many ways.

Arthur Schopenhauer
(1788-1860)

Hayagrīva dāsa: For Schopenhauer, happiness is inactive satisfaction, inactivity, *nirvāṇa*. Since the will to live is the irrational urge that brings about all suffering, he advocates the extinction of this world. In *The World As Idea*, he writes: "The Vedas and Purāṇas have no better simile than a dream for the whole knowledge of the actual world, which they call the web of māyā....Indeed, life is a long dream....What is this world of perception besides being my idea? Is that of which I am conscious only as idea, exactly like my own body, of which I am doubly conscious, in one aspect as idea, in another aspect as will?" He goes on to conclude that life is a projection of the will.
Śrīla Prabhupāda: Yes, life is a projection of the will, or material desire. The living entity cannot be desireless. *Nirvāṇa* means that material desires are finished, but because the living entity is an eternal spiritual being, he has spiritual desires. Now these spiritual desires are covered by material desires, but in any case, desire is the constant companion of the living entity. Because he is materially covered, he considers the temporary world to be reality, but because it is constantly changing, it is not. According to the type of body we get, we have

different desires. The soul transmigrates in this material world from one body to another, and he creates desires accordingly. The supreme will affords him different bodies in order to fulfill his will or material desires. The living entity is willing, and the supreme will, God, or Kṛṣṇa, understanding the finite will, gives him facilities to fulfill his particular desire. Therefore will is the cause of this material existence. However, we say that since you are a living being, you must have desires. If your desires are stopped, you become like a stone. Instead of trying to put an end to all desire, you should try to cleanse this diseased form of desire. That is the process of *bhakti.*

sarvopādhi-vinirmuktaṁ
tat-paratvena nirmalam
hṛṣīkena hṛṣīkeśa-
sevanaṁ bhaktir ucyate

"*Bhakti,* or devotional service, means engaging all our senses in the service of the Lord, the master of all the senses. When the spirit soul renders service unto the Supreme, there are two side effects. He is freed from all material designations, and, simply by being employed in the service of the Lord, his senses are purified." (*Bhakti-rasāmṛta sindhu,* 1.1.12) Presently, our desires are desires of the body (*upādhi*). When the living entity acquires the body of an American, a European, a Chinaman, or whatever, he thinks in a certain way. When he changes his body to that of a dog, he spends his time barking. According to his desires, he has received a particular type of body. These desires are temporary, and the living entity moves from one body to another. Therefore in one sense this is all a dream. It is a fact that we cannot fulfill our material desires, which come and go like dreams. Now all material activities, subtle or gross, are manifestations of different desires, and therefore the Māyāvādī philosophers say *brahma satyaṁ jagan mithyā.* The dreamer is a fact, but the dream is false. Our Vaiṣṇava philosophy agrees that the dreamer is the factual living entity, and the dream is temporary; therefore the dreamer has to be brought to the real spiritual platform so that his material dreams can be extinguished. When we abandon the dream and awaken to reality, that is Kṛṣṇa consciousness, or *bhakti.*

Śyāmasundara dāsa: Then will or desire can never be annihilated?

Śrīla Prabhupāda: No, not even for a second. Because we are living, we must will and desire. It is stated in *Bhagavad-gita* that we cannot live for a second without will, without desires.

na hi kaścit kṣaṇam api
jātu tiṣṭhaty akarmakṛt
kāryate hy avaśaḥ karma
sarvaḥ prakṛti-jair guṇaiḥ

"All men are forced to act helplessly according to the impulses born of the modes of material nature; therefore no one can refrain from doing something, not even for a moment." (*Bg.* 3.5)

Śyāmasundara dāsa: Don't the Buddhists advocate a state of desirelessness, or nonwillingness?

Śrīla Prabhupāda: They believe that if you dismantle this material combination, this material body, there will no longer be will, desire, or suffering. But this is not a fact. You are the eternal servant of Kṛṣṇa, and you do not die after the destruction of the body. Thinking, feeling, and willing are carried from this body to another body in the process of transmigration. When the body dies, the living entity is carried away by his will. According to our will, we receive another body at the time of death. That body may be the body of a demigod, dog, human, or whatever. In any case, will, or desire, is the carrier.

Hayagrīva dāsa: Schopenhauer was profoundly influenced by some of the Vedic literatures. For example, he writes: "Every keen pleasure is an error and an illusion, for no attained wish can give lasting satisfaction; and moreover, every possession and every happiness is but lent by chance for an uncertain time, and may therefore be demanded back the next hour. All pain rests on the passing away of such illusion; thus both arise from defective knowledge. The wise man therefore holds himself equally aloof from joy and sorrow, and no event disturbs his composure."

Śrīla Prabhupāda: Yes, in this material world, people say, "This is good, and this is bad," but factually there is no question of good and bad. This is all on the temporary platform. The Māyāvādīs use the word "false," but we say "temporary." It is also stated in *Bhagavad-gītā* that the pains and pleasures experienced in the material world do not touch the spirit soul. Under illusion, a spirit soul, concerned with a material body, thinks that the pains and pleasures are his, but this is not a fact. Therefore Kṛṣṇa instructs that the pleasures and pains simply touch the body, not the soul. Kṛṣṇa says:

mātrā-sparśās tu kaunteya
śītoṣṇa-sukha-duḥkha-dāḥ
āgamāpāyino'nityās

tāṁs titikṣasva bhārata

"O son of Kuntī, the nonpermanent appearance of happiness and distress, and their disappearance in due course, are like the appearance and disappearance of winter and summer seasons. They arise from sense perceptions, and one must learn to tolerate them without being disturbed." (*Bg.* 2.14) Since pleasures and pains come and go in due course, they are not the reality. So why bother about them? If I feel pain, let me tolerate it and go about my business.

Śyāmasundara dāsa: Schopenhauer sees happiness in the world as a negative state at best, a momentary suspension of suffering.

Śrīla Prabhupāda: Yes, that is also explained by Caitanya Mahāprabhu. Sometimes when a man is to be punished, he is held under water to the point of suffocation. Then he is let up, and when he comes up for temporary relief, he thinks, "Ah! Happiness at last!" The point is, he should do something that will relieve him of his unhappiness permanently.

Śyāmasundara dāsa: Schopenhauer says, "Human life must be some kind of mistake." The greatest crime of man was that he was ever born.

Śrīla Prabhupāda: When you understand that there is a crime, you must understand that someone is there to punish you. If you suffer because of that crime, you must understand that there is someone who has judged you to be criminal.

Śyāmasundara dāsa: He concludes, however, that because the world is mad or irrational, it could not possibly have an author. If there were a God, He would have set the world in order.

Śrīla Prabhupāda: We have certainly experienced that there are madmen in the world, but there are also hospitals where such men can be treated. The world may be mad, but there is hospitalization. Unfortunately, Schopenhauer has no knowledge of the hospital or of the treatment. He speaks of sinful life, but he does not accept the judge who gives the punishment for sinful life. He sees that the world is mad, but he does not know the treatment for madmen.

Hayagrīva dāsa: In *The World As Will*, Schopenhauer writes: "My body is the objectivity of my will.... Besides will and idea, nothing is known to us or thinkable.... The genitals are properly the focus of the will, and consequently the opposite pole of the brain, the representative of knowledge.... In this respect... they were worshipped by the Hindus in the *liṅgam*, which are thus the symbol of the assertion of the will. Knowledge, on the other hand, affords the possibility of the suppression of willing, of salvation through freedom, of conquest and annihilation of the world."

Śrīla Prabhupāda: As I said before, willing is done in accordance with the body, but we should understand that we have nothing to do with this material world, which is the production of the material will. We are spiritual, and when we will spiritually, we are Kṛṣṇa conscious. When we will materially, we get different types of material bodies. It is true that the basis of material life is sex. We always say:

yan maithunādi-gṛhamedhi-sukhaṁ hi tucchaṁ
kaṇḍūyanena karayor iva duḥkha-duḥkham
tṛpyanti neha kṛpaṇā bahu-duḥkha-bhājaḥ
kaṇḍūtivan manasijaṁ viṣaheta dhīraḥ

"Sex life is compared to the rubbing of two hands to relieve an itch. *Gṛhamedhis*, so-called *gṛhasthas* who have no spiritual knowledge, think that this itching is the greatest platform of happiness, although actually it is a source of distress. The *kṛpaṇas*, the fools who are just the opposite of *brāhmaṇas*, are not satisfied by repeated sensuous enjoyment. Those who are *dhīra*, however, who are sober, and who tolerate this itching, are not subjected to the sufferings of fools and rascals." (*Bhāg*. 7.9.45). The basic principle of those who are addicted to the material world is *maithuna*, sexual intercourse. This strong desire for sex continues as long as we are in material existence, because that is the center of all pleasure. However, when we get a taste of Kṛṣṇa's pleasure, we can give this up.

viṣayā vinivartante
nirāhārasya dehinaḥ
rasa-varjaṁ raso'py asya
paraṁ dṛṣṭvā nivartate

"The embodied soul may be restricted from sense enjoyment, though the taste for sense objects remains. But, ceasing such engagements by experiencing a higher taste, he is fixed in consciousness." (*Bg*. 2.59)

Śyāmasundara dāsa: Schopenhauer considers sex to be selfishness, whereas real love means sympathy.

Śrīla Prabhupāda: Sex is animalistic. It is not love but lust. Sex means the mutual satisfaction of senses, and that is lust. All this lust is taking place under the name of love, and out of illusion, people mistake this lust for love. Real love says, "People are suffering from a lack of Kṛṣṇa consciousness. Let us do something for them so that they can understand the value of life."

Śyāmasundara dāsa: He also considered immoral acts to result from a

sense of egoism.
Śrīla Prabhupāda: Yes, that is so. People think, "Why should I surrender to Kṛṣṇa? Kṛṣṇa is a person, and I am also a person." Such thinking is demoniac. Rascals cannot understand that by surrendering unto the supreme will and satisfying the supreme will, salvation can be attained.
Śyāmasundara dāsa: Yet Schopenhauer felt that it is possible to crush egoism and desire by love and sympathy for others.
Śrīla Prabhupāda: Yes, without love, nothing can be sustained. If I do not love Kṛṣṇa, I cannot surrender unto Him. A small child naturally surrenders unto his parents because there is love for the parents. The more you love, the more your surrender is perfect. When there is a lack of love, the mentality by which you can surrender will not develop. If you have some love for me, you will carry out my orders. There is no question of forcing one to surrender. The living entity is free to love or to reject. Without freedom, there cannot be love. Kṛṣṇa consciousness means learning to love Kṛṣṇa.
Śyāmasundara dāsa: Schopenhauer looked on love as compassionate sympathy for one who is suffering. Through this compassionate love, we can lose desire.
Śrīla Prabhupāda: Why should you love those who are suffering and not those who are enjoying?
Śyāmasundara dāsa: Schopenhauer sees everyone as suffering.
Śrīla Prabhupāda: Yes, we agree to this. Everyone within material nature is suffering. Therefore Kṛṣṇa descends and delivers *Bhagavad-gītā.* Kṛṣṇa is described as the deliverer of all fallen souls. A Vaiṣṇava takes *sannyāsa*, the renounced order, out of compassion for others, because his only duty is to preach the message of Kṛṣṇa consciousness. People in the world are suffering due to their ignorance. They think, "Oh, now I have a nice car, apartment, and girl friend; therefore I am happy." Actually, this is not happiness but suffering. Because the Vaiṣṇava loves Kṛṣṇa and understands that he is part and parcel of Kṛṣṇa, he realizes that the conditioned living entities are suffering for want of Kṛṣṇa consciousness. Therefore, out of compassion, the Vaiṣṇava takes *sannyāsa* and goes forth to preach.
Hayagrīva dāsa: As for the nature of the world, Schopenhauer is vague, but he sees material life as basically irrational and whimsical.
Śrīla Prabhupāda: Yes, that is a fact, and therefore we are changing bodies. This means that our material mind is not fixed; it is constantly rejecting and accepting. Māyāvādī philosophers and Buddhists say that since these material pleasures and pains arise from this material combi-

nation, the best course is to dismantle it. They do not say that the soul is the basis, but that the material body is nothing but a combination of the material elements. They therefore advise us to let the earth return to earth, the water return to water, and so on. In this way, they tell us that we should strive to become zero, to attain *nirvāṇa*.

Śyāmasundara dāsa: Leibnitz claimed that this is the best of all possible worlds, and you agreed because the world is God's arrangement. But Schopenhauer sees this as the worst of all possible worlds.

Śrīla Prabhupāda: There is no doubt that whatever Kṛṣṇa creates is perfect. However, since the nature of this world is material, there are three modes working: goodness, passion, and ignorance. As you work, you receive the results, the reactions. We do not agree that this is the worst of worlds. Why should God create the worst of anything?

Śyāmasundara dāsa: Schopenhauer believes this because the world is so full of madness and frustration.

Śrīla Prabhupāda: Had he taken his frustration seriously, it might have made him successful. We receive many letters from frustrated students who understand that frustration is another hell, and eventually they come to understand that they should seek the real shelter. So frustration is really not so bad. If you are put in a dangerous position, and you know how to save yourself from it, that very danger will later give you pleasure.

Śyāmasundara dāsa: Schopenhauer claims that the working of the world is ethically evil.

Śrīla Prabhupāda: To some extent that is right because when you are in prison, you will find that there is evil. But that evil is good for you. It is there so that you can learn a lesson. When you are out of the prison, you will be able to love someone.

Hayagrīva dāsa: For Schopenhauer, there is frustration behind all material pleasures and endeavors. Happiness eludes us. As soon as we attain the objects of our desires, they no longer appear the same. "They soon grow stale or forgotten," he writes, "and though not openly disowned, are yet always thrown aside as vanished illusions."

Śrīla Prabhupāda: Yes, all this is going on, and therefore the living entity acquires one body after another.

Hayagrīva dāsa: He sees us moving through a constant transition from desire to satisfaction and then to a new desire, "the rapid course of which is called happiness, and the slow course sorrow...." It is this flux from desire to satisfaction that characterizes the will's activities in the phenomenal world. Outside of this, there is only *nirvāṇa*, extinction.

Śrīla Prabhupāda: That is not a fact. We have to understand that behind the will and its satisfaction is a person who is willing. Schopenhauer does not take that person into consideration; he considers only the will and its satisfaction. It is the individual soul who is willing. If he succeeds in stopping this flickering willing, what next? Even the stopping of the will is temporary. One kind of willing may be stopped, but there will be another kind of willing and satisfaction. We must understand that behind the whimsical will is the spirit soul. When that spirit soul understands his real identification as the eternal servant of Kṛṣṇa, his will is purified. We should not be satisfied by simply trying to annihilate the whimsical will. We should understand the real will of the real person. That is the beginning of spiritual life.

Hayagrīva dāsa: Schopenhauer believes that voluntary and complete chastity is the first step in asceticism, or in the denial of the will to live. "Chastity denies the assertion of the will which extends beyond the individual life," he writes, "and gives the assurance that with the life of the body, the will, whose manifestation it is, ceases."

Śrīla Prabhupāda: Yes, but he must understand that behind the will there is a person who is willing. It will not help us simply to negate the temporary material will. We have to will in reality, and that is our eternal willing, that is Kṛṣṇa consciousness. In the material world, the will is directed toward sense satisfaction because the living entity has forgotten the spiritual field of willing. When the same will is directed towards satisfying the senses of the Supreme, that is the eternal willing of the living entity. *Jīvera 'svarūpa' haya—kṛṣṇera 'nitya-dāsa'* (*Caitanya-caritāmṛta,* Madh. 20.108). When we come to the platform of real knowledge, we understand that we are the eternal servants of God. When our will is concentrated on how to serve God, we attain our real position of eternity, bliss, and knowledge.

Hayagrīva dāsa: Although Schopenhauer officially takes an atheistic stand, he writes: "If a man fears death as his annihilation, it is just as if he were to think that the sun cries out at evening, 'Woe is me! For I go down to eternal night....' Thus suicide appears to us as a vain and therefore foolish action...."

Śrīla Prabhupāda: Yes, because the will is there, death is not the stoppage of life. One simply gets another life.

dehino'smin yathā dehe
kaumāraṁ yauvanaṁ jarā
tathā dehāntara-prāptir
dhīras tatra na muhyati

"As the embodied soul continually passes, in this body, from boyhood to youth to old age, the soul similarly passes into another body at death. The self-realized soul is not bewildered by such a change." (*Bg*. 2.13) This is proof that the life of the person who is willing is eternal. His desire and will are eternal, but Schopenhauer does not know what his eternal willing is. His eternal will is to serve Kṛṣṇa always. It is a fact that suicide is no solution. One just implicates himself more and more. If we kill the body given by God, we have to accept another body, or remain a ghost. If I live in this body eighty years, and then commit suicide, I have to remain a ghost for five years before I get a chance to receive another body. Of course, you may argue that since the soul is everlasting, it makes no difference whether the body is killed. It is all right if the body is annihilated, but you cannot deliberately kill the body because that is hindering its progress. The living entity is destined to live in a particular body, and if you destroy that body, he has to wait for another. This means that you are interfering with his spiritual evolution, his spiritual progress. Therefore you are liable for punishment.

Hayagrīva dāsa: Schopenhauer also looked on Indian philosophy as a philosophy of the denial of the will, and he cited many examples of suicide as a religious act.

Śrīla Prabhupāda: But he did not study Vedic philosophy and religion perfectly. He has some idea of some portions of the Māyāvādī and Buddhist philosophies, but evidently he did not know about Vaiṣṇavism. Although he has touched *Bhagavad-gītā*, he did not study it thoroughly, because in *Bhagavad-gītā*, Kṛṣṇa tells Arjuna that if he only tried to attain knowledge of God, his life and will would be purified, and he would return back to Godhead upon giving up the body.

janma karma ca me divyam
evaṁ yo vetti tattvataḥ
tyaktvā dehaṁ punar janma
naiti mām eti so'rjuna

"One who knows the transcendental nature of My appearance and activities does not, upon leaving the body, take his birth again in this material world, but attains My eternal abode, O Arjuna." (*Bg*. 4.9) Either Schopenhauer did not study *Bhagavad-gītā* thoroughly, or he could not understand for want of a real spiritual master. According to *Bhagavad-gītā* itself, we should go to a bona fide guru who has seen the truth. Schopenhauer is speculating on the basis of his own experience; therefore, although everything is there in *Bhagavad-gītā*, he could not see it.

Hayagrīva dāsa: As examples of the denial of the will to live, Schopenhauer cites the religious suicides under the wheels of the Jagannātha carts, and the ritual of *satī*.
Śrīla Prabhupāda: These are not suicides. These are acts based on the understanding that because we are getting different types of bodies, we are suffering a variety of miseries. When one voluntarily accepts death in these ways, he thinks of his spiritual life while dying, and he attains it.

yaṁ yaṁ vāpi smaran bhāvaṁ
tyajaty ante kalevaram
taṁ tam evaiti kaunteya
sadā tad-bhāva-bhāvitaḥ

"Whatever state of being one remembers when he quits the body, that state he will attain without fail." (*Bg*. 8.6) Therefore King Kulaśekhara prayed that Kṛṣṇa take him while he was in good health and remembering Kṛṣṇa, because he feared forgetting Kṛṣṇa when dying in a diseased condition. Often, when death comes, a person is in a coma, his bodily functions are impeded, he dreams in various ways, and so on. Therefore an intelligent man sometimes thinks that it would be more desirable to meet death in sound health so that he can think of his next life and go back to Godhead. If a person thinks of Lord Jagannātha while dying, he goes back to Lord Jagannātha. That is not suicide but the voluntary acceptance of death so that one can immediately transfer to the spiritual world.
Hayagrīva dāsa: And that is effective?
Śrīla Prabhupāda: Yes.
Hayagrīva dāsa: What of Caitanya Mahāprabhu's throwing Himself in the ocean?
Śrīla Prabhupāda: No, that was different. That was an act of ecstasy.
Śyāmasundara dāsa: Schopenhauer noted that the will forces a person to live even when he has nothing to live for. It impels him to suffer day after day. He compares it to the alms which a beggar receives one day just so he can live in hunger the next day. All this misery and frustration are not partaken by a few men, but by all.
Śrīla Prabhupāda: That is certainly a good point, but why does the individual hanker after something when he is being frustrated? The point is that there is a goal, and the individual is hankering after that goal. In order to understand what that goal actually is, we should approach a spiritual master.
Hayagrīva dāsa: According to Schopenhauer, the man of knowledge is

not perturbed in any condition. "Such a man would regard death as a false illusion," he writes, "an impudent specter which frightens the weak but has no power over him who knows that he is himself the will of which the whole world is the objectification or copy, and that therefore he is always certain of life and also of the present...."

Śrīla Prabhupāda: This is contradictory. On the one side there is a desire for the certainty of life, and on the other he says that *nirvāṇa* is the only answer. Which does he want? He is simply trying to adjust things. He cannot understand the philosophy behind purification of the will.

Hayagrīva dāsa: One of the first major Western philosophers to have read *Bhagavad-gītā*, Schopenhauer feels that it was Kṛṣṇa's assurance of immortality that brought Arjuna to fight.

Śrīla Prabhupāda: Yes, but what is Schopenhauer's philosophy of the immortal living being? He does not understand that just as the living entity is immortal, his will is also immortal. If the soul is immortal, how can his will be stopped? How is *nirvāṇa* possible?

Hayagrīva dāsa: He offers no solution other than suppression of the will.

Śrīla Prabhupāda: But that is not possible. He must change the quality of his willing in order to be happy. That is the process of *bhakti.*

sarvopādhi-vinirmuktaṁ
tat-paratvena nirmalam
hṛṣīkena hṛṣīkeśa-
sevanaṁ bhaktir ucyate

"*Bhakti*, or devotional service, means engaging all our senses in the service of the Lord, the master of all the senses. When the spirit soul renders service unto the Supreme, there are two side effects. He is freed from all material designations, and, simply by being employed in the service of the Lord, his senses are purified." (*Bhakti-rasāmṛta-sindhu*, 1.1.12) *Bhakti* is the purification process: *śravaṇaṁ kīrtanaṁ viṣṇoḥ*. Chanting and hearing the pastimes of the Lord will purify us. Schopenhauer misses the point of *Bhagavad-gītā*. Although he accepts the fact that life is eternal, he thinks that its purpose is *nirvāṇa*. Unfortunately, he does not know what real *nirvāṇa* is. *Nirvāṇa* means putting an end to the whimsical will and coming to the platform of willing in Kṛṣṇa consciousness.

Hayagrīva dāsa: Schopenhauer was impressed that the religion of India has endured for more than four thousand years. He writes that such a religion "cannot be arbitrarily invented superstition, but must have its foundation in the nature of man."

Śrīla Prabhupāda: Within the Vedic religion there are two basic sects: Māyāvādī and Vaiṣṇava. Both acknowledge the fact that the material world is flickering and transient and that there is another life in the spiritual world. For the Māyāvādīs, spiritual life means merging into the Brahman effulgence, and for the Vaiṣṇava it means associating personally with God in His abode, Goloka Vṛndāvana, Vaikuṇṭha. Both envision a spiritual life attainable after death.

Hayagrīva dāsa: Schopenhauer considered Indian religion to be based on the denial of the will.

Śrīla Prabhupāda: Yes, denial of the will for material happiness, but it is not the will itself that is denied. While denying the will for material happiness, we must assert the will for spiritual happiness. When denying one thing, we must accept something else. No one can remain in a neutral position. *Paraṁ dṛṣṭvā nivartate (Bg.* 2.59). We give up the inferior for the superior.

Śyāmasundara dāsa: For Schopenhauer, there are three means of salvation: aesthetic, ethical, and religious. Through aesthetic salvation, contemplation of the Platonic ideals through poetry, music, and art, we are transported above passion, desire and willing.

Śrīla Prabhupāda: This is nothing new. It is mentioned in *Bhagavad-gītā*, and the students of this Kṛṣṇa consciousness movement abandoned their abominable living habits because they received a better life with superior thoughts, philosophy, food, song, poetry, and art. When the mind is filled with Kṛṣṇa, there is no chance in its engaging in the contemplation of nonsense.

Śyāmasundara dāsa: Aesthetic salvation is a temporary experience. When we look at a beautiful painting, for instance, we momentarily transcend the lower levels of consciousness and become desireless.

Śrīla Prabhupāda: Yes, we admit that this may be the case, but we wish to remain in that higher consciousness continually, not momentarily. This is possible through practice. By practice, a child learns to read and write, and thus becomes educated. It is not a momentary thing. If we practice Kṛṣṇa consciousness daily, lower consciousness will automatically vanish. *Śrī-vigrahārādhana-nitya-nānā-śṛṅgāra-tan-mandira-mārjanādau (Śrī Gurv-aṣṭaka* 3). The spiritual master engages his disciples in the temple worship of the Lord. You cannot derive benefit from worshipping the Deities unless the aesthetic sense is applied with reverence and respect.

Śyāmasundara dāsa: According to ethical salvation, we should attempt to satisfy the will. When it is satisfied, no new desires can arise. This brings permanent happiness.

Śrīla Prabhupāda: Apart from the individual will, there is the supreme will. If we satisfy the supreme will, we are happy. *Yasya prasādād bhagavat-prasādo* (*Śrī Gurv-aṣṭaka* 8). Our philosophy is that by satisfying the spiritual master, the representative of God, we satisfy the supreme will. It is not our will that is to be satisfied, but the will of God.

Śyāmasundara dāsa: By religious salvation, the most effective type of salvation, the will is denied through asceticism. In this way, Schopenhauer believed that we could attain the state of *nirvāṇa*, nothingness.

Śrīla Prabhupāda: Such people claim that when there is no longer any sense of pleasure and pain, there is no world. The fact is, there are three stages: waking, sleeping, and total unconsciousness. In all three stages, the will is there. A person can emerge from a state of total unconsciousness and immediately remember his waking state and his dreams. Therefore the will is there. The will cannot be killed because it is the function of the soul. Since the soul is eternal, willing is also eternal. The will may be suppressed for some time, however. For instance, after death, when a living entity enters a womb, he spends the next nine months developing his next body, and there is a suspension of the will. However, according to your will, you develop a certain type of body. When you emerge from your mother's womb, the willing process resumes. Death means a suspension of the will for a few months, that's all. If you train your willing process improperly, you have to suffer life after life, but if you train it properly, you can go to Vaikuṇṭha immediately after death.

Hayagrīva dāsa: Concerning religious practices, Schopenhauer writes that "the Christian mystic and teacher of Vedanta agree that all outward works and religious exercises are superfluous for him who has attained to perfection." But doesn't Kṛṣṇa recommend just the opposite?

Śrīla Prabhupāda: Yes. In *Bhagavad-gītā*, He says:

yajña-dāna-tapaḥ-karma
na tyājyaṁ kāryam eva tat
yajño dānaṁ tapaś caiva
pāvanāni manīṣiṇām

"Acts of sacrifice, charity, and penance are not to be given up but should be performed. Indeed, sacrifice, charity, and penance purify even the great souls." (*Bg.* 18.5) If we give up the ritualistic ceremonies, there is every chance that we will fall down. Even though we may be liberated, we should continue performing sacrifices, charities, and penance in

order to keep our position secure.
Hayagrīva dāsa: In discussing the functions of the brain, Schopenhauer notes that the need for sleep is directly proportionate to the intensity of our mental activities. Dull creatures like reptiles and fish sleep little and lightly; the more intelligent animals sleep deeply and long. "The more completely awake a man is," he writes, "the clearer and more lively his consciousness, the greater for him is the necessity of sleep, and thus the deeper and longer he sleeps."
Śrīla Prabhupāda: No. Those who are ignorant, materially covered, sleep more, and those who are spiritually enlightened sleep less. Sleep is a necessity of the body, not of the soul; therefore those who are spiritually advanced do not require a lot of sleep. *Nidrāhāra-vihārakādi-vijitau.* We understand that Rūpa Gosvāmī conquered sleeping, eating, and mating. When we are spiritually engaged, we consider sleep a waste of time. Those who are interested in spiritual life adjust their lives in such a way that their sleep is practically nil. Arjuna was addressed as Guḍākeśa, "one who has conquered sleep."
Hayagrīva dāsa: Schopenhauer recommends about eight hours of sleep a night. How many are recommended in the Vedic tradition?
Śrīla Prabhupāda: Sleep should be avoided, but since that is not possible, it should be adjusted to the minimum. The Gosvāmīs did not sleep more than two hours daily. Even some *karmīs* are so absorbed in their work that they practically don't sleep at all. It is said that Napolean slept while riding his horse, and Gandhi slept while riding in a car. Generally, six hours is sufficient.
Hayagrīva dāsa: In *The Ages of Life*, Schopenhauer writes: "A complete and adequate notion of life can never be attained by anyone who does not reach old age, for it is only the old man who sees life whole and knows its natural course....He alone has a full sense of its utter vanity, whereas others never cease to labor under the false notion that everything will come out right in the end."
Śrīla Prabhupāda: This may seem to be the case, but in Western countries we observe old men still following the path of sense gratification. So what is the use of their experience? Unless one receives training, it is not sufficient to become an old man in order to understand the purpose of life. Training is required from early childhood. According to the Vedic plan, an old man should take the renounced order of *sannyāsa* and completely devote his time and energy to understanding and serving God. We do not become spiritually mature just by growing old. We should be trained from the very beginning as *brahmacārī*.

Hayagrīva dāsa: Schopenhauer points out that it is customary to call youth the happy part of life and old age the sad part, but factually this is not the case. "This would be true if it were the passions that made a man happy," he writes, "but a man feels happy just insofar as his intellect is the predominating part of him."

Śrīla Prabhupāda: For modern civilization, happiness means sense gratification. Desire for sense gratification continues even when one is an old man; therefore early training is required. It is said that one can become an old man even without advancing in age. This means that it is knowledge that is important, not age. If one is not educated properly, he becomes an old fool.

Hayagrīva dāsa: Schopenhauer notes that in the *Upaniṣads,* the natural human life span is set at a hundred years. "To come to one's end before the age of ninety means to die of disease," he writes. "In other words, prematurely."

Śrīla Prabhupāda: Yes. In this millennium, the maximum age is one hundred years, but in former millennia, men used to live for a thousand years. In the Tretā-yuga, the life span was ten thousand years, and in the Satya-yuga, it was one hundred thousand years. Presently, in Kali-yuga, life has become so degraded that people expect to live only about seventy years. As one becomes more sensuous, his life span decreases. That is the law of nature.

VIII
EVOLUTIONARY NATURALISM

Charles Robert Darwin
(1809-1882)

Hayagrīva dāsa: Darwin's conception of evolution rests on the premise that there is a real genetic change from generation to generation. In other words, he rejects the Platonic *eidos* (idea, type, or essence) for a species. Whereas Kṛṣṇa says that He is the generating seed of all existences, Darwin would reject the existence of a particular seed for a particular type. There are no fixed species, but shifting, evolving, physical forms, constantly changing.

Śrīla Prabhupāda: No. The forms are already there from the beginning of creation. There is evolution, however, but Darwin thinks that this is an evolution of the body. That is incorrect. The body never evolves, but the soul within the body evolves and transmigrates from one body to another. The soul is within the body, and as he desires, he evolves. A man may desire to change apartments, and he may move from one apartment to another, but it is the man who is doing the changing, not the apartment. According to the Vedic conception, the soul evolves, not the body.

Śyāmasundara dāsa: Darwin originated the doctrine of natural selection and survival of the fittest. An animal, he maintains, will develop in a way that is best suited for survival in his environment, and he will pass on his superior qualities to his offspring. Some species survive, and others, not so suitable to the environment, die out.

Śrīla Prabhupāda: A snake gives birth to many hundreds of snakes at a time, and if so many snakes are allowed to exist, there will be a disturbance. Therefore, according to nature's law, the big snakes eat up the small snakes. Nature's law is not blind, because behind it there is a brain, and that brain is God.

mayādhyakṣeṇa prakṛtiḥ
sūyate sa-carācaram
hetunānena kaunteya
jagad viparivartate

"This material nature is working under My direction, O son of Kuntī, and it is producing all moving and unmoving beings. By its rule this manifestation is created and annihilated again and again." (*Bg.* 9.10) Whatever is taking place in material nature is being directed by the Supreme Lord, who maintains everything in order. When one species becomes overly dominant, nature arranges to curb it. According to the theory of Malthus, whenever there is overpopulation, there must be some war, epidemic, or earthquake. These natural activities do not take place by chance but are planned. If Darwin says it is a matter of chance, his knowledge is insufficient.

Śyāmasundara dāsa: Darwin also sees a plan or design in nature.

Śrīla Prabhupāda: If you see a plan or design, you must ask, "Whose design?" As soon as you admit that there is a design, you must admit a designer. It is nonsense to say that nature is simply working mechanically. If so, there must be some mechanic to set it in motion. The sun rises exactly to the minute, to the second, and the seasons also come according to plan. Behind the great machine of nature there is a brain that has set it in order. We explain the original source of everything as Brahman, the Absolute Truth, Kṛṣṇa. Scientists admit that they do not know where things are coming from, but when they see them, they suddenly claim to have invented them. But that is not invention. These things are already there.

Śyāmasundara dāsa: From scientific research, it is concluded that through the years, animals have evolved toward more and more complex forms, from very simple forms found in the sea to more complex forms, such as dinosaurs and so on. These forms eventually died out, and other forms evolved from them.

Śrīla Prabhupāda: When you say they died out, you mean that those animals no longer exist on this earth. But how can you say that they are not existing somewhere else? Now, according to Darwin's theory of evolution, the human body evolved from the simians.

Śyāmasundara dāsa: He claims that they are related, that they come

from the same ancestor.
Śrīla Prabhupāda: That is another thing. Everything is related. But he claims that the ape's body or monkey's body developed into a human body. If that is the case, why haven't the simians ceased to exist? We can see that apes, monkeys, and human beings are existing simultaneously. Scientists cannot prove that no human being existed aeons ago. If man evolved from the ape, the ape should no longer exist. *Kārya-kāraṇa.* When the effect is there, the cause is finished.
Śyāmasundara dāsa: It is not that the monkey caused the man to exist; rather, they came from a common ancestor.
Śrīla Prabhupāda: We say that we all come from God, the same ancestor, the same father. The original father is Kṛṣṇa.

sarva-yoniṣu kaunteya
mūrtayaḥ sambhavanti yāḥ
tāsāṁ brahma mahad yonir
ahaṁ bīja-pradaḥ pitā

"It should be understood that all species of life, O son of Kuntī, are made possible by birth in this material nature, and that I am the seed-giving father." (*Bg.* 14.4)
Śyāmasundara dāsa: Any any rate, according to Darwin's theory, there is an evolution from simpler forms to more complex forms, from small one-celled animals to more complex animals like man.
Śrīla Prabhupāda: But at the present moment, the simple forms are existing along with the complex. It is not that the simplest developed into the most complex. My present body has developed from my childhood body, but that childhood body is no longer existing. Presently, the species are simultaneously existing.
Śyāmasundara dāsa: But they find no evidence that all these complex forms existed in earlier times.
Śrīla Prabhupāda: Earlier times or modern times are not in question. When I see all the 8,400,000 species still existing, where is the question of development? You may not know or have evidence that these forms existed long ago, but that is due to your imperfect knowledge. These species are all existing now, and they were existing millions of years ago. You may not have evidence of this, but that is a different thing. We accept evolution, but we also accept the fact that the species are all existing simultaneously now. If they are not existing on this planet, they are existing on some other. Of course, Darwin had no chance to study that. We accept the proposition that there is an evolutionary process from aquatics to insects to birds to animals and to humans, but we do not accept Darwin's theory that one species becomes extinct as another survives. All are existing simultaneously.

Śyāmasundara dāsa: But there are many forms that are extinct on this planet.
Śrīla Prabhupāda: But has Darwin seen all the planets and all the universes? Has he the power to see everything? Since our powers are limited, we cannot conclude that a particular species is extinct. Of course, the scientists do not accept the fact that our senses, by which we are gathering information, are limited. But they are. It is not possible to excavate the entire earth. We can only take samples. Our first charge against Darwin is that human life was always existing. He cannot prove that at a certain time there was no human life. It is not that the bodies of the species are changing. These bodies are already there. Rather, the soul is changing bodies, transmigrating from one body to another, and this is actual evolution. It is the evolution or progress of the soul from one body to another.
Hayagrīva dāsa: Concerning the soul, Darwin writes: "A few persons feel anxiety from the impossibility of determining at what precise period in the development of the individual, from the first trace of a minute germinal vesicle, man becomes an immortal being, and there is no greater cause for anxiety because the period cannot possibly be determined in the gradually ascending organic scale." That is, it is impossible to know at what point the immortal soul inhabits these species.
Śrīla Prabhupāda: The soul is the most important factor, and in order to understand the soul, education is required. It is the soul that moves the body, whether that body be that of an ant, bacteria, a human being, animal, or whatever. Nothing can move without the presence of the soul, and each and every individual soul is immortal.
Śyāmasundara dāsa: As mentioned, Darwin doesn't accept the fact that there are a fixed number of species. Rather, he maintains that the species may vary at different times according to natural selection. There are new species always evolving.
Śrīla Prabhupāda: But what does he know of all the species? Does he have a complete list of all the species in the universe? From *Padma Purāṇa*, we learn that there are 8,400,000 species. First of all, we must understand what all these species are. You may walk through a market and see many different types of people. As you walk, you continue to see different types of people, but you cannot say that a particular type no longer exists because you do not see it anymore. The point is that you can neither see nor comprehend the beginning or the end.
Śyāmasundara dāsa: Well, they claim that everything started with a one-celled animal.
Śrīla Prabhupāda: But where did that animal come from?
Śyāmasundara dāsa: From chemical combinations.
Śrīla Prabhupāda: Then who supplied the chemicals?

Śyāmasundara dāsa: Scientists are not so concerned with who, but with the existing phenomena.

Śrīla Prabhupāda: Mere study of phenomena is childish. Real science means finding the original cause. Darwin may have studied this island or that island, or he may have dug holes in this desert or that desert, but he has not seen the other millions of planets that are existing in the universe. He has not excavated and dug into the depths of all the other planets. How, then, can he conclude that this is all? He speaks of natural selection, but he has not perfectly studied nature. He has only studied nature functioning in a particular place, and a very small place at that. When we speak of nature, we refer to *prakṛti*. We refer to the universe. There are millions of universes, and Darwin has not studied them, yet he is drawing all these conclusions. There is certainly natural selection, but Darwin does not know how it is working. Darwin's defect is that he has no information of the soul.

Śyāmasundara dāsa: The fact remains that excavations throughout the world prove the existence of species that no longer exist on this planet.

Śrīla Prabhupāda: But nature is not confined to this one planet. When you speak of material nature, you must include all the planets in the universe.

Śyāmasundara dāsa: But the scientists have no evidence that all the species have been existing from time immemorial.

Śrīla Prabhupāda: You cannot give evidence that the sun existed millions of years ago; still, we conclude that it did. The sun was not just created this morning. Within the sun, everything is existing, and if the sun is existing, other things must be existing also. Darwin draws conclusions about nature from a limited study of this one planet. This is not full knowledge. If your knowledge is not perfect, why should we accept your theories? Whether complex life-forms were existing on this planet millions of years ago is not really the point. All these forms are existing in nature. According to the Vedas, the species in nature are fixed at 8,400,000. These may or may not be existing in your neighborhood, but that is not important. The number is fixed, and they are simultaneously existing. There may be an evolution from simpler forms to more complex, but it is not that a species becomes extinct. Real evolution is the evolution of the soul through the existing species. Now, we admit that with the changes of seasons, or with extreme heat or cold, differences may arise, but it is not that the species are new. If there is a great flood, and all the men on earth are drowned, the human species is not extinct. Man may or may not survive certain catastrophes; this does not affect the species. We cannot say that the human species is extinct, but that under these circumstances man has survived or not survived. Whatever the case, human beings are existing somewhere else.

Śyāmasundara dāsa: When the *Padma Purāṇa* says that there are 400,000 species of human life, what does it mean?
Śrīla Prabhupāda: There are differences in culture and in body types. Scientists will say that human beings are all of one species, but when they speak of species, they mean something different. The Vedas, for instance, would consider the Negroes and Aryans to belong to different species. As far as Kṛṣṇa consciousness is concerned, bodies may differ; it doesn't matter. Our classification is on the basis of the soul. The soul is equal despite different types of bodies. The soul is one and does not change.

vidyā-vinaya-sampanne
brāhmaṇe gavi hastini
śuni caiva śvapāke ca
paṇḍitāḥ sama-darśinaḥ

"The humble sage, by virtue of true knowledge, sees with equal vision a learned and gentle *brāhmaṇa*, a cow, an elephant, a dog, and a dog-eater [outcaste]." (*Bg.* 5.18) One who sees to the bottom, sees the soul. Because Darwin and other material scientists have no information of the soul, they have missed the whole point. On the material platform, one material form may be superior to another, just as one apartment may be better than another, but these are material considerations . Now, according to our position, we may evolve from lower apartments to higher, but it can also work the other way around. If we are not able to pay the rent or price for a higher apartment, we have to enter a lower one. It is not that the soul is necessarily progressing from lower to higher forms.
Śyāmasundara dāsa: Darwin would claim that all living things on earth are evolving from lower to higher.
Śrīla Prabhupāda: Generally, that may be accepted because at certain periods people may be constructing certain types of apartments, but the apartments themselves are not evolving. Evolution takes place within the apartment according to the desire of the *jīva*, the living entity. Darwin thinks that it is the apartment that is changing, but actually it is the desire of the *jīva*. According to our mentality at the time of death, we get a certain type of apartment. In any case, the apartment is already there. It is not that I have to create it. The types of apartments are fixed at 8,400,000, and we can enter into any of them. You cannot conceive of a type of apartment beyond this number. A hotel keeper knows that different customers want different types of facilities; therefore he makes arrangements to receive all kinds of customers. Similarly, this is God's creation, and God knows how many different ways a living entity can think and desire; therefore God has created all these species. If the living entity thinks in a certain way, God says, "Come on. Here is the body

that you want."

prakṛteḥ kriyamāṇāni
guṇaiḥ karmāṇi sarvaśaḥ
ahaṅkāra-vimūḍhātmā
kartāham iti manyate

"The bewildered spirit soul, under the influence of the three modes of material nature, thinks himself to be the doer of activities, which are in actuality carried out by nature." (*Bg.* 3.27) Nature is giving us all facilities. God, as the Paramātmā within the heart of everyone, knows what the living entity wants, and orders nature to give it to him.

Śyāmasundara dāsa: But presently we see that on this planet there are no longer any dinosaurs. That type of apartment is no longer available.

Śrīla Prabhupāda: As I said before, you may or may not have seen dinosaurs. In any case, you have certainly not seen all the 8,400,000 species of life. This does not mean that these species are no longer existing. They may be existing on some other planet. You have no information of this. Scientists are experimenting with their imperfect senses, but we are receiving knowledge from a different source. Regardless of the amount of scientific research, the conclusions will always be imperfect because the senses are imperfect.

Hayagrīva dāsa: At first, Darwin was a Christian, but his faith in the existence of a personal God eventually faded. He finally wrote: "The whole subject is beyond the scope of man's intellect....The mystery of the beginning of things is insoluble by us, and I for one must be content to remain an agnostic...." He based *The Origin of Species* on evidence he had amassed on a voyage around the world from 1830 to 1836.

Śrīla Prabhupāda: In any case, his research was limited. He certainly could not have investigated all the species on the planet.

Hayagrīva dāsa: He spent the rest of his life writing about the information he gathered during this voyage. According to his theory of natural selection, the best and fittest survive, and therefore the race necessarily and steadily improves. But then, in Kali-yuga, isn't there steady degeneration?

Śrīla Prabhupāda: Yes, we can actually see that the human race has become degraded.

Hayagrīva dāsa: What is the cause of this?

Śrīla Prabhupāda: Improper education. Every individual person is a soul, and each has a particular type of body. The human body in particular requires education. The soul evolves through various species according to his desires. Material nature supplies the bodies, acting under the orders of God. God exists within the core of everyone's heart, and when the individual soul desires something, material nature, following the orders of God, gives him a machine in the form of a body. When we attain the human form, we can either regress to the animal form, or make spiritual progress. Animals also have desires, but they change bodies and species according to the laws of nature. The human body in particular is meant for understanding God, acting accordingly, and returning home, back to Godhead. If we do not utilize this opportunity, we regress to lower species.

Śyāmasundara dāsa: According to the Vedic version, were there higher life forms on this planet millions of years ago?

Śrīla Prabhupāda: Yes. The Vedas inform us that the first created creature within this universe is also the most intelligent—Lord Brahmā. How, then, can we accept the theory that the intellect develops over so many millions of years? We receive Vedic knowledge from Brahmā, who was instructed by Kṛṣṇa. Darwin's theory that intellect developed is not scientific. It is merely a suggestion, a guess.

Śyāmasundara dāsa: When Brahmā created, were there also other developed life-forms beside man?

Śrīla Prabhupāda: All the forms have been existing since the creation.

Śyāmasundara dāsa: What evidence do we have that higher life-forms existed on this planet millions of years ago?

Śrīla Prabhupāda: The authority of Vedic literature.

Śyāmasundara dāsa: But what other authority is acceptable? If we dig up a bone and make a test with our senses, isn't that authoritative?

Śrīla Prabhupāda: That is bone authority. You may be satisfied with such authority, but we have our own. You will accept your authority, and I will accept mine. That is a different matter. Scientific authority is always relative, just like scientific knowledge. Theories are always being contradicted by other theories. Has Darwin gone down to the bottom of the sea and excavated there? Who has dug into the layers of the earth below the sea to find out what is there? All Mr. Frog knows is that his well is only three feet deep and three feet wide. If you tell him of the existence of the Atlantic Ocean, he will say, "How big is it? Twice as big as my well? Ten times as big?" Since he can never conceive of the Atlantic Ocean, what good will his investigations do? What knowledge can he have of the vast ocean? Therefore we must take knowledge from one who has created the Atlantic Ocean. In this way, our knowledge will be perfect.

Śyāmasundara dāsa: But certain of Darwin's theories appear factual. For instance, no one can deny the fact that the fittest survive.

Śrīla Prabhupāda: We may try to adjust things, but if our adjustments are not approved by the Supreme, they will not be successful. According to nature's way, parents have affection for their children, but if parents do not take care of them, the children will not survive. Still, the parents' care is not the last word. If the child is condemned by the Supreme Lord, he will not exist despite the parents' care. In other words, we have to go to the Supreme Lord if we ultimately want to survive. If Kṛṣṇa does not want us to survive, we will not be able to survive, despite all our attempts. All these natural laws are working under one controller, God. Electricity may serve many purposes, but the powerhouse is one. It is generating energy for all. We may utilize the same electrical current to serve different purposes, but the power is the same.

Śyāmasundara dāsa: Well, the same current may be working in both the deer and the tiger, but the tiger is able to kill the deer. In this case, one survives, and the other does not.

Śrīla Prabhupāda: According to the law of karma, no one will survive. The body is the field of activity, and we are given license to act within this body for some time. That is all. There is no question of survival.

Śyāmasundara dāsa: By survival, Darwin means that the species will survive.

Śrīla Prabhupāda: There is no question of survival. The species are always there.

Śyāmasundara dāsa: But why is there no evidence that human civilizations existed on this earth millions of years ago?

Śrīla Prabhupāda: Our evidence for a previous Vedic civilization is *śruti*, spoken evidence. For instance, Vyāsadeva received Vedic knowledge from Nārada, and Nārada received Vedic knowledge from Lord Brahmā millions and millions of years ago. We can hardly calculate one of Brahmā's days in which fourteen Manus come and go. Each Manu lives for 306,720,000 years. According to the Vedic calculations, millions, billions, and trillions of years are not very astonishing. When Brahmā was born, he was educated by God. This means that this Vedic philosophy was existing then.

Śyāmasundara dāsa: But if the earth is so old, it must have undergone many transformations.

Śrīla Prabhupāda: Yes, but this doesn't matter. After one day of Brahmā, there is devastation. Brahmā lives for a hundred years composed of his incredibly long days, and at the end of each day there is devastation. So there are many devastations, and we are not very amazed to hear about them. Nor are we amazed at hearing about the passage of millions and trillions of years. This is nothing. According to Vedic historical methods, trillions and trillions of years account for nothing. Even though we do not find evidence of civilization existing on this earth millions of years ago, we cannot conclude that there was no civilization. We can only conclude that our knowledge is imperfect.

Hayagrīva dāsa: Debating against Darwinism, William Jennings Bryan, a famous lawyer and politician, said, "They [the Darwinists] do not dare to tell you that it began with God and ended with God....Darwin says the beginning of all things is a mystery unsolvable by us. He does not pretend to say how these things started."

Śrīla Prabhupāda: The material world is created, and the living entities are allowed to act within it. Since the living entities all come from God, God says *bījaṁ māṁ sarva-bhūtānāṁ viddhi pārtha sanātanam.* "O son of Pṛthā, know that I am the original seed of all existences." (*Bg.* 7.10) Material nature is the mother, and God, the father, gives the *bījam,* the seed. The mother's womb cannot produce in itself, but when the spiritual seed is given, the body can form and develop. The living entity, an eternal part and parcel of God, is put into material nature and develops a body according to his desire. This is the actual beginning of life.

Hayagrīva dāsa: According to the Biblical version, God created man in His image some six thousand years ago.

Śrīla Prabhupāda: It was not so recent. According to the Vedas, this creation goes back millions and millions of years. Whatever the case, God created this cosmic manifestation and impregnated it with living entities to appear in different species according to their desires. The individual soul proposes, and God disposes. All the species have been existing from the very beginning. It is not that there was no human form in the beginning of the creation. This is very easy to understand. The body is created by material nature, and the soul, part and parcel of God, is placed into the body according to his desires. Material energy is called the inferior energy of God, and the living entity, the individual soul, is called the superior energy. Both come from God, and therefore it is said that God, the Absolute Truth, is He from whom everything flows.

Hayagrīva dāsa: In *The Descent of Man,* Darwin writes: "The idea of a universal and beneficent creator does not seem to arise in the mind of man until he has been elevated by a long continued culture."

Śrīla Prabhupāda: Yes, culture is very important, because we can be elevated by spiritual association. According to our cultural life, we can go to higher planetary systems, remain where we are, or go back home, back to Godhead. Therefore culture is most important.

Śyāmasundara dāsa: Darwin felt that if we could sufficiently understand

the evolutionary process, we could control it. Today, people speak of conquering nature, and claim that man is now living a longer, healthier life than ever before.
Śrīla Prabhupāda: That is just more nonsense. My grandmother lived ninety-six years, but I don't expect to live that long. The life span is decreasing. People are not sufficiently healthy because they are not getting proper food. Where is the medicine that puts an end to all disease? Every time you discover new medicines, new diseases come along. There is no question of stopping them. Even if you find a cure for cancer, you cannot put an end to death. However great our scientific advancements may be, we can never put an end to birth, old age, disease, and death. The attempt is a waste of time. Our business is to utilize our time in such a way that after giving up this material body, we can return home, back to Godhead.
Śyāmasundara dāsa: Darwin made the evolution of species seem so mechanically arranged that God is removed from the picture. It appears as if combinations of ingredients created animals, and that they evolved from one another.
Śrīla Prabhupāda: Combination means God, because it is God who is combining. It is not that the combination takes place automatically. A cook combines many ingredients when he is making a preparation. It is not that the ingredients can combine themselves. Darwin should have asked how the combination comes about, but it appears that he did not even raise this question. Material elements, ingredients, do not combine automatically. There must be a living entity who combines them.
Śyāmasundara dāsa: One theory is that everything emanates from some energy.
Śrīla Prabhupāda: That energy must belong to the energetic. When a computer works, there must be someone pushing the button. According to the Vedas, as soon as God wishes, material energy is immediately set into action. Then things emerge automatically. A man may say that there is no God behind the material energy, but if God withdrew such a man's speaking power, he would not even have the ability to deny God's existence. In order to support Darwin's theories, Western philosophers and historians reject the fact that the Vedic literatures were composed thousands of years ago. But the discovery of the Ajanta Caves proves that there were very intelligent people living many thousands of years ago. But these scientists are simply searching after bones. What is more important? Vālmīki's *Rāmāyaṇa*, or a pile of bones?

In ages past, the memories of the students were very sharp because they were pure *brahmacārīs*, strictly celibate. There was no need to write these literatures down. According to the *śruti* system, the student heard the subject matter once from the spiritual master, and after that he could recall every word. Now Darwin and other material scientists are trying to understand phenomena, Kṛṣṇa's energy, but they are not interested in knowing the source of this energy. Kṛṣṇa says, *ahaṁ sarvasya prabhavaḥ*. "I am the source of all spiritual and material worlds." (*Bg.* 10.8) If we are Kṛṣṇa conscious, we know that Kṛṣṇa is the original source of all energy. If a person becomes a chemist or physicist, his duty should be to prove that Kṛṣṇa is the original source of all energy. Then his knowledge of chemistry and physics is perfect. People want knowledge through the modern scientific method; therefore if one is a real scientist, it is his duty to prove that this material energy is coming from Kṛṣṇa. If one is a biologist, or naturalist, it is his duty to prove that all life-forms are coming from Kṛṣṇa. Unfortunately, scientists are thinking, "Oh, we shall create something." But they cannot create anything because God is doing all the creating. They are trying to imitate God just as a child seeing his mother cooking. "Oh, I shall cook too!" It is childish play, and for this play they are spending much labor and many billions of dollars. They try to create a human in a test tube, but every day many humans are being born. They are trying to create something artificial, that's all. By God's multi-energies, everything is being created automatically. All ingredients are given by Kṛṣṇa. Your intelligence and your body are given by Kṛṣṇa. He gives us everything, and we cannot do anything without Him. When we act, we should try to satisfy Kṛṣṇa; then our action will be successful. It is not possible to go outside the boundaries of Kṛṣṇa.

Thomas Henry Huxley
(1825-1895)

Hayagrīva dāsa: Huxley felt that the main difference between man and the animals is the ability to speak. In his essay "Man and the Lower Animals," he writes: "Man alone possesses the marvelous endowment of intelligible rational speech, whereby...he has slowly accumulated and organized the experience which is almost lost with the cessation of every individual life and other animals...."

Śrīla Prabhupāda: That is another misconception. Everyone speaks his own language. Animals have theirs, and human beings theirs.

Hayagrīva dāsa: He specifically mentions "intelligible, rational speech."

Śrīla Prabhupāda: Animals have rational speech.

Hayagrīva dāsa: They may be able to articulate certain basic facts to one another, but they have no culture or history. They have not been able to accumulate and organize the experience of their species.

Śrīla Prabhupāda: According to the Vedic tradition, the Sanskrit language is the mother of all languages and is spoken in the higher planetary systems, but this is not to say that one is an animal if he doesn't speak Sanskrit. Everyone has his own language—Englishmen, Indians, animals, birds, whatever. It is education that is really important, not language. A human being with developed consciousness can receive a spiritual education, whereas animals cannot. That is the main difference. It is not basically a question of language, because knowledge can be imparted in any language, just as we are imparting Vedic knowledge in English and other languages. It is not language that distinguishes man from the lower species, but knowledge. Animals cannot receive knowledge of God, but a human being, regardless of his language, can understand God if knowledge is properly imparted to him.

Hayagrīva dāsa: Although Huxley defended Darwin's theory of evolution, he differed in his belief in the survival of those who are "ethically the best." In *Evolution and Ethics*, he writes: "Social progress means a checking of the cosmic process at every step and the substitution for it of another, which may be called the ethical process; the end of which is not the survival of those who may happen to be the fittest...but of those who are ethically the best."

Śrīla Prabhupāda: The cosmic process cannot be checked. It continues functioning in different modes: goodness, passion, and ignorance. In the mode of goodness, there is advancement, but ultimately the individual has to transcend the mode of goodness to come to the platform of the all-good, the platform of pure goodness. In the material world, whatever process we accept for advancement is conditioned by goodness, passion, and ignorance. It is very difficult in the material world to keep a process pure; therefore the soul must come to the platform of goodness and then transcend it. The platform of pure goodness is called *bhakti*, and on that platform our transactions are only with God. It is only when we come to that platform that we can survive. Otherwise, no one survives, because everyone has to continue transmigrating from one body to another. *Tathā dehāntara-prāptir (Bg.* 2.13). However, when we come to the platform of pure goodness, we can understand God and transcend repeated birth and death.

janma karma ca me divyam
evaṁ yo vetti tattvataḥ
tyaktvā dehaṁ punar janma
naiti mām eti so'rjuna

"One who knows the transcendental nature of My appearance and activities does not, upon leaving the body, take his birth again in this material world, but attains My eternal abode, O Arjuna." (*Bg.* 4.9) Apart from this, there is no meaning to survival. Survival means that the soul remains pure in its original position and does not transmigrate. Survival is only in the spiritual world, where there is no change.

Śyāmasundara dāsa: Huxley believed that it is within our own hands to guide our ethical evolution.

Śrīla Prabhupāda: It is certainly within our hands. First of all, you hear that it is wrong to steal and that those who steal go to jail. Then it is up to you to steal or not.

Śyāmasundara dāsa: Huxley believed that we have to qualify ourselves ethically to be worthy to survive. It is not just a question of the physically fittest.

Śrīla Prabhupāda: Nobody is fit to survive. This idea of survival is simply nonsense. However, we can elevate our consciousness and that of all human society by this Kṛṣṇa consciousness process. This is a question of education. When we become Kṛṣṇa conscious, we become worthy to survive. We no longer have to undergo the process of transmigration.

Śyāmasundara dāsa: Huxley maintains that the most morally worthy ought to survive.

Śrīla Prabhupāda: The most morally worthy is he who is Kṛṣṇa conscious. There is no question of ought; rather, he will survive. But as far as morality is concerned, what is Huxley's morality? We say that cow killing is immoral, but others say that it is moral because by eating beef, the body is developed. Which morality is more worthy for us to select? There are many questions like this, and one person says that this is moral, whereas another says it is immoral. Of course, the meat eaters claim that morality depends on what the majority wants—that is, the majority of meat eaters. Such people will naturally agree that cow killing is very nice, but does this make cow killing moral?

Śyāmasundara dāsa: Huxley believes that because nature is amoral, man must not imitate but must combat nature.

Śrīla Prabhupāda: There is no question of combatting nature. You cannot conquer nature. Of course, everyone is perpetually trying to fight nature, but in *Bhagavad-gītā*, Kṛṣṇa says:

daivī hy eṣā guṇamayī
mama māyā duratyayā
mām eva ye prapadyante
māyām etāṁ taranti te

"This divine energy of Mine, consisting of the three modes of material nature, is difficult to overcome. But those who have surrendered unto Me can easily cross beyond it." (*Bg.* 7.14) It is impossible to defeat material nature. You are trying to live, but material nature deals death to everyone. This combat is going on, but nature is always stronger. No one has ever been successful in battling nature.

Śyāmasundara dāsa: Is it true that nature is amoral?

Śrīla Prabhupāda: Nature is most moral because she is abiding by the order of Kṛṣṇa. How can nature be mistaken? In *Brahma-saṁhitā* (5.44) it is said: *sṛṣṭi-sthiti-pralaya-sādhana-śaktir-ekā chāyeva yasya bhuvanāni vibharti durgā.* Durgā, material nature, is so powerful that she can create, maintain, and annihilate.

Śyāmasundara dāsa: Huxley based his morality on sympathy, and he claimed that nature has no sympathy.

Śrīla Prabhupāda: Nature has all sympathy because she is working under the orders of Kṛṣṇa. Nature is very much like the police. When a person breaks the law, he thinks that the police are most unsympathetic, but if a person abides by the law, the police are friends and protectors. In any case, this is the proposal.

Śyāmasundara dāsa: It would appear that if one man's house burns down and another man's doesn't, there is no sympathy involved—just arbitrariness and chance.

Śrīla Prabhupāda: It is not arbitrary. It is not by chance. It is clearly stated that material nature is working under the orders of Kṛṣṇa. Since Kṛṣṇa is not immoral, one carrying out His orders cannot be immoral. The apparent punishment dealt by nature is also sympathy. Mother Durgā is always seen with a trident in her hand, and she is always punishing, but this is indirectly moral. She is punishing living entities so that they will become Kṛṣṇa conscious. She puts them in all kinds of miserable conditions in order to bring them to awareness of Kṛṣṇa, to the consciousness whereby they can understand that if they surrender unto Kṛṣṇa, they will be free. It is not possible to conquer nature by material contrivances. We can conquer nature only by rendering devotional service to the Lord. The material attempt to conquer or control nature is man's disease, his attempt to imitate Kṛṣṇa. Such imitation is never perfection.

Śyāmasundara dāsa: Still, Huxley felt that man could improve his environment. Agriculturally, for instance.

Śrīla Prabhupāda: Yes, but although the governments are promising people more and more, the people are becoming more miserable. They give man food to eat, facilities to sleep, to have sex life, and assurance from danger. These are the primary necessities, and even an animal can be satisfied with these. But man cannot. Because he has developed consciousness, man wants something more. Therefore in human society there is music, art, philosophy, and religion. But if man utilizes his developed consciousness simply to eat, sleep, defend, and mate, he will never be satisfied. Man's higher consciousness should be utilized to develop Kṛṣṇa consciousness. The material struggle for survival is not natural. Struggle is unnatural. Our natural condition is enjoyment.

Śyāmasundara dāsa: But, by use of intelligence, can't man come to understand the world, and in this way make his own world?

Śrīla Prabhupāda: It is stated in *Bhagavad-gītā:*

antavat tu phalaṁ teṣāṁ
tad bhavaty alpa-medhasām
devān deva-yajo yānti
mad-bhaktā yānti mām api

"Men of small intelligence worship the demigods, and their fruits are limited and temporary. Those who worship the demigods go to the planets of the demigods, but My devotees ultimately reach My supreme planet." (*Bg.* 7.23) It is up to you. If you want to remain here, you can. Kṛṣṇa has given us intelligence and all facilities. It is now up to us to make our choice, whether to go to heaven, hell, or to Kṛṣṇa.

Hayagrīva dāsa: Huxley looked on civilization as something of an attempt to give order to nature. Civilization might be defined then as a complex ethical understanding between men enabling as many men as possible to survive.

Śrīla Prabhupāda: That is not possible. You cannot dictate to nature; rather, nature will dictate death to you. According to the laws of material nature, there is no question of survival. When you can actually dictate to material nature, then you can survive. This is possible only through Brahman realization, as explained in *Bhagavad-gītā:*

māṁ ca yo'vyabhicāreṇa
bhakti-yogena sevate
sa guṇān samatītyaitān
brahma-bhūyāya kalpate

"One who engages in full devotional service, who does not fall down in any circumstance, at once transcends the modes of material nature and thus comes to the level of Brahman." (*Bg.* 14.26)

Hayagrīva dāsa: Huxley saw the Indian philosopher as buckling under a stronger cosmos. He writes: "By the Ganges, ethical man admits that the cosmos is too strong for him—"

Śrīla Prabhupāda: Yes.

Hayagrīva dāsa: "—and destroying every bond which ties him to it by ascetic discipline, he seeks salvation in absolute renunciation."
Śrīla Prabhupāda: That is correct.
Hayagrīva dāsa: However, Huxley saw this attempt as "flight from the battlefield." Exhorting Englishmen to cosmic battle, he writes, "We are grown men, and must play the man 'strong in will to strive, to seek, to find, and not to yield.'"
Śrīla Prabhupāda: And at last to die. He may not yield, but nature will kick him and say, "You must die." In any case, Mr. Huxley is no longer surviving. Whether we be Englishmen, Frenchmen, Americans, or whatever, we cannot survive but have to succumb to the dictations of material nature. According to *Bhagavad-gītā:*

prakṛteḥ kriyamāṇāni
guṇaiḥ karmāṇi sarvaśaḥ
ahaṅkāra-vimūḍhātmā
kartāham iti manyate

"The bewildered spirit soul, under the influence of the three modes of material nature, thinks himself to be the doer of activities, which are in actuality carried out by nature." (*Bg.* 3.27) It is false ego that says, "I shall survive. I am an Englishman." According to the law of nature, death is unavoidable for everyone; therefore the intelligent man first of all considers how he can transcend death. It is explained in *Bhagavad-gītā* that if we understand Kṛṣṇa, we can survive.
Hayagrīva dāsa: It is not that Huxley believed in any kind of material immortality. In *Evolution and Ethics*, he writes of transmigration and karma: "Every sentient being is reaping as it has sown; if not in this life, then in one or other of the infinite series of antecedent existences of which it is the latest term." Also, of Indian philosophy: "The substance of the cosmos was Brahman, that of individual man Ātman; and the latter was separated from the former only, if I may so speak, by its phenomenal envelope, by the casing of sensations, thoughts, and desires, pleasures and pains, which make up the illusive phantasmagoria of life."
Śrīla Prabhupāda: Brahman is not separated from *ātmā*; rather, they are eternally co-existing. That is explained in the Thirteenth Chapter of *Bhagavad-gītā,* wherein Śrī Kṛṣṇa discusses the body, *kṣetra,* which is the field of action, and the *ātmā,* the individual soul, who is the owner of the field and who works in it. It is also pointed out that there is another owner:

upadraṣṭānumantā ca

bhartā bhoktā maheśvaraḥ
paramātmeti cāpy ukto
dehe'smin puruṣaḥ paraḥ

"Yet in this body there is another, a transcendental enjoyer who is the Lord, the supreme proprietor, who exists as the overseer and permitter, and who is known as the Supersoul." (*Bg.* 13.23) The *ātmā,* the individual soul, knows only his own body, but the Supersoul knows everything about everybody. I may know the pains and pleasures of my body, but I am ignorant of the pains and pleasures of another. The Supersoul, Paramātmā, knows everything about all bodies in the universe. There is no question of separation; rather, the two are eternally co-existing.

Hayagrīva dāsa: Huxley's understanding is similar to that of the Śaṅkarites: the *ātmā* is imprisoned within the body, and when he attains enlightenment, "the bubble of illusion will burst, and the freed individual *Ātman* will lose itself in the universal Brahman."

Śrīla Prabhupāda: This does not mean that the *ātmā* becomes Paramātmā. A drop of water may merge into the sea, but it does not become the sea. The sea remains the same, whether a drop of water merges with it or not. When a green bird enters a green tree, you may not be able to see the bird anymore, but it is foolish to think that the bird has become one with the tree. The individual *ātmā* retains his individuality, although our defective vision may not be able to perceive it. The Śaṅkarites mistakenly think that the individual soul merges with the Supreme and becomes the Supreme, but this is not the case. In all cases, he retains his individuality.

Hayagrīva dāsa: Huxley writes: "There was no external power which could effect the sequence of cause and effect which gives rise to karma; none but the will of the subject of the karma which could put an end to it."

Śrīla Prabhupāda: As long as the individual soul acts according to bodily designations, he is not free. When he gives up these designations and agrees to become Kṛṣṇa-*dāsa,* the servant of Kṛṣṇa, he saves himself.

Hayagrīva dāsa: But is there any question of liberation independent of Kṛṣṇa?

Śrīla Prabhupāda: No. It is explained in *Bhagavad-gītā (Bg.*3.9) that we should work only for Kṛṣṇa. Otherwise, we become entangled. Freedom means acting on behalf of the Supreme. By acting in this way, we are not bound by karma. When a soldier follows his orders and kills on the battlefield, he receives medals, but as soon as he kills one man on his own behalf, he is considered a murderer and is subject to be hanged. This is *karma-bandhanaḥ,* bondage to karma. The act may be the same, but in one instance the soldier is acting under the orders of the state, and in the other he is acting for his own sense gratification. Similarly, when you act for Kṛṣṇa, you act in freedom, and when you act for yourself, you are bound by karma. That is the main teaching throughout *Bhagavad-gītā*. Arjuna was thinking of leaving the battlefield due to personal considerations, but when he understood that it was his duty to fight on Kṛṣṇa's behalf, he agreed.

Hayagrīva dāsa: In *Evolution and Ethics*, Huxley tries to relate karma to evolution: "In the theory of evolution, the tendency of a germ to develop according to a certain specific type...is its karma....The snowdrop is a snowdrop and not an oak, and just that kind of snowdrop, because it is the outcome of the karma of an endless series of past existences."

Śrīla Prabhupāda: That is correct. This process is called *karma-bandhanaḥ*. One takes on one body after another until he reaches the human form. He is then capable of deciding whether he should continue or put an end to this process of *karma-bandhanaḥ* by surrendering to Kṛṣṇa. If he surrenders to Kṛṣṇa, the process stops, and if he does not, the process continues according to the laws of nature.

Hayagrīva dāsa: As soon as Huxley became a Darwinist, he rejected a supernatural God and the Bible, proclaiming that "argument from design" had "received its death blow." Unlike Spinoza, he did not accept a pantheistic God, but believed in "the Divine government of the universe," and felt that the cosmic process is rational and not accidental. Still, he rejected a personal God concerned with morality.

Śrīla Prabhupāda: That is a mistake. Nature in itself is not rational; it is simply dead matter. A piece of wood is not rational, but the carpenter who shapes it is. The cosmic process may be rational, but this is only because there is a rational being behind it. That rational being is the Supreme Personality of Godhead. Nature cannot be rational out of its own accord any more than a piece of wood can become a table without a carpenter.

Śyāmasundara dāsa: Huxley felt that man must remain an agnostic because he cannot know God, even though God may exist.

Śrīla Prabhupāda: Why can man not know Him?

Śyāmasundara dāsa: Because He does not appear in phenomenal form.

Śrīla Prabhupāda: But what if He appears? You say that you cannot see Him in a phenomenal form, but God can appear and teach you. Then you can know Him. We don't try to attain knowledge of God by speculating, nor do we try to get knowledge of God from fools, rascals, and philosophers. We take knowledge directly from God Himself. God appears and gives us the instructions of *Bhagavad-gītā*, and we take our knowledge from this.

Śyāmasundara dāsa: In any case, Huxley agreed that we can never realize God by the empiric method.

Śrīla Prabhupāda: That is nice. We agree that God cannot be known by our present senses. However, we do not agree that God cannot be known at all. The present senses can be purified by Kṛṣṇa consciousness, and with purified senses, we can come to know God.

Śyāmasundara dāsa: Huxley also introduced the conception called epiphenomenalism, the belief that the mind and consciousness are products of the physical process.

Śrīla Prabhupāda: We also accept the fact that the mind is physical and that consciousness is also physical and yet subtle.

Śyāmasundara dāsa: For Huxley, when the body dies, the mind and consciousness also die.

Śrīla Prabhupāda: But he has no information of the soul. Wherever there is the soul, there is mind, consciousness, and everything else. The mind, consciousness, and intelligence are all present, but now they are materially contaminated. What we have to do is to purify them. It is not that we are to try to make our mind, consciousness and intelligence nil. That is not possible.

Śyāmasundara dāsa: But when the body dies, does the individual consciousness also die with it?

Śrīla Prabhupāda: No. How can you die? Your consciousness simply carries you to another body.

Henri Bergson
(1859-1941)

Hayagrīva dāsa: Bergson maintained that God's reality can be intuited only by mystical experience. The creative effort "is of God if it is not God Himself." This knowledge of God leads to activity, not passivity.
Śrīla Prabhupāda: Yes, knowledge of God certainly leads to activity. For instance, in *bhakti-yoga* we are engaged twenty-four hours daily in Kṛṣṇa's service. It is not that we just sit down and meditate. In *Bhagavad-gītā*, Kṛṣṇa says that the best activity is to preach the message of *Bhagavad-gītā:*

ya idaṁ paramaṁ guhyaṁ
mad-bhakteṣv abhidhāsyati
bhaktiṁ mayi parāṁ kṛtvā
mām evaiṣyaty asaṁśayaḥ

"For one who explains the supreme secret to the devotees, devotional service is guaranteed, and at the end he will come back to Me." (*Bg.* 18.68) This is also Caitanya Mahāprabhu's order: "Become a guru by spreading Kṛṣṇa consciousness." To be a guru means to be active.
Hayagrīva dāsa: The word "mystic" can have many different meanings.

When Bergson says that God's reality can be intuited only by mystical experience, what is meant?

Śrīla Prabhupāda: God is mystical for one who does not know God, but for one who knows God and receives orders from Him, God is a perceivable person. The word "mystic" may imply something vague or obscure.

Śyāmasundara dāsa: Bergson believed that the mystic who has contact with God can lead others and teach them to become godly.

Śrīla Prabhupāda: That is very nice. Then by "mystic," he means God's representative. That is the spiritual master who is following in the disciplic succession. The *Bhagavad-gītā* tells us to approach a guru who has realized the truth, God. It is not that the mystic poses himself to be God. No, he surrenders unto Kṛṣṇa and teaches others to do so. In this way, he teaches us how to become godly. Actually, it is better to say God conscious instead of godly. One who is God conscious is a true mystic.

Śyāmasundara dāsa: According to modern interpretations, a mystic is someone mysterious or magical.

Śrīla Prabhupāda: Yes, the meaning has degraded to that because so many gurus come over, display miracles, and claim to be God. So these rascals are misleading the unintelligent who want to see miracles, and the unintelligent look on these miracles as mysticism. It is another case of the cheaters and the cheated.

Hayagrīva dāsa: Originally, the Greek word *mystikos* referred to one initiated in secret religious rites, and today the word has degenerated to mean something obscure or occult. For Bergson, a mystic is one who can commune with God through contemplation and love, participate in God's love for mankind, and aid the divine purpose. This is the real meaning of "creative evolution."

Śrīla Prabhupāda: Yes, everyone is in ignorance due to a long separation from God. In the material world, the living entity has forgotten his relationship with God; therefore he acts only for sense gratification. He awakens to his real life when he is given instructions on how to become God conscious; otherwise, he lives like an animal. Sentiment is one thing, but when religion is understood in the light of good logic and philosophy, we can attain a perfect understanding of God. Without philosophy, religion is simply sentiment. Sentiment in itself does not help very much. A sentimentalist may be interested one day and disinterested another. As stated in *Śrīmad-Bhāgavatam*, religion means learning how to love God. At the present moment, in our physical condition, we cannot see God, but by hearing about Him, we can develop our dormant love.

Śyāmasundara dāsa: Bergson envisioned two types of religion: static and dynamic. Static religion is comprised of myths devised by human intelligence as a means of defense against life's miseries. Fearful of the future, man attempts to overcome his condition by constructing religious myths.

Śrīla Prabhupāda: Whatever is created by human beings is not acceptable. We do not follow such faiths because human beings are always imperfect. We cannot accept anything manufactured by human beings; we must take our information directly from God, as it is given in *Śrīmad-Bhāgavatam*, *Bhagavad-gītā* and other scriptures. *Dharmaṁ tu sākṣād bhagavat-praṇītam.* "Real religious principles are enacted by the Supreme Personality of Godhead." (*Bhāg.* 6.3.19) Kṛṣṇa says, "Surrender unto Me." This is real religion. It is not man-made. Man is constantly creating so many ism's, but these are not perfect. Religion that leads us to surrender to God is real religion. Otherwise it is bogus.

Śyāmasundara dāsa: For Bergson, real religion is dynamic.

Śrīla Prabhupāda: Yes, that is so. It is not static because it is on the spiritual platform. The spirit is the dynamic force in this body. There is no question of the spirit being static.

Śyāmasundara dāsa: Bergson says that prompted by the vital impulse, by dynamic religion, the human will identifies with the divine will in a mystical union.

Śrīla Prabhupāda: Yes, that is the process of Kṛṣṇa consciousness. We are teaching people to agree with the divine will, which means surrendering to God. Oneness means agreeing with this teaching.

Śyāmasundara dāsa: Real religion is a mystic oneness with God.

Śrīla Prabhupāda: Yes, oneness means that I agree with God. God says, "Surrender," and I say, "Yes, I surrender." God tells Arjuna, "Fight," and Arjuna fights. Oneness means that we agree with God on all points.

Hayagrīva dāsa: Bergson felt that the greatest obstacle to creative evolution is the struggle with materialism. He believed that politics and economic reforms cannot help matters.

Śrīla Prabhupāda: Politics and economic reforms can help provided they are properly guided—that is, provided they aim at helping our understanding of our relationship with God. Vedic civilization was divided into four *varṇas* and four *āśramas*, and these divisions were meant to help people develop their dormant God consciousness. Unfortunately, today the *kṣatriyas,* the administrators, have forgotten the real objective of human life. Now they are thinking only of caring for the body, living comfortably, and gratifying their senses. But that is not the real purpose of human civilization.

Hayagrīva dāsa: Bergson believed that the spirit of mysticism must be kept alive by the fortunate few who know God "until such time as a profound change in the material conditions imposed on humanity by nature should permit, in spiritual matters, of a profound transformation."

Śrīla Prabhupāda: Yes, and this Kṛṣṇa consciousness movement is dedicated to bringing about this change. I have already said that a perfect society is centered in love of God. This love is without motive. It is a natural love, like the love between a son and his father or mother. The material conditions provoke certain bodily demands: eating, sleeping, mating, and defending. At present, people are interested only in these four activities.

Hayagrīva dāsa: How are these material conditions going to change?

Śrīla Prabhupāda: These daily bodily necessities will remain, but in addition, people should understand God and His instructions. That will bring about change. We are not neglecting the bodily necessities, but we realize that our main business is advancing in Kṛṣṇa consciousness. Presently, Kṛṣṇa consciousness is not supported by the state or social leaders. People are busy thinking of eating, sleeping, mating, and defending. It is not that these activities stop when we are Kṛṣṇa conscious; rather, they are regulated.

Hayagrīva dāsa: Bergson was optimistic in his belief that the mystics, through love, would eventually help mankind return to God.

Śrīla Prabhupāda: Yes, this is the real purpose of human life. Man has the opportunity afforded by nature to understand the instructions of the Vedas and the spiritual master. Only a suicidal civilization remains in darkness, concerned only with the bodily necessities.

Śyāmasundara dāsa: For Bergson, the nature of God is love, through which the world comes into being.

Śrīla Prabhupāda: Yes, of course God loves. Unless He loves, why does He come down personally to give us instructions through the scriptures?

Hayagrīva dāsa: In *Creative Evolution,* Bergson writes: "For an ego which does not change does not endure, and a psychic state which remains the same so long as it is not replaced by the following state does not endure either." He sees all psychic states of the individual, including the ego, as constantly changing.

Śrīla Prabhupāda: This is the false ego that says, "I am this body." By education, we can come to understand that we are spirit soul. Then the activities of the soul begin. The first lesson of *Bhagavad-gītā* instructs us that the living entity is not the material body but the soul within. That soul is Brahman, pure spirit. Once we understand that we are not the body, our struggle to maintain the body stops. *Brahma-bhūtaḥ prasannātmā (Bg.* 18.54). Once we understand that we are spirit soul, we concern ourselves with elevating the spirit soul to the highest perfection. We then come to understand that we are not only spirit soul, but that everyone else is spirit soul as well. We then want everyone to be given a chance to attain perfect understanding.
Śyāmasundara dāsa: Bergson's Vitalism states that the life force cannot be explained by physics and chemistry or the other sciences. It is separate from Darwin's mechanical laws. Science will never be able to accurately explain the source of life, which is nonmaterial.
Śrīla Prabhupāda: That is very nice. He is speaking of the soul, but he is unable to capture the idea positively. It is true that the soul is not controlled by physical laws, and that is verified by *Bhagavad-gītā* itself:

nainaṁ chindanti śastrāṇi
nainaṁ dahati pāvakaḥ
na cainaṁ kledayanty āpo
na śoṣayati mārutaḥ

"The soul can never be cut into pieces by any weapon, nor can he be burned by fire, nor moistened by water, nor withered by the wind." (*Bg.* 2.23) The vital force, or the soul, can be temporarily covered by physical elements, but the soul itself does not belong to any of the physical elements. The soul is a living force, and it has a little independence. The supreme living force is God, and the individual soul is part and parcel of God, just as sparks are part of a great fire. The individual soul misuses his independence when he himself wants to become God and lord it over material nature. He then falls from his purely spiritual position into the physical encagement, and, forgetting his real identity, he thinks that he is the body. But he is not. The body is a circumstantial covering, a dress. The living, vital force is different.
Śyāmasundara dāsa: Bergson says that the reality, the living force, is always in a state of becoming and never at rest. Logical or scientific explanations are ineffective because they deal with static problems.
Śrīla Prabhupāda: Yes, so-called scientists do not know the real basic

principle; therefore they are misled and misleading. The soul is living force. The soul has a little independence, and he wants to enjoy the material world, which he cannot do. By running after phantasmagoria and trying to lord it over material nature, he becomes more and more entrapped.

Śyāmasundara dāsa: Being constantly dynamic, changing, and unpredictable, the life force is too elusive for scientific investigation.

Śrīla Prabhupāda: Yes, this is so. Because it is living force, it must be dynamic. Living force is not dead stone. We are all living force. We may be sitting here now, or we may be leaving. No one can check these movements in time. Not even God interferes with our dynamic force. He allows us to do whatever we like. If God interferes with our independence, we are no longer living entities. We become dead stones. Therefore God does not interfere; He gives us full freedom. At the same time, He comes down to instruct us, saying, "Why are you so engaged in this foolish activity? Please come to Me, back home, back to Godhead. Then you will be happy."

Śyāmasundara dāsa: For Bergson, the unpredictable life force is constantly creating new things.

Śrīla Prabhupāda: Yes, it is creating new things in the material phenomena, but when the life force is spiritually situated, there are no such changes. Our only business is to serve Kṛṣṇa. And even in the service of Kṛṣṇa, there are many varieties, but those are spiritual varieties. At the present moment, we are creating material varieties and a variety of bodies, all subject to the threefold miseries and to birth, death, old age, and disease. As long as we are materially entrapped, our dynamic force is creating trouble, and we are becoming more and more entangled.

Śyāmasundara dāsa: Can we ever predict the movements of the life force?

Śrīla Prabhupāda: Yes, it is moving in a variety of dresses, but its ultimate future is to return home, back to Godhead. But because the individual soul is acting unintelligently, he has to be kicked in the face very strongly by material nature. Then he will come to his senses. That is his position. When he thinks intelligently, he realizes that it is his duty to serve Kṛṣṇa instead of his own material body. In this material world, we see that everybody is trying to be happy, but everyone is constantly being frustrated. This is because material happiness ultimately means frustration. This is māyā's way of kicking.

Śyāmasundara dāsa: In any case, the life force will eventually return

to Godhead?
Śrīla Prabhupāda: Yes, everyone will sooner or later. Some sooner, and some later.
Śyāmasundara dāsa: But can we predict that the process of punishment will have some permanent effect? Many prisoners leave the prison, but some come back.
Śrīla Prabhupāda: There is nothing permanent. Because we have a little independence, we have the freedom to misuse our independence again and return to the prison; otherwise there is no meaning to independence. Independence means that you can do what you like.
Śyāmasundara dāsa: Bergson spoke of the soul as *elan vital*, "vital impulse."
Śrīla Prabhupāda: The soul is a living, vital force, and is therefore dynamic. It is never at rest, but is always working through the mind, intelligence, and body.
Śyāmasundara dāsa: Is the soul present in the same quantity in every living body?
Śrīla Prabhupāda: Yes. Its measurement is the same: one ten thousandth part of the tip of a hair.
Śyāmasundara dāsa: But what about its amount of energy?
Śrīla Prabhupāda: Yes, the same amount of spiritual energy is everywhere, in the ant and in the elephant.
Śyāmasundara dāsa: When you say that the soul is one ten thousandth part of the tip of a hair, this seems to denote a physical size. That is, this seems to be a physical concept.
Śrīla Prabhupāda: Material size and spiritual size are not the same. Spiritual size is permanent, and material size is changing. We give this example of the tip of a hair because you have no spiritual vision. Therefore you have to understand by a material example.
Śyāmasundara dāsa: Bergson believes that the qualities of the soul can be perceived only by intuition, not by the senses.
Śrīla Prabhupāda: That is correct. The soul cannot be experienced by the senses, but we can understand that the soul is absent from a dead man. We see the dead body, and this is called perception. Then we understand that there is something intangible that is absent, and we call that the soul. This is the process of intuition.
Hayagrīva dāsa: Concerning remembering and forgetting, Bergson writes: "The cerebral mechanism is arranged just so as to drive back into the unconscious almost the whole of this past, and to admit beyond the threshold only that which can cast light on the present situation or

further the action now being prepared—in short, only that which can give useful work."

Śrīla Prabhupāda: The cerebral mechanism is a machine, just like this microphone. This machine has nothing to do with my voice, but it amplifies it so that others may hear. In this way, the machine can help. Similarly, the brain is a machine that can help us understand God. Human beings have a good machine, but they do not know the use of it. That is their misfortune.

Hayagrīva dāsa: Doesn't Kṛṣṇa arrange this cerebral mechanism, causing remembrance and forgetfulness?

Śrīla Prabhupāda: Yes, because He is the supreme power, He can do this. If we persistently want to forget Kṛṣṇa, despite Kṛṣṇa's instructions, Kṛṣṇa, who is within the heart, gives us a chance to become more and more forgetful so that we completely forget our relationship with God. Kṛṣṇa says:

tān ahaṁ dviṣataḥ krūrān
saṁsāreṣu narādhamān
kṣipāmy ajasram aśubhān
āsurīṣv eva yoniṣu

"Those who are envious and mischievous, who are the lowest among men, are cast by Me into the ocean of material existence, into various demoniac species of life." (*Bg.* 16.19) He also says:

sarvasya cāhaṁ hṛdi sanniviṣṭho
mattaḥ smṛtir jñānam apohanaṁ ca

"I am seated in everyone's heart, and from Me come remembrance, knowledge, and forgetfulness." (*Bg.* 15.15) It is Kṛṣṇa's punishment that the living entity remains in perpetual darkness, but it is the mercy of Kṛṣṇa's devotee, the Vaiṣṇava, that he remembers his relationship with Kṛṣṇa. Therefore Bhaktivinoda Ṭhākura says, "O Vaiṣṇava, please accept me as your dog." The cerebral mechanism, the brain, is a machine, and according to one's desires, he remembers Kṛṣṇa or forgets Him. Just as Kṛṣṇa enables the demoniac to be punished, He gives the devotee the intelligence by which he can remember and understand.

teṣāṁ satata-yuktānāṁ
bhajatāṁ prīti-pūrvakam
dadāmi buddhi-yogaṁ taṁ
yena mām upayānti te

"To those who are constantly devoted and worship Me with love, I give the understanding by which they can come to Me." (*Bg.* 10.10)

Hayagrīva dāsa: Can we forget Kṛṣṇa eternally?

Śrīla Prabhupāda: No, it is not possible. A son may be separated from his father, but it is not possible for him to forget his father eternally. Sometimes he remembers his father. The father is always remembering the son, and looking forward to the time when the son will obey his orders. So there is no question of forgetting perpetually.

Śyāmasundara dāsa: Because the living entity has independence, at one moment he may be liberated, and at another moment, conditioned?

Śrīla Prabhupāda: Kṛṣṇa has given you liberation. When you misuse your liberation, you become entrapped.

Śyāmasundara dāsa: But is this all predictable? Can we know it beforehand?

Śrīla Prabhupāda: What is the use of all this prediction? The prediction is that the living entity will be kicked, kicked, kicked, and kicked, until someday he will come to Kṛṣṇa.

Śyāmasundara dāsa: So after falling down many times, the living entity will eventually come to Kṛṣṇa and remain permanently. Is that right?

Śrīla Prabhupāda: No, there is no question of permanence. Because the living entity has independence, he can misuse that independence and fall down again. A man is not permanently free just because he's released from prison. He can return to prison again. There is no guarantee. This is what is meant by eternally conditioned. The living entities in the spiritual sky who are eternally liberated will never be conditioned because they never choose to misuse their independence. They are very experienced.

Hayagrīva dāsa: Concerning karma and transmigration, Bergson writes: "What are we, in fact, what is our character, if not the condensation of the history that we have lived from our birth—nay, even before our birth, since we bring with us prenatal dispositions. Doubtless we think with only a small part of our past, but it is with our entire past, including the original dint of our soul, that we desire, will, and act." Although we cannot recall much of the past, our present state has grown out of it.

Śrīla Prabhupāda: It is our defect that we cannot recall the past; therefore little tests are there to remind us of our opportunity to take advantage of Vedic knowledge. We have forgotten, but our forgetfulness is not perpetual. When we are reminded, we can come to our real consciousness, Kṛṣṇa consciousness. Forgetting Kṛṣṇa, God, people are thinking that they are masters of everything. Many so-called scientists are decrying God, and claiming that they can do everything independently. This attitude is demoniac. *Sādhu, śāstra,* and guru are here to remind us that we are under the clutches of māyā and that we are not to remain in this position.

Hayagrīva dāsa: Bergson is essentially saying that our past activities have determined what we are today.

Śrīla Prabhupāda: Yes, that is karma. According to our past karmas, we are in a particular position. However, this position can be changed; it is not that it will have to continue indefinitely. Kṛṣṇa says that we are suffering due to our past misdeeds, and this suffering was caused by our not surrendering to Him. If we surrender to Kṛṣṇa, He will put an end to all the reactions of karma. So we do not have to continue to suffer the reactions of our past activities.

Hayagrīva dāsa: Bergson writes: "From this survival of the past, it follows that consciousness cannot go through the same state twice. Circumstances may still be the same, but they will act no longer on the same person, since they find him at a new moment of his history. Our personality, which is being built up each instant with its accumulated experience, changes without ceasing."

Śrīla Prabhupāda: There is no cessation because the soul is eternal. Consciousness is also eternal, but it is changing according to the circumstances, association, time, place, and personalities involved. Good association is required, because by it, our consciousness can be changed from material to spiritual. The purpose of this Kṛṣṇa consciousness movement is to change our consciousness from absorption in material things to Kṛṣṇa. This requires guidance, which is provided by Kṛṣṇa's instructions and the spiritual master. Kṛṣṇa is so kind that He has given us *śāstra, sādhu,* and guru.

Hayagrīva dāsa: But if the personality is determined by experience, and experience is forgotten at death, then a new personality must emerge at rebirth. How can the personality be built up with accumulated experience?

Śrīla Prabhupāda: We may forget our deeds in the past, but Kṛṣṇa does not forget them. He therefore gives us a chance to fulfill previous desires. At death, the body changes, but the soul does not change. The soul continues and brings with him reactions of past deeds. Even though the soul forgets what he has done in the past, Kṛṣṇa is there to remind him that he wanted to do this or that.

Hayagrīva dāsa: So the person is the same, but the personality changes?

Śrīla Prabhupāda: Yes. This personality can be perfected if we follow the instructions of Kṛṣṇa.

Hayagrīva dāsa: But personality, as we understand it, changes from life to life, doesn't it?

Śrīla Prabhupāda: Yes, but according to your work, your body will be selected. It is not that you select your body. Because you have acted in a certain way, superior authorities select your body according to your activities.

Hayagrīva dāsa: If at death the soul takes the mind, intelligence, and ego with it into a new body, isn't it possible for the mind to remember past lives?

Śrīla Prabhupāda: Yes, and there are many instances of this. Bharata Mahārāja received the body of a deer, but by the grace of Kṛṣṇa he remembered everything about his past life. Although Bharata Mahārāja was a devotee, he neglected his devotional service due to being overly attached to a deer. Since he was thinking of the deer at the time of death, he received the body of a deer, but out of His great mercy, Kṛṣṇa reminded him of his situation. In his next birth, therefore, Mahārāja Bharata was born into a good *brāhmaṇa* family.

Hayagrīva dāsa: Bergson says that "our personality shoots, grows, and ripens without ceasing." If this is so, how can the *jīva* regress to a lower form of life? How could a greater experience be confined to a lesser one?

Śrīla Prabhupāda: According to nature's process, everything is calculated at the time of death. Here in Hawaii we see that there are many boys addicted to the water sport called surfing. Now they are creating a mentality which will enable them to become aquatics. So naturally at the time of death they will think of all these things, and nature will give them a body accordingly. We cannot check this process. After death, we are completely under nature's control. We cannot dictate. Since people cannot or will not understand this, they conclude that there is no life after death.

Hayagrīva dāsa: How could a great personality like Indra, with his mind, intelligence, and ego all intact, possibly become a hog?

Śrīla Prabhupāda: Yes, this can be done, because as long as we are materially existing, our thoughts are under the modes of material nature. Sometimes our thoughts are in the mode of goodness, sometimes in passion, and sometimes in ignorance. Accordingly, we go up and down the scale in different species. In order to keep ourselves on the proper platform, we should engage in devotional service. This is confirmed in *Bhagavad-gītā:*

māṁ ca yo'vyabhicāreṇa
bhakti-yogena sevate
sa guṇān samatītyaitān
brahma-bhūyāya kalpate

"One who engages in full devotional service, who does not fall down in any circumstance, at once transcends the modes of material nature and thus comes to the level of Brahman." (*Bg.* 14.26) If we stay on the Brahman platform, there is no degradation. We are trying to do this by engaging ourselves every moment in Kṛṣṇa consciousness.
Hayagrīva dāsa: Bergson saw change as maturation. He writes: "We are seeking only the precise meaning that our consciousness gives to this word, 'exist,' and we find that, for a conscious being, to exist is to change, to change is to mature, to mature is to go on creating oneself endlessly."
Śrīla Prabhupāda: It is not necessary to struggle to attain our highest position, because that position is indicated by Śrī Kṛṣṇa: "Abandon all dharmas, and surrender unto Me. I will give you all protection." (*Bg.* 18.66) Unfortunately, the living entity thinks that Kṛṣṇa is an ordinary human being and therefore incapable of granting the topmost position. Therefore he goes on with his plan making. After many, many births, he finally comes to the conclusion that everything is Kṛṣṇa. *Vāsudevaḥ sarvam iti sa mahātmā surdurlabhaḥ* (*Bg.* 7.19). But why go through many births of struggle? If we at once accept Kṛṣṇa's instructions, we can become perfect immediately.
Śyāmasundara dāsa: Bergson sees the life impulse moving through the universe and creating new forms and varieties, just as an artist creates different paintings. The creations progressively improve.
Śrīla Prabhupāda: Yes, you might call that evolution. The living entity moves through 8,400,000 species, and each is better than the last, until one comes to the human form. Once he has reached the human platform, he may choose to become a demigod like Lord Brahmā. Brahmā is also a living entity; he is not in the Viṣṇu category. Yet Brahmā has such power that he can create this universe. God can create infinite universes, but Brahmā can create at least one universe. Of course, from the human form, one can also regress to lower forms.
Śyāmasundara dāsa: For Bergson, world evolution moves progressively through history as instinct, intelligence, and intuition.
Śrīla Prabhupāda: Then he agrees that one moves from the lower stages to the higher.
Śyāmasundara dāsa: To realization?
Śrīla Prabhupāda: Realization means arriving at the truth.
Śyāmasundara dāsa: Bergson says that understanding through intuition is superior to understanding through the intelligence.
Śrīla Prabhupāda: That is correct.
Śyāmasundara dāsa: He sees the creative process as advancing up to

the level of immortality.
Śrīla Prabhupāda: Yes, we are receiving different types of bodies, and when we are perfectly situated in Kṛṣṇa consciousness, we no longer receive material bodies.
Śyāmasundara dāsa: Then although the life force itself is eternal, the forms advance up to the form of immortality?
Śrīla Prabhupāda: The forms are changing, but the living force is not changing. The forms are changing, but the person within the forms is permanent. When he identifies with the body, he thinks that he is changing.
Śyāmasundara dāsa: Is the progress toward human immortality a creative process? By creative, Bergson implies that we are creating our immortality.
Śrīla Prabhupāda: No, you are always immortal. You are immortal by constitution, but you are changing bodies. The process is creative in the sense that you create your own body or your next body as you desire. If you create within yourself the mentality of a dog, you will get the body of a dog in the next life. Similarly, if you create the mentality of a servant of God, you return to Kṛṣṇa.
Hayagrīva dāsa: In *Creative Evolution*, Bergson writes: "We may conclude, then, that individuality is never perfect, and that it is often difficult, sometimes impossible, to tell what is an individual, and what is not, but that life nevertheless manifests a search for individuality, as if it strove to constitute systems naturally isolated, naturally closed."
Śrīla Prabhupāda: Why is there a search for individuality? We are all naturally individuals.

na tv evāhaṁ jātu nāsaṁ
na tvaṁ neme janādhipāḥ
na caiva na bhaviṣyāmaḥ
sarve vayam ataḥ param

"Never was there a time when I did not exist, nor you, nor all these kings; nor in the future shall any of us cease to be." (*Bg*. 2.12) We are individuals in the past, present, and future. Our individuality is always there, but in quantity we are not as great as Kṛṣṇa. Compared to Him, our intelligence is very meager. When we utilize our individuality properly and follow Kṛṣṇa's instructions, we perfect our lives. Māyāvādī philosophers want to annihilate this individuality, but this is not possible. We are perpetually individuals, and God is also an individual. It is incorrect to think that by killing individuality, we become one with God.

Our individuality is retained. Even though for a time we may think, "I will merge into the existence of God," we will fall down again due to individuality. In any case, there is no need for a search for individuality because we are always individuals.

Hayagrīva dāsa: According to Bergson, we can see the creation as either coming from God, or moving toward Him. Depending on our viewpoint, "we perceive God as efficient cause or as final cause."

Śrīla Prabhupāda: God is always there. He was there before the creation, and when the creation is finished, He will be there. God is not part of the creation. Being the creator, He exists before, during, and after His creation. This is standard Vedic knowledge.

aham evāsam evāgre
nānyad yat sad-asat param
paścād ahaṁ yad etac ca
yo'vaśiṣyeta so'smy aham

"It is I, the Personality of Godhead, who was existing before the creation, when there was nothing but Myself. Nor was there the material nature, the cause of this creation. That which you see now is also I, the Personality of Godhead, and after annihilation, what remains will also be I, the Personality of Godhead." (*Bhāg.* 2.9.33)

Hayagrīva dāsa: Bergson is saying that God is the beginning, middle, and end, depending on our point of view.

Śrīla Prabhupāda: It is not dependent on our viewpoint. God is always there, but because we are imperfect, we are thinking in this limited way. This cosmic manifestation is a temporary creation to give the individual soul a chance to develop his consciousness. If he does not do so, and there is universal annihilation, he must remain in an unconscious position. When there is creation, he again comes to consciousness. This is the cycle that is going on. But God is always there.

Hayagrīva dāsa: Bergson further writes: "If life realizes a plan, it ought to manifest a greater harmony the further it advances, just as a house shows better and better the idea of the architect as stone is set upon stone. If, on the contrary, the unity of life is to be found solely in the impetus that pushes it along the road of time, the harmony is not in front but behind. The unity is given at the start as an impulsion, not placed at the end as an attraction."

Śrīla Prabhupāda: This is what is called nature's course. First of all, something is created, it develops, stays for a while, leaves some by-products, grows old, dwindles, and finally vanishes. These are the changes that all material things are subject to, but the spirit soul is not material and therefore has nothing to do with bodily changes. The soul has his perpetual duty and activity, which is devotional service. If we are trained in our perpetual duty, we can put an end to bodily changes, remain in our eternal, spiritual body, and return home, back to Godhead.

Hayagrīva dāsa: So creative evolution must necessarily be the evolution of the soul?

Śrīla Prabhupāda: No, since the soul is ever existing, there is no question of evolution. As long as the soul is entangled in material existence and bodily conceptions, he thinks that a superior body evolves from an inferior one. However, if his consciousness is changed, there is no changing bodies. He remains in his eternal body.

Śyāmasundara dāsa: Bergson thinks that it is the vital force that is guiding everyone and creating its own evolution.

Śrīla Prabhupāda: Yes, the vital force will determine this. But the individual must be educated to know how to make progress. It is ultimately up to the spirit soul whether to surrender to Kṛṣṇa or not. The living entity has the right to accept or reject. If he takes the right path, he progresses, but if he rejects this path, he will regress. This depends on him.

Hayagrīva dāsa: There seems to be a basic contradiction between Bergson and the Vedas, as far as the evolution of the universe is concerned.

Śrīla Prabhupāda: Anything material, be it the universe or whatever, undergoes the basic changes I mentioned. Since its birth, this universe has been increasing in volume, and that is material change. This has nothing to do with the spiritual. Just as we have a soul within this body, the universe also has a soul within, and that is the Garbhodakaśāyī Viṣṇu. Viṣṇu is not changing, but the universe is.

Hayagrīva dāsa: Bergson theorizes that the further life advances, the greater harmony is being realized.

Śrīla Prabhupāda: There is harmonious change, just as a child's body harmoniously changes into a boy's body. In any case, change is there.

Hayagrīva dāsa: So there is harmony in the beginning, middle, and end?

Śrīla Prabhupāda: Everything is in harmony, be it material or spiritual. That is God's law.

Hayagrīva dāsa: If everything is always in harmony, evolution has an incidental meaning.

Śrīla Prabhupāda: This is harmony: One is an aquatic, then an insect, then a plant, then a tree, and so on up to the body of a human being.

Change is there, but there is harmony. Once one has attained a human body, he can decide whether or not to stop this evolutionary process, or to remain in it. If one accepts the instructions of Kṛṣṇa, he can put an end to this bothersome evolution. If not, he remains. This is the version of *Bhagavad-gītā:*

aśraddadhānāḥ puruṣā
dharmasyāsya parantapa
aprāpya māṁ nivartante
mṛtyu-saṁsāra-vartmani

"Those who are not faithful on the path of devotional service cannot attain Me, O conqueror of foes, but return to birth and death in this material world." (*Bg.* 9.3) By following Kṛṣṇa's instructions, we can become completely detached from the cycle of birth and death.

Hayagrīva dāsa: Bergson sees man as the culmination of earth's evolution. He writes: "Man might be considered the reason for the existence of the entire organization of life on our planet."

Śrīla Prabhupāda: On this planet there are different types of men. Not everyone is in the same position. There are fools and sages, rich men and poor.

Hayagrīva dāsa: He is speaking of mankind in general.

Śrīla Prabhupāda: What does he mean by all mankind? Everyone is an individual. In any case, man is not the highest form of life.

Hayagrīva dāsa: Bergson sees the material worlds as being basically isolated from one another. He writes: "It is not artificially, for reasons of mere convenience, that we isolate our solar system: Nature itself invites us to isolate it."

Śrīla Prabhupāda: We feel isolated because we are individuals. In a prison, every criminal is different from every other criminal, and everyone has to suffer the consequences of his criminal activities. Thus every individual is suffering or enjoying according to his past deeds. If there is combination, you forget individuality. But that is not possible.

Hayagrīva dāsa: We feel isolated as individuals, but in addition we feel isolated communally on this planet. Man has never been able to communicate with beings on other planets.

Śrīla Prabhupāda: What is the point in communicating with other planets? They are also like this planet. People there have their individuality also.

Hayagrīva dāsa: Well, man has always had the desire to communicate with something outside of this world, something higher. Basically, this must be a desire to reach God.

Śrīla Prabhupāda: Since God is there, why not communicate with Him? There is no point in communicating with other planets. Other living entities cannot help us. If we communicate with God, Kṛṣṇa, we automatically understand everything else. If you hear people talking on other planets, what benefit will you derive? It is better to listen to Kṛṣṇa speaking *Bhagavad-gītā*.

Hayagrīva dāsa: Is this isolation between worlds characteristic only of the lower and middle planetary systems? Is there as much isolation between the higher systems?

Śrīla Prabhupāda: Isolation is always there. Even in this world, crows remain to themselves, and swans remain to themselves. This isolation is natural because everyone is functioning under the different modes of material nature. However, if people come to Kṛṣṇa consciousness, there is no longer isolation because everyone is engaged in the Lord's service.

Hayagrīva dāsa: Bergson sees the universe itself as expanding and evolving. He writes: "For the universe is not made, but is being made continually. It is growing, perhaps indefinitely, by the addition of new worlds."

Śrīla Prabhupāda: Yes, the universes emanate from the breathing of Mahā-viṣṇu. If we accept the fact that the universe is increasing, then universes may come out like particles and then begin to develop. We see that for everything material, there is a small beginning. When the living entity enters the womb, he is very small indeed. A banyan tree begins to grow from a small seed. This is the way of nature. It is a fact that the universe is increasing, but not perpetually. It increases to a certain extent, stops, dwindles, and vanishes.

Hayagrīva dāsa: Modern astronomers theorize that the universe is expanding and that the systems are exploding outward into space and moving proportionately further and further from one another, just like raisins expanding in dough when it is heated in the oven.

Śrīla Prabhupāda: That expansion goes on to a certain extent. Then it stops.

Hayagrīva dāsa: But Bergson sees the universe as evolving toward some grand harmony.

Śrīla Prabhupāda: What does he mean by grand harmony? Everything is increasing, and everything will eventually dwindle and be annihilated. That is the course of material nature, and the harmony is in this process.

Hayagrīva dāsa: In attempting to relate God to the universe, Bergson speaks of "a center from which worlds shoot out like rockets in a fireworks

display."
Śrīla Prabhupāda: The creation is like a wheel rotating. There are spokes, and there is a rim. There is also a center around which everything revolves. *Ahaṁ sarvasya prabhavo mattaḥ sarvaṁ pravartate.* "I am the source of all spiritual and material worlds. Everything emanates from Me." (*Bg.* 10.8) That center is God, and all the parts are revolving around Him. In any case, the center remains where it is, and is always the same.
Śyāmasundara dāsa: Bergson spoke of the world as "a machine for the making of gods." In a sense, this world is a training ground wherein we can make ourselves immortal.
Śrīla Prabhupāda: You are immortal already. You have just forgotten.

mamaivāṁśo jīva-loke
jīva-bhūtaḥ sanātanaḥ
manaḥ ṣaṣṭhānīndriyāṇi
prakṛti-sthāni karṣati

"The living entities in this conditioned world are My eternal, fragmental parts. Due to conditioned life, they are struggling very hard with the six senses, which include the mind." (*Bg.* 15.7) There is bewilderment, but no change. We are fixed as spirit soul. It is as if we are dreaming: "Oh, I have fallen into the Pacific Ocean. I am drowning. Save me!" We may dream so many troublesome things, but actually there is no Pacific Ocean, and we are not drowning. It is simply a dream. The temporary covering of the body is just like a dream, and as soon as you come to Kṛṣṇa consciousness, you wake up. When you are awake, the dream has no value. However, when the dream is happening, you are thinking that it is real, but since it has no value, it is called māyā. Māyā means "that which has no real existence but appears to."
Śyāmasundara dāsa: Does māyā mean nothingness?
Śrīla Prabhupāda: You cannot say that. It is nothing appearing like something, but we do not say that it is nothing. Māyāvādīs say that it is nothing, but we say that it is temporary. How can you say that a cloud is nothing? A cloud appears, remains for a while, and then goes. The body is there temporarily for a few years, or a few hours. It is like a cloud. We cannot say that it is nothing, but that it is temporary.
Śyāmasundara dāsa: Bergson thought that the life force, passing through different bodies, will eventually become immortal on this planet.
Śrīla Prabhupāda: At present, people are living for an average of seventy years, at the utmost a hundred. They are thinking that they would like to live for a hundred and seventy years, but in this material world, seventy, a hundred and seventy, or seventeen million years are the same.

The years will eventually end. However, one who only lives for seventy years thinks that a million years is immortality.

Śyāmasundara dāsa: Bergson is interested in knowing the course of future evolution. He feels that because man has progressed from the instinctive stage to the intelligent and then to the intuitive stages, he will eventually attain the immortal stage.

Śrīla Prabhupāda: That is very nice, the idea that man will attain perfection. Progress means that you go forward, that you do not remain stagnant. The Vedas say:

tad viṣṇoḥ paramaṁ padaṁ
sadā paśyanti sūrayaḥ
divīva cakṣur ātataṁ
viṣṇor yat paramaṁ padạm

"The lotus feet of Lord Viṣṇu are the supreme objective of all the demigods. These lotus feet of the Lord are as enlightening as the sun in the sky." (*Ṛg Veda* 1.22.20) Those who are learned and advanced in knowledge are called *sūrayaḥ*. Modern scientists are looking forward to going to other planets, but those who are learned are looking forward to going to the lotus feet of Viṣṇu. They are thinking, "When will I reach You?" The goal is there, and those who know it do not miss it. One who is Kṛṣṇa conscious knows the goal and attempts to reach it. Those who do not know the goal waste their time philosophizing and misleading others. This is the blind leading the blind.

Hayagrīva dāsa: So when Bergson refers to the universe as "a machine for the making of gods," in what sense is he correct?

Śrīla Prabhupāda: Well, in one sense there is no making of gods, because the demigods are already there. All the parts of the wheel are there complete. Our normal life is a life in Kṛṣṇa consciousness. That is *mukti*, liberation. It is not a question of becoming something different, but of returning to normal health, to our constitutional position. In māyā, a man is diseased, and in his delirium, he speaks all kinds of nonsense.

Hayagrīva dāsa: Then instead of speaking of the universe as a machine for the making of gods, it would be better to call it a hospital for the curing of souls.

Śrīla Prabhupāda: Yes, it is a hospital. When we are cured, we are freed from all designations, which begin with the body. People are thinking, "I am European, American, Christian, Hindu," and so on. These are all misconceptions. Our real position is that we are part and parcel of Kṛṣṇa and are His eternal servants. It is not that a man can be made into a demigod or God. Man is already part and parcel of God. He has

to understand his position in order to attain *mukti*. After all, what is a demigod? There is no difference between a demigod and a man. A demigod is in a better position, that's all. A high court judge and a layman are both human beings, but the judge is in a superior position. The demigods are elevated due to their being situated in a higher mode, in *sattva-guṇa*. On this earth, *rajo-guṇa* and *tamo-guṇa*, passion and ignorance, are prominent. Being spirit soul, however, we are not subject to any *guṇa*. We are transcendental. If we keep ourselves in our constitutional transcendental position by engaging in devotional service, we are above all the *guṇas*, including *sattva-guṇa*. This is the liberation attained by devotional service. The devotees are not interested in becoming demigods. After all, the demigods are also rotting in this material world. For a devotee, Brahmā, Indra, Candra, and the other demigods are no better than small insects. Everyone has a different type of body according to karma, whether it be Brahmā's body or an ant's body. One who has attained liberation is not at all concerned with the body; therefore devotees are not interested in being elevated to higher planetary systems. In fact, one devotee prays, "I don't care to be a Brahmā. I would prefer to be a small ant in the house of a devotee." This is the Vaiṣṇava position.
Śyāmasundara dāsa: Bergson conceived of two types of morality: closed and open. Closed morality depends on prevailing conventions, or social pressures. This is traditional morality.
Śrīla Prabhupāda: That kind of morality changes according to time and circumstance. What is moral in one society may be considered immoral in another.
Śyāmasundara dāsa: Open morality is determined by individuals and is guided by intuition. Bergson saw this as the morality of saints like St. Paul or St. Francis.
Śrīla Prabhupāda: If we are God conscious, we can tell what is real morality. Because St. Paul was a *sādhu*, he could say what morality is. Our process is *sādhu*, guru, *śāstra*. We have to accept knowledge through saintly persons, and this knowledge has to be confirmed by the scriptures and explained by the guru. In this way, our knowledge can be perfect. The scriptures are already there. We have to read them and understand how they have been realized and followed by saintly persons. If there is any difficulty in understanding, we should inquire from the spiritual master. In this way, *sādhu*, guru, and *śāstra* confirm one another. It is not that we try to understand these scriptures directly. We have to see how the scriptural injunctions are being followed by saintly persons.

Samuel Alexander
(1859-1938)

Śyāmasundara dāsa: Alexander is the philosopher of emergent evolution. For him, external objects have an existence independent of consciousness. Unlike many other philosophies, Alexander's neo-realism contends that something may exist even though it is not perceived.
Śrīla Prabhupāda: Yes, that is so. God exists whether we perceive Him or not. God is the original creator, and just as everyone has a father, all living entities are coming originally from this original father. The father is there. Fact is fact, whether anyone perceives it or not. You may not have seen my father, but you know that I had a father. You do not have to perceive him directly to know that he is a fact. Because I exist, my father is essential. That is understood and assumed by everyone. Therefore people say, "What is your father's name?" instead of, "Do you have a father?" It is assumed that one has a father, even though this father is not immediately perceived.
Śyāmasundara dāsa: Alexander uses the example of a house: whether we are conscious of a house or not, the house itself is a real entity unaffected by our awareness of it. It has a real, objective existence.

Śrīla Prabhupāda: Yes, as far as that proposition is concerned, if we accept the fact that we are eternal, it is very natural to assume that we have an eternal house, an eternal home. That is back home, back to Godhead. When people ask, "Where do you live?" they are asking for your residence. Your present address may not be your birthplace, but it is a fact that we must live somewhere. No one may be interested in knowing where I live, but everyone knows that I have a place to live.

Śyāmasundara dāsa: Alexander believes that our consciousness of an object gives us only limited perspective. When we shift our position, our perspective changes. If I see a table, that table has an objective reality; it is not just a mental image.

Śrīla Prabhupāda: Yes, you cannot say that the table is just a mental image. If someone throws the table and knocks you down, you will bleed. That is not simply mental.

Śyāmasundara dāsa: Alexander also claims that even illusions or hallucinations are genuinely real objects. If I think I see a snake, which is really a rope, the illusion of that snake is real.

Śrīla Prabhupāda: There is in reality a snake, otherwise how can the image of a snake come to the imagination? I may falsely take a rope to be a snake, but that doesn't matter. In reality, the snake exists.

Śyāmasundara dāsa: For Alexander, the mind never creates anything new, but rearranges things. Since everything already exists, there is no question of creating anything.

Śrīla Prabhupāda: Yes, you cannot create anything. You can only transform. This table is nothing but wood. The wood is not my creation; it is already there. I have only transformed the wood into a shape called a table. It is said that necessity is the mother of invention. When I need something to sit on, I invent a chair.

Śyāmasundara dāsa: Some philosophers reason that because man feels a necessity for God, he has invented God.

Śrīla Prabhupāda: Not invented. He knows God. And this is perfectly natural. Any sane man would ask, "Who is the original father?" There is no question of inventing the original father. Anyone can understand that there is an original father by philosophical research. The *Vedānta-sūtra* states, *janmādy asya yataḥ*. "God is the original father of everyone." Invention refers to a thing that I create which was not in existence, and discovery refers to something I find that is already there. Invention and discovery practically convey the same idea because nothing is new. In the case of God, it is discovery. There is no question of invention.

Hayagrīva dāsa: In his major work, *Space, Time and Deity*, Alexander writes: "Religion leans on metaphysics for the justification of its indefeasible conviction of the reality of its object (God); philosophy leans on religion to justify it in calling the possessor of deity by the religious name of God. The two methods of approach are therefore complementary."

Śrīla Prabhupāda: We have often said that philosophy without religion is mental speculation, and religion without philosophy is sentiment. The combination of the two is most desirable. *Bhagavad-gītā* is religion and philosophy combined. Religion is explained in terms of worship of God, and philosophy is explained in terms of the immortality of the soul, and other subjects. Thus *Bhagavad-gītā* is the supreme combination of religion and philosophy.

Hayagrīva dāsa: If religion is like hunger, God is the food for that hunger. Alexander writes: "This religious appetite may either be stirred in us directly by the impact of the world with its tendency to deity, or it may first be felt by us as a need of our nature...."

Śrīla Prabhupāda: We are seeking love of God beginning with our own body. We love this body because we live within it, and as long as the living soul is there, the body has value. The living soul is valuable because he is part and parcel of God. We also understand from *Bhagavad-gītā* that within the body God is also living. So within there are two *kṣetra-jñas*, one who knows the individual body, and the other who knows all bodies. The ultimate conclusion is that because the Supreme Living Entity, God, is within the body and within the universe, we are attracted by love, society, friendship, communalism, and nationalism. When all this culminates in love for God, we attain perfection. We are searching for love of God, but we are moving by degrees from one platform to another.

Hayagrīva dāsa: Alexander writes: "It is idle to hope that by defining God in conceptual terms, whether as the sum of reality, or the perfect being, or the first cause, or by other device, we can establish the connection between such a being and the rest of our experience. We do but start with an abstraction, and we do but end with one. Proofs of God's existence in nature there are none, if such a God is to be identified with the object of worship."

Śrīla Prabhupāda: We can understand the presence of God in nature, and we can certainly see His presence there. We can understand that there is a proprietor of the land, sea, and air. We may not be able to see the proprietor of the universe, but from our present experience with proprietorship, we can understand that there must be an ultimate proprietor. God is the proprietor of the sun, moon, and the sky itself.

Vedic literatures describe the moon as the mind of God, the sun as the eyes of God, the land as the food of God, and the waters as the semina of God. This is the beginning of impersonal realization, but we should understand that there is a person in the background. Although we have not seen the Governor of Hawaii, we can understand that he is present by seeing the different branches of government. Similarly, as long as we are not qualified to see the Supreme Personality of Godhead, we can understand that this is God's hand, this is God's heart, His mind, His eyes, and so on. When we are qualified, we can personally see God, face to face.

Hayagrīva dāsa: Alexander felt that "even the description of God...is full of figurative language." For him, it is impossible to describe God.

Śrīla Prabhupāda: If it is impossible, why is he trying? Why shouldn't we accept the Vedic descriptions? In *Bhagavad-gītā*, Arjuna tells Kṛṣṇa:

paraṁ brahma paraṁ dhāma
pavitraṁ paramaṁ bhavān
puruṣaṁ śāśvataṁ divyam
ādi-devam ajaṁ vibhum

āhus tvām ṛṣayaḥ sarve
devarṣir nāradas tathā
asito devalo vyāsaḥ
svayaṁ caiva bravīṣi me

"You are the Supreme Brahman, the ultimate, the supreme abode and purifier, the Absolute Truth and the eternal divine person. You are the primal God, transcendental and original, and You are the unborn and all-pervading beauty. All the great sages such as Nārada, Asita, Devala, and Vyāsa proclaim this of You, and now You Yourself are declaring it to me." (*Bg.* 10.12-13) If all authorities accept Kṛṣṇa as the Supreme Personality of Godhead, what further evidence do we need? No further argument is necessary. Things should be simplified.

Śyāmasundara dāsa: The mind is always reorganizing existing things, new comes from old, and from this, Alexander draws his idea of evolution.

Śrīla Prabhupāda: Since there is gold and mountains, I can imagine a gold mountain. I can combine many ideas with my imagination. The mind creates some ideas, and then rejects them to create others, and then rejects them also. The mind is not satisfied with creating something final. The mind by nature is creative. It creates something, then thinks, "Oh, this is not perfect," and then begins again. That is the mind's business: accepting and rejecting.

Śyāmasundara dāsa: For Alexander, the mind has two functions: contemplation and enjoyment. Contemplation involves perceiving the qualities of an object— for instance, an apple's redness.
Śrīla Prabhupāda: Or, if I see a tamarind, I immediately salivate.
Śyāmasundara dāsa: Enjoyment involves a mental awareness of inner, physiological activity.
Śrīla Prabhupāda: Yes, there are many examples. One may dream of a sex object and have a nocturnal discharge. The mind creates things in this way, and there are actual physical reactions. In a dream, the mind may create a tiger, and the dreamer may cry aloud in fright. But actually there is no tiger.
Śyāmasundara dāsa: Alexander believes that even these dream images have an objective reality in our consciousness.
Śrīla Prabhupāda: Yes, when I dream of a woman or a tiger, they exist in objective reality. The impressions in my mind are created hallucinations, but they may evoke physical reactions.
Śyāmasundara dāsa: Alexander describes time as an infinity of single instants, and space as an infinity of points. Together, they constitute primordial reality.
Śrīla Prabhupāda: Yes, we also consider time and space to be reality. Time is eternal, and therefore we take time to be another feature of God. Space is a later creation. Space is *prakṛti. Prakṛti* refers to nature, the elements like earth, water, fire, ether, space. Space or sky is one of the fundamental factors of *prakṛti. Prakṛti, kāla, jīva,* Bhagavān: nature, time, the individual soul, and God. These are all realities, and they are all eternal. There is only one ultimate creator, Bhagavān, and the *jīvātmā*, the individual soul, is the subsequent creator. God creates wood, and from this wood I create a table or a chair. Thus I am the subsequent, not the ultimate creator. Both creators, Bhagavān and *jīvātmā*, are eternal. Because the creation has a past, present, and future, time is also eternal.
Śyāmasundara dāsa: Is there such a thing as spiritual space?
Śrīla Prabhupāda: Of course. If not, how could there be a spiritual world? The quality is different, but the ingredients are exactly the same.
Śyāmasundara dāsa: Alexander, like Bergson, also believes that nothing remains at rest, that everything is in perpetual transition.
Śrīla Prabhupāda: Yes, we also accept that. Everything is going forward. That is called *jagat*.
Śyāmasundara dāsa: Can this be said of the activities in the spiritual world?

Śrīla Prabhupāda: We are speaking of the material world. The spiritual world is different. In the spiritual world, activities are eternal. In the material world, they are not.
Śyāmasundara dāsa: But isn't the motion of everything eternal?
Śrīla Prabhupāda: That motion is the interaction of the three modes: goodness, passion, and ignorance. In course of time, these modes react, and creation takes place. There is certainly motion. Without motion, there cannot be creation. Material nature is composed of earth, water, fire, ether, and space. Whatever you see is composed of one or more of these ingredients. There are also subtler ingredients: mind, intelligence, and ego. These are the eight material elements given in *Bhagavad-gītā*, and they are considered the differentiated energy of Kṛṣṇa.
Śyāmasundara dāsa: Alexander's primary category is more abstract. He says that it is motion.
Śrīla Prabhupāda: But where does the motion come from? Motion means that there must be someone there to push.
Śyāmasundara dāsa: Another major category is identity, or diversity. Everything has a personal identity and individuality differentiating it from every other thing.
Śrīla Prabhupāda: Yes, that is called *sajātīyo vijātīya* in Sanskrit. There is difference *(vijātīya)* even between like things. There may be two mango trees, but there is still a difference between them. They may be one as mango trees, but there is still individuality. Similarly, my fingers are one, but each finger is different from the other. *Sajātīya* refers to the same category, but even within that category there is a difference.
Śyāmasundara dāsa: Existence, or being, is another major category.
Śrīla Prabhupāda: That existence is composed of one or more of the five elements. One ingredient may be more prominent than the other, but there is at least one ingredient.
Śyāmasundara dāsa: Relation and order are other categories. Everything relates to everything else, and there is order in everything.
Śrīla Prabhupāda: Yes, there is certainly order in *prakṛti*. The sun rises and sets at designated times. There is order everywhere.
Śyāmasundara dāsa: The mind also occupies space and works in time.
Śrīla Prabhupāda: Yes, we are occupying space, and since the mind is within us, the mind also occupies space. From practical experience we can understand that the mind can immediately travel thousands of miles with no difficulties.

Śyāmasundara dāsa: But is that distance within me, or does my mind actually travel there?
Śrīla Prabhupāda: It travels. It actually occupies space. Unless it occupies space, how could it travel? It travels so fast that you can't exactly remember how it is going, but as soon as it reaches its destination, you can apprehend it. In any case, it occupies space.
Śyāmasundara dāsa: The mind can leave the body and go somewhere?
Śrīla Prabhupāda: Not leave. It is just like a shoot: it extends. At night, when we are dreaming, the subtle body also extends and comes back again. In fact, we may take the subtle bodies in dreams to be very important at the time.
Śyāmasundara dāsa: Alexander maintains that new categories are constantly being uncovered because evolution is progressing. The living entity can evolve into new forms that we now know nothing about.
Śrīla Prabhupāda: No, we do not agree. We know that the days are going on now, and will continue, just as we have experienced them in the past. In the past there was summer, autumn, winter, and spring, and in the future these will also be experienced. Of course, the old order changes and yields to the new, but from our past experience we know what will be there.
Śyāmasundara dāsa: Then in the future there will be nothing unpredictable appearing, such as an entirely new form of existence?
Śrīla Prabhupāda: No. Why should there be? Why should there be a winter without spring, or a spring without summer? Why should there be a new type of man? A new species? According to the Vedic version, everything is here. The number of species in the water, in air, and on land is fixed. There is no question of the species increasing.
Śyāmasundara dāsa: Some scientists predict that the future man will have no bodily hair, that his head will be very large due to increased brain capacity, that the rest of his body will be atrophied, that he may lose some of his toes, and so on.
Śrīla Prabhupāda: This is more foolishness. There has never been such a thing, nor will there ever be. Man has always had ten toes, and he always will.
Śyāmasundara dāsa: Alexander believes that man may evolve to the demigod platform in the future, that he may have super consciousness.
Śrīla Prabhupāda: Yes, that is possible. *Yānti deva-vratā devān (Bg.* 9.25). If you are fond of the demigods, you will go to the demigods. *Pitṝn yānti pitṛ-vratāḥ (Bg.* 9.25). Or you can go to the ancestors. Or remain within this material world.

Śyāmasundara dāsa: But Alexander thinks that evolution is moving in this way, progressing from inorganic life, to organic, to mental, and to demigod.

Śrīla Prabhupāda: How can life come from inorganic matter? That is nonsense. What evidence do we have that life is developing from inorganic matter? If that is the case, why don't they manufacture life in the laboratory? Living force cannot be produced from matter. Matter is different from living force, or soul. Of course, in one sense, they are both the energy of God, but categorically they are different. You cannot even manufacture an ant. You may have all the chemicals, but you cannot inject the soul. The soul appears in different ways. For instance, fermentation, perspiration. When rock and water decompose, there may be fermentation, and it may be possible that the soul takes advantage of this and comes out, being born in some life form. In any case, life never comes from matter. It is thought by the foolish that scorpions are born out of rice, but actually the scorpion lays its eggs within the rice, and by the fermentation, or heating of the rice, the eggs incubate, and scorpions are born. But this does not mean that matter itself is producing life. The Vedas accept the fact that living creatures can arise from fermentation, but this is only because the soul finds refuge there.

Śyāmasundara dāsa: But what of the idea that nature is progressing? Will man some day evolve to the demigod stage?

Śrīla Prabhupāda: According to the Vedas, the demigods were created before men. First, Lord Brahmā was created, and from Lord Brahmā, Lord Śiva was created. By created, I mean born. Similarly, from Brahmā, others came, the Prajāpatis, and then the Manus. There were many. There is no question of these personalities emerging from inorganic life. Lord Brahmā came from the navel of Viṣṇu. You may ask, What is the origin of Viṣṇu? We have no information of this because Viṣṇu is the origin, and it was from Him that Brahmā and all the other demigods came. Then the animals and others came. The first created being is Lord Brahmā, and he is also the most intelligent. It is not that he evolved from animals or man. These evolutionists propose that life evolves from the lowest to the highest, but we believe that it begins with the highest, with Viṣṇu. Kṛṣṇa says, *ahaṁ sarvasya prabhavaḥ*. "I am the origin of everything." (*Bg.* 10.8) How can you say that higher species will develop from the lower? God is the origin. *Vedānta-sūtra* also says, "The Absolute Truth is He from whom everything is generating." The Absolute Truth is the supreme life, and from Him all life is coming. What evidence do we have of a dead stone giving birth to a

man or animals?
Śyāmasundara dāsa: Alexander felt that in the future, the race of man will evolve into super-conscious beings, into demigods.
Śrīla Prabhupāda: No, we have no information of this. Why is he so anxious about the planet earth? These super-conscious beings are already existing on Siddha-loka, Gandharva-loka, and many other higher planets. There are millions of planets with super-human beings. From the *śāstras* we learn that the inhabitants of Siddha-loka can fly from one planet to another without the aid of a space vehicle.
Śyāmasundara dāsa: Alexander proposes that nature develops bodies to that point.
Śrīla Prabhupāda: No. Bodies never develop in that way. There are different types of bodies, and the soul takes shelter of a particular type, selecting bodies just as a person selects clothes in a store. When we are within a suit, the suit moves. Bodies are selected according to the soul's desires. By your karma, you get a particular type of body. We have already discussed this.
Śyāmasundara dāsa: Then demigods will not evolve on this planet in the natural course of things?
Śrīla Prabhupāda: No.
Śyāmasundara dāsa: How is genius accounted for?
Śrīla Prabhupāda: When one is born a genius, we must understand that in his previous life he cultivated a particular faculty, and that knowledge is being manifested in this life. In *Bhagavad-gītā*, Kṛṣṇa says that if a yogī does not complete the yoga process, he is given another chance (*Bg.* 6.41). It is not that these things happen accidently.
Śyāmasundara dāsa: Then, through the practice of yoga, a higher consciousness can be developed?
Śrīla Prabhupāda: Yes. For instance, we are practicing *bhakti-yoga* to develop Kṛṣṇa consciousness. As far as your spiritual development is concerned, you must understand that you are spirit soul. Then you can qualify yourself to return to the spiritual world. There you can associate with the Lord and engage in spiritual activities. The *śāstras* tell us that we should try for spiritual perfection and not waste our time endeavoring for material comforts. Material comforts and distresses automatically come; there is no need in wasting time striving for them. In nature, there are many millions of living entities without business or profession, yet they are living, eating, sleeping, mating, and defending. These things will come automatically. Our endeavor should be for spiritual emancipation.

Śyāmasundara dāsa: According to Alexander, on the mental level, we are capable of enjoying objects and receiving pleasure from them, but cannot understand them as they are. On the higher level, we can contemplate objects and understand them as they are, as well as enjoy them.

Śrīla Prabhupāda: Yes, that is our philosophy. A common man may see a rose and think, "Oh, I will offer this nice flower to my girl friend." But when a devotee sees a rose, he thinks, "How wonderfully God's energy is acting!" He understands that it is through Kṛṣṇa's energy that such a wonderful flower exists, and therefore he knows that the flower should be offered to Kṛṣṇa. After all, since Kṛṣṇa produced it, it is Kṛṣṇa's property. After offering the rose to Kṛṣṇa, the devotee smells it. Then it is *prasādam*, the Lord's mercy. This is higher consciousness. Lower consciousness thinks, "Let me pick it and enjoy it!" That is mere enjoyment without understanding. An animal eats just as man eats, but a man should have sufficiently developed consciousness to understand that what he is eating is given by Kṛṣṇa. The Vedas state: *eko bahūnāṁ yo vidadhāti kāmān.* "The Supreme Lord is supplying all necessities of life to everyone." (*Kaṭha-upaniṣad* 2.2.13). When one understands that Kṛṣṇa is supplying everything, he thinks, "First, let me offer this to Kṛṣṇa." If everything is not offered in sacrifice to the Supreme Lord, we will be entangled. Higher consciousness is mature consciousness. It is like a flower that has blossomed and is emitting a fragrance. That full blossom of consciousness is Kṛṣṇa consciousness.

Śyāmasundara dāsa: Alexander believes that the entire world is moving to that point.

Śrīla Prabhupāda: Well, nature is giving us the chance, but because we have independence, we may or may not take the opportunity.

Śyāmasundara dāsa: Will only certain individuals attain that higher consciousness, or will the whole world attain it?

Śrīla Prabhupāda: That is a nonsensical question. Sometimes rascals inquire, "Swāmījī, if everyone becomes God conscious and goes back to Godhead, then who will remain here?" What is the meaning of such a nonsensical question? Why is a fool anxious for everyone? Why is he not anxious for himself? It is the same to ask, "If everyone is honest, then who will go to jail?" As if maintaining the jail is a very important business!

Śyāmasundara dāsa: During Alexander's day, people were very optimistic about man's future, thinking that everyone would be benefitted by scientific discoveries.

Śrīla Prabhupāda: People think that by nature's way, they will be promoted, that once they have attained the status of man, they cannot be degraded. But if one can go up, he can also go down. The rich can become poor again. Theosophists and others think that everything goes up, progresses. They don't even have the common sense to look around them.

Hayagrīva dāsa: Alexander distinguished between deity and God Himself. For him, deity is a relative term for the next highest level of existence. For an ant, a dog may be a deity; for a dog, a man may be a deity; for a man, a demigod may be a deity. Deity is always one evolutionary step ahead of us. Alexander defines God as "the being which possesses deity in full." That is, God is always one step ahead of every creature.

Śrīla Prabhupāda: He does not know the exact Vedic science of God, but as a philosopher he is suggesting a very nice method. For an ant, a bird is a deity; for a bird, a cat is a deity, and so on according to one's position. And if you continue searching, you will find someone who has no one to worship. The ant must worship the bird, the bird worship the cat, and so on, but when we arrive at a person who has no one to worship, we have arrived at God. In the lower stages, there are always higher living beings, but when we come to the highest living being, we come to God Himself. This is explained in the Vedic literatures:

īśvaraḥ paramaḥ kṛṣṇaḥ
sac-cid-ānanda-vigrahaḥ
anādir ādir govindaḥ
sarva-kāraṇa-kāraṇam

"Kṛṣṇa, who is known as Govinda, is the Supreme Godhead. He has an eternal, blissful, spiritual body. He is the origin of all. He has no other origin, and He is the prime cause of all causes." (*Brahma-saṁhitā* 5.1) And in *Bhagavad-gītā*, Kṛṣṇa says:

mattaḥ parataraṁ nānyat
kiñcid asti dhanañjaya
mayi sarvam idaṁ protaṁ
sūtre maṇi-gaṇā iva

"O conqueror of wealth, there is no Truth superior to Me. Everything rests upon Me, as pearls are strung on a thread." (*Bg.* 7.7) There is no authority superior to Kṛṣṇa. As long as one has a superior, he is not God, but a servant of God.

Śyāmasundara dāsa: Alexander believes that lower organisms strive to emulate higher. Animals strive to become like men, and men strive to become like gods.

Śrīla Prabhupāda: There is no question of striving. It is by nature's way that the lower animals come to the platform of men. The living entity evolves from one life form to another, but this is with the help of nature. This law holds, up to the human platform. Having developed consciousness, the human being has the power of discrimination. Originally, the soul is given independence. Kṛṣṇa tells Arjuna, "Whatever you like, you do." (*Bg*. 18.63) God is the Supersoul, and we are the *jīva* souls subordinate to Him. Therefore we are called *taṭastha*, which means that we are marginal; we can go either way. We may take God's side, or māyā's side. That is our choice. When we don't want to serve God, we are sent to māyā to serve her. Man's position as a subordinate remains the same, but in māyā he thinks, "I am the master." This is just like a child trying to act against his father's wishes. When he is given a chance to do as he likes, the child thinks, "Oh, I am independent now." Actually he is never independent, but he thinks that he is. When death comes, no one is independent. Although man continually serves māyā life after life, he still thinks of himself as independent. Only when we surrender to Kṛṣṇa do we enjoy our real independence.

Śyāmasundara dāsa: But don't lower forms try to emulate higher ones?

Śrīla Prabhupāda: That is natural. Everyone wants a higher position because everyone is trying to be master. That is the whole problem. One can be a master to some extent: a head clerk in an office, a president, or prime minister. There is much ambition in the material world because materialistic men are guided by the idea that "I shall become like Kṛṣṇa." When their efforts fail in the material world, they strive to merge into Kṛṣṇa. This is Māyāvādī philosophy. Not knowing that they are already Brahman, spirit soul, they consider themselves the Supreme Brahman, God Himself. Therefore they sit and meditate, thinking, "I am moving the sun. I am moving the moon." This is simply imagination. This is the last snare of māyā. Māyā first of all allures us to become a big merchant, a prime minister, a president. Māyā is always saying, "Become this, become that, become, become." Māyā is always telling us to work under her direction. Finally, she says, "Now you have failed in all these things. It is better now that you become God, and attain your real status again." So the living entity begins to think, "I am God," but māyā is still kicking him. As soon as this so-called God gets some toothache, he runs to the doctor. He does not stop to think, "What kind of God am I?"

Śyāmasundara dāsa: But what is that urge for promotion?
Śrīla Prabhupāda: It is not the individual's urge. Nature is giving the impetus. For instance, when you were a child, there was no sex urge, but when you attained adolescence, immediately the sex urge became manifest. Similarly, the perfection of consciousness is there, but unless you come to the platform of human life, it will not develop.
Śyāmasundara dāsa: Is there also an urge among lower animals to improve themselves, to be promoted?
Śrīla Prabhupāda: Yes, but all that is being carried out by nature. That is evolution. Darwin has taken this idea from the Vedas, but he has no idea of the soul. The only business of animals is eating, sleeping, mating, and defending. You may call this the struggle for existence. They are simply trying to live; they have no other ambition. If a man, having attained the human stage, is interested only in these things, he is no better than an animal. Nowadays, these are being taught by modern civilization. They teach you how to live comfortably with a car, a bungalow, a girl friend, and restaurants. All living entities in this material world have the propensity to enjoy. On one platform, the living entity enjoys certain types of pleasure, but he is always wanting more. It is the spirit of material enjoyment that brings about the disease of materialistic life.
Śyāmasundara dāsa: So the urge to advance is perverted by the urge to enjoy?
Śrīla Prabhupāda: Yes, perverted. The living entity's position is to serve Kṛṣṇa, but instead he is serving his senses and thinking that he is enjoying. You can see how everyone is working hard day and night in order to enjoy. Everyone is thinking that he will be happy if he just becomes a millionaire. Animals work hard to get some food, and as soon as they acquire food, they are satisfied. But human beings are not so easily satisfied. They are so passionate that they are constantly working very hard to be happy. People do not understand that in material life, they cannot be happy in any position.
Śyāmasundara dāsa: Can the urge to advance be the desire to become godly?
Śrīla Prabhupāda: Desire means that one has lost his real happiness dancing with God like the *gopīs*. *Ānandamayo 'bhyāsāt*. The *Vedānta-sūtra* says that by nature, the living entity wants *ānanda*, bliss. Because he seeks *ānanda* in a perverted way, he is confused and frustrated; therefore he thinks, "Not this state but that will give me happiness." However, when he goes to his desired state, he again finds unhappiness.

This is because he is seeking *ānanda* in a perverted way. In Vaikuṇṭhaloka, there is eternal happiness because everyone is surrendered to Kṛṣṇa. In Vṛndāvana, all the cowherd boys, *gopīs*, cows, trees, and other living entities are centered about Kṛṣṇa. They are all concerned with making Kṛṣṇa happy. Only on that platform will we avoid confusion and frustration.

Śyāmasundara dāsa: Alexander says that at this point, we cannot know the qualities of the next stage of evolution.

Śrīla Prabhupāda: He may not know, but we know. One who has Kṛṣṇa as his master and teacher knows everything. *Yasmin vijñate sarvam eva vijñataṁ bhavanti.* If you understand Kṛṣṇa, you understand everything.

Hayagrīva dāsa: Again, concerning the conception of deity, which is so central, Alexander writes: "The infinitude of God's deity marks the difference between Him and all other empirical beings....Not only is God infinite in extent and duration, but His deity is also infinite in both respects."

Śrīla Prabhupāda: If God is infinite deity, He is not subject to created living beings. It is incorrect to think of God's deity as one of the deities within this material world. A person who thinks in this way is condemned as a *mūḍha*. "Because I appear as an ordinary human being," Kṛṣṇa tells us, "*mūḍhas*, asses, consider Me an ordinary human." (*Bg.* 9.11)

Hayagrīva dāsa: Alexander states that God is both body and soul, and that His soul is His deity. "All finites are included in Him," he writes, "and are fragments of God's body, though their individuality is not lost in it....God is...an individual being just as man or any other finite is, only that He is infinite."

Śrīla Prabhupāda: That is right. God is a person, but not like us. People mistake Him to be like an ordinary human being, but this is due to illusion. Kṛṣṇa is infinite, and Arjuna is finite. It is explained in *Bhagavad-gītā* that Kṛṣṇa, being infinite, knows everything in the past, present, and future (*Bg.* 4.5). That is one of the differences between an ordinary living entity and God. The living entity forgets, but God does not.

Hayagrīva dāsa: Alexander sees God's body as neither spaceless nor timeless, for it is space-time itself.

Śrīla Prabhupāda: Yes, since everything emanates from Him, there is nothing separate from Him. God includes everything. Everything is part and parcel of God. The Māyāvādīs say that everything is one, but they do not accept the variety. The wheel is one, but there are different parts: the rim, the spokes, and the hub.

Hayagrīva dāsa: Alexander writes: "Now the body of God is the whole universe, and there is no body outside His. For Him, therefore, all objects are internal, and the distinction of organic and special senses disappears."

Śrīla Prabhupāda: For the impersonalists who are not familiar with the personal form of God, Arjuna in *Bhagavad-gītā* requested Kṛṣṇa to show His universal form, the *virāṭ-rūpa*. Arjuna himself was accepting the person Kṛṣṇa as the Supreme, but he knew that those with a poor fund of knowledge would not accept Him. For this reason, in the Eleventh Chapter of *Bhagavad-gītā,* the universal form of God is very elaborately explained. However, we should understand that since the universal form was shown by Kṛṣṇa, Kṛṣṇa is the originator. It is not that the universal form is the origin. It was manifested by Kṛṣṇa, and Lord Kṛṣṇa's natural form is that of Kṛṣṇa Himself. The universal form is a feature. This is also confirmed in *Bhagavad-gītā: ahaṁ sarvasya prabhavo mattaḥ sarvaṁ pravartate*. "I am the source of all spiritual and material worlds. Everything emanates from Me." (*Bg*. 10.8) Since everything emanates from Him, the universal form has also emanated from Him. One who understands this becomes Kṛṣṇa's devotee.

Hayagrīva dāsa: For Alexander, theism is equated with personalism, and pantheism with impersonalism. He writes: "For theism, God is an individual being distinct from the finite beings which make up the world....For pantheism, God is eminent in the universe of finite things...."

Śrīla Prabhupāda: When we cannot understand the Supreme Personality of Godhead, God is impersonal. The sunshine is impersonal, but the sun god is in the background. Because we are on a lower platform, we cannot talk with the sun god; we can experience only the sunshine. Similarly, the expansion of God's energy is impersonal, but the personality is in the background. Because we are in the material energy, we are not in direct touch with God; therefore we say that God is impersonal. If we become devotees, we can talk with God in person, just as the cowherd boys and girls did in Vṛndāvana. It is also stated, *nityo nityānāṁ cetanaś cetanānām (Kaṭha-upaniṣad* 2.2.13). God is an eternal, living being, and we are also eternal, living beings. Yet He is different from us in that He is the chief. He has arranged everything for us in both the material and spiritual worlds. He has given us air, water, and fire in order to live. He is the maintainer, and we are subordinate *jīvas.*

Hayagrīva dāsa: Alexander seems to acknowledge both theistic and pantheistic views.

Śrīla Prabhupāda: Yes, as I said, because water has come from God, we say that it is God's semina. Because light has come from Him, we say that the sun is his eye. In that everything is an emanation from God, everything is related to God. In any case, the impersonal features are subordinate to the personal.

mayā tatam idaṁ sarvaṁ
jagad avyakta-mūrtinā
mat-sthāni sarva-bhūtāni
na cāhaṁ teṣv avasthitaḥ

"By Me, in My unmanifested form, this entire universe is pervaded. All beings are in Me, but I am not in them." (*Bg.* 9.4) Just as the sunshine depends on the sun itself, so the entire cosmic manifestation depends on God. Kṛṣṇa says that although everything is resting on Him, He is personally not present. Queen Kuntī also says, "You are within and without, yet fools cannot see You." These verses spoken by Queen Kuntī are given in *Śrīmad-Bhāgavatam:*

namasye puruṣaṁ tvādyam
īśvaraṁ prakṛteḥ param
alakṣyaṁ sarva-bhūtānām
antar bahir avasthitam

māyā javanikācchannam
ajñādhokṣajam avyayam
na lakṣyase mūḍha-dṛśā
naṭo nāṭyadharo yathā

tathā paramahaṁsānāṁ
munīnām amalātmanām
bhakti-yoga-vidhānārthaṁ
kathaṁ paśyema hi striyaḥ

"O Kṛṣṇa, I offer my obeisances unto You because You are the original personality and are unaffected by the qualities of the material world. You are existing both within and without everything, yet You are invisible to all. Being beyond the range of limited sense perception, You are the eternally irreproachable factor covered by the curtain of deluding energy. You are invisible to the foolish observer, exactly as an actor dressed as a player is not recognizable. You Yourself descend to propagate the transcendental science of devotional service unto the hearts of the advanced transcendentalists and mental speculators, who are purified by being able to discriminate between matter and spirit. How, then, can we women know You perfectly?" (*Bhāg.* 1.8.18-20)

This is a very good example. Kṛṣṇa is playing on the stage, and His son is seeing Him, and another friend is saying, "Do you see your father?" But the son does not recognize his father. A devotee can understand, but a speculator with limited sense perception cannot.

Hayagrīva dāsa: Alexander writes: "It is not so much that God is in everything but rather that everything is in God."

Śrīla Prabhupāda: Since there is nothing but God, how can anything be without God? Since everything is God's expansion, how can we be sometimes with God and sometimes without Him? When we are not in God, we are in māyā, but māyā is also God's. It is illusion to think that we are without God.

Hayagrīva dāsa: After analyzing both theism and pantheism, the personal and impersonal, Alexander finds them both defective in themselves, but he concludes, "if a choice must be made, it is theistic."

Śrīla Prabhupāda: This means that when one comes to the personal aspect of God, he sees that everything refers to God and that there is nothing independent. To the unintelligent, it appears that the cosmic manifestation is different from Bhagavān, but actually nothing can exist without the Supreme Personality of Godhead.

Hayagrīva dāsa: At times, Alexander takes the Aristotelian view in maintaining that "there is no reciprocal action from God. For though we speak, as we inevitably must, in human terms of God's response to us, there is no direct experience of that response except through our own feeling that devotion to God or worship carries with it its own satisfaction."

Śrīla Prabhupāda: This means that he does not understand God's omnipotence. God is omnipotent, and He comes before Arjuna to speak *Bhagavad-gītā*. Being all powerful, God can come and speak to His devotee. If He cannot, what is the meaning of His omnipotence? Kṛṣṇa reciprocates with the advanced devotees.

teṣāṁ satata-yuktānāṁ
bhajatāṁ prīti-pūrvakam
dadāmi buddhi-yogaṁ taṁ
yena mām upayānti te

"To those who are constantly devoted and worship Me with love, I give the understanding by which they can come to Me." (*Bg.* 10.10) God talks to His devotee who is fully in love with Him, but He does not talk with ordinary men.

premāñjana-cchurita-bhakti-vilocanena
santaḥ sadaiva hṛdayeṣu vilokayanti
yaṁ śyāmasundaram acintya-guṇa-svarūpaṁ
govindam ādi-puruṣaṁ tam ahaṁ bhajāmi

"I worship the primeval Lord, Govinda, who is always seen by the devotee whose eyes are anointed with the pulp of love. He is seen in His eternal form of Śyāmasundara situated within the heart of the devotee." (*Brahma-saṁhitā* 5.38) Just as a king talks with his immediate officers and ministers and not with the ordinary man in the street, God personally talks to His devotees but not to the nondevotees or atheists. We understand that Kṛṣṇa talked to the *gopīs* and *gopas* in Vṛndāvana and reciprocated with His parents, Mother Yaśodā and Mahārāja Nanda. The cowherd boys who played with Kṛṣṇa amassed many pious activities in their previous lives to arrive at a position where they could play with God. This is not an ordinary position. People generally think that such play is inconceivable, but when we come to that platform of devotion, we can play with God, ride on God's shoulders, and talk with Him just as with an ordinary friend. Of course, one comes to that position of perfection after many millions of pious births.

Hayagrīva dāsa: Within the same book, *Space, Time and Deity*, Alexander contradicts himself on this issue of reciprocation. "God reciprocates the worship man pays Him and the confidence he reposes in Him," he writes. "There is always the double relationship of need. If man wants God and depends upon Him, God wants man, and is so far dependent."

Śrīla Prabhupāda: God is not dependent on anyone. God is independent, but that statement is acceptable in the sense that sometimes God wants to become dependent. That is according to His pleasure. Sometimes He accepts some of His devotees in ways that He can depend on them. He became dependent on Mother Yaśodā, just as an ordinary child becomes dependent on his mother. Although everything is dependent on God, and He is not dependent on anyone, He takes pleasure in this kind of relationship.

Hayagrīva dāsa: I don't think Alexander understood it in that way.

Śrīla Prabhupāda: This is not a very ordinary thing to understand. It cannot be understood by mental speculation.

Hayagrīva dāsa: Alexander also writes that God Himself is involved in our acts and their issues. "Not only does He matter to us, but we matter to Him." Is this actually so?

Śrīla Prabhupāda: Yes, although we are sons of God, we are fallen conditioned souls and are suffering. Therefore God is very compassion-

ate, and He comes personally to teach us. He says, "Why are you rotting in this material world? Surrender to Me and go back to Godhead. Then you will be happy." God is the father of everyone, and it is natural for a father to be concerned about his sons. Presently we are conditioned by material nature because we are disobedient. God, being the Supreme Father, feels for our suffering. But He is not suffering. The devotees of God also feel for the conditioned souls, and Kṛṣṇa's devotees are very dear to Him because they are trying to spread His instructions, *Bhagavad-gītā*. The devotees are acting on behalf of God to deliver conditioned souls.
Śyāmasundara dāsa: Alexander believed that man, being part of God, is capable of cooperating with God to make further progress in the universe.
Śrīla Prabhupāda: Yes, that is real life, cooperating with God. But in this material world, man is uncooperative. Kṛṣṇa says, "Surrender unto Me," but no one wants to do this. Even when people attain the highest levels of human life wherein their karma is regulated and they possess knowledge and yogic abilities, they still will not surrender to Kṛṣṇa.

kṛṣṇa-bhakta—niṣkāma, ataeva 'śānta'
bhukti-mukti-siddhi-kāmī—sakali 'aśānta'

"Because a devotee of Lord Kṛṣṇa is desireless, he is peaceful. Fruitive workers desire material enjoyment, *jñānīs* desire liberation, and yogīs desire material opulence; therefore they are all lusty and cannot be peaceful." (*Caitanya-caritāmṛta*, Madh. 19.149) The *karmīs* want sense enjoyment, the *jñānīs* want *mukti*, liberation, and the yogīs want *yoga-siddhis*, the yoga powers. All these people are demanding various things: sense gratification, liberation, mystic powers. Only the Kṛṣṇa-*bhakta* makes no demands. He says, "Dear Lord, I am Your eternal servitor. I surrender unto You. Now do whatever You like with me."

bhoktāraṁ yajña-tapasāṁ
sarva-loka-maheśvaram
suhṛdaṁ sarva-bhūtānāṁ
jñātvā māṁ śāntim ṛcchati

"The sages, knowing Me as the ultimate purpose of all sacrifices and austerities, the Supreme Lord of all planets and demigods, and the benefactor and well-wisher of all living entities, attain peace from the pangs of material miseries." (*Bg.* 5.29) By understanding that Kṛṣṇa is the supreme enjoyer, the supreme proprietor, and the supreme friend, we can become *śānta*, peaceful.

Śyāmasundara dāsa: Alexander felt that man should cooperate with God in order to usher in a higher stage of consciousness, the next stage of evolution. This is man's responsibility.

Śrīla Prabhupāda: But what is the next stage of evolution? When man is prepared to cooperate with God, he has already attained the highest position. Unfortunately, no one wants to cooperate. There is simply enjoyment; there is no more evolution. If you come to the point of worshipping the Supreme Lord, there is no question of evolution. You have already attained the highest form of evolution.

māṁ ca yo'vyabhicāreṇa
bhakti-yogena sevate
sa guṇān samatītyaitān
brahma-bhūyāya kalpate

"One who engages in full devotional service, who does not fall down in any circumstance, at once transcends the modes of material nature and thus comes to the level of Brahman." (*Bg.* 14.26) The Brahman platform is already attained; he doesn't have to strive to become Brahman. He immediately transcends the three *guṇas* and comes to the platform of spirit. Without being Brahman, how can you serve the Supreme Brahman?

Alexander speaks of the higher stages of evolution, but he has no real knowledge of them. According to the Vaiṣṇava philosophy, there are five basic stages: *śānta, dāsya, sākhya, vātsalya,* and *mādhurya.* When you attain the *brahma-bhūta* stage and understand that you are not the body but spirit soul, you have attained the *śānta* platform. On that platform, you think, "Oh, God is so great!" From the *śānta* stage, you can progress to the *dāsya* stage, wherein you realize that God is so great that some service must be rendered to Him. In the *sākhya* stage, you not only know that God is great and render service to God, but you also serve God as a friend, like Arjuna. On the *vātsalya* platform, service is rendered to Kṛṣṇa as a father or a mother. Yaśodā, for instance, rendered service to Kṛṣṇa as a mother, and she was always thinking, "Kṛṣṇa is hungry. I must feed Him. I must protect Him from monkeys and fire." On the platform of *mādhurya-rasa,* the highest platform, you can enter into intimate pastimes with Kṛṣṇa. Although there are many stages in spiritual life, there is actually no difference between them. It is not that those who serve Kṛṣṇa as friends are inferior to Rādhārāṇī, who serves Kṛṣṇa as His consort.

Śyāmasundara dāsa: Alexander sees the freedom of the will operating as an activity not subject to extraneous forces. It is the expression of a person acting to serve not only his own interests but those of society as well.

Śrīla Prabhupāda: In a state, a citizen also cooperates in two ways. When he does not break the law, he cooperates as a free citizen, and when he breaks the law, he cooperates by going to prison. He either cooperates by free will or by force. Forceful cooperation is inferior. Caitanya Mahāprabhu said:

jīvera 'svarūpa' haya—kṛṣṇera 'nitya-dāsa'
kṛṣṇera 'taṭasthā-śakti', 'bhedābheda-prakāśa'

sūryāṁśa-kiraṇa yaiche agni-jvālā-caya
svābhāvika kṛṣṇera tina-prakāra 'śakti' haya

"It is the living entity's constitutional position to be an eternal servant of Kṛṣṇa because he is the marginal energy of Kṛṣṇa, and a manifestation simultaneously one and different from the Lord, like a molecular particle of sunshine or fire. Kṛṣṇa has three varieties of energy." (*Caitanya-caritāmṛta*, Madh. 20.108-109) By his constitutional position, the living entity is the eternal servant of Kṛṣṇa. In the Vaikuṇṭha planets, cooperation is voluntary, and here in this material world, cooperation is forced. In the material world, we are serving māyā, working under her force. We can avoid that force only by voluntarily cooperating with Kṛṣṇa.

daivī hy eṣā guṇamayī
mama māyā duratyayā
mām eva ye prapadyante
māyām etāṁ taranti te

"This divine energy of Mine, consisting of the three modes of material nature, is difficult to overcome. But those who have surrendered unto Me can easily cross beyond it." (*Bg.* 7.14) Automatic cooperation is *bhakti*, and forced cooperation is karma. These may appear to be the same, but they are not. The *karmī* may be typing, and the *bhakta* may be typing, but the *karmī* is typing under the force of māyā, to earn money for sense gratification, and the *bhakta* is typing for the glorification of Kṛṣṇa. The activity is the same, but the consciousness is different.

Śyāmasundara dāsa: Alexander believed that when one has attained the higher levels of evolution, he can see that everything on the lower levels is determined.

Śrīla Prabhupāda: Yes. For instance, we should not try to improve our economic condition because it is already decided. Why is one man born rich, and another born to work so hard? *Śrīmad-Bhāgavatam* (1.5.18) says that we should not strive hard for material happiness, because material happiness and distress come automatically. An intelligent man utilizes his time to develop his Kṛṣṇa consciousness.

Śyāmasundara dāsa: Alexander accepted Plato's three greatest values in life—truth, beauty, and goodness—as values to be accepted by the majority.

Śrīla Prabhupāda: Unfortunately, in the material world, no one likes the truth. At least in this age, the majority of people are not truthful. As soon as one becomes truthful, he becomes a *brāhmaṇa.* Where are the *brāhmaṇas* in this age? *Kalau śūdra sambhava.* In Kali-yuga, everyone is a *śūdra.* If Alexander thinks that everyone will accept truthfulness as a great value, he is mistaken.

Śyāmasundara dāsa: For Alexander, there is a practical criterion for truth, but he preferred the coherence principle by which the majority opinion determined truth by mutual agreement.

Śrīla Prabhupāda: Because he is European, he is thinking in a democratic way. The hard fact is that truth is not accepted by ordinary men. Truth is truth. Either it is in your mind or not; truth is absolute. Only highly elevated persons can understand the truth. Out of many truthful men, perhaps only one can understand Kṛṣṇa as He is.

Śyāmasundara dāsa: Alexander defines a good person as one who integrates and controls his impulses for the best interests of himself and society.

Śrīla Prabhupāda: This is also described in Vedic literatures:

tapasā brahmacaryeṇa
śamena ca damena ca
tyāgena satya-śaucābhyāṁ
yamena niyamena vā

"To concentrate the mind, one must observe a life of celibacy and not fall down. One must undergo the austerity of voluntarily giving up sense enjoyment. One must then control the mind and senses, give charity, be truthful, clean and nonviolent, follow the regulative principles, and regularly chant the holy name of the Lord." (*Bhāg.* 6.1.13) These are the processes by which we may become perfect, but if we become devotees of Kṛṣṇa, we immediately attain all the good qualities. *Yasyāsti bhaktir bhagavaty akiñcanā sarvair guṇais tatra samāsate surāḥ.* "All the demigods and their exalted qualities, such as religion, knowledge, and renunciation, become manifest in the body of one who has developed unalloyed devotion for the Supreme Personality of Godhead." (*Bhāg.* 5.18.12).

Śyāmasundara dāsa: In the second sense of the word "good," Alexander says that whatever enhances man's welfare or happiness is good.
Śrīla Prabhupāda: That is not necessarily so. One may open hospitals to help people, but spreading Kṛṣṇa consciousness is greater welfare work. What is really good for man is Kṛṣṇa *bhakti*. Nothing else.
Śyāmasundara dāsa: Alexander maintains that goodness consists of modifications in the environment that will aid man in his spiritual pursuits.
Śrīla Prabhupāda: That is what we are trying to do in this Kṛṣṇa consciousness movement. It is not that everyone can follow the regulative principles strictly. We are proposing that people chant Hare Kṛṣṇa. Whatever the situation, somehow or other, we must engage our mind in Kṛṣṇa. Rūpa Gosvāmī said: *yena tena prakāreṇa manaḥ kṛṣṇe niveśayet.* "Never mind the rules and regulations. Just fix your mind on Kṛṣṇa! As soon as you become Kṛṣṇa conscious, the regulative principles will be your servants."
Hayagrīva dāsa: As for the existence of evil and suffering in the world, Alexander writes: "God is not responsible for the miseries endured in working out His providence, but rather we are responsible for our acts...."
Śrīla Prabhupāda: Yes, we create our own miserable condition, just as a silkworm creates a cocoon, becomes entrapped and dies.

aśraddadhānāḥ puruṣā
dharmasyāsya parantapa
aprāpya māṁ nivartante
mṛtyu-saṁsāra-vartmani

"Those who are not faithful on the path of devotional service cannot attain Me, O conqueror of foes, but return to birth and death in this material world." (*Bg.* 9.3) Because the living entity acts independently, not caring for God's instructions, he is entangled, and he suffers. In this way, he creates his own suffering.

Friedrich Wilhelm Nietzsche
(1844-1900)

Hayagrīva dāsa: Whereas Schopenhauer spoke of the blind will of the individual as being the basic propelling force that keeps us tied to material existence, to transmigration, Nietzsche spoke of *der wille zur macht,* "the will to power," which is a different type of will. This will is not so much a subjugating of others as a mastering of one's lower self. It is characterized by self-control and an interest in art and philosophy. Most people are envious of others, but it is the duty of the philosopher to transcend this envy by sheer willpower. In Nietzsche's words, the philosopher "shakes off with one shrug much vermin that would have buried itself deep in others." When the philosopher has rid himself of resentment and envy, he can even embrace his enemies with a kind of Christian love. An example of such a powerful man in action would be that of Socrates meeting his death with good cheer and courage.

Śrīla Prabhupāda: This is called spiritual power. Envy is a symptom of conditioned life. In *Śrīmad-Bhāgavatam,* it is stated that the neophyte who is beginning to understand the Vedic literatures should not be envious. In this material world, everyone is envious. People are even envious of God and His instructions. Consequently, people do not like to accept Kṛṣṇa's instructions. Although Kṛṣṇa is the Supreme Personality of Godhead and is accepted as such by all *ācāryas*, there are men called *mūḍhas* who either reject Kṛṣṇa's instructions or try to eschew some contrary meaning from them. This envy is symptomatic of conditioned souls. Unless we are liberated from conditioned life, we will remain confused under the influence of the external material energy. Until we come to the spiritual platform, there is no possibility of escaping from envy and pride by so-called power. The transcendental stage is described in *Bhagavad-gītā* as *brahma-bhūtaḥ prasannātmā samaḥ sarveṣu bhūteṣu* (18.54). When we attain that stage, we can look at everyone with the same spiritual understanding.

Hayagrīva dāsa: Nietzsche calls the man who possesses such spiritual power the *Ubermensch*, a word literally meaning "above man," and often translated as "the superman." The *Ubermensch* is totally self-possessed, fearless of death, simple, self-knowing, and self-reliant. He does not need any props, and he is so powerful that he can change the lives of others simply on contact. Neitzsche never referred to any historical person as the *Ubermensch*, and he did not consider himself such.

Śrīla Prabhupāda: We accept the guru as the superman because he is worshipped like God. *Yasya prasādād bhagavat-prasādaḥ (Śrī Gurvaṣṭaka* 8). By the mercy of the superman, one can get in touch with the Supreme Personality of Godhead. Caitanya Mahāprabhu also accepts this:

brahmāṇḍa bhramite kona bhāgyavān jīva
guru-kṛṣṇa-prasāde pāya bhakti-latā-bīja

"According to their karma, all living entities are wandering throughout the entire universe. Some of them are being elevated to the upper planetary systems, and some are going down into the lower planetary systems. Out of many millions of wandering living entities, one who is very fortunate gets an opportunity to associate with a bona fide spiritual master by the grace of Kṛṣṇa. By the mercy of both Kṛṣṇa and the spiritual master, such a person receives the seed of the creeper of devotional service." (*Caitanya-caritāmṛta*, Madh. 19.151) By the mercy of Kṛṣṇa and the guru, or the superman, we receive information about spiritual life so that we can return home, back to Godhead. Śrī Caitanya Mahāprabhu requested everyone to become gurus, or supermen. The superman distributes transcendental knowledge strictly according to the authorized version he has received from his superior. This is called *paramparā*, the disciplic succession. One superman delivers this supreme knowledge to another superman, and this knowledge was originally delivered by God Himself.

Hayagrīva dāsa: In *Thus Spake Zarathustra,* Nietzsche concludes that all men want power. At the top of the hierarchy in the quest for power is the ascetic and the martyr. The *Ubermensch* would be one who has conquered his passions and attained all good qualifications. His actions are creative, and he does not envy others. He is constantly aware that death is always present, and he is so superior to others that he is almost like God in the world.

Śrīla Prabhupāda: In Sanskrit, the *Ubermensch* or superman is called a *svāmī*, or *gosvāmī*. He is described by Rūpa Gosvāmī:

vāco vegaṁ manasaḥ krodha-vegaṁ
jihvā-vegam udaropastha-vegam
etān vegān yo viṣaheta dhīraḥ
sarvām apīmāṁ pṛthivīṁ sa śiṣyāt

"A sober person who can tolerate the urge to speak, the mind's demands, the actions of anger, and the urges of the tongue, belly, and genitals, is qualified to make disciples all over the world." (*Upadesāmṛta* 1) These forces that drive men are six in number: speech, the tongue, mind, anger, belly, and genitals. A *gosvāmī* can control these forces, especially the genitals, belly, and tongue, which are very hard to control. Bhaktivinoda Ṭhākura says: *tā'ra madhye jihwā ati, lobha moy sudurmati, tā'ke jetā kaṭhina saṁsāre.* "Among the senses, the tongue is the most voracious and uncontrollable; it is very difficult to conquer the tongue in this world." (*Gītāvalī, Prasāda-sevāya* 1) The force of the tongue is very great, and for its gratification we create many artificial edibles. Nonsensical habits like smoking, drinking, and meat eating have entered society due to the urges of the tongue. There is no real need for these undesirable things. A person does not die because he cannot smoke, eat meat, or drink intoxicants. Rather, without these indulgences, he can elevate himself to the highest platform. Due to the urges of the tongue, people have become addicted to drinking, smoking, meat eating, and frivolous conversation. It is therefore said that one who can control the tongue can control the urges of the other senses also. One who can control all the senses, beginning with the tongue, is called a *gosvāmī* or *svāmī*, or, as Nietzsche would say, the *Ubermensch.* But this is not possible for an ordinary man.

Hayagrīva dāsa: Nietzsche believed that everyone seeks power, but that the weak seek it vainly; instead of trying to conquer themselves, they attempt to conquer others, and this is the will to power misdirected or misinterpreted. For instance, in his will to power, Hitler sought to subjugate the world, but was ultimately unsuccessful, and he brought disaster upon himself and Germany. The *Ubermensch*, on the other hand, strives to overcome himself, and demands more of himself than others. In this striving for perfection, he transcends the ordinary man.

Śrīla Prabhupāda: Politicians like Hitler are not able to control the force of anger. A king or politician has to use anger properly. Narottama dāsa Ṭhākura says that we should control our powers and apply them in the proper cases. We may become angry, but our anger must be controlled. We should utilize anger at the proper place and in the proper circumstances. Although a king may not be angry by nature, he has to display his anger toward a criminal. It is not good for a king to try to control his anger when a criminal act is performed; therefore Narottama dāsa Ṭhākura says that anger is controlled when it is properly used. *Kāma-krodha-lobha-moha. Kāma* refers to lust; *krodha* means anger; *lobha* means greed; and *moha* means illusion. These can all be properly utilized. For instance, *kāma*, which is great eagerness, or lusty desire, can be utilized in attaining the lotus feet of Kṛṣṇa. If we desire Kṛṣṇa, our strong desire is very laudable. Similarly, anger can be properly utilized. Although Caitanya Mahāprabhu taught that we should be very submissive, humbler than the grass and more tolerant than a tree, He became angry upon seeing Nityānanda Prabhu hurt by Jagāi and Mādhāi. Everything can be properly utilized in the service of Kṛṣṇa, but not for personal aggrandizement. In the material world, everyone is certainly after power, but the real superman is not after power for himself. He himself is a mendicant, a *sannyāsī*, but he acquires power for the service of the Lord. For instance, I came to the U.S.A. not to acquire material power but to distribute Kṛṣṇa consciousness. By the grace of Kṛṣṇa, all facilities have been afforded, and now, from the material point of view, I have become somewhat powerful. But this is not for my personal sense gratification; it is all for the spreading of Kṛṣṇa consciousness. The conclusion is that power for Kṛṣṇa's service is very valuable, and power for our own sense gratification is to be condemned.

Hayagrīva dāsa: Nietzsche was not very clear about the utilization of power, but he concluded that power results from self-control. According to him, no one has ever attained the level of the superman.

Śrīla Prabhupāda: You cannot do anything without power. Power is required for Kṛṣṇa's service, not for sense gratification. One who can act according to this principle is a superman. Generally, people use power for their own sense gratification, and therefore it is not easy to find anyone on the level of the superman.

Hayagrīva dāsa: Nietzsche claims that because the *Ubermensch* subjugates his own passions, he is beyond good and evil and not subject to mundane dualities.

Śrīla Prabhupāda: Yes, because the superman acts on behalf of God, he is transcendental. At the beginning of *Bhagavad-gītā*, Arjuna was thinking like an ordinary person in his reluctance to kill his kinsmen. From the material point of view, nonviolence is a good qualification. Arjuna was excusing the others, although they had insulted him and his wife and usurped his kingdom. He pleaded on their behalf before Lord Kṛṣṇa, arguing that it would be better to let them enjoy his kingdom. "I am not going to fight." Materially, this appears very laudable, but spiritually it is not, because Kṛṣṇa wanted him to fight. Finally, Arjuna carried out Kṛṣṇa's order and fought. Clearly, this kind of fighting was not for personal aggrandizement, but for the service of Kṛṣṇa. By using his power for the service of the Lord, Arjuna became a superman.

Hayagrīva dāsa: Concerning religion, Nietzsche felt that because Christ's own disciples misunderstood him, Christianity as such never existed. "The last Christian died on the cross," he wrote. Although Christ was totally pure and free from all resentment and envy, Christianity has had envy and resentment as its focal point from its very beginning, even though it calls itself the religion of love. Thus Nietzsche proclaimed, "God is dead," in the sense that the God of the Christian religion is dead.

Śrīla Prabhupāda: If you create an artificial god, it is better that he is dead so that he cannot inflict more injuries.

Hayagrīva dāsa: Then it is better to have no conception of God than a bad conception?

Śrīla Prabhupāda: Yes, better. But Christ was the embodiment of tolerance. There is no doubt about this.

Hayagrīva dāsa: It is not that Nietzsche criticizes Christ himself, but his followers.

Śrīla Prabhupāda: Yes, actually we can see that the Christians hate the Jews because the Jews crucified Christ. They even utilize the symbol of the cross to remind people that the Jews crucified him. Even in the churches there are pictures of Lord Jesus, with thorns on his head, being forced to carry his cross. In this way, the people are reminded of all the troubles that the Jews gave to Christ. Emphasizing Christ on the cross is a way of prolonging resentment against the Jews. But the fact is that Christ had many other activities, which are not brought into prominence. Actually, it is very painful for a devotee to see his master being crucified. Even though Christ was crucified, that scene in his life should not be emphasized.

Hayagrīva dāsa: Neitzsche considered Buddhism and Hinduism superior to Christianity, but he disliked the nihilism of the Buddhists and the caste system of the Hindus, especially the Hindu treatment of the untouchables.

Śrīla Prabhupāda: That is a later concoction by the caste Hindus. The true Vedic religion does not speak of untouchables. Caitanya Mahāprabhu Himself demonstrated His system by accepting so-called untouchables like Haridāsa Ṭhākura, who was born in a Mohammedan family. Although Haridāsa Ṭhākura was not accepted by Hindu society, Caitanya Mahāprabhu personally indicated that he was most exalted. Haridāsa Ṭhākura would not enter the temple of Lord Jagannātha because he did not want to create commotion, but Caitanya Mahāprabhu Himself came to see Haridāsa Ṭhākura every day. It is a basic principle in the Vedic religion that we should not be envious of anyone. Kṛṣṇa Himself says in *Bhagavad-gītā:*

māṁ hi pārtha vyapāśritya
ye'pi syuḥ pāpa-yonayaḥ
striyo vaiśyās tathā śūdrās
te'pi yānti parāṁ gatim

"O son of Pṛtha, those who take shelter in Me, though they be of lower birth—women, *vaiśyas* [merchants], as well as *śūdras* [workers]—can approach the supreme destination." (*Bg.* 9.32) Despite birth in a lower family, if one is a devotee, he is eligible to practice Kṛṣṇa consciousness and return to God, provided the necessary spiritual qualifications are there.

Hayagrīva dāsa: Nietzsche believed that by stressing the transcendental world, a person would come to resent this world. He therefore personally rejected all formal religions.

Śrīla Prabhupāda: This material world is described as a place of suffering. *Ābrahma-bhuvanāl lokāḥ punar āvartino'rjuna.* "From the highest planet in the material world down to the lowest, all are places of misery, wherein repeated birth and death take place." (*Bg.* 8.16) We do not know whether Nietzsche realized this or not, but if one really understands the soul, he can realize that this material world is a place of suffering. Being part and parcel of God, the soul has the same qualities possessed by God. God is *sac-cid-ānanda-vigraha,* eternal, full of knowledge and bliss, and He is eternally enjoying Himself in the company of His associates. The living entities have the same nature, but in material life, eternity, knowledge, and bliss are absent. It is therefore better that we learn to detest material existence and try to give it up. *Paraṁ dṛṣṭvā nivartate (Bg.* 2.59). The Vedas advise us to understand the spiritual world and try to return there. *Tamasi mā jyotir gama.* The spiritual world is the kingdom of light, and this material world is the kingdom of darkness. The sooner we learn to avoid the world of darkness and return to the kingdom of light, the better it is.

Hayagrīva dāsa: Nietzsche was greatly influenced by the ancient Greeks, and he was astounded that out of so few men, so many great individuals emerged. He believed that mankind ought to be constantly striving to produce such great men, men who conquer their evil instincts, and he considered this to be mankind's only duty.

Śrīla Prabhupāda: Everyone is trying to be a great man, but one's greatness is accepted when he becomes God realized. The word *veda* means "knowledge," and a person is great when he is conversant with the lessons of the Vedas. The object of knowledge, as described in *Bhagavad-gītā,* is God, or the self. Since the individual is part and parcel of God, one is self-realized whether he realizes himself or God. There are different methods for self-realization, which is difficult. However, if one realizes God, he automatically realizes himself. If the sun is out, we can see everything very clearly. In the Vedas, it is said, *yasmin vijñate sarvam eva vijñataṁ bhavanti.* By understanding God, we understand all other things and automatically become jolly. *Brahma-bhūtaḥ prasannātmā (Bg.* 18.54). The word *prasannātmā* means "jolly." *Samaḥ sarveṣu bhūteṣu (Bg.* 18.54). At that time, we can see that everyone is exactly like ourselves, because everyone is part and parcel of the Supreme Lord. At this point, service of the Lord begins, and we attain the platform of knowledge, bliss, and eternity.

Hayagrīva dāsa: Nietzsche emphatically states that there has never been a superman. "All too similar are men to each other," he writes. "Verily, even the greatest found I all too human." Nor does the superman evolve in the Darwinian sense. The *Ubermensch* is a possibility at present if man uses all of his spiritual and physical energies. But how is the superman possible without an object for his spiritual energies?

Śrīla Prabhupāda: We become supermen if we engage in the service of the Supreme Person. The Supreme Being is a person, and the superman is also a person. *Nityo nityānāṁ cetanaś cetanānām (Kaṭha-up-*

aniṣad 2.2.13). God is the chief amongst all personalities. The superman has no other business than carrying out the orders of the Supreme Being.

anyābhilāṣitā-śūnyaṁ
jñāna-karmādy-anāvṛtam
ānukūlyena kṛṣṇānu-
śīlanaṁ bhaktir uttamā

"*Uttama bhakti*, or unalloyed devotion unto the Supreme Personality of Godhead, Śrī Kṛṣṇa, involves the rendering of devotional service in a way that is favorable to the Lord. This devotional service should be free from any extraneous motive and devoid of fruitive karma, impersonal *jñāna*, and all other selfish desires." (*Bhakti-rasāmṛta-sindhu* 1.1.11) Kṛṣṇa comes to make everyone a superman. He therefore orders, *sarva-dharmān parityajya mām ekaṁ śaraṇaṁ vraja*. "Just give up everything and surrender to Me." (*Bg*. 18.66) Unless we are supermen, we cannot understand this instruction. If we can surrender to Kṛṣṇa, we are supermen.

bahūnāṁ janmanām ante
jñānavān māṁ prapadyate
vāsudevaḥ sarvam iti
sa mahātmā sudurlabhaḥ

"After many births and deaths, he who is actually in knowledge surrenders unto Me, knowing Me to be the cause of all causes and all that is. Such a great soul is very rare." (*Bg*. 7.19) The ordinary man thinks, "I have my independence and can do something myself. Why should I surrender?" However, as soon as he realizes that his only duty is to surrender to Kṛṣṇa, and that he has no other duty in this material world, he becomes the superman. This consciousness is attained after many, many births.

Hayagrīva dāsa: Nietzsche would reject dependence on anything exterior to the superman himself. That is, he would reject props. But isn't it impossible for a man to elevate himself to that platform independent of the Supreme Lord?

Śrīla Prabhupāda: Of course, and therefore Kṛṣṇa says, "Depend upon Me." You have to be dependent, and if you do not depend on Kṛṣṇa, you have to depend on the dictations of māyā, illusion. There are many philosophers and politicians dependent on others, or dependent on their own whimsical ideas, but we should depend on the perfect instructions of God. The fact is that every living being is dependent; he cannot be independent. If he voluntarily depends on the instructions of God, he becomes the superman.

Hayagrīva dāsa: Nietzsche's superman seems to resemble the *haṭha-yogī* who elevates himself seemingly independent of God.
Śrīla Prabhupāda: Yes, seemingly. As soon as a *haṭha-yogī* gets some extraordinary mystic powers, he thinks that he has become God. This is another mistake, because no one can become God. To some extent, a yogī may attain some mystical powers by practice, or by the favor of the Lord, but these powers are not sufficient to enable him to become God. There are many who think that through meditation, or *haṭha-yoga*, it is possible to become equal to God, but this is another illusion, another dictation of māyā. Māyā is always saying, "Why depend on God? You can become God yourself."
Hayagrīva dāsa: Independence seems to be central to Nietzsche's philosophy. In a sense, his superman is somewhat like Hiraṇyakaśipu, who made the demigods tremble to see his austerities.
Śrīla Prabhupāda: Yes, and ultimately he was outwitted by the Supreme Himself. It is not good to struggle for material power and control over others. If one becomes a servant of God, he becomes the superman automatically and acquires many subordinate followers. One does not have to undergo severe austerities to control others. Everything can be mastered in one stroke. As soon as you become a devout servant of God, many people will follow you. Separate endeavor is not required.
Hayagrīva dāsa: And what of sense control?
Śrīla Prabhupāda: Control of the senses is automatically there.

yasyāsti bhaktir bhagavaty akiñcanā
sarvair guṇais tatra samāsate surāḥ
harāv abhaktasya kuto mahad-guṇā
manorathenāsati dhāvato bahiḥ

"All the demigods and their exalted qualities, such as religion, knowledge, and renunciation, become manifest in the body of one who has developed unalloyed devotion for the Supreme Personality of Godhead, Vāsudeva. On the other hand, a person devoid of devotional service and engaged in material activities has no good qualities. Even if he is adept at the practice of mystic yoga, or the honest endeavor of maintaining his family and relatives, he must be driven by his own mental speculations and must engage in the service of the Lord's external energy. How can there be any good qualities in such a man?" (*Bhāg.* 5.18.12) If one becomes a devotee of the Supreme Lord, he controls his senses and many other living entities. But he never thinks that he has become God or the actual controller. Rather, he receives his power automatically.

Hayagrīva dāsa: One last point on Nietzsche. He believed in eternal recurrence—that is, after this universe has been destroyed, it will be repeated again after many aeons.

Śrīla Prabhupāda: In *Bhagavad-gītā*, it is stated, *bhūtvā bhūtvā pralīyate (Bg.* 8.19). This material world is manifest at a certain point, maintained for a certain period, then destroyed. Brahmā, Viṣṇu, and Śiva are in charge of creation, maintenance, and destruction. Above them is Kṛṣṇa, the Supreme Personality of Godhead. It is the nature of everything material to be created, maintained, and annihilated.

Hayagrīva dāsa: Well, that's one type of general repetition, but Nietzsche believed that everything will be repeated infinitely in every detail. That is, the detailed arrangements of this world will eventually recur sometime in the future.

Śrīla Prabhupāda: The creation will be repeated in detail in that the twenty-four elements will again be assembled. There are the five gross elements—earth, water, fire, air, and ether—and three subtle elements: mind, intelligence, and ego. There are the ten senses, and the five sense objects. All these will be created again.

Hayagrīva dāsa: That's one type of detail, but he believes that eventually, Friedrich Nietzsche will live again from 1844 to 1900.

Śrīla Prabhupāda: The year 1844 is an element of time, and from the moment of creation, we may begin to assign dates. In this way, the date may again be repeated. For instance, every day is a new day, but in every day there is six o'clock, eight o'clock, and so on. There is automatic repetition.

Hayagrīva dāsa: If this is the case, if one has to continue being Friedrich Nietzsche, or whoever, how is liberation possible?

Śrīla Prabhupāda: This material world is created for the conditioned soul, who is put here in order to learn his position as the eternal servant of God. Lord Brahmā, the first created being in the universe, is given the Vedic instructions, and he distributes them through the disciplic succession, from Brahmā to Nārada, from Nārada to Vyāsadeva, from Vyāsadeva to Śukadeva Gosvāmī, and so on. These instructions encourage the conditioned soul to return home, back to Godhead. If the conditioned soul rejects them, he remains in the material world until it is annihilated. At that time, he remains in an unconscious state, just like a child within the womb of his mother. In due course of time, his consciousness revives, and he again takes birth. The point is that anyone can take advantage of the Vedic instructions and go back to Godhead. Unfortunately, the conditioned living entities are so attached to the material world that they repeatedly want to take up material bodies. In this way, history repeats. There is again creation, maintenance, and destruction.

Hayagrīva dāsa: Nietzsche believes that even the minute details will recur. That is, he would again be Friedrich Nietzsche, living in Germany, going through the same actions, writing the same books, and so on.

Śrīla Prabhupāda: Why is he so attached to Germany? That is his attachment for māyā. Under māyā's influence, we think that we will again return in these same bodies and do the same things. Sometimes when people hanker after this repetition, they go to an astrologer and ask, "Can we again come back as husband and wife?" This is all due to attachment. There may be an accidental recurrence, and one will again be a husband and have a wife, but he will not have exactly the same wife. That is an illusion. What is the point in combining the same husband and wife? The living entities combine for some sense gratification, and they get it, be it this husband or that wife. The purpose is the same, though the minute details are different.

Hayagrīva dāsa: Sometimes people claim to have experiences of deja-vu, thinking that they have been at the same spot before doing the same thing. This convinced Nietzsche of the doctrine of eternal recurrence.

Śrīla Prabhupāda: People simply want the same atmosphere. This is due to māyā's influence.

IX

UTILITARIANISM AND POSITIVISM

John Stuart Mill
(1806-1873)

Hayagrīva dāsa: In *Essay on Nature,* Mill writes: "The order of nature, insofar as unmodified by man, is such as no Being whose attributes are justice and benevolence would have made with the intention that his rational creatures should follow it as an example....It could only be as a designedly imperfect work which man, in his limited sphere, is to exercise justice and benevolence in amending."
Śrīla Prabhupāda: Man is called a rational animal; he has a rational nature and an animal nature. Eating, sleeping, mating, and defending are activities common to animals, but a man should cultivate his rational nature. For instance, by his reason, man can understand that it is not necessary to eat meat in order to live a healthy life. It is not that man should be carried by nature's way, which says that man can eat anything. Human beings are accustomed to eating the most abominable foods, and in so doing, they become implicated. Beyond eating, sleeping, mating, and defending, man should search out the Absolute Truth. In this way, man's rationality is properly used. Otherwise, he remains an animal.
Śyāmasundara dāsa: Mill claimed that the world, or nature, can be improved by man's efforts, but that perfection is not possible.

Śrīla Prabhupāda: In one sense, that is correct. This world is so made that although you make it perfect today, tomorrow it will deteriorate. Nonetheless, the world can be improved by this Kṛṣṇa consciousness. You can better the world by bringing people to Kṛṣṇa consciousness and delivering the message of Kṛṣṇa to whomever you meet. That is the best social activity you can perform.
Śyāmasundara dāsa: The goal of the utilitarians was more specifically to obtain whatever the people desire or require.
Śrīla Prabhupāda: The people desire happiness. The utilitarians try to give people artificial happiness, happiness separate from Kṛṣṇa, but we are trying to give direct happiness, happiness that is connected with Kṛṣṇa. If we purify our existence, we can attain spiritual, eternal happiness and bliss. Everyone is working hard for happiness, but how can happiness be attained in a diseased condition? The material disease is an impediment to happiness. This disease has to be cured.
Hayagrīva dāsa: Mill felt that virtues like courage, cleanliness, and self-control are not instinctive in man but have to be cultivated. In *Nature*, he writes: "The truth is that there is hardly a single point of excellence belonging to human character which is not decidedly repugnant to the untutored feelings of human nature...."
Śrīla Prabhupāda: Yes. Therefore there are educational systems in human society. Men should be educated according to the instructions given in the Vedic literatures. *Bhagavad-gītā* is the grand summation of all Vedic literature, and therefore everyone should read it as it is. It is not necessary to interpret.
Śyāmasundara dāsa: For Mill, there are several ways to ascertain knowledge. For instance, we can determine the cause and the effects of things by determining whether the phenomena under investigation have only one circumstance in common. If so, we can conclude that the circumstance alone is the cause of the effect.
Śrīla Prabhupāda: Certainly there is the natural law of cause and effect, but if we go further to determine the cause, we ultimately arrive at Kṛṣṇa. Everything has an original source, a cause. If you try to find out the cause of this and that, and conduct research, that is called *darśana*, which means "to find the cause." Therefore philosophy is called *darśana-śāstra*, which means "finding the cause of the cause." The idea is that we ultimately arrive at Kṛṣṇa, the original cause of everything.
Śyāmasundara dāsa: But what kind of test can we apply to phenomena to find out the cause? How can we determine that God is the cause behind everything?

Śrīla Prabhupāda: For every phenomenon, there is a cause, and we know that God is the ultimate cause. Mill may give many methods for studying immediate causes, but we are interested in the ultimate cause of everything. The ultimate cause has full independence to do anything and everything beyond our calculation. Everything that we see is but an effect of His original push.
Śyāmasundara dāsa: If we see rain falling and want to prove that God is the cause of rain, what test can we apply?
Śrīla Prabhupāda: The *śāstras*, the Vedic literatures. We are advised to see through the *śāstras* because we cannot see directly. Since our senses are defective, direct perception has no value. Therefore we have to receive knowledge through authoritative instruction.
Śyāmasundara dāsa: In other words, when we see an apple fall from a tree, we have to see through the eyes of the *śāstras* in order to see God in that act?
Śrīla Prabhupāda: God has made His laws so perfect that one cause effects one thing, and that in turn effects another, and so on. We may see an apple grow and explain it as "nature," but this nature is working according to certain laws. An apple has a certain color and taste because it is following specific laws set down by Kṛṣṇa. Kṛṣṇa's energies are perfect and are working perfectly. Everything is being carried out under systematic laws, although we may not perceive these laws.
Śyāmasundara dāsa: Scientists admit that nothing can come out of nothing.
Śrīla Prabhupāda: If something emerges, there must be a cause in the background. We say that the root cause of everything is Brahman, the Absolute Truth.
Hayagrīva dāsa: Mill certainly did not see God as the cause of evil. In fact, he considered God at war against it. Man's role is to help God end this war. He writes: "If Providence is omnipotent, Providence intends whatever happens, and the fact of its happening proves that Providence intended it. If so, everything which a human being can do is predestined by Providence and is a fulfillment of its designs. But if, as is the more religious theory, Providence intends not all which happens, but only what is good, then indeed man has it in his power, by his voluntary actions, to aid the intentions of Providence...."
Śrīla Prabhupāda: Providence desires only the good. The living entity is in this material world due to the improper utilization of his will. Even though he wants to enjoy this material world, God is so kind that He gives him facilities and directions. When a child wants to play in a

certain way, he is guided by some nurse or servant hired by the parents. Our position is something like that. We have given up the company of God to come to this material world to enjoy ourselves. So God has allowed us to come here, saying, "All right, enjoy this experience, and when you understand that this material enjoyment is ultimately frustrating, you can come back." Thus the Supreme Lord is guiding the enjoyment of all living beings, especially human beings, so that they may again return home, back to Godhead. Nature is the agent acting under the instructions of God. If the living entity is overly addicted to misuse his freedom, he is punished. This punishment is a consequence of the living entity's desire. God does not want a human being to become a pig, but when one develops such a mentality by eating anything and everything, God gives the facility by providing the body of a hog. God is situated in everyone's heart, and is noting the desires of the living entity from within. According to one's desires, God orders material nature to provide a particular body.

Hayagrīva dāsa: Mill further writes: "Limited as, on this showing, the divine power must be by inscrutable but insurmountable obstacles, who knows what man could have been created without desires which never are to be, and even which never ought to be, fulfilled?" Thus Mill concludes that the existence of evil, or pain and death, excludes the existence of an omnipotent God. He sees man in a position to "aid the intentions of Providence" by surmounting his evil instincts. God is not infinite in His power, because if He were, there would be no evil.

Śrīla Prabhupāda: Evil is undoubtedly created by God, but this was necessary due to the human being's misuse of his free will. God gives man good directions, but when man is disobedient, evil is naturally there to punish him. Evil is not desired by God, yet it is created because it is necessary. Although a government constructs prisons, it prefers to construct universities so that people can attain an education and become highly enlightened. Because some people misuse their independence, prisons are necessary. We suffer due to our evil activities. Thus God, being supreme, punishes us. When we are under the protection of God, nothing is evil; everything is good. God does not create evil, but man's evil activities provoke God to create an evil situation.

Hayagrīva dāsa: In the Judeo-Christian tradition, God is at war with Satan. In Vedic literatures, there are also wars between the demigods and the demons, as well as Kṛṣṇa and the demons, but these wars do not seem to be taken as serious confrontations between God and His enemies. Isn't Kṛṣṇa's mood always playful?

Śrīla Prabhupāda: Since Kṛṣṇa is all powerful, when He is fighting with demons, He is actually playing. This fighting does not affect His energy. It is like a father fighting with his small child. One slap is sufficient. Kṛṣṇa gives the demons a chance to play by fighting Him, but one strong slap is sufficient. There is no question of fighting with God. He is omnipotent. However, when a living entity is disobedient and harasses the devotees, God kills him. *Paritrāṇāya sādhūnāṁ vināśāya ca duṣkṛtām (Bg.* 4.8). When Kṛṣṇa descends on this earth, He chastises the demons and protects His devotees. Whenever there is a fight between the demons and the demigods, God takes the side of the demigods.

Hayagrīva dāsa: Mill saw it more like an actual struggle between God and Satan, or evil.

Śrīla Prabhupāda: There is struggle because the demons are always transgressing God's rules. A demon is one who rejects God's rules, and a demigod is one who accepts them. That is the main difference, as stated in the *śāstras.*

Hayagrīva dāsa: But Mill pictures God Himself as struggling hard in the fight to conquer the demons.

Śrīla Prabhupāda: God has no reason to struggle. According to the Vedas, He is so powerful that He has nothing to do. Just as a king may have many servants, ministers, and soldiers to carry out his desires, Kṛṣṇa has many energies that act according to His order. Kṛṣṇa Himself has nothing to do. He is playing His flute and enjoying Himself. That is *ānanda.* Although He is enjoying Himself, the universe is going on in accordance with His orders, through the agencies of His multi-energies. There is no question of God struggling. He doesn't even have to fight. His various agents can easily enough kill all the evil elements in the world.

Śyāmasundara dāsa: Mill believed that God is good, but that He is involved in a world not of His own making.

Śrīla Prabhupāda: Is God to be judged by Mr. Mill? God is good, but not as good as Mr. Mill thinks He ought to be? Is this his opinion of God? Is God good in all conditions? Or is God only good when Mr. Mill considers Him good? What is God's position?

Śyāmasundara dāsa: Mill says that the presence of evil indicates that if God were everything, He would not be completely good.

Śrīla Prabhupāda: Therefore God has to depend on the opinion of Mr. Mill. Is it that Mr. Mill does not approve of all God's activities?

Śyāmasundara dāsa: He maintains that God is good, but that He is limited in His power. If His power were absolute, everything would be good.

Śrīla Prabhupāda: How nonsensical! Everything *is* good! That is our philosophy. When God kills a demon, immediately flowers are showered from the sky. Whatever God does is good. Kṛṣṇa danced with other men's wives in the dead of night, and this activity is worshipped as *rāsa-līlā*. However, if an ordinary man does this, he is immediately condemned as a debauchee. In all circumstances, God is good and worshipable. It is not that we subject God to our judgement, saying, "Oh yes, You are good, but not so good." Fools think, "I am better than God. I can create my own God." God creates us; we cannot create God. Unfortunately, Mill did not know what is evil and what is good. He should have known that whatever is created by God is good, even if it appears to be evil to us. We may think that such and such is evil, but actually it is good. If we do not know how it is good, that is our fault. God cannot be placed under our judgement. In all circumstances, God is good.

Hayagrīva dāsa: Mill was particularly interested in the role of authority. In *Utility of Religion*, he writes, "Consider the enormous influence of authority on the human mind.... Authority is the evidence on which the mass of mankind believe everything which they are said to know except facts of which their own senses have taken cognizance. It is the evidence on which even the wisest receive all those truths of science, or facts in history or in life, of which they have not personally examined the proofs...."

Śrīla Prabhupāda: You can neither defy nor deny real authority. We are presenting our Kṛṣṇa consciousness movement on this principle. We should carry out the orders of the authority, and Kṛṣṇa, or God, is the Supreme Authority. Whatever He says must be accepted without interpretation. In this way, everyone can be happy. Those who are sane do not hesitate to accept God's authority, and they become happy abiding by His orders. Those who exactly follow the instructions of the Supreme Authority are also authorities. The spiritual master is the authoritative servant, and God is the authoritative master. If we follow the instructions of the authoritative servant, we in turn become authoritative servants of the spiritual master.

Hayagrīva dāsa: Concerning morality, Mill writes: "Belief, then, in the supernatural, great as are the services which it rendered in the earlier stages of human development, cannot be considered to be any longer required either for enabling us to know what is right and wrong in social morality, or for supplying us with motives to do right and to abstain from wrong."

Śrīla Prabhupāda: Morality means abiding by the orders of God. That is real morality. Other moralities are manufactured, and they differ in different countries. Religion and real morality, however, function according to the same principle. Religion means carrying out the orders of God, and morality means following those principles whereby we can fulfill the desires of God. Before the battle of Kurukṣetra, Arjuna considered killing to be immoral, but when he understood from the instructions of Kṛṣṇa that the fight was necessary, he decided to carry out his duty as a *kṣatriya*. So this is morality. Ultimately, morality means carrying out the desires of God.

Śyāmasundara dāsa: For Mill, there are two moral sanctions of conduct. One is internal, which is our conscience and sense of duty.

Śrīla Prabhupāda: What does he mean by conscience? A sense of duty is different from the conscience. It is our duty to receive instructions from higher personalities. If we do not, how can we know our duty?

Śyāmasundara dāsa: Mill felt that our duty is that which produces the most good for the most people.

Śrīla Prabhupāda: That is all so vague. What if everyone wants to take drugs? Is it our duty to help them? How can a rascal understand what his duty is? One has to be trained to know.

Śyāmasundara dāsa: Mill would say that there is a rational or guiding principle for action, and this is the golden rule of the Christians: "Do unto others, as you would have them do unto you."

Śrīla Prabhupāda: This means that you have to approach Christ. You cannot manufacture golden rules yourself. You have to abide by the orders of Christ, and that means approaching a superior authority.

Śyāmasundara dāsa: The second sanction of moral conduct is external: the fear of displeasing other men or God. We hope to win favor through acting morally.

Śrīla Prabhupāda: This also means accepting authority. Therefore the Vedas tell us that if we want to be really learned, we must approach a guru. Did John Stuart Mill have a guru?

Śyāmasundara dāsa: His father, James Mill, was also a great philosopher.

Śrīla Prabhupāda: In any case, we must accept some authority, be it Christ or Kṛṣṇa. Our duty lies in following the orders of the higher authority. Of course, we accept Kṛṣṇa, the Supreme Personality of Godhead, as our authority.

Hayagrīva dāsa: Mill himself rejected many basic Christian tenets, and he even believed that there is no intrinsic value in the belief in the immortality of the soul. He writes: "Those who believe in the immortality of the soul generally quit life with fully as much if not more reluctance as those who have no such expectation."

Śrīla Prabhupāda: We have daily experience of how the soul continues, even though the body changes. In our own family we can see that the body of an infant changes into the body of a boy, a young man, a middle-aged man, and then an old man. In any condition, the soul is the same. Why is it difficult to understand the immortality of the soul? If we cannot understand it, we are not very intelligent.

yasyātma-buddhiḥ kuṇape tridhātuke
sva-dhīḥ kalatrādiṣu bhauma ijya-dhīḥ
yat-tīrtha-buddhiḥ salile na karhicij
janeṣv abhijñeṣu sa eva go-kharaḥ

"A human being who identifies this body made of three elements with his self, who considers the by-products of the body to be his kinsmen, who considers the land of birth worshipable, and who goes to the place of pilgrimage simply to take a bath rather than meet men of transcendental knowledge there is to be considered like an ass or a cow." (*Bhāg.* 10.84.13) If a person does not understand the immortality of the soul, he is an animal. There is no question of belief. It is a fact. If a man says, "I don't believe that I will grow old," he is ignorant of facts. If he does not die when he is young, he necessarily grows old. This is a question of common sense, not of beliefs. In *Bhagavad-gītā*, Kṛṣṇa says that there was never a time when we did not exist, nor will there ever be a time when we will cease to exist (*Bg.* 2.12). The soul is immortal; he never takes birth, and he never dies. This is the beginning of knowledge. First of all, we must understand what we are. If we do not, we will surely be wrongly directed. We will take care of the body just as a foolish man might take care of a bird cage, and neglect the bird within it.

Hayagrīva dāsa: Mill was not only a utilitarian but a humanist, and he felt that a religion of humanity can have a greater effect than a supernatural religion. The religion of humanity would foster unselfish feelings and would have man at the center.

Śrīla Prabhupāda: Without God, how can it be a religion? As I have already explained, religion means carrying out the orders of God.

Hayagrīva dāsa: Concerning immortality, Mill asserts that there is no evidence for the immortality of the soul, and none against it.

Śrīla Prabhupāda: What does he need to be convinced? There is a great deal of evidence. It is mankind's misfortune that a person like Mill cannot understand a simple truth that even a child can understand.

Hayagrīva dāsa: Ultimately, Mill considered the whole domain of the supernatural as removed from the region of belief into that of simple hope.
Śrīla Prabhupāda: It is neither hope nor belief, but a fact. At any rate, to those who are Kṛṣṇa conscious, it is a fact. Kṛṣṇa came and gave Arjuna instructions, and those instructions are recorded.
Hayagrīva dāsa: Mill was such a staunch humanist that he wrote: "I will call no being good who is not what I mean when I apply that epithet to my fellow creatures, and if such a being can sentence me to hell for not so calling him, to hell I will go."
Śrīla Prabhupāda: God is always good, and if one does not know the goodness of God, he is imperfect. According to all Vedic literatures, God is always good and always great. What does Mill consider to be a good man?
Hayagrīva dāsa: One who works for what he calls "the greatest happiness principle," that is, the greatest happiness for everyone on earth.
Śrīla Prabhupāda: Is there any man who can do good for all?
Hayagrīva dāsa: Christ said that no man is good, that there is only one good, and that is God.
Śrīla Prabhupāda: Yes, that is a fact. You may think that this man is good, but he is limited in his power. He may still think in terms of his nation or society. Only a pure devotee of Kṛṣṇa can be good because he abides by the order of the Supreme Good. Even if one has the desire to be a good man, it is not possible independent of God. In any case, these are all mental concoctions: good and bad. One who is not God conscious is necessarily bad, and one who is God conscious is good. This should be the only criterion.
Śyāmasundara dāsa: But what of Mill's contention that the good gives the greatest pleasure to the greatest number of people?
Śrīla Prabhupāda: And what if the people are fools and rascals? The greatest number of people may say that cigarettes are very nice, but does this mean that they are desirable?
Śyāmasundara dāsa: Mill makes a distinction between the quality and the quantity of pleasure. Certain pleasures are superior to others.
Śrīla Prabhupāda: When you have quality, the quantity naturally decreases. For instance, ordinary people take pleasure in eating, sleeping, mating, drinking, smoking, and so on. The pleasure of Kṛṣṇa consciousness is a transcendental pleasure, but the people who take to it are very few. Generally, since conditioned souls are fools, the pleasure that is most popular is the one followed by the greatest number of fools. According to our Vedic philosophy, man is born a fool, but he can be made

intelligent through education and culture.

Śyāmasundara dāsa: Mill advocated utilizing those principles that can give the pleasure of highest quality to the maximum people. He also wrote: "It is better to be a human being dissatisfied than a pig satisfied. It is better to be Socrates dissatisfied than a fool satisfied."

Śrīla Prabhupāda: But how often will you find a Socrates? You cannot find Socrates loitering on every street. There will only be one in millions. There is no question of the maximum number of people. Men of Socrates's caliber are a minimum. In *Bhagavad-gītā*, Kṛṣṇa says:

manuṣyāṇāṁ sahasreṣu
kaścid yatati siddhaye
yatatām api siddhānāṁ
kaścin māṁ vetti tattvataḥ

"Out of many thousands among men, one may endeavor for perfection, and of those who have achieved perfection, hardly one knows Me in truth." (*Bg*. 7.3) This is not a question of quantity, but of quality.

Śyāmasundara dāsa: Mill felt that the highest quality of pleasure might also be enjoyed by a larger number. All men should be trained to find pleasure according to this higher standard.

Śrīla Prabhupāda: This means that the maximum pleasure should be introduced to the maximum number of people. Unfortunately, it is not accepted by the greatest number but by a few only. This Kṛṣṇa consciousness movement, for instance, cannot be understood by the masses. Only a few who are fortunate can understand. There may be millions of stars in the sky, but there is only one moon, and that is sufficient to drive away the darkness. It is not possible to have many moons, although there may be many glowworms.

Śyāmasundara dāsa: Mill was trying to ascertain that standard of pleasure which is most desirable.

Śrīla Prabhupāda: That he does not know. That he has to learn from the Vedas. Ordinary men take sex to be the highest pleasure, and the entire material world is existing because of sex, but how long does this sex pleasure last? A few minutes only. A man who is wise does not want pleasure that lasts only a few minutes but pleasure that continues perpetually. *Nitya* means "eternal," and *ānanda* means "bliss." The Vedas state that those who are intelligent are not interested in transient pleasure but in eternal pleasure. They know their constitutional position; they know they are not the body. The pleasures of the body are transient and are sought by rascals. If one identifies with the body, he naturally seeks

bodily pleasure. One who knows that he is not the body but eternal spirit soul seeks eternal spiritual pleasure.
Śyāmasundara dāsa: Mill believed that a small amount of a higher type of pleasure is superior to a greater amount of a lower type.
Śrīla Prabhupāda: Yes, that is our philosophy. In *Bhagavad-gītā* it is said:

nehābhikrama-nāśo'sti
pratyavāyo na vidyate
svalpam apy asya dharmasya
trāyate mahato bhayāt

"In this endeavor there is no loss or diminution, and a little advancement on this path can protect one from the most dangerous type of fear." (*Bg.* 3.40) Even if one falls down from Kṛṣṇa consciousness, he still gains from what little he has experienced. On the other hand, if one works according to the *varṇāśrama dharma* but does not take to devotional service, all his labors go in vain. There are many students who come to Kṛṣṇa consciousness for a few days and then go away, but they return again because the quality is so great. Hare Kṛṣṇa is so potent. Save for Kṛṣṇa consciousness, everything is being dissipated by time, by the sun's progress through the sky. Everything in this world is transient, but because we are eternal spirit souls, we should accept only that which has permanent value. It is foolishness to be satisfied with anything else.
Śyāmasundara dāsa: Mill would have said that the only standard we have for understanding what is desirable is the fact the people desire it.
Śrīla Prabhupāda: We should desire Kṛṣṇa, but people do not know about Kṛṣṇa. People are thinking, "I love my country," or, "I love my body." What is this love? Because we are spirit soul and are within the body, we say, "I love."
Śyāmasundara dāsa: But Mill reasons that if something is desired, it is desirable per se.
Śrīla Prabhupāda: Living entities desire many things. A hog desires stool, but is that desirable? The men on the Bowery are interested only in drinking. Is that very desirable? Caitanya Mahāprabhu desires Kṛṣṇa, and that is a different type of desire. That should be the real standard for desire. We should know what the greatest personalities, the *mahājanas*, are desiring, and we should make that our standard. We may desire something that is harmful for us, and not desire the good. In *Bhagavad-gītā*, Kṛṣṇa wanted Arjuna to fight, but this was not Arjuna's desire. Arjuna initially wanted to leave the battlefield, but he changed

his mind because Kṛṣṇa wanted him to fight. The point is that we should desire what is desired by the great personalities, not by ourselves. After all, what are we? We should always consider ourselves to be fools.

Śyāmasundara dāsa: Mill advocated complete freedom so that everyone can express himself as he pleases.

Śrīla Prabhupāda: That is nonsense. No one has that freedom.

Śyāmasundara dāsa: But he felt that everyone should be free.

Śrīla Prabhupāda: Then everyone should be a philosopher. Mill has his own philosophy, and everyone else has his.

Śyāmasundara dāsa: He believed that if everyone is free to compete, the best will emerge.

Śrīla Prabhupāda: That is not freedom but competition. Our viewpoint is that everyone is ultimately dependent on Kṛṣṇa. Of course, in illusion we are dependent on māyā, but in any case, we must be dependent.

Auguste Comte
(1798-1857)

Hayagrīva dāsa: Comte is the French founder of Positivism. He felt that theology dealt solely with the heart, or sentiments, and that metaphysics dealt solely with the intellect, but that Positivism reconciled the two. In *A General View of Positivism,* he writes: "It is a fundamental doctrine of Positivism...that the heart preponderates over the intellect. The intellect should devote itself exclusively to the problems which the heart suggests, the ultimate object being to find proper satisfaction for our various wants."

Śrīla Prabhupāda: From *Bhagavad-gītā,* we understand that above the gross senses are the mind, intelligence, or intellect, and then the soul. The soul is the original principle of all activities, which are manifest in grosser and grosser ways. First, there are the gross activities of the body, then the subtle activities of the mind, and then the still more subtle activities of the intellect, and finally the spiritual activities. In this way, the different platforms of knowledge and understanding are categorized.

Śyāmasundara dāsa: Comte believed that theology, metaphysics and Positivism constitute three stages through which the perfect society evolves. In the beginning, the theological stage, man moves from polytheism to monotheism. In the second stage, the metaphysical, man abandons the first stages and places his faith in impersonal forces, like cause and effect, gravity, and so on.

Śrīla Prabhupāda: This philosophy is imperfect. From the personal platform, you have to reach the person, the Supreme Personality of Godhead. How can the law of gravitation save you? It is an energy of God, a natural law. When we speak of law, we predicate the fact that someone makes the law.

Śyāmasundara dāsa: Comte suggests that primitive man worships personal forms in nature, and that as man becomes more sophisticated, he worships impersonal forms.

Śrīla Prabhupāda: That is backwards. The personal aspect is higher. Of course, if one does not know the Supreme Personality of Godhead, that is a different matter. Foolish men attempt to worship the impersonal. Primitive man by nature wants to worship a person. Because people do not know who that person is, out of frustration they turn to impersonalism. As far as our philosophy is concerned, we know the person because the personal God has told us, "Here I am." When He is present, He proves that He is God, the Supreme Lord. When people see Him, they write books about Him. When Vyāsadeva saw Kṛṣṇa, He abandoned all other literatures to write of Kṛṣṇa's activities in *Śrīmad-Bhāgavatam*. He knew by personal, meditative, and authoritative knowledge that Kṛṣṇa is God. One who does not know Kṛṣṇa may turn to impersonalism.

Śyāmasundara dāsa: Comte believed that above the metaphysical platform is the Positivist stage wherein man abandons theological and metaphysical explanations in order to acquire positive knowledge. In this stage, man is sufficiently competent to ascertain facts and amass scientific data.

Śrīla Prabhupāda: We don't agree with this. It is not that science is above metaphysics; rather, real scientific knowledge is metaphysical.

Śyāmasundara dāsa: Comte maintained that the more facts that we discover through science, the more complicated science becomes. Thus science advances toward the positive stage.

Śrīla Prabhupāda: We say that it becomes more superficial. Complete knowledge means finding the original cause. Sense perception is considered scientific, but the Vedas state that sense perception is misleading and is not independent. For instance, at the moment you can see me, but if there were no sunlight, you would not be able to see me. Your seeing is dependent on the sun, but you have not supplied the sun. The sun has come into being by someone else's arrangement, and your seeing is dependent on that arrangement. Therefore your seeing has no intrinsic value.

Śyāmasundara dāsa: Comte considered sociology to be the most complex science because it depends on all the other sciences for its understanding. It is the science of human behavior, of group relations.

Śrīla Prabhupāda: Sociology is already given by Kṛṣṇa. It is not Comte's gift. In *Bhagavad-gītā*, Kṛṣṇa says:

cātur-varṇyaṁ mayā sṛṣṭaṁ
guṇa-karma-vibhāgaśaḥ
tasya kartāram api māṁ
viddhy akartāram avyayam

"According to the three modes of material nature and the work ascribed to them, the four divisions of human society were created by Me. And, although I am the creator of this system, you should know that I am yet the non-doer, being unchangeable." (*Bg.* 4.13) This is perfect sociology. If you try to create some system, that system will be imperfect because you are imperfect. There will not be peace. Certainly, human groups are necessary, but they must have a scientific basis. Kṛṣṇa says that He has created the *varṇas;* therefore we have to accept the system as it is given. Just as different parts of your body work in order to sustain the body, the different parts of society should work to maintain the social order. It is not that you can artificially create social orders. When people attempt this, they create only havoc.

Hayagrīva dāsa: Comte believed that man's scientific attempt to improve nature is more desirable than a passive belief in God. He writes: "Even the laws of the solar system are very far from perfect...the increasing imperfection of the economy of nature becomes a powerful stimulus to all our faculties, whether moral, intellectual, or practical.... The conception of man becoming, without fear or boast, the arbiter within certain limits, of his own destiny, has in it something far more satisfying than the old belief in Providence, which implied our remaining passive."

Śrīla Prabhupāda: This means that he has no knowledge of God. There is no question of passivity. God is the ultimate controller of everything, and although He may act through different agents, the ultimate decision is given by Him. He is sitting in everyone's heart observing the activities of the individual soul, and without His permission, no one can act. He gives intelligence, and He also causes one to forget. By God's grace, we can have the power to remember activities long past. In any case, God is the ultimate director. Man cannot be independent, because man's actions are impelled by the three modes of material nature.

prakṛteḥ kriyamāṇāni
guṇaiḥ karmāṇi sarvaśaḥ
ahaṅkāra-vimūḍhātmā
kartāham iti manyate

"The bewildered spirit soul, under the influence of the three modes of material nature, thinks himself to be the doer of activities, which are in actuality carried out by nature." (*Bg.* 3.27) The ultimate director is the Supersoul situated in the heart of every living entity and within every atom.

Śyāmasundara dāsa: Comte believed that social reforms are implemented more by love than anything else. His motto was: "Love for the principle, order for the basis, progress for the end."

Śrīla Prabhupāda: Unfortunately, he does not know what the end is. He is simply theorizing. The end is Viṣṇu. *Śrīmad-Bhāgavatam* states:

na te viduḥ svārtha-gatiṁ hi viṣṇuṁ
durāśayā ye bahir-artha-māninaḥ
andhā yathāndhair upanīyamānās
te 'pīśa-tantryām uru-dāmni baddhāḥ

"Persons who are strongly entrapped by the consciousness of enjoying material life, and who have therefore accepted as their leader or guru a similar blind man attached to external sense objects, cannot understand that the goal of life is to return home, back to Godhead, and engage in the service of Lord Viṣṇu. As blind men guided by another blind man miss the right path and fall into a ditch, materially attached men led by another materially attached man are bound by the ropes of fruitive labor, which are made of very strong cords, and they continue again and again in materialistic life, suffering the threefold miseries." (*Bhāg.* 7.5.31) Unless we know the end, all our theorizing will not help. All their humanitarian work will never be successful because they have missed the main point: Kṛṣṇa.

Hayagrīva dāsa: Comte would agree with Protagoras's saying, "Man is the measure of all things." He writes: "The universe is to be studied not for its own sake, but for the sake of man, or rather of humanity. To study in any other spirit would not only be immoral, but also highly irrational."

Śrīla Prabhupāda: Our view is that man should be anxious to understand the Absolute Truth. Human intelligence is meant for searching out the ultimate source of everything. It is useless to try to improve man's material situation. Every living being is destined to undergo a certain amount of happiness and distress. By virtue of our past activities, we get a particular type of body destined to suffer or enjoy. That cannot be changed. You may call this either fatalism or destiny, but it is a fact that every man is destined in this way, and his destiny cannot be changed. However, his intelligence can change his position in reference to God. Presently, man is forgetful of God and his relationship with God. Human life is meant for changing this position. Man's economic position is already fixed by destiny and cannot be changed. This is also confirmed in *Śrīmad-Bhāgavatam.* When we engage in devotional service, we can change our destiny. Otherwise, destiny is fixed.

Hayagrīva dāsa: Comte distinguishes between atheism and Positivism in this way: "Atheism, even from the intellectual point of view, is a very imperfect form of emanicipation; for its tendency is to prolong the metaphysical stage indefinitely by continuing to seek for new solutions to theological problems instead of setting aside all inaccessible researches on the grounds of their utter inutility.... The true Positivist spirit consists in studying the How instead of the Why." Since religious questions can never be answered, they had best be forgotten.

Śrīla Prabhupāda: How can man forget? If man does not believe in God, God comes as death. How can man counteract death? From *Bhagavad-gītā* we understand that God appears as death for the atheists, and in this way God convinces the atheists, "Here I am." No one can avoid this. No one can become independent by atheistic speculation.

Hayagrīva dāsa: Comte equated intellectual and moral improvement with material progress. He writes: "A nation that has made no efforts to improve itself materially will take but little interest in moral or mental improvement."

Śrīla Prabhupāda: The standard of material improvement is not actually fixed. One person may be satisfied with certain material conditions, while another may be dissatisfied with the same conditions. The question is, "What should the standard of material life be?" As far as Vedic civilization is concerned, the material necessities are eating, sleeping, mating, and defending. These are present in both the animal and human kingdoms. Standards, however, vary, according to different cultures.

Śyāmasundara dāsa: Comte felt that we should deal only with information that can be verified by experiment, or demonstration.

Śrīla Prabhupāda: Then, how are these planets floating in the air? What is the scientific explanation for that? Who made this cosmic arrangement? If they don't know, then what is the value of their scientific knowledge? Because they cannot answer these questions, they say that they are not worth knowing.

Śyāmasundara dāsa: Comte would feel that such knowledge is not very useful.
Śrīla Prabhupāda: But knowledge means finding out the source of knowledge, the source of everything. You are seeing only a portion of someone's actions and reactions, but you do not know who that someone is. If you don't know, you cannot pose as a man of knowledge.
Śyāmasundara dāsa: Comte is interested in knowledge dealing with sense phenomena, knowledge that can be directly, scientifically utilized.
Śrīla Prabhupāda: Well, naturally you can perceive a tree growing, but a man interested in knowledge wants to know the origin of that tree. One who does not or cannot know says, "It doesn't matter," but if you are serious about knowledge, it matters. Knowledge of the tree's origin is certainly practical. We understand that a tree comes from a seed, but where does the seed come from? How is it that so much potency is given to the seed? Who gives that seed such potency?
Śyāmasundara dāsa: Is that knowledge useful?
Śrīla Prabhupāda: Yes. Of course, it may not be useful for a fool. For a fool, such scientific knowledge is of no use, but for a real scientist, knowledge of the origin of things is most essential. Only a fool would say that such knowledge is useless. A scientific man wants to find the cause of things, whether knowledge of that cause is immediately useful or not. Higher knowledge has no value for an ordinary man. In this Kali-yuga, the ordinary man is a fool. He thinks, "Why are people wasting their time searching for God?" For a fool, the search for God is unimportant, but for a scientist, it is most important.
Hayagrīva dāsa: Comte felt that it was the working man, the *śūdra*, who is most apt to be the arbiter of Positivism, not the scientist or philosopher. He writes: "The occupations of working men are evidently far more conducive to philosophical views than those of the middle classes, since they are not so absorbing as to prevent continuous thought, even during the hours of labor."
Śrīla Prabhupāda: How can the working man become an arbiter? Every working man requires some manager to direct him, and in Communist countries we have seen that there is a managerial class as well as a working class. If this is the case, how can the worker help us? He is always subordinate to some manager.
Hayagrīva dāsa: Comte wanted to form working men's clubs that would be dedicated to the philosophy of Positivism. These would form "a provisional substitute for the church of old times, or rather to prepare the way for the religious building of the new form of worship, the worship of

humanity."

Śrīla Prabhupāda: His conception of humanity is not very clear. What does he mean by humanity? What does the working class know of humanity? If by "humanity" he means the totality of all human beings, he must still admit that every human being has some individuality. Even if you consider all humanity to be the same, how will you account for individuality?

Hayagrīva dāsa: Well, it is his contention and that of Communism in general that all men are basically the same in relation to the state.

Śrīla Prabhupāda: Yes, they are all under the laws of the state, but their thinking, feeling, and willing are not under the state. Men think, feel, and will differently. How, then, can they be one? Of course, human beings have two arms, two legs, and one head, but the working of the brain differs according to the individual. It is not possible to adjust these differences and reconcile all humanity as a whole. Everyone will not be in total agreement. People have their own tastes even in eating, sleeping, mating, and defending—to say nothing of thinking, feeling, and willing. If you try to force uniformity, you will create dissatisfaction.

Hayagrīva dāsa: Comte felt that Positivism and Communism—which was then in its formative stage—could go hand in hand. He writes: "Positivism has nothing to fear from Communism; on the contrary, it will probably be accepted by most Communists among the working classes...."

Śrīla Prabhupāda: He speaks of a working class but not a managerial class. He wants a classless society, but he wants it populated only by working men. But the fact is that working men require direction, just as the legs and hands require directions from the brain. That is quite natural. It is not possible for the working classes not to be under someone's direction.

Hayagrīva dāsa: Concerning the different qualities of men and women, Comte wrote: "In all kinds of force, for the physical, intellectual or practical, it is certain that men surpass women, in accordance with a general law which prevails throughout the animal kingdom....If there were nothing else to do but to love...women would be supreme."

Śrīla Prabhupāda: This is a natural distinction between men and women. How can it be changed? Women are meant for certain activities, just as men are. You may try to change this artificially, but basically it cannot be changed. A woman becomes pregnant, but a man does not. How can this be changed?

Hayagrīva dāsa: Well, from this he concludes that women, being dominated by love, are morally superior to men. He envisioned woman as "the spontaneous priestess of humanity. She personifies in the purest

form the principle of love upon which the unity of our nature depends."
Śrīla Prabhupāda: This is Comte's imagination. When a woman is misguided, she becomes dangerous, and there is no question of love. According to the Vedic conception, women and children are on the same level, and they should both be protected by men. In childhood a woman is protected by her father, in youth by her husband, and in old age by her grown sons. Women should never be given independence, but they should be given protection. In this way, their natural love for father, husband, and children will develop very smoothly. Thus the relationship between women and men should be established very happily so that both can execute their real function: cooperative spiritual life. The woman should look after the comfort of the man, and the man, who works hard, should also look after her comfort. Then both will be satisfied, and their spiritual lives will progress. A man is meant to work hard, and a woman is meant to give comfort and love in the home. In this way, man and woman can combine so that both can progress in spiritual life.
Hayagrīva dāsa: Comte felt that love of God is inconsistent with love for our fellow men, and that it has always interfered with man's love of woman. He writes: "It was impiety for the knight to love his lady better than his God; and thus the best feelings of man's nature were repressed by his religious faith. Women, therefore, are not really interested in perpetuating the old system [of religion]; and the very instincts by which their nature is characterized will soon incline them to abandon it."
Śrīla Prabhupāda: Generally, women are interested in a comfortable home life. That is their nature. They are not spiritually very advanced or interested, but if a man has spiritual interests, and the woman helps the man—either as a mother, wife, or daughter—both can make spiritual progress. However, the woman must remain subordinate, and the man must make spiritual progress. Because the woman helps the man, she shares his spiritual benefits.
Hayagrīva dāsa: Comte envisioned women primarily as companions of men. He writes: "The first aspect then, under which Positivism considers woman, is simply as the companion of man, irrespective of her maternal duties.... For perfect friendship, difference of sex is essential, as excluding the possibility of rivalry."
Śrīla Prabhupāda: According to the bodily demands, there are sexual necessities. Women should not only give sex pleasure to their husbands, but should also prepare good food. After coming home from a day of hard work, the man should be supplied good food, comfort, and sex. Then the home becomes very happy, and both husband and wife are satisfied.

Then they can improve their real business, which is spiritual understanding. Human life is meant for progressing spiritually, and people must first of all know that the spirit soul is at the basis even of material life. The body is built upon the soul. Although women are generally less intelligent, this understanding is required of both men and women. With the help of the husband, a woman can become more intelligent. In Vedic history, we have the example of Kapila-deva giving spiritual instructions to his mother Devahūti. Whether the woman is a daughter, wife, or mother, if she remains subordinate, she can receive knowledge from either her father, husband, or son. In the *Purāṇas*, there is the example of Lord Śiva answering the spiritual questions of Pārvatī. Women supply the comforts of the tongue, belly, and genitals, and, remaining submissive, they are instructed in spiritual life. Thus there is cooperative advancement.

Hayagrīva dāsa: Comte felt that at least in the beginning stages of Positivism, women should take the place of God as an object of man's affection and love. He writes: "From childhood, each of us will be taught to regard women's sex as the principal source of human happiness and improvement, whether in public life or in private.... In a word, man will kneel to women, and to women alone.... She will be regarded by man as the most perfect personification of humanity.... The worship of women, when it has assumed a more systematic shape, will be valued for its own sake as a new instrument of happiness and moral growth.... The worship of women satisfies this condition, and is so far of greater efficacy, than the worship of God."

Śrīla Prabhupāda: It is the duty of men to protect women and maintain them comfortably, not worship them. It is not a very good proposal to worship a woman as God. Then man will be henpecked. Worship is reserved for God only, and is not meant for others. However, cooperation between men and women for the sake of worshipping God is desirable. It is not that a man or a woman should be worshipped as God. Sometimes, affection is so strong that a person may see another person as God, but that is sentimentalism. God is different from men and women, who are but living entities meant to worship God. A woman should always be engaged in assisting a man in every respect in his religious, social, and family life. That is the real benefit of conjugal life.

Hayagrīva dāsa: Comte writes that "the whole effect of Positivist worship will be to make men feel clearly how far superior in every respect is the synthesis founded on the love of humanity to that founded on the love of God."

Śrīla Prabhupāda: Love of humanity means raising humanity to the point where people can understand the real goal of life. We do not serve humanity by keeping people in darkness. We must enlighten others with knowledge, and ultimate knowledge means understanding God, our relationship with God, and the activities of that relationship. That is real humanitarian work. Mankind must be informed of the nature of the body and the soul and the necessities and goal of the soul. In this way, we can really serve humanity. We do not serve it by encouraging the animal propensities.

X
COMMUNISM

Karl Marx

(1818-1883)

Hayagrīva dāsa: Marx was a descendent of rabbis on both sides of his family, but Marx's father was converted to Christianity, and Marx received a Christian education. In any case, Marx himself opposed both Christianity and Judaism. At the age of twenty-three, after having studied some philosophy in his university classes, Marx became an avowed atheist. It was Hegel who wrote: "Because the accidental is not, God or the Absolute is." On this, Marx commented: "Obviously the reverse can also be said." That is, because God is not, the accidental is.

Śrīla Prabhupāda: How can any sensible man accept the view that everything is accidental? Is a child taking birth accidental? There must have been unity between a father and a mother. Marx, for instance, may not have wanted to die, but he was forced to. How can this take place accidentally? There must be some superior force. We may not wish to have an accident, but accidents happen nonetheless. This is a question of common sense. In nature, we see that there are many planets in the sky, and they are not accidentally colliding, but are remaining in their positions. The sun rises according to precise calculations. Since universal functions are going on very systematically, there must be some brain behind them, and we call this supreme brain God. How can you deny this?

Hayagrīva dāsa: Marx felt that true philosophy would say: "In simple truth, I bear hate for any and every God." He saw this as philosophy's "own avowal, its own judgement against all heavenly and earthly gods who do not acknowledge human self-consciousness as the supreme divinity. There must be no other on a level with it."

Śrīla Prabhupāda: How can human intelligence be perfect unless it comes to the point of understanding the Absolute Truth, the original cause of everything? Our consciousness must progress, and progress means moving toward the ultimate goal. If a human being is ignorant of the ultimate cause and the ultimate goal, of what value is his intelligence?

Hayagrīva dāsa: Marx considered religion to be the pastime of degraded men who attempt to escape reality. He writes: "Religion is the sigh of the distressed creature, the soul of a heartless world, as it is also the spirit of a spiritless condition. It is the opium of the people." Being an illusion, religion cannot solve any of man's problems, but can only complicate them. "The more man puts into God," Marx wrote, "the less he retains in himself."

Śrīla Prabhupāda: We can actually see that the Communists are not being so greatly favored without God. Now the Chinese and Russians are disagreeing. Differences of opinion will still be there, whether people deny God or not. So how have they improved matters? Both Communists and capitalists need to understand the nature of God. We have seen that denying God and acting independently have not brought peace.

Śyāmasundara dāsa: Marx believed that everything is produced from economic struggle, and that religion is a technique invented by the bourgeoisie or the capitalists to dissuade the masses from revolution by promising them a better existence after death.

Śrīla Prabhupāda: He himself has created a philosophy that is presently being enforced by coercion and killing. As we have often explained, religion is that part of our nature which is permanent, which we cannot give up. No one can give up his religion. And what is that religion? Service. Marx desires to serve humanity by putting forward his philosophy; therefore that is his religion. Everyone is trying to render some service. The father is trying to serve his family, the statesman is trying to serve his country, and the philanthropist is trying to serve all humanity. Whether you are Karl Marx, or Stalin, or Gandhi, a Hindu, a Muslim, or a Christian, you must serve. Because we are presently rendering service to so many people and concepts, we are becoming confused. Therefore Kṛṣṇa advises us to give up all other service and serve Him alone.

Hayagrīva dāsa: Like Comte, Marx hoped that the worker would eventually eliminate religion. He wrote: "The political emancipation of the Jew, the Christian, the religious man in general, is the emancipation of the state from Judaism, from Christianity, from religion generally." Thus the worker would become the savior of mankind by freeing man from a religion that worships a supernatural being.

Śrīla Prabhupāda: Has that actually happened? Marx is dead and gone, yet his Communist theory is being exhibited in practice, and still we see that they have not liberated anyone. Now the Russians are not relating congenially with the Chinese. Why is this? They have abolished God, and the working class is there. Why, then, is there dissension and desire?

Hayagrīva dāsa: Marx felt that religion was blocking man's path to happiness. He wrote: "The abolition of religion as the illusory happiness of the people is the demand for their real happiness. The demand to abandon the illusions about their condition is the demand to give up a condition that requires illusion. Hence criticism of religion is...criticism of this vale of tears whose halo is religion."

Śrīla Prabhupāda: A religious system deteriorates when there is no understanding of its philosophical basis. People are apt to reject such sentimental religions. We must understand in fact that God is at the top of all cosmic manifestations and activities. Laws given by the supreme head of the cosmic manifestation constitute what we call religion. If we create our own religious systems on the basis of sentiments, we create only troubles and will be misunderstood. We must understand that there is a brain behind all the cosmic manifestations, and if we know the nature of this brain and how it is working, we attain real scientific understanding.

Hayagrīva dāsa: Marx encouraged labor not for the construction of temples but for the benefit of man himself. He writes: "The alien being, to whom labor and the produce of labor belong, and in whose service labor is done and for whose benefit the produce of labor is provided, can only be man himself."

Śrīla Prabhupāda: We must come to the understanding that it is beneficial for man to abide by the orders of God. If there is any organization at all, there is a director, even in Communist countries. Leaders are necessary, and the supreme leader is called God. It is not that the Communists can do without leaders. Even Karl Marx provided leadership. Now it is up to people to decide whether to work under the leadership of God, or under Marx and Lenin. We cannot avoid leadership; so now the question remains, "Whose leadership is perfect?" That we must decide.

Hayagrīva dāsa: Like Comte, Marx believed that atheism was unnecessary because it was negative denial, whereas socialism is positive assertion. Marx writes: "Socialism is man's positive self-consciousness, no longer mediated through the annulment of religion, just as real life is man's positive reality through Communism."

Śrīla Prabhupāda: We have made our point that real religion is not sentiment and that leadership has to be accepted, be it Communist, theist, or atheist. When leadership is selected, and directions are given by the leader, we can call it some "ism," but in any case, religion means accepting the leadership of God and His directions. I don't think that even the Communists can basically change this concept. They also have a leader—Marx, Lenin, or Stalin—and they are giving directions for the people to follow. Similarly, Kṛṣṇa is there, and we are following His instructions. So factually what is the difference? In either case, there is authority. We have to select the best leader, and we also have to select a criterion for establishing him.

Hayagrīva dāsa: For Marx, there is nothing spiritual in the universe. He writes: "An incorporeal substance is just as much a contradiction as an incorporeal body. Body, being, substance are one and the same real idea. One cannot separate the thought from matter which thinks."

Śrīla Prabhupāda: When there is no spirit soul within the body, the body is considered dead. Otherwise, what is the difference between a dead body and a living body?

Hayagrīva dāsa: He further writes: "Since only what is material is perceptible, knowable, nothing is known of the existence of God. I am sure only of my own existence."

Śrīla Prabhupāda: But if he does not know of the spirit soul, how can he be certain of his own existence? What is his idea of life? Why is the body like a dead stone when life has ended? He must first understand what life is.

Hayagrīva dāsa: He felt that consciousness is basically social. "Life is not determined by consciousness," he writes, "but consciousness by life.... Consciousness is therefore from the very beginning a social product, and remains so as long as men exist at all."

Śrīla Prabhupāda: Then why does life have an end? Why does he cease to exist? What is the answer to this? The soul of man exists, but why does he die? Death is a fact, and it cannot be denied. During this lifetime, he may speak very loudly, but as soon as he is dead, he can speak no more. Where is consciousness then?

Hayagrīva dāsa: Marx opposed Comte's recommendation of the worship of women, and also the worship of God in nature. "There is no question," he writes, "that modern sciences, which along with modern industry, have revolutionized the whole of nature and put an end to man's childish attitude toward nature, as well as to other forms of childishness....The position as regards to the worship of female is the same as nature worship."

Śrīla Prabhupāda: But how has science overcome the basic laws of nature? Has man put an end to birth, death, old age, and disease? If not, what is the meaning of revolutionizing or conquering nature? Nature's laws are going on just as before. Before Marx died, his father and mother died, and their parents died before them, and so on. How has man then conquered nature? Death, old age, and disease continue. Where is the improvement?

Hayagrīva dāsa: If there is no improvement, he would feel that it is because religion has been an impediment.

Śrīla Prabhupāda: This has nothing to do with religion. This is the work of nature. When a man takes birth, he faces death. How has science revolutionized this matter? Nature's work is going on despite all the theories of Marx and others. So how have they surpassed the laws of nature?

Hayagrīva dāsa: Marx felt that religion is the cause of constant antagonism between men. "The most persistent form of antagonism between the Jew and the Christian is religious antagonism," he writes. "How does one solve an antagonism? By making it impossible. And how is a religious antagonism made impossible? By abolishing religion."

Śrīla Prabhupāda: The question of antagonism is solved if we know God and God's desires. If we know the government and its laws, there is no antagonism. Antagonism is there when so-called religious systems do not know of God and His desires. God and His regulations are clearly described in the *Bhagavad-gītā,* and therefore we are advocating the reading of *Bhagavad-gītā* so people will know God and His instructions. As I have said before, religion means understanding God according to a system. God is the supreme proprietor and the supreme friend of everyone. He is the enjoyer of everything. People claim that their religion is better than others, but first of all we must know what religion is. It is knowing the orders of the supreme proprietor, and living according to them. If we do not know what religion is, why criticize religion and create antagonisms?

Hayagrīva dāsa: Marx felt that both Christian and Jew should cast off their respective religions, "as nothing more than different stages of evolution of the human spirit, as different snakeskins shed by history." Then man will no longer be bothered by religious antagonisms but will be able to enjoy a scientific and human relationship.

Śrīla Prabhupāda: When people stamp themselves Christians, Jews, Hindus, and Moslems without knowing God and His desires, there will naturally be antagonism. Therefore we should scientifically understand what is religion and who is God. Then this antagonism will cease.

Hayagrīva dāsa: Marx believed that the state should eventually assume the role of Christ. He writes: "Religion is merely the indirect recognition of man through a mediator. The state is the mediator between man and the freedom of man. As Christ is the mediator on whom man unburdens all his own divinity and his whole religious burden, so also the state is the mediator on which man places all his unholiness and his whole human burden."

Śrīla Prabhupāda: Christ gave the knowledge by which we can be relieved of the material body, and that is the function of all religious scripture. Religious scriptures should give information about God's exact position. When people learn scientifically of God's existence and their relationship with God, everything will be adjusted. Our Kṛṣṇa consciousness movement is trying to give people an exact idea of God, exact definitions, and exact instructions.

Hayagrīva dāsa: Here is a point that most Communists would choose to ignore: "To practice one's own particular religion is explicitly included among the rights of man," Marx writes. "The privilege of religion is a universal human right."

Śrīla Prabhupāda: It is always the state's duty to see that there is freedom of religion. It is also the state's duty to see that when a person is propagating a particular type of religion, he is acting according to it.

Hayagrīva dāsa: Marx felt, however, that religion should be individual, not communal. "But liberty as a right of man is not based on the association of man with man, but rather on a separation of man from man. It is the right of the separation, the right of the limited individual, limited to himself."

Śrīla Prabhupāda: There is no question of separation. When we accept God as the Supreme Father, we accept His sons as brothers who should be obedient to Him. If we all obey the Supreme Father, how will there be differences of opinion? When we do not know the Supreme Father and do not obey Him, there is dissension. It is the son's duty to obey the father and enjoy his property. It is a question of the father being the center.

Hayagrīva dāsa: Marx believed that if man persists in worshipping God, he should do so privately and not communally.

Śrīla Prabhupāda: If God is a fact, and man must worship Him, then why not communally? Does he think that every individual should manufacture his own God and worship Him? God is the Supreme Father, the Father of every man, of every living entity. How can He be different? There may be ten sons in a family, but the father is one. It is not that the different sons say, "Oh, I will select my own father." It is not possible. The difficulty is that no one knows the Supreme Father, and no one is prepared to obey His orders. That is the difficulty.

Hayagrīva dāsa: Marx was hoping that the isolation of religion would lead to its dissolution.

Śrīla Prabhupāda: The dissolution of religion means animalism, and we have come to that point in human history. That is the defect in modern society. If people are serious about religion, they should sit down together and acknowledge God as the Supreme Father. Once people do this, they will not fight among themselves. In any case, religion will not dissolve because it is an inherent quality within every living entity. When I was in Russia, I saw that even the young men there were also interested in God. Belief in God cannot be avoided.

Śyāmasundara dāsa: As far as Marx's political philosophy is concerned, we should try to change the world, not interpret it. Dialectic materialism is based on the Hegelian dialectic of thesis, antithesis, and synthesis, which he applied to economics and sociology. The thesis is the capitalist bourgeoisie; the antithesis is the proletariat; and the synthesis is a classless, or Communistic, society.

Śrīla Prabhupāda: But how is it possible to have a classless society? We find that there are different classes of men by nature. Kṛṣṇa says: *Cātur-varṇyaṁ mayā sṛṣṭaṁ guṇa-karma- vibhāgaśaḥ.* "According to the three modes of material nature and the work ascribed to them, the four divisions of human society were created by Me." (*Bg.* 4.13) Also:

brāhmaṇa-kṣatriya-viśāṁ
śūdrāṇāṁ ca parantapa
karmāṇi pravibhaktāni
svabhāva-prabhavair guṇaiḥ

"*Brāhmaṇas, kṣatriyas, vaiśyas*, and *śūdras* are distinguished by their qualities of work, O chastiser of the enemy, in accordance with the modes of nature." (*Bg.* 18.41) Since this is the case, how can we bring different natures to the same level?

Śyāmasundara dāsa: Marx felt that it was the mode of production that determined our beliefs and ideas. He wrote: "It is not the consciousness of men that determines their being, but, on the contrary, their social being that determines their consciousness."

Śrīla Prabhupāda: That is a question of training. The next question is, What is the center of that training? What is the motto?

Śyāmasundara dāsa: The motto is: "From each according to his abilities, to each according to his needs."

Śrīla Prabhupāda: The contributions of different living entities are different. A scientific man contributes one thing, a philosopher another, and a worker something else. Trees are also contributing, as well as birds and beasts. The cow contributes milk, and the dog contributes its service as a watchdog. Everyone is contributing, giving, and taking. This arrangement is already there by nature. But what is Marx's idea of a classless society?

Śyāmasundara dāsa: He felt that the means of production should be owned in common so that there would be no exploitation of workers.

Śrīla Prabhupāda: What is the question of exploitation? I am a religious preacher, and my contribution is spiritual knowledge. Where is the exploitation? As far as a classless society is concerned, I have been to Moscow and have seen women sweeping the streets while the big bosses sit in their cars and watch. So where is this classless society? As long as you maintain a society, you have to make some distinction between upper and lower. However, if the central point is one, it doesn't matter on what level we work. Our bodies have different parts, which are all working to contribute to the whole.

Śyāmasundara dāsa: They claim to look on it the same way. The scientist or manager is in a top position, but the worker is considered to occupy as glorious a position.

Śrīla Prabhupāda: But we have seen in Moscow that not everyone is satisfied. One boy came to us and lamented that he was not allowed to leave the country. The point is that you will never be able to make everyone happy. Nor will there ever be a classless society because the mentalities of people differ. How can you say that your mentality is the same as mine?

Śyāmasundara dāsa: Marx believed that it was possible to have a uniformity of ideas and purpose if the means of production are controlled. The problem is that the capitalists, who own the means of production, control people's ideas.

Śrīla Prabhupāda: It is not possible for everyone to think uniformly, but it is possible to find a central interest. For instance, in our Society for Kṛṣṇa Consciousness, our central interest is Kṛṣṇa. People are working in different ways, but everyone is convinced that he is working to render service to Kṛṣṇa.

Śyāmasundara dāsa: For Marx, the center is the state, which in time will wither away. Then a classless society will emerge.

Śrīla Prabhupāda: But if you make the state the center, there is no question of a classless society. In the state, there is always a leader, a president or prime minister. Khruschev was the head, and when people were dissatisfied, they drove him from office. This means that the head was not perfect and that people were dissatisfied with him. This is going on even in noncommunist countries. So what is the difference between Marx's theory and others? What is taking place inside Russia is also taking place outside. First of all, the person in the center must be perfect; then his dictations can be considered perfect. If you put a lot of imperfect men in office, what is the point in changing governments? The same corruption will go on.

Śyāmasundara dāsa: Presumably, the perfect leader would be one who follows Marx's philosophy perfectly.

Śrīla Prabhupāda: But his philosophy is not perfect. He proposes a classless society, but that will never emerge. When you run a government, there must be administrators, and also people to sweep the streets. So how will a classless society come about? When will the street sweeper be satisfied to see someone enjoying an administrative position? Now, in this Kṛṣṇa consciousness society, I sit on a *vyāsāsana*, and you offer me garlands. Why is this? You do this willingly because you see that there is a perfect man you can follow. Unless you are convinced that the leader is perfect, there is no question of bowing down and working hard like menial servants.

Śyāmasundara dāsa: For Communists, Lenin was a perfect man.

Śrīla Prabhupāda: But who is following Lenin? Lenin's perfection was in overthrowing the royal family. What other perfection has he given? People are not happy simply reading books. You cannot make people happy artificially, by force. Unless there is a perfect ideal man in the center, there cannot be a classless society. It is not possible. We have seen in Russia that people do not feel that there is perfection in the center.

Śyāmasundara dāsa: Well, the goal is the production of goods for the material well being of all people.

Śrīla Prabhupāda: That is useless. We have seen that production in America is beyond comparison in the world, and that is a capitalist society. Yet despite so much production, people are not satisfied. The young men especially are confused. It is nonsensical to think that by increasing production you will satisfy people. Man is not created simply to eat. Man also has a brain and spiritual and intellectual necessities. In India, we have seen people sitting silently in a solitary place and practicing yoga. There is no question of production satisfying them. The proposition that everyone will be satisfied by increasing production is a proposition for animals. The basic principle is nonsensical and due to insufficient knowledge. Perhaps Marx was thinking like that because he was coming from a country where people were starving. This means that he has no conception of what happiness actually is.

Happiness is in understanding the truths given in *Bhagavad-gītā*. We are happy when we know that God is the proprietor of everything and that He is the supreme enjoyer. We are not enjoyers; we are all workers. By nature there are enjoyers and workers. In your body, for instance, the stomach enjoys, and all the other parts work to satisfy the stomach. When the stomach is satisfied, all other parts of the body are nourished. Everywhere we look, we see that there are those who are enjoying, and those who are working. There is no question of a Communist or capitalist society. You cannot avoid the fact that there must be directors, or enjoyers, and workers. We therefore have to find out how both the manager and the worker can feel equal happiness. There must be cooperation for a central purpose, and a classless society is possible only when Kṛṣṇa is at the center. Then the *brāhmaṇas, kṣatriyas, vaiśyas,* and *śūdras* all work for His satisfaction.

yataḥ pravṛttir bhūtānāṁ
yena sarvam idaṁ tatam
svakarmaṇā tam abhyarcya
siddhiṁ vindati mānavaḥ

"By worship of the Lord, who is the source of all beings, and who is all pervading, man can, in the performance of his own duty, attain perfection." (*Bg*. 18.46) Each class works in his own way for the satisfaction of Kṛṣṇa. The *brāhmaṇa* contributes one thing, and the *kṣatriyas, vaiśyas,* and *śūdras,* something else:

śamo damas tapaḥ śaucaṁ
kṣāntir ārjavam eva ca

jñānaṁ vijñānam āstikyaṁ
brahma-karma svabhāva-jam

śauryaṁ tejo dhṛtir dākṣyaṁ
yuddhe cāpy apalāyanam
dānam īśvara-bhāvaś ca
kṣātraṁ karma svabhāva-jam

kṛṣi-gorakṣya-vāṇijyaṁ
vaiśya-karma svabhāva-jam
paricaryātmakaṁ karma
śūdrasyāpi svabhāva-jam

"Peacefulness, self-control, austerity, purity, tolerance, honesty, wisdom, knowledge, and religiousness—these are the qualities by which the *brāhmaṇas* work. Heroism, power, determination, resourcefulness, courage in battle, generosity, and leadership are the qualities of work for the *kṣatriyas*. Farming, cow protection, and business are the qualities of work for the *vaiśyas*. And for the *śūdras*, there is labor and service to others." (*Bg*. 18.42-44)

Śyāmasundara dāsa: How does this differ from the Communist state wherein the street sweepers, the managers, the farmers, and the military all contribute for the central purpose, the state?

Śrīla Prabhupāda: If the state is not perfect, no one will be willing to contribute to it. Of course, you may force people to contribute to it; that is a different thing. But voluntary contribution will be there only when people are satisfied that the center is perfect. In any case, there will never be a classless society because there will always be an intellectual class, an administrative class, a mercantile class, and a working class. People will never find perfection in the state; therefore the workers will always remain dissatisfied. If not, why are they always running their leaders out of office?

Śyāmasundara dāsa: In examining history, Marx noted that the main production amongst the ancient Greeks and Romans was carried out by slaves, and in feudal times by serfs.

Śrīla Prabhupāda: But the Communists have also created slaves; they call them workers. When you have workers, you must also have people directing them. Therefore a dictator is needed. There must be directors and workers in any society, but they should be so satisfied that they forget their differences. That is, there should be no envy. If you make the center anything other than Kṛṣṇa, you will have nothing but materialistic activity. Materialism necessarily means exploitation. The only solution is Kṛṣṇa consciousness. We must make Kṛṣṇa the center, and work for Him. This is the formula: pour water on the root of the tree, and all the branches, twigs, and leaves will be satisfied. By satisfying Kṛṣṇa, we satisfy everyone. Arjuna had many problems, but by satisfying Kṛṣṇa, all his problems were resolved. When we put Kṛṣṇa at the center, everything we do is absolute. We may either write books or wash the dishes; our activities will not collide because they are on the absolute platform. In Vṛndāvana, some living entities are cowherd boys, some are cows, some are trees, and so on, but they are all satisfied because Kṛṣṇa is the center, and they are happy by loving Him. When people become Kṛṣṇa conscious and understand how to love Kṛṣṇa, there will be a classless society. Otherwise, it is not possible. It is all bogus, humbug.

Śyāmasundara dāsa: Marx felt that in the capitalistic state, a few men control at the expense of many.

Śrīla Prabhupāda: But there are only a few men in the Kremlin. What is the difference? Marx was interested in changing society, but we can see there is no difference. Society can be changed only when the center is Kṛṣṇa. The people in this International Society for Kṛṣṇa Consciousness have actually changed their lives. Unless the consciousness of people is changed, how can the social structure change? First of all, we must change the consciousness; then society will change. If the consciousness of people does not change first, how will they accept a new theory? First, we must change the heart, and that is the process of Kṛṣṇa consciousness. *Ceto-darpaṇa-mārjanam* (*Śikṣāṣṭaka* 1). By chanting, we cleanse the mirror of the mind.

If the consciousness is the same, what do you gain by changing the form of government? You will have the same situation. When you see stool on the ground, one side is dry, and the other side is moist. If you think, "Oh, this side is very nice because it is dry," you are very foolish. After all, any way you look at it, it is stool. There will always be people who are hungry, and people who are wealthy. There will always be people with different ideas and capacities. People will never become the same. Temporary situations are created by materialistic men or by the laws of nature; they come and they go. Kṛṣṇa tells us in *Bhagavad-gītā* that we should be fixed on the absolute platform and not worry about these temporary things. *Āgamāpāyino 'nityās tāṁs titikṣasva* (*Bg*. 2.14). A sane man should not bother with these temporary "ism's." We do not support capitalism or Communism, this idea or that idea. Our only concern is how to satisfy Kṛṣṇa. We know perfectly well that all these systems will come and go, that if they are existing now, in the future they will not continue to exist. We must fix ourselves up with that system which is eternal.

Śyāmasundara dāsa: In Marx's society, private property would be abolished, and there would be common ownership of the means of production. That is, everything would be state owned.

Śrīla Prabhupāda: Well, we have seen in Moscow that the people do not like to go shopping because they are obliged to stand in line for hours. So that system does not appear to be working very well. If you cannot get what you want, what is the use of the stores? Besides, what is the state but an extension of the individual self? The self is extended in the form of one's family, children, community, and nation. So-called nationalism and Communism are just extensions of the self. The labels are different; the quality remains the same. We may steal ourselves, or have others steal for us. What is the difference? We may say, "Nothing is mine." That much is a fact. But we also say, "Everything belongs to God." We can live very comfortably in this world with the consciousness that everything belongs to God. God has given us the opportunity to live here, and we should satisfy and glorify God.

Śyāmasundara dāsa: Marx saw the capitalists as parasites living at the cost of the workers.

Śrīla Prabhupāda: But the Communists are also living at the cost of the workers. They are drawing big salaries while others are sweeping the streets. So what is the difference?

Śyāmasundara dāsa: Marx felt that the price of a product should equal the labor expended on it.

Śrīla Prabhupāda: Well, we see that in India the price of ghee has risen, but people are still buying ghee. The price may be two hundred rupees a kilo, or two rupees a kilo. The man who is destined to purchase it will do so, regardless of price.

Śyāmasundara dāsa: Marx would say that no profit should be made off the ghee.

Śrīla Prabhupāda: He is simply pointing out some anomalies, but these anomalies cannot be checked even by the Communists. They will appear in different ways because that is the nature of material existence. Material existence means exploitation, and these anomalies can be checked only when there is Kṛṣṇa consciousness. You may say that one should not make a profit, but no one will accept this theory. The tendency to make a profit is there, and you cannot stop it. The exploitative mind is there, whether one is a Communist or a capitalist.

In Bengali, this is called *māyā-tattva*. It is a bug's business to suck the blood of others. In the winter, the bug dries up, but as soon as summer comes, he immediately starts sucking again. In the material world, the mentality is to exploit others and become fat like a bug. Whether you are a Commmunist in the winter, or a capitalist in the summer, your tendencies are the same. As soon as you have an opportunity, you will become fat by extracting the blood of others. Unless there is a change in heart, this cannot be stopped.

Śyāmasundara dāsa: Marx felt that only the workers are entitled to the surplus value of a product.

Śrīla Prabhupāda: But as soon as a worker gets some money, he becomes a proprietor, takes advantage of his position, and becomes a capitalist. What is the point in changing your designation? A change in mentality is needed.

Śyāmasundara dāsa: Since capital is unnecessary for production, Marx urged the workers to unite and violently overthrow the capitalists.

Śrīla Prabhupāda: When one is very poor, he favors his brothers who are also poor and working hard. But as soon as one gets a little money, he immediately becomes a capitalist. This is because everyone in this material world is thinking, "I shall become the Lord." In material life, everyone is searching for a profit, for some adoration, for a position. How can you equalize people forcibly? It is not possible.

Śyāmasundara dāsa: The Communists have played upon this profiteering tendency. If the worker produces more, he is glorified by the state and given a small bonus as incentive.

Śrīla Prabhupāda: This means that he has a tendency to lord it over the creation, and he wants some profit, some bribe. Everyone wants some profit, and the state cannot destroy this tendency, neither by law nor by force.

Śyāmasundara dāsa: The Communists are trying to centralize everything—money, communications, and transport—by putting everything in the hands of the state.

Śrīla Prabhupāda: To what benefit? As soon as all the wealth is centralized, the members of the central government will appropriate it just as Stalin and Khruschev did. All these ideas are useless as long as the tendency for exploitation is not reformed. The Russians have organized their country according to Marx's theories, yet all their leaders have turned out to be cheaters. Where is their program for reforming this cheating propensity? In any case, the leaders will never be able to train the people to think that everything belongs to the state. This idea is simply Utopian nonsense.

Śyāmasundara dāsa: Another slogan of Marx is: "Human nature has no reality." He believes that man's nature changes through history according to material conditions.

Śrīla Prabhupāda: What does he know of human nature? It is certainly true that everything in this cosmic creation, or *jagat*, is changing. Your body changes daily. Everything is changing, just like the waves in the ocean. It does not take a very advanced philosophy to understand this. Marx's theory is also changing. It cannot last. Man does, however, have a fundamental nature that never changes, and that is his spiritual nature. We are teaching people to act according to their changeless spiritual nature, and this means serving Kṛṣṇa. If we try to serve Kṛṣṇa now, we will continue to serve Him when we go to Vaikuṇṭha, the spiritual world. Therefore loving service to Lord Kṛṣṇa is called *nitya*, eternal.

satataṁ kīrtayanto māṁ
yatantaś ca dṛḍha-vratāḥ
namasyantaś ca māṁ bhaktyā
nitya-yuktā upāsate

"Always chanting My glories, endeavoring with great determination, bowing down before Me, these great souls perpetually worship Me with devotion." (*Bg.* 9.14) The Communists try to replace Kṛṣṇa with the state, expecting people to think, "Nothing in my favor; everything in favor of the state." But people will never accept this. It is impossible. All the rascals can do is force the people to work, as Stalin did. As soon as someone opposed Stalin, Stalin immediately had his throat cut. The same disease is there today. So how will their program be successful?

Śyāmasundara dāsa: Marx believed that human nature is a product of environment. By putting a man in a factory and getting him to identify with the state, he would be transformed into a selfless person.

Śrīla Prabhupāda: The basic disease of man is envy, and as long as he is envious, he will remain selfish. When a man sees that he is working very hard but that the profits are not coming to him, his enthusiasm will immediately slacken. In Bengal, there is a proverb: "As a proprietor, I can turn sand into gold, but as soon as I am no longer the proprietor, the gold becomes sand." The Russian people are in this position. They are not as rich as the Europeans and Americans, and because of this, they are unhappy. If people cannot make a profit from their work, they will eventually lose all interest in their country. The average man will think, "Whether I work or not, I get the same result. I cannot adequately feed

and clothe my family." Thinking in this way, he will lose his incentive to work. A scientist will see that despite his high position, his wife and children are dressed just like common laborers.
Śyāmasundara dāsa: Marx felt that industrial and scientific work constitute the highest kind of activity.
Śrīla Prabhupāda: But unless the scientists and industrialists receive sufficient profit, they will be reluctant to work for the state.
Śyāmasundara dāsa: The Russian goal is the production of material goods for the enhancement of human well-being.
Śrīla Prabhupāda: Their human well-being actually means, "If you don't agree with me, I'll cut your throat." This was Stalin's idea of human well-being, and anyone who disagreed with him was killed or imprisoned. They say that a few must suffer for the sake of many, but we have personally seen that Russia has achieved neither general happiness nor prosperity. In Moscow, for instance, none of the big buildings have been recently built. They are old and ravaged, or poorly renovated. And there are also long lines in the stores. These are indications that the economic condition is unsound.
Śyāmasundara dāsa: Lenin reinforced all of Marx's ideas and added a few of his own. He saw history moving in leaps and progressing toward the Communistic era. He wanted Russia to leap into the dictatorship of the proletariat, which he called the final stage of historical development.
Śrīla Prabhupāda: We can say with confidence—and they may note it carefully—that after the Bolshevik Revolution, there will be other revolutions, because as long as people live on the mental platform, there will be revolutions. Our proposition is to give up all these mental concoctions and come to the spiritual platform where there are no longer revolutions. As Dhruva Mahārāja said: "Now that I am seeing God, I am completely satisfied. Now all kinds of theories are finished." God consciousness is the final revolution. There will be repeated revolutions in this material world until people come to Kṛṣṇa consciousness. People are trying to approach an objective, but they do not know that the final objective is Kṛṣṇa. They are trying to make adjustments with materialistic revolutions, not knowing that they are spiritual beings and that without God, there is no question of happiness. We are part and parcel of the Supreme Spirit, Kṛṣṇa, but we have left His association and fallen from the spiritual world because of our desire to enjoy this material world. Unless we reawaken the understanding of our spiritual position and return to the spiritual world, we can never be happy, just as a fish can never be happy out of water. We may theorize for many lifetimes, but we will

continue to see one revolution after another. History repeats itself. The old orders change, yielding their places to the new.

Śyāmasundara dāsa: Marx believed that the Communist revolution would be the final revolution because it is the perfect answer to all social contradictions.

Śrīla Prabhupāda: As long as the Communist idea remains materialistic, it cannot be the final revolution. It must be spiritualized. They believe that the state is the owner of everything, but the real owner is God. When they come to this conclusion, the Communistic idea will be perfect. In our International Society for Kṛṣṇa Consciousness, we are practicing perfect spiritual Communism by doing everything for Kṛṣṇa. We know that Kṛṣṇa is the supreme enjoyer of the result of all work. *Bhoktāraṁ yajña-tapasām (Bg.* 5.29). The Communist philosophy as it is now practiced is vague, but it can become perfect if the conclusion of *Bhagavad-gītā* is accepted: that is, Kṛṣṇa is the supreme proprietor, the supreme enjoyer, and the supreme friend of everyone. Now people mistrust the state, but if people accept Kṛṣṇa as their friend, they will have perfect confidence in Kṛṣṇa, just as Arjuna had on the battlefield of Kurukṣetra. The great victory of Arjuna and his associates on the battlefield showed that his confidence in Kṛṣṇa was justified.

yatra yogeśvaraḥ kṛṣṇo
yatra pārtho dhanur-dharaḥ
tatra śrīr vijayo bhūtir
dhruvā nītir matir mama

"Wherever there is Kṛṣṇa, the master of all mystics, and wherever there is Arjuna, the supreme archer, there will also certainly be opulence, victory, extraordinary power, and morality. That is my opinion." (*Bg.* 18.78) If Kṛṣṇa is at the center of society, the people will be perfectly secure and prosperous. The Communist idea is welcomed, provided they are prepared to replace the so-called state with God. That is religion.

XI
AMERICAN PRAGMATISM

William James
(1842-1910)

Hayagrīva dāsa: In his most famous book, *The Varieties of Religious Experience*, James writes: "Were we to limit our view to it, we should have to define religion as an external art, the art of winning the favor of God.... The relation goes direct from heart to heart, from soul to soul, between man and his maker."

Śrīla Prabhupāda: There are varieties of living beings living everywhere from the water up to the higher planetary systems. In fact, *Padma Purāṇa* informs us that there are 8,400,000 species: plants, creepers, trees, insects, aquatics, birds, animals, and so forth. God is concerned with all of them, because they are all part and parcel of God. In one word, God is the Father and maintainer of all living entities. He has two subordinate energies—material and spiritual. In the material world, material nature is the mother, God is the Father, and the various living entities are all sons maintained by the Supreme Father. This is the basis of universal brotherhood. It is also confirmed in *Bhagavad-gītā (sarva-yoniṣu, Bg.* 14.4) that material nature is the mother and that Kṛṣṇa is the seed-giving father. If we understand these relationships, we will attain peace and advanced knowledge.

Hayagrīva dāsa: Concerning the founding of religions, James writes: "The founders of every church owed their power originally to the fact of their direct personal communion with the divine. Not only the superhuman founders, the Christ, the Buddha, Mohammed, but all the originators of Christian sects have been in this case;—so personal religion should seem the primordial thing, even to those who continue to esteem it incomplete."

Śrīla Prabhupāda: Yes, the Supreme Father is a person. We have no experience of a father being anything but a person. Just as in the material world, all fathers are persons, the ultimate Father is also a person. The personal conception of God is there in every religion: Christian, Mohammedan, and Vedic. In the Vedic religion, it is stated, *oṁ tad viṣṇoḥ paramaṁ padam.* Those who are spiritually advanced know that the Supreme Father is Lord Viṣṇu. Lord Viṣṇu and Kṛṣṇa are the same. Impersonal realization is imperfect and incomplete, whereas Bhagavān, the personal God, is the ultimate end of realization. Our first business is to know God and our relationship with Him. Then we can act accordingly to perfect our lives. This is the process of God realization.

Hayagrīva dāsa: James considered religion to be the source of philosophy. He writes: "Since the relation [of man to God] may be either moral, physical, or ritual, it is evident that out of religion in the sense in which we take it, theologies, philosophies, and ecclesiastical organizations may secondarily grow."

Śrīla Prabhupāda: Philosophy means advancing knowledge, and we are perfecting our knowledge when we begin our understanding of God. Due to foolishness, we sometimes deride God's existence. Sometimes we concoct some imaginary idea, and sometimes we have impersonal and pantheistic conceptions. Philosophy is the search for God, but due to our imperfection, we have different opinions and conceptions of Him. God is a person, and when we know God, talk with Him, see Him, feel His presence, and play with Him, we have attained the highest platform of God realization. We then come to realize that God is great and that we are small and always subordinate. Carrying out God's orders is religion, and the more we realize this, the more we perfect our religion.

Śyāmasundara dāsa: James noted that there are two fundamental philosophical temperaments. One is called tender-mindedness, and this is typified by the rationalist, the idealist, the optimist, the religionist, and the dogmatist. Tough-mindedness is typified by the empiricist, the materialist, the pessimist, the atheist, the fatalist, and the skeptic.

Śrīla Prabhupāda: This depends upon our education, whether we become tender or tough-minded. In either case, we propose that originally the soul is good. Tenderness and toughness are developed later on. They are not the standard. When you come to the platform of the soul, everything is good. From *Bhagavad-gītā*, we understand that every living entity is part and parcel of God, and God is good. Arjuna accepts Kṛṣṇa as *paraṁ brahma paraṁ dhāma pavitram* (*Bg*. 10.12). The word *pavitra* means "pure." Because we are part of God, we are pure. Impurities are acquired due to contamination in this material world. We may be either tender or tough-minded: this is due to our impurity acquired in this material world. We don't credit a person either way, being tender or tough. A man suffering from a headache thinks that it is better to be suffering from indigestion instead, and vice versa. Because the pure soul is affected by the three *guṇas*—*sattva*, *rajas*, and *tamas*—he is suffering. He must be relieved from all suffering. From the material point of view, one may be a *brāhmaṇa* contaminated by *sattva-guṇa*, or a *śūdra* contaminated by *tamo-guṇa* or *rajo-guṇa*, but from the spiritual platform, both are contaminated by material nature. Because of this, both are suffering. It is explained in *Bhagavad-gītā* that the *brāhmaṇa* thinks, "Oh, I am so pure and learned. I am so this, I am so that." This is called contamination by *sattva-guṇa*. He is not thinking that he is part and parcel of Kṛṣṇa. As long as we are affected by these material modes of nature, our position is the same.

Śyāmasundara dāsa: James called himself a radical empiricist. He did not see the universe as a neat set of relationships because direct experience informs us that facts are mosaic and discontinuous in their design. Thus for him the universe is a composition of facts which do not form a perfect unity.

Śrīla Prabhupāda: Because he is seeing the universe with imperfect eyes, it appears imperfect. Actually, everything is complete. According to the first verse of *Īśopaniṣad:*

oṁ pūrṇam adaḥ pūrṇam idaṁ
pūrṇāt pūrṇam udacyate
pūrṇasya pūrṇam ādāya
pūrṇam evāvaśiṣyate

"The Personality of Godhead is perfect and complete, and because He is completely perfect, all emanations from Him, such as this phenomenal world, are perfectly equipped as complete wholes. Whatever is produced of the complete whole is also complete in itself. Because He is the complete whole, even though so many complete units emanate from Him,

He remains the complete balance." (*Īśopaniṣad*, Invocation) God is perfect, and whatever is created by God is perfect. James thinks that it is imperfect because he cannot see it through the eyes of God.

Śyāmasundara dāsa: For James, the ultimate unification of the universe is never fully attained. He writes: "The universe continually grows in quantity by new experiences that graft themselves upon the older mass; but these very new experiences often help the mass to a more consolidated form."

Śrīla Prabhupāda: This conception results from a poor fund of knowledge. The universe is complete, but man alone is not complete. Because the universe is created by a perfect being, it is also perfect. It is not that the universe is evolving. It has been perfect since its creation. Since our knowledge is imperfect, we think that it is evolving.

Śyāmasundara dāsa: Is this because my observations of the universe are evolving toward a unity?

Śrīla Prabhupāda: Yes.

Śyāmasundara dāsa: Well, this is James's criterion for truth: that which I perceive is true. Truth is what one can experience.

Śrīla Prabhupāda: But what you can perceive may also be wrong because you are not perfect. You may think an imperfect thing perfect, or a perfect thing imperfect. In the *śāstras* it is stated that because human beings are controlled by the mode of passion, they love to work very hard, and thus they think that hard work is happiness. At the same time, the *śāstras* point out that hard work for sense gratification is also being carried on by hogs and dogs. Animals are also working hard for some remuneration, for food, or sense enjoyment. This is called māyā, illusion.

Śyāmasundara dāsa: James felt that truth is more than just an agreement of idea with reality. It also has practical significance. What is practical is true.

Śrīla Prabhupāda: Yes, the truth must be practical. From the verses of Prabodhānanda Sarasvatī, we can understand that one who receives but the slightest merciful glance of Lord Caitanya Mahāprabhu considers Brahman and liberation to be hellish. *Kaivalyaṁ narakāyate.* Such a person also considers the heavenly planets to be mere phantasmagoria, and the *yoga-siddhis*, the yoga potencies, to be unimportant. Materialists suffer in this material condition, but a devotee is always satisfied. Although others are full of anxiety, a devotee sees everything as pleasing. All of this is possible by a fragment of the merciful glance of Caitanya Mahāprabhu. This is practical. As soon as we become Kṛṣṇa conscious, all this takes place.

Śyāmasundara dāsa: For James, truth means experience.
Śrīla Prabhupāda: That is also our proposal. *Bhaktiḥ pareśānubhavo viraktir anyatra caiṣa (Bhāg.* 11.2.42). One who is advanced in *bhakti* is no longer interested in material enjoyment. Unless we come to detest material things, it is to be understood that we are not making progress. When a hungry man eats, he feels satisfied, and his body gains strength. Similarly, when we advance in Kṛṣṇa consciousness, we feel spiritually strong and lose our taste for material enjoyment.
Śyāmasundara dāsa: James felt that truths can be created or developed in the same way as wealth or health.
Śrīla Prabhupāda: Health may be created, but truth cannot. It is not that truth is developing; rather, you are gradually progressing towards truth. It is not that the sun is developing, but as the clouds disappear, your ability to see the sun develops. The sun is fixed in its position.
Śyāmasundara dāsa: Well, for James, truth is a system of verification. That is, ideas become true or are made true through our experience of them.
Śrīla Prabhupāda: No, as you make progress, truth is revealed. In *Bhagavad-gītā,* Kṛṣṇa says that as we surrender unto Him, He reveals Himself proportionately (*Bg.* 4.11).
Śyāmasundara dāsa: But if an idea works, and is applied to concrete facts of experience, we can accept it as a true idea. As our experiences develop, our life progresses. If an idea works in my experience, it becomes true for me.
Śrīla Prabhupāda: Yes, that is our process. In the beginning, it is through faith that we enter into the Kṛṣṇa consciousness movement. In the beginning, we have no practical experience of Kṛṣṇa consciousness. We may see that people who are Kṛṣṇa conscious appear to have very bright faces, and our interest may increase on seeing this. Thus we first come with a little faith and interest, and as we associate with the devotees, our interest increases.
Śyāmasundara dāsa: So our experiences prove that the ideas are true.
Śrīla Prabhupāda: Yes, otherwise how can European and American boys be satisfied with so few material possessions? They are realizing in practice that a simple life is better than an artificial one.
Śyāmasundara dāsa: But what is practical for one person may not be for another. What is the criterion?
Śrīla Prabhupāda: There are relative truths, and there is the Absolute Truth. Some people are interested in one, and some in the other. We may accept some temporary means to attain a goal; however, the ultimate

goal is to please Kṛṣṇa, and for this end we may adopt some temporary, relative means.
Śyāmasundara dāsa: According to James, one who believes has a greater chance to discover the truth than one who doubts.
Śrīla Prabhupāda: That is so.

ajñaś cāśraddadhānaś ca
saṁśayātmā vinaśyati
nāyaṁ loko'sti na paro
na sukhaṁ saṁśayātmanaḥ

"But ignorant and faithless persons who doubt the revealed scriptures do not attain God consciousness. For the doubting soul, there is happiness neither in this world nor in the next." (*Bg.* 4.40) Those who are doubters are finished. Is James a believer or a doubter?
Śyāmasundara dāsa: He was a believer, a New England Protestant. He says that one who disbelieves faces the risk of losing any chance of discovering the truth.
Śrīla Prabhupāda: That is so. This means that we accept the fact that God is truth and that He is existing. He believes that we have a better chance to get at the truth by believing in God, and God is truth; therefore God is existing. If you believe that you can become warm by getting next to fire, you are asserting the existence of fire. Unless there is a fire, how can there be warmth? So the belief itself is the proof.
Śyāmasundara dāsa: For James, the mind must survive the body, since the mind is not dependent on the body for its existence.
Śrīla Prabhupāda: That is a fact. When the gross body is finished, the subtle body consisting of the mind, intelligence, and ego remains. These guide us to another gross body. They are like the aroma coming from a rose. We can see the rose, but we cannot see the aroma. Still, the aroma is being scattered by the air. Similarly, when the spirit soul gives up the gross body, it is carried by the mind, intelligence, and ego. According to our desire, that subtle body enters another gross body.
Śyāmasundara dāsa: If the mind and intelligence are not material, do they not die?
Śrīla Prabhupāda: To die means to disappear. The mind disappears when you are liberated.
Śyāmasundara dāsa: Then I carry my mind with me throughout all my lifetimes?
Śrīla Prabhupāda: Yes, as long as you are not liberated.
Śyāmasundara dāsa: Is this the same mind I have now and have always

had?
Śrīla Prabhupāda: Yes, but the body, which is material and gross, changes. The subtle material body—mind, intelligence, and false ego—accompanies us until we are liberated.
Hayagrīva dāsa: Concerning nondevotional religions, James gives the following estimation of impersonalism and Buddhism: "There are systems of thought which the world usually calls religious, and yet do not positively assume a God. Buddhism is in this case. Popularly, of course, the Buddha himself stands in place of a God; but in strictness the Buddhistic system is atheistic."
Śrīla Prabhupāda: Yes, and that is also the description given in *Śrīmad-Bhāgavatam.* Lord Buddha appeared at a time when people were atheistic and accustomed to killing many animals in sacrificial offerings. Lord Buddha was very much aggrieved to see poor animals being killed unnecessarily; therefore he preached a religion of nonviolence. Because the people were atheists, Lord Buddha, in order to bring them under his control, agreed with them and said, "Yes, there is no God, but listen to me." This is a kind of transcendental cheating. In the beginning he said there is no God, but he is God Himself. In this way, people accepted his words and instructions. Animal killers cannot understand God and religion, although they may have some vague idea. Lord Buddha wanted to stop their sinful activities and reestablish a system of religion dedicated to nonviolence. Therefore he rejected the Vedas, which allow restricted animal sacrifice.
Hayagrīva dāsa: For James, religion means surrender and total involvement. He writes: "In the religious life...surrender and sacrifice are positively espoused: even unnecessary givings-up are added in order that the happiness may increase. Religion thus makes easy and felicitous what in any case is necessary....It becomes an essential organ of our life, performing a function which no other portion of our life can so successfully fulfill."
Śrīla Prabhupāda: Yes, society without religion is animalistic. We have already defined religion as understanding, loving, and obeying God. These principles are personally taught by God Himself in *Bhagavad-gītā:*

manmanā bhava mad-bhakto
mad-yājī māṁ namaskuru
mām evaiṣyasi satyaṁ te
pratijāne priyo'si me

"Always think of Me and become My devotee. Worship Me and offer your homage unto Me. Thus you will come to Me without fail. I promise you this because you are My very dear friend." (*Bg.* 18.65) We may think of God either as a personal God or a localized or all-pervading God, but in any case, God has form. It is easier to think of the form of the Lord. Attempting to meditate on the impersonal aspect is very troublesome (*Bg.* 12.5). Although Kṛṣṇa has different incarnations and forms, He is the Supreme; therefore we meditate upon Him. In our Kṛṣṇa consciousness movement, we can think of Kṛṣṇa easily because His form, the Deity, is in the temple. We also have the perfect instructions of *Bhagavad-gītā*. God gives perfect instructions in everything: religion, politics, sociology, philosophy, science, physics, and history. Those who are fortunate will see the actual form of God according to His instructions, and perfect their lives. This is what is wanted.

Hayagrīva dāsa: James sees happiness as an integral part of religion.

Śrīla Prabhupāda: When you know and follow God, you become happy.

brahma-bhūtaḥ prasannātmā
na śocati na kāṅkṣati
samaḥ sarveṣu bhūteṣu
mad-bhaktiṁ labhate parām

"One who is transcendentally situated at once realizes the Supreme Brahman. He never laments nor desires to have anything; he is equally disposed to every living entity. In that state, he attains pure devotional service unto Me." (*Bg.* 18.54) As soon as we are God realized, we transcend duality and all distress, and become immediately happy. There is no longer hankering and lamentation. We no longer distinguish between men and nations. We see everyone within the material world—whether man, animal, or a tree—as a living entity, a part and parcel of God. In this way, we have a clear understanding and a perfect life.

Hayagrīva dāsa: In *The Varieties of Religious Experience*, James further writes: "If a creed makes a man feel happy, he almost inevitably adopts it. Such a belief ought to be true; therefore it is true—such rightly or wrongly, is one of the immediate inferences of the religious logic used by ordinary men."

Śrīla Prabhupāda: Yes, if you have a clear conception of God, and have decided to obey Him and love Him, you will be happy. This is the process utilized by this Kṛṣṇa consciousness movement. We have no other business than obeying the orders of God. God has told us to preach this confidential philosophy of *Bhagavad-gītā* everywhere. Since we are trying to love God and obey His orders, we are eager to spread this Kṛṣṇa consciousness movement. Otherwise, it is Kṛṣṇa's business. Why should we bother about Him? We are attempting to spread this movement because we love Kṛṣṇa, and He is happy that His message is being spread throughout the world. That is our happiness also. Since we are serving God without a doubt, we also feel happiness. This is reciprocation with God. This is religion. Religion is not sentiment, but actual realization of God, the actual carrying out of His orders. Our progressive life is secure if we are happy when God is happy.

Hayagrīva dāsa: James sees the lover of God as being a morally free person. He writes: "St. Augustine's maxim, 'If you but love God, you may do as you incline—' is morally one of the profoundest of observations, yet it is pregnant, for such persons, with passports beyond the bounds of conventional morality."

Śrīla Prabhupāda: Yes, that is very nicely put. If God is satisfied with our action, our action is moral. Conventional morality, which says, "This is good, and this is bad," is a mental concoction. Morality refers to the activities which satisfy God. If our action dissatisfies God, it is immoral. We therefore sing every day, *yasya prasādād bhagavat-prasādo (Śrī Gurv-aṣṭaka* 8). The orders of God are carried out by the representative of God, the spiritual master. When we have no direct connection with God, the spiritual master serves as a transparent intermediary between God and ourselves. In the perfectional stage, of course, we can talk with God directly, but in the beginning, the neophyte must receive instructions from the spiritual master who is directly connected with God. If we satisfy the spiritual master, we have satisfied God, and this is our happiness.

Hayagrīva dāsa: Concerning evil, James writes: "Evil is a disease; and worry over disease is itself an additional form of disease, which only adds to the original complaint....The best repentence is to up and act for righteousness, and forget that you ever had relations with sin."

Śrīla Prabhupāda: When you are in a diseased condition, your suffering increases. When no one attempts to extinguish a fire, it increases. Debts unpaid will compound interests. Therefore diseases, fire, and debts should not be left unattended. They should be completely extinguished. We must know that our suffering is due to our disobedience to the orders of God, to our being irreligious. We have a relationship with God, but because we are now covered by material contamination, we are ignorant of it. We are thinking of ourselves as independent, and that is our foolishness. The demoniac and atheistic incorrectly think themselves independent of the orders of God; therefore they are forced to accept what they do not want: the punishments of birth, old age, disease, and death. Despite this punishment, the atheists still deny God's existence. God is there, and His orders are there. We should accept the instructions of a bona fide spiritual master, the representative of God, and execute them. Then we become happy and overcome the results of evil.

Śyāmasundara dāsa: Like Mill and others, James felt that due to the existence of evil in the universe, God is not unlimited.

Śrīla Prabhupāda: He did not know that evil does not exist independent of God. According to the *śāstras,* evil is the back side of God. Back side or front side, God is God. God is absolute. It is not that I can neglect or deny my back. I cannot say, "Beat me on my back side." The back is as important as the front. Those who are sinful cannot stand the front of God. Therefore Kṛṣṇa says:

yeṣāṁ tv anta-gataṁ pāpaṁ
janānāṁ puṇya-karmaṇām
te dvandva-moha-nirmuktā
bhajante māṁ dṛḍha-vratāḥ

"Persons who have acted piously in previous lives and in this life, whose sinful actions are completely eradicated, and who are freed from the duality of delusion, engage themselves in My service with determination." (*Bg.* 7.28) Unless we are completely uncontaminated, we cannot come to Kṛṣṇa consciousness. Once we surrender unto Kṛṣṇa and accept His orders, Kṛṣṇa immediately relieves us from all sinful reactions.

Śyāmasundara dāsa: James defines the world as the "stuff of pure experience," and says that experience is sometimes manifest as mind, and sometimes as matter.

Śrīla Prabhupāda: It is made up of experience, but whose experience? It is not due to your experience that these flowers are here. You have not created these flowers. He speaks of pure experience, but he does not know that it is Kṛṣṇa's experience.

na tasya kāryaṁ karaṇaṁ ca vidyate
na tat-samaś cābhyadhikaś ca dṛśyate
parāsya śaktir vividhaiva śrūyate
svā-bhāvikī jñāna-bala-kriyā ca

"He does not possess bodily form like that of an ordinary living entity. There is no difference between His body and His soul. He is absolute. All His senses are transcendental. Any one of His senses can perform the action of any other sense. Therefore, no one is greater than Him or equal to Him. His potencies are multifarious, and thus His deeds are automatically performed as a natural sequence." (*Śvetāśvatara Upaniṣad* 6.7-8) According to the Vedas, the Supreme is equipped with different kinds of energies, and those energies can be experienced. This universe and everything within the cosmic manifestation is designed by the Supreme. Everything is a result of His multi-energies. In order for a man to create a flower on canvas, he must be thoroughly experienced in his art, but we can see that the multi-energies of Kṛṣṇa are working so nicely that flowers appear automatically.

Hayagrīva dāsa: James divides religion into two basic types. One he calls the "sky-blue optimistic gospel," and the other "pessimistic" in its recognition of the futility and miseries of materialistic life. He felt that the completest religions take a pessimistic view of material existence, and offer liberation from it.

Śrīla Prabhupāda: Yes, only an animal is not pessimistic about life in this material world. A man is capable of knowing the threefold sufferings of material life. There are sufferings of the mind and body, sufferings offered by other living entities, and sufferings forced upon us by natural catastrophes and the laws of nature. The world is full of suffering, but under the spell of māyā, illusion, we think we are progressing. Ultimately, whatever we do, death is there to annihilate the results. Under these circumstances, there is no happiness within this material world. We may make all arrangements for happiness, but at any moment, death may capture us. So what happiness can we have here? Therefore an intelligent man is always pessimistic about material life. He knows that he will not be allowed to be happy here. As we further advance, we understand the orders of Kṛṣṇa: *sarva-dharmān parityajya mām ekaṁ śaraṇaṁ vraja*. "Abandon all religions and just surrender unto Me." (*Bg.* 18.66) We must surrender to the Supreme Personality of Godhead, and after surrendering and understanding Him fully, we can go to the world that is full of bliss, knowledge, and eternal life. Unless we take a pessimistic view of this material world, we will remain attached to it, and the repetition of birth and death will ensue. In this world, everyone is attempting to live permanently, but nature does not allow this. People work very hard, and sometimes get good results, bad results, or frustration. So where is happiness? Happiness is understanding God, acting according to His advice, and returning home, back to Godhead.

Hayagrīva dāsa: James believes that there is a certain composite picture of universal saintliness, which is the same in all religions, and of which

the features can be easily traced. He has noted that holymen possess: "One, a feeling of being in a wider life than that of this world's selfish little interest; and a conviction...of the existence of an Ideal Power."
Śrīla Prabhupāda: Yes, that feeling is there because the greatness of God is experienced. God is great in six opulences: wealth, strength, fame, knowledge, beauty, and renunciation.
Hayagrīva dāsa: Secondly, holymen possess "a sense of the friendly continuity of the Ideal Power with our own life, in a willing self-surrender to its control."
Śrīla Prabhupāda: Yes, there is a friendly continuity. There are five basic relationships. In the first, the relationship is between master and servant, then friend to friend, son to father, father to son, and beloved to beloved. All of these are friendly relationships, and every living entity has a natural instinct to accept any one of them. Thus our friendly relationships with God can be chosen. Someone may like to relate to Him as a servant, a friend, a father, a son, or a conjugal lover. When we are free from material contamination, our particular relationship is revived, and we understand ourselves as eternal parts and parcels of God.
Hayagrīva dāsa: Thirdly, the holyman experiences "an immense elation and freedom, as the outlines of the confining selfhood melt down."
Śrīla Prabhupāda: Yes, material selfishness is māyā. Those who are enchanted by the spell of māyā do not know that their real self-interest is in knowing their relationship with God. Our first duty is to have a complete idea of God and our relationship with Him. According to the Vedic process, whether we take up the *haṭha-yoga, jñāna-yoga,* or *bhakti-yoga* system, the purpose is realization of God. A perfect human being knows that God is supplying his necessities and that he need not try to improve his economic condition. A *sādhu,* or holyman, is not interested in improving his material condition, but his spiritual condition.
Hayagrīva dāsa: Lastly, James speaks of the holyman experiencing "a shifting of the emotional center toward loving and harmonious affections, toward 'yes' and away from 'no' where the claims of the non-ego are concerned."
Śrīla Prabhupāda: Yes, God is always asking us to obey His orders, and as soon as we do so, as soon as we agree with Him, we become liberated. *Śrīmad-Bhāgavatam* describes liberation as giving up everything except devotional life.

nārāyaṇa-parāḥ sarve
na kutaścana bibhyati
svargāpavarga-narakeṣv

api tulyārtha-darśinaḥ

"Devotees solely engaged in the devotional service of the Supreme Personality of Godhead, Nārāyaṇa, never fear any condition of life. For them, the heavenly planets, liberation, and the hellish planets are all the same, because such devotees are interested only in the service of the Lord." (*Bhāg.* 6.17.28) Life is meant for rendering devotional service to the Lord, and as soon as we understand this and commit ourselves to the rendering of such service, we are liberated. That is called *mukti.*

Hayagrīva dāsa: James believes that the existence of many religions in the world is not regrettable because different types of men necessitate different types of religion. "Some may really be the better for a religion of consolation and reassurance," he writes, "whilst others are better for one of terror and reproof...."

Śrīla Prabhupāda: I have said that religion means accepting God as the Supreme Father, material nature as the mother, and all living entities as sons of God. The father is the maintainer, and all his sons have the right to live at his expense. Every living being should be satisfied with his condition, which is given by God. No one should encroach upon the rights of others, including the rights of animals to live peacefully. According to Bhaktivinoda Ṭhākura, a happy life means living in the family of Kṛṣṇa without violating the rules and regulations. In a family, the sons can live very happily by obeying their father. So there may be many types of religion, but awareness of this basic relationship with God and His creation should be there.

Hayagrīva dāsa: Since James was acquainted only with the impersonalist Vedānta school of Hinduism, he wrote of *samādhi* instead of devotional service. "When a man comes out of *samādhi,*" he writes, "...he remains 'enlightened, a sage, a prophet, a saint, his whole character changed, his life changed, illumined.'"

Śrīla Prabhupāda: *Samādhi* means ecstasy, and if we are in God consciousness, we are in *samādhi.* In *Bhagavad-gītā,* Kṛṣṇa speaks of the yogī in *samādhi:*

yoginām api sarveṣāṁ
mad-gatenāntarātmanā
śraddhāvān bhajate yo māṁ
sa me yuktatamo mataḥ

"And of all yogīs, he who always abides in Me with great faith, worshipping Me in transcendental loving service, is most intimately united with Me in yoga and is the highest of all." (*Bg.* 6.47) In *samādhi,* the mind is always absorbed in God. If we continue in Kṛṣṇa consciousness, we are in *samādhi.*

Hayagrīva dāsa: James describes *samādhi* to be a union in which the individual has lost contact with the external world.

Śrīla Prabhupāda: Yes.

Hayagrīva dāsa: And he therefore concludes that "Mystical states cannot be sustained for long. Except in rare instances, half an hour, or at most an hour or two, seems to be the limit beyond which they fade into the light of common day. Often, when faded, their quality can but imperfectly be reproduced in memory; but when they recur, it is recognized; and from one recurrence to another it is susceptible of continuous development in what is felt as inner richness and importance."

Śrīla Prabhupāda: Yes, that richness is perfected when we think of Kṛṣṇa constantly. That is recommended in the Sixth Chapter of *Bhagavad-gītā,* which I quoted previously. Consequently, in our Kṛṣṇa consciousness movement, we are devoted to thinking of Kṛṣṇa twenty-four hours daily. When we do not fall down from the yoga principle, we experience *samādhi.*

Hayagrīva dāsa: James himself claims to have experienced such a state momentarily, under the influence of ether. And today, people claim to induce mystical states through psychedelic drugs.

Śrīla Prabhupāda: These are artificial means, and they cannot be sustained. It is better to engage in the bona fide devotional process—*śravaṇaṁ kīrtanaṁ viṣṇoḥ smaraṇaṁ pāda-sevanam (Bhāg.* 7.5.23)—always hearing about Kṛṣṇa, talking about Him, remembering Him, serving Him in the temple, distributing His literatures, and so on. There are many services we can render in order to be fully absorbed in Kṛṣṇa consciousness.

Hayagrīva dāsa: After analyzing many different religious experiences, James arrives at five basic conclusions. One: "That the visible world is part of a more spiritual universe from which it draws its chief significance."

Śrīla Prabhupāda: Yes, the material universe is existing on the spiritual effulgence of the Lord, just as all the planets are resting upon the sunshine. Everything rests on the spiritual effulgence of the Lord, but when we forget the Lord, we call this the material world. Actually, the material world is in the spiritual world, but forgetfulness of God is material. When we revive our dormant God consciousness, the material world no longer exists. For a person truly advanced in God consciousness, there is nothing material. Everything is spiritual.

Hayagrīva dāsa: You are anticipating James's second conclusion, which

is: "Union or harmonious relation with that higher universe is our true end."
Śrīla Prabhupāda: Yes, that is so. When we no longer forget our eternal relationship with God, nothing is material.
Hayagrīva dāsa: Third, prayer, or communion with God, "is a process wherein work is really done, and spiritual energy flows in and produces effects, psychological or material, within the phenomenal world." And, fourth, religion produces "a new zest which adds itself like a gift to life."
Śrīla Prabhupāda: Yes, realizing God's creation with awe, veneration, and appreciation constitutes one type of relationship called *śānta-rasa.* From there, we can progress to the point of *dāsya-rasa,* which involves serving God, and finally to the *mādhurya-rasa,* which includes accepting God as our most beloved object. The devotee may choose whichever relationship he likes; the result is the same. However, by comparative study, the *sādhus* have decided that the *mādhurya-rasa,* our relationship with God as lover and beloved, is the highest relationship.
Hayagrīva dāsa: Finally, religion produces "an assurance of safety and a temper of peace, and, in relation to others, a preponderance of loving affections."
Śrīla Prabhupāda: Yes, that is very nice. A devotee is always at peace because he is always confident that since he is sincerely serving Kṛṣṇa, Kṛṣṇa will save him from all danger. Prahlāda Mahārāja was always peaceful, although his demoniac father, Hiraṇyakaśipu, attempted to kill him in so many ways. God always protects His devotee, and therefore the pure devotee is not disturbed by any material condition. He has firm faith in God, and this is called surrender. Full surrender means accepting everything favorable to God consciousness and rejecting everything unfavorable. When we enter the family of God, we have firm faith and security under the protection of God.
Hayagrīva dāsa: James then concludes that "in opening ourselves to God's influence, our deepest destiny is fulfilled."
Śrīla Prabhupāda: Yes, that fulfillment is what is wanted. God demands that we fully surrender unto Him, and when we do so, our lives are perfected.

John Dewey
(1859-1952)

Hayagrīva dāsa: Dewey believed that religions are basically myths and that experience is of the utmost necessity. He considered philosophy superior to religion. "The form [in philosophy] ceases to be that of the story told in imaginative and emotional style," he writes, "and becomes that of rational discourse observing the canons of logic." For him, the Vedic accounts of Kṛṣṇa's pastimes would be purely mythical.
Śrīla Prabhupāda: Kṛṣṇa is a historical fact; He is not imaginary. The *Mahābhārata* is accepted by all Indian authorities, especially by the *ācāryas* who control the spiritual life of India. They do not, however, accept Mr. Dewey's imaginative thinking.
Hayagrīva dāsa: When science began to investigate the phenomenal universe without admitting the proprietorship of God, a breakdown in morality and value ensued. Dewey tried to reassemble these shattered values in a philosophical way, but he, like science, attempted to do so without acknowledging the proprietorship of a Supreme Being.
Śrīla Prabhupāda: That is simply a form of lunacy because everything has a proprietor. Why should this great cosmic manifestation not have a proprietor? It is natural and logical to accept a proprietor. Who would

think that an organized nation has no government? How can a logical man come to such conclusions?

Hayagrīva dāsa: He felt that science dealt a death blow to the orthodox, historical religions as we know them.

Śrīla Prabhupāda: As I have repeatedly explained, religion means accepting the laws of God. The whole cosmic manifestation has a date of creation and is therefore historical. Anything material that has a beginning has a history, but long before this cosmic manifestation was created, religion existed. We are tiny people and know the small history of this world, which extends for some thousands of years, but the history of Brahmā is far different. That history covers billions and billions of earth years. At the same time, our history is different from an ant's history. So, historically speaking, everything is relative according to the living entity computing or experiencing the history. Most people have no information of greater personalities, which we call the demigods, but Vedic literatures inform us that in the higher planetary systems, the standard of life is different and the duration longer. Unless one has thorough knowledge of the entire universe, religions may seem imaginary, but what is imaginary to one may be factual to another. For an ant, the history of man is imaginary. Unfortunately, scientists and philosophers on this planet are thinking in their own terms and taking everything they think to be factual. On the other hand, whatever they cannot conceive, they consider mythological.

Hayagrīva dāsa: Writing in the early part of this century, Dewey felt that it was high time to set aside all superstitious religions. According to him, logic "demands that in imagination we wipe the slate clean and start afresh by asking what would be the idea of the unseen...." In other words, we must define God and religion anew.

Śrīla Prabhupāda: Yes, that is required. *Śrīmad-Bhāgavatam* rejects all religions considered to be "cheating religions," because they do not contain perfect knowledge.

dharmaḥ projjhita-kaitavo'tra paramo nirmatsarāṇāṁ satāṁ
vedyaṁ vāstavam atra vastu śivadaṁ tāpa-trayonmūlanam
śrīmad bhāgavate mahāmuni-kṛte kiṁ vā parair īśvaraḥ
sadyo hṛdy avarudhyate 'tra kṛtibhiḥ śuśrūṣubhis tat-kṣaṇāt

"Completely rejecting all religious activities which are materially motivated, this *Bhāgavata Purāṇa* propounds the highest truth, which is understandable by those devotees who are pure in heart. The highest truth is reality distinguished from illusion for the welfare of all. Such truth uproots the threefold miseries. This beautiful *Bhāgavatam*, compiled by the great sage Śrī Vyāsadeva, is sufficient in itself for God realization. As soon as one attentively and submissively hears the message of *Bhāgavatam*, he becomes attached to the Supreme Lord." (*Bhāg.* 1.1.2)

The sum and substance of the *Bhāgavata* religion is the acceptance of God as supreme controller. *Janmādy asya yato 'nvayād itarataś cārtheṣv abhijñaḥ svarāṭ (Bhāg.* 1.1.1). That is the principle: Brahman is He from whom everything emanates. Unless we know the ultimate source of emanation, our knowledge is imperfect. Our experience tells us that everything has a source of emanation. Similarly, this entire creation has a history and a source from which it has emanated. Just because we are unable to reach that source, we should not think that it is imaginary. There is no question of starting a new religion because religion is always there. Someone must be the supreme controller, and that someone is called God. Dewey may ask, "Well, what is your experience?" We experience inert matter without consciousness, and we experience consciousness. We cannot go beyond this. Above these, there is one controller, a third element, which is the Absolute Truth, the controller of all visible animate and inanimate objects. Why is it difficult to understand this?

Hayagrīva dāsa: In *A Common Faith*, Dewey writes: "What I have been criticizing is the identification of the ideal with a particular Being, especially when that identification makes necessary the conclusion that this Being is outside of nature, and what I have tried to show is that the ideal itself has its roots in natural conditions...."

Śrīla Prabhupāda: God does not arise out of nature. God is the supreme controller in charge of nature. How can anyone think that this great phenomenon which we call nature has no controller? How can anyone think that everything is happening automatically?

Hayagrīva dāsa: Dewey sees God emerging out of man's striving for perfection.

Śrīla Prabhupāda: God is already there, and man's perfection depends on his ability to understand God. It is not that a perfect man can create God through his imagination. Anything created by man is controlled, but God is the supreme controller. If man dies under the control of the Supreme, how can he be said to create or control the Supreme? If he cannot control what is already imposed by God—birth, old age, disease, and death—how can he imagine or create God? First, one should become independent of the laws of God before thinking of creating God.

Hayagrīva dāsa: It appears that Dewey wants to use the word "God" to serve his own ends: promoting his philosophic conception of "the working union of the ideal and actual." He writes: "Use of the words God or divine to convey the union of actual with ideal may protect man from a sense of isolation and from consequent despair or defiance."

Śrīla Prabhupāda: Of course, one may define God, but one must be a *muni*, a very learned man, to define Him properly. For instance, one may say, "God is there," or, "God is great." We can go on from there to define His greatness. This greatness includes ultimate greatness in six opulences: power, wealth, knowledge, fame, beauty, and renunciation. Only God possesses these opulences in complete fullness. When Kṛṣṇa was present on this planet, He proved that He was the strongest, the most influential, the most beautiful and pure, and the most supremely wise. Kṛṣṇa's teachings, *Bhagavad-gītā*, are still being studied all over the world. Great *ācāryas* like Rāmānujācārya, Madhvācārya, Nimbārka, Śaṅkarācārya, and Caitanya Mahāprabhu have all accepted Kṛṣṇa as the Supreme Lord. There is complete agreement among the authorities that Kṛṣṇa is God. There is no question of mythology. Kṛṣṇa's lifting of Govardhana Hill is described in *Śrīmad-Bhāgavatam*, and when speculators read it, they consider it to be mythological. But, really, is it difficult for God to lift a hill? If He is all powerful, what is the difficulty? When God comes and shows His godly powers, we should not consider it mythical.

Hayagrīva dāsa: Unlike Marx and Comte, Dewey rejects humanity as an object of worship. He writes: "Nature produces whatever gives reinforcement and direction but also what occasions discord and confusion. The divine is thus a term of human choice and aspiration."

Śrīla Prabhupāda: There is no question of human choice. Can you say that death is your choice? Obviously there is force, and where is that force coming from? No one wants to die, but everyone dies. No one wants to grow old, but everyone grows old. We must understand the origin of this enforcement. The supreme authority, the supreme force, is God. You may call this God "nature," or whatever, but you must admit that there is something supreme controlling you. How can we philosophize and imagine that man can become God?

Hayagrīva dāsa: Dewey writes that "a humanistic religion, if it excludes our relationship to nature, is pale and thin, as it is presumptuous, when it takes humanity as an object of worship."

Śrīla Prabhupāda: For a God conscious person, everything is worshipable, even an ant. But the supremely worshipable is God: *īśvaraḥ paramaḥ kṛṣṇaḥ*. Some people think that nature is the supreme, but those who are aware of God know that God is the controller of nature also. *Mayādhyakṣeṇa prakṛtiḥ sūyate sa-carācaram.* "This material nature is working under My direction, and it is producing all moving and unmoving beings." (*Bg.* 9.10) Nature is only matter, and matter cannot act independently. Matter is being handled and controlled by a living being, who is the superior nature. *Bhūmir āpo'nalo vāyuḥ khaṁ mano buddhir eva ca (Bg.* 7.4). Earth, water, air, fire, and so forth constitute inferior nature. Above and beyond this is the superior nature. The living entities are finite controllers, but above them is another controller, the supreme controller who is God. It is very easy to understand. There are two natures: an active and an inactive nature. Above both of these natures is an active personality who is controlling both.

Śyāmasundara dāsa: As far as his methodology is concerned, Dewey believed that practical consequences are the only valid test of truth. He claimed that the proof of an idea consists in its being subject to predictable results.

Śrīla Prabhupāda: If an idea is concocted, its results cannot be ascertained. If it is factual, the results can be predicted.

Śyāmasundara dāsa: For Dewey, the object of inquiry is belief itself. Because we want something to believe in, we ask questions. This is the nature of inquiry.

Śrīla Prabhupāda: The *Vedānta-sūtra* advises us to find out the ultimate cause of everything, to inquire into the Absolute Truth. But inquiries should be directed to a person who knows. Otherwise, what is the use in inquiring? The Vedas advise us to approach a bona fide spiritual master, a guru, if we want to find the truth. Unfortunately, at the present moment, there are many pseudo gurus; therefore we have to add this word "bona fide." Otherwise, the word guru means bona fide, because one who is not bona fide cannot be a guru. Now, when we speak of inquiry, we mean learning the truth. Therefore we should inquire from one who knows the truth, otherwise our inquiry has no validity. *Tad viddhi praṇipātena paripraśnena sevayā.* "Just try to learn the truth by approaching a spiritual master. Inquire from him submissively and render service unto him." (*Bg.* 4.34) This is the Vedic injunction. The inquiry should be genuine, and the answer should come from a genuine person.

Śyāmasundara dāsa: Dewey believes that the final outcome of inquiry is the fulfillment of human needs. By practical action, we can change the external environment.

Śrīla Prabhupāda: Unless a human being inquires about the Absolute

Truth, he is not considered sufficiently developed in his human form. For the consciousness to be developed, one must inquire about the self, asking, "What am I?" If this question is not asked, he is still in ignorance.

Śyāmasundara dāsa: Dewey felt that by inquiry, we can determine what is wrong with our environment, act to change it, and fulfill human needs.

Śrīla Prabhupāda: If a person is serious, inquiry will clear up everything. If he inquires about the aim of human life, he is intelligent. It is not possible for animals to ask these questions. Animals are only eating, sleeping, defending, and mating.

Śyāmasundara dāsa: But should the aim of our inquiry be to change our external environment?

Śrīla Prabhupāda: If you are seriously inquiring, and if you know things as they are, you will change your activities. We are preaching that it is our business to know Kṛṣṇa. If people take this movement seriously, their entire mode of living will be changed. This is happening now. Previously, our students were leading a certain undesirable type of life, and since they have come to Kṛṣṇa consciousness, their entire lives have been changed.

Śyāmasundara dāsa: Then, setting aside trying to improve the environment, we should first try to change our consciousness?

Śrīla Prabhupāda: It is the consciousness that needs to be changed, either by hearing from authority, or by circumstances. There are two processes by which knowledge can be attained—by hearing, and by direct experience. An intelligent person can understand by hearing. He knows that if he acts in a such a way, he will fall into danger. So he learns by listening to authorities. A less intelligent man has to experience an awkward or dangerous position in order to change his consciousness. For him, hearing is not sufficient. Of the two processes, learning by hearing is better. It is therefore our process to approach the bona fide teacher and learn from him. That is the process of *brahmacarya*. It is not that we have to learn by practical experience. The experience is already there. We only have to hear of it and accept it; then it becomes easier. We should not say, "Let me fall into the ditch, then I shall cry." Better we take good advice and avoid the ditch altogether.

Hayagrīva dāsa: In the realm of philosophy and religion, Dewey believes that certainty is impossible. He writes: "Any philosophy that in its quest for certainty ignores the reality of the uncertain in the ongoing processes of nature, denies the conditions out of which it arises."

Śrīla Prabhupāda: There is uncertainty when you do not accept the reality. The reality is God, and God explains how nature is working. If we do not accept His explanation, our position is very precarious, very uncertain. But if God comes and reveals Himself and His activities, and we consider them mythological, how can we be convinced? How can we ever be certain?

Hayagrīva dāsa: For Dewey, there is but one sure road of access to truth: what he calls "the road of patient, cooperative inquiry operating by means of observation, experiment, record, and controlled reflection."

Śrīla Prabhupāda: The record is there in the *Mahābhārata*, and those who have seen have confirmed it. Vyāsadeva, Nārada, and Arjuna all confirm that everything is there in the record, but if people do not believe, how can they be convinced? Conditioned living entities do not have the perfect senses to see, and if they remain unconvinced, they will always live in darkness. They may go on imagining in the dark, but they will never attain perfect knowledge in this way.

Śyāmasundara dāsa: Dewey set down five steps for solving problems and attaining truths: we observe a problem and consider its nature; we intellectualize and analyze it; we hypothesize and consider solutions; we analyze our hypothesis according to past experience, and choose possible solutions; and we put the solutions into practice.

Śrīla Prabhupāda: Our process for solving problems is Kṛṣṇa. Kṛṣṇa says, *kaunteya pratijānīhi na me bhaktaḥ praṇaśyati*. "O son of Kuntī, declare it boldly that My devotee never perishes." (*Bg*. 9.31) When we take shelter of Kṛṣṇa, our problems are solved. *Yatra yogeśvaraḥ kṛṣṇaḥ* (*Bg*. 18.78). Kṛṣṇa is the reservoir of all mystic power. He is *yogeśvaraḥ*. It is not the *bhakta's* business to strive to become a yogī; rather, he takes shelter of the Supreme Personality of Godhead, who is *yogeśvaraḥ*, the master of all mystic power. We consider this to be the solution to all our problems.

daivī hy eṣā guṇamayī
mama māyā duratyayā
mām eva ye prapadyante
māyām etāṁ taranti te

"This divine energy of Mine, consisting of the three modes of material nature, is difficult to overcome. But those who have surrendered unto Me can easily cross beyond it." (*Bg*. 7.14) There are various methods for solving problems, but the best method is to surrender unto Kṛṣṇa. Then all problems are solved.

Śyāmasundara dāsa: On the social platform as well?

Śrīla Prabhupāda: Yes. Everything is solved. For instance, the Pāṇḍavas had a political problem, and when they took shelter of Kṛṣṇa, their political and social problems were solved.
Śyāmasundara dāsa: For Dewey, truth must satisfy human needs and improve social conditions. He sees truth as a practical tool.
Śrīla Prabhupāda: We are the ones who have created social problems. Kṛṣṇa is perfect, and whatever Kṛṣṇa has created is perfect. *Oṁ pūrṇam adaḥ pūrṇam idam (Īśopaniṣad,* Invocation). Things appear to be imperfect because we disobey Kṛṣṇa's orders. If we remain faithful to Kṛṣṇa, there are no problems. People speak of truth, but unfortunately, they do not know the truth.

na te viduḥ svārtha-gatiṁ hi viṣṇuṁ
durāśayā ye bahir-artha-māninaḥ
andhā yathāndhair upanīyamānās
te 'pīśa-tantryām uru-dāmni baddhāḥ

"Persons who are strongly entrapped by the consciousness of enjoying material life, and who have therefore accepted as their leader or guru a similar blind man attached to external sense objects, cannot understand that the goal of life is to return home, back to Godhead, and engage in the service of Lord Viṣṇu. As blind men guided by another blind man miss the right path and fall into a ditch, materially attached men led by another materially attached man are bound by the ropes of fruitive labor, which are made of very strong cords, and they continue again and again in materialistic life, suffering the threefold miseries." (*Bhāg.* 7.5.31) The ultimate truth, the ultimate objective, is Viṣṇu. Unfortunately, people are trying to solve the problems of this world without referring to Viṣṇu. Of course, this is not possible.
Śyāmasundara dāsa: How does worship of Viṣṇu solve social problems?
Śrīla Prabhupāda: Man who executes this *varṇāśrama-dharma* satisfies Viṣṇu. The *brāhmaṇas, kṣatriyas, vaiśyas,* and *śūdras* have various prescribed duties. If they follow them, all problems are solved. Unfortunately, in India this *varṇāśrama-dharma* has been killed. Now everyone is a *śūdra.* The word *śūdra* refers to an unintelligent person. Since everyone is unintelligent, how can they solve problems? What can they do? They are trying to run a democratic government according to the votes of *śūdras,* but *śūdras* cannot solve anything. Once, America belonged to the red Indians, but they did not develop it. Why couldn't they improve their condition? The land and everything else was there. But when the Europeans came, they developed the land. *Śūdras* cannot ac-

tualize anything. If we once again establish the *varṇāśrama-dharma*, all problems will be solved. That was the plan of my Guru Mahārāja. *Daiva-varṇāśrama* refers to that which is stated by Kṛṣṇa. The *varṇas* are not established by birth, but by qualification. By qualification, one is a *brāhmaṇa* or a *śūdra*. By following the course prescribed for our *varṇa*, we can satisfy Lord Viṣṇu and in this way be happy.

Śyāmasundara dāsa: Dewey writes: "The good man is the man who no matter how morally worthy he has been, is moving to become better. Growth itself is the only moral end."

Śrīla Prabhupāda: In the beginning, a devotee may still do something wrong, but because he has taken to Kṛṣṇa consciousness, he is accepted as a *sādhu*.

api cet sudurācāro
bhajate mām ananya-bhāk
sādhur eva sa mantavyaḥ
samyag vyavasito hi saḥ

"Even if one commits the most abominable actions, if he is engaged in devotional service, he is considered saintly because he is properly situated." (*Bg.* 9.30) There may be many discrepancies in one's life, but if one's heart is in the right place, if he is working for Kṛṣṇa consciousness, he is considered a *sādhu*, even though he has not corrected his bad habits. *Kṣipraṁ bhavati dharmātmā śaśvac-chāntiṁ nigacchati.* "He quickly becomes righteous and attains lasting peace." (*Bg.* 9.31) Because he has taken to Kṛṣṇa consciousness, all his bad habits will be rectified very soon.

Śyāmasundara dāsa: In other words, he is striving to improve his moral condition?

Śrīla Prabhupāda: Yes. If one takes to Kṛṣṇa consciousness, his morality will gradually develop.

yasyāsti bhaktir bhagavaty akiñcanā
sarvair guṇais tatra samāsate surāḥ

"All the demigods and their exalted qualities, such as religion, knowledge, and renunciation, become manifest in the body of one who has developed unalloyed devotion for the Supreme Personality of Godhead, Vāsudeva." (*Bhāg.* 5.18.12) All good qualities will automatically come. We should stick to the four regulative principles: avoiding illicit sex, intoxication, meat eating, and gambling. And we should chant the Hare Kṛṣṇa *mahā-mantra*. By abiding by the orders of the spiritual master, everything will automatically develop. All good moral qualities will follow. It is not that we have to develop these qualities separately or independently. All good qualities are already there in the spirit soul, but presently they are covered by material contamination. When we are purified by Kṛṣṇa consciousness, all these original qualities emerge. *Hṛṣīkeṇa hṛṣīkeśa-sevanaṁ bhaktir ucyate (Bhakti-rasāmṛta sindhu* 1.1.12). We should purify our senses by engaging them in the service of the master of the senses, Kṛṣṇa. That is the process of *bhakti.*

Śyāmasundara dāsa: Dewey did not believe in absolute good or evil; each situation must be treated individually.

Śrīla Prabhupāda: Whatever is done in Kṛṣṇa consciousness is good, and whatever is done for something other than Kṛṣṇa's satisfaction is useless, although it may be ethically correct.

Śyāmasundara dāsa: He felt that the greatest good is the elimination of the greatest evil. It is the fulfillment of man's greatest needs.

Śrīla Prabhupāda: The highest objective is Kṛṣṇa, Viṣṇu. By becoming a Vaiṣṇava, we attain the highest perfection of human life. The greatest need is Kṛṣṇa consciousness, pure, supreme consciousness. Every living entity is Kṛṣṇa's part and parcel. *Mamaivāṁśo jīva-loke jīva-bhūtaḥ sanātanaḥ.* "The living entities in this conditioned world are my eternal, fragmental parts." (*Bg.* 15.7) Therefore we must always remember that, being part and parcel of Kṛṣṇa, it is our duty to serve Kṛṣṇa. In perverted consciousness, we think, "I am Kṛṣṇa. I am God." That is not Kṛṣṇa consciousness.

Śyāmasundara dāsa: Dewey believed that we should not choose good or evil simply on the basis of some theory. We should choose in order to alleviate specific evils.

Śrīla Prabhupāda: The *virāṭ-rūpa,* the universal form of the Lord, was manifest before Arjuna. Arjuna then saw that everything within the universe is part and parcel of that *virāṭ-rūpa,* within which everything has a function, a duty. When we work according to that function, problems are automatically solved.

Śyāmasundara dāsa: For Dewey, we can never attain absolute certainty or perfection. We can only attain higher levels of moral progress.

Śrīla Prabhupāda: This means that he has no knowledge of absolute perfection.

Śyāmasundara dāsa: The world can be made better by man's efforts, but perfection in the world is not possible.

Śrīla Prabhupāda: That is a different thing. This world is so made that if you perfect it today, tomorrow it will deteriorate. Therefore in one sense you cannot make it perfect. But you can improve it.

paritrāṇāya sādhūnāṁ
vināśāya ca duṣkṛtām
dharma-saṁsthāpanārthāya
sambhavāmi yuge yuge

"In order to deliver the pious and to annihilate the miscreants, as well as to reestablish the principles of religion, I appear Myself millennium after millennium." (*Bg.* 4.8) Any bad condition can be improved by Kṛṣṇa consciousness. Kṛṣṇa and Kṛṣṇa consciousness are the same. If you are in Kṛṣṇa consciousness, you are living with Kṛṣṇa, and if you are living with Kṛṣṇa, then what is your fear? On the battlefield of Kurukṣetra, Arjuna was fearless because Kṛṣṇa was beside him.

samāśritā ye padapallava-plavaṁ
mahat-padaṁ puṇya-yaśo murāreḥ
bhavāmbudhir vatsa-padaṁ paraṁ padaṁ
padaṁ padaṁ yad vipadāṁ na teṣām

"For one who has accepted the boat of the lotus feet of the Lord, who is the shelter of the cosmic manifestation and is famous as Mukunda, the giver of liberation, the ocean of the material world is like the water contained in a calf's hoofprint. Vaikuṇṭha is his goal, not the place where there is danger at every step." (*Bhāg.* 10.14.58) In this material world, there is danger at every step, but as soon as we understand Kṛṣṇa, we become eligible to be transferred to the spiritual world.

janma karma ca me divyam
evaṁ yo vetti tattvataḥ
tyaktvā dehaṁ punar janma
naiti mām eti so'rjuna

"One who knows the transcendental nature of My appearance and activities does not, upon leaving the body, take his birth again in this material world, but attains My eternal abode, O Arjuna." (*Bg.* 4.9)

Śyāmasundara dāsa: So people are removed from all danger, or evil, by becoming Kṛṣṇa conscious?

Śrīla Prabhupāda: Certainly. Therefore this is the best welfare activity for the entire world. By other means, people may be able to give some temporary benefit or temporary relief, but the situation will again deteriorate. You may give charity to a needy man, and this charity will serve him for a temporary period, but if you give him Kṛṣṇa *premā*, he is immediately transferred to the spiritual world. Therefore Caitanya Mahāprabhu is called the most munificent incarnation because He has

delivered Kṛṣṇa *premā* to the world. *Namo mahā-vadānyāya kṛṣṇa-prema-pradāya te kṛṣṇaya kṛṣṇa-caitanya-nāmne gaura-tviṣe namaḥ.*
Śyāmasundara dāsa: But the goal of the utilitarians is to achieve what the people desire and require.
Śrīla Prabhupāda: The people desire and require happiness, but they are searching for it in temporary things.

ṛṣabha uvāca
nāyaṁ deho deha-bhājāṁ nṛloke
kaṣṭān kāmān arhate viḍ-bhujāṁ ye
tapo divyaṁ putrakā yena sattvaṁ
śuddhyed yasmād brahma-saukhyaṁ tv anantam

"Lord Ṛṣabhadeva told His sons: My dear boys, of all the living entities who have accepted material bodies in this world, one who has been awarded this human form should not work hard day and night simply for sense gratification, which is available even for dogs and hogs that eat stool. One should engage in penance and austerity to attain the divine position of devotional service. By such activity, one's heart is purified, and when one attains this position, he attains eternal, blissful life, which is transcendental to material happiness, and which continues forever." (*Bhāg*. 5.5.1) Purify your existence, and you will attain eternal happiness and bliss. Everyone is working hard for happiness, but how can happiness be attained in a diseased condition? First the disease must be cured because it is an impediment to happiness. The real disease is *janma-mṛtyu-jarā-vyādhi (Bg*. 13.9): birth, old age, disease, and death. Cure these, and you will attain real happiness. Whatever you may desire, the ultimate end is happiness. Unfortunately, a diseased person is thinking, "I am happy." This is false happiness. Although you are dying, you are thinking that you are happy. This is called a fool's paradise.
Śyāmasundara dāsa: Dewey felt that the desirable course of action should meet certain conditions subject to prediction, and should be based on judgments or appraisals that might serve as guidelines to future activity.
Śrīla Prabhupāda: This is predictable: You say, "I don't want to die." I say, "Come to this position, and you will not die."
Śyāmasundara dāsa: Is there some experience that would show this to be a predictable result?
Śrīla Prabhupāda: Yes. You might not have the experience, but your superiors do.

ābrahma-bhuvanāl lokāḥ

punar āvartino'rjuna
mām upetya tu kaunteya
punar janma na vidyate

"From the highest planet in the material world down to the lowest, all are places of misery wherein repeated birth and death take place. But one who attains to My abode, O son of Kuntī, never takes birth again." (*Bg.* 8.16) If we go to Kṛṣṇa, we will never come back to this material world again. Who can excel Kṛṣṇa's experience? Since He knows past, present, and future, it is to our good to accept His instructions.

Śyāmasundara dāsa: Dewey would recommend basing our judgments on personal experience.

Śrīla Prabhupāda: We may not have personal experience, but we can take the advice of a person who does. Such experience is as good as our own. You may not have gone to New York, but because others have purchased tickets there and gone and returned, you can take advantage of their experience and learn something about that place.

Śyāmasundara dāsa: Dewey claims that value exists only where there is satisfaction.

Śrīla Prabhupāda: Unless you have faith in a person, how can you be satisfied? You should find a person in whom you can place your faith. Who can be a better person than Kṛṣṇa?

Śyāmasundara dāsa: If certain conditions are met, satisfaction is transformed into value. If my hunger is satisfied by eating certain food, that food is given value.

Śrīla Prabhupāda: It is Kṛṣṇa who gives that value. In the beginning of *Bhagavad-gītā*, Arjuna was refusing to fight, but because he valued Kṛṣṇa and was satisfied by his faith in Kṛṣṇa, he was victorious.

Śyāmasundara dāsa: For Dewey, moral laws may serve as guidelines for action. They are comparable to physical laws, in that if I act in a certain way, I can expect a certain result.

Śrīla Prabhupāda: We prescribe:

ādau śraddhā tataḥ sādhu-saṅgo 'tha bhajana-kriyā
tato 'nartha-nivṛttiḥ syāt tato niṣṭhā rucis tataḥ
athāsaktis tato bhāvas tataḥ premābhyudañcati
sādhakānām ayaṁ premṇaḥ prādurbhāve bhavet kramaḥ

"In the beginning, the neophyte devotee must have a preliminary desire for self-realization. This will bring him to the stage of trying to associate with persons who are spiritually elevated. In the next stage, he becomes initiated by an elevated spiritual master, and, under his instruction, begins the process of devotional service. By execution of devotional service under the guidance of the spiritual master, he becomes free from all material attachment, attains steadiness in self-realization, and acquires a taste for hearing about the Absolute Personality of Godhead, Śrī Kṛṣṇa. This taste leads him further forward to attachment for Kṛṣṇa consciousness, which is matured in *bhāva,* or the preliminary stage of transcendental love of God. Real love for God is called *premā,* the highest perfectional stage of life." (*Bhakti-rasāmṛta-sindhu*) If you follow one step after the other, you get the results. If you have faith, and associate with the devotees, you will be eager to execute devotional service. Then all misgivings are eradicated, and your faith becomes firm. Unless you experience the next result, how can you make progress? Moral guidelines are also given by Rūpa Gosvāmī:

utsāhān niścayād dhairyāt
tat-tat-karma-pravartanāt
saṅga-tyāgāt sato vṛtteḥ
ṣaḍbhir bhaktiḥ prasidhyati

"There are six principles favorable to the execution of pure devotional service: being enthusiastic, endeavoring with confidence, being patient, acting according to regulative principles [such as *śravaṇaṁ kīrtanaṁ viṣṇoḥ smaraṇam*—hearing, chanting, and remembering Kṛṣṇa], abandoning the association of nondevotees, and following in the footsteps of the previous *ācāryas.* These six principles undoubtedly assure the complete success of pure devotional service." (*Upadesāmṛta* 3) We should be patient, enthusiastic, and firmly convinced. We should be fair in our dealings, and should associate with saintly persons. In this way, we can advance.

Śyāmasundara dāsa: Then the results follow these guidelines predictably and automatically?

Śrīla Prabhupāda: Yes, one after another. A teacher instructs his students, and when they realize one instruction, he gives another, then another. In this way, the students can make progress. Consider the guidelines. First of all, we must be enthusiastic. Unless we are enthusiastic, how can we enter into any activity? We should also be patient. We should not think, "Oh, I am working so hard, but am getting no results." The results will come in time. We should also have firm conviction that because we have taken the path of the *mahājanas,* the path prescribed by Kṛṣṇa, success is imminent. Although success may be delayed, it doesn't really matter. We must know that success will definitely come. We must also perform our prescribed duties fairly and in good faith. And we should also associate with saintly people. This will give us impetus. If we follow these guidelines, the result is certain and predictable.

Śyāmasundara dāsa: Dewey believes that moral laws are not inflexible absolute rules that never permit exceptions.

Śrīla Prabhupāda: The real moral law is the law of the Supreme. In *Bhagavad-gītā*, Kṛṣṇa described many different types of yoga: *dhyāna-yoga, jñāna-yoga, haṭha-yoga*, and so on. However, at the end, He said, *sarva-dharmān parityajya*. "Abandon all these dharmas and surrender unto Me." (*Bg*. 18.66) Kṛṣṇa's word is the ultimate morality. Vaiṣṇavas do not consider this or that moral or immoral. Whatever Kṛṣṇa or His representative orders is moral. That is our position.

Śyāmasundara dāsa: Dewey claims that we place value upon that which we must act on.

Śrīla Prabhupāda: Yes, there is certainly value in Kṛṣṇa, and because Arjuna followed the decision of Kṛṣṇa, he became victorious, enjoyed his kingdom, and became a famous devotee. These were practical results of his activities. Parīkṣit Mahārāja compared the battle of Kurukṣetra to a great ocean in which Bhīṣma, Droṇa, Karṇa, and others were like great sharks. It was important for his grandfather, Arjuna, to cross that ocean, which was dangerously infested with many ferocious fish. Although this was very difficult, by the grace of Kṛṣṇa it was possible.

yatra yogeśvaraḥ kṛṣṇo
yatra pārtho dhanur-dharaḥ
tatra śrīr vijayo bhūtir
dhruvā nītir matir mama

"Wherever there is Kṛṣṇa, the master of all mystics, and wherever there is Arjuna, the supreme archer, there will also certainly be opulence, victory, extraordinary power, and morality. That is my opinion." (*Bg*. 18.78)

XII
EXISTENTIALISM

Soren Aabye Kierkegaard
(1813-1855)

Hayagrīva dāsa: Kierkegaard, a Danish philosopher, a Christian, is often called the father of existentialism. He believed that if the truths of religions are not innate within man, they must be transmitted by a teacher. Since man would be overawed by God, if God Himself came to teach as He is, God comes instead as a servant of God in human form, or, for a Christian, as Jesus Christ.

Śrīla Prabhupāda: Generally, because men are on the animal platform, some system of education is required. When man's consciousness is advanced, he can be educated in the understanding of God through the teachings of the authorities. That is the Vedic system. In the human form, the living entity is sometimes very inquisitive, and wants to understand God. That is technically called *brahma-jijñāsā*: interest in the Absolute. That is possible only in the human form. If we are anxious to know about God, we have to approach a guru, otherwise we cannot understand the nature of God or of our relationship with Him. Accepting a guru is not a fashion but a necessity. A guru is one who is fully trained in the ocean of spiritual knowledge, or Vedic knowledge. Vedic words or sound vibrations are not ordinary, material vibrations. They are completely spiritual. The Hare Kṛṣṇa *mahā-mantra*, for instance, is a purely spiritual sound. Once a person is fully trained in the ocean of spiritual sound, he is no longer interested in materialistic life. Nor does such a person manufacture gold, or juggle words to attract foolish people and make money. A guru by definition is one who is no longer interested in material things. He has taken shelter of the Supreme Lord, and his material desires have completely ceased. We should approach such a bona fide guru, surrender unto him, serve him, and then question him about God and our relationship with God.

Hayagrīva dāsa: Is Kierkegaard correct in maintaining that man would be overawed if God came to teach as He is? Didn't Kṛṣṇa, as He is, come to teach *Bhagavad-gītā*?

Śrīla Prabhupāda: Kṛṣṇa came as He is, but people misunderstood Him because He appeared to them as an ordinary human being. Because they could not surrender unto Him, He came later as a devotee, Caitanya Mahāprabhu, to teach men how to approach God. That is the concept of Śrī Caitanya Mahāprabhu. Sarvabhauma Bhaṭṭācārya understood His activities and wrote about a hundred verses in appreciation. Two of these verses read:

vairāgya-vidyā-nija-bhakti-yoga-
śikṣārtham ekaḥ puruṣaḥ purāṇaḥ
śrī-kṛṣṇa-caitanya-śarīra-dhārī
kṛpāmbudhir yas tam ahaṁ prapadye

kālān naṣṭaṁ bhakti-yogaṁ nijaṁ yaḥ
prāduṣkartuṁ kṛṣṇa-caitanya-nāmā
āvirbhūtas tasya pādāravinde
gāḍhaṁ gaḍhaṁ līyatāṁ citta-bhṛṅgaḥ

"Let me take shelter of the Supreme Personality of Godhead, Śrī Kṛṣṇa, who has descended in the form of Lord Caitanya Mahāprabhu to teach us real knowledge, His devotional service, and detachment from whatever does not foster Kṛṣṇa consciousness. He has descended because He is an ocean of transcendental mercy. Let me surrender unto His lotus feet. Let my consciousness, which is like a honeybee, take shelter of the lotus feet of the Supreme Personality of Godhead, who has just now appeared as Śrī Kṛṣṇa Caitanya Mahāprabhu to teach the ancient system of devotional service to Himself. This system had almost been lost due to the influence of time." (*Caitanya-caritāmṛta*, Madh. 6.254-255) Sarvabhauma Bhaṭṭācārya thus understood that Caitanya Mahāprabhu is the very same Kṛṣṇa come to teach *bhakti-yoga* and the process of renunciation. Śrī Caitanya Mahāprabhu taught the very same philosophy: *Bhagavad-gītā.* However, instead of coming as Kṛṣṇa, He came as a devotee of Kṛṣṇa. Rūpa Gosvāmī also appreciated Caitanya Mahāprabhu as the most munificent incarnation because He not only gives Kṛṣṇa, but pure love of Kṛṣṇa. *Namo mahā vadānyāya kṛṣṇa-prema-pradāya te.* In order to give Himself to the devotee, Kṛṣṇa demands full surrender, but Caitanya Mahāprabhu, without making any demands, gives pure love of Kṛṣṇa. Because we are all His sons, Kṛṣṇa, the Supreme Lord, is affectionate towards us. Because we are rotting in this material world, Kṛṣṇa comes Himself, or as a devotee, and leaves His instructions. He is always anxious to enlighten a human being and show him how to return home, back to Godhead.

Hayagrīva dāsa: Concerning God's personality, Kierkegaard writes: "God is certainly personal, but whether He wishes to be so in relation to the individual depends upon whether it pleases God. It is the grace of God that He wishes to be personal in relation to you; if you throw away His grace, He punishes you by behaving objectively [impersonally] towards you."

Śrīla Prabhupāda: That is a very good point. As stated in *Bhagavad-gītā:*

kleśo'dhikataras teṣām
avyaktāsakta-cetasām
avyaktā hi gatir duḥkhaṁ
dehavadbhir avāpyate

"For those whose minds are attached to the unmanifested, impersonal feature of the Supreme, advancement is very troublesome. To make progress in that discipline is always difficult for those who are embodied." (*Bg.* 12.5)

Hayagrīva dāsa: Because the ordinary man does not wish to have a personal relationship with God, "in that sense one may say that the world does not have a personal God, despite all the proofs....There are no longer the men living who could bear the pressure and weight of having a personal God."

Śrīla Prabhupāda: Yes, a personal God makes demands, just as Kṛṣṇa demands in *Bhagavad-gītā:*

man-manā bhava mad-bhakto
mad-yājī māṁ namaskuru
mām evaiṣyasi yuktvaivam
ātmānaṁ mat-parāyaṇaḥ

"Engage your mind always in thinking of Me, offer obeisances and worship Me. Being completely absorbed in Me, surely you will come to Me." (*Bg*. 9.34) This is God's demand, and if we carry it out, we attain perfection. *Tyaktvā dehaṁ punar janma naiti mām eti (Bg.* 4.9) It is clearly stated that when a devotee gives up his material body, he does not accept another, but returns back to Godhead in his original spiritual body.

Śyāmasundara dāsa: Kierkegaard observed three basic stages in a typical life: the aesthetic, the ethical, and the religious. In the aesthetic stage, a person may be either a hedonist in search of pleasure or romantic love, or an intellectual interested in philosophical speculation. Kierkegaard says that both are uncommitted because they do not have specific goals.

Śrīla Prabhupāda: How can a philosopher have no ultimate goal?

Śyāmasundara dāsa: On this platform, they are only mental speculators. They become bored, and their lives become empty.

Śrīla Prabhupāda: This is the result of impersonalism and voidism. Impersonalists or voidists are not necessarily overcome by despair, but they are often disgusted with their present lives because they do not know the aim of life. When one has no goal, he becomes disappointed in life, and that is the cause of despair.

Śyāmasundara dāsa: Kierkegaard sees men as indulging in sense gratification and mental speculation in order to cover up their basic despair.

Śrīla Prabhupāda: In the material world, when a man's business fails, or when he experiences some great shock, he takes to intoxication in order to forget.

Śyāmasundara dāsa: Kierkegaard suggests that this despair may serve as the first stepping stone toward self-realization. Understanding that the aesthetic life ends in despair, a person abandons it for the next stage.

Śrīla Prabhupāda: We agree with this. According to the *Vedānta-sūtra*, people begin to inquire about self-realization after they have worked very hard and still have not attained life's goal. At this point, people begin to think, "What is the purpose of life?" That is called *brahma-jijñāsā*, inquiry into the ultimate truth of life. Such an inquiry is natural, and necessary for further development.

Śyāmasundara dāsa: In order to attain self-realization, we must face certain choices. For Kierkegaard, life is an "either/or" decision. Realizing this, we advance to the ethical stage. The emphasis here is on action.

Śrīla Prabhupāda: First of all, we must understand how action or activity comes about. What is the origin of action? Modern science is interested in describing or witnessing life's activities, and scientists claim that life develops automatically due to nature's interactions, but from *Bhagavad-gītā* we understand that behind all these material activities, there is God. Material nature is a machine working under God's directions. *Vedānta-sūtra* explains that the Absolute Truth is that from which all things emanate, and *Śrīmad-Bhāgavatam* discusses the nature of that origin. First, we must understand that the origin is consciousness. Life does not arise from bones and stones. Once we understand that the creation does not take place automatically, we must admit that there is a creator.

Śyāmasundara dāsa: At the ethical stage, man may perform pious works or humanitarian deeds, and Kierkegaard sees this as a step in the right direction toward authentic selfhood. By making the proper ethical decisions, we can approach self-awareness and the religious stage.

Śrīla Prabhupāda: But what is the ultimate decision? Why do people become moral? Simply to feed the poor and become humanitarians?

Śyāmasundara dāsa: For Kierkegaard, it does not much matter what we choose, but the fact that we make the choice. Through choosing, we discover our own integrity.

Śrīla Prabhupāda: But it is not clear how a person makes the right decisions. One man may choose to slaughter, and another may choose to help others. A man may give charity to others, and at the same time encourage killing animals. What are the ethics involved? On the one hand, Vivekananda was advocating feeding the poor, but on the other hand he was suggesting feeding them with Mother Kālī's prasādam, with bulls. So what kind of ethics are these? What is the value of ethics if they are based on imperfect knowledge?

Śyāmasundara dāsa: Kierkegaard would say that by turning inward, we would make the proper decision. This entails self-knowledge and self-commitment.

Śrīla Prabhupāda: But what is that inwardness? One may simply think, "I will protect my brother by killing another." What are the ethics involved? We must have some standard by which to make the right decision.

Śyāmasundara dāsa: His standard would be, "Choose thyself."

Śrīla Prabhupāda: But without knowing yourself, how can you make a choice? And how can you know yourself unless you go to one who knows things as they are? Most people think that they are the body. What kind of self-knowledge is this? If one identifies with the body, he is no better than an ass. Then what is the value of his philosophy?

yasyātma-buddhiḥ kuṇape tridhātuke

sva-dhīḥ kalatrādiṣu bhauma ijya-dhīḥ
yat-tīrtha-buddhiḥ salile na karhicij
janeṣv abhijñeṣu sa eva go-kharaḥ

"A human being who identifies this body made of three elements with his self, who considers the by-products of the body to be his kinsmen, who considers the land of birth worshipable, and who goes to the places of pilgrimage simply to take a bath rather than meet men of transcendental knowledge there, is to be considered like an ass or cow." (*Bhag.* 10.84.13)

Śyāmasundara dāsa: Kierkegaard emphasizes the very act of deciding, not the decision.

Śrīla Prabhupāda: But unless we know the aim of life, how can we make the right decision? It is childish to say that we become enlightened by choosing either this or that. A child chooses to play sometimes with one toy and sometimes with another, but where is his enlightenment? Animals also make their decisions. The ass decides to eat a morsel of grass and work all day carrying loads. If the decision is not important, why not decide for unrestricted sense gratification?

Śyāmasundara dāsa: Kierkegaard would say that unrestricted sense gratification ultimately leads to boredom and despair.

Śrīla Prabhupāda: But if we think that it is the aim of life, it is not boring. If we choose according to our whims, we can make any decision. A man on the Bowery may decide to purchase a bottle of whiskey as soon as he gets some money.

Śyāmasundara dāsa: Kierkegaard would say that there is no commitment to a higher ethic there. On the ethical level, we would have to take up a good cause and make decisions based on that.

Śrīla Prabhupāda: But such good causes are relative. Who is to decide what's a good cause?

Śyāmasundara dāsa: If we begin to anticipate death, we will make the right decision, considering each act to be our last. In this way, the truth will emerge.

Śrīla Prabhupāda: Yes, a man should think, "I do not wish to die, but death is overcoming me. What is the cause of this? What should I do?" No one wants to die, but death overcomes everyone. No one wants to be diseased, but diseases are inevitable. These are real human problems that cannot be overcome simply by making some whimsical decisions. We should decide, "I do not wish to suffer, but suffering is coming upon me. Now, I must make a permanent solution to this problem." This is the real decision: putting a permanent end to suffering. We should understand that the body exists for a few years and then is doomed to perish, that the body is external, and that we should not make our decisions on the basis of the body, but the soul.

Śyāmasundara dāsa: For Kierkegaard, a man whose consciousness is unhappy is alienated from both past and future. He wishes to forget the past, and the future holds no hope. In proper consciousness, when the personality is integrated, the past and future are unified, and we can make the proper decision.

Śrīla Prabhupāda: Your decision should be based on the fact that you are part and parcel of Kṛṣṇa. Kṛṣṇa told Arjuna that in the past he was existing, and that he would continue to exist in the future. Our decision should be based on the platform of the soul.

Śyāmasundara dāsa: Kierkegaard sees the self as unifying past and future and thus establishing its integrity as an integrated whole. Then the self is capable of making decisions.

Śrīla Prabhupāda: If he comes to the platform of the self, he must accept the fact that the self is eternal in order to integrate past, present, and future.

Śyāmasundara dāsa: Yes, this is the highest stage, the religious. On this platform, one commits himself to God and obeys God.

Śrīla Prabhupāda: That would be the stage of Kṛṣṇa consciousness.

Śyāmasundara dāsa: Kierkegaard believed that in the religious stage, there is intense suffering, comparable to the suffering of Job.

Śrīla Prabhupāda: Why is this? If one is Kṛṣṇa conscious, why should he suffer?

Śyāmasundara dāsa: Well, Kierkegaard was a Christian. Christ suffered for our sins, and the process of overcoming sin is a kind of suffering.

Śrīla Prabhupāda: But that is a wrong theory. If Christ is God, or the son of God, why should he suffer? What kind of God is subjected to suffering? Why should either God or man suffer? The whole point is that if there is suffering, you must put an end to it. Many so-called Christians think that because they have some contract with Christ, because Christ suffered for their sins, they can go on sinning. Is this a very good philosophy?

Śyāmasundara dāsa: As an existentialist, Kierkegaard believed that existence is prior to essence, and that to attain self-realization, we must pass through these various stages.

Śrīla Prabhupāda: That is correct. We are transmigrating through different species and eventually arriving at the human form wherein we can understand the purpose of life. At the perfectional stage, we become

Kṛṣṇa conscious; therefore existence precedes essence.

Śyāmasundara dāsa: For Kierkegaard, the culmination of commitment is religious life, which is epitomized in the inwardness of suffering.

Śrīla Prabhupāda: Suffering arises because we identify with the body. When a person has an automobile accident, he may not actually suffer, but because he identifies himself with matter, with the body, he suffers. Because God is always in full knowledge and is always transcendental to the material world, God never suffers. It is a question of knowledge whether there is suffering or not.

Śyāmasundara dāsa: But don't penance and austerity involve suffering?

Śrīla Prabhupāda: No. For those who are advanced in knowledge, there is no suffering. Of course, there may be some bodily pain, but a person in knowledge understands that he is not the body; therefore, why should he suffer? He thinks, "Let me do my duty. Hare Kṛṣṇa." That is the advanced stage. Suffering is due to ignorance.

Śyāmasundara dāsa: But doesn't one forsake bodily comforts by serving God?

Śrīla Prabhupāda: Rūpa and Sanātana Gosvāmī were high government ministers, but they abandoned their material opulence in order to bestow mercy upon the common people. Thus they accepted a mere loincloth and slept under a different tree every night. Of course, foolish people might say that they were suffering, but they were merged in the ocean of transcendental bliss writing about Kṛṣṇa's pastimes with the *gopīs*. They engaged their minds in thoughts of Kṛṣṇa and the *gopīs*, and they wrote books from day to day. There was no question of their suffering, although a fool may think, "Oh, these men were ministers, high government officials, and they were so comfortable with their families and homes. Now they have no home, and are going about in loincloths, and eating very little." A materialist would think that they were suffering, but they were not suffering. They were enjoying.

Śyāmasundara dāsa: Some Christians emphasize the value of suffering, thinking that to abandon worldly life is to abandon pleasure and to suffer.

Śrīla Prabhupāda: This is due to a poor fund of knowledge. They have developed this philosophy after the demise of Jesus Christ. It is more or less concocted.

Hayagrīva dāsa: Apart from suffering, Kierkegaard emphasized the importance of love in the religious life. In his book *Works of Love*, he considers God to be the hidden source of all love. "God you must love in unconditional obedience," he writes, "even if that which He demands of you may seem injurious to you....For God's wisdom is incomparable with respect to your own...."

Śrīla Prabhupāda: Yes, that is also the instruction of *Bhagavad-gītā*. God demands that we give up all our plans as well as the plans of others, and accept His plan. *Sarva-dharmān parityajya (Bg.* 18.66). "Abandon all varieties of religion and just surrender unto Me." If we fully depend on Kṛṣṇa, the Supreme Personality of Godhead, He will guide us home.

Hayagrīva dāsa: In defining love, Kierkegaard points out that St. Paul considered love to be "the fulfillment of the law." "Love is a matter of conscience," Kierkegaard writes, "and hence it is not a matter of impulse and inclination; nor is it a matter of emotion, nor a matter for intellectual calculation.... Christianity really knows only one kind of love, spiritual love...."

Śrīla Prabhupāda: Yes, love in the material world is impossible, because everyone is interested only in his own sense gratification. The love experienced between men and women is not actually love, but lust, because both parties are interested in their own sense gratification. Love means that one does not think of his own sense gratification, but of the sense gratification of his beloved. That is pure love, and that is not possible in the material world. We see examples of pure love, however, in the Vedic depictions of Vṛndāvana, a village wherein men, animals, fruits, flowers, water, and everything else exist only for the sake of loving Kṛṣṇa. They are not interested in any return from Kṛṣṇa. Now, that is real love. *Anyābhilāṣitāśūnyam.* If one loves God with some motive, that is material love. Pure love is interested only in satisfying the desires of the Supreme Personality of Godhead. When we speak of love in the material world, we are misusing the word. Lusty desires take the place of real love. Real love applies only to God—individually, collectively, or any other way. Kṛṣṇa, the Supreme Personality of Godhead, is the supreme object of love, and this love can be expressed through adoration, service, or friendship. Or we can love Him as a child, or as a conjugal lover. There are five basic relationships expressing true love of Godhead.

Hayagrīva dāsa: For Kierkegaard, love of God is the decisive factor, and from it stems love of neighbor. "If you love God above all else," he writes, "then you also love your neighbor, and in your neighbor, every man....To help another man to love God is to love the other man; to be helped by another man to love God is to be loved."

Śrīla Prabhupāda: That is the basis of our Kṛṣṇa consciousness movement. We're learning how to love God, and teaching the same principle to the whole world. We're teaching that God is one, and that no one is equal to Him, nor greater than Him. God is never dead. If love of God is taught by a religion, that religion should be considered first class, be it Christian, Hindu, Moslem, or whatever. The test of a religion is this: "Have the followers learned how to love God?" God is the center of love, and since everything is God's expansion, a lover of God is a lover of everyone. He does not discriminate by thinking that only man should be loved and given service. No. He is interested in all living entities, regardless of the forms in which they are existing. A lover of God loves everyone, and his love reaches everyone. When we water the root of a tree, we are nourishing all parts of the tree: the trunk, branches, twigs, and leaves. When we give the stomach food, we satisfy the entire body. God is everything. As stated in *Bhagavad-gītā, mayā tatam idaṁ sarvam* (*Bg.* 9.4). Nothing can exist without God because everything is His expansion. *Viṣṇu Purāṇa* says that God is present everywhere, although situated in His own abode, just as the light and heat of the sun are present everywhere, although the sun is situated in one place. God is all pervading. Nothing can exist without Him. At the same time, this does not mean that everything is God. Rather, everything is resting on His energy. Despite His expansions, He maintains His personality.

Śyāmasundara dāsa: Kierkegaard also considered faith to be an important part of religion. For him, the opposite of faith is sin, which is the same as despair.

Śrīla Prabhupāda: If you are in Kṛṣṇa consciousness, there is no question of sin. It is not a question of faith, but of fact. At the beginning of *Bhagavad-gītā,* Arjuna did not want to fight, but he finally decided to abide by the order of Kṛṣṇa. That is piety: satisfying the higher authority, God. In the material world, we imagine this or that to be sinful or pious, but these are mental concoctions. They have no value.

Śyāmasundara dāsa: Kierkegaard would define piety as faith in the orders of God.

Śrīla Prabhupāda: That means he must receive God's orders. But if a person has no conception of God, if he conceives of God impersonally, there is no question of God's orders. If God is impersonal, He has no mouth with which to speak, no eyes with which to see. Therefore there is no question of His giving orders.

Hayagrīva dāsa: In his *Journals,* Kierkegaard writes: "There is a God; His will is made known to me in holy scripture and in my conscience. This God wishes to intervene in the world. But how is He to do so except with the help of man?"

Śrīla Prabhupāda: *Sādhu-śāstra-guru.* We can approach God by understanding a saintly person, studying the Vedic scriptures, and following the instructions of the bona fide spiritual master. *Sādhu, śāstra,* and guru should corroborate. A *sādhu* is one who talks in terms of the scriptures, and the guru is one who teaches according to the scriptures. A guru cannot manufacture words that are not in the *śāstras*. When we receive instructions from all three, we can progress perfectly in our understanding of the Supreme Personality of Godhead.

Hayagrīva dāsa: Kierkegaard writes: "The only adequate way to express a sense of God's majesty is to worship Him....It is so easy to see that one to whom everything is equally important and equally insignificant can only be interested in one thing: obedience."

Śrīla Prabhupāda: Yes, and God demands that full obedience: *sarva-dharmān parityajya mām ekaṁ śaraṇaṁ vraja (Bg.* 18.66). Our original obedience should be to the Supreme Personality of Godhead, and we should obey the spiritual master because he is God's representative. If a person does not directly receive the orders of God, he cannot be a bona fide guru. A guru cannot manufacture anything; he simply presents what God speaks in the *śāstras*. When God comes as an incarnation, He also gives references to the scriptures, just as Kṛṣṇa referred to the *Brahma-sūtra* in *Bhagavad-gītā*. Although Kṛṣṇa is God, and His word is final, He still gives honor to the *Brahma-sūtra* because in that work spiritual knowledge is set forth logically and philosophically. It is not that we accept just anyone's proclamations about God. Statements must be corroborated by the standard scriptures.

Hayagrīva dāsa: Kierkegaard says that we should "renounce everything as an act of worship offered to God, and not so because He needs to use us as an instrument; but to renounce everything as the most insignificant superfluity and article of luxury—that means to worship."

Śrīla Prabhupāda: Yes, worship begins with the renunciation of ulterior motives. Our only business is to love God, and a first-class religious system teaches its followers to love God without ulterior motive. Such worship cannot be checked by material considerations. We can love God in any condition, and God will help.

Śyāmasundara dāsa: Kierkegaard lamented the disintegration of Christianity as an effective form of worship. He considered modern Christendom to be a kind of sickness, a corruption of Christ's original message.

Śrīla Prabhupāda: Christianity is Christianity, and you cannot call it modern or ancient, nor can you say that God is modern or ancient. We say that either a person is a Christian or not. Either he follows the orders of Christ, or he doesn't. If you do not follow the tenets of your religion, how can you claim to belong to that religion? This applies to all religions. For instance, there are many so-called Hindus who do not believe in anything, yet they consider themselves Hindus and *brāhmaṇas*. This is insulting.

Śyāmasundara dāsa: Kierkegaard saw Christian despair as a "sickness unto death." The wish to die is the result of despair.

Śrīla Prabhupāda: People try to avoid the results of their sinful activities by killing themselves, but this is not possible. Suicide is just another sin. Therefore those who commit suicide become ghosts.

Śyāmasundara dāsa: Kierkegaard believed that a man should live as if he were to die at any moment. He should act as if each act were to be his last.

Śrīla Prabhupāda: This requires practice, and therefore we are recommending the chanting of Hare Kṛṣṇa without cessation. Of course, death may come at any moment, and if we are chanting Hare Kṛṣṇa, that death is a happy death.

Śyāmasundara dāsa: According to Catholicism, at the time of death, a priest can absolve you of your sins.

Śrīla Prabhupāda: Provided you have the consciousness to understand the words of the priest.

Śyāmasundara dāsa: Even though one has committed many sins throughout his life, he can be absolved of his sins on his deathbed.

Śrīla Prabhupāda: That is quite possible because a priest can remind you of God at the time of death. Your thoughts at the time of death are very important. There are so many examples: Ajāmila, and Bharata Mahārāja. Therefore King Kulaśekhara prays, "Let me die immediately while I am thinking of Kṛṣṇa." Of course, unless we are practiced, it is not possible to think of Kṛṣṇa at the time of death, because at that time there are many bodily disturbances. Therefore from the beginning, austerities are required.

Hayagrīva dāsa: Kierkegaard writes: "The true relation in prayer is not when God hears what is prayed for, but when the person praying continues to pray until he is the one who hears what God wills."

Śrīla Prabhupāda: Yes, that is very nice. Through prayer, one becomes qualified to understand God, talk with God, and receive His directions.

teṣāṁ satata-yuktānāṁ
bhajatāṁ prīti-pūrvakam
dadāmi buddhi-yogaṁ taṁ
yena māṁ upayānti te

"To those who are constantly devoted and worship Me with love, I give the understanding by which they can come to Me." (*Bg.* 10.10) Our ultimate goal is to give up this material world and return to God. Prayer is just one form of service. There are nine basic processes we can follow in the rendering of devotional service:

śravaṇaṁ kīrtanaṁ viṣṇoḥ
smaraṇaṁ pāda-sevanam
arcanaṁ vandanaṁ dāsyaṁ
sakhyam ātma-nivedanam

"Hearing and chanting about the holy name, form, qualities, paraphernalia and pastimes of Lord Viṣṇu, remembering them, serving the lotus feet of the Lord, offering the Lord respectful worship with sixteen types of paraphernalia, offering prayers to the Lord, becoming His servant, considering the Lord one's best friend, and surrendering everything unto Him—these nine processes are accepted as pure devotional service." (*Bhāg.* 7.5.23) Prayer is *vandanam.* If we accept all nine processes, or just one of them, we can progress in spiritual life. Christians and Mohammedans offer prayers, and Hindus render service in the temple. The Deities are decorated, the temples are cleansed, and food is offered. This is called *arcanam*, and through this process we can engage in devotional service. God is within, and when He sees that we are sincere in His service, He takes charge and gives directions by which we can swiftly approach Him. God is complete in Himself; He is not hankering after our service, but if we offer Him service, we can become purified. When we are purified, we can talk with God and see Him. We can receive His instructions personally, just as Arjuna did.

Śyāmasundara dāsa: For Kierkegaard, faith is revealed in the self's relation to its own self, through its willingness to be its authentic self and to stand transparently before God in full integrity.

Śrīla Prabhupāda: For the Māyāvādīs, self-realization means becoming one with the Supreme Self, but such merging is not possible. Standing transparent before God means engaging in God's service. To engage in God's service, you must understand that you are part and parcel of the Supreme. A part of the body engages in the service of the entire body. As soon as you engage in God's service, you are self-realized. That is *mukti*, liberation. The *karmīs*, *jñānīs*, and yogīs are trying to realize the self, but because they are not engaged in rendering service to the Supreme Self, they are not liberated. We are therefore pushing this Kṛṣṇa consciousness for the ultimate self-realization of everyone.

Śyāmasundara dāsa: Kierkegaard sees self-realization arising out of the expression of the will. The more self-realized a person is, the more will he has. When we are fully ourselves, we are fully willed, and able to make the proper decisions.
Śrīla Prabhupāda: But if you are part and parcel of the whole, you have to take decisions from the whole. You cannot make the decisions. A finger does not make decisions for the entire body. The only decision you can make is the decision to serve Kṛṣṇa. The orders come from the superior. Arjuna was ordered by Kṛṣṇa to fight, and at the conclusion of *Bhagavad-gītā,* he decided to abide by Kṛṣṇa's will. This is the only decision we can make: to abide by Kṛṣṇa's will or not. Kṛṣṇa or His representative makes all the other decisions.
Śyāmasundara dāsa: Then what is the meaning of full will?
Śrīla Prabhupāda: Full will means to surrender fully, to follow absolutely the orders of the Supreme.
Śyāmasundara dāsa: Kierkegaard saw that even despair can bear fruit in that it can lead us to desire a genuine life of self-realization. It can be a springboard for a higher consciousness.
Śrīla Prabhupāda: When one despairs, that is a great happiness. Then everything is finished. All responsibility is gone, and the person is relieved. Out of despair, Arjuna was thinking of becoming a mendicant. When we despair of all happiness in material life, we may then turn to spiritual life. Sometimes Kṛṣṇa smashes all of our material resources so that out of despair we may fully engage in Kṛṣṇa's service. Kṛṣṇa sometimes wrecks a person materially when a person wants to become God conscious but at the same time wants material enjoyment due to strong attachment. Sometimes, when God smashes a person's material hopes, the person thinks that God is unkind to him, and the person despairs. He doesn't realize that this is God's mercy, that God is removing impediments so that the person can fully and absolutely surrender.

Once Indra, the king of heaven, was forced to be a hog, and he had to enter the material world as a lowly animal. As a hog, he had a hog-wife, hog-children, and so on. Finally, Lord Brahmā came down and told him, "My dear Indra, you have forgotten your position. You were once a heavenly king and possessed great opulence. Now that you are a hog, you have forgotten your previous exalted existence. Please leave this filthy life and come with me." Yet, despite all Brahmā's pleadings, Indra was not convinced. He said, "Why should I go with you? I am very happy. I have my wife, children, and home." Seeing that Indra had become very much attached to his hog-existence, Brahmā began to kill all his hog-children, and eventually his hog-wife. When Indra saw that his wife was killed, he despaired: "Oh! You have killed all my family!" It was only then that Indra agreed to go with Lord Brahmā. Similarly, Kṛṣṇa sometimes creates a situation in which the living entity will despair, and, out of despair, turn to Kṛṣṇa and fully surrender unto Him.

Śyāmasundara dāsa: Kierkegaard was considering the despair of thinking, "Oh, I am a sinner," and believing that we will never be relieved of sin. He claims that this leads us even further into a sinful life.

Śrīla Prabhupāda: There is no question of despair because of sin. A person sins out of ignorance. If you ask a butcher, "Why are you committing sins?" he will say, "This is my business. What is sinful about it?" When Nārada informed the hunter that killing animals was sinful, the hunter did not despair, but was elevated to Kṛṣṇa consciousness by Nārada's instructions.

Śyāmasundara dāsa: Kierkegaard believes that faith conquers sin and despair.

Śrīla Prabhupāda: Faith means faith in God. To strengthen our faith in God, we have to give up all hope of happiness in this material life. We have to despair of material happiness.

Śyāmasundara dāsa: For Kierkegaard, existence is continuous and therefore forever incomplete.

Śrīla Prabhupāda: The system is complete when we surrender unto Kṛṣṇa. God has a complete system by which we can progress to God consciousness. When we become fully conscious, we have attained completion. As long as we have not reached that point, we are progressing.

Hayagrīva dāsa: "God is the wellspring of all individuality," Kierkegaard writes. "To have individuality is to believe in the individuality of everyone else; for the individuality is not mine; it is the gift of God through which He permits me to be, and through which He permits everyone to be."

Śrīla Prabhupāda: This fact is also explained in *Kaṭha-upaniṣad: nityo nityānāṁ cetanaś cetanānām.* God is a living being, and we are also living beings. Just as He is eternal, we are also eternal. Qualitatively, we are one; but quantitatively, we are different. God is maintaining everyone, and all the living entities are being maintained. We are all individual, eternal parts of God, and our natural position, being parts of Him, is to love Him.

Śyāmasundara dāsa: Kierkegaard sees the individual in a continuous state of becoming.

Śrīla Prabhupāda: Becoming what? What is the goal? The goal is Kṛṣṇa consciousness. Therefore in *Bhagavad-gītā*, Kṛṣṇa says:

mattaḥ parataraṁ nānyat
kiñcid asti dhanañjaya
mayi sarvam idaṁ protaṁ
sūtre maṇigaṇā iva

"O conqueror of wealth, there is no truth superior to Me. Everything rests upon Me as pearls are strung on a thread." (*Bg.* 7.7) Kṛṣṇa is the ultimate truth, the supreme goal, and completion means coming to Kṛṣṇa consciousness.

Śyāmasundara dāsa: But isn't there still a process of becoming, even when we are fully Kṛṣṇa conscious and in association with Kṛṣṇa?

Śrīla Prabhupāda: No. The becoming process ends. There are, however, varieties, which are spiritual. Everything is complete, but varieties are enjoyed. Sometimes, Kṛṣṇa is a cowherd boy, sometimes He is Yaśodā's child, sometimes He is Rādhārāṇī's consort, sometimes He is in Mathurā, sometimes He is in Vṛndāvana. There are many spiritual varieties, but everything is complete in itself. There is no question of becoming. We reach the point where we are simply enjoying variety. That is all.

Śyāmasundara dāsa: What is the difference between spiritual variety and material variety?

Śrīla Prabhupāda: Material variety is artificial. It is like a man satisfied with a plastic flower. Enjoyment of a plastic flower cannot be the same as the enjoyment of a real flower. A plastic flower has no aroma. It is artificial, bluff.

Śyāmasundara dāsa: Whereas Hegel emphasized speculative thought, Kierkegaard emphasized action. He saw freedom in proper action.

Śrīla Prabhupāda: Yes, spiritual life means proper action. It is improper to think that one is inactive when he attains the perfectional stage. That is the Māyāvādī theory. Māyāvādīs contend that a jug will make a big sound if it is not full of water. They equate fullness with silence. But from *Bhagavad-gītā*, we understand that the soul is never inactive. Sometimes, however, we see that inactivity is recommended. This means that we should not speak or act foolishly. If we cannot talk intelligently, we had better stop talking. But that inactivity cannot be equated with perfection.

Śyāmasundara dāsa: Kierkegaard found truth in the relative and subjective, in personal, individual reflection, in what he calls "inward passion."

Śrīla Prabhupāda: Truth is truth, and that is absolute. You may manufacture relative truths, but the Absolute Truth is one. If we have no knowledge of the Absolute Truth, we emphasize relative truths. There may be inward passion, or whatever, but if we do not know the ultimate goal, we may be misled. It is all right to say that passion is truth, but passion means activity. Where will your activity end? What is the purpose of your activity? You may drive your car, but if you do not know where to go, what is the point? You are wasting your energy. Of course, one may say, "I do not know where to go, but that doesn't matter. Just let me start my car and go." But is this a very good proposal?

Śyāmasundara dāsa: For Kierkegaard, it is not what is done, but how it is done.

Śrīla Prabhupāda: This is a dog's obstinacy.

Śyāmasundara dāsa: This is a kind of subjectivity that is always uncertain. Uncertainty creates anxiety.

Śrīla Prabhupāda: One who does not know life's aim will always be in anxiety.

Śyāmasundara dāsa: For Kierkegaard, this anxiety and uncertainty are dispelled by what he calls "the leap of faith."

Śrīla Prabhupāda: Yes, but the leap must be made when there is a goal. Unless you know the goal, the fixed point, your passion and energy may be misused, misdirected.

Śyāmasundara dāsa: As a Christian, Kierkegaard felt that our energy should be used to reach God through Christ.

Śrīla Prabhupāda: That is a good position. That is our process. But it is not necessary to pass through the lower stages. Why not take to God immediately, if you can reach God through Jesus Christ? Our process is that you must surrender yourself to the guru in order to understand the highest truth.

tad viddhi praṇipātena
paripraśnena sevayā
upadekṣyanti te jñānaṁ
jñāninas tattva-darśinaḥ

"Just try to learn the truth by approaching a spiritual master. Inquire from him submissively and render service unto him. The self-realized soul can impart knowledge unto you because he has seen the truth." (*Bg.* 4.34) *Śrīmad-Bhāgavatam* also states:

tasmād guruṁ prapadyeta
jijñāsuḥ śreya uttamam
śābde pare ca niṣṇātaṁ

brahmaṇy upaśamāśrayam

"Any person who is seriously desirous of achieving real happiness must seek out a bona fide spiritual master and take shelter of him by initiation. The qualification of a spiritual master is that he must have realized the conclusion of the scriptures by deliberation and arguments and thus be able to convince others of these conclusions. Such great personalities who have taken complete shelter of the Supreme Godhead, leaving aside all material consideration, are to be understood as bona fide spiritual masters." (*Bhāg.* 11.3.21) This is the process. It is not that we continue in our own way, hoping to take the right path through experience. In the middle of the vast ocean, you do not know where to direct your ship. You may go one way, and then you may go another. If you do not know the direction, your endeavors will be frustrated. A captain, a compass, and a sextant are needed. The captain is the guru who gives directions. If you have a ship without a captain, you will go one way and then another, and waste your energy. If Kierkegaard accepts Christ, he is accepting some guidance.

Śyāmasundara dāsa: Kierkegaard says: "God does not think, He creates; God does not exist, He is eternal. Man thinks and exists, and existence separates thought and being."

Śrīla Prabhupāda: What does he mean that God is eternal and does not exist?

Śyāmasundara dāsa: For him, the word "existence" refers to that which is coming into being. God does not "exist" in the sense that He is always the same.

Śrīla Prabhupāda: That means He is perfect. God does not progress from one state to another. If that is Kierkegaard's philosophy, he should agree to follow the orders of God. Why experiment? God is omnipotent and all powerful. We agree that He does not have to make plans. He creates automatically. His energies are so perfect and subtle, that as soon as He thinks, a thing is realized. It is created perfectly.

Śyāmasundara dāsa: Kierkegaard sees man's existence as a state of constantly becoming. Man's thought is separate from his being.

Śrīla Prabhupāda: Then why not unite thought and being by surrendering to Kṛṣṇa?

Jean-Paul Sartre
(1905-1980)

Hayagrīva dāsa: Descartes and Leibnitz believed that before the creation, the concept of man existed in essence in the mind of God, just as a machine exists in the mind of its manufacturer before it is constructed. Sartre takes exception to this. In *The Humanism of Existentialism,* he writes: "Atheistic existentialism, which I represent, is more coherent. It states that if God does not exist, there is at least one being in whom existence precedes essence, a being who exists before he can be defined by any concept, and that this being is man, or, as Heidegger says, human reality."

Śrīla Prabhupāda: But where does human reality come from? There are also other realities. Why is he stressing human reality?

Hayagrīva dāsa: As for man's origin, Sartre would say that man is "thrown into the world."

Śrīla Prabhupāda: Thrown by whom? The word "throw" implies a thrower.

Hayagrīva dāsa: Sartre isn't really interested in a thrower. "Existentialism isn't so atheistic that it wears itself out showing God doesn't exist," he writes. "Rather, it declares that even if God did exist, that would change nothing. There you've got our point of view. Not that we believe that God exists, but that we think that the problem of His existence is not the issue."

Śrīla Prabhupāda: But if you and others exist, why doesn't God exist? Why deny God and His existence? Let them all exist.

Śyāmasundara dāsa: Since Sartre sees man as having been thrown into the world and abandoned, for him, God is dead.

Śrīla Prabhupāda: Abandoned by God does not mean that God is dead. You have to admit that you are condemned to the material world, but just because you are condemned, you should not think that God is also condemned. God is always in Vaikuṇṭha. He is not dead.

Śyāmasundara dāsa: Sartre believes that because we have been abandoned, we must rely on ourselves alone.

Śrīla Prabhupāda: But God has not abandoned us. God is not partial. He does not accept one person and abandon another. If you feel abandoned, it is because you have done something that has brought this condition about. If you rectify your position, you will be accepted again.

Hayagrīva dāsa: But Sartre would deny God's existence, particularly that of a personal God.

Śrīla Prabhupāda: But his denial should be based on some logic or reason. Why mention the word "God," if God does not exist? God is there, but Sartre denies God's existence. This is inconsistent. If God does not exist, why even mention the word? His proposal is that he does not want God to exist.

Hayagrīva dāsa: He wants to set the whole question aside in order to place emphasis on man, on human reality.

Śrīla Prabhupāda: If you believe in your existence, why not believe in the existence of another? There are 8,400,000 different species existing in multifarious forms. Why shouldn't God exist? According to the Vedic understanding, God is also a living being, but He is different in that He is the chief, supreme living being. According to *Bhagavad-gītā*, *mattaḥ parataraṁ nānyat (Bg.* 7.7). There is no living being superior to God. We all experience the fact that there are beings more intelligent than we. God is the ultimate intelligence. Why can't a person who exceeds all others in intelligence exist? There is no question of "if God exists." God must exist. In the *śāstras* He is described as the superlative personality, as the super powerful, the super intelligent. We can see in this world that everyone is not on an equal level, that there are varying degrees of perfection. This indicates that there is a superlative, and if we go on searching—either for wealth, intelligence, power, beauty, or whatever—

we will find that God possesses all qualities to the superlative degree, and that every other living entity possesses qualities in degrees relative to Him. How, then, can we rationally deny His existence?

Hayagrīva dāsa: According to Sartre, the first principle of existentialism is that "man is nothing else but what he makes of himself." This can be true only if there is no God to conceive of human nature.

Śrīla Prabhupāda: If man is what he makes of himself, why doesn't man exist as a superman? If his capacities are completely independent of anyone else, why is he in his present situation?

Hayagrīva dāsa: That is also Sartre's question. He therefore emphasizes man's responsibility. "But if existence really does precede essence," he writes, "man is responsible for what he is. Thus existentialism's first move is to make every man aware of what he is and to make the full responsibility of his existence rest on him."

Śrīla Prabhupāda: If man is responsible, who gave him this responsibility? What does he mean by responsibility? You feel responsible to someone when someone gives you duties to discharge. If there is no duty, or overseer, where is your responsibility?

Śyāmasundara dāsa: Sartre sees man as being overwhelmed by his very responsibility. He is in anguish and anxiety because he has the freedom to change himself and the world.

Śrīla Prabhupāda: This means that man is in an awkward position. He wants peace, but he does not know how to attain it. But this does not mean that peace is not possible. Peace is not possible for a man in ignorance.

Śyāmasundara dāsa: Anxiety arises from responsibility. Man thinks that he has to choose properly in order to enjoy something. If he chooses wrongly, he must suffer.

Śrīla Prabhupāda: Yes, responsibility is there, but why not take it to transfer yourself to a safe place where there is no anxiety? It may be that you do not know of a safe place, but if there is such a place, why not ask someone who knows? Why constantly remain disappointed and anxious? The safe place where there is no anxiety is called Vaikuṇṭha. The word Vaikuṇṭha means "no anxiety."

Hayagrīva dāsa: Sartre believes that the task of existentialism is "to make every man aware of what he is and to make the full responsibility of his existence rest on him..... And when we say that a man is responsible for himself, we do not only mean that he is responsible for his own individuality, but that he is responsible for all men."

Śrīla Prabhupāda: Suppose I want to benefit you, and you are free. Your freedom means that you can accept or reject my good intentions. How can I be responsible for you if you don't obey? How can you be responsible for me? Sartre claims that you are responsible for others, but if others do not follow your instructions, how can you be considered responsible? This is all contradictory. Unless there is some standard, there must be contradiction. According to the Vedic version, God is the Supreme Person, and we should all be His obedient servants. God gives us some duty, and we are responsible to carry that duty out. Our real responsibility is to God. If we reject God, society becomes chaotic. Religion means avoiding chaos and meeting our responsibility to God by fulfilling our duty. Responsibility rests on us, and it is given by God. If we make spiritual progress by fulfilling our duty, we can finally live with God personally.

Hayagrīva dāsa: Sartre claims that the existentialist does not actually want to deny God's existence. Rather, "the existentialist thinks it very distressing that God does not exist because all possibility of finding values in a heaven of ideas disappears along with Him.... If God didn't exist, everything would be possible. That is the very starting point of existentialism. Indeed, everything is permissible if God does not exist...."

Śrīla Prabhupāda: This means that he does not know the meaning of God. As we have many times said, God is the Supreme Being, the Supreme Father who impregnates material nature with countless living entities. As soon as we accept material nature as the mother, we must accept some father. Therefore there is a conception of God the Father in all human societies. It is the father's duty to maintain his children, and therefore God is maintaining all the living entities within the universe. There is no question of rationally denying this.

Hayagrīva dāsa: Well, Sartre at least makes the attempt. He writes: "Since we have discarded God the Father, there has to be someone to invent values. You've got to take things as they are. Moreover, to say that we invent values means nothing else but this: Life has no meaning a priori. Before you become alive, life is nothing; it's up to you to give it a meaning, and value is nothing else but the meaning that you choose."

Śrīla Prabhupāda: Therefore everyone invents his own meaning? If this is the case, how will people ever live peacefully in society? Since everyone has his own idea of life, there can be no harmony. What kind of government would exist?

Hayagrīva dāsa: Recently, Sartre has turned to Marxism.

Śrīla Prabhupāda: But in Communist countries, there are very strong governments. It is not possible for a people to avoid government or leadership.

Śyāmasundara dāsa: Regardless of the form of government, Sartre believes that man is basically free.

Śrīla Prabhupāda: As soon as you speak of freedom, you refer to some living being. Matter itself has no freedom. It is the active principle that is free.

Śyāmasundara dāsa: Sartre maintains that man is condemned to be free, that this is a fate from which man cannot escape.

Śrīla Prabhupāda: If man is condemned, who has condemned him?

Śyāmasundara dāsa: Man is condemned by accident, thrown into the world.

Śrīla Prabhupāda: Is it simply by accident that one person is condemned and another blessed? Is it an accident that one man is in jail and another is not? What kind of philosophy is this? Such so-called philosophy simply misleads people. Nothing is accidental. We agree that the living entity is condemned to this material world, but when we speak of condemnation, we also speak of blessedness. So what is that blessedness?

Śyāmasundara dāsa: Sartre argues that man is condemned in the sense that he cannot escape this freedom. Since man is free, he is responsible for his activities.

Śrīla Prabhupāda: If you are responsible, then your freedom is not accidental. How is it you are accidentally responsible? If there is responsibility, there must be someone you are responsible to. There must be someone who is condemning you or blessing you. These things cannot happen accidentally. His philosophy is contradictory.

Śyāmasundara dāsa: Man's nature is an indefinite state of freedom. Man has no definite nature. He is continually creating it.

Śrīla Prabhupāda: This means that he is eternal. But the living entity does not change accidentally. His changes take place under certain regulations, and he attains specific bodies according to his karma, not by accident.

Śyāmasundara dāsa: But we have no fixed nature in the sense that today I may be happy and tomorrow unhappy.

Śrīla Prabhupāda: That is true to some extent. When you are placed into the sea, you have no control. You move according to the waves. This means that there is a power that is controlling you. However, if you put yourself in better circumstances, you will be able to control. Because you have placed yourself under the control of material nature, you act according to the modes of material nature.

prakṛteḥ kriyamāṇāni
guṇaiḥ karmāṇi sarvaśaḥ
ahaṅkāra-vimūḍhātmā
kartāham iti manyate

"The bewildered spirit soul, under the influence of the three modes of material nature, thinks himself to be the doer of activities, which in actuality are carried out by nature." (*Bg.* 3.27) Because you are conditioned, your freedom is checked. When you are thrown into the ocean of material existence, you essentially lose your freedom. Therefore it is your duty to get yourself liberated.

Śyāmasundara dāsa: Because we are one thing today and something else tomorrow, Sartre says that our essential nature is "no-thingness."

Śrīla Prabhupāda: You are nothing in the sense that you are under the full control of a superior power, being carried away by the waves of māyā. In the ocean of māyā, you may say, "I am nothing," but actually you are something. Your something-ness will be very much exhibited to you when you are put on land. Out of despair, you conclude that your nature is that of nothingness. Sartre's philosophy is a philosophy of despair, and we say that it is unintelligent because despair is not the result of intelligence.

Śyāmasundara dāsa: Although the basis of our nature is nothingness, Sartre maintains that man chooses or creates his own nature.

Śrīla Prabhupāda: That is a fact. Therefore you should create your nature as something, not nothing. In order to do that, however, you have to take lessons from a higher personality. Before philosophizing, Sartre should have taken lessons from a knowledgeable person. That is the Vedic injunction.

tad-vijñānārthaṁ sa gurum evābhigacchet
samit-pāṇiḥ śrotriyaṁ brahma-niṣṭham

"In order to learn the transcendental science, one must approach the bona fide spiritual master in disciplic succession, who is fixed in the Absolute Truth." *(Muṇḍaka-upaniṣad* 1.2.12)

Śyāmasundara dāsa: Sartre sees our nature as always in the making, as continually becoming.

Śrīla Prabhupāda: It is not in the making. It is changing. But man can make his nature in the sense that he can decide not to change. He can understand that changes are taking place despite the fact that he does not want them. Man can mold his nature by deciding to serve Kṛṣṇa, not by dismissing the whole matter, and, out of confusion and disappointment, claiming it to be nothing. The attempt to make life zero is due to a poor fund of knowledge.

Śyāmasundara dāsa: Sartre sees that we are constantly choosing or making our life, but that everything ends at death. That is, man is always in the process of becoming until death. At death, everything is finished.

Śrīla Prabhupāda: Death means changing into another body. The active principle on which the body stands does not die. Death is like changing apartments. A sane man can understand this.

Hayagrīva dāsa: Although man has no determined nature other than nothingness, Sartre sees man as a being striving to be God. He writes: "To be man means to reach toward being God. Or if you prefer, man fundamentally is the desire to be God."

Śrīla Prabhupāda: On the one hand, he denies the existence of God, and on the other, he tries to be God. If there is no God, there is no question of desiring to be God. How can one desire to be something that does not exist?

Hayagrīva dāsa: He is simply stating that man wants to be God. As far as God's existence is concerned, he prefers to set this question aside.

Śrīla Prabhupāda: But that is the main question of philosophy! God has created everything: your mind, intelligence, body, existence, and the circumstances surrounding you. How can you deny His existence? Or set it aside as not relevant? In the Vedas, it is stated that in the beginning, God existed, and the Bible also states that in the beginning there was God. In this material universe, existence and annihilation are both temporary. According to the laws of material nature, the body is created on a certain day, it exists for some time, and then is eventually finished. The entire cosmic manifestation has a beginning, middle, and end. But before this creation, who was there? If God were not there, how could the creation logically be possible?

Hayagrīva dāsa: As far as we've seen, most philosophers are concerned with resolving this question.

Śrīla Prabhupāda: Not all philosophers are denying God's existence, but most are denying His personal existence. We can understand, however, that God is the origin of everything, and that this cosmic manifestation emanates from Him. God is there, nature is there, and we are also there, like one big family.

Hayagrīva dāsa: Sartre would not admit the existence of an originator in whom things exist in their essence prior to creation. He would say that man simply exists, that he just appears.

Śrīla Prabhupāda: A person appears due to his father and mother. How can this be denied? Does he mean to say, "I suddenly just dropped from the sky."? Only a fool would say that he appeared without parents. From our experience we can understand that all species of life are manifest from some mother. Taken as a whole, we say that the mother is material nature. As soon as a mother is accepted, the father must also be accepted. It is most important to know where you came from. How can you put this question aside?

Śyāmasundara dāsa: Sartre believes that man's fundamental desire is the "desire to be." That is, man seeks existence rather than mere nothingness.

Śrīla Prabhupāda: That is so. Because man is eternal, he has the desire to exist eternally. Unfortunately, he puts himself under certain conditions that are not eternal. That is, he tries to maintain a position that will not endure eternally. Through Kṛṣṇa consciousness, we attain and retain our eternal position.

Śyāmasundara dāsa: Sartre feels that man wants solidity. He is not satisfied with being a mere being-for-itself. He also desires to be being-in-itself.

Śrīla Prabhupāda: Nothing in the material world exists eternally. A tree may exist for ten thousand years, but eventually it will perish. In the material world, nothing stays forever. What he is seeking is actual spiritual life. In *Bhagavad-gītā*, Kṛṣṇa speaks of another nature, a nature that is permanent, *sanātana.*

paras tasmāt tu bhāvo'nyo
'vyakto'vyaktāt sanātanaḥ
yaḥ sa sarveṣu bhūteṣu
naśyatsu na vinaśyati

"Yet there is another nature, which is eternal and is transcendental to this manifested and unmanifested matter. It is supreme and is never annihilated. When all in this world is annihilated, that part remains as it is." (*Bg.* 8.20) After the annihilation of this material universe, that *sanātana* nature will abide.

Śyāmasundara dāsa: This desire to be being-in-itself is the desire to be God, which Sartre maintains is man's fundamental desire.

Śrīla Prabhupāda: This is more or less Māyāvādī philosophy. The Māyāvādīs believe that when they attain complete knowledge, they become God. Because man is part and parcel of God, he wants to be united with God. It is like a man who has been away from home for a long time. Naturally he wants to go home again.

Śyāmasundara dāsa: Sartre believes that this desire to be God is bound to fail.
Śrīla Prabhupāda: Certainly, because man is not God. If he is God, how has he become something else? His very desire to be God means that he is not God at the present moment. A man cannot become God, but he can become godly. Existing in darkness, we desire light. We may come into the sunshine, but this does not mean that we become the sun. When we come to the platform of perfect knowledge, we become godly, but we do not become God. If we are God, there is no question of being something other than God. There is no question of being ignorant. Another name for Kṛṣṇa is Acyuta, which means, "He who never falls down." This means that He never becomes not-God. He is God always. You cannot become God through some mystic practice. This passion to become God is useless because it is doomed to frustration.
Śyāmasundara dāsa: Therefore Sartre calls man a "useless passion."
Śrīla Prabhupāda: A man is not useless if he attempts to be Kṛṣṇa conscious. The attempt to be Kṛṣṇa conscious and the attempt to be Kṛṣṇa are totally different. One is godly, the other asuric.
Śyāmasundara dāsa: Sartre then reasons that because it is impossible to become God, everything else is useless.
Śrīla Prabhupāda: That is foolishness. You are not God, but God's servant. You have chosen to attempt to become God, but you have found this to be impossible. Therefore you should give up this notion and decide to become a good servant of God, instead of a servant of māyā. That is the proper decision.
Śyāmasundara dāsa: Sartre concludes that since things have no reason to exist, life has no essential purpose.
Śrīla Prabhupāda: Nothing can exist without a purpose. There is also a supreme cause. The defect in such philosophers is that they do not have sufficient brain substance to go further than what they superficially see. They are not capable of understanding the cause of causes. Many modern scientists also maintain that nature, *prakṛti,* is the sole cause of existence, but we do not ascribe to such a theory. We understand that God is behind nature, and that nature is not acting independently. Nature is phenomena, but behind or beyond nature is noumena, God, Kṛṣṇa.

In *Bhagavad-gītā,* philosophy like Sartre's is called asuric, or demoniac. Demons do not believe in a superior cause. They consider that everything is accidental. They say that a man and a woman unite accidentally, and that their child is the result of sex, and nothing more. Therefore they claim that there is no purpose to existence.

asatyam apratiṣṭhaṁ te
jagad āhur anīśvaram
aparaspara-sambhūtaṁ
kim anyat kāma-haitukam

"They say that this world is unreal, that there is no foundation, and that there is no God in control. It is produced of sex desire, and has no cause other than lust." (*Bg.* 16.8) This type of philosophy is called asuric, demoniac, because it is of the nature of darkness, ignorance.

Śyāmasundara dāsa: For Sartre, being-for-itself refers to human consciousness, which is subjective, individual, incomplete, and indeterminate. It is nothingness in the sense that it has no density or mass.

Śrīla Prabhupāda: Because he is so materialistic, his senses cannot perceive anything that is not concrete. According to Vedic philosophy, the senses and their objects are created simultaneously. Unless there is an aroma, the sense of smell has no value. Unless there is beauty, the eyes have no value. Unless there is music, the ears have no value. Unless there is something soft, the sense of touch has no value. There is no question of nothingness. There must be interaction.

Śyāmasundara dāsa: Since man's essential nature is an undetermined nothingness, Sartre believes that man is free to choose to be either a coward or a hero. Our situation is in our own hands.

Śrīla Prabhupāda: If you claim that you were tossed into the world by some superior power, or by accident, what can you do? How can you become a hero? If you try to become a hero, you will be kicked all the more because you are placed here by a superior power. If a culprit under police custody attempts to become a hero, he will be beaten and punished. Actually, you are neither a coward nor a hero. You are an instrument. You are completely under the control of a superior power.

Śyāmasundara dāsa: Well, if someone is attacking you, you have the power to choose to be a hero and defend yourself, or to run.

Śrīla Prabhupāda: It is not heroic to defend oneself. That is natural. If that is the case, even a dog can be a hero when he is attacked. Even an ant can be a hero. Heroism and cowardice are simply mental concoctions. After all, you are under the control of a power that can do what He likes with you. Therefore there is no question of your becoming a hero or a coward.

Śyāmasundara dāsa: Suppose someone is in danger, and you rescue him. Isn't that being heroic?

Śrīla Prabhupāda: All you can rescue is the exterior dress. Saving that

dress is not heroism. It is not even protection. One can be a real hero only when he is fully empowered or fully protected. Such a person can only be a devotee, because only Kṛṣṇa can fully protect or empower.
Śyāmasundara dāsa: Being free, man is subject to what Sartre calls "bad faith," a kind of self-deception. Through bad faith, man loses his freedom and responsibility.
Śrīla Prabhupāda: You certainly have limited freedom to choose, but if you choose improperly, you have to suffer. Responsibility and freedom go hand in hand. At the same time, there must be discrimination. Without it, our freedom is blind. We cannot understand right from wrong.
Śyāmasundara dāsa: A man in bad faith drifts along from day to day without being involved, avoiding responsible decisions.
Śrīla Prabhupāda: This means that he has decided to drift. His drifting is a decision.
Śyāmasundara dāsa: Sartre believes that bad faith must be replaced by a solid choosing, and by faith in that choice.
Śrīla Prabhupāda: But if he makes the wrong decision, what is the value of his action? Moths fly very valiantly and courageously into the fire. Is that a very good decision?
Śyāmasundara dāsa: Due to bad faith, people treat others as objects instead of persons. Sartre advocates rectifying this situation.
Śrīla Prabhupāda: He speaks of bad faith, but what about good faith?
Śyāmasundara dāsa: If bad faith is the avoidance of decisions, good faith would mean making decisions courageously and following them out, regardless of what these decisions are.
Śrīla Prabhupāda: But what if your decision is wrong?
Śyāmasundara dāsa: For Sartre, it is not a question of right or wrong.
Śrīla Prabhupāda: Then whatever decision I make is final and absolute? This means that the insect's decision to enter the fire is a proper decision. This is the philosophy of insects. If man can do as he pleases, where is his responsibility?
Śyāmasundara dāsa: Sartre believes that the fate of the world depends on man's decisions. Obviously, if man decides properly, the world would be a better place.
Śrīla Prabhupāda: Therefore we are trying to introduce this Kṛṣṇa consciousness in order to make the world into Vaikuṇṭha, into a place where there is no anxiety. But this is not a blind decision. It is the decision of a higher authority; therefore it is perfect.
Śyāmasundara dāsa: Many people call Sartre's philosophy pessimistic because he maintains that man is a "useless passion" vainly striving in

a universe without a purpose.

Śrīla Prabhupāda: Sartre may be a useless passion, but we are not. No sane man is useless. A sane man will follow a superior authority. That is Vedic civilization. If one approaches a bona fide spiritual master, he will not be bewildered. Sartre believes that the universe is without a purpose because he is blind. He has no power to see that there is a plan. Therefore, according to *Bhagavad-gītā,* his philosophy is asuric, demoniac. Everything in the universe functions according to some plan. The sun and moon rise, and the seasons change according to plan.

Śyāmasundara dāsa: For Sartre, man stands alone in the world, yet he is not alone if he is a being-for-others. Man needs others for his own self-realization.

Śrīla Prabhupāda: This means that man requires a guru.

Śyāmasundara dāsa: Sartre does not speak of a guru but of interaction with others for self-understanding.

Śrīla Prabhupāda: If this is required, why not interact with the best man? If we require others to understand ourselves, why should we not seek the best man for our own understanding? We should receive help from the man who knows. If you take the advice of one who can give you the right direction, your end will be glorious. That is the Vedic injunction. *Tad-vijñānārthaṁ sa gurum evābhigacchet (Muṇḍaka-upaniṣad* 1.2.12).

Śyāmasundara dāsa: Sartre feels that in the presence of others, man is ashamed.

Śrīla Prabhupāda: Man is ashamed if he is not guided by a superior. If you are guided by a superior, you will be glorious, not ashamed. Your superior is that person who can lead you to the glory of Kṛṣṇa consciousness.

XIII
PSYCHOANALYSIS

Sigmund Freud
(1856-1934)

Śyāmasundara dāsa: Freud saw a conflict between the primal self, which he called the id, and the ethical self, the ego. It is the id that attempts to gratify all needs, and its basic motivating force is the libido, the sexual instinct. When the id comes in contact with the senses, the ego is formed. The superego is a modified part of the ego, which is formed through experiences related to one's parents. The superego is characterized by the feelings of conscience, and it is the principal repressive factor in the ego's striving to curb the primitive, sex-motivated, lawless tendencies of the id.

Śrīla Prabhupāda: We also agree that everyone has a sexual appetite, and it is stated in *śāstras* that sex is the principal bond to the material world. Actually, everyone has a tendency not only for sex, but for intoxication and meat eating also. These tendencies are inherent in the living entity. According to the *śāstras*, we are allowed sexual intercourse in marriage, but we are prohibited from having any other sex. Kṛṣṇa says, *dharmāviruddho bhūteṣu kāmo'smi.* "I am sex life which is not contrary to religious principles." (*Bg.* 7.11) This means that sex life has to be regulated. Of course, people have a perverted tendency to have sex against the Vedic injunctions. The Vedas give regulations for all undesirable activities, not only sex, but meat eating and intoxication as well. The idea is to restrict these *anarthas*, these unwanted things, so that the living entity may eventually be freed of them. In the conditioned state, everyone creates a false ego, thinking, "I am American, I am Hindu, I am Christian, Moslem, Russian, I am a human being, I am this body, I am this and that." This is false ego. Superior ego says, "I am Brahman. I am the eternal servant of Kṛṣṇa." If we understand the self in this way, false ego automatically vanishes. Our senses are gross, but they are controlled by the mind. The mind is part of the subtle body, and the mind in turn is controlled by the intelligence. The intelligence is controlled by the ego, and if this ego is false, the entire structure is false. False ego thinks, "I am this body." This is false identification. When the ego is thus deluded, everything subordinate to it is also illusioned because everything else is standing on a false platform. Therefore the Vedas advise us to come to the platform of knowledge, and this is called *brahma-jñāna*. As *Bhagavad-gītā* states:

brahma-bhūtaḥ prasannātmā
na śocati na kāṅkṣati
samaḥ sarveṣu bhūteṣu
mad-bhaktiṁ labhate parām

"One who is thus transcendentally situated at once realizes the Supreme Brahman. He never laments nor desires to have anything; he is equally disposed to every living entity. In that state, he attains pure devotional service unto Me." (*Bg*. 18. 54) When we come to the knowledge that we are not the body but pure spirit soul, we immediately become happy. All the neuroses and problems that Freud is trying to cure are due to false ego. When we understand our actual position, the blazing fire of material existence is immediately extinguished. Freud is describing this blazing fire, and he is trying to treat people within this fire. But how can a person be happy when there is fire all about? It is the fire itself that must be extinguished, or the person himself must be removed from the fire. Then there will be happiness.

I recall some years ago in India, when a criminal was pleading insanity to a murder charge, a psychiatrist was called to judge whether this person was sane during the time of the murder. The psychiatrist said, "I have examined many people, and I have concluded that more or less, everyone is insane. If his innocence depends upon his sanity, then I would say that he should be excused, but as far as I know, everyone is more or less insane." This is also our conclusion. Whoever is infected with this material nature is more or less insane. When the living entity takes on the material body, he must be crazy. Therefore everyone is speaking in different ways.

Śyāmasundara dāsa: Freud believed that painful or traumatic experiences, often repressed by forgetfulness, lie deep in our subconscious. By recalling them, we may be able to overcome the neuroses that they inflict.

Śrīla Prabhupāda: Our process is different. When you give a man a better thing, he will forget inferior things.

viṣayā vinivartante
nirāhārasya dehinaḥ
rasa-varjaṁ raso'py asya
paraṁ dṛṣṭvā nivartate

"The embodied soul may be restricted from sense enjoyment, though the taste for sense objects remains. But, ceasing such engagements by experiencing a higher taste, he is fixed in consciousness." (*Bg.* 2.59) Fear is created when we are not in Kṛṣṇa consciousness. This is a characteristic of the conditioned soul. As soon as we become Kṛṣṇa conscious, our fears and anxieties automatically vanish.

nārāyaṇa-parāḥ sarve
na kutaścana bibhyati
svargāpavarga-narakeṣv
api tulyārtha-darśinaḥ

"Devotees solely engaged in the devotional service of the Supreme Personality of Godhead, Nārāyaṇa, never fear any condition of life. For them the heavenly planets, liberation, and the hellish planets are all the same, for such devotees are interested only in the service of the Lord." (*Bhāg.* 6.17.28) When we are God conscious, we don't fear anything. Although Prahlāda Mahārāja's demonic father threatened him with death and put him in all kinds of frightful circumstances, Prahlāda remained quiet and peaceful. Indeed, his father asked him, "Prahlāda, how is it that you are so proud and fearless when I am trying to chastise you?" Prahlāda replied, "The person who gives you your power is the same person who is protecting me." Forgetfulness of painful experiences is in itself artificial. People forget because they are not properly trained. There is no usefulness in forgetting painful experiences. When we are Kṛṣṇa conscious, we are not afraid to remember them. We actually thank Kṛṣṇa, and say, "Kṛṣṇa, You are so kind that You have saved me from so many frightful situations. Now I am sure that I am pure and have my safety in You." A

Kṛṣṇa conscious man is not frightened by any of his past experiences. Rather, he laughs at them, thinking, "What a fool I was to have been afraid of all these things!"

Śyāmasundara dāsa: Freud did not believe that forgetfulness is artificial. He felt that it is a natural instinct to forget painful experiences.

Śrīla Prabhupāda: Well, that is so. For instance, when you were in the womb of your mother, you were in a very, very painful situation. Now you have forgotten that experience, and that forgetfulness is certainly natural. It is a fact that you were confined to a womb, but you cannot remember this. When you think about it, you can understand what a horrible situation that was. However, the *śāstras* say that even though you have forgotten this, you have not escaped the situation. You are waiting for a similar painful experience.

Śyāmasundara dāsa: Freud contends that anxieties and tensions are caused by the id's primitive instincts that are always forcing us to act contrary to the rational, moral ego and superego.

Śrīla Prabhupāda: Anxieties will continue as long as you are in the material condition. In conditioned life, you cannot be freed from anxiety.

Śyāmasundara dāsa: Is this because we are always desiring something and being frustrated?

Śrīla Prabhupāda: Frustration must be there because you do not desire the right thing. You are desiring something that is not permanent, and this is a cause for anxiety. We wish to live forever, but we have accepted this temporary material body. Therefore there is no question of living forever, and we are always anxious because we fear that death is coming. We fear death and the destruction of the body, and this is the main cause of our anxiety. Anxiety is due to our acceptance of something which will not exist, which is temporary.

Śyāmasundara dāsa: The ego develops strategies of defense against this anxiety engendered by the id. Whenever there is a strong animalistic desire, the ego represses it for self-preservation.

Śrīla Prabhupāda: Repression is always there. If we are diseased, and the doctor advises us not to take solid food, we have to repress our appetite. In the system of *brahmacarya*, the *brahmacārī* represses his desire for sex. This is called *tapasya*, voluntary repression. Of course, this is very difficult without some better engagement. Therefore, as I said, we have to replace an inferior engagement with a superior one. When you are captivated by seeing the beautiful form of Kṛṣṇa, you naturally no longer desire to see the beautiful form of a young woman.

Śyāmasundara dāsa: The Buddhists speak not only of the repression of desires, but of their extinction.

Śrīla Prabhupāda: We don't advocate that. There will always be desires, and sometimes we have to repress them. My Guru Mahārāja used to say that as soon as you rise from bed, you should beat your mind a hundred times with your shoes, and when you go to bed at night, you should beat your mind a hundred times with a broomstick. In this way, you will be able to control your mind. Wild tigers have to be controlled by repression, but when the tigers are under control, there is no question of repression. Then you can play with the tigers, and they will be your friends. So repression is not always bad.

Hayagrīva dāsa: Freud considered sexual repression to be harmful, but sublimation to be often beneficial. He didn't advocate total sexual freedom; rather, he suggested that instead of trying to deny the sex drive, we should try to redirect it, perhaps to some artistic activity, or positive study.

Śrīla Prabhupāda: This means diverting our attention, and that is recommended in the Vedic culture for the *brahmacārī*. If we are taught Kṛṣṇa from the very beginning of life, we will forget sex. Even if an adult takes to Kṛṣṇa consciousness seriously, he can also forget sex. That is the experience of Yāmunācārya: *Yadāvadhi mama cetaḥ kṛṣṇa-padāravinde.* "Since I have been engaged in Kṛṣṇa consciousness, every time I think of sex, I spit." If we engage in sex without restriction, we will eventually become impotent. That is nature's way of punishment. Sex cannot be artificially repressed, but there is a proper training process.

Hayagrīva dāsa: Freud believed that sex could not be stamped out, and that if one tried, it would manifest itself in undesirable neurosis.

Śrīla Prabhupāda: He did not know the training process of Kṛṣṇa consciousness. According to our philosophy, as long as we have sexual inclinations, we have to accept a material body and become entangled in the miseries of material existence. However, there is such a thing as spiritual life, and if we are trained spiritually, we will no longer be bothered by material desires.

Hayagrīva dāsa: In exploring the realm of infantile sexuality, Freud discovered a definite sexual nature in the early stages of childhood. He concluded that sexual activities in childhood were normal, and this led him to write that "in a normal sex life, no neurosis is possible."

Śrīla Prabhupāda: It all depends on the child's training. If a child is trained as a *brahmacārī*, he will have no inclination for sex. Sometimes a father enjoys sex before his children, and the children imitate. It is the nature of a child to imitate, especially his parents. According to

Vedic civilization, as soon as a child is four or five years old, he is sent to a *gurukula*, where he is disciplined. There, he practically forgets sex life. But when he becomes a young man, he may naturally have a little tendency for sex, and if this is the case, the guru suggests marriage. If, on the other hand, one can perfectly control his sexual tendencies, he can become a *sannyāsī*. My Guru Mahārāja, for instance, never married. This is all a matter of education.

Śyāmasundara dāsa: Freud believed that many of our present unconscious wishes and conflicts have their origins in these infantile experiences.

Śrīla Prabhupāda: That may be, but you are not going to be an infant again. So why not forget all this? After this life, you will be placed in the womb of another mother, and all those experiences will happen again. It is therefore the duty of the guru and the parents to save the living entity from rebirth.

gurur na sa syāt sva-jano na sa syāt
pitā na sa syāj jananī na sā syāt
daivaṁ na tat syān na patiś ca sa syān
na mocayed yaḥ samupeta-mṛtyum

"One who cannot deliver his dependents from the path of repeated birth and death should never become a spiritual master, a father, a husband, a mother, or a worshipable demigod." (*Bhāg.* 5.5.18) *Janma-mṛtyu-jarā-vyādhi.* At the time of death, we will again experience this horrible situation. We will again have to enter a womb, be confined, and undergo birth. Whether we forget these experiences or not, we will have to undergo them again and again if we do not become Kṛṣṇa conscious.

Śyāmasundara dāsa: Freud felt that most of our problems, which are sexual in nature, can be cured by recalling painful experiences and objectively analyzing them.

Śrīla Prabhupāda: We must understand why this sex problem is there. If we tolerate a little itching sensation, we will be spared much pain. *Yan maithunādi-gṛhamedhi-sukhaṁ hi tucchaṁ kaṇḍūyanena karayor iva duḥkha-duḥkham.* "Sex life is compared to the rubbing of two hands to relieve an itch. *Gṛhamedhis*, householders without spiritual knowledge, think that this itching is the greatest platform of happiness, although it is actually a source of distress." (*Bhāg.* 7.9.45) When ordinary men are overly attached to materialistic life, their only happiness is sexual intercourse. The *śāstras* say that happiness derived from sexual intercourse is very, very insignificant. Indeed, it is not even happiness. At best, it may be considered a tenth-class happiness. Because people have no idea of the happiness of Kṛṣṇa consciousness, they think that sex is the highest happiness. But if we analyze it, what kind of happiness is it? When we have an itch, we scratch it and feel some pleasure, but after that pleasure passes, the effects are abominable. The itch becomes worse. The *śāstras* tell us that if we just try to tolerate this itching sensation, we will be spared a great deal of pain. This is possible if we practice this Kṛṣṇa consciousness.

Śyāmasundara dāsa: Freud believed that neuroses, disorders, anxieties, and frustrations have their origin in repression.

Śrīla Prabhupāda: And I am telling you that all these are due to sex. But we are not advocating repression. We give facility in the form of a wife. The sex impulse is to be directed to the wife.

Śyāmasundara dāsa: But Freud insisted that the sex impulse is present at the very beginning of life.

Śrīla Prabhupāda: We also admit that. We say that as soon as the living being is embodied, he experiences hunger and sex. Why is that? *Āhāra-nidra-vyavāyaḥ*. We find these impulses even in animals. These drives are already there. What is the use in philosophizing about them?

Śyāmasundara dāsa: Through psychoanalysis, pent-up emotions can be released, and the original shock mitigated by remembering and confessing.

Śrīla Prabhupāda: But what guarantee is there that we will not receive another shock? The living entity is receiving shock after shock. You try to cure him of one, and another comes. It is a fact that material life is painful. As soon as you receive this material body, you must suffer the threefold miseries. Everyone is seeking happiness, but unless materialistic life is stopped, unless we put an end to birth, old age, disease, and death, there is no question of happiness. Materialistic life is a disease, and Vedic civilization attempts to cure this disease. Our program is total cure. No more shock. Freud's treatment is useless because he cannot guarantee that there will not be another shock. If you are situated in real Kṛṣṇa consciousness, the worst type of misery may face you, and you will not be disturbed. You will not experience any shock at all. Freud was trying to cure his patients of the results of some shock they had experienced years ago , but there is no guarantee that a similar shock will not come again. Rather, the living entity will receive one shock after another after another.

daivī hy eṣā guṇamayī
mama māyā duratyayā

mām eva ye prapadyante
māyām etāṁ taranti te

"This divine energy of Mine, consisting of the three modes of material nature, is difficult to overcome. But those who have surrendered unto Me can easily cross beyond it." (*Bg.* 7.14) As soon as we try to solve one problem, another problem comes, then another. If we are in Kṛṣṇa consciousness, there are no more shocks.

Śyāmasundara dāsa: Freud believed that our present personality is greatly influenced by our sexual experiences in infancy and childhood.

Śrīla Prabhupāda: Therefore we are trying to train our boys as *brahmacārīs*. Of course, there is the tendency for sex, but by practicing *brahmacarya*, by diverting our attention to Kṛṣṇa, there will be very little chance that a shock will come about. If the Vedic system is followed by human society, these shocks will not be there.

Hayagrīva dāsa: Freud also tied infantilism in with the religious impulse. He wrote: "Psychoanalysis, which has taught us the intimate connection between the father complex and belief in God, has shown us that the personal God is psychologically nothing but an exalted father.... Youthful persons lose their religious belief as soon as the authority of the father breaks down." Thus Freud sees God as a father figure arising out of the helplessness experienced by the little child.

Śrīla Prabhupāda: How can a little child invent his father? Was he not born of his father? And how can he abandon the idea of his father? Without a father, how can one come into being? Even Freud had a father, grandfather, great grandfather, and so on back. We speak of God as the first father because there is no one beyond Him.

Hayagrīva dāsa: Still, Freud considers belief in God as infantile. In *The Future of an Illusion*, he writes: "Man cannot remain a child forever; he must venture at last into the hostile world." Instead of continuing to dwell in such a nursery, man should try to rid himself of the psychic crutch of religion.

Śrīla Prabhupāda: What is his definition of childishness? Everyone must be a child, and everyone must have a father. Just as we cannot deny our biological father, we cannot deny the ultimate Supreme Father.

Hayagrīva dāsa: It is not that he is denying biological fathers, but the idea of a Supreme Father, which he felt arose out of man's initial helpless state.

Śrīla Prabhupāda: Helplessness is always there, because the threefold miseries will always exist in material life. There will always be miseries arising from the body and mind, miseries inflicted by other living entities, and natural catastrophes. In addition, there is always birth, old age, disease, and death. It is only a fool or a rascal who hopes against hope and makes plans to overcome all these difficulties. However we may plan, nature is so strong that it will smash our plans to pieces with the kick of death. Man hopes against hope to adjust material things so that he can be happy in this world, but this is foolishness. Man is helpless at every step.

Hayagrīva dāsa: Freud felt that belief in God the Father is "so patently infantile, so incongruous with reality, that to one whose attitude to humanity is friendly, it is painful to think that the great majority of mortals will never be able to rise above this view of life."

Śrīla Prabhupāda: So what is his reality? Belief in God may be infantile to him, but what is he except a child? He also makes plans, and that in itself is childish. How is it that he is more than a child? Can he give an ultimate solution that will rid man of his helplessness?

Hayagrīva dāsa: Well, he personally hoped that psychoanalysis would provide the answers.

Śrīla Prabhupāda: How can a common man understand psychoanalysis? The fact is that there is a supreme controller who is present everywhere. Psychoanalysis should begin with this point. Why is he defying this fact?

Hayagrīva dāsa: He sincerely believed that the maturation process necessarily entails ridding oneself of religion. He writes: "If one attempts to assign religion its place in man's evolution, it seems not so much to be a lasting acquisition as a parallel to the neurosis which the civilized individual must pass through on his way from childhood to maturity."

Śrīla Prabhupāda: He has reached this conclusion because he has seen so many sentimental religions, but first of all he must understand what religion actually is. Religion is not possible without an understanding of God, and a religion without God cannot truly be called a religion. According to the Vedic system, religion refers to the orders of God; therefore if we have no conception of God, we cannot be said to have a religion. If we do not know God or His nature, how can we know the orders God is giving?

Hayagrīva dāsa: It has often been noted—initially by Jung—that Freud tried to repress religious feelings within himself. In a letter, he once confided, "I cannot rid myself of certain materialistic prejudices, and I would carry them over into the research of the occult."

Śrīla Prabhupāda: Religion is neither occult nor obscure. Of course, everything is obscure for an unintelligent person who has no idea of either God or religion.

Hayagrīva dāsa: In the same letter, Freud continues: "Thus I am entirely incapable of considering the 'survival of the personality' after death, even as a mere scientific possibility.... I think, therefore, it is better if I continue confining myself to psychoanalysis."
Śrīla Prabhupāda: But if he cannot understand the eternity of the soul, he will be deficient in psychoanalysis as well. Even within one lifetime, we can see that the body changes while the soul remains the same. We go through the changes of childhood, youth, manhood, middle age, and old age, but the soul, the person, is always there.
Hayagrīva dāsa: In *Beyond the Pleasure Principle*, Freud theorizes on the death instinct. Equating a child's fondness to repeat a certain act that gives him pleasure with the tendency to restore a previous state of affairs, he concludes that if instincts aim at the past, they would necessarily tend to regress to the prenatal state. This is a desire to "return to the womb" that brought Freud to write: "The goal of all life is death." For him, death is the cessation of suffering.
Śrīla Prabhupāda: If this is the case, why are people afraid of death? Why do people go to a doctor when they fear some disease? If death is ultimate happiness, why do people try to avoid it?
Hayagrīva dāsa: Once, after an argument with Jung, Freud fainted, and his words when he came to were, "How sweet it must be to die."
Śrīla Prabhupāda: Now, what pleasure does one derive from being dead? What is the pleasure of extinction? That is the pleasure of a stone.
Hayagrīva dāsa: Well, he did speak of return to the "quiescence of the inorganic world."
Śrīla Prabhupāda: Then why bother philosophizing or psychoanalyzing? Just commit suicide and become like a stone. Why take up so much time? If it is better to die, then become a stone, and be happy. If ultimate happiness is extinction, why write so many books?
Hayagrīva dāsa: Freud considered the quietude that follows the sexual act to be very much like death, because desires are extinguished. Thus sleep often follows sexual intercourse. In this sense, the pursuit of pleasure is a drive to extinction.
Śrīla Prabhupāda: If this is the purpose of life, we should pray to God to make us dogs and hogs because these animals have very good facilities for sex life. They all consider sex to be the ultimate goal, and then sleep.

ṛṣabha uvāca
nāyaṁ deho deha-bhājāṁ nṛloke
kaṣṭān kāmān arhate viḍ-bhujāṁ ye
tapo divyaṁ putrakā yena sattvaṁ

śuddhyed yasmād brahma-saukhyaṁ tv anantam

"Lord Ṛṣabhadeva told His sons: My dear boys, of all the living entities who have accepted material bodies in this world, one who has been awarded this human form should not work hard day and night simply for sense gratification, which is available even for dogs and hogs that eat stool. One should engage in penance and austerity to attain the divine position of devotional service. By such activity, one's heart is purified, and when one attains this position, he attains eternal, blissful life, which is transcendental to material happiness, and which continues forever." (*Bhāg.* 5.5.1) Human life is meant for *tapasya*, for putting an end to sex. This is the process of *brahmacarya*.

Śyāmasundara dāsa: For Freud, the sexual energy, or libido, is not only manifest through sexual intercourse. It is associated with a wide variety of pleasurable sensations relating to bodily activities and including pleasures of the mouth and the different organs.

Śrīla Prabhupāda: We have already said that the only happiness in this material world is considered to be sexual. *Yan maithunādi (Bhāg.* 7.9.45). The word *ādi* means the basic principle, which, in the material world, is sex. What is materialistic happiness? It is enjoying this life with one's friends and family. But what kind of pleasure is this? It is compared to a drop of water in the desert. Actually, we are seeking unlimited pleasure. *Ānandamayo 'bhyāsāt.* How can this drop of water in the desert, which is materialistic pleasure, ever satisfy us? No one is satisfied, although people are having sex in so many different ways. And now young girls are almost going naked, and the female population is increasing everywhere. As soon as there is an increase in the female population, the women say, "Where are the men?" There then must be disaster because every woman is trying to attract a man, and men will take advantage of this situation. When milk is available in the market, what is the use in keeping a cow? The more men become attached to women, the more the female population will increase.

Śyāmasundara dāsa: How is that?

Śrīla Prabhupāda: When you have more sex, your power to beget a male child is diminished. When the man is less potent, a girl is born, and when a man is more potent, a boy is born. If a man's discharge is larger, there will be a male child. If the woman's discharge is larger, there will be a female child. When women are easily available, men become weak, and they beget female children because they lose their power from over-indulgence. Sometimes they even become impotent. If you don't restrict your sex life, there will be so many disasters. Yāmunācārya says:

yadāvadhi mama cetaḥ kṛṣṇa-padāravinde
nava-nava-rasa-dhāmanudyata rantum āsīt
tadāvadhi bata nārī-saṅgame smaryamāne
bhavati mukha-vikāraḥ suṣṭu niṣṭhīvanaṁ ca

"Since I have been engaged in the transcendental loving service of Kṛṣṇa, realizing ever-new pleasure in Him, whenever I think of sex pleasure, I spit at the thought, and my lips curl with distaste."

Śyāmasundara dāsa: Freud would consider this a form of repression.

Śrīla Prabhupāda: His idea of repression is different from ours. Our repression means rising early in the morning, attending *maṅgala-āratik*, chanting the Hare Kṛṣṇa *mahā-mantra*, and engaging in devotional service. In this way, we repress material propensities.

Śyāmasundara dāsa: In other words, it's repression with awareness and knowledge.

Śrīla Prabhupāda: Actual knowledge will come later. In the beginning, there is obedience to the spiritual master. In this way, we will not become habituated to undesirable activity.

Śyāmasundara dāsa: Yet by remembering some traumatic or shocking experience, our tensions are often relieved, and personality disorders rectified. This is a fact of psychoanalysis.

Śrīla Prabhupāda: That may be, but when a seed has fructified and grown into a tree, it is no longer possible to rectify the seed. The seed is no longer there. It has changed into a tree. Freud may be able to find out the cause, but does he know the cure? Our cure is to divert the attention to Kṛṣṇa. By understanding Kṛṣṇa, we automatically forget our problems. Kṛṣṇa is the panacea for all diseases.

Śyāmasundara dāsa: Freud also investigated projection, that is attributing one's own personality onto others. A man may regard others as a thief because he's a thief himself.

Śrīla Prabhupāda: We accept that. *Ātmanā manyate jagat.* Everyone thinks others to be like himself.

Śyāmasundara dāsa: Freud also felt that children act in different ways to win the love and affection of their parents.

Śrīla Prabhupāda: Children imitate. In Agra, I have seen two and three-year-old children try to imitate the sexual intercourse of their parents. They did not know anything about sex pleasure, but they were imitating what they had seen. Children do not know the value of things, but they imitate their parents. There is no fixed pattern of development for the personality of children. You can mold children in any way. They are like soft dough, and you can make out of them what you like. All you have

to do is put them into the mold. Many of the neuroses Freud talked about are not experienced in Indian families. If you place a child in good association, he will act properly, and if you place him in bad association, he will act improperly. A child has no independence in that sense.
Śyāmasundara dāsa: Freud believed that our behavior must be understood in terms of our entire life history.
Śrīla Prabhupāda: That is so. Therefore in our Vedic system, it is forbidden for the husband and wife to speak of sex even jokingly before a small child, because the child cannot understand. If children know of sexual intercourse, it is because they have learned about it from their parents.
Hayagrīva dāsa: Although often avoiding the very subject of religion, Freud sometimes took an agnostic stand. He writes: "Of the reality value of most religions we cannot judge; just as they cannot be proved, neither can they be refuted."
Śrīla Prabhupāda: First of all, he does not know what religion is. As we have said, religion means the orders given by God. Since he has no conception of God, how can he know anything of God's orders? He is acquainted only with fictitious religions, which have been described in *Śrīmad-Bhāgavatam* as *kaitava*—cheating religions. Real religion is law. Just as you cannot manufacture laws in your home, you cannot manufacture religion.
Hayagrīva dāsa: Freud further writes: "The riddles of the universe only reveal themselves slowly to our inquiry. To many questions science can as yet give no answer; but scientific work is our only way to the knowledge of external reality....No, science is no illusion. But it would be an illusion to suppose that we can get anywhere else what it cannot give us."
Śrīla Prabhupāda: First of all, we have to learn what the object of knowledge is. The word *veda* means "knowledge," and *anta* means "ultimate." Unless you come to the ultimate point of knowledge, or Vedānta, your knowledge is imperfect or insufficient. The ultimate object of knowledge is God, and if we cannot define God or explain His nature, we have not reached the ultimate point of knowledge. God is a fact, but unfortunately we have no clear idea of Him. This means that our knowledge has not reached the ultimate point—that is, it is imperfect. If the knowledge of a philosopher or scientist is imperfect, of what value is it? According to the Vedic method, we receive our knowledge from the perfect person: Kṛṣṇa, the Supreme Personality of Godhead.
Hayagrīva dāsa: As for the origin of religions, Freud writes: "As it is a delicate task to decide what God has Himself ordained and what derives rather from the authority of an all-powerful parliament or a supreme

judicial decision, it would be an indubitible advantage to leave God out of the question altogether, and to admit honestly the purely human origin of all cultural laws and institutions."

Śrīla Prabhupāda: God does not derive power from anyone. As stated in the beginning of *Śrīmad-Bhāgavatam: janmādy asya yato 'nvayād itarataś cārtheṣv abhijñaḥ sva-rāṭ (Bhāg.* 1.1.1). The Supreme God, the Absolute Truth, knows everything in complete detail. The word *abhijñaḥ* means "complete awareness." How is it God has complete knowledge? From whom has He received this knowledge? The answer is: *sva-rāṭ*. He does not receive it from anyone. He is completely independent. If God has to receive knowledge from Mr. Freud, He is not God. God is the only person who is completely independent.

na tasya kāryaṁ karaṇaṁ ca vidyate
na tat-samaś cābhyadhikaś ca dṛśyate
parāsya śaktir vividhaiva śrūyate
svā-bhāvikī jñāna-bala-kriyā ca

"He does not possess bodily form like that of an ordinary living entity. There is no difference between His body and His soul. He is absolute. All His senses are transcendental. Any one of His senses can perform the action of any other sense. Therefore, no one is greater than Him or equal to Him. His potencies are multifarious, and thus His deeds are automatically performed as a natural sequence." (*Śvetāśvatara Upaniṣad* 6.7-8) God is naturally all perfect, and He doesn't have to adopt some process in order to become perfect. Anyone who is trying to be perfect is not God. When Kṛṣṇa was only three months old, He could kill the big giant Pūtanā. His potencies are there automatically, whether He appears as a child or as a young man. Nowadays, so-called yogīs are trying to become God by meditating, but Kṛṣṇa did not have to meditate. If God is always God, He doesn't have to learn anything from anyone. That is the true meaning of independence. If we want to know something about God, we should receive knowledge from Him directly, or from a person who knows Him. This is the direction given in *Bhagavad-gītā:*

tad viddhi praṇipātena
paripraśnena sevayā
upadekṣyanti te jñānaṁ
jñāninas tattva-darśinaḥ

"Just try to learn the truth by approaching a spiritual master. Inquire from him submissively and render service unto him. The self-realized soul can impart knowledge unto you because he has seen the truth." (*Bg.*

4.34) The word *tattva-darśinaḥ* refers to one who factually knows about God. It is necessary to learn about God from one who has seen Him eye to eye. Arjuna, for instance, was talking to God on the battlefield of Kurukṣetra. If we wish to understand God, we should understand Him as Arjuna did. What was Arjuna's understanding? That is found in the Tenth Chapter of *Bhagavad-gītā:*

paraṁ brahma paraṁ dhāma
pavitraṁ paramaṁ bhavān
puruṣaṁ śāśvataṁ divyam
ādi-devam ajaṁ vibhum

āhus tvām ṛṣayaḥ sarve
devarṣir nāradas tathā
asito devalo vyāsaḥ
svayaṁ caiva bravīṣi me

"You are the Supreme Brahman, the ultimate, the supreme abode and purifier, the Absolute Truth, and the eternal divine person. You are the primal God, transcendental and original, and You are the unborn and all-pervading beauty. All the great sages such as Nārada, Asita, Devala, and Vyāsa proclaim this of You, and now You Yourself are declaring it to me." (*Bg*. 10.12-13)

Hayagrīva dāsa: Concerning early religious training, Freud writes: "So long as a man's early years are influenced by the religious thought-inhibition and by the lower one derived from it, as well as by the sexual one, we cannot really say what he is actually like." Freud strongly believed that early religious education warps a man's natural development.

Śrīla Prabhupāda: What is wrong with informing a child that there is a Supreme Being controlling the whole cosmic situation? Is it that Freud did not believe in education?

Hayagrīva dāsa: He felt that children should not be indoctrinated with religious "thought-inhibitions."

Śrīla Prabhupāda: But there must be some form of education, and spiritual education is the most important. The only business of human life is to learn about God. Lower species cannot understand God, but understanding is possible in the human form. Therefore spiritual education is primary.

Hayagrīva dāsa: Marx called religion "the opiate of the people," and Freud similarly says that "the consolations of religion may be compared to that of a narcotic."

Śrīla Prabhupāda: As I have said before, neither Marx nor Freud know

what religion is, and that is their difficulty. First, they have to learn what religion is before they can discuss it intelligently.
Hayagrīva dāsa: Freud writes: "The believer will not let his faith be taken from him neither by arguments nor by prohibitions. And even if it did succeed with some, it would be a cruel thing to do. A man who has for decades taken a sedative is naturally unable to sleep if he is deprived of it...."
Śrīla Prabhupāda: It is also cruel to mislead people by telling them that God the Father is simply an infantile conception. That is real cruelty. It is cruel to stress sex and death and deny the conception of God as the Supreme Father.
Hayagrīva dāsa: Freud would not think that it is cruelty to disenchant man with an illusion. He writes: "I disagree with you when you go on to argue that man cannot in general do without the consolation of the religious illusion, that without it he would not endure the troubles of life, the cruelty of reality."
Śrīla Prabhupāda: Without a spiritual education, man remains an animal. A man's life should be more than merely eating, sleeping, mating, defending, and dying. Man should strive to advance in spiritual knowledge. Spiritual education means understanding God. Freud may deny the existence of God, but in any case the conception of God is there in human society. One may accept or reject different conceptions of God, but the fact is undeniable that in every civilized country, there is some form of religion. One may be Christian, Buddhist, Hindu, or Moslem: the designation is not very important. Understanding God is the important factor, because that ultimate understanding is Vedānta, the ultimate conclusion of all knowledge. *Athāto brahma-jijñāsā (Vedānta-sūtra).* Now, in this human form, is the time to inquire, "What is Brahman?" Brahman, the Absolute Truth, is the goal of real knowledge. Man does not have to be educated to understand sex. According to a Bengali proverb, you do not have to be taught how to cry, or how to enjoy sex. When you lament, you automatically cry, and when there is the impulse to enjoy sex, you enjoy it automatically. This doesn't require the help of an educator like Mr. Freud. Everyone, animals and human beings, knows how to enjoy sex. There is no question of a "sex philosophy." Philosophy means inquiring into the Absolute Truth, Brahman, the supreme controller, He from whom everything has emanated. Philosophy is concerned with understanding where things come from. We may inquire into the origin of life on earth, and conclude that life comes from water, earth, or fire. Then, where do earth, water, and fire come from?

He who is the source of everything is the Absolute Truth. In *Bhagavad-gītā*, Lord Kṛṣṇa says:

ahaṁ sarvasya prabhavo
mattaḥ sarvaṁ pravartate
iti matvā bhajante māṁ
budhā bhāva-samanvitāḥ

"I am the source of all spiritual and material worlds. Everything emanates from Me. The wise who know this perfectly engage in My devotional service and worship Me with all their hearts." (*Bg.* 10.8) You become a devotee of Kṛṣṇa when you perfectly understand that Kṛṣṇa is the ultimate source. This knowledge comes after many lifetimes of searching and searching.

bahūnāṁ janmanām ante
jñānavān māṁ prapadyate
vāsudevaḥ sarvam iti
sa mahātmā sudurlabhaḥ

"After many births and deaths, he who is actually in knowledge surrenders unto Me, knowing Me to be the cause of all causes and all that is. Such a great soul is very rare." (*Bg.* 7.19) After understanding that Vāsudeva, Kṛṣṇa, is everything, the *mahātmā*, the great soul, begins his *bhajana*, his worship.

mahātmānas tu māṁ pārtha
daivīṁ prakṛtim āśritāḥ
bhajanty ananya-manaso
jñātvā bhūtādim avyayam

"O son of Pṛthā, those who are not deluded, the great souls, are under the protection of the divine nature. They are fully engaged in devotional service because they know Me as the Supreme Personality of Godhead, original and inexhaustible." (*Bg.* 9.13)

Hayagrīva dāsa: Freud admits that without religion man will "find himself in a difficult situation. He will have to confess his utter helplessness and his insignificant part in the working of the universe." Yet he goes on to say that without religion, man will venture at last into the hostile world, and this venture is his "education to reality."

Śrīla Prabhupāda: And what service has Mr. Freud rendered? He has misled the world and made it more difficult for people to accept the words of God. Men who are innocent accept the words of God, but now many have become "over intelligent," and they think that sex is God. It will take some time to counteract this type of mentality, but man must eventually learn that his happiness is found in understanding and accepting the way of life defined by God Himself.

Hayagrīva dāsa: Christ pointed out that unless one becomes as a little child, he shall not enter into the kingdom of God, but Freud advocates "growing up" and setting this illusion aside.

Śrīla Prabhupāda: He may advocate so many things, but if he does not know the meaning of God, or God's nature, what is the value of his knowledge? According to the Vedic philosophy, we should receive knowledge from a person who knows God. If one has not known God, his knowledge is useless, or, even worse, misleading. It is a fact that there is a supreme controller, and real education means understanding how the supreme controller is working. Denying Him is useless. He is there beyond our control, and we cannot avoid His control. We may make plans to live here very happily, but today or tomorrow, we may die. How can we deny the fact that we are being controlled? Knowledge means understanding how the supreme controller is controlling. People who defy religion and deny the existence of a supreme controller are like the jackal that keeps jumping and jumping, trying to reach grapes on a high vine. After seeing that he cannot reach the grapes, he says to himself, "Oh, there is no need to reach them. They are sour anyway." People who say that we do not need to understand God are indulging in sour-grape philosophy.

Carl Gustav Jung
(1875-1961)

Hayagrīva dāsa: Jung gave the following criticism of Sigmund Freud: "Sexuality evidently meant more to Freud than to other people. For him it was something to be religiously observed....One thing was clear; Freud, who had always made much of his irreligiosity, had now constructed a dogma, or rather, in the place of a jealous God whom he had lost, he had substituted another compelling image, that of sexuality."
Śrīla Prabhupāda: Yes, that is a fact. He has taken sexuality to be God. It is our natural tendency to accept a leader, and Freud abandoned the leadership of God and took up the leadership of sex. In any case, we must have leadership. That is our position. In Russia, I pointed out that there is no difference in our philosophic processes. However, whereas they accept Lenin as their leader, we accept Kṛṣṇa. It is the nature of human beings to accept a leader. It is unfortunate that Freud lost God's leadership and took up instead the leadership of sex.
Hayagrīva dāsa: Jung concluded: "Freud never asked himself why he was compelled to talk continually of sex, why this idea had taken such possession of him. He remained unaware that his 'monotony of interpretation' expressed a flight from himself, or from that other side of him

which might perhaps be called mystical. So long as he refused to acknowledge that side, he could never be reconciled with himself."

Śrīla Prabhupāda: Yes, that was because he was accepting the leadership of sexuality. If we accept the leadership of Kṛṣṇa, our life becomes perfect. All other leadership is māyā's leadership. There is no doubt that we have to accept a leader, and therefore he was constantly speaking about sex. Those who have taken God as their leader will speak only of God, nothing else. *Jīvera 'svarūpa' haya—kṛṣṇera 'nitya-dāsa' (Caitanya-caritāmṛta,* Madh. 20.108) According to Caitanya Mahāprabhu's philosophy, we are all eternal servants of God, but as soon as we give up God's service, we have to accept the service of māyā.

Śyāmasundara dāsa: For Freud, the unconscious process, the id, was invariably animalistic and lawless, whereas for Jung, these unconscious energies were potentially sources of positive creative activity.

Śrīla Prabhupāda: The subconscious state is covered by our present consciousness, and it can also be covered by Kṛṣṇa consciousness. In that case, the subconscious states will no longer be able to react. For instance, the subconscious sex drive is there, but because Yāmunācārya was in Kṛṣṇa consciousness, he could overcome it. The subconscious experiences, which have been gathering for life after life, which are stored, as it were, will not be able to overcome the individual if he is fully Kṛṣṇa conscious.

Śyāmasundara dāsa: Jung sees the mind as being composed of a balance of the conscious and the unconscious, or subconscious. It is the function of the personality to integrate these. For instance, if one has a strong sex drive, he can sublimate or channel that drive into creative art or religious activity.

Śrīla Prabhupāda: That is our process. The sex impulse is natural for everyone in the material world. If we think of Kṛṣṇa embracing Rādhārāṇī, or dancing with the *gopīs,* our material sex impulse is sublimated and weakened. If we hear about the pastimes of Kṛṣṇa and the *gopīs* from the right source, lusty desire within the heart will be suppressed, and we will be able to develop devotional service. What we must understand is that Kṛṣṇa is the only *puruṣa,* enjoyer. If we help Him in His enjoyment, we also receive enjoyment. We are predominated, and He is the predominator. On the material platform, if a husband wants to enjoy his wife, the wife must voluntarily help him in that enjoyment. By helping him, the wife also becomes an enjoyer. The predominator, the enjoyer, is Kṛṣṇa, and the predominated, the enjoyed, are the living entities. Actually, both enjoy, but one enjoys as the predominated, and the other as the predominator. When the predominated helps the predominator, that is the perfection of enjoyment. We must admit that sex desire is present in everyone, both male and female, and from an impartial point of view, it appears that the male is the enjoyer and the female the enjoyed, but if the female agrees to be enjoyed, she naturally becomes the enjoyer. All living entities are described as *prakṛti*, female. Kṛṣṇa is *puruṣa*, male. When the living entities agree to help Kṛṣṇa's sex desire, they become enjoyers.

Śyāmasundara dāsa: What is meant by Kṛṣṇa's sex desire?

Śrīla Prabhupāda: You might more correctly say "sense enjoyment." Kṛṣṇa is the supreme proprietor of the senses, and when we help Kṛṣṇa in His sense enjoyment, we also naturally partake of it. The sweet *rasagulla* is to be enjoyed, and therefore the hand takes it and puts it into the mouth so that it can be tasted and go to the stomach. It is not that the hand tries to enjoy it directly. Kṛṣṇa is the only direct enjoyer; all others are indirect enjoyers. By satisfying Kṛṣṇa, we also satisfy others. We cannot possibly satisfy others directly. For instance, when a wife sees her husband eating and enjoying himself, she becomes happy. Upon seeing the predominator happy, the predominated becomes happy.

Śyāmasundara dāsa: In the individual, should the unconscious state be predominated by the conscious?

Śrīla Prabhupāda: That is being done. Unconscious or subconscious states sometimes emerge; we are not always aware of them. But consciousness is always there. Actually, the word "unconscious" is not a good word because it implies a lack of consciousness. "Subconscious" is a better word.

Śyāmasundara dāsa: Psychologists say that the unconscious or subconscious often acts through the conscious, but that we do not know it.

Śrīla Prabhupāda: Yes, that is what I am saying. The subconscious is there, but it is not always manifest. Sometimes it is suddenly manifest, just as a bubble will suddenly emerge in a pond. The energy was there within all the time, but suddenly it comes out, just like a bubble popping to the surface of the water. You may not be able to understand why it emerges, but it is assumed that it was in the subconscious state and then suddenly manifests. That subconscious state does not necessarily have any connection with our present consciousness. It is like a stored impression, a shadow, or a photograph. The mind takes many snapshots, and they are stored.

Śyāmasundara dāsa: Does the subconscious mind think like the conscious mind?

Śrīla Prabhupāda: No, but the impressions are there, and they may suddenly come to the surface.

Śyāmasundara dāsa: For Jung, there are two types of subconscious states. One is the personal unconscious, consisting of those personal items stored from our individual childhood, a repressed history of stored impressions that can be aroused to consciousness in dreams and through psychoanalysis. The second is what Jung calls the collective unconscious, consisting of the collective experience of the race, archetypal images passed on from generation to generation, and common to men all over the globe.

Śrīla Prabhupāda: Yes, we might even call that tradition. Of course, we emphasize *paramparā*, which is different. *Paramparā* means receiving proper knowledge from the Supreme. This is not something archetypal. Archetypes may change, but the knowledge received from Kṛṣṇa is different. Spiritual knowledge imparted in *Bhagavad-gītā* is not knowledge coming from tradition. Rather, we learn it from a great authority like Kṛṣṇa.

Hayagrīva dāsa: Jung could see that the soul is always longing for light, and he wrote of the urge within the soul to rise out of primal darkness, making note of the pent-up feelings in the eyes of primitive people, and even a certain sadness in the eyes of animals, "a poignant message which speaks to us out of that existence."

Śrīla Prabhupāda: Yes, every living entity, including man, is constitutionally a servant. Therefore everyone is seeking some master, and that is our natural propensity. You can often see a puppy attempt to take shelter of some boy or man, and that is his natural tendency. He is saying, "Give me shelter. Keep me as your friend." A child or a man also wants some shelter in order to be happy. That is our constitutional position. When we attain the human form, when our consciousness is developed, we should take Kṛṣṇa as our shelter and our leader. In *Bhagavad-gītā*, Kṛṣṇa tells us that if we want shelter and guidance, we should take Him. "Abandon all varieties of religion and just surrender to Me." (*Bg.* 18.66) This is the ultimate instruction of *Bhagavad-gītā*.

Śyāmasundara dāsa: Jung would say that our understanding of Kṛṣṇa as the Supreme Father and the cause of all causes is an archetypal understanding that is shared by all humans. People may represent Him in different ways, but the archetype is the same.

Śrīla Prabhupāda: Yes, it is exactly the same. Kṛṣṇa, or God, is the Supreme Father. A father has many sons, and all men are sons of God,

born of their father. This is an experience common to everyone at all times.
Śyāmasundara dāsa: There are certain common archetypes in the dream life of all men, and even similar symbols found among the Incas of South America, or the Vaiṣṇavas of India, or inhabitants of the Pacific Islands. Could this be due to a common ancestry in the original Vedic culture?
Śrīla Prabhupāda: Vedic culture or no Vedic culture, there are many similarities experienced in human existence. Because we are all living beings, the similarities are there. Every living being eats, sleeps, mates, fears, and dies. These are experiences common to everyone; therefore there must be similarities in representations, or whatever.
Śyāmasundara dāsa: Jung believes that the unconscious sometimes emerges in the form of a superiority or inferiority complex, by which we react in inhibited or arrogant fashions.
Śrīla Prabhupāda: What are we? Inferior or superior? In Kṛṣṇa consciousness, we consider ourselves servants of God. We are not guided by impulses or complexes; we are guided directly by the superior.
Śyāmasundara dāsa: Jung states that there are two basic attitudes: extrovertive and introvertive.
Śrīla Prabhupāda: The introvert is called a *muni* because he is introspective. The extrovert is generally guided by *rajas*, the mode of passion.
Śyāmasundara dāsa: The personality and behavior of a living entity are determined by the interaction between the unconscious and the conscious mind.
Śrīla Prabhupāda: Full consciousness in Sanskrit is called *jāgaraṇam*. Dreaming is called *svapnaḥ*, and *suṣuptiḥ* refers to no consciousness, as in an anesthetized state.
Śyāmasundara dāsa: Jung would call the dreaming state the unconscious also. The contents of the unconscious spill over into the conscious mind during dreams.
Śrīla Prabhupāda: I do not like the word "unconscious" because it implies lack of consciousness. When you are anesthetized, you are unconscious. In such a state, you can be cut open and not even know it. However, when you sleep or dream, a mere pinch will awake you. As I said before, "subconscious" is a better word.
Śyāmasundara dāsa: Both Jung and Freud used the word "unconscious" to refer to the subconscious mind that determines our personality.
Śrīla Prabhupāda: When the living entity is in the womb of the mother, he is unconscious. Death means remaining unconscious for seven or nine months. The living entity does not die; he simply remains unconscious

for that duration. That is called *suṣuptiḥ*. When you have an operation, an anesthetic is administered, and you are unconscious for a period. When the anesthetic wears off, you emerge into the dream state. That dream state is actually a state of consciousness. When you dream, the mind works.

Śyāmasundara dāsa: Jung believes that if we don't awaken to the many unconscious factors governing our personality, we will remain slaves to our unconscious life. The point of psychoanalysis is to reveal them to us and enable us to face them.

Śrīla Prabhupāda: That is what we are teaching. We say that presently the soul is in an unconscious state, and we are telling the soul, "Please wake up! You are not this body!" It is possible to awaken the human being, but other living entities cannot be awakened. A tree, for instance, has consciousness, but he is so packed in matter that you cannot raise him to Kṛṣṇa consciousness. Jagadish Candra Bose proved that a tree feels pain when it is cut, although this pain is very slightly manifest. A human being, on the other hand, has developed consciousness, which is manifest in different stages. Lower life forms are more or less in a dream state, or unconscious.

Hayagrīva dāsa: In his autobiography, *Memories, Dreams, Reflections*, Jung writes: "I find that all my thoughts circle around God like the planets around the sun, and are as irresistibly attracted by Him. I would feel it to be the grossest sin if I were to oppose any resistance to this force." Jung also sees all creatures as parts of God, and at the same time unique in themselves. "Like every other being," he writes, "I am a splinter of the infinite Deity...."

Śrīla Prabhupāda: It is also our philosophy that we are part and parcel of God, just as sparks are part of a fire.

Hayagrīva dāsa: "It was obedience which brought me grace," he writes. "One must be utterly abandoned to God; nothing matters but fulfilling His will. Otherwise all is folly and meaningless."

Śrīla Prabhupāda: Very good. Surrender unto God is real spiritual life. *Sarva dharmān parityajya (Bg.* 18.66). Surrender to God means accepting that which is favorable to God and rejecting that which is unfavorable. The devotee is always convinced that God will give him all protection. He remains humble and meek, and thinks of himself as one of the members of God's family. This is real spiritual communism. Communists think, "I am a member of a certain community," but it is man's duty to think, "I am a member of God's family." God is the Supreme Father, material nature is the mother, and living entities are all sons of God.

There are living entities everywhere: on land, and in the air, and water. There is no doubt that material nature is the mother, and according to our experience, we can understand that a mother cannot produce a child without a father. It is absurd to think that a child can be born without a father. A father must be there, and the Supreme Father is God. In Kṛṣṇa consciousness, a person understands that the creation is a spiritual family headed by one Supreme Father.

Hayagrīva dāsa: Jung writes: "According to the Bible...God has a personality and is the ego of the universe, just as I myself am the ego of my psychic and physical being."

Śrīla Prabhupāda: Yes, the individual is conscious of his own body, but not the bodies of others. Beside the individual soul, or consciousness in the body, there is the *Paramātmā*, the Supersoul, the super consciousness present in everyone's heart. This is discussed in *Bhagavad-gītā:*

kṣetrajñaṁ cāpi māṁ viddhi
sarva-kṣetreṣu bhārata
kṣetra-kṣetrajñayor jñānaṁ
yat taj jñānaṁ mataṁ mama

"O scion of Bharata, you should understand that I am also the knower in all bodies, and to understand this body and its owner is called knowledge. That is my opinion." (*Bg.* 13.3)

Hayagrīva dāsa: Recalling his difficulties in understanding God's personality, Jung writes: "Personality, after all, surely signifies character...certain specific attributes. But if God is everything, how can He still possess a distinguishable character...? Moreover, what kind of character or what kind of personality does He have? Everything depends on that, for unless one knows the answer, one cannot establish a relationship with Him."

Śrīla Prabhupāda: God's character is transcendental, not material. He also has many attributes. For instance, He is very kind to His devotees, and this kindness may be considered one of His characteristics or attributes. He also has unlimited qualities, and sometimes He is described according to these transcendental qualities. His qualities, however, are permanent. Whatever qualities or characteristics we have are but minute manifestations of God's. God is the origin of all attributes and characteristics. As indicated in the *śāstras*, He also has a mind, senses, feelings, sense perception, sense gratification, and everything else. Everything is there unlimitedly, and since we are part and parcel of God, we possess His qualities in minute quantities. The original qualities in God are manifest minutely in ourselves. According to the Vedas, God is a person just like us, but His personality is unlimited. Just as my consciousness is limited to this body, and His consciousness is super consciousness within everybody, so I am a person confined to this particular body, and He is the super person living within all. As Kṛṣṇa tells Arjuna in *Bhagavad-gītā,* the personality of God and that of the individual are eternally existing.

na tv evāhaṁ jātu nāsaṁ
na tvaṁ neme janādhipāḥ
na caiva na bhaviṣyāmaḥ
sarve vayam ataḥ param

"Never was there a time when I did not exist, nor you, nor all these kings; nor in the future shall any of us cease to be." (*Bg.* 2.12) Both God and the living entity are persons, but God's personality is unlimited, and the individual personality is limited. God has unlimited power, strength, influence, knowledge, beauty, and renunciation. We have limited, finite power, knowledge, influence, and so on. That is the difference between the two personalities.

Hayagrīva dāsa: Seeing that philosophies and theologies could not give him a clear picture of God's personality, Jung concludes: "What is wrong with these philosophers? I wondered. Evidently they know of God only by hearsay."

Śrīla Prabhupāda: Yes, that is also our complaint. None of the philosophers we have discussed has given us any clear idea of God. Because they are speculating, they cannot give concrete, clear information. As far as we are concerned, our understanding of God is clear because we receive the information given by God Himself to the world. Kṛṣṇa is accepted as the Supreme Person by Vedic authorities; therefore we should have no reason not to accept Him as such. Nārāyaṇa, Lord Śiva, and Lord Brahmā possess different percentages of God's attributes, but Kṛṣṇa possesses all the attributes cent per cent, in totality. Rūpa Gosvāmī has analyzed this in his *Bhakti-rasāmṛta-sindhu,* which we have translated as *The Nectar of Devotion.* God is a person, and if we study the attributes of man, we can also know something of God's. Just as we enjoy ourselves with friends, parents, and others, God also enjoys Himself in various relationships. There are five primary and seven secondary relationships that the living entities can have with God. Since we take pleasure in these relationships, God is described as *akhila-rasāmṛta-sindhu,* the reservoir of all pleasure. There is no need to speculate about

God, or try to imagine Him. The process for understanding is described in *Bhagavad-gītā:*

mayy āsakta-manaḥ pārtha
yogaṁ yuñjan mad-āśrayaḥ
asaṁśayaṁ samagraṁ māṁ
yathā jñāsyasi tac chṛṇu

"Now hear, O son of Pṛthā, how by practicing yoga in full consciousness of Me, with mind attached to Me, you can know Me in full, free from doubt." (*Bg.* 7.1) You can learn about God by always keeping yourself under His protection, or under the protection of His representative. Then, without a doubt, you can perfectly understand God. Otherwise, there is no question of understanding Him.

Hayagrīva dāsa: Jung continues: "At least they [the theologians] are sure that God exists, even though they make contradictory statements about Him....God's existence does not depend on our proofs....I understand that God was, for me at least, one of the most certain and immediate of experiences."

Śrīla Prabhupāda: Yes, that is a transcendental conviction. One may not know God, but it is very easy to understand that God is there. We have to learn about God's nature, but there is no doubt that God is there. Any sane man can understand that he is being controlled. So, who is that controller? The supreme controller is God. This is the conclusion of a sane man. Jung is right when he says that God's existence does not depend on our proof.

Hayagrīva dāsa: Recalling his early spiritual quests, Jung writes: "In my darkness...I could have wished for nothing better than a real, live guru, someone possessing superior knowledge and ability, who would have disentangled from me the involuntary creations of my imagination...."

Śrīla Prabhupāda: Yes, according to Vedic instructions, we must have a guru in order to acquire perfect knowledge.

tad vijñānārthaṁ sa gurum evābhigacchet
samit-pāniḥ śrotriyaṁ brahma-niṣṭham

"In order to learn the transcendental science, one must approach the bona fide spiritual master in disciplic succession, who is fixed in the Absolute Truth." (*Muṇḍaka Upaniṣad* 1.2.12) The guru must factually be a representative of God. He must have seen and experienced God in fact, not simply in theory. We have to approach such a guru, and by service, surrender, and sincere inquiry, we can come to understand what is God. The Vedas inform us that a person can understand God when he has received a little mercy from His Lordship; otherwise, he may speculate for millions and millions of years. *Bhaktyā mām abhijānāti.* "One can understand the Supreme Personality as He is only by devotional service." (*Bg.* 18.55) This process of *bhakti* includes *śravaṇaṁ kīrtanaṁ viṣṇoḥ*, hearing and chanting about Lord Viṣṇu and always remembering Him. *Satataṁ kīrtayanto māṁ* (*Bg.* 9.14). The devotee is always glorifying the Lord. *Śrīmad-Bhāgavatam* says:

naivodvije para duratyaya-vaitaraṇyās
tvad-vīrya-gāyana-mahāmṛta-magna-cittaḥ
śoce tato vimukha-cetasa indriyārtha-
māyā-sukhāya bharam udvahato vimūḍhān

"O best of the great personalities, I am not at all afraid of material existence, for wherever I stay I am fully absorbed in thoughts of Your glories and activities. My concern is only for the fools and rascals who are making elaborate plans for material happiness and maintaining their families, societies, and countries. I am simply concerned with love for them." (*Bhāg.* 7.9.43) The devotee's consciousness is always immersed in the ocean of the pastimes and unlimited activities of the Supreme Lord. That is transcendental bliss. The spiritual master trains his disciple to remain always in the ocean of God consciousness. One who works under the directions of the *ācārya* knows everything about God.

Hayagrīva dāsa: When in Calcutta in 1938, Jung met some celebrated gurus, but generally avoided so-called holymen. "I did so because I had to make do with my own truth," he writes, "not to accept from others what I could not attain on my own."

Śrīla Prabhupāda: On the one hand, he says he wants a guru, and then on the other, he doesn't want to accept one. Doubtless, there are many cheating gurus in Calcutta, and Jung might have seen some bogus gurus he did not like. In any case, the principle of accepting a guru cannot be avoided. It is absolutely necessary.

Hayagrīva dāsa: Concerning consciousness after death, Jung feels that the individual must pick up the level of consciousness which he left.

Śrīla Prabhupāda: Yes, and therefore according to that consciousness, we have to accept a body. That is the process of the soul's transmigration. An ordinary person can see only the gross material body, but accompanying this body is the mind, intelligence, and ego. When the body is finished, these remain, although they cannot be seen. A foolish man thinks that everything is finished at death, but the soul carries the mind, intelligence, and ego—that is, the subtle body—with it into another body. This is confirmed by *Bhagavad-gītā: na hanyate hanyamāne śarīre.* "He is not slain when the body is slain." (*Bg.* 2.20)

Hayagrīva dāsa: Jung believes that individual consciousness cannot supersede world consciousness. He writes: "If there were to be a conscious existence after death, it would, so it seems to me, have to continue on the level of consciousness attained by humanity, which in any age has an upper thought variable limit."

Śrīla Prabhupāda: It is clearly explained in *Bhagavad-gītā* that although the body is destroyed, the consciousness continues. According to one's consciousness, he acquires another body, and again in that body, the consciousness begins to mold its future lives. If a person were a devotee in his past life, he would again become a devotee after his death. Once the material body is destroyed, the same consciousness begins to work in another body. Consequently, we find that some people quickly accept Kṛṣṇa consciousness, whereas others take a longer time. *Bahūnāṁ janmanām ante (Bg.* 7.19) This indicates that the consciousness is continuing, although the body is changing. Bharata Mahārāja, for instance, changed many bodies, but his consciousness continued, and he remained fully Kṛṣṇa conscious. We may see a person daily, but we cannot visualize his intelligence. We can understand that a person is intelligent, but we cannot see intelligence itself. When one talks, we can understand that there is intelligence at work. When the gross body is dead and no longer capable of talking, why should we conclude that the intelligence is finished? The instrument for speech is the gross body, but when the body is finished, we should not conclude that consciousness and intelligence are finished. After the destruction of the gross body, the mind and intelligence continue. Because they require a body to function, they develop a body, and that is the process of the soul's transmigration.

Hayagrīva dāsa: Still, what of Jung's contention that the individual's level of consciousness cannot supersede whatever knowledge is available on this planet?

Śrīla Prabhupāda: No, it can supersede, provided we acquire knowledge from authority. You may not have seen India, but a person who has seen India can describe it to you. We may not be able to see Kṛṣṇa, but we can learn of Him from an authority who knows. In *Bhagavad-gītā*, Kṛṣṇa tells Arjuna that there is an eternal nature:

paras tasmāt tu bhāvo'nyo
'vyakto'vyaktāt sanātanaḥ

yaḥ sa sarveṣu bhūteṣu
naśyatsu na vinaśyati

"Yet there is another nature, which is eternal and is transcendental to this manifested and unmanifested matter. It is supreme and is never annihilated. When all in this world is annihilated, that part remains as it is." (*Bg.* 8.20). On this earth, we encounter temporary nature. Here, things take birth, remain for some time, change, grow old, and are finally destroyed. There is dissolution in this material world, but there is another world in which there is no dissolution. We have no personal experience of this other world, but we can understand that it exists when we receive information from authority. It is not necessary to know it by personal experience. *Parokṣāparokṣa.* There are different stages of knowledge, and not all knowledge can be acquired by direct perception. That is not possible.

Hayagrīva dāsa: Jung believed in the importance of consciousness elevation. He writes: "Only here, in life on earth, can the general level of consciousness be raised. That seems to be man's metaphysical task...."

Śrīla Prabhupāda: Yes, our consciousness should be developed. As stated in *Bhagavad-gītā:*

prāpya puṇya-kṛtāṁ lokān
uṣitvā śāśvatīḥ samāḥ
śucīnāṁ śrīmatāṁ gehe
yoga-bhraṣṭo 'bhijāyate

athavā yoginām eva
kule bhavati dhīmatām
etaddhi durlabhataraṁ
loke janma yad īdṛśam

tatra taṁ buddhi-saṁyogaṁ
labhate paurva-dehikam
yatate ca tato bhūyaḥ
saṁsiddhau kuru-nandana

"The unsuccessful yogī, after many, many years of enjoyment on the planets of the pious living entities, is born into a family of righteous people, or into a family of rich aristocracy. Or he takes his birth in a family of transcendentalists who are surely great in wisdom. Verily, such a birth is rare in this world. On taking such a birth, he again revives the divine consciousness of his previous life, and he tries to make further progress in order to achieve complete success." (*Bg.* 6.41-43)

So if one's yoga practice is incomplete, or if he dies prematurely, his consciousness accompanies him, and in the next life, he begins at the point where he left off. His intelligence is revived. In an ordinary class, we can see that some students learn very quickly, while others cannot understand. This is evidence for the continuation of consciousness. If a person is extraordinarily intelligent, his previously developed consciousness is being revived. The fact that we have undergone previous births is also evidence for the immortality of the soul.

Hayagrīva dāsa: Jung speaks of the paradox of death: from the point of view of the ego, death is a horrible catastrophe, "a fearful piece of brutality." Yet from the point of view of the psyche, the soul, death is "...a joyful event. In the light of eternity, it is a wedding."

Śrīla Prabhupāda: Yes, death is horrible for one who is going to accept a lower form of life, and it is a pleasure for the devotee, because he is returning home, back to Godhead.

Hayagrīva dāsa: Death is not always a joyful event for the soul?

Śrīla Prabhupāda: No. How can it be? If one has not developed his spiritual consciousness, death is very horrible. The tendency in this life is to become very proud, and often people think, "I don't care for God. I am independent." Crazy people talk in this way, but after death, they have to accept a body according to the dictations of nature. Nature says, "My dear sir, since you have worked like a dog, you can become a dog. Since you have been surfing in the sea, you can now become a fish." These bodies are awarded according to a superior order.

karmaṇā daiva-netreṇa
jantur dehopapattaye
striyāḥ praviṣṭa udaraṁ
puṁso retaḥ-kaṇāśrayaḥ

"Under the supervision of the Supreme Lord and according to the result of his work, the living entity, the soul, is made to enter into the womb of a woman through the particle of male semina and to assume a particular type of body." (*Bhāg.* 3.31.1) When we are in touch with the modes of material nature, we are creating our next body. How can we stop this process? This is nature's way. If we are infected by some disease, we will necessarily get that disease. There are three modes of material nature—*tamo-guṇa, rajo-guṇa,* and *sattva-guṇa*—and our bodies are acquired according to our association with them. As far as the unsuccessful yogī is concerned, he is given a chance to revive his spiritual consciousness in his next life. In general, the human form affords us a chance to make progress in Kṛṣṇa consciousness, especially when we are born in an aristocratic, *brāhmaṇa,* or Vaiṣṇava family.

Hayagrīva dāsa: Concerning *saṁsāra,* Jung writes: "The succession of birth and death is viewed [in Indian philosophy] as an endless continuity, as an eternal wheel rolling on forever without a goal. Man lives and attains knowledge and dies and begins again from the beginning. Only with the Buddha does the idea of a goal emerge, namely, the overcoming of earthly existence."

Śrīla Prabhupāda: Overcoming earthly existence means entering into the spiritual world. The spirit soul is eternal, and it can pass from this atmosphere into another. That is clearly explained in *Bhagavad-gītā:*

janma karma ca me divyam
evaṁ yo vetti tattvataḥ
tyaktvā dehaṁ punar janma
naiti mām eti so 'rjuna

"One who knows the transcendental nature of My appearance and activities does not, upon leaving the body, take his birth again in this material world, but attains My eternal abode, O Arjuna." (*Bg.* 4.9) Those who continue to revolve in the cycle of birth and death require another material body, but those who are Kṛṣṇa conscious go to Kṛṣṇa. They do not acquire another material body. Those who are not envious of Kṛṣṇa accept His instructions, surrender unto Him, and understand Him. For them, this is the last material birth. For those who are envious, however, transmigration is continuous.

Hayagrīva dāsa: Concerning karma, Jung writes: "The crucial question is whether a man's karma is personal or not. If it is, then the preordained destiny with which a man enters life presents an achievement of previous lives, and a personal continuity therefore exists. If, however, this is not so, and an impersonal karma is seized upon in the act of birth, then that karma is incarnated again without there being any personal continuity."

Śrīla Prabhupāda: Karma is always personal.

Hayagrīva dāsa: When Buddha was asked whether karma is personal or not, he avoided answering. He said that knowing this would not contribute to liberation from the illusion of existence.

Śrīla Prabhupāda: Buddha refused to answer because he did not teach about the soul or accept the personal soul. As soon as you deny the personal aspect of the soul, there is no question of a personal karma. Buddha wanted to avoid this question. He did not want his whole philosophy dismantled.

Hayagrīva dāsa: Jung asks, "Have I lived before in the past as a specific personality, and did I progress so far in that life that I am now able to seek a solution?"
Śrīla Prabhupāda: Yes, that is a fact.
Hayagrīva dāsa: Jung admits that he doesn't know.
Śrīla Prabhupāda: That is explained in *Bhagavad-gītā:*

tatra taṁ buddhi-saṁyogaṁ
labhate paurva-dehikam
yatate ca tato bhūyaḥ
saṁsiddhau kuru-nandana

"On taking such a birth, he again revives the divine consciousness of his previous life, and he tries to make further progress in order to achieve complete success, O son of Kuru." (*Bg.* 6.43)
Hayagrīva dāsa: "I could well imagine that I might have lived in former centuries and there encountered questions I was not yet able to answer," Jung writes. "I had to be born again because I had not fulfilled the task that was given to me."
Śrīla Prabhupāda: That is a fact.
Hayagrīva dāsa: "When I die, my deeds will follow along with me—that is how I imagine it."
Śrīla Prabhupāda: That is personal karma.
Hayagrīva dāsa: "I will bring with me what I have done," Jung concludes. "In the meantime it is important to insure that I do not stand at the end with empty hands."
Śrīla Prabhupāda: If you are making regular progress in Kṛṣṇa consciousness, your hands will not be empty at the end. Completeness means returning home, back to Godhead. This return is not empty. Because the Māyāvādīs cannot understand the positivity of God's kingdom, they try to make it empty. Eternal life with Kṛṣṇa is our aspiration. A Vaiṣṇava does not want emptiness. Since materialists are thinking that everything will be empty at the end of life, they conclude that they should enjoy themselves now as much as possible. Therefore sense enjoyment is at the core of material life, and materialists are mad after it.
Hayagrīva dāsa: Jung believes that we are reborn because we relapse again into desires, feeling that something remains to be completed. "In my case," he writes, "it must have been primarily a passionate urge toward understanding....for that was the strongest element in my nature."
Śrīla Prabhupāda: That understanding for which he is longing is understanding of Kṛṣṇa. That is explained in *Bhagavad-gītā:*

bahūnāṁ janmanām ante
jñānavān māṁ prapadyate
vāsudevaḥ sarvam iti
sa mahātmā sudurlabhaḥ

"After many births and deaths, he who is actually in knowledge surrenders unto Me, knowing Me to be the cause of all causes and all that is. Such a great soul is very rare." (*Bg.* 7.19) Our understanding is complete when we come to the point of understanding Kṛṣṇa. Then our material journey comes to an end. *Tyaktvā dehaṁ punar janma naiti mām eti so'rjuna.* "Upon leaving the body, he does not take birth again into this material world, but attains My eternal abode." (*Bg.* 4.9) Lord Kṛṣṇa Himself gives instructions by which He can be understood.

mayy āsakta-manaḥ pārtha
yogaṁ yuñjan mad-āśrayaḥ
asaṁśayaṁ samagraṁ māṁ
yathā jñāsyasi tac chṛṇu

"Now hear, O son of Pṛthā, how by practicing yoga in full consciousness of Me, with mind attached to Me, you can know Me in full, free from doubt." (*Bg.* 7.1) If we can understand Kṛṣṇa completely, we will take our next birth in the spiritual world.

Hayagrīva dāsa: Concerning scripture, Jung writes: "The word of God comes to us, and we have no way of distinguishing to what extent it is different from God."

Śrīla Prabhupāda: The word of God is not at all different from God. Since God is absolute, both He and His words are the same. God's name and God are the same. God's pastimes and God are the same. God's Deity and God are the same. Anything related to God is God. For instance, *Bhagavad-gītā* is God. *Mayā tatam idaṁ sarvam (Bg.* 9.4). Everything is God, and when we are complete in God realization, we can understand this. Otherwise we cannot. Everything is God, and without God, nothing can exist.

Hayagrīva dāsa: Jung conceived of the false ego in terms of *persona.* "The *persona,*" he writes, "is the individual's system of adaptation to, or the manner he assumes in dealing with, the world.... The *persona* is that which in reality one is not, but which oneself as well as others think one is."

Śrīla Prabhupāda: Our real *persona* is that we are eternal servants of God. When we realize this, our *persona* becomes our salvation and perfection. The person must be there, but as long as we are in the material world, our *persona* identifies with our family, community, body, nation, ideal, and so on. The person is there and must continue, but proper understanding is realizing that we are eternal servants of Kṛṣṇa. As long as we are in the material world, we labor under the delusion of the false ego, thinking, "I am American. I am Russian. I am Hindu, etc." This is false ego at work. In reality, we are all servants of God. When we speak of false ego, we also admit a real ego, a purified ego, who understands that he is the servant of Kṛṣṇa.

Hayagrīva dāsa: Jung envisioned the self as a personality composed of the conscious and also the subconscious. He writes: "The self is not only the center but also the whole circumference which embraces both conscious and unconscious."

Śrīla Prabhupāda: Everything depends on the personality, and it is the personality that is surrounded by so many conceptions. In conditional life, we may have many different types of dreams, but when we are purified—like Lord Caitanya Mahāprabhu—we dream of Kṛṣṇa's pastimes. In the purified state, we dream about Kṛṣṇa and His activities and instructions.

Hayagrīva dāsa: Although the self can never be fully known by the individual, it does have individuality.

Śrīla Prabhupāda: We can know that we are individual persons with our own ideas and activities. The problem is purifying our ideas and activities. When we understand our role as servants of Kṛṣṇa, we are purified.

Śyāmasundara dāsa: For Jung, the purpose of psychoanalysis is to come to grips with our unconscious shadow personality in order to know completely who we are.

Śrīla Prabhupāda: That means attaining real knowledge. When Sanātana Gosvāmī approached Śrī Caitanya Mahāprabhu, he said, "Please reveal to me who and what I am." In order to understand our real identity, we require the assistance of a guru.

Śyāmasundara dāsa: Jung says that in the shadow personality of all males, there is a bit of the female, and in all females there is a bit of the male. Because we repress these aspects of the shadow personality, we do not understand our actions.

Śrīla Prabhupāda: We say that every living entity is by nature a female, *prakṛti. Prakṛti* means female, and *puruṣa* means male. In this material world, although we are *prakṛti*, we are posing ourselves as *puruṣa*. Because the *jīvātmā*, the individual soul, has the propensity to enjoy as a male, he is sometimes described as *puruṣa*, but actually the *jīvātmā* is not *puruṣa*. He is *prakṛti*. As I said before, *prakṛti* means dominated, and *puruṣa* means predominator. The only predominator is Kṛṣṇa; therefore originally we are all female by constitution.

Śyāmasundara dāsa: In the male species, at any rate, the temperament is different, isn't it? There is dominance and aggression.

Śrīla Prabhupāda: There is no different temperament. We can see that the female also has the same temperament because she wants to be treated equally, just like a man. In any case, the real position is that every living entity is originally female, but under illusion he attempts to become a male, an enjoyer. This is called māyā. Although a female by constitution, the living entity is trying to imitate the supreme male, Kṛṣṇa. When we come to our original consciousness, we understand that we are not the predominator but the predominated.

Śyāmasundara dāsa: Jung noticed male and female characteristics reflected in nature. For instance, a mountain may be considered male because it is strong and dominant, whereas the sea is female because it is passive and is the womb of life.

Śrīla Prabhupāda: These are all mental concoctions. They have no real scientific value. You may imagine things like this, but the real identity of these things is different. Life is not generated from the ocean; rather, everything is generated from the breathing of Lord Viṣṇu, who lies in the causal ocean. If I am lying on this bed, and something emanates from my breathing, does this mean that something is emanating from the bed?

Śyāmasundara dāsa: But aren't there specific male and female characteristics?

Śrīla Prabhupāda: The only male is God. Male means enjoyer, and female means enjoyed. But for God, no one is the enjoyer. Therefore He is the only male.

Śyāmasundara dāsa: Then is it false to think of anything as masculine besides God?

Śrīla Prabhupāda: Masculine is different. We speak of the masculine gender. The *liṅga* is the symbol of masculinity in the material body. In Bengali, it is said that one can tell if an animal is male or female simply by raising its tail. But these are material considerations. The real male is Kṛṣṇa.

Śyāmasundara dāsa: But couldn't you refer to the ocean as "mother ocean"?

Śrīla Prabhupāda: You may in the sense that the ocean contains so many living entities, just as the female contains a child within her womb. Or you may speak of a mountain as being male because of its strength and durability. In that sense, you may make these comparisons, but you should not think that these are the real identities of these things.

Śyāmasundara dāsa: For Jung, the soul, or self, is the center of organization within the personality, and seeks a harmonious balance between the conscious and the unconscious.

Śrīla Prabhupāda: When we speak of personality, we must admit the existence of the soul. Because you are a living entity, you have a separate identity called personality. Unless there is an individual soul, there is no possibility of personality.

Śyāmasundara dāsa: Jung said that the self is rarely completely balanced. But don't we say that the self is always stable?

Śrīla Prabhupāda: No, when the self is under the influence of māyā, he is not balanced. He is imbalanced and ignorant. His true consciousness is covered. When rain falls from the sky, it is clear, but as soon as it touches the earth, it becomes muddy. Originally, the soul's consciousness is clear, but when it comes in contact with the three modes of material nature, it is muddied.

Hayagrīva dāsa: "If the soul is anything," Jung writes, "it must be of unimaginable complexity and diversity, so that it cannot possibly be approached through a mere psychology of instinct."

Śrīla Prabhupāda: According to Caitanya Mahāprabhu, we can understand the soul through training. By negation, we can understand, "I am not this, I am not that." Then we can come to understand.

nāhaṁ vipro na ca nara-patir nāpi vaiśyo na śūdro
nāhaṁ varṇī na ca gṛha-patir no vanastho yatir vā
kintu prodyan-nikhila-paramānanda-pūrṇamṛtābdher
gopī-bhartuḥ pada-kamalayor dāsa-dāsānudāsaḥ

"I am not a *brāhmaṇa*, I am not a *kṣatriya*, I am not a *vaiśya* or a *śūdra*. Nor am I a *brahmacārī*, a householder, a *vānaprastha*, or a *sannyāsī*. I identify Myself only as the servant of the servant of the servant of the lotus feet of Lord Śrī Kṛṣṇa, the maintainer of the *gopīs*. He is like an ocean of nectar, and He is the cause of universal transcendental bliss. He is always existing with brilliance." (*Caitanya-caritāmṛta*, Madh. 13.80) That is our real identification. As long as we do not identify ourselves as eternal servants of Kṛṣṇa, we will be subject to various false identifications. *Bhakti*, devotional service, is the means by which we can be purified of false identification.

Hayagrīva dāsa: "I can only gaze with wonder and awe at the depths and heights of our psychic nature," Jung writes. "Its non-spatial universe conceals an untold abundance of images which have accumulated over millions of years of living development and become fixed in the or-

ganism."
Śrīla Prabhupāda: Since we are constantly changing bodies, constantly undergoing transmigration, we are accumulating various experiences. However, if we remain fixed in Kṛṣṇa consciousness, we do not change. There is none of this fluctuation once we understand our real identification, which is, "I am the servant of Kṛṣṇa, and my duty is to serve Him." Arjuna realized this after hearing *Bhagavad-gītā*, and he told Śrī Kṛṣṇa:

naṣṭo mohaḥ smṛtir labdhā
tvat prasādān mayācyuta
sthito 'smi gata-sandehaḥ
kariṣye vacanaṁ tava

"My dear Kṛṣṇa, O infallible one, my illusion is now gone. I have regained my memory by Your mercy, and I am now firm and free from doubt and am prepared to act according to Your instructions." (*Bg.* 18.73) So after hearing *Bhagavad-gītā*, Arjuna comes to this conclusion, and his illusion is dispelled by Kṛṣṇa's mercy. Arjuna is then fixed in his original position. And what is this? *Kariṣye vacanaṁ tava*. "Whatever you say, I will do." At the beginning of *Bhagavad-gītā*, Kṛṣṇa told Arjuna to fight, and Arjuna refused. At the conclusion, Arjuna's illusion is dispelled, and he is situated in his original constitutional position. Thus our perfection lies in executing the orders of Kṛṣṇa.
Hayagrīva dāsa: Jung classifies five types of rebirth. One is metempsychosis, by which "...one's life is prolonged in time by passing through different bodily existences; or, from another point of view, it is a life-sequence interrupted by different reincarnations....It is by no means certain whether continuity of personality is guaranteed or not: there may be only a continuity of karma."
Śrīla Prabhupāda: A personality is always there, and bodily changes do not affect it. However, one identifies himself according to his body. When the soul, for instance, is within the body of a dog, he thinks according to that particular bodily conception. He thinks, "I am a dog, and I have my particular duty." In human society, when one is born in America, for instance, he thinks, "I am an American, and I have my duty." According to the body, the personality is manifest, but in all cases, personality is there.
Hayagrīva dāsa: But is this personality continuous?
Śrīla Prabhupāda: Certainly the personality is continuous. At death, the same soul passes into another gross body, along with its mental and intellectual identifications. The individual acquires different types of bodies, but the person is the same.

Hayagrīva dāsa: This would correspond to what Jung calls reincarnation, the second type of rebirth: "This concept of rebirth necessarily implies the continuity of personality," he writes. "Here the human personality is regarded as continuous and accessible to memory, so that when one is incarnated or born, one is able, at least potentially, to remember that he has lived through previous existences and that these existences were one's own, i.e., that they had the same ego-form as the present life. As a rule, reincarnation means rebirth in a human body."
Śrīla Prabhupāda: Not necessarily into a human body. From *Śrīmad-Bhāgavatam,* we learn that Bharata Mahārāja became a deer in his next life, and after being a deer, he became a *brāhmaṇa.* The soul is changing bodies just as a man changes his dress. The man is the same, although his dress may be different.

vāsāṁsi jīrṇāni yathā vihāya
navāni gṛhṇāti naro 'parāṇi
tathā śarīrāṇi vihāya jīrṇāny
anyāni saṁyāti navāni dehī

"As a person puts on new garments, giving up old ones, similarly, the soul accepts new material bodies, giving up the old and useless ones." (*Bg.* 2.22) When a dress is old and cannot be used anymore, one has to exchange it for another. In a sense, you purchase a new dress with the money, or karma, you have accumulated in your life. The man is the same, but his dress is supplied according to the price he can pay. According to your karma, you receive a certain type of body.
Hayagrīva dāsa: For Jung, the third type of rebirth, called resurrection, may be of two types: "It may be a carnal body, as in the Christian assumption that this body will be resurrected." That is, according to Christian doctrine, at the end of the world, the gross bodies will reassemble themselves and ascend into heaven, or descend into hell.
Śrīla Prabhupāda: And what will the person do in the meantime?
Hayagrīva dāsa: I don't know. Obviously the material elements disperse.
Śrīla Prabhupāda: The material body is finished, but the spiritual body is always there. This type of resurrection talked about is applicable to God and His representatives, not to all. In this case, it is not a material body, but a spiritual one. When God appears, He appears in a spiritual body, and this body does not change. In *Bhagavad-gītā,* Kṛṣṇa says that He spoke to the sun god millions of years ago, and Arjuna questioned how this could be possible. Kṛṣṇa replies that although Arjuna had been

present, he could not remember. Remembrance is possible only if one does not change bodies. Changing bodies means forgetting.
Hayagrīva dāsa: Jung admits that on a higher level, the process is not material. "It is assumed that the resurrection of the dead is the raising up of the *corpus gloriaficationis*, the subtle body, in the state of incorruptibility."
Śrīla Prabhupāda: This is the spiritual body, which never changes. According to the Māyāvādī conception, the Absolute Truth is impersonal, and when He comes as a person, He accepts a material body. Those who are advanced in spiritual knowledge, who accept the *Bhagavad-gītā*, understand that this is not the case.

avajānanti māṁ mūḍhā
mānuṣīṁ tanum āśritam
paraṁ bhāvam ajānanto
mama bhūta-maheśvaram

"Fools deride Me when I descend in the human form. They do not know My transcendental nature and My supreme dominion over all that be." (*Bg.* 9.11) Because Kṛṣṇa appears like a human being, the unintelligent think that He is nothing but a human being. They have no knowledge of the spiritual body.
Hayagrīva dāsa: The fourth form of rebirth is called *renovatio,* and this refers to "the transformation of a mortal into an immortal being, of a corporeal into a spiritual being, and of a human into a divine being." As an example, Jung cites the ascension of Christ into heaven.
Śrīla Prabhupāda: We say that the spiritual body never dies, and the material body is subject to destruction. *Nāyaṁ hanti na hanyate (Bg.* 2.19). After the material body's destruction, the spiritual body is still there. It is neither generated nor killed.
Hayagrīva dāsa: But aren't there examples of a kind of ascension into heaven? Didn't Arjuna ascend?
Śrīla Prabhupāda: Yes, and Yudhiṣṭhira. There are many instances. The special instance is Kṛṣṇa Himself and His associates. But we should never consider their bodies material. They didn't go through death of any sort, although their bodies traveled to the higher universe. But it is also a fact that everyone possesses a spiritual body.
Hayagrīva dāsa: The fifth type of rebirth is indirect, like an initiation ceremony, or the twice-born ceremony of transformation. "Through his presence at the rite, the individual participates in divine grace."
Śrīla Prabhupāda: Yes, one's first birth is by his father and mother, and

the next birth is by the spiritual master and Vedic knowledge. When one takes his second birth, he comes to understand that he is not the material body. That is spiritual education. That birth of knowledge, or birth into knowledge, is called *dvijaḥ*.

Hayagrīva dāsa: In one of his last books, *The Undiscovered Self*, Jung writes: "The meaning and purpose of religion lie in the relationship of the individual to God (Christianity, Judaism, Islam) or to the path of salvation and liberation (Buddhism). From this basic fact all ethics is derived, which without the individual's responsibility before God can be called nothing more than conventional morality."

Śrīla Prabhupāda: First of all, we understand from *Bhagavad-gītā* that no one can approach God without being purified of all sinful reactions. Only one who is standing on the platform of pure goodness can understand God and engage in His service. From Arjuna, we understand that God is *paraṁ brahma paraṁ dhāma pavitraṁ paramaṁ bhavān (Bg.* 10.12). He is the Supreme Brahman, the ultimate, the supreme abode and purifier. *Paraṁ-brahma* indicates the Supreme Brahman. Every living being is Brahman spiritually, but Kṛṣṇa is the *Paraṁ-brahma*, the Supreme Brahman. He is also *paraṁ-dhāma*, the ultimate abode of everything. And *pavitraṁ paramaṁ*, the purest of the pure. In order to approach the purest of the pure, one must become completely pure, and to this end, morality and ethics are necessary. Therefore in our Kṛṣṇa consciousness movement, we prohibit illicit sex, meat eating, intoxication, and gambling, the four pillars of sinful life. If we can avoid these, we can remain on the platform of purity. Kṛṣṇa consciousness is based on this morality, and one who cannot follow these principles falls down from the spiritual platform. Purity is the basic principle of God consciousness, and is essential for the reestablishment of our eternal relationship with God.

Hayagrīva dāsa: Jung sees atheistic Communism as the greatest threat in the world today. He writes: "The state has taken the place of God; that is why, seen from this angle, the socialist dictatorships are religions, and state slavery is a form of worship."

Śrīla Prabhupāda: Yes, I agree with him. Atheistic Communism has contributed to the degradation of human civilization. The Communists supposedly believe in the equal distribution of wealth. According to our understanding, God is the Father, material nature the mother, and living entities the sons. The sons have a right to live at the cost of the father. The entire universe is the property of the Supreme Personality of Godhead, and living entities are being supported by the Supreme Father.

However, we should be satisfied with the supplies allotted to us. According to *Īśopaniṣad, tena tyaktena bhuñjīthā (Īśopaniṣad* 1). We should be satisfied with our allocation, and not envy another or encroach upon his property. We should not envy the capitalists or the wealthy because everyone is given his allotment by the Supreme Personality of Godhead. Therefore everyone should be satisfied with what he receives. On the other hand, no one should exploit others. One may be born in a wealthy family, but he should not interfere with the rights of others. Whether one is rich or poor, he should be God conscious, accept God's arrangement, and serve God to his fullest. This is the philosophy of *Śrīmad-Bhāgavatam,* and it is confirmed by Śrī Caitanya Mahāprabhu. We should be content with our allocations from God, and concern ourselves with advancing in Kṛṣṇa consciousness. If we become envious of the rich, we will be tempted to encroach upon their allotment, and in this way we are diverted from our service to the Lord. The main point is that everyone, rich or poor, should engage in God's service. If everyone does so, there will be real peace in the world.

Hayagrīva dāsa: In the socialist state, the goals of religion are turned into worldly promises of bread, "the just distribution of material goods, universal prosperity in the future, and shorter working hours."

Śrīla Prabhupāda: This is because they have no understanding of spiritual life, nor can they understand that the person within the body is eternal and spiritual. Therefore they recommend immediate sense gratification.

Hayagrīva dāsa: Jung believed, however, that Marxism cannot possibly replace religion. "A natural function which has existed from the beginning...cannot be disposed of with rationalistic and so-called enlightened criticism."

Śrīla Prabhupāda: The Communists are concerned with adjusting material things that can never be adjusted. They imagine that they can solve problems, but ultimately their plans will fail. The Communists do not understand what religion is. It is not possible to avoid religion. Everything has a particular characteristic. Salt is salty, sugar is sweet, and chili is hot and pungent. These are intrinsic characteristics. Similarly, the living entity has an intrinsic quality. His characteristic is to render service, be he a Communist, a theist, a capitalist, or whatever. In all countries, people are working and rendering service to their respective governments—be they capitalists or Communists—and the people are not profiting. Therefore we say that if people follow the footsteps of Śrī Caitanya Mahāprabhu by serving Kṛṣṇa, they will be happy. In the material world, people are rendering service, and they are not happy doing so because their service is actually meant for Kṛṣṇa. Therefore, for the sake of happiness, people should individually and collectively render service to Kṛṣṇa. When that service is misplaced, we are never happy. Both Communists and capitalists are saying, "Render service to me," but Kṛṣṇa says, *sarva-dharmān parityajya (Bg.* 18.66). "Just render Me service, and I will free you from all sinful reactions."

Hayagrīva dāsa: Jung feels that materialistic capitalism cannot possibly defeat a pseudo-religion like Marxism. The only solution is to adopt a nonmaterialistic religion. "The antidote should in this case be an equally potent faith of a different and nonmaterialistic kind...."

Śrīla Prabhupāda: That religion is this Kṛṣṇa consciousness movement. Kṛṣṇa has nothing to do with any materialistic "ism," and this movement is directly connected with Kṛṣṇa, the Supreme Personality of Godhead. God demands complete surrender, and we are teaching, "You are servants, but your service is being wrongly placed. Therefore you are not happy. Just render service to Kṛṣṇa, and you will find happiness." We neither support Communism nor capitalism, nor do we advocate the adoption of pseudo religions. We are for Kṛṣṇa only.

Hayagrīva dāsa: Jung laments the absence of a potent nonmaterialistic faith in the West that "could block the progress of a fanatical ideology" like Marxism. He sees mankind as desperately in need of a religion that has immediate meaning.

Śrīla Prabhupāda: That nonmaterial religion which is above everything—Marxism and capitalism—is this Kṛṣṇa consciousness movement. If we cultivate Kṛṣṇa consciousness, we will transcend sinful reactions and make spiritual progress. *Janma karma ca me divyam (Bg.* 4.9). Kṛṣṇa says that just by knowing of His transcendental appearance and pastimes, we will not take birth in this material world again.

Hayagrīva dāsa: Jung writes: "It is unfortunately only too clear that if the individual is not truly regenerated in spirit, society cannot be either, for society is the sum total of individuals in need of redemption."

Śrīla Prabhupāda: True, the basis of change is the individual. Now there are a few disciples individually initiated into Kṛṣṇa consciousness, and if a large percentage can thus become invigorated, the face of the world will change. There is no doubt of this.

Hayagrīva dāsa: For Jung, the salvation of the world consists in the salvation of the individual soul. "His individual relation to God would be an effective shield against these pernicious influences."

Śrīla Prabhupāda: Yes, those who seriously take to Kṛṣṇa consciousness are never troubled by Marxism, this-ism, or that-ism. A Marxist may take to Kṛṣṇa consciousness, but a Kṛṣṇa conscious devotee would never become a Marxist. That is not possible. It is explained in *Bhagavad-gītā* that when one knows the highest perfection of life, he cannot be misled by a third or fourth-class philosophy.

Hayagrīva dāsa: Jung also felt that materialistic progress could be a possible enemy to the individual. "A favorable environment merely strengthens the dangerous tendency to expect everything to originate from outside," he writes, "even that metamorphosis which external reality cannot provide, mainly, a deep-seated change of the inner man...."

Śrīla Prabhupāda: Yes everything originates from inside, from the soul. It is confirmed by Bhaktivinoda Ṭhākura and others that material progress is essentially an expansion of the external energy, māyā, illusion. We are all living in illusion, and so-called scientists and philosophers cannot even understand God and their relationship to Him, despite their material advancement. Material advancement and knowledge are actually hindrances to the progressive march of Kṛṣṇa consciousness. To live a saintly life, we minimize our necessities. We are not after luxurious living. We feel that life is meant for spiritual progress and Kṛṣṇa consciousness, not for material advancement.

Hayagrīva dāsa: To inspire this deep-seated change in the inner man, Jung feels that a proper teacher is needed, someone to explain religion.

Śrīla Prabhupāda: Yes, according to the Vedic injunction, it is essential to seek out a guru, who, by definition, is a representative of God. *Sākṣād-dharitvena samasta-śāstrair (Śrī Gurv-aṣṭaka* 7). The representative of God is worshipped as God, but he never says, "I am God." Although he is worshipped as God, he is the servant of God. God Himself is always master. Caitanya Mahāprabhu requested everyone to become a guru. "Whatever you are, it doesn't matter. Simply become a guru and deliver all these people who are in ignorance." One may say, "I am not very learned. How can I become a guru?" Caitanya Mahāprabhu said that it is not necessary to be a learned scholar, for there are many so-called learned scholars who are fools. It is only necessary to impart Kṛṣṇa's instructions, which are already there in *Bhagavad-gītā*. Whoever explains *Bhagavad-gītā* as it is is a guru by definition. If one is fortunate enough to approach such a guru, his life becomes successful.

Hayagrīva dāsa: Jung points out that "our philosophy is no longer a way of life, as it was in antiquity; it has turned into an exclusively intellectual and academic affair."

Śrīla Prabhupāda: That is also our opinion. Mental speculation has no value in itself. We must be directly in touch with the Supreme Personality of Godhead, and, using all reason, assimilate the instructions given by Him. We can then follow these instructions in our daily life and do good to others by teaching *Bhagavad-gītā*.

Hayagrīva dāsa: He sees on the one hand an exclusively intellectual philosophy, and on the other, denominational religions with "archaic rites and conceptions," which have "become strange and unintelligible to the man of today...."

Śrīla Prabhupāda: That is because preachers of religion are simply dogmatic. They have no clear idea of God; they make only official proclamations. When one does not understand, he cannot make others understand. But there is no such vanity in Kṛṣṇa consciousness, which is clear in every respect. This is the expected movement Mr. Jung wanted. Every sane man should cooperate with this movement and liberate human society from the gross darkness of ignorance.

Hayagrīva dāsa: He describes the truly religious man as one "who is accustomed to the thought of not being sole master of his own house. He believes that God, and not he himself, decides in the end."

Śrīla Prabhupāda: Yes, that is the natural situation. What decisions can we make? Since there is already a controller over us, how can we be absolute? Everyone should depend on the supreme controller and fully surrender to Him.

Hayagrīva dāsa: Jung feels that modern man should ask himself, "Have I any religious experience and immediate relation to God, and hence that certainty which will keep me, as an individual, from dissolving in the crowd?" Our relationship with God ultimately assures our own individuality.

Śrīla Prabhupāda: Yes, all living entities are individuals, and God is the supreme individual. According to the Vedic version, all individuals are subordinate to Him. *Nityo nityānāṁ cetanaś cetanānām (Kaṭha-upaniṣad* 2.2.13). The supreme individual is one, and the subordinate are many. The supreme individual is maintaining His subordinates, just as a father maintains his family. When the children learn to enjoy their father's property without encroaching upon one another, accepting what is allotted them, they will attain peace.

Hayagrīva dāsa: That ends our session on Jung.

Śrīla Prabhupāda: So far, he seems the most sensible.

GLOSSARY

(A note on Sanskrit Pronunciation:

Throughout the centuries, the Sanskrit language has been written in a variety of alphabets. The mode of writing most widely used throughout India, however, is called *devanāgarī*, which means, literally, the writing used in "the cities of the demigods." The *devanāgarī* alphabet consists of forty-eight characters, comprising thirteen vowels and thirty-five consonants. Ancient Sanskrit grammarians arranged the alphabet according to practical linguistic principles, and this order has been accepted by all Western scholars. The system of transliteration used in this book conforms to a system that scholars in the last fifty years have accepted to indicate the pronunciation of each Sanskrit sound.

The short vowel **a** is pronounced like the **u** in b**u**t, long **ā** like the **a** in far, and short **i** like the **i** in p**i**n. Long **ī** is pronounced as in p**i**que, short **u** as in p**u**ll, and long **ū** as in r**u**le. The vowel **ṛ** is pronounced like the **ri** in **ri**m. The vowel **e** is pronounced as in th**e**y, **ai** as in **ai**sle, **o** as in g**o**, and **au** as in h**ow**. The *anusvāra* (**ṁ**), which is a pure nasal, is pronounced like the **n** in the French word *bo***n**, and *visarga* (**ḥ**), which is a strong aspirate, is pronounced as the final **h** sound. Thus **aḥ** is pronounced like **aha**, and **iḥ** like **ihi**.

The guttural consonants—**k, kh, g, gh,** and **ṅ**—are pronounced from the throat in much the same manner as in English. **K** is pronounced as in **k**ite, **kh** as in Ec**kh**art, **g** as in **g**ive, **gh** as in di**g h**ard, and **ṅ** as in si**ng**. The palatal consonants—**c, ch, j, jh** and **ñ**—are pronounced from the palate with the middle of the tongue. **C** is pronounced as in **ch**air, **ch** as in staun**ch-h**eart, **j** as in **j**oy, **jh** as in he**dgeh**og, and **ñ** as in ca**ny**on. The cerebral consonants—**ṭ, ṭh, ḍ, ḍh and ṇ**—are pronounced with the tip of the tongue turned up and drawn back against the dome of the plate. **Ṭ** is pronounced as in **t**ub, **ṭh** as in ligh**t-h**eart, **ḍ** as in **d**ove, **ḍh** as in re**d-h**ot, and **ṇ** as in **n**ut. The dental consonants—**t, th, d, dh** and **n**—are pronounced in the same manner as the cerebrals, but with the forepart of the tongue against the teeth. The labial consonants—**p, ph, b, bh** and **m**—are pronounced with the lips. **P** is pronounced as in **p**ine, **ph** as in u**ph**ill, **b** as in **b**ird, **bh** as in ru**b-h**ard, and **m** as in **m**other. The semivowels—**y, r, l** and **v**—are pronounced as in **y**es, **r**un, **l**ight, and **v**ine respectively. The sibilants—**ś, ṣ** and **s**—are pronounced, respectively, as in the German word **s***prechen* and the English words **sh**ine and **s**un. The letter **h** is pronounced as in **h**ome.)

A

ĀCĀRYA: a spiritual master who teaches by his personal example.

ACINTYA-BHEDĀBHEDA-TATTVA: Lord Caitanya's doctrine of the "inconceivable oneness and difference" of God and His creation, establishing the Absolute Truth as both personal and impersonal.

AGNI: the demigod controlling fire.

AHAṀ BRAHMĀSMI: "I am Brahman." The spiritual identity of the living entity.

AHIṀSĀ: nonviolence.

AKARMA: Kṛṣṇa conscious activities that carry no reactions, either good or bad.

ĀNANDA: transcendental bliss.

AṆU: atomic, minute.

ARCA-VIGRAHA: the incarnation of the Lord in the form of material elements, such as a statue (Deity or *mūrti*), or painting, or even a mental image. It is manifest to facilitate worship by the devotees in the material world.

ARTHA: economic development.

ĀSANAS: bodily postures used in yoga discipline.

ĀŚRAMA: a spiritual order according to the Vedic social system: *brahmacarya* (student life), *gṛhastha* (householder), *vānaprastha* (retirement), and *sannyāsa* (renunciation).

AṢṬĀṄGA-YOGA: the eightfold path consisting of *yama* and *niyama* (moral practices), *āsana* (bodily postures), *prāṇāyāma* (breath control), *pratyāhāra* (sensory withdrawal), *dhāraṇa* (steadying the mind), *dhyāna* (meditation), and *samādhi* (deep concentration on Viṣṇu within the heart).

ASURA: not godly; demon, or one opposed to God.

ĀTMĀ: the self, or soul.

ĀTMA-HAN: killer of the soul; one who neglects spiritual life.

ĀTMĀRĀMA: self-satisfied; one who delights in the Self.

B

BALARĀMA: Lord Kṛṣṇa's first expansion, appearing as elder brother of Kṛṣṇa, manifestation of spiritual strength.

BHAGAVĀN: the possessor of all opulences, the Supreme Lord.

BHAKTISIDDHĀNTA SARASVATĪ: founder of India's famous Gauḍīya Math mission, and spiritual master of His Divine Grace A. C. Bhaktivedanta Swami Prabhupāda.

BHAKTIVINODA ṬHĀKURA: a great devotee, father of Bhaktisiddhānta Sarasvāti.

BHAKTI-YOGA: linking with the Supreme Lord through devotional service.

BRAHMĀ: the first created living being in the universe, empowered by Lord Viṣṇu to further create the material manifestation and rule the mode of passion.

BRAHMA-BHŪTA: state of being freed from material contamination, and transcendentally happy by virtue of devotional service.

BRAHMACĀRĪ: celibate student; the first *āśrama.*

BRAHMA-JIJÑĀSĀ: inquiry into spiritual matters.

BRAHMAJYOTI: the impersonal effulgence emanating from the transcendental body of Lord Kṛṣṇa and illuminating the spiritual world.

BRAHMALOKA: the abode of Lord Brahmā, highest planet in the material universe.

BRAHMAN: (1) the Supreme Personality of Godhead; (2) the impersonal, all pervasive aspect of God; (3) the total material substance (*mahat-tattva*); (4) the individual soul.

BRĀHMAṆA: the intellectual, or priestly class, according to the Vedic social system of *varṇas.*

BRAHMA-SAṀHITĀ: an ancient Sanskrit scripture of the prayers of Brahmā to Govinda.

C

CAITANYA-CARITĀMṚTA: a scripture by Kṛṣṇadāsa Kavirāja Gosvāmī describing Lord Caitanya Mahāprabhu's teachings and pastimes.

CAITANYA MAHĀPRABHU: Lord Kṛṣṇa's incarnation in the age of Kali, appearing in Bengal, India, in the late Fifteenth Century, to inaugurate the dharma of this age: the congregational chanting of Hare Kṛṣṇa.

CAṆḌALA: a dog-eater, outcaste.

D

DHARMA: true nature, religious principles; the rendering of service to God.

DHRUVA MAHĀRĀJA: a great boy-devotee, renowned for his firm determination and penance. He later ruled this planet and was finally given the polestar, Dhruvaloka.

DHYĀNA: Meditation

DURGĀ: the personification of the material energy.

DUṢKṚTINA: miscreant; one who does not surrender to Kṛṣṇa.

DVĀPARA-YUGA: the third age of the cycle of *yugas*. It ended with the disappearance of Lord Kṛṣṇa from this earth, five thousand years ago.

G

GAṆEŚA: one of the demigods, son of Lord Śiva, often worshipped for success in material affairs.

GARBHODAKAŚĀYĪ VIṢṆU: the Viṣṇu expansion of the Supreme Lord entering each universe to create diversity.

GO-MĀTĀ: mother cow.

GOPAS: the cowherd boy friends of Kṛṣṇa, highly elevated devotees who enjoy sporting with Kṛṣṇa in Vṛndāvana.

GOPĪS: the cowherd girl friends of Kṛṣṇa, highly elevated devotees who enjoy transcendental feelings with Kṛṣṇa in the conjugal rasa.

GOVARDHANA HILL: a hill near Vṛndāvana lifted by Lord Kṛṣṇa to protect His devotees from the torrents of Indra.

GOVINDA: name of Kṛṣṇa, meaning one who gives pleasure to the cows.

GṚHASTHA: householder; the second *āśrama*.

GUṆAS: the three material modes, or qualities, of the material universe: goodness, passion, and ignorance.

H

HARE: the spiritual energy of the Lord by which the Lord is reached.

HARI: the Supreme Lord, Kṛṣṇa.

HARI-KĪRTANA: chanting of the names of God.

HAṬHA-YOGA: a system of bodily postures (*āsanas*) to help control the senses and mind and thereby aid meditation.

HIRAṆYAKAŚIPU: a great demon, father of the devotee Prahlāda Mahārāja, killed by Kṛṣṇa in His incarnation as Nṛsiṁhadeva.

HṚṢĪKEŚA: master of the senses, Lord Kṛṣṇa.

I

INDRA: a great demigod, the king of heaven and presiding deity of rain.

ĪŚOPANIṢAD: one of the most important of the 108 Upaniṣads, establishing the proprietary rights of the Supreme Personality of Godhead.

J

JAPA: chanting of the holy names of God.

JĪVA, JĪVĀTMĀ: the individual soul, or living entity.

JÑĀṆAVĀN: wise man.

JÑĀNA-YOGA: the predominantly empirical, intellectual process of linking with the Supreme, generally executed when one is still attached to mental speculation.

K

KĀLA: the manifestation of Kṛṣṇa as eternal time.

KĀLĪ: a goddess personifying the ghastly form of material nature.

KALI-YUGA: the age of quarrel and ignorance, the fourth and most degraded age in the cycle of four yugas. Five thousand years of this current Kali-yuga have expired; 428,000 years remain.

KALKI-AVATĀRA: incarnation of Kṛṣṇa, manifest at the end of Kali-yuga. Appearing on a white horse, He will annihilate all the demons with His sword.

KĀMA: desire, lust.

KĀRAṆODAKAŚĀYĪ VIṢṆU: the Mahā-viṣṇu who lies within the causal ocean and breathes out innumerable universes.

KARMA: (1) material action performed according to scripture; (2) the chain of action and reaction.

KARMA-KĀṆḌA: the division of the Vedas dealing with fruitive activities performed by materialists for purification and material success.

KARMA-YOGA: linking to God by dedicating the fruits of action to Him.

KARMĪ: a materialist; one attached to the fruits of his labor.

KṚPAṆA: a miser; one who does not spend his life on spiritual realization.

KṢATRIYA: a warrior or administrator in the Vedic social system. Literally, a *kṣatriya* is one who protects others from harm.

KṢĪRODAKAŚĀYĪ VIṢṆU: the Supersoul entering into the heart of every living being. He exists in and between every atom, and He is the source of many incarnations.

KUṆṬHA: the material universe. Literally, the place of anxiety.

KUNTĪ: mother of the five Pāṇḍavas, and great devotee of Lord Kṛṣṇa.

KURUKṢETRA: place of pilgrimage, north of modern New Delhi, where *Bhagavad-gītā* was spoken and the great battle between the Kurus and Pāṇḍavas took place.

KURUS: the one hundred sons of Dhṛtarāṣṭra.

M

MAHĀBHĀRATA: the great epic of 100,000 verses composed by Vyāsadeva, narrating the history of the Pāṇḍavas and including *Bhagavad-gītā.*

MAHĀMANTRA: the great chanting for deliverance: Hare Kṛṣṇa, Hare Kṛṣṇa, Kṛṣṇa Kṛṣṇa, Hare Hare, Hare Rāma, Hare Rāma, Rāma Rāma, Hare Hare.

MAHĀTMĀ: a great soul who understands that Kṛṣṇa is everything and therefore surrenders unto Him.

MAHAT-TATTVA: the total material energy.

MAHĀVIṢṆU: the Kāraṇodakaśāyī Viṣṇu who lies within the causal ocean and breathes out innumerable universes.

MAṄGALA-ĀRĀTRIKA: early morning (4:30 a.m.) offering to the Lord in the temple, accompanied by chanting and bells.

MANU: the father of mankind, the demigod who set forth *Manu-saṁhitā*, the law book for humanity.

MĀYĀ: illusion; the external energy of Kṛṣṇa that deludes the living entity into forgetfulness of Kṛṣṇa.

MĀYĀDEVĪ: personification of the illusory material energy.

MĀYĀVĀDĪ: impersonalist or voidist maintaining that God is ultimately formless and without personality.

MOKṢA: liberation from the cycle of birth and death.

MŪḌHA: hard-working ass; gross materialist.

MUKUNDA: the granter of liberation (*mukti*), Kṛṣṇa.

MUNI: sage or self-realized soul.

N

NANDA MAHĀRĀJA: a great devotee, who served as foster father of Kṛṣṇa in the Vṛndāvana pastimes.

NĀRADA: one of the Lord's greatest devotees, author of *Nārada-bhakti-sūtras.* He spreads love of God throughout the universe.

NĀRĀYAṆA: four-handed expansion(s) of Viṣṇu presiding over the Vaikuṇṭha planets.

NITYA: eternal; refers both to the Lord and the living entity.

NṚSIṀHADEVA: incarnation of Lord Kṛṣṇa in the form of half-man, half-lion, savior of Prahlāda Mahārāja.

O

OṀ TAT SAT: the transcendental syllables chanted by *brāhmaṇas* for satisfying the Supreme when chanting Vedic hymns or offering sacrifices. They indicate the Supreme Absolute Truth, the Personality of Godhead.

OṀKARA: *Oṁ*; the transcendental syllable representing the impersonal aspect of Kṛṣṇa.

P

PĀṆḌAVAS: the five sons of King Pāṇḍu: Yudhiṣṭhira, Arjuna, Bhīma, Nakula, and Sahadeva.

PARAMAHAṀSA: the topmost devotee of the Lord. Literally, swanlike.

PARAMĀTMĀ: the Supersoul, the localized aspect of the Supreme Lord within the heart of all living entities, accompanying everyone as witness and guide.

PARAṀ-BRAHMA: the Supreme Brahman, the Personality of Godhead, Śrī Kṛṣṇa.

PARAMPARĀ: the disciplic succession through which spiritual knowledge is transmitted.

PĀTĀLA-LOKA: lowest planet in the material universe.

PAVITRAM: pure.

PRAHLĀDA MAHĀRĀJA: a great devotee, persecuted by his demonic father, Hiraṇyakaśipu, and saved by Lord Nṛsiṁhadeva.

PRAKṚTI: material nature. Literally, that which is predominated.

PRASĀDAM: food offered in devotion to Lord Kṛṣṇa. Literally, mercy.

PREMĀ: pure, spontaneous love of God.

PŪJĀ: worship.

PURĀṆAS: the eighteen historical supplements to the Vedas.

PURUṢA: the enjoyer, the dominator, the Supreme Lord. Sometimes the word refers to the individual soul.

PUTRA: son.

R

RĀDHĀ(RĀṆĪ): eternal consort of Kṛṣṇa, His own internal pleasure potency.

RAJO-GUṆA: the material mode of passion.

RĀMA: (1) a name of God meaning the enjoyer; (2) Lord Rāmacandra, the incarnation, hero of Vālmīki's *Rāmāyaṇa;* (3) Lord Balarāma, the expansion of Kṛṣṇa.

RĀSA: Lord Kṛṣṇa's transcendental pastime of dancing with the *gopīs* in the forests of Vṛndāvana.

RASA: relationship.
ṚṢI: saint or sage.
RŪPA GOSVĀMĪ: one of the principal disciples of Lord Caitanya Mahāprabhu, author of many authoritative books on *bhakti-yoga*, including *Bhakti-rasāmṛta-sindhu.*

S

SAC-CID-ĀNANDA: eternal being, knowledge, and bliss.
SĀDHANA-BHAKTI: devotional service executed by regulative principles, as opposed to spontaneous love.
SĀDHU: holyman or sage.
SAHAJIYĀ: a type of impersonalist who takes things cheaply and mistakenly identifies the finite living entity with Kṛṣṇa.
SAMĀDHI: trance, absorption in Kṛṣṇa consciousness.
SANĀTANA-DHARMA: the eternal religion; devotional service.
ŚAṄKARĀCĀRYA: (AD 788-820) the great philosopher who established the doctrine of *advaita* (nondualism), stressing the impersonal nature of God and the identity of all souls with the undifferentiated Brahman.
SĀṄKHYA-YOGA: (1) analytical discrimination between spirit and matter, soul and body; (2) devotional yoga taught in *Śrīmad-Bhāgavatam* by Lord Kapila, son of Devahūti.
SAṄKĪRTANA-YAJÑA: the congregational chanting of the names of God, the prescribed sacrifice for this age of Kali.
SANNYĀSA: the renounced order of life, the fourth *āśrama* in the Vedic social system.
ŚĀNTI: transcendental peace.
ŚĀSTRA: scripture.
SATTVA-GUṆA: the material mode of goodness.
SATYA-YUGA: the age of goodness and wisdom, first of the four ages of the universe, characterized by virtue and religion.
SIDDHALOKA: a higher planet inhabited by perfected yogīs.
ŚIVA: Qualitative incarnation of Kṛṣṇa in charge of the mode of ignorance and responsible for the annihilation of the material universe; demigod worshipped commonly for material benedictions.
ŚLOKA: a Sanskrit verse.
SMRITI: realization of sages, written in the Purāṇas and Vedic commentaries. They complement *śruti.*

ŚRĪMAD-BHĀGAVATAM: the scripture composed by Vyāsadeva to explain and describe Kṛṣṇa's pastimes.

ŚRUTI: the Vedas directly spoken by the Supreme Personality of Godhead.

ŚUDDHA-SATTVA: purified goodness above the three guṇas.

ŚŪDRA: a member of the working class in the Vedic social system.

ŚYĀMASUNDARA: a name of the original form of Lord Kṛṣṇa as manifest in the Vṛndāvana pastimes.

T

TAMO-GUṆA: the material mode of ignorance.

TAPASYA: penance or austerity voluntarily accepted for spiritual progress.

TILAKA: clay markings worn on the forehead and other places to sanctify the body as a temple of the Supreme Lord.

TRETĀ-YUGA: the second age in the cycle of *yugas*, renowned for great sacrifices.

V

VAIKUṆṬHA: the eternal planets of the spiritual sky. Literally, without anxiety.

VAIṢṆAVA: a devotee of the Supreme Lord.

VAIŚYA: the merchant or farmer class according to the Vedic social system.

VĀLMĪKI: author of the *Rāmāyaṇa*.

VĀNAPRASTHA: retired life, in which one quits home and travels to places of pilgrimage in preparation for the renounced order of *sannyāsa*.

VARṆA: social class, or occupational division.

VARṆĀŚRAMA: the Vedic social system arranged into four occupations (*varṇas): brāhmaṇa*, *kṣatriya*, *vaiśya*, and *śūdra;* and four spiritual divisions (*āśramas): brahmacārī*, *gṛhastha*, *vānaprastha*, and *sannyāsa*.

VĀSUDEVA: Kṛṣṇa, the son of Vasudeva.

VEDĀNTA: the philosophical system based on the *Vedānta-sūtra*, the treatise written by Vyāsadeva.

VEDAS: the four original scriptures (*Ṛg*, *Yajur*, *Sāma*, and *Atharva)*. Also, in a larger sense, their supplements, the Purāṇas, *Mahābhārata*, *Vedānta-sūtra*, etc.

VIKARMA: unauthorized or sinful activity performed against the injunctions of revealed scriptures.

VIRĀṬ-RŪPA: the universal form of Lord Kṛṣṇa, as described in the Eleventh Chapter of *Bhagavad-gītā.*

VIṢṆU: the Personality of Godhead.

VIṢṆU-MĀYĀ: the internal energy of the Lord, which hides Him from material vision. Also called *yoga-māyā.*

VIṢṆU-TATTVA: innumerable primary or Viṣṇu expansions of Kṛṣṇa.

VṚNDĀVANA: the transcendental abode of Lord Kṛṣṇa. Also called Goloka Vṛndāvana or Kṛṣṇaloka.

VYĀSADEVA: literary incarnation who compiled the Vedas and wrote the Purāṇas, *Mahābhārata,* and *Vedānta-sūtra.*

Y

YAJÑA: sacrifice

YAJÑA-PURUṢA: Kṛṣṇa, the Lord and enjoyer of all sacrifices.

YAMARĀJA: the god of death; demigod who punishes sinful living entities after death.

YAMUNĀ: Holy river flowing by Vṛndāvana, site of Kṛṣṇa's pastimes. Also spelled Jamunā.

YOGA-MĀYĀ: the internal energy of the Lord, which hides Him from one's material vision.

YOGĪ: one engaged in the practice of yoga, linking up with the Supreme.

YUDHIṢṬHIRA: the eldest Pāṇḍava brother, the son of Dharma. To install him on his rightful throne, the battle of Kurukṣetra was fought.

YUGAS: the four ages of the universe: Satya-yuga, Tretā-yuga, Dvāpara-yuga, and Kali-yuga. As the ages proceed from Satya to Kali, religion and goodness decline, and ignorance predominates.

INDEX

J

K

L

ABOUT THE AUTHOR

His Divine Grace A.C. Bhaktivedanta Swami Prabhupāda was born into a family of Kṛṣṇa devotees in Calcutta, India, in 1896. From early childhood, he showed signs of pure devotion to Lord Kṛṣṇa. In 1922, he met his spiritual master, Śrīla Bhaktisiddhānta Sarasvatī, the founder of India's Gauḍīya Maṭha. At their first meeting, Prabhupāda received the instructions that would later win him world recognition: "Go to the West and spread Kṛṣṇa consciousness in the English language." Taking this instruction to heart, Prabhupāda studied his spiritual master's teachings, and in the 1940s established *Back To Godhead*, an English-language magazine dealing with the science of Kṛṣṇa consciousness. Using his own money, and working with no assistance, he wrote, edited, printed, and distributed *Back To Godhead* on a modest basis in and around New Delhi.

During the years that followed, he dreamed several times that Śrīla Bhaktisiddhānta was telling him to give up household life and formally take up the spiritual order of *sannyāsa*. When he had the dream again in Vṛndāvana, India, the place of Lord Kṛṣṇa's childhood pastimes, Śrīla Prabhupāda accepted the challenge. In September, 1959, he was given the *sannyāsa* order and the name A.C. Bhaktivedanta Swami. This put him in an ideal social position to fulfill his spiritual master's order, but first he needed books, and passage to America.

At this time, Śrīla Prabhupāda began his life's main literary work: an English translation, with commentaries, of the *Śrīmad-Bhāgavatam*, an encyclopedic scripture often called the "cream of the Vedic literature" because it deals exclusively with Lord Kṛṣṇa's personality and activities. Śrīla Prabhupāda struggled alone, writing and collecting money to print the first three volumes. "I did not know anything about writing," he later said humbly. "But my spiritual master told me to spread Lord Kṛṣṇa's glories in English, and this is what I tried to do, following in the footsteps of my Guru Mahārāja. He was such a transcendental aristocrat. I had no great personal qualifications. I just tried to follow his instructions."

In 1965, the way was finally cleared for Prabhupāda's now historic journey to the West. The Scindia Steamship Line gave him free passage aboard the freighter *Jaladūta*, and in August, Śrīla Prabhupāda left India with a crate of his *Śrīmad-Bhāgavatams*, a pair of *karatālas* (cymbals) and seven dollars.

Śrīla Prabhupāda's forty-day journey was arduous. A few days out at sea, the *Jaladūta* passed through heavy storms, and Prabhupāda suffered from seasickness and heart attacks. For two consecutive nights, the attacks came, and at age sixty-nine, Prabhupāda knew that they could prove fatal. On the third night, he dreamed that Lord Kṛṣṇa Himself was rowing the ship to America, urging him on, and offering him all protection. The next day, the storms and heart attacks subsided.

When the *Jaladūta* finally docked in New York City, Śrīla Prabhupāda wrote: "My dear Lord Kṛṣṇa, You are so kind upon this useless soul, but I do not know why You have brought me here. Now You can do whatever You like with me. How will I make them understand the message of Kṛṣṇa consciousness? I am very unfortunate, unqualified, and most fallen. Therefore, I am seeking Your benediction so I can convince them, for I am powerless to do so on my own."

Then, with his books, his cymbals, and seven dollars, Śrīla Prabhupāda entered the anonymity of Manhattan. Throughout the winter of 1965-1966, he continued writing in cold tenements, and managed to sell only a few copies of *Śrīmad-Bhāgavatam.* Despite the difficulties, he began lecturing to visitors in his small room. A few yoga students attended, and the word spread that an Indian svāmī was in town with a unique yoga method: chanting Hare Kṛṣṇa. After his room was ransacked by thieves, Prabhupāda moved to Manhattan's Lower East Side, renting an apartment and a small storefront at 26 Second Avenue.

In July, 1966, Śrīla Prabhupāda formed the International Society for Kṛṣṇa Consciousness (ISKCON), and initiated his first disciples. In the autumn, in nearby Tompkins Square Park, he led the first public chanting of Hare Kṛṣṇa in the Western world, and gained quick notice on the Lower East Side. Though he had only a dozen disciples—his strict regimen allowed no meat eating, illicit sex, intoxication, or gambling—Prabhupāda was well on his way to realizing his mission.

Within months, he opened centers in San Francisco, Montreal, Boston, Los Angeles, and Buffalo. In 1968, he founded the New Vrindaban Community in the West Virginia hills, and in 1969 he went to Europe to visit new centers in London and Hamburg. In the 1970s, as Śrīla Prabhupāda made no less than fourteen world tours, the Hare Kṛṣṇa movement rapidly swept around the world, and centers opened in all the major cities of the Americas, Europe, Africa, and Asia.

Even though constantly travelling, Śrīla Prabhupāda never stopped writing on the science of Kṛṣṇa consciousness. His Society has published and distributed over eighty volumes of his works, totalling millions of copies. These include *Bhagavad-gītā As It Is* (1968), *Teachings of Lord Caitanya* (1968), *Kṛṣṇa, The Supreme Personality of Godhead* (1970),

Nectar of Devotion (1970), *Caitanya-caritāmṛta* (1970-1975, seventeen volumes), and thirty volumes of *Śrīmad-Bhāgavatam*. Wherever Śrīla Prabhupāda stayed, whether in a London manor, an Indian hut, or a West Virginia shack, he translated Vedic literature at night, and guided ISKCON by day.

Śrīla Prabhupāda accomplished his mission between the ages of seventy and eighty-two through great personal effort and unshakable faith in Kṛṣṇa. Although he had thousands of disciples, he continued to carry the burden of counselling them and managing the Society's affairs. In India, he supervised the establishment of magnificent Rādhā-Kṛṣṇa temples in holy places like Vrndāvana and Māyāpura, and at Juhu Beach, Bombay. Today, at New Vrindaban, Prabhupāda's Palace of Gold has become a major tourist attraction, and New Vrindaban's "Land of Kṛṣṇa" project has introduced millions of pilgrims and visitors to Vedic culture.

Obviously, Śrīla Prabhupāda was no ordinary person. Before passing away on November 14, 1977, he had nurtured his Society into a worldwide confederation of more than one hundred *āśramas*, schools, temples, institutes, and farm communities. Today, still expanding under the guidance of his words and example, ISKCON has become one of the world's most dynamic religious movements.